The Singing Turk

LARRY WOLFF

The Singing Turk

OTTOMAN POWER *and*

OPERATIC EMOTIONS

on the EUROPEAN STAGE

from the SIEGE OF VIENNA

to the AGE OF NAPOLEON

STANFORD UNIVERSITY PRESS

Stanford, California

Stanford University Press
Stanford, California

Printed in the United States of America on acid-free, archival-quality paper

Library of Congress Cataloging-in-Publication Data
Names: Wolff, Larry, author.
Title: The singing Turk : Ottoman power and operatic emotions on the
    European stage from the siege of Vienna to the age of Napoleon /
    Larry Wolff.
Description: Stanford, California : Stanford University Press, 2016. |
    Includes bibliographical references and index.
Identifiers: LCCN 2015047458 | ISBN 9780804795777 (cloth : alk. paper)
Subjects: LCSH: Opera—Europe—18th century. | Turks in opera. |
    Exoticism in opera. | Operas—Characters.
Classification: LCC ML1720.3 .W65 2016 | DDC 782.1094—dc23
LC record available at http://lccn.loc.gov/2015047458

ISBN 9780804799652 (electronic)

Text composition: by Stanford University Press in 10/14 Minion

Cover design: by Bruce Lundquist

Cover image: Mahomet II, costume design for Le siège de Corinthe by artist
Hippolyte Lecomte. Courtesy of the Bibliothèque Nationale de France

Operatic excerpts relevant to this text are indicated with appropriate links
on the web site www.singingturk.com

Beaver: Are ya' finished yet, Wally?
Wally: Well, I don't know if I'm finished, but I think I better stop.
—*Leave It to Beaver,* "Beaver's Haircut"

"*Pappataci dee mangiar! Pappataci dee dormir!*"
Pappataci must eat! Pappataci must sleep!
—Rossini, *L'italiana in Algeri*

Tintin: Klow at last!
Milou: When are we going to eat?
—Hergé, *King Ottokar's Sceptre*

"*Arrive Renard en costume de religieuse.*"
Renard arrives in the costume of a nun.
—Stravinsky, *Renard*

"It's none of my business, but I think there's a brace of woodpeckers in the orchestra."
—Otis B. Driftwood in *A Night at the Opera*

"A man never gets so old that he forgets how it was being a little boy."
—Ward Cleaver in *Leave It to Beaver*

Contents

Acknowledgments

The Singing Turk is the first book that I have fully conceived, researched, and written since moving to New York and NYU in 2006, a move that also brought me a much greater involvement in the world of opera than my previous life in Boston (a life much more focused on symphony, baseball, and parking). At NYU I was from the very beginning beholden to and inspired by the brilliance, originality, and generosity of my friend Mike Beckerman, in the Music Department. He encouraged me to be brave about taking on this project involving music and gave me hugely helpful comments on several of the chapters. My colleagues in the NYU History Department have also helped me to think outside my usual comfort zone. I am grateful to Stef Geroulanos who has encouraged me to think more creatively about the history of ideas. I owe so much to Leslie Peirce who has generously offered me her guidance and insight as I have tried to find my way around Ottoman subjects about which she knows so much and I so little—and especially the subject of Suleiman and Roxelana. I thank Katy Fleming who co-taught with me a course on the eastern Mediterranean at exactly the moment when I was thinking through the Mediterranean issues of this book. I have also benefited greatly from her own analysis of the web of cultural constructions surrounding the Ottoman figure of Ali Pasha of Ioannina, himself the subject of an opera.

I have been exceptionally lucky to work in the NYU History Department under a series of chairs whose friendship and support have made it possible for me to research and write this book: many thanks to Laurie Benton, Joanna Waley-Cohen, and Barbara Weinstein. I am also hugely grateful to my associates at the NYU Center for European and Mediterranean Studies, and want to mention especially my assistant director, Mikhala Stein, with whom I am so happy to be working again, in New York as previously in Boston, and our assistant Anastasia Skoybedo, whose help was invaluable in the final stages of preparing the manuscript. My colleague Tamsin Shaw has wonderfully managed to make musical culture an important part of what we do at the Center. Jennifer Homans has helped me to think much more seriously about what it means to write about the arts, and I've been inspired by her commitment to thinking historically about ballet. I remember gratefully my late friend and brilliant colleague Tony Judt who played such a large role in bringing me to NYU and with whom I discussed this project in its early stages. Finally, I am very happy to acknowledge the support for my research and publication by the NYU Dean for the Humanities, Joy Connolly, and the NYU Center for the Humanities, directed by Jane Tylus and Uli Baer.

My first attempt to address the material in this book occurred at a conference at the Österreichische Akademie der Wissenschaften in Vienna, in 2007, on the question "*Wie europäisch ist die Oper?*" The conference was organized by Peter Stachel and Philipp Ther. I have also greatly benefited from the encouragement of the scholars at the marvelous Don Juan Archiv in Vienna, including Hans Weidinger, Michael Hüttler, Matthias Pernerstorfer, and Suna Suner; I traveled to Istanbul in 2009 to participate in one of the very stimulating Don Juan Archiv conferences on the Ottoman empire and European theater. I have learned so much from the thoughts and erudition of my colleagues in the Mozart Society of America and want to mention especially Isabelle Emerson, Ed Goehring, and Bruce Brown; Bruce very generously read a part of the manuscript. I was also very happy to have a chance in 2009 to present some of my research closer to home—uptown at Columbia—where I benefited from valuable comments and criticisms from Elaine Sisman and Walter Frisch. In 2010 I participated in the very stimulating Princeton seminar on Turquerie, organized by Alexander Bevilacqua and Helen Pfeifer. In 2014 I was honored to be able to present some of this research in Warsaw in a lecture established to commemorate the late great early modern historian Antoni Mączak. Later in 2014 I had the opportunity to present some of this work at Yale, and much appreciated the comments of Adam Tooze, Tim Snyder, and Rick Cohn. I owe a special debt of gratitude to composer Scott Wheeler, who not only helped me prepare the musical quotations for publication in this book, but also, in our discussions, has transformed and deepened my whole sense of what opera is and how it works.

I am particularly grateful for the invaluable assistance of librarians at the

Biblioteca Marciana and the Casa Goldoni in Venice; the Biblioteca Braidense in Milan; the Österreichische Nationalbibliothek in Vienna; the Houghton Library at Harvard; the New York Public Library for the Performing Arts; and the NYU Bobst Library; and in Paris at the Bibliothèque-Musée de l'Opéra at the Palais Garnier; the Bibliothèque nationale de France at the François-Mitterand site; and the Music Department of the BnF at the Richelieu-Louvois site.

While working on this project, I frequently had reason to remember important friends, teachers, and colleagues, now deceased. I have thought fondly and gratefully about my friends Tom Perry and Steve Gould; back in Boston in the 1980s and 1990s they both helped make me into a Handelian who could begin to appreciate the brilliant complexities of *Tamerlano*. I have also thought often and with deepest gratitude about my doctoral adviser at Stanford, Wayne Vucinich, who believed that every East Europeanist needed to know Ottoman history and who, subscribing to the throw-them-in-the-water approach, assigned me to lecture to his Ottoman history class in the fall of 1980 so that I could begin to learn something about the sultans and their extraordinary empire.

As so often before, I am grateful in a thousand ways to Perri Klass, who went to Istanbul with me in 1976, crossing Europe in a van with farcical company, in the spirit of *opera buffa*. Over the last forty years she has lived with so many of my odd obsessions, including the operatic ones, and so many aspects of my academic life, always in the spirit of *opera buffa*. For sure, I would have managed to achieve nothing—including this book—without her.

I am, as ever, profoundly grateful to my parents, Bob and Renee Wolff, for their love and support in everything I do, and I must thank my father above all for raising me in a house where opera was always to be heard, for taking me to the opera for the first time—to the Old Met, in 1963—and for telling me the stories of the operas, including *The Abduction from the Seraglio*, when I was a child. What a pleasure it has been for me to move to New York and to see my parents at the opera!

While working on this book, I have, as always, been greatly assisted in keeping my balance by the humorous perspective of my three children, Orlando, Josephine, and Anatol. *The Singing Turk* emerges from a family matrix in which everyone has strong feelings about music and theater and how they fit together, but nobody actually stands up and performs on stage. Over these last ten years I've enjoyed watching music and theater find their places in Orlando's and Josephine's increasingly adult lives. As for Anatol, he made the move to New York with Perri and me, and has therefore been indulgently involved in every aspect of my work on *The Singing Turk* during these years when we all became, to some degree, New Yorkers. Musical fellow that he is, he knows that when he's not around I am always singing a certain song for him.

The Singing Turk

INTRODUCTION

Operatic Representation and the Triplex Confinium

Operas on Turkish subjects were performed all over Europe in the eighteenth century. The figure of the singing Turk recurred in every decade on every stage, and constituted an enormous cultural phenomenon, with Ottoman characters and stories constantly recycled, set to new music, and presented in Turkish costumes and on Turkish stage sets. The most famous such opera was Mozart's *The Abduction from the Seraglio*, first performed in Vienna in 1782, enormously popular in German theaters in the 1780s and 1790s, and continuing to hold some place in the repertory thereafter—though never as perennially revivable as *The Marriage of Figaro*, *Don Giovanni*, or *The Magic Flute*. Much more than any of these latter masterpieces, however, Mozart's *Abduction* was purposefully composed to fit with a particular trend, by focusing on an Ottoman subject, as Mozart intended the work to be his vehicle for introducing himself to Vienna as an opera composer. Mozart's own celebrity later guaranteed the long-term survival of the *Abduction*, which therefore comes down to us as the magnificently visible tip of a vast submerged repertory that has been largely forgotten. This book will attempt to recover some of the bulk of that repertory, while exploring its relation to more general aspects of eighteenth-century culture, and considering the context of European-Ottoman international relations.

The century of Turkish subjects in European opera was a long eighteenth century, dating from the 1680s to the 1820s, a distinctive period in European-Ottoman relations from the wars of the Holy League in the 1680s, when the Habsburgs withstood the siege of Vienna and then conquered Hungary, until the Greek War of Independence in the 1820s, which produced the modern "Eastern Question" of how to regulate the ongoing territorial displacement of the Ottomans. In the mid-seventeenth century, the Ottoman empire might still have been denounced in Europe according to the rhetoric of early modern epithets—as the Enemy of God or the Infidel Scourge—consistent with the spirit of religious crusading. In the mid-nineteenth century, the European perspective on the Ottoman empire, according to the logic of the Eastern Question, had become a clinical problem of modern diplomatic pathology: the empire seen as the Sick Man of Europe.[1] Neither as the Infidel Scourge, a punishment sent by God, nor as the Sick Man of Europe, an ongoing international crisis, was the Ottoman empire particularly fit for operatic compositions. In the intervening, long eighteenth century, however, the century of the European Enlightenment, when religious prejudice was somewhat moderated, and intellectual curiosity about other cultures was greatly stimulated, the Ottoman empire inspired a balance of fear, interest, curiosity, titillation, entertainment, and even sympathy—which made it entirely suitable as a subject for European operas. At the same time it became one of the most important operatic subjects through which Europeans explored what it meant to be European.

Even as the Christian armies broke the Ottoman siege of Vienna in 1683 and began to push into Hungary, the siege itself was transformed into opera in Hamburg in 1686 with an opera about the Ottoman Grand Vizier Kara Mustafa, who was executed for his failure to take Vienna. In 1689 in Venice there was performed an opera *Il gran Tamerlano*, echoed in Hamburg in 1690 by another opera on the same subject called *Bajazeth und Tamerlan*. Both dramatized the humiliating captivity of the Ottoman sultan Bajazet at the hands of Tamerlane in the early fifteenth century, and allowed the Ottoman sultan to sing for sympathy from the operatic stage. The most celebrated treatment of this constantly composed and recomposed operatic subject was created by Handel for London in 1724 under the title *Tamerlano*, though the central dramatic figure was certainly the Ottoman sultan Bajazet. Thus, the first inklings of the recession of the Ottoman empire in the 1680s almost immediately produced in response an outburst of baroque operatic dramatization that centered on the figure of a singing Ottoman sultan.

At the other end of the long eighteenth century, as the age of Napoleon gave way to the Restoration, Rossini created a whole series of works with Turkish themes and singing Turks. *L'italiana in Algeri* was created for Venice in 1813, and Stendhal believed that "never has a people enjoyed a spectacle that better fit its character; and of all the operas that have ever existed, it is this which must have most pleased the Venetians."[2] The huge success of *L'italiana* led Rossini to compose *Il turco in Italia* for La Scala the next year, in 1814. It was, finally, Rossini's *Maometto Secondo* in Naples in 1820, revised as *Le siège de Corinthe* for Paris in 1826, which marked the culmination and conclusion of the whole Turkish tradition in European opera: a grand opera about Mehmed the Conqueror in the fifteenth century presented on the nineteenth-century stage in the decade of the Greek War of Independence. The advent of the modern Eastern Question in international relations, along with the beginning of modern Mediterranean colonialism when the French occupied Ottoman Algeria in 1830, altered the geopolitical circumstances that had made Turkish subjects so important for such a long time at the opera. In 1813 it was delightful to applaud Rossini's Italian girl as she undertook an operatic conquest of Algiers, which was represented by a painted stage set; in 1830, when the French army undertook the military conquest of Algiers, the prospect of empire was compelling, but no longer operatic.

The urban contexts of Vienna for Mozart's *Abduction* and Venice for Rossini's *L'italiana* suggest the particular importance of these two cities, which were both major operatic capitals and also the political capitals of the two states—the Habsburg monarchy and the Venetian republic—which maintained long land borders with the Ottoman empire, adjoining the Ottoman *pashalik* of Bosnia. These three polities—the Habsburg, Ottoman, and Venetian states—all met at a single point in the eighteenth century, making their frontier into the so-called Triplex Confinium, or triple border, militarized and sometimes belligerent but also permeable in peacetime and conducive to a certain intimacy among the neighboring states.[3]

Both the Venetian republic and the Habsburg monarchy were sites of some familiarity with Islamic culture, Ottoman politics, and Turkish people, and in fact the Viennese of 1683 could actually contemplate the besieging Turks at very close proximity, just outside the city walls. The perspective of Venice involved not only the long border between Venetian Dalmatia and Ottoman Bosnia but a vast commercial network of contacts across the Mediterranean, extending from the Fondaco dei Turchi in Venice to the Venetian community in the Galata quarter of Istanbul. This book will consider Vienna and Venice as particularly important operatic sites for the production of works with Ottoman subjects, while recognizing that opera in Vienna may be considered in relation to operatic production at other German courts, and opera in Venice in relation to other important Italian operatic centers such as Milan and Naples. In fact, even Handel's *Tamerlano* in London emerged from a Venetian libretto and Italian operatic tradition. At the other end of the long eighteenth century Rossini's Adriatic origin at Pesaro conditioned the final flowering of European operas with Ottoman subjects.

While Venice and Vienna, capitals of the Triplex Confinium, neighbors and enemies of the Ottomans, serve as two of the principal sites for this study, the third and contrasting focal site is Paris, a crucial capital for eighteenth-century opera but with an altogether different relation to the Ottoman world. France was an implicit ally of the sultans against the common Habsburg enemy, dating back to the sixteenth century. The French did not face the Turks in battle, and Paris, unlike Vienna, could scarcely imagine the reality of an Ottoman siege. For all these reasons Paris became the site of a more whimsical operatic relation to Turkishness: anticipated with Molière and Lully's Turkish ceremony in *Le bourgeois gentilhomme* in the age of Louis XIV. In the popular musical comedies of the Paris fairs in the early eighteenth century, there were performed such works as *Arlequin au serail* or *Arlequin sultane favorite*—with Harlequin disguising himself as a sultana to enter the harem. In 1735 Jean-Philippe Rameau created at the Paris Opéra, within the larger frame of *Les Indes galantes*, the operatic model of "Le Turc généreux" (The generous Turk) whose unexpected magnanimity toward his Christian captives would be replayed in numerous operatic scenarios, including the final scene of Mozart's *Abduction*. In a more fully farcical approach, Charles-Simon Favart's *Les trois sultanes* (The three sultanas), performed at the Comédie-Italienne in 1761, was set at the court of Suleiman the Magnificent and represented the great sultan becoming infatuated, domesticated, and ultimately civilized according to French tastes and values by a singing French sultana. The concept of the generous Turkish master and the captivating captive sultana circulated all over Europe, reflecting both in content and influence the sway of Paris as the capital of the European Enlightenment. In fact, the singing Turk on stage, like the European public in the opera house, was crucially conditioned by and susceptible to the enlightened values of the eighteenth century.

Operatic Turkishness and the
Musical Confrontation of Cultures

This is not a musicological study but rather a study in cultural and intellectual history, exploring how ideas about the Ottoman empire and representations of Turkishness took operatic form. Musicologists have long noted the
most striking musical features of operatic Turkishness, namely the adoption
of percussion instrumentation inspired by Turkish Janissary bands—cymbals, jingling bells, bass drums—and the cultivation of a musical style *alla
turca* that codified certain rhythms, intervals, and note patterns as recognizably Turkish to the ears of the European public. While the *alla turca* style
and Janissary percussion were not identical to musical performance within
the Ottoman empire, they were not entirely Orientalist inventions, musical
fantasies of Otherness. In Vienna, Turkish Janissary bands played outside the
walls of the city during the siege of 1683, but later there would be Janissary
bands present at European courts in the eighteenth century, often influencing
the musical styles of European military bands. Mozart probably had some
opportunity to hear a Janissary band and could have drawn upon his perfect
musical ear to recreate some of its aural components in the overture and
Turkish choruses of the *Abduction*, the most famous examples of European
operatic music *alla turca*. He would also, however, have been familiar with
similar passages that had already been used in operas by composers he admired, such as Gluck and Haydn.

Beyond the matters of *alla turca* style and Janissary instrumentation, this
study pays particular attention to the figure of the singing Turk and how song
became expressive of Turkishness in different operatic contexts. Voice and
range were certainly meaningful, and it is particularly notable that the singing Turk tended, over the course of the eighteenth century, to gravitate toward the deepest masculine tones of the basso register. Mozart's Osmin in the
Abduction affirms his human understanding with the words "*Ich hab' auch
Verstand*" (I also have a mind) in a musical phrase that descends to a very
low F, and the composer carefully crafted the part to suit the dramatically low
range of one particular German basso in Vienna, Ludwig Fischer. Rossini's
Turks were all performed by one particular Italian basso, Filippo Galli, in one
opera after another, so that it would be very difficult to separate the question
of vocal type from any discussion of operatic Turkishness.

Galli became a sort of Turkish specialist, singing as the Italian in Turkish disguise in *La pietra del paragone* of 1812, as the comical Mustafa, Bey of Algiers, in *L'italiana in Algeri* in 1813, as the romantic Prince Selim in *Il turco in Italia* in 1814, and finally as the charismatic historical conqueror Sultan Mehmed II in *Maometto Secondo* in 1820. The consistency of casting in these Turkish roles suggests that the operatic representation of Turkish characters was not treated altogether casually, and therefore the basso voice (for Rossini, as for Mozart) also had some dramatic Turkish significance. Handel assigned the role of Sultan Bajazet to a tenor, Francesco Borosini, who had previously, in Italy, sung the role of the same sultan in another operatic treatment of the same subject. He too was a sort of Turkish specialist, and Handel emphasized his tenor masculinity by placing him between two castrati stars, while the basso Galli, in Rossini's *Maometto Secondo*, faced a Venetian romantic rival sung in dramatic travesty by a female contralto. The musical masculinity of the operatic Turk was an essential aspect of his operatic representation.

This study will bring together diverse approaches to music, opera, and exoticism in the eighteenth century, and place them, first, in the cultural context of the Enlightenment and, second, in the international context of European-Ottoman relations. The principal concerns will be to recover the dimensions of a largely forgotten body of operas on Turkish themes, to understand the significance of the singing Turk in eighteenth-century culture, and to study the connections between opera and international relations—the singing Turk on the operatic stage and the fighting Turk as a figure in European affairs. The arguments will address the particular cultural importance of three periods of warfare. First, there was an epoch of warfare dating from the siege of Vienna and the campaigns of the Holy League in the 1680s through the treaties of Karlowitz in 1699 and Passarowitz in 1718. It was during these decades that European operas with Ottoman subjects were first created and presented. Second, the midcentury Russian-Ottoman war of 1768 to 1774, closely watched by Europeans of the Enlightenment at the moment that Franco Venturi has described as the first crisis of the ancien régime, gave an enormous stimulus to operatic production on Ottoman themes.[4] Finally, the Napoleonic wars of the early nineteenth century, dating from Napoleon's invasion of Ottoman Egypt in 1798, provided the context for the last flowering of operas on Turkish subjects.

Musicologists have pointed the way toward the historical appreciation of this operatic repertory. Particularly important are Thomas Betzwieser's study of French operas and Turkish exoticism, Bruce Brown's book on Gluck's work in Vienna, Thomas Bauman's account of Mozart's *Abduction* in the Cambridge Opera Handbooks series, and Matthew Head's study of Orientalism and Mozart's "Turkish" music.[5] Fatma Müge Göçek's account of France and the Ottoman empire in the eighteenth century, *East Encounters West*, has been exceptionally valuable for considering the cultural implications of international relations, as have been Daniel Goffman's study *The Ottoman Empire and Early Modern Europe* and Juan Cole's book *Napoleon's Egypt*.[6] Because of the importance of European captives in operas with Ottoman scenarios, the history of piracy and captivity is particularly relevant, including the recent books of Linda Colley, Robert Davis, and Molly Greene.[7] The issues of opera, politics, and society have been engaged by a set of extremely original and thoughtful works, including *Opera and Sovereignty* by Martha Feldman, *Listening in Paris* by James Johnson, *Backstage at the Revolution* by Victoria Johnson, *Napoléon et l'opéra* by David Chaillou, *Rossini in Restoration Paris* by Benjamin Walton, and *Listening to Reason* by Michael Steinberg.[8]

Because of the prominence of issues of exoticism, European opera on Turkish subjects can scarcely be discussed without reference, implicit or explicit, to the insights of Edward Said. His ideas have been especially important for this project, inasmuch as he not only produced the pioneering study of modern Orientalism, and not only created a critical approach to issues of culture and empire, but also wrote with great insight about music in all these regards. The singing Turks of the eighteenth century, however, were not simply the manifestations of fantasized, exotic Otherness, produced by imperial projects of mastery, but rather reflected a sense of intimacy, and even identity, between Turks and other Europeans, between the singing subjects and the listening public.

Martin Luther wrote of the Ottomans as "God's Scourge" (*Gottes Rute*), sent to punish Christian sinners, and sixteenth-century accounts, at the time of the first siege of Vienna in 1529, saw the Turks in apocalyptic terms as the armies of Gog and Magog.[9] In the seventeenth century a crusading Christian perspective still tended to regard the Ottoman-European encounter in binary terms—framed as a "clash of civilizations" in the phrase of Samuel Huntington. Likewise, in the nineteenth century, Turkishness came to be regarded from a perspective closer to Said's model of Orientalism, for this was the age of modern empire that Said saw as the particular condition of Orientalist thinking. During the eighteenth century, however, though the Habsburgs, Venetians, and especially the Romanovs all had designs on Ottoman territory, it was also true that the Ottomans had reciprocal ambitions. The Ottoman empire was as much an active and aggrandizing empire as it was the object of imperialist designs and annexations. While Said rightly notes the importance of the Napoleonic invasion of Ottoman Egypt in 1798 as an important turning point, it is also useful to keep in mind that that invasion was a failure, that Napoleon and the French had to retreat from Egypt, and that Napoleon ended up forming a tactical alliance with the Ottomans—the traditional French alliance—against the British.

The Ottoman empire finally became the object of consummated imperialist aggression in 1830 with the French occupation of Algeria, and one might argue that this also inaugurated the age of high Orientalism in French culture, with Eugène Delacroix arriving in 1832, right behind the occupation. This was, however, the very moment that European operas on Ottoman subjects ceased to play a major role in the repertory, just after the production of Rossini's *Le siège de Corinthe* in Paris in 1826. In other words, far from being produced as a cultural consequence of European Orientalism, these operas could no longer flourish in an age of high Orientalism, the age of European colonization of Ottoman territory, the age of the Ottoman empire as the Sick Man of Europe.

Opera and the Ottoman Aspects of European Identity

The anthropology of the Enlightenment involved an engagement with other societies that was not simply a matter of constructing a binary system of Self and Other. In fact, many writers of the Enlightenment were both deeply interested in understanding different societies and notably self-aware of their own relative cultural perspectives as shaping their observations. This was true from the very beginning of the eighteenth century, with Montesquieu's *Persian Letters* in 1721 and Swift's *Gulliver's Travels* in 1726, both foundational works of the Enlightenment and studies in the dynamics of cultural relativism.[10] The *Persian Letters* concerned the balance of difference and resemblance between Christian Europe and Muslim Persia, and served as an implicit model for later reflections on the Ottoman empire, with the qualification that Turkey, as compared to Persia, was even closer and more familiar to Europe. A large part of the Ottoman empire was actually in Europe, and much of the rest confronted Europe directly along and across the Mediterranean Sea.

In his classic historical account of the Mediterranean region in the sixteenth century, Fernand Braudel argued that the sea was divided politically between Ottoman Muslim and Habsburg Christian forces, but that its shores were united by a variety of social, economic, and cultural common factors.[11] In the eighteenth century the premise of European operas with Ottoman subjects was the very near resemblance of Europeans and Turks, so much so that one might well conclude that the Turks on the European operatic stage were intended to be taken as members of the European family. European performers became Turks on stage simply by donning an exotic costume, a turban, and sometimes a beard or moustache. The difference between Turks and Europeans was thus assumed to be fundamentally cosmetic, a matter of costumes and props, and this was often emphasized within the operas themselves with the theme of Ottoman disguises: from the Turkish ceremony of *Le bourgeois gentilhomme,* to the mock Albanians in Mozart's *Così fan tutte.* The premise of Rossini's *Maometto Secondo* illustrates the reverse procedure, since before the curtain rises the European heroine has already fallen in love with the Ottoman sultan in the successfully disguised persona of an Italian student.

The voices of the singing Turks in European operas proclaimed emotions readily recognized by Europeans, though sometimes in more extreme, passionate, or even violent forms—such that Turkishness became a vehicle for expressing the extreme passions that were, anyway, the domain of operatic drama. In the history of emotions, the long eighteenth century, from the 1680s to the 1820s, witnessed on the one hand an emphasis on emotional discipline, as suggested by Norbert Elias's account of mannerly restraint in the "civilizing process," but on the other hand the cultural articulation of emotions in a variety of styles from baroque passions, to Rousseauist sensibility, to Sturm und Drang, right up to the age of Romanticism.[12] The dynamics of emotional expression and emotional control were therefore implicit in operatic representations, comic or tragic, and the singing Turk became a prominent protagonist in this enlightened exploration of emotional development and the civilizing process.

Just as the emotional excesses of the singing Turk referred to generally European emotions, so the political implications of operas with Ottoman subjects reflected on generally acknowledged European issues: usually connected to the manifestations of power and authority, between men and women, between rulers and subjects. The political scenarios of operas about Turks—from Handel's *Tamerlano* to Rossini's *Maometto Secondo*, both presenting historical Ottoman sultans—explored the issue of "despotism," with its supposed pertinence to Oriental regimes. Lucette Valensi, however, has argued that the Venetian perspective on Ottoman government was especially relevant for articulating enlightened conceptions of despotism within a discourse on European political institutions. Joan-Pau Rubiés has likewise shown that the European attribution of despotism to the Ottomans was not merely a matter of Orientalist fantasy but was based on the empirical observations of early modern travelers and was applied to the European problem of evaluating the French monarchy following the death of Louis XIV in 1715. Rubiés emphasizes "a link between the issue of Oriental despotism and the European debate about limited versus absolute monarchies," such that representation of the Ottoman empire was always, in part, a reflection upon Europe itself.[13] Juan Cole has observed that the young Napoleon in Egypt was "playing the role of a Muslim sultan"—which thus became a sort of rehearsal for imperial rule in Europe.[14] These political issues of despotism and authority could be culturally explored through opera by giving voice to the singing Turk.

Daniel Goffman has suggested that between the late seventeenth century and early nineteenth century it is possible to speak of the European "integration" of the Ottoman empire:

> By the last decades of the seventeenth century, the Ottoman empire was as integrated into Europe as it would ever be. Earlier, it had been perceived as too much the belligerent outsider for Christendom to integrate the empire into its political, economic, and social body. Later as the "sick man of Europe" (a phrase that does suggest at least its geographic and political acceptance as a part of Europe) it was to become supposedly too weak to be taken seriously.[15]

This chronology of Ottoman integration precisely matches the age of the singing Turk in European opera. As the Ottoman empire drew closer to Europe, and vice versa, it became plausible for particular cultural representations of Turkishness to reflect upon Europe more generally.

Opera is an art form closely associated with European civilization, and for that reason the operatic perspective offers particular insight into the supposedly "civilized" view of the world in the age of Enlightenment, in the age that invented the neologism "civilisation" in French and "civilization" in English. The operatic stage may be viewed as a forum for the musically and dramatically inflected mental mapping of places and peoples located according to the geography and ethnography of European cultural consciousness. In this sense, European opera in the age of Enlightenment, from the generation of Handel to the generation of Rossini, helped to put Turkey and the Turks on the map of Europe, by setting them on the stage.

While the profusion of European operas about Ottoman subjects is immediately detectable from a study of eighteenth-century repertory, the phenomenon receives its most emphatic confirmation from the undeniable fact of its disappearance in the nineteenth century. The masterpieces of the modern operatic repertory—the works of Bellini, Donizetti, Verdi, Wagner, Gounod, Bizet, Massenet, Puccini, and Strauss—which have appeared night after night in opera houses all over the world, up until the present day, have featured Druids and Gypsies, Babylonians and Egyptians, Chinese and Japanese, but none of them include Ottoman Turks. The disappearance of the singing Turk in the nineteenth century thus further emphasizes both the importance of the phenomenon during the long eighteenth century and its historically contingent nature. This book will seek to explore and understand the particular dramatic power and musical charisma of the singing Turk during the long eighteenth century, when the palaces and harems of sultans and pashas were regularly recreated on the European operatic stage.

1

THE CAPTIVE SULTAN

Operatic Transfigurations of the
Ottoman Menace after the Siege of Vienna

Introduction: Bajazet the Tenor

In 1724, as Handel was completing his opera *Tamerlano* for performance by the Royal Academy of Music at the King's Theater in the Haymarket, the Venetian tenor Francesco Borosini arrived in London to star in the opera as Tamerlane's vanquished enemy, the Ottoman sultan Bajazet. The historical conqueror Timur, or Tamerlane, defeated and captured the historical Bajazet (Bayezid) at the battle of Ankara in 1402. He died in 1403 as Tamerlane's captive, possibly by suicide as represented in Handel's opera. This major setback for the Ottomans could only be redressed after Tamerlane's own death in 1405 during his Chinese campaign, which was followed by an Ottoman resurgence under Bajazet's son Mehmed I, his grandson Murad II, and his great-grandson Mehmed II, who conquered Constantinople in 1453.

When the tenor Borosini came to England to sing the part of Bajazet for Handel, he was probably carrying with him an operatic score by the composer Francesco Gasparini, a setting of the libretto by the poet and Venetian patrician Agostino Piovene.[1] This was basically the same libretto that Handel would use, though lightly adapted for him by Nicola Francesco Haym. Gasparini's *Tamerlano* had been performed in Venice in 1711 and was then significantly revised and revived in Reggio Emilia (near Parma) in 1719 with the prominence of the Ottoman sultan considerably enhanced and the title accordingly changed to *Il Bajazet*. The revision also allowed the sultan, very dramatically, to poison himself and die on stage. The tenor Borosini had performed the expanded part of Bajazet in Reggio Emilia in 1719, and he

Francesco Borosini was the tenor who sang the expanded role of Bajazet in Gasparini's *Il Bajazet* in Reggio Emilia in 1719, including Bajazet's death scene which may have been composed partly according to the tenor's own conception. He then traveled to London to create the role of Bajazet in Handel's *Tamerlano* in 1724. Artist unknown, Wikimedia Commons.

therefore had some stake in helping Handel to appreciate the importance of Bajazet's role.[2]

Piovene's Venetian libretto, originally for Gasparini, would be set to music by some twenty different composers all over Europe during the course of the eighteenth century, alternately titled for Tamerlano or Bajazet. It was still being recomposed for performance in Venice as *Bajazette* by Gaetano Marinelli as late as 1799, at the century's end. Piovene's libretto of 1711, however, was not even the first Venetian version of the subject, as an earlier libretto was composed and performed as *Il gran Tamerlano* at the Teatro Grimani of the church of San Giovanni e Paolo in 1689. The operatic elaborations of the history of the Ottoman sultan Bajazet thus played out over the course of more than a century in Venice.

Handel in 1724 had the opportunity to tailor the part of Bajazet to Borosini's tenor skills, as demonstrated in rehearsal, but also to study the Gasparini score in which Borosini's Turkish character had already been endowed with heroic stature. When Handel's opera opened, Borosini performed the part of a noble tragic hero, as complex as any that had ever been composed for a tenor on the operatic stage; this was all the more remarkable for the fact that the character was an Ottoman sultan, whose dynastic descendants were still widely regarded as the enemies of Christendom in the early eighteenth century. Borosini himself had to be imported from Venice, because Handel did not have a tenor in his regular company, and he wanted to create a tragic tenor role that would sound particularly striking among the rival leads, the Mongol or Tartar conqueror Tamerlano and the Greek Byzantine prince Andronico, both of them performed by castrati. The figure of Bajazet, especially as conceived for Borosini, became the earliest important incarnation of the singing Turk, and numerous composers and performers would recreate the role, making the sultan sing in captivity through most of the eighteenth century and across much of the European continent.

The Drama of Bajazet in the Seventeenth Century

Operas about Turks emerged as a European phenomenon at the very end of the seventeenth century, after the siege of Vienna. They were, however, anticipated and conditioned by earlier spoken dramas on Ottoman subjects, sometimes with incidental music, and there were even some early instances of musical cantatas for singing Turks. In the mid-seventeenth century the baroque composer Luigi Rossi composed the "Lamento di Mustafà e Bajazet," a cantata in which two Ottoman princes plead in vain for their lives as they are about to be executed by their brother the sultan, in a classic instance of Ottoman political fratricide. These princes already demonstrated the musical nobility that Gasparini and Handel would invest in the tragic figure of Sultan Bajazet in *Tamerlano*. Rossi, who received his musical training in Naples and worked principally in Rome, came originally from Torremaggiore in Apulia, on the Adriatic Sea, looking toward the Ottoman empire. In 1656 there was performed in London, under Cromwell's Protectorate, an opera on *The Siege of Rhodes*, based on the historical siege by Suleiman the Magnificent in 1522. Jointly composed by several English composers to a libretto by William Davenant, and including Suleiman himself among the singing parts, *The Siege of Rhodes* was probably the very first British opera—though its music has not survived.[3] In France in 1670 Molière's *Le bourgeois gentilhomme* was performed for Louis XIV; its exotic Turkish disguises, mock-Turkish ceremonies, and pseudo-Turkish phrases were employed to make a fool out of the titular bourgeois gentleman while also entertaining the king. The work as a whole was classified as a *comédie-ballet*, and was accompanied with music by Lully, including the musical composition of the Turkish scene.[4]

The Ottoman sultan Bajazet in particular emerged as an important dramatic subject as early as the sixteenth century. Christopher Marlowe's *Tamburlaine* came to the Elizabethan stage in the 1580s, with Bajazet presented as a tyrant no less arrogant than Tamerlane himself. Before the great battle, the Ottoman sultan addresses his pashas and Janissaries, and promises not only to defeat Tamerlane but to castrate and humiliate him:

> BAJAZET: By Mahomet my kinsman's sepulchre,
>   And by the holy Alcoran I swear,
>   He shall be made a chaste and lustless eunuch,
>   And in my sarell [seraglio] tend my concubines . . .[5]

It is, however, Tamerlane who wins the battle of arms. He takes Bajazet captive and, according to the conventional tale, imprisons him in a cage. Marlowe's Tamerlane already imagines Bajazet singing like a caged bird: "If thou wilt have a song, the Turk shall strain his voice."[6] Bajazet, however, defiantly commits suicide by battering his skull against the bars of the cage—on stage.

This presentation of Bajazet in Elizabethan drama in the 1580s followed the first major European defeat of the Ottomans in the naval battle of Lepanto in 1571. In the 1590s Shakespeare, in *Henry IV, Part 2*, had Prince Hal, upon his succession, reassure his brothers:

> Brothers, you mix your sadness with some fear:
> This is the English, not the Turkish court;
> Not Amurath an Amurath succeeds,
> But Harry Harry.[7]

Shakespeare meant that Prince Hal would not barbarously put his brothers to death, as a newly enthroned Ottoman sultan might have done.

Marlowe's Bajazet was as much a barbarian as Tamerlane, and it was not until a century later that French classical drama, in the age of Louis XIV, began to rethink the relation between these two figures, and to reconsider their respective political qualities. Racine's *Bajazet* of 1672 concerned a completely different Bajazet, an executed Ottoman prince of the seventeenth century who fell victim to romantic jealousy and political feuding within the sultan's family and household. The crucial work for provoking operatic interest in the

Ottomans was that of Racine's less successful rival Jacques Pradon, author of the drama *Tamerlan, ou la mort de Bajazet* in 1676. Pradon believed his play's lack of success was due to a hostile cabal manipulated by Racine.

In a preface to the play, Pradon clearly stated that he did not intend for Tamerlane to be a mere exemplar of barbarism: "I have made a gentleman [*honnête homme*] of Tamerlane, contrary to the opinions of some people who would have him be completely brutal." Tamerlane is therefore capable of looking upon Bajazet in captivity with "a pitying gaze" (*un regard pitoyable*)—which might also have conditioned the response of the audience.[8] The representation of his humiliations rendered the sultan sympathetic: In Vienna, also in the 1670s, a set of Flemish tapestries on the theme of Bajazet and Tamerlane was ordered from Antwerp for St. Stephen's Cathedral, including a tapestry of Bajazet in his cage and another of Tamerlane using the sultan as a stool for mounting a horse.[9]

The problem of Pradon's play is Bajazet's sense of his own profound superiority, which leads to his furious defiance and open contempt for Tamerlane, and the utter rejection of the conqueror's pity. Bajazet, who rhymes "Tartare" with "barbare" in French couplets, insults Tamerlane to his face, as if trying to provoke him to appear openly as a barbarian. It is Tamerlane who ends up speaking with the voice of reason and moderation:

> TAMERLANE: Bajazet, modérez cette rage inutile.
> Devant moi reprenez une âme plus tranquille.
>
> Bajazet, moderate this useless rage.
> Before me recover a more tranquil spirit.[10]

Yet over the course of the opera, Bajazet achieves a stoical resolve and, finally committing suicide, he welcomes his own death:

> BAJAZET: Je sens déjà la mort & secourable & prompte,
> Qui m'enlève à la vie, & m'arrache à la honte.
>
> I already feel death, helpful and prompt,
> Which takes me from life and removes me from shame.[11]

This tragic and stoical death already suggested the kind of hero Bajazet would become on the operatic stages of the eighteenth century.

English drama returned to Tamerlane more than a century after Marlowe, when Nicholas Rowe presented his play *Tamerlane* in 1701, just two years after the peace of Karlowitz—but also the same year as the outbreak of the War of the Spanish Succession. The play's huge success and constant revival was in fact conditioned by the British war against Louis XIV over the course of the following decade, as the drama became ever more detached from the Ottoman setback that probably conditioned its initial presentation. For Rowe's characterization of a noble Tamerlane and an impossibly arrogant Bajazet reflected both a very negative view of the Ottoman sultan and, as was generally supposed, a literary conflation of Bajazet with the French king Louis XIV, Britain's long-standing enemy. A hostile British publication of 1690 made the Turkishness of the French monarch more explicit: *The Most Christian Turk; or, A view of the life and bloody reign of Lewis XIV.*[12]

In Rowe's dramatic conception, Bajazet was a tyrant dedicated to war and destruction, while Tamerlane, fundamentally a man of peace, was hailed for having discovered "a nobler way to empire," becoming "Lord of the willing world." That nobler way to empire was supposed to suggest a British way to empire, contrasting with French aggression and militarism, and Rowe's Tamerlane was taken by contemporary audiences as the effigy of the British king William III, hero of the Glorious Revolution, who died in 1702. The play thus became a kind of royal commemoration. It was regularly revived on November 4, for King William's birthday, and on November 5, the anniversary of William's arrival in England in 1688.[13] Tamerlane's victory over Bajazet at the battle of Ankara takes place in the interval between Rowe's first and second acts, which begins with a "Symphony of Warlike Music," according to the stage direction. Even outside the operatic genre the encounter seemed to call for some sort of musical accompaniment.

The Ottoman sultan is indicted in Rowe's drama for making war and practicing political tyranny, but Tamerlane also diagnoses and denounces Bajazet's overweening pride:

> Thou vain, rash thing,
> That, with gigantic insolence, hast dar'd
> To lift thy wretched self above the stars . . .[14]

All dramatic and operatic representations of Bajazet would acknowledge his pride, and even in Rowe's very negative conception it was impossible to deny absolutely the sultan's dignity. When Bajazet laments his "loss of sacred honour, the radiancy of majesty eclips'd," there is some echo of Shakespeare's Richard II, with the righteous Tamerlane now looking something like the usurper Bolingbroke. Bajazet in captivity affirms that "death shall free me at once from infamy," but Rowe did not permit him the noble suicide on stage that Handel later composed.[15] Rowe's drama ended instead with Bajazet finally exhausting Tamerlane's goodhearted indulgence and being condemned to a humiliating confinement in the legendary cage.

Pradon's Bajazet of 1676 was not yet unequivocally the tragic hero of the drama, and Rowe's Bajazet of 1701 was far from admirable, but the Ottoman sultan would acquire a more noble character in Piovene's libretto for Gasparini. The conditioning factor of this metamorphosis was decades of warfare, which definitively transformed the Ottoman sultanate from a fearful power in Europe, still aiming to extend its borders at the expense of Christian European states, to a defeated political force capable of arousing in the European public some of the same pity that Tamerlane was supposed to be feeling for Bajazet in Pradon's drama. When the Ottomans were beaten outside Vienna on September 12, 1683, by an army of Christian allies under the supreme command of Polish king Jan Sobieski, there began a whole generation of aggressive Habsburg, Polish, and Venetian wars against the Turks, ending with the peace settlements of Karlowitz in 1699 and Passarowitz in 1718.

The Siege of Vienna and the Captivity of Bajazet

The breaking of the Turkish siege of Vienna in September 1683 was celebrated all over Catholic Europe, and there were fireworks and illuminations in Rome, Madrid, and Bologna, while in Ferrara the Sultan Mehmed IV and the Grand Vizier Kara Mustafa were festively hanged in effigy.[16] In Habsburg Madrid there was a theatrical piece performed in December 1683 with allegorical figures of Fame and Music celebrating the Habsburg dynasty, and by December 1684 the Jesuit College in Vienna presented a drama with music about the reconquest of Spain from the Moors in 1492, thus heralding the reconquest of southeastern Europe from the Ottomans.[17] In 1684 Pope Innocent XI decreed that September 12, the day of the Ottoman defeat and the name day of the Virgin Mary, should always be celebrated on the Catholic calendar throughout Europe. Kara Mustafa became the subject of a popular entertainment at Hernals, near Vienna, where there was established an annual reenactment of a donkey ride representing his humiliating retreat from Vienna, a sort of charivari in which the Grand Vizier was mockingly serenaded with an Austrian imitation of Janissary music in the Turkish style.[18]

Kara Mustafa at the siege of Vienna became an operatic subject in Hamburg in 1686, only three years after the conclusion of the siege. The composer was Johann Wolfgang Franck, the librettist was Lukas von Bostel (later the mayor of Hamburg), and the opera was conceived in two parts: "Der glückliche Gross-Vezier Cara Mustapha" and then, on another night, "Der unglückliche Cara Mustapha." The vizier is "fortunate" (*glücklich*) only up until the failure of the siege, and then "unfortunate" (*unglücklich*) as he is promptly executed. The first part of the opera covers the "gruesome siege" of Vienna, while the second part dramatizes the "joyous relief" of the city.[19] Thus, the Ottoman military assault on Vienna was almost immediately reenacted as operatic entertainment in Hamburg, with the Turkish commander as the titular protagonist. Interestingly, the opera has the Turkish Janissaries themselves singing a chorus of celebration when the "tyrant" Kara Mustafa is executed, so that the Turks as well as the Viennese are shown to be liberated by the outcome of the siege and of the opera:

| So endet sich Trübsahl und Noth: | So ends distress and need: |
| Mustapha, der Bluthund ist todt! | Mustafa the bloodhound is dead![20] |

The research of Andrea Sommer-Mathis suggests that the opera was an "extraordinarily great stage success" in Hamburg, not only for its timely staging of the recent crisis but perhaps especially on account of its spectacular theatrical settings of the siege.[21] A related musical work was performed in Venice in 1686 at the theater of San Moisè. The Venetian title compared Kara Mustafa to the excessively powerful Roman officer Sejanus who was executed by Emperor Tiberius: *Il Seiano moderno della Tracia overo La caduta dell'ultimo Gran-Visir* (The modern Sejanus of Thrace; or, the fall of the recent Grand Vizier).[22]

The first prominent operatic treatment of Tamerlane and Bajazet was *Il gran Tamerlano*, performed in Venice in 1689—six years after the siege, in the period of ongoing warfare which included Venice as one of the belligerent allies of the Holy League against the Ottomans. The text was by Giulio Cesare Corradi, the music by Marc'Antonio Ziani, and the dances were advertised as including "Turkish instruments," thus promising Ottoman authenticity. The opera was dedicated to Ferdinando, Grand Prince of Tuscany, whose father, the reigning Grand Duke Cosimo III de' Medici, had sent assistance to Vienna during the Ottoman siege in 1683.

Ferdinando was a major collector of paintings and patron of musicians, instrument makers, and composers—including the young Handel in Italy. Ferdinando's patronage clearly extended beyond Florence to Venice, and he was supposed to have contracted syphilis at the Venetian Carnival. The year of *Il gran Tamerlano*, 1689, was also the year of Ferdinando's marriage to a Bavarian Wittelsbach princess, though the prince was also known to have been romantically involved with a series of castrati opera singers, principally the artists known as Petrillo and Cecchino.[23]

Corradi's dedication of *Il gran Tamerlano* sought to establish the "representation of the ruin of Baiazette under the victorious scimitar of Tamerlano" as an operatic endeavor particularly fitting for a Medici prince: "the former [Bajazet] could not better console himself for his misfortunes than by having recourse to the magnanimous protection of Your Serene Highness, nor the latter [Tamerlane] better increase the glory of his triumphs than by crowning them with your most fortunate name." Ferdinando was an artistically important patron but not a major political force—he would die from syphilis before he could succeed his father as Grand Duke of Tuscany—so it was ingratiatingly hyperbolic for Corradi to place the prince in political alignment with such titanic historical rulers as Tamerlane and Bajazet: "I know of no more noble way to renew the memory [*rinnovare la memoria*] of two great monarchs if not by stirring the ashes of oblivion beneath the auspices of a great prince." Within a generation Tamerlane and Bajazet would become such celebrated subjects of European opera that there would be no need to apologize for their historical obscurity, but in 1689 Corradi could still flatter Ferdinando that nothing was grander than the glory of the Medici family: "Therefore it is no wonder that even from the tombs of Tartary the crowned shades of Baiazette and Tamerlano come to seek protection, and are sure of receiving it at a time when the most happy marriage of Your Serene Highness brings the dispensation of favors with a generous hand."[24] The marriage would be childless, but the joining of Tamerlane and Bajazet in music and drama would produce numerous operatic progeny.

In spite of the Florentine patronage of Grand Prince Ferdinando, the production of 1689 was performed for the Venetian public at the Teatro Grimani. Though Tamerlano gave his name to the opera, the introductory statement of the "Argomento" presented Bajazet to the Venetian public as the principal subject of interest:

> The world has never seen a greater spectacle than that of Baiazette. Great
> monarch, base servant. Great soldier, base slave. Defeated in battle by
> Tamerlano he was subject to the constant mockery of the conqueror, even to
> becoming his footstool, an entertainment on view [*trastullo al guardo*] . . . He
> was enclosed in a cage of iron.[25]

Bajazet was the object of fascination because of the disparity between his
former power and his ensuing humiliation. In 1689 the "Argomento" that advertised Bajazet as an "entertainment" surely reflected the military campaigns
of the 1680s: the Ottomans had been driven back from the siege of Vienna
in 1683, and then put to flight and driven out of Hungary by the Habsburg
imperial forces.

Venice had also had great victories against the Turks during this decade,
enjoying a military comeback after the Turks had taken Crete from the Venetians as recently as 1669. In the 1680s, with Francesco Morosini commanding
the Venetian army, the Greek Peloponnesus or Morea was completely conquered, with Corinth falling in 1687 and even Athens—though only briefly and at great cost, since it was at this time that Venetian shelling brought
about the explosion that partly destroyed the Parthenon. Some of this territory would be regained by the Ottomans at the peace of Karlowitz in 1699, and
the whole Peloponnesus would revert to Turkish rule at the peace of Passarowitz in 1718. In 1689, however, the Venetians, with Morosini now the doge,
would have had good reason to believe that they had humiliated the Turks in
Greece and reversed the imbalance of centuries. The operatic presentation of
Bajazet—formerly a great monarch, now ignominiously humbled—would
have seemed entirely relevant to the current events of the day. The probably
apocryphal iron cage (which would disappear in Piovene's later libretto) in
some sense suggested the operatic stage on which Bajazet was held up as an
"entertainment on view" for the Venetian public.

Accordingly, the curtain rose in 1689 upon the figure of Bajazet sleeping
on the ground among the other slaves of Tamerlane. He wakes and sings the
lament of his captivity in hyperbolic baroque phrases:

Fin che haurò pupilla in fronte	As long as I have eyes in my face
Sarò visto a lacrimar:	I will be seen crying:
Sian pur vasti e vasti i Fiumi,	However vast the rivers may be,
Da miei lumi	From my eyes
Ha maggior tributo il Mar.[26]	The sea has a greater tributary.

From the beginning the Ottoman sultan is the central "spectacle" of the opera, and the climactic scene shows him committing suicide by banging his head on the iron bars of his cage. According to one of the conventions of baroque opera, *Il gran Tamerlano* includes a comical servant, Ali, who witnesses Bajazet's suicide and appropriately exclaims, "*Povero Baiazette!*" Ali resolves to make a pilgrimage to Mecca, but only after fortifying himself with a forbidden glass of wine and singing a cheerful aria to celebrate the vintage: "*O che dolce liquor.*" As an additional comical and musical element the dramatis personae specified clowns (*buffoni*) with Turkish instruments.[27] While later libretti, and especially Piovene's, would frame the operatic drama with greater clarity and power, worthy of Handel's genius in 1724, *Il gran Tamerlano* of 1689 introduced Bajazet to the operatic stage at precisely the moment when European-Ottoman relations made his story most compelling. From its opening scene the opera suggested that the Ottoman sultan's reversal of fortune could be most powerfully expressed if he sang of his tragic captivity.

By 1690, the following year, there was already an opera entitled *Bajazeth und Tamerlan* being performed in Hamburg, with music by Johann Philipp

Bajazeth und Tamerlan, was presented as a Singspiel in Hamburg in 1690, only seven years after the Ottoman siege of Vienna, with music by Johann Philipp Förtsch. In Venice there was an opera on this subject just one year earlier in 1689, *Il gran Tamerlano*. With kind permission of the Österreichische Nationalbibliothek.

Förtsch and libretto by Christian Heinrich Postel, probably based on Corradi's Venice libretto. It was performed at the Hamburg Opera "am Gänsemarkt," the goose market, with tickets available to the urban public, rather than in a closed and courtly context. Hamburg, like Venice, was an urban republic, though as a Hanseatic city it was oriented toward the Baltic, remote from the Ottoman empire. The work was characterized as a Singspiel, with spoken dialogue and musical numbers, and the preface, addressed to the reader and therefore the theatrical public, acclaimed the story of Bajazet and Tamerlane as "one of the most famous histories in the world"— but presented only quite recently (*gar neulich*) as an operatic subject. The public was offered a bit of Ottoman erudition in the form of Bajazet's Ottoman epithet Yildirim (rendered here as Gilderum), meaning thunderbolt, because he was "so heated and quick in all things." While in Corradi's libretto for Venice Tamerlane humiliated Bajazet's wife by having her stripped almost naked to serve him, the Hamburg libretto by Postel more judiciously supposed that Tamerlane meant to honor her according to Tartar custom by allowing her to serve him.[28] Here too, as in Pradon, the source of the tragedy lay not so much in Tamerlane's barbarism as in Bajazet's "heated" temper and obstinate pride.

To better emphasize Bajazet's reversal of fortune, the librettist Postel made the unusual decision—differing from Pradon and Corradi—to begin the opera before the battle of Ankara, and thus to represent Bajazet before his downfall. In the opening scene a chorus of Turkish soldiers sings their enthusiasm for battle and confidence in Bajazet's military leadership:

Unendliches Glück	Endless fortune
Begleite des blitzenden	Accompany the flashing
Gilderums Waffen	Thunderbolt's weapons
Ihm Sieg zu verschaffen . . .	To bring him victory . . .[29]

Bajazet Gilderum responds in kind with an aria rousing his army to fight for victory against Tamerlane. Postel the librettist rhymed *Blut* (blood) and *Wuth* (fury), so that Förtsch the composer could give operatic expression to Bajazet's extreme emotion:

Eifer entzünde dich!
Raset und tobet ihr zorniger Geister.
Flammet ihr blitzenden Augen von Wuth.
Strebe du lechzende Seele nach Blut.

Zeal, catch fire!
Rage and storm, you angry spirits.
Flame with fury, you flashing eyes.
Strive for blood, you thirsty soul.[30]

Bajazet's wife, however, here Hellenized under the name of Despina, is already wary of his temper and pride, and they sing a duet about fortune:

BAJAZET: Die Tapfern erhebet.	It raises up the brave.
DESPINA: Die Trotzigen fället.	It strikes down the defiant.
BAJAZET: Die Mutigen stärket.	It strengthens the bold.
DESPINA: Die Stolzen zerschellet.	It smashes the proud.[31]

Such pointed demonstration of the moral lesson of Bajazet's pride, his absence of humility, may perhaps be understood in the context of Protestant Hamburg, for the librettist Postel was the son of a Protestant minister, probably familiar with the spirit of sermonizing. Still there was a place in the libretto and score for a comical Muslim servant, Hassan, scolded by his wife for his drinking.[32]

By the opening of the second act, the battle has been fought, and Bajazet is in his cage—from which he intemperately denounces Tamerlane as a *Bluthund* (bloodhound). The plot, however, maintains a strong comic aspect, with Bajazet's daughter disguised as a young man, "Murat," and Tamerlane's son in female clothes disguised as Despina's servant, "Iris." In the third act, Bajazet batters himself to death on the bars of his cage, and then, incongruously, the young people step out of their disguises to marry each other and seal the peace between Turks and Tartars. The happy ending was dedicated to "Amor." Bajazet's death scene, however, already showed some signs of the musical and dramatic innovation that would become so prominent in Gasparini's and Handel's treatments. Bajazet recites a monologue of rage and humiliation, while "the instruments begin to play sad music," thus emotionally mingling the sultan's rage with the pathos of his situation.[33]

Operatic interest in the Ottoman sultans was further developed in 1696, in Hamburg, with an opera on the subject of Mehmed the Conqueror, titled *Mahumeth II*, composed by Reinhard Keiser, dramatizing the Turkish conquest of Greece in the fifteenth century. Mehmed, as the conqueror of Constantinople in 1453, had traumatized Renaissance Europe, and it perhaps appeared fitting to revisit his conquests at the opera in the 1690s at a time when the Venetian armies had retaken the Greek Peloponnesus. In *Mahumeth II* the sultan appears as a frustrated lover, in love with the daughter of a Venetian official (as in Rossini's *Maometto Secondo* of 1820), but in the end Mehmed is compelled to kill the woman he loves in order to satisfy the bloodthirsty Janissaries.[34] The subject of Mehmed the Conqueror was a problematic one that European opera would not take up again for a very long time; his celebrated triumphs hardly fit the spirit of the late seventeenth century as neatly as the humiliations of Bajazet.

Bajazet in Chains and Europe Unafraid

The treaty of Karlowitz was signed on January 26, 1699, and almost immediately afterward, at Carnival in Bologna, the priests of the Somaschi Order sponsored a performance of a tragedy titled *Tamerlano* at the Accademia degli Ardenti. Though it may not have been fully operatic, it included music and dance, specified as ballet, minuet, and chaconne, which taken in the spirit of Carnival suggested that the tragedy was also some sort of cheerful celebration.[35] The subject of Tamerlano and Bajazet thus continued to receive musical attention in Italy, and particularly the interest of Grand Prince Ferdinando de' Medici. In 1689 he had generously helped to fund the creation of *Il gran Tamerlano* for the Venetian public, and in 1706 he sponsored a new version for his own theater, for his villa at Pratolino outside Florence. This time the composer was Alessandro Scarlatti (the father of Domenico), born in Palermo, who spent much of his career composing operas and cantatas in Naples and Rome but was also favored by Ferdinando. The libretto by Antonio Salvi, clearly based on Pradon, showed great sympathy for Bajazet, whose part was sung by one of the regular members of Ferdinando's company, Giuseppe Canavese, a tenor. So already in 1706 the role belonged to a tenor voice, and would continue to remain tenorial for Gasparini and Handel. Canavese was criticized by one contemporary for a lack of subtlety in his singing, a lack of naturalness in his acting (favoring "attitudes of academic painting, with forced gestures, with a frown and a stern face"), and a voice of variable beauty, but he was considered to have "great success, particularly in dramatic roles."[36] Canavese performed at Pratolino from 1684 to 1707, so the role of Bajazet came late in his career, a kind of dramatic culmination.

In the second act Bajazet is brought out of his cage and taken before Tamerlane, so that the Turk might sing his humiliation and his defiance before his captor:

Vieni, o Tiranno, e della mia sventura
Trionfa, esulta, e godi . . .

Come, oh tyrant, and over my misfortune,
Triumph, exult, and enjoy . . .[37]

It was as if Bajazet were singing not only to Tamerlane but, across the fourth wall, to the audience at Pratolino, inviting them to triumph, exult, and enjoy the spectacle of the Ottoman disaster at this particular moment in European-Ottoman relations. The humiliation of Bajazet in 1403 might have seemed almost contemporary in 1703 with the dethronement and death of Mustafa II by the Janissaries following the disastrous treaty of Karlowitz.

In Scarlatti's opera of 1706 Bajazet scorns the "base cage" (*indegna gabbia*) in which Tamerlane keeps him, and perhaps as well the entire operatic framework that made his captivity into a musical entertainment. He sings out that he will "never be broken or conquered by you" (*da te domato o vinto*), meaning Tamerlane of course—but his defiance surely also addressed the European audience, and spoke to some ongoing European anxiety about the Ottoman empire.[38] Grand Prince Ferdinando seems to have been uncertain about how to respond to the opera, and wrote to Scarlatti asking that the music be made "more easy and noble in style," and, furthermore, "if in such places as is permissible, you will make it rather more cheerful."[39] Such a reaction testifies to the tragic intensity of Scarlatti's treatment of the subject.

Though Scarlatti's Tamerlane comments on his captive's "haughty pride" and urges the sultan to control himself—"*modera la tua rabbia*" (moderate your rage)—Bajazet remains emotionally immoderate, denouncing Tamerlane as "obscure of birth" and "barbarous of nation."[40] This irrepressible contempt for Tamerlane, present in Pradon and preserved in Salvi and Scarlatti as an aspect of the sultan's outraged arrogance, would become in Piovene's libretto and notably in Handel's opera the basis for a fully developed and thoroughly dignified representation of Ottoman pride. That pride could be more easily acknowledged, and enjoyed, by Europeans when it occurred in the operatic context of Bajazet's captivity and the contemporary international context of Ottoman defeat.

Gasparini's *Tamerlano* of 1711 in Venice signaled a newly sympathetic treatment of Bajazet, but that spirit of sympathy for the Ottomans was not unanimously adopted by European composers across the continent. In Weimar in 1713 Johann Sebastian Bach composed a cantata (BWV 18) that included a line of traditional Lutheran animus, asking God for protection against the "horrible murder and blasphemy, fury and rage of Turks and Papists" (*des Türken und des Papsts grausamen Mord und Lästerungen, Wüten und Toben*).[41] These lines were intoned by the boy soprano and then endorsed by the chorus, the text echoing Luther's litany of the early sixteenth century from the time of Suleiman the Magnificent and the first siege of Vienna in 1529. While the Ottomans were becoming less fearsome at the very moment that Bach composed his cantata, the traditional reference to Turkish fury and rage would persist as an emotional key to operas about Turks, including the case of the raging Bajazet.

In Rome in 1717, the year that Prince Eugene of Savoy conquered the Ottoman fortress at Belgrade for the Habsburgs, there was performed at the Collegio Romano of the Jesuits an operatic piece by Gasparini entitled *Intermezzi in derisione della setta maomettana* (Intermezzi in derision of the Mohammedan sect). Such musical derision of Islam was consistent with the triumphalist sentiment of Rome but notably contrasted with Gasparini's deeply sympathetic operatic treatment of Bajazet in defeat. In 1717, also in Rome, a cantata was performed celebrating "The Present Victories achieved by Imperial Arms against the Turk," dedicated to Count Jan Vaclav Gallas, the Habsburg ambassador in Rome, with text by Ignazio di Bonis and music by Giuseppe Amadori who generally specialized in sacred compositions.[42] There were only two singing "characters" in this cantata, Fama (Fame) and Tebro (the Tiber), neither of them sacred. The dialogue between them involves Tebro asking Fama for the reassuring news that the Turks really have been defeated:

Dell'Asia il fier Tiranno,	The proud tyrant of Asia,
Dimmi, ch'è in ceppi avvinto,	Tell me that he is in chains,
Dimmi, ch'Eugenio ha vinto.	Tell me Eugene is victorious.[43]

This was a musical celebration of Prince Eugene at Belgrade, victorious over the Turks, with the contemporary cantata echoing the historical operas of Scarlatti and Gasparini, which had already dramatized Bajazet in chains. Handel would soon follow their example: "*Son tra ceppi, e m'insulta il mio ne-*

mico" (I am in chains, and my enemy insults me), declared Handel's Bajazet.[44] In Rome in 1717 there was also performed an opera by Gasparini entitled *Il Trace in catena* (The Thracian in chains) at the Teatro Capranica, near the Pantheon. The librettist was Antonio Salvi, and the libretto was roughly the same that Alessandro Scarlatti had composed in 1706 in Florence as *Il gran Tamerlano*. In other words, the eponymous Thracian in chains was none other than the Ottoman sultan Bajazet in another treatment by Gasparini.[45]

In the Roman cantata of 1717 Fama confirms the happy report of victory against the Turks, and praises both Prince Eugene and the Habsburg emperor Charles VI, before asking Tebro a question:

Temesti o Tebro? e come	Were you afraid, Oh Tiber? and how
Puoi dar luogo al timor . . .	Can you give way to fear . . .[46]

While the ideology of the cantata celebrated Habsburg victory, its emotional content concerned the reassurance of long-standing European fears about the Turks. After the recent wars it was possible for Europe to stop being afraid of Ottoman advances and look forward to a future of Ottoman retreats. This suspension of fear was precisely the cultural condition for the sudden appearance of Turkish subjects on the European operatic stage. "*Austria vinse, Asia piange, e il mondo gode,*" announces Fama (Austria is victorious, Asia weeps, and the world enjoys). The world here could also be construed as the emerging European public, both readers of the gazettes and *avvisi* (the Italian reports) and the audiences in the theater and at the opera. Tebro salutes the Habsburg emperor who by defeating the Turks is bringing peace to the whole universe:

Per lui respira	For him breathes
Italia bella,	Beautiful Italy
Ne più sospira	And no more sighs
Per lo timor.	For fear.[47]

With the passing of the age of fear, an age that dated back to the fifteenth century when an Ottoman army did actually invade the Italian peninsula at Otranto, Italians no longer needed to feel a real terror of the Turks, and following the reassuring message of the cantata, Italian opera was about to inaugurate an age of Turkish figures on the European operatic stage.

Ottoman Suicide on Stage:
Piovene, Gasparini, Borosini, and Handel

Agostino Piovene's libretto, using Pradon's characters and basic dramatic scenario, was published with a date of 1710 according to the Venetian calendar (which, eccentrically, began the year in March), but was actually performed in early 1711, set to music by Francesco Gasparini for the Teatro Tron of San Cassiano. The role of the Ottoman sultan Bajazet was performed by the Genoese tenor Giovanni Paita, sometimes called the Orpheus of Liguria, who was making a career for himself in Venice.[48] In Vienna in 1711 a giant bell was consecrated—the Pummerin—cast from captured Turkish siege cannons for the tower of St. Stephen's cathedral, so that the Habsburg victory of 1683 continued to be commemorated in musical form whenever the bell was rung. The year 1711 was in fact one of modest resurgence for the Ottomans, as they defeated the Russian army of Peter the Great on the Pruth River in Moldavia and improved their position on the Black Sea.

In the immediately following years, operas with the title *Tamerlano*, probably based on Piovene's libretto with Gasparini's music, were staged in Verona (1715), Florence (1716), and Ancona and Livorno (1719).[49] Clearly, this was a popular subject during the years of Venetian and Habsburg war against the Ottomans, from 1714 to 1718, ending with the peace of Passarowitz. With the coming of that peace, however, Venice embarked upon a policy of international neutrality which ultimately meant that the republic would never go to war against the Ottomans again. It was in the pacific context of this long-term Venetian neutrality, beginning after Passarowitz, that a fully sympathetic interest in Turkishness—even a fashionable interest, what historian Paolo Preto has called Turcheria—could develop and thrive.[50] The recreation of Gasparini's *Tamerlano* as *Il Bajazet* in 1719 might thus be taken as one signal of the inauguration of this new era.

Gasparini not only retitled but very substantially revised his opera for Reggio Emilia in 1719, with the tenor Francesco Borosini singing as the now eponymous Ottoman sultan in *Il Bajazet*, performing a new and dramatic death scene. The work returned to Venice in 1723 as *Bajazette*, with Giovanni Paita again—while Borosini would go to England to work with Handel in 1724.[51] By the convention that dated back at least as far as Canavese's perfor-

Bajazette was performed in Venice in 1723 at the important Venetian festival of the Ascension. The production was dedicated to Prince Joseph von Hessen-Darmstadt, later Bishop of Augsburg. The Gasparini score set to the Piovene libretto was used, and the tenor in the role of the Ottoman sultan was Giovanni Paita, who originally sang the role in Venice in 1711—when the opera was called *Tamerlano*. With kind permission of the German Historical Institute in Rome, Department of Music History.

mance at Pratolino in 1706, Borosini had every reason to feel confident that Handel needed a tenor like himself for the role.

Later in the 1720s Borosini, still holding on to the Gasparini score of 1719, presented it to a German duke, and it is preserved today in Meiningen. A page was attached to the score noting that Piovene wrote the libretto, "except for the last scene that was composed by Zanella according to the idea of Signore Borosini."[52] The poet Ippolito Zanella thus extended Piovene's work, presumably writing Bajazet's climactic death scene, but the note suggests that it was Borosini himself who conceived of that scene in Reggio Emilia, just as it was probably Borosini who persuaded Handel that such a scene was essential for London.

Handel completed a first version of *Tamerlano* in July 1724 (never performed), before Borosini arrived in England with the 1719 score; the composer then prepared another version in October which was performed at the premiere on October 31. The biggest difference between the two Handel versions (reflecting the difference between the two Gasparini treatments of 1711 and 1719) was the expansion and highlighting of the part of Bajazet, the composition of a death scene on stage as the dramatic high point of the last act, and the tailoring of the part to the specific vocal range and dramatic talent of Borosini. Musicologist C. Steven LaRue, studying the two versions, has concluded that Handel must have had another singer originally in mind for the part, probably the Scottish tenor Alexander Gordon, with a higher vocal range than Borosini, but that the part was then lowered, expanded, featured, and dramatized for Borosini, to make him the star of the show. His range extended over two tenor octaves, and both Gasparini and Handel had him leaping vocally across that range—as if to demonstrate the precipitous peaks and descents of political fortune.[53]

The Piovene libretto, adapted for Reggio Emilia in 1719, was further adapted in London by Nicola Francesco Haym who collaborated with Handel in 1724. The foundation of the whole work, however, was the original Piovene libretto, which also became the basis for operas about Tamerlane and Bajazet all over Europe in the decades to follow. There were more than twenty different musical settings, and Piovene's libretto long outlived Piovene himself (who probably died in the 1720s). These operas regularly recurred in Venice over the course of the whole century. The 1723 Gasparini *Bajazette* was performed for the festival of the Ascension that marked Venice's legendary wedding with the Adriatic Sea—as was the 1765 *Tamerlano* with music by Pietro

Guglielmi and an impressive wardrobe of 104 costumes. In 1799 the Piovene libretto, having outlived the Republic of Venice, was set to music once again by the Neapolitan composer Gaetano Marinelli, and performed as *Bajazette* in Venice at the Teatro San Benedetto.[54]

The extraordinary operatic resilience of this historical encounter—between Tamerlane and Bajazet, especially as formulated in Piovene's libretto—made the tragic Ottoman hero into one of the pillars of eighteenth-century opera in Europe. Already at the beginning of the century Piovene provided a preface to the libretto suggesting that the story would be altogether familiar to operagoers, and explaining that his treatment sought to strip away the sensational and apocryphal details:

> So well known is the history of Tamerlano and Bajazet that instead of laboring to instruct the reader, I should try to efface certain opinions that have become accredited as true. It is commonly believed that after taking Bajazet prisoner, Tamerlano used him as a footstool for mounting his horse, that he locked him up in an iron cage, and that he made his wife serve naked in the mess hall. The most accredited authors make no mention of any of this; on the contrary many assert that all this is fable. Nevertheless, I, who am not trying to write a history, but to represent a tragedy, have taken from the above-mentioned fables, reduced to the decorum of the theater and to possible probability, the motive for a plot which leads to the death of Bajazet.[55]

Making Ottoman history operatic thus involved making it less fabulous, more plausible, and persuasively tragic. From the beginning Piovene's purpose was not to exoticize the history of Bajazet, but rather the reverse.

While the "base cage" still played a part at Pratolino in 1706, Piovene eliminated even the word from his libretto, which begins with Bajazet being freed from some unspecified condition of imprisonment. In the first line of Piovene's libretto, Bajazet therefore offers thanks for this temporary liberty. Handel and Haym, however, inserted another first line of recitative preceding this one, so that the Byzantine prince Andronico would now begin the opera by urging Bajazet, "*Esci, esci, o Signore*" (Come out, come out . . .). The cage is never mentioned, but it would have been possible either to stage or to imagine a cage from which the sultan "came out" at the very beginning of the opera. Handel's musical setting had the first syllable of "*esci*" moving from F up to B-flat with the repetition, almost as if the prisoner were ascending as he emerged.[56]

an die Gräntze der Landschafft Armenien, rück= | ansichtig ward, wie seine Gemahlin, des
te von dannen auf Galatien, und schickte sich | Herrn in Servien Tochter, dem Tamerlan
zum Streit. Bajazeth war mit aller Macht | halb nacket vor der Tafel aufwarten, und wie

261.
Tamerlan
sperret
Bajazeth
in einen
eisernen
Kesig ein.

1402. ein Page einschencken muste, verdroß ihn die= | figs, bis er kranck ward, und starb. Dieses zerstö
Bajazeth se Schmach dermassen, daß er nicht länger zu | war der Ausgang und die Folge der so grau= sich d

"Tamerlane locks Bajazet in an iron cage" (*Tamerlan sperret Bajazeth in einen eisernen Kefig [Käfig] ein*). Copper engraving from the seventeenth-century *Historische Chronik* of Johann Ludwig Gottfried, as republished in Frankfurt in 1743. Bajazet's captivity remained an important cultural theme, though Piovene eliminated the cage itself from his libretto. With kind permission of the Österreichische Nationalbibliothek.

Piovene's commitment to accuracy meant that his setting was geographically precise and historically correct: "The scene is set in Prusa, the capital of Bithynia, today Bursa, and the first city occupied by Tamerlane after the defeat of the Turks." Prusa was its classical name, and Piovene was sufficiently conscious of classicizing Ottoman history to excuse himself in the preface: "The references to fate, the stars, the gods [*Numi*], etc. should be understood with the mind of a good Christian, as he who wrote them also professes to be."[57] Historically, the religious framework of the encounter between Tamerlane and Bajazet ought to have been Muslim, but Bajazet, in Piovene's conception, was to be a Muslim Ottoman tragic hero rendered in fully classical and pagan style, reflecting the intersection of late baroque classicism with the philosophical paganism of the early Enlightenment.[58]

Though the title of Handel's work remained *Tamerlano*, Bajazet was un-questionably the tragic hero of the opera, as was really the case already for Gasparini in 1711, for Scarlatti in 1706, and for Ziani in 1689. Bajazet is deter-mined to die rather than live in the dishonor of captivity, but also defiantly refuses to consent to the indignity of his daughter's marriage to the conquer-or. These sentiments of defiance and dignity inform his first aria, the stoical acceptance of death tempered only by protective paternal affection and ex-pressed in the affirmative key of C major:

Forte e lieto a morte andrei,	Strong and glad I would go to death
se celassi ai pensier miei	if I could hide from my thoughts
della figlia il grande amor.	my great love for my daughter.
Se non fosse il suo cordoglio,	If not for her affliction
tu vedresti in me più orgoglio,	you would see more pride in me,
io morrei con più valor.[59]	I would die with greater valor.[59]

The first word of the aria, "*forte*," descends a full octave to emphasize the grounding of Bajazet's strength. A trill in the violin accompaniment expresses the gladness with which he will meet death, and the aria ends with the elabo-rate ornamentation of "*valor*." Winton Dean notes that Handel was generally inspired by Gasparini's setting of this aria in the score of 1719. Dean further comments on the Handelian ornamentation: "Triadic rather than stepwise coloratura is characteristic of Handel's writing for natural male voices, as op-posed to castratos and women, and of Bajazet's music in particular; it is tax-ing but never showy, a tribute to Borosini's technique and dramatic commit-ment."[60] In fact, Gasparini's setting had made much greater use of trilling in the vocal line, presenting the aria as a frenetic display piece, whereas Handel, with a simpler, steadier vocal line, produced a greater sense of poignancy and steadfast purpose. Masculine, stoical classicism was the emotional and philo-sophical key to Handel's Turkish hero. The Ottomans had not yet conquered Constantinople in Bajazet's time, though he himself had captained a long siege of the city. Handel's musical rhythms suggested that the Ottoman sultan might already be considered as a dramatically legitimate heir to the Romans.

The most striking musical precedent for the stoical Bajazet of Pradon, Pio-vene, Gasparini, and Handel would have been the undated cantata "Lamento di Mustafà e Bajazet" by Luigi Rossi, who died in 1653, and his lament may have been altogether unknown to the creators of *Tamerlano* in the early eighteenth century. This cantata, twenty-five minutes long, was almost operatic in its dramatic aspect: the sultan Amarat or Murad (sung by a basso) condemns two princes, his brothers, to death, and they (sung by tenor and baritone) plead with dignity and pathos their innocence of any treason against the Ottoman state. The precise historical reference remains somewhat uncertain. Murad II executed his younger brother Mustafa in 1422 for rebellion. Murad III, who reigned from 1574 to 1595, had five of his brothers strangled when he came to the throne, a not unconventional Ottoman maneuver to secure the succession. Murad IV had his younger brother Bajazet killed in 1635 (and later two other brothers), during Rossi's actual lifetime and career; this was in fact the instance of fratricide that Racine made into his tragic drama *Bajazet* in 1672.

What is certain is that Rossi's Bajazet, like Racine's, was not modeled on the same historical figure as Handel's Bajazet, the prisoner of Tamerlane, but Rossi's baritone prince is similarly stoical in the face of death: "*Soffro la morte mia con ciglio asciutto*" (I suffer death with dry eyes). His brother Mustafa is a tenor, like Handel's Bajazet, and faces death with comparable stoicism:

Numi del Turco Impero,	Gods of the Turkish empire,
Allor che sarò morto	When I am dead,
Fate fede al mio Re ch'io moro a torto!	Tell my king I die wrongly.[61]

The plural "gods" of the Turkish empire suggest that this was a classical and pagan world, not a Muslim civilization. The chorus immediately responds with pity, as the audience was also presumably intended to do:

Dar morte agl'innocenti	Putting the innocent to death,
Chi non move a pietà?	Who is not moved to pity?[62]

The text further suggested some familiarity with Turkish society and institutions as specified in the description of the Turks affected by the scene:

Né vi fu Giannizzero o Spagi,	There was no Janissary or Sipahi,
Agà né Capigi	Nor Aga nor Kapici
Ch'il pianto trattener potesse più.	Who could keep from weeping.[63]

The cantata concludes by condemning the execution of the princes: "*Opra fu d'un crudel barbaro atroce!*" (It was the work of a cruel atrocious barbarian!).[64] Sultan Amarat is an Ottoman barbarian, but the princes face death with noble courage, and every other Turkish figure in Rossi's piece, from the actually singing chorus to the implicitly present Janissaries and Sipahis, demonstrates the highly civilized capacity for sympathetic pity. In Handel's opera this sympathy is focused on the Ottoman sultan Bajazet as he prepares to meet his death "*forte e lieto*," strong and glad.

As in Rossi's seventeenth-century cantata, so in Handel's eighteenth-century opera, Muslim faith seemed to play no role whatsoever in the drama or the characterizations, not even as a possible point of resemblance between Tamerlane and Bajazet, both historically Muslim rulers. Instead, Handel's opera presented them ethnographically as a Tartar and a Turk, with Andronico principally characterized not as a Christian but as a Greek. Tamerlane, whom modern historians might describe as a Turkic Mongol, was classified in the eighteenth century as a Tartar alongside Genghis Khan; the name Tartar served as a byword for Asiatic barbarism, as summed up for the Enlightenment in the 1750s in the *Histoire générale des Huns, des Mongoles, des Turcs et des autres Tartares occidentaux*, by Joseph de Guignes. Handel's Tamerlane is truly a magnificent barbarian, dazzling in his castrato vocal display which expresses both the thrilling exultation of triumph and his furious outrage at his captive's defiance.[65]

When Tamerlane demands Bajazet's daughter in marriage, the Ottoman sultan articulates his outrage in terms of blood and descent:

BAJAZET: Tua sposa? non è vero;
    degli Ottomani il sangue
    non puo accoppiarsi al sangue
    d'un pastore.
TAMERLANE: Infelice superbo
    non sai, ch'io sono tuo signor ancora?
BAJAZET: Eh! fortuna non toglie,
    o lieto, o avversa
    a te viltà di sangue,
    a me grandezza.

Your wife, it is not true;
the blood of the Ottomans
cannot be coupled with the blood
of a shepherd.
Unfortunate arrogant man,
don't you know I'm your lord?
Eh! Fortune does not remove,
whether favorable or averse,
from you base blood,
from me greatness.[66]

Both Piovene's libretto and Handel's music seemed to suggest that in spite of Tamerlane's rejoinder—"*infelice superbo*"—Bajazet was right to take pride in his Ottoman blood. In fact, during Bajazet's reign in the late fourteenth century, the Ottoman dynasty was still young, and he was only the fourth sultan in the family line. By Handel's time, however, the Ottomans had become one of the venerable dynasties in Europe, preserving their rule over the course of four centuries. If the Ottoman empire appeared less fearsome in the early eighteenth century, and more readily conceivable as an object of musical sympathy, the dynasty could certainly be accorded the dignity of long endurance across the centuries, having evolved in image from an alien and infidel scourge to become Europe's most familiar and intimate enemy. The pride of Bajazet was expressed as European pride, and Handel made him sound accordingly sympathetic as the singing Turk.

The Handelian Death of Bajazet

Handel arrived in Italy in 1706, at the age of twenty-one, and since he received the Medici patronage of Grand Prince Ferdinando, it is possible that he was present at Pratolino for the performance of Scarlatti's *Il gran Tamerlano*, starring the tenor Canavese as Bajazet. Handel remained in Italy until 1710, leaving one year before he might have had the chance to hear Gasparini's *Tamerlano* in Venice in 1711. Spending time in Florence, Venice, and Rome, Handel probably met Gasparini and Scarlatti, and also knew the librettist Salvi.[67] These youthful years in Italy certainly put Handel in the same circles with the musicians who were involved in the performance of operas about Tamerlane and Bajazet.

While the London Haymarket was as distant as any major European opera theater could be from the Ottoman empire, Handel's operatic conception of Bajazet was by no means arbitrarily exotic, for he himself had experienced the Italian climate in the aftermath of Karlowitz, and his work on *Tamerlano* was thoroughly shaped by the Venetian influences of Gasparini, Piovene, and Borosini. Furthermore, England itself was not untouched by the new eighteenth-century interest in Turkishness, and particularly relevant to Handel's London were the open-minded and sympathetic letters from the Ottoman empire written by Lady Mary Wortley Montagu in 1717 and 1718 when her husband was ambassador in Constantinople to the court of Ahmed III. Though published formally as the *Turkish Embassy Letters* only in 1763, after Lady Mary's death, the manuscript letters circulated informally when they were received by her friends in London's cultural elite. In Constantinople she admiringly contemplated the tombs of the "fierce warlike sultans" of the past, and she composed these lines of verse which suggested that their ferocity had been put to rest:

> The marble mosques, beneath whose ample domes
> Fierce warlike sultans sleep in peaceful tombs.[68]

In fact, the early sultans were generally buried in Bursa (where the mausoleum or *türbe* of Bajazet also stands), but the writer's sympathetic imagination put them to rest in the Ottoman capital. Handel would bring Bajazet back to life in 1724, and then stage his death in a scene of deeply sympathetic operatic intensity.

Bajazet concludes a suicide pact with Asteria at the beginning of the third act, and a tender exchange between them in recitative is followed by an aria for the tenor sultan. He offers an appointment to meet his daughter in another world:

Su la sponda del pigro Lete	On the bank of the lazy Lethe
Là m'aspetta	Wait for me there
Se vi giungi pria di me.	If you arrive before me.[69]

A slowly winding figure in the tenor line and the string accompaniment, with the tempo marked as *largo*, seemed to represent the lazy river. There was, however, no trace of Islam to be found in the sultan's intention to meet his daughter in the underworld of the ancient Greeks, by the Lethe River. According to Winton Dean, Handel brought something of Bach's style and harmony to Bajazet's music, which was comparable at moments to the Christian intensity of the St. Matthew Passion of 1727.[70]

Asteria, the Turkish heroine of Handel's opera, is by no means completely passive in the face of Ottoman defeat, and if she hesitates to carry out her side of the suicide pact, it is only because she plans first to poison Tamerlane in order to avenge her father's defeat, to resist "tyranny," and for the sake of Ottoman honor. When she fails in her plot, Tamerlane determines, in forceful recitative, that her punishment will be her sexual humiliation, to be carried out in front of her father: "and let Bajazet be the spectator." She is to be brought to "the seraglio of the slaves" and there offered up as "prey" (*preda*) to the "mob" (*turba*).[71] The horrified "spectator" Bajazet also represented the crowd of spectators who would have been watching from the audience of the Haymarket theater, sympathizing with Asteria from Bajazet's paternally Ottoman perspective. The audience, of course, was not always sympathetic, and when Lady Mary Wortley Montagu attended Handel's *Tamerlano* in 1724, to witness one of her "fierce warlike sultans" in operatic captivity, she pronounced the whole production to be "execrable."[72]

Bajazet denounces Tamerlane in an aria of brassy, rapid, and rhythmical rage, but the captive is powerless for the present and can only threaten to make war from beyond the grave:

Empio, per farti guerra,	Impious one, to make war on you,
dal regno di sotterra	from the underground kingdom
l'ombra ritornerà.	my shade will return.[73]

The forceful tenor line was accompanied by hammering, warlike eighth notes in the orchestra, characterized by a rising figure that ended by sounding five times in fanfare the highest note of the series. The tenor's vocal part, according to Winton Dean, suggest that this aria was composed before Handel had actually heard Borosini's voice and recognized his restricted upper range. The composer in this case did not transpose downward but preferred to give the aria an extra intensity by challenging the tenor.[74] Thus the accompaniment suggested the rising of Bajazet's shade from the underworld to assault his nemesis, while the tenor line ended with dramatic ornamentation on the accented last syllable of his promise to return: *ritornerà*. Bajazet also invokes the multiple deities who he hopes will pour down their wrath upon Tamerlane—"*l'ira degli Dei*" (the wrath of the gods)—demonstrating once again the irrelevance of Islamic monotheism in Handel's opera.[75]

Bajazet's death scene is often considered to be one of Handel's greatest musical dramatic accomplishments, making use of *recitativo secco*, *recitativo accompagnato*, and aria forms in unprecedented combination, the better to achieve the dramatic impact of the sultan's death. It was this scene which made Bajazet indisputably the dramatic hero of the opera.[76] The sultan begins with the gentlest recitative, lovingly embracing the prospect of his own death: "*Oh per me lieto, avventuroso giorno!*" (Oh for me what a glad and fortunate day!). He then shifts to defiance as he calls Tamerlane a tyrant, and declares himself freed from the bonds of tyranny: "*E 'l sai, tiran? da' lacci tuoi son sciolto*" (Do you know, tyrant? I am freed from your bonds).[77] While early modern political theorists generally associated the Ottoman empire with issues of Asiatic despotism, Bajazet in captivity became the Handelian spokesman for liberty against tyranny.

With the entrance of the orchestra to create *recitativo accompagnato*, Bajazet explains in the language of classical philosophy that by taking his own life he will reclaim his liberty. This is Bajazet's triumph over Tamerlane's threats, with each of the sultan's lines punctuated by fierce orchestral semiquavers of defiance:

Fremi, minaccia!	Shake, threaten!
mi rido del tuo furor, di tue minaccie.	I laugh at your fury, at your threats.
Ho vinto l'orgoglio tuo	I have defeated your pride
con mio velen;	with my poison;
né puoi farmi morire,	you can neither kill me,
né far si ch'io non mora;	nor prevent me from dying;
è questa morte il mio trionfo eletto.	this death is my chosen triumph.[78]

Death was the particular triumph that the European public could most exultantly celebrate for an Ottoman sultan in the aftermath of Karlowitz and Passarowitz. Handel excised from the opera a long final scene for Asteria (originally composed in the July version before Borosini's arrival), so that Bajazet became indisputably the star, his death the definitive dramatic climax.

At the sultan's death, the cautious Greek Andronico finally finds his political voice and denounces Tamerlano in the single word that summed up the philosophical perspective of the opera: "*Barbaro!*" If Tamerlane was a barbarian, Bajazet then represented his civilized antithesis: the Ottoman sultan as the demonstrative model of classical civilization. This was one important part of the perspective that Borosini brought with him from Italy along with the Gasparini score, indeed what Handel himself may have brought back from his Italian years in the first decade of the century: the Venetian cultural perspective by which the Ottoman Turks, whatever else one might say about them, were not to be simply dismissed as barbarians. Rather, Bajazet in the opera represented the civilized perspective on Tamerlane's ferocity and barbarism, and brought about, by the dramatic example of his death, the complete reform of Tamerlane's Tartar nature: in effect, the civilizing of Tamerlane. Like the operatic public, Tamerlane is moved by Bajazet's death—so much so that he renounces both his vindictive and romantic intentions toward Asteria, and magnanimously bestows her upon her beloved Andronico.

"*e 'l sai, tiran? da' lacci tuoi son sciolto*"—Bajazet's death scene, from Handel's *Tamerlano*, 1724. "Do you know, tyrant? I am freed from your bonds," the sultan sings to Tamerlane. The *recitativo secco* shifts to *recitativo accompagnato*, as illustrated by the figures of beamed sixteenth notes in the orchestration, as Bajazet sings, "*Fremi, minaccia! mi rido del tuo furor*" (Shake, threaten! I laugh at your fury). He tells Tamerlane that he has taken poison, and that "this death is my chosen triumph."

"*io vado le furie a scatenar per tuo tormento*"—Handel's *Tamerlano*, 1724. Bajazet's death scene continues with the music marked "*furioso*" by Handel, to express the dying sultan's rage at his captor: "I will unleash the furies to torment you." This is followed by a dramatic shift in dynamics (marked *piano*) and tone as he sings, "*già miro il dì mancar; morte, ti sento*" (already I see the day fading; death, I feel you). The variations in form and emotion made Bajazet's long death scene a landmark in expressive operatic composition for tenor voice.

Tamerlane and Andronico then together celebrate the happy ending with a duet:

Coronata di gigli e di rose,   Crowned with lilies and roses,
con gli amori ritorni la pace.   may peace return with love.[79]

They celebrate the advent of peace, with the implausible implication that Bajazet's suicide has had such an edifying effect on Tamerlane as to cause him to give up warfare and conquest altogether. The strings supplied a cheerful dotted rhythm and almost frivolous runs of semidemiquavers. Musically, however, what was missing from this concluding duet for two castrati was all too evident: the masculine register of the tenor voice, which disappeared from the score with Bajazet's death. The two castrati could harmonize beautifully in thirds, with Andronico on the upper line of the score (the celebrated Senesino for Handel in 1724), but their registers were close enough so that they could easily trade top note for bottom. The classical dignity of Bajazet's Ottoman masculinity was made strikingly evident in the conclusion by his musical absence. His tenor voice had reflected his maturity as a concerned father, not an ardent lover, as a philosophical prince, not a ferocious conqueror. The extinguishing of that tenor voice was particularly notable in the concluding music, just as the effacement of the Ottoman presence was correspondingly suggestive in relation to contemporary international politics.

In the sequence of Handel's operas of the 1720s, *Tamerlano* of October 1724 immediately followed *Giulio Cesare* of February 1724 and directly preceded *Rodelinda* of February 1725. Together they constituted a set of politically preoccupied operatic masterpieces which belong to what might be called—borrowing the phrase of historian J.G.A. Pocock—an operatic "Machiavellian moment." All three works were deeply concerned with the issues of legitimacy, usurpation, and conquest articulated in Machiavelli's *Prince*, and central to political discussion ever after. Handel's *Tamerlano* offered a sort of operatic commentary on Machiavelli, with Tamerlano the conqueror and usurper represented as barbarous, and Bajazet the deposed, legitimate sultan as the object of musical and dramatic sympathy. In *Rodelinda*, the political perspective would be even more sharply defined, with Bertarido the virtuous and legitimate king of the Lombards returning to find his throne occupied by the wicked usurper Grimoaldo. Borosini lent his tenor voice to the cause of legitimacy in *Tamerlano*, but then sang the role of Grimoaldo in *Rodelinda*.

In British dramatic culture these preoccupations with legitimacy and usurpation dated back to the sixteenth century, the century of Machiavelli, as exemplified in Shakepeare's *Richard II*. In Handel's operas of the 1720s these themes recur with particular force, and in 1727, when George I was legitimately succeeded by George II, it was Handel who composed the coronation anthems to celebrate the legitimacy of British monarchical rule. Musicologist Ellen Harris has delineated the musical and dramatic dimensions of East and West in Handel's operas and has noted the "repeated opposition of courageous and virtuous Western heroes and tyrannical Eastern despots."[80] In *Tamerlano*, however, the sultan Bajazet was presented on stage as a deposed Ottoman despot, and for that reason was able to sing with poignant regret and righteous fury about outraged political legitimacy.

Vivaldi's Pasticcio in Verona

As in the conceptions of Scarlatti in 1706 and Gasparini in 1711, Handel's Bajazet expressed himself in the register of tenorial masculinity. Throughout the eighteenth century, and in spite of the huge popularity of castrati singers, Turkish protagonists on European operatic stages would remain almost exclusively in the masculine vocal registers, generally descending as the decades passed. Antonio Vivaldi, who also set a version of Piovene's libretto for operatic performance, was supposed to have hesitated over which voice to use for Bajazet: tenor, baritone, or bass.[81] He finally settled on a baritone, and restored the sultan's name to the title of the opera, *Bajazet*, which was performed in Verona within the Venetian republic in 1735. In that same year Rameau's opera-ballet *Les Indes galantes* was performed in Paris, opening with an Ottoman act, "Le Turc généreux" (The generous Turk), which inaugurated a new chapter in the history of Turkish subjects in European opera. The 1730s also saw the return of European warfare with the Ottomans for the first time since the peace of Passarowitz in 1718; in 1735 Russia and Turkey went to war, and in 1737 the Habsburgs joined in, though Venice remained neutral. With the treaty of Belgrade in 1739 the Ottomans regained the city of Belgrade which they had lost at Passarowitz. So the heroic return of Bajazet to the operatic stage in 1735 coincided with the return of the Ottomans to the stage of international affairs.

The 1730s, furthermore, was a crucial literary decade for the Enlightenment's treatment of Islam, with the first performance of Voltaire's drama *Zaïre* in 1732 at the Comédie-Française in Paris. The heroine Zaïre is the Christian-born slave of Orosmane, sultan of Jerusalem in the age of the Crusades; the drama concerns the tragic outcome of their love for one another. Like Bajazet, Voltaire's Orosmane was a tragic Muslim hero on the European stage and by no means remote from enlightened European values.

Luigi Ferdinando Marsigli, the Bolognese military engineer and natural historian, was the author of a work published posthumously in Amsterdam and The Hague in 1732, in both Italian and French, a study of *L'état militaire de l'Empire Ottoman, ses progrès et sa décadence* (The military condition of the Ottoman empire, its progress and its decline). Marsigli, who had participated in the Habsburg-Ottoman wars of the late seventeenth century, had been taken prisoner by the Turks, and when freed had assisted in the mapping of the Habsburg-Ottoman border for the peace of Karlowitz; he argued strongly for the significance of Ottoman military decline as a fact of international relations in the early eighteenth century.[82] That perceived decline and consequent vulnerability provided the contemporary context for the ongoing representation of Bajazet's captivity on the operatic stage in the 1730s.

Vivaldi's *Bajazet* of 1735 came a decade after Handel's *Tamerlano* in London, and more than two decades after Gasparini's first setting of Piovene's libretto in 1711. Vivaldi's baritone sultan, however, was actually less dramatically central to the drama than was Handel's tenor sultan, and most notably Vivaldi did not compete with Handel's extraordinary death scene for the sultan. Instead, Vivaldi's Bajazet dies quietly offstage, a discretion that eliminated from the opera what could have been considered the story's most dramatic moment. Yet Vivaldi in his own way was certainly a Turkish partisan in the composition of the opera. Bajazet was constructed as a "pasticcio," making use of recycled music by Vivaldi but also of music by other composers. It was principally for the Turkish characters—Bajazet and his daughter Asteria—that the Venetian Vivaldi reserved his own musical compositions, while the Tartar Tamerlano and the Greek Andronico had to make do with the music of rival composers in the Neapolitan style (such as Johann Adolph Hasse and Riccardo Broschi). The opera's ethnographic rivalries were thus subtly emphasized by the underlying musical opposition between Venetian and Neapolitan music, and Vivaldi's own musical triumph reinforced the moral victory of the Turks within the opera.[83]

As in Handel's *Tamerlano*, so Vivaldi's *Bajazet* emphasized the vocal masculinity of the Ottoman sultan, in this case by setting him alongside a female contralto (singing the role of Tamerlane) and a male castrato (as Andronico). Though the Piovene libretto provided a roughly similar dramatic basis for Handel and Vivaldi, the character of Bajazet emerged as rather different in the hands of the Venetian composer. The classical stoicism of the libretto—as expressed in the sentiment of the sultan's first aria, "Del destin non dee lagnarsi" (One must not complain about destiny)—was undercut by Vivaldi's determination that Bajazet, singing Vivaldi's own music, should actually outsing his dramatic rivals in dazzling display. Not only was the role conceived more conventionally by Vivaldi in the use of the forms of recitative and aria, but Handel's complex representation of tragic resignation, introspective fortitude, and the renunciation of life itself gave way to brilliant, energetic, and extravagantly ornamented display in Vivaldi's conception of Bajazet.

In spite of sentiments of stoical resignation in the libretto, the frenzied accompaniment to Bajazet's aria "Dov'è la figlia? dov'è il mio trono?" (Where is my daughter? where is my throne?) suggest that he is no less emotionally overwrought than Tamerlane. In the second act quartet "Sì crudel!" the rivals find themselves balanced in the ensemble, as mutual charges of cruelty and barbarism mingle in harmony. It is actually Tamerlane who denounces Bajazet for his barbarous pride (*barbara fierezza*). Deprived of a death scene on stage, Vivaldi's Bajazet takes his leave with a tiny, brilliant aria, less than a minute long, in which he promises to unleash the furies upon Tamerlane from the other world—and the music is appropriately furious. While Handel's Bajazet almost fades away, under the influence of poison, Vivaldi's sultan exits with an aria of intense passion and fierce ornamentation.

It falls to Asteria to announce her father's offstage death, to speak for the Ottomans and bring the charge of tyranny against Tamerlane:

È morto sì, tiranno,   He is dead, yes, tyrant,
io stessa il vidi.   I myself saw it.[84]

Her testimony is essential, since neither Tamerlane nor the audience have witnessed Bajazet's death themselves. In Vivaldi's concluding music—"crowned with lilies and roses"—the baritone voice of the Ottoman sultan, even more than Handel's tenor, is notable by its absence.

Conclusion: The Operatic Recurrence of Bajazet

Asteria's announcement of Bajazet's death in Vivaldi's opera would have made no sense in Handel's opera, since that death took place on stage. Yet, referring back to Piovene's original libretto of 1711 for Venice (before the revision for Reggio Emilia in 1719), one sees that Asteria sang exactly the same words in 1711. The revision of 1719 by Piovene and Gasparini, championed by Borosini and then remade into a new masterpiece by Handel in 1724, was not the text for Vivaldi's pasticcio, which reverted to the older version. Musicologist Giovanni Morelli has argued that with Vivaldi's opera in Verona in 1735— offering a diminished role for Bajazet and a woman performing the role of Tamerlane, singing borrowed arias from other men's operas—the whole subject of Bajazet and Tamerlane had lost its "thematic function" in the operatic culture of the early eighteenth century.[85] Bajazet's captivity was perhaps most

meaningful in the theater when staged in the international epoch of Karlowitz and Passarowitz, from the 1680s to the 1720s.

Yet Vivaldi's pasticcio was certainly not the end of the operatic road for
Bajazet. Piovene's libretto was composed, not only by Gasparini, Handel, and
Vivaldi but also (titled variously as *Tamerlano, Bajazet,* or *Bajazette*) by Fortu-
nato Chelleri in 1720 (for Treviso); Leonardo Leo in 1722 (for Naples); Nicola
Porpora in 1730 (for Turin); Giovanni Porta in 1730 (for Florence); Giuseppe
Clemente Bonomi in 1732 (for Ljubljana); Andrea Bernasconi in 1742 (for
Venice); Egidio Duni in 1743 (for Florence); Giovanni Battista Lampugnani
in 1746 (for Milan); Niccolò Jommelli in 1753 (for Turin); Gioachino Cocchi
and Giovanni Battista Pescetti together in 1754 (for Venice); Giuseppe Sarti in
1764 (for Copenhagen); Giuseppe Scarlatti in 1765 (for Verona); Ferdinando
Bertoni in 1765 (for Parma); Pietro Alessandro Guglielmi in 1765 (for Venice,
at Ascension); Josef Mysliveček in 1771 (for Milan); Antonio Sacchini in 1773
(for London); and Gaetano Marinelli in 1799 (for Venice).[86] When Marinelli composed his *Bajazette* for Venice in 1799, it is possible that the death of
the Ottoman Bajazet on stage might have been interpreted as an allegory of
the demise of the Republic of San Marco in 1797. It is even possible that the
Ottoman indictment of Tamerlane as a barbarian might have been silently
considered by some Venetians to be a comment on the conqueror Napoleon.

Piovene's libretto never went out of fashion in the eighteenth century,
created in Venice in 1711 and concluding its career in Venice in 1799. Certainly,
Venice and the Venetian republic stood at the center of the Bajazet phenomenon, though from there it extended its domain all over Italy and Europe, as
far as Handel's London. The death of Bajazet did not reach Paris. Nor was
Piovene's scenario enacted in Vienna, though it was operatically present in
the Habsburg cities of Milan and Ljubljana. A variant libretto by Antonio
Denzio was set to music for Prague in 1728 by Matteo Lucchini: *La caduta di
Baiazetto imperatore de' Turchi* (The fall of Bajazet, emperor of the Turks).

Bonomi's *Tamerlano* for Ljubljana in 1732 was the earliest documented
and identifiable performance of an opera in Habsburg Ljubljana, staged in
the private palace of Count Franz Anton Thurn-Valsassina. This occasion
brought the drama of the sultan Bajazet daringly close to the Triplex Confinium, the triple border where the Habsburg, Ottoman, and Venetian empires
all met. The composer's dedication to Count Thurn-Valsassina mentioned
the military service of the count's family, probably under the Habsburgs

against the Ottomans, while Bonomi also noted his own family ties to the border region of Carniola which included Ljubljana.[87] Mysliveček's *Il gran Tamerlano*, composed for Milan in 1771, was dedicated to the Habsburg archduke Ferdinand, the governor of Milan, the son of Empress Maria Theresa and Emperor Francis Stephen.

Handel's *Tamerlano* of 1724 was immediately translated into German and performed in Hamburg in 1725. Yet *Tamerlano* could not be automatically revived in London in future seasons, because Handel's company lacked a regularly employed tenor to sing the role. Borosini had come all the way from Italy, carrying the revised Gasparini score that suggested just how important the dramatic tenor role of Bajazet could be. Handel clearly appreciated this when he composed the role, but without Borosini he had no tenor to fill it. The opera was eventually revived in 1731; at that time the duke of Lorraine was present in London, and at an early rehearsal of *Tamerlano* the duke "sang a part" prior to attending the performance.[88] The duke of Lorraine was none other than Francis Stephen, who would marry into the Habsburg family as the husband of Maria Theresa in 1736 and then become the Holy Roman Emperor in 1745, reigning alongside Maria Theresa in Vienna until his death in 1765. Though it was not specified what part he sang at the rehearsal, the future father of Maria Theresa's eleven children could not possibly have been a castrato, and therefore probably sang the major male role composed in a normal masculine register, the tenor, that is the Sultan Bajazet.

The future Holy Roman Emperor thus presumably impersonated the tragically heroic Ottoman sultan of Handel's opera, constituting a remarkable temporary interplay of political identities and suggesting the ways in which Ottoman Turks might not have seemed altogether alien to the European opera public of the eighteenth century. Francis Stephen's son Joseph would be imperially present in the Burgtheater in Vienna in 1782 for the first performance of Mozart's *Abduction*. In that opera an enlightened Turkish pasha, conceived partly in tribute to Joseph himself, would be saluted for his magnanimity by all the European characters in the opera. Just as Francis Stephen might have tried on the role of the Turkish sultan Bajazet in 1731, his son Joseph would have seen his own political reflection in the character of the Turkish pasha Selim in 1782.

While the operatic setting of Tamerlane and Bajazet seems never to have come to Paris in the eighteenth century, there was an intended production of a sequel in the 1780s, to be titled *Tamerlan*, about the conqueror's reconciliation with the Ottomans after the death of Bajazet. A libretto was prepared by Étienne Morel de Chédeville and a score was being composed by the Prussian composer Johann Friedrich Reichardt, but the work never came to fruition and a different setting of the libretto was eventually performed in Paris only in 1802 with music by Peter von Winter. The opera was not supposed to dramatize Bajazet himself upon the stage, as it began only after his death, with a chorus of mufti announcing the news—*"Bajazet et mort!"*—and a chorus of Turks then responding:

O perte irréparable!	Oh irreparable loss!
O malheur effroyable!	Oh horrifying misfortune![89]

Bajazet's death was one of the great events of eighteenth-century European opera, and the French sequel was thus supposed to begin by expressing the same grief that audiences all over Europe had felt while actually watching the death of Bajazet on the operatic stage.

In Milan in 1771 *Il gran Tamerlano*, composed by Mysliveček, still used Piovene's libretto, sixty years after he first wrote it, but following the downward trend of Turkish voices in European opera, Bajazet now became a basso. Mysliveček was born in Prague, and the opera was revived in communist Czechoslovakia, two centuries after the Milan premiere. In Prague the role of Bajazet was given to the great Czech Jewish basso Karel Berman, who had survived Theresienstadt and Auschwitz during World War II.[90] Eighteenth-century librettists, composers, performers, and audiences had responded to the Ottoman sultan Bajazet, not as a figure of religious or cultural difference but rather in the spirit of the early Enlightenment, by attempting to comprehend the human dimensions of his tragic captivity. Karel Berman could vocalize that experience of captivity with new understanding that derived from the tragic history of the twentieth century.

2

The Generous Turk

Captive Christians and
Operatic Comedy in Paris

Introduction: Comedy versus Tragedy

While the Habsburg view of the Ottomans was shaped by centuries of military encounter in southeastern Europe and the Venetian view involved alternating bouts of naval warfare with long periods of commercial intimacy with the Ottomans, the perspective of France was entirely different. When the figure of "the generous Turk" stepped forward on the Parisian stage to sing his magnanimity in Jean-Philippe Rameau's *Les Indes galantes* of 1735, that performance followed upon two centuries of extremely cordial Franco-Ottoman relations. This cordiality accompanied the scandalous alliance of "the Lily and the Crescent"—formed by King François I and Sultan Suleiman I in the 1530s, aimed at their common Habsburg enemy. While Paris was geographically more remote from the Ottoman empire than Venice or Vienna, both as a political capital and later as an operatic center, the French-Ottoman association created a special relationship that involved, not the frontier intimacy of the Triplex Confinium, but rather the formal ceremonial rituals of political entente. Back at the beginning of the alliance in the 1530s there took place an unprecedented Ottoman embassy to France and the establishment of a French ambassador, Jean de La Forêt, in Istanbul. More important for French theatrical history was the embassy of Müteferrika Suleiman Aga to the court of Louis XIV in 1669, directly inspiring the Turkish ceremonial of Molière and Lully's *Le bourgeois gentilhomme* of 1670. Still more important was the year-long embassy of Yirmisekiz Mehmed Çelebi Efendi to France in 1720–21, encouraging a fashionable interest in

Turkishness, called Turquerie, which helped to create the operatic fantasy of "the generous Turk."

While the Ottoman operatic subject in Venice emerged as fundamentally tragic, with the Sultan Bajazet singing in captivity and ultimately killing himself rather than submitting to the will of Tamerlane, Turkish operatic scenarios in Paris evolved along largely comical lines. Molière and Lully created an entirely comical travesty of Turkishness in the late seventeenth century, and then in the early eighteenth century a new genre of musical Turkishness emerged in the popular comedies of the Paris fairs, combined with characters of the commedia dell'arte tradition. In 1735 "the generous Turk" of *Les Indes galantes* at the Paris Opéra offered the first important operatic treatment of European captives in the Ottoman empire, exploiting the dramatic premise of European women in the power of Turkish men. Yet this was a situation that almost never turned tragic in the eighteenth century, instead offering the occasion for romance and comedy with an almost inevitably happy ending. The staging of captivity received its most whimsically entertaining form in 1761 with Charles-Simon Favart's Parisian musical comedy *Les trois sultanes* (The three sultanas) about the harem of Sultan Suleiman the Magnificent.

While the tragedy of Bajazet allowed Europeans to sympathize with the defeated Turkish sultan in the early eighteenth century, operatic comedies of Turkishness seemed to go one step further in allowing Europeans to respond with laughter to the no-longer-invincible Ottomans. At the same time, comic opera also had the effect of humanizing its Turkish subjects and encouraging European audiences to sympathize with the singing Turks on stage as participants in a common human comedy that encompassed both the characters of the opera and the members of the public. Audiences might sympathize with Bajazet, but they would be unlikely to identify with the Ottoman sultan in captivity. In comic opera the audience more readily recognized themselves when they laughed at the foibles of the singing figures on stage, and that identification could be sustained even when the figures were Turkish.

Lully and Campra: Mamamouchi in the Seventeenth Century

Turkishness in musical comedy dated back to the performance in 1670 of Molière's comedy *Le bourgeois gentilhomme*—specified as a "*comédie-ballet*"—with music by Lully, concluding with a farcical "Turkish ceremony."

Influenced by the presence of the Ottoman embassy of 1669, Molière created a Turkish ceremony that made use of exotic Turkish costumes and a
mock-Turkish jargon of comical words and phrases that Jean-Baptiste Lully
set to music. The work was first performed in October 1670 for Louis XIV at
the Chateau de Chambord, and a performance in Paris followed in November
at the Théâtre du Palais-Royal. There are no actual Turks among the dramatis personae, for the farce consists of the impersonation of Turks, which
is intended to deceive the bourgeois gentleman and obtain his daughter in
marriage for the visiting "Turkish prince" (her French suitor in disguise). The
travesty serves to ridicule the bourgeois protagonist by providing a farcical
mock-Turkish ceremony of ennoblement to indulge his longing for social
elevation. Inasmuch as *Le bourgeois gentilhomme* was about impersonating
Turks and staging Turkishness, it represented the dynamics of creating an
opera about Turks without actually constituting such an opera.

The single musical scene of the Turkish ceremony begins with a march
characterized by strong percussive rhythm; the vocal music features one
low-singing baritone role for the presiding mufti. There is also a chorus of
Turks and a troupe of Turkish dancers. The singing and dancing Turks of
1670 performed their ceremony around the figure of Monsieur Jourdain, the
bourgeois gentleman (played by Molière himself in 1670), dressed in Turkish costume. Following the Turkish march, the Turkish chorus intoned with
mock solemnity the name of Allah in comical repetition, and the Turkish
mufti (played by Lully) addressed Monsieur Jourdain in a comical sort of
pidgin language that may in fact have represented the Mediterranean lingua
franca of the seventeenth century. He sang in an ungrammatical but not incomprehensible Italianate jumble, using only verbal infinitives:

Se ti sabir,	If you know,
Ti respondir;	You answer;
Se non sabir,	If you don't know,
Tazir, tazir.	Stay silent, stay silent.[1]

Monsieur Jourdain is then invested with a turban and saber—"*per defender
Palestina*"—while the mufti and chorus of Turks celebrate in repetitive nonsense syllables: "*He la ba, ba la chou, ba la ba, ba la da.*"

The French infatuation with Turkishness brings about the farcical thwart-
ing of the bourgeois gentleman, who is thrilled to receive the title of "Mamamouchi," and the young lovers are then able to marry happily in the spirit of

the comedy. Georgia Cowart has observed that Molière and Lully made use of Turkishness to create an "ultraburlesque" spectacle that allowed for the "carnivalesque" transcendence of categories of class and nation.[2] *Le bourgeois gentilhomme* contained only this one Turkish musical scene, but because of the prestige of Molière and Lully, that scene became a precedent and point of reference for later French musical entertainments.

While "Mamamouchi" was perhaps a purely nonsensical title, and some of the spoken dialogue of the false Turks was intended as pseudo-Oriental nonsense (*"ossa binamen sadoc babally oracaf ouram"*), the comical language of the Turks, as well as their exotic costumes and even some of their movements and instruments, may have been copied from the authentic Turkish embassy of 1669. Michèle Longino, in her study of Orientalism in French classical drama, has emphasized the role of the chevalier Laurent d'Arvieux, a merchant and traveler to the Ottoman empire who actually knew Turkish and Arabic and had some knowledge of Middle Eastern customs. Louis XIV himself was aware of his expertise, and in 1670 d'Arvieux worked with Molière and Lully as a consultant on Ottoman details for the construction of their Turkish ceremony.[3] Even in Paris, far from the Triplex Confinium, there was familiarity and expertise that facilitated the theatrical construction of farcical Turkishness and permitted the audience to appreciate the musical comedy.

In 1669, the year of the Turkish embassy, Louis XIV created the Académie d'Opéra, which became the Académie Royale de Musique in the 1670s under the direction of Lully, and which later came to be known as the Paris Opéra. It was there, at the Académie Royale, that André Campra's opera-ballet, *L'Europe galante*, was performed in 1697. The work consisted of an allegorical prologue followed by four acts, each one a treatment of love with arias and dances in a different national context: France, Spain, Italy, and Turkey. The inclusion of Turkey—in the opera and in "gallant Europe"—coincided with the conclusion of the long war in southeastern Europe, during which Louis XIV had been tacitly allied with the Ottomans against the Habsburgs.

Campra's work, with a libretto by Antoine Houdar de La Motte and musical contributions by André Cardinal Destouches, featured French shepherds, Spanish serenaders, and masked Venetians. The fourth and final act was set in Turkey in the harem of Zuliman, probably intended to represent Sultan Suleiman the Magnificent, and the role of the sultan was sung by a basso. In a comical drama of harem rivalry, Roxane and Zaide vie for the sultan's favor, and whereas the historical Suleiman supposedly loved Roxane (or Roxela-na, Hürrem Sultan) above all others, Campra's treatment concluded with the romantic triumph of the self-abasing Zaide. While the French, Spanish, and Italian acts generally involved male suitors pursuing their female loves, the Turkish act reversed those terms. Zaide sings as a slave infatuated with her master in an aria that may have been composed by Destouches rather than Campra:

Et je me trouvay trop heureuse	And I found myself too happy
D'être captive auprès de lui.	To be his captive.

While Turkey was thus included as a part of gallant Europe in Campra's work, it was also clearly a different part of Europe, in which the structure of gallant-ry was inverted to fit the paradigm of Ottoman despotism while nevertheless remaining within the genres of comedy and romance. According to the li-brettist La Motte, "We have expressed, within the limitations of the stage, the haughtiness and supreme authority of the sultan and the passionate nature of the sultanas."[4] In fact, it was through song that the sultana expressed both the emotional depth of her passion and the operatic intensity of her abasement before the turbaned embodiment of supreme authority.

The Paris Fairs: Harlequin in the Harem

Lully's Turkish ceremony and Campra's harem romance set seven-teenth-century precedents for later operatic works on Ottoman themes. In the opening decades of the eighteenth century, however, while operas on the tragedy of Bajazet were being created in Italy, Turkish subjects followed a very different musical and dramatic course in France. Sultans and sultanas began to play a part in popular musical dramas at the commercial fairs of Paris, en-tirely within the genre of comedy and even combined with elements of com-media dell'arte. In the theatrical life of British fairs there was also a place for Turkish tragedy, and William Hogarth's painting and print of the Southwark Fair in London from the 1730s included a theatrical company advertising its performance of "The Fall of Bajazet."

At the Paris fairs of the early eighteenth century, at Saint-Germain and at Saint-Laurent, the popular theatrical entertainments—*théâtre de la foire*—in-cluded musical comedies, puppet shows, and acrobatic performances. Musicologist Thomas Betzwieser has studied the particular prevalence of exotic themes, including Turkish and more generally Oriental settings, in the theater pieces of the fairs. Of particular relevance was the elimination of the Comédie-Italienne in Paris in 1697 by Louis XIV, under the moral influence of Mme de Maintenon, followed by the publication of the *Thousand and One Nights* in French translation by Antoine Galland between 1704 and 1717. This coincidence of events meant that the Italian commedia dell'arte could be adopted by French performers at the Paris fairs at the same time that a thousand and one Oriental scenarios could be adapted to the French theater. As a result, there was a proliferation of musical comedies featuring the figure of Harlequin (or Arlequin, in French), such as *Arlequin Grand Vizir* and *Arlequin Roi de Serendib* at Saint-Germain in 1713, *Arlequin Mahomet* at Saint-Laurent in 1714, *Arlequin sultane favorite* at Saint-Germain in 1715, and *Arlequin Hulla ou la femme repudiée* (a comedy of Muslim divorce and the "repudiated woman") at Saint-Laurent in 1716. Such comedies could also extend to the more remote Orient, as in *Arlequin invisible chez le roi de Chine* (Invisible Arlequin visiting the king of China), performed at Saint-Laurent in 1713.[5] Theater historian Bent Holm estimates, from the collected texts, that generally "Turkish" subjects made up as much as 20 percent of the theatrical repertory of the fairs.[6]

Arlequin Grand Vizir was a work that originated in the late seventeenth century, and echoed some of the mock-mufti singing of Lully's Turkish ceremony: "*vivir vivir, gran vizir.*" Arlequin first enters the Turkish harem in female disguise and eventually ends up becoming the sultan's Grand Vizier.[7] At the Paris fairs such works of commedia dell'arte became increasingly parodic and irreverent as popular entertainment. In *Arlequin Roi de Serendib* there is scatological humor with Arlequin proposing to use his turban as a chamber pot. In *Arlequin Mahomet* he is casually mistaken for the Muslim Prophet, takes advantage of his prestige to arrange a happy marriage for an unhappy Oriental princess, and then chooses a "Houri" for himself before the final dance of slaves and eunuchs.[8] At the fairs the music was provided on the principle of the "vaudeville," as new lyrics were composed for old songs with well-known popular tunes, specified by their opening lines. Such confections were artfully contrived to evade the monopoly of the Paris Opéra on singing, and that of the Comédie-Française on reciting in French. Musicologist Daniel Heartz has observed that the hybrid entertainments of the Paris fairs were particularly important for the evolution of the eighteenth-century *opéra comique*. Art historian Thomas Crow has further noted the significance of the Paris fairs for the emergence of an eighteenth-century public sphere.[9]

The Ottoman harem was to become one of the great operatic subjects of the eighteenth century, and it was prominent at the Paris fairs. *Arlequin sultane favorite* (Arlequin, the favorite sultana), was performed at the fair of Saint-Germain in 1715. Roughly contemporary with Gasparini's operatic tragedy of Bajazet in Venice (1711) and Reggio Emilia (1719), the French comedy was set in the seraglio of the Grand Seigneur, the Ottoman sultan. There the captive Arlequin encounters his old friend and rival Pierrot, both of them characters from the commedia dell'arte. Likewise a captive, Pierrot is already "dressed à la Turque" and installed as a clown in the service of the sultan. Pierrot sings:

> Non, de mon sort je ne dois pas me plaindre,
> Et le malheur à quelque chose est bon.
> Les Turcs m'ont pris mais je n'ai rien à craindre.
> Le Grand Seigneur m'a choisi pour bouffon.

> No, I should not complain of my fate,
> And in every misfortune there is some good.
> The Turks have taken me but I have nothing to fear.
> The sultan has chosen me to be a clown.[10]

Pierrot promises that he can be useful to Arlequin, can even obtain for him the office of "black eunuch"—for the popular theater of the fairs was bold enough to make jokes about castration. As the title suggests, however, Arlequin was destined to enter the harem not as a eunuch but rather as a sultana. In Paris, as in Venice, there was nothing to be feared from the Turks in the decade of Passarowitz.

In 1715, the year of the death of Louis XIV, Arlequin sang a song of Ottoman tyranny in *Arlequin sultane favorite*, though the song was labeled "*joconde*," reflecting the lighthearted treatment of the subject:

Sous la puissance d'un Tyran	Under the power of a tyrant
Nous voici donc Esclaves	Here we are slaves
Dans un Pays ou l'Alcoran	In a land where the Koran
Ne souffre point de caves.	Tolerates no wine cellars.
On n'y voit point de Cabarets,	There one sees no taverns,
O misère inouïe!	Unheard of misery!
Me voilà serré pour jamais	Here I am shut off forever
De vin & d'eau de vie.	From wine and from brandy.[11]

The earnest rhyming of "Tyran" and "Alcoran" quickly gives way to Arlequin's alcoholic concerns, reflecting the supposed perspective of a popular audience at the fair. Arlequin himself, in spite of his reservations, seems inclined to convert to Islam at Pierrot's suggestion, and is very ready to admire himself in a Turkish robe, singing, "*J'aurai l'air d'un Mamamouchi*" (I will have the air of a Mamamouchi).[12] It was Molière who created the title of Mamamouchi in order to ridicule Monsieur Jourdain in the Turkish ceremonial scene of *Le bourgeois gentilhomme* in 1670, and by the beginning of the eighteenth century it was already a sufficiently familiar point of reference to be cited in the musical comedies of the Paris fairs. Arlequin actually aspires to more authentic titles: "*Je veux devenir Bacha*" (I want to become a pasha).[13] Though only a servant at home in Europe, in the Ottoman empire Arlequin can imagine himself achieving high rank.

In *Arlequin sultane favorite* the Ottoman sultan himself appears on stage to court his Christian captive, Isabelle—who turns out to be the lost beloved of Arlequin's Christian master Léandre. The Sultan sings his passion, while also emphasizing his absolute power:

Astre brillant, que sur mon coeur	Brilliant star who over my heart
Avez pris tant d'empire,	Has established such an empire,
J'attends de vous mon bonheur	I expect my happiness from you,
C'est assez vous en dire.	It suffices to tell you that.
Il faut bannir la rigueur	One must ban all severity
Quand un Sultan soupire.	When a sultan is sighing.[14]

The issues of absolutism were very well understood in 1715, the final year in the reign of Louis XIV, and these were the same issues that would be explored over the next century in the various genres of opera about Turks.

The Christian lovers in *Arlequin sultane favorite* can only escape from the seraglio by distracting the sultan with the irresistible presence of Arlequin himself, veiled and costumed as a lady of the harem. When the concupiscent sultan finally succeeds in removing the lady's veil to discover Arlequin behind it, Arlequin himself understands that the situation only requires him to do what he can do best: make the sultan laugh. "*Riez donc* [so laugh], *Monsieur Mustapha*," he urges, treating the sultan as a familiar type with a generic name.[15] Mustafa II had reigned in Istanbul until 1703 but was then succeeded by Ahmed III. Within the comedy the sultan shows that he has both a sense

Arlequin sultane favorite—Arlequin the favorite sultana—was performed as a musical comedy at the Paris fair of Saint-Germain in 1715, the year of the death of Louis XIV. Veiled and costumed as a sultana of the harem, Arlequin comically deceives the sultan in order to facilitate an escape from the seraglio. In the end, when unveiled and revealed, he has to try to make the sultan laugh: "*Riez donc, Monsieur Mustapha.*" With kind permission of the Teylers Museum, Haarlem, The Netherlands.

of humor and a sense of magnanimity, acting as a "generous Turk" twenty years before that type and epithet were definitively established with *Les Indes galantes*. He liberates the Europeans to return to Europe, and though Arlequin is invited to remain in Turkey, he prefers to return to France, where he can drink more freely.

Arlequin was the star of the comedy, and the sultan, invited to laugh at Arlequin along with the audience, was not himself made into an object of ridicule. In this Turkish farce Turkishness itself was not farcical; Turkish costume, for instance, was only comical when it was being inappropriately worn by Arlequin, who represented Europe. In *Arlequin au sérail* of 1747, Arlequin and his master, Octave, grow long beards and pretend to be dervishes in order to rescue from the local pasha Octave's love Angelique and Arlequin's Columbine. Such works continued to be performed throughout the eighteenth century, and not only in France. *Harlekin Hulla*, based on the French original, was performed in Copenhagen in 1751, and *Arlekin der Türkensklave* (Harlequin the Turkish slave) appeared in Vienna for the siege centennial of 1783. *Arlequin esclave à Baghdad* (Harlequin slave in Baghdad) by Citoyen Vallier, in prose and vaudeville, was performed in Paris in year VII of the republic (1798–99), while *Arlequin odalisque*, by Citoyen Auger, was performed on the fifteenth day of Messidor in the revolutionary year VIII: July 4, 1800.[16] The musical escapades of Arlequin at the Paris fairs had a major influence on operatic comedies with singing Turks throughout the eighteenth century.

The Ottoman Embassy of Mehmed Efendi and the Rise of French Turquerie

The Turkish embassy to France in 1720–21 by Yirmisekiz Mehmed Çelebi Efendi inaugurated an era of French Turquerie, coinciding as it did with the flowering of rococo style and a new cultural openness following the death of Louis XIV and the advent of the Enlightenment. Historian Fatma Müge Göçek argues that this cultural Franco-Turkish engagement had reciprocal consequences in the Ottoman empire that were even more meaningful and durable: "The impact in France was temporary; it manifested itself as a fashion that gradually faded away. In the Ottoman Empire, the impact was permanent."[17]

The Ottoman sultan Ahmed III came to the throne in 1703, after the peace of Karlowitz, and reigned until 1730. He had broad interests in art, literature, and gardening, presiding over the so-called Tulip Period in Constantinople in the 1720s. The gardening of the Tulip Period was partly influenced by French horticultural style, which became known in the Ottoman empire following the embassy of Mehmed Efendi. He brought home some knowledge of things French, while leaving behind a French fascination with things Turkish. In *Arlequin Grand Vizir*, at the Saint-Germain fair of 1713, the fictive sultan asked Arlequin to reform the empire:

Puisque vous nous faites la grace	Since you do us the grace
De venir reformer ces lieux,	Of coming to reform this place,
Du Grand Visir prenés la place.	Take the job of the Grand Vizier.[18]

The year that Mehmed Efendi went to France, 1720, was around the time of the establishment of the first printing press in Constantinople, the work of the Hungarian convert Ibrahim Müteferrika. While European operatic stages were open to the representation of a sympathetically "generous Turk" in the early eighteenth century, it was also true that during the reign of Ahmed III the Ottomans were increasingly interested in European culture.[19]

Western influence became a vector of modernization in the East, while the influence of Turquerie lasted through the eighteenth century and affected several arenas of French culture, beginning with the visual and decorative arts. The popular interest in Turkish theatrical themes at the Paris fairs was complemented, after 1720, by elite Turquerie, an interest in Turkish costumes and styles inspired by the embassy of Mehmed Efendi. The Turkish ambassador himself observed that "as no one in Paris had ever seen either a Turk, or the dress of a Turk, we were observed with admiring eyes." According to Mehmed Efendi, "The desire of people to view us was such that they would make excursions from four or five-hour distances to the riverside to watch us. Striving to get in front of each other, they would fall into the water." One Frenchwoman, the wife of a former French ambassador to Istanbul, chose to dress in Ottoman costume in order to entertain Mehmed Efendi. This fashion soon made its mark on the visual arts, as subjects posed for portraits in Turkish clothing, while painters chose Ottoman subjects that involved turbans, plumes, divans, floor cushions, and tassels. Art historian Marianne Roland Michel has noted the influence of Charles de Ferriol's collection of engravings of the peoples of the Levant, published in 1707 and 1708; the images were based on the paintings of Jean-Baptiste Van Mour and depicted a great variety of Ottoman figures in their appropriate costumes.[20] The publication of these engravings also coincided with the first appearance in 1704 of Galland's translation of the *Thousand and One Nights*, to which the "Oriental" costumes seemed vaguely relevant. These tales became a European phenomenon, with an English translation in 1706 known as the *Arabian Nights*, a German edition in 1712, and an Italian version in 1722 published in Venice.[21]

Even more closely associated with the embassy of Mehmed Efendi in 1720–21 was the publication in 1721 of Montesquieu's *Persian Letters*, a foundational work of the European Enlightenment. This epistolary fiction explored the reciprocal perspectives of European Christians and Oriental Muslims at the moment of the Ottoman embassy, and acknowledged the rational validity of the Muslim perspective on Europe. The work was immediately translated from French into English in 1722, and would have shaped the cultural context for Handel's *Tamerlano* in 1724. In Paris in 1724 there also appeared a new edition of the score for Campra's *L'Europe galante*, presumably in association with new performances, including the Turkish act.[22] The Ottoman embassy helped to stimulate this interest in the Muslim world in the 1720s.

Mehmed Efendi, who was himself taken to the opera in France to see Lully's tragedy *Thésée*, appreciated the crowds who came to watch him, as if it were they and not he who constituted the spectacle—and even a comic spectacle as they pushed one another into the water. The French genres, of course, were not familiar to the Turks, and it was reported that one of Mehmed Efendi's men, while attending *Thésée*, "was not able to prevent himself from laughing during the whole performance." Göçek suggests that in this Franco-Turkish encounter both sides were watching each other with a sense of theatrical appreciation.[23]

The figure of the "generous Turk" took center stage when Rameau's *Les Indes galantes* was performed in Paris in 1735, the same year that Vivaldi's *Bajazet* was introduced in Verona. In fact, a few months after *Les Indes galantes*, the Paris Opéra presented yet another work with a Turkish subject in that same year: the opera *Scanderberg*, composed by François Francoeur and François Rebel, dramatizing the encounter between the fifteenth-century Albanian warrior Scanderbeg and the Ottoman sultan Murad II. If 1735 was thus a year of multiple Ottoman subjects at the opera, it was also a year when Russia and the Ottoman empire went to war again, with Austria later joining in—which guaranteed that singing Turks would be invested with a certain degree of current political interest. Though Venice remained neutral, the Habsburg and Venetian states that bordered the Ottoman empire relayed the news of the ongoing war to the rest of Europe. Historian Orhan Kologlu has observed that for obtaining Turkish news in Paris in the eighteenth century, "the two most important cities in Europe that played the role of centers of information for the *Gazette* were Vienna and Venice."[24] The Parisians thus followed Ottoman affairs at one remove from the Viennese and Venetians.

The Ottoman military effort in the 1730s was notably assisted by guidance in artillery from the renegade French officer Claude-Alexandre de Bonneval. He had served Prince Eugene in the taking of Belgrade in 1717 but then defected from Habsburg service, converted to Islam, and served the sultan in his war against the Habsburgs. As the Ottoman wars of the 1730s were also intricately related to the simultaneous War of the Polish Succession, the Ottomans were fighting in tacit cooperation with the French. France and the Ottoman empire both supported the same (ultimately unsuccessful) candidate for the Polish throne, Stanisław Leszczyński, whose daughter was the queen of France.

Art historian Nebahat Avcioğlu notes that Leszczyński expressed his aspirations to power by having himself painted in the costume of an Ottoman sultan, in the style of Ahmed III. In 1737, when Leszczyński had lost Poland but gained in compensation the duchy of Lorraine, he built at his palace in Lunéville a kiosk in the Ottoman style, acknowledging his own history of friendly Turkish relations while advancing the architectural progress of European Turquerie.[25] From a French perspective, both policy and culture combined to create a sympathy for the Ottomans that manifested itself operatically in the figure of the generous Turk.

In 1732 Voltaire's drama *Zaïre* was performed at the Comédie-Française, just three years before the first performance of Rameau's opera-ballet *Les Indes galantes* at the Académie Royale in 1735. Both would be hugely successful in France and influential all over Europe for the rest of the century. *Zaïre* was a drama of the Crusades, set in thirteenth-century Jerusalem, and the central figure of Sultan Orosmane, therefore, could not have been an

Ottoman Turk, though he was Muslim, Middle Eastern, possibly Mameluke, certainly sultanic—and therefore suggestive of Ottomanism and related to the contemporary spirit of Turquerie. Orosmane was an almost fully enlightened Muslim ruler, beyond religious prejudice in the spirit of the eighteenth century. The more narrow-minded Christians of the drama, however, attempt to persuade Zaïre, the sultan's slave who loves and is loved by him, that she should not marry a Muslim, since she was born a Christian in the age of the Crusades. Orosmane ends by murdering Zaïre out of mistaken jealousy—his tragic flaw, with the tragedy probably modeled in some degree on Shakespeare's *Othello*.

The relevance of Voltaire's *Zaïre* of 1732 for Rameau's "Le Turc généreux" in 1735 was partly a matter of contrasting genres: the resonance of tragedy in a Muslim context for drama, even as comedy was about to establish its generic dominance for operas about Turks. Both Voltaire's declaiming Sultan Orosmane and Rameau's singing Osman Pasha were sympathetically represented on the French stage, but their virtues were different. Orosmane's jealousy could not ultimately be considered to be generous, while Osman's generosity acknowledged that he was not the romantic hero of his own story. He merely permitted the Christian lovers to live happily ever after. What really linked the two works was the context of Turquerie in the 1730s and the fact that Voltaire's tragedy was also a drama of the seraglio: "*La scène est au sérail de Jérusalem.*"[26] The costumes and staging thus became matters of contemporary Turquerie, in *Zaïre* as in "Le Turc généreux," encouraging the construction of theatrical kiosks like those that Leszczyński built at Lunéville. The problem of Muslim male authority over captive slaves in the seraglio, introduced by the Enlightenment as political parable in Montesquieu's *Persian Letters* and appropriated by Voltaire for exploring the tragic implications of crusading religious conflict, was about to become the theme for countless variations in eighteenth-century operatic comedy.

Rameau's Generous Turk: "Remember Osman"

Rameau's "Le Turc généreux," first performed in Paris in August 1735, was closely contemporary with Vivaldi's *Bajazet*, performed during Carnival 1735 in Verona. The contrast in operatic genre between tragedy and comedy was clearly evident in the dynamics of captivity, which were neatly inverted from

Vivaldi to Rameau. The drama of *Bajazet*, with its first operatic setting dating back to 1689, represented an Ottoman sultan in tragic captivity, but "Le Turc généreux" would inaugurate a tradition of operatic comedies in which the Turk himself was the master of captives and slaves. His mastery, over the course of the opera, would be ingeniously undermined and overturned—possibly in the end with his own generous acquiescence. This structural inversion from captive to captor did not therefore necessarily place the operatic Turk in an unsympathetic light, though it usually underlined the limits of his authority. As an operatic plot it also fit some aspects of Mediterranean social circumstances, for the taking of European captives by Muslim corsairs was a fact of maritime life, and Robert Davis has even estimated that there could have been a million European captives taken between 1530 and 1780. Though such captivity was declining as a phenomenon by the eighteenth century, Linda Colley estimates that six thousand British subjects were taken captive between the 1670s and the 1730s—the period that roughly concluded with Handel's *Tamerlano* in London—and more than two thousand of those captives were ransomed and redeemed.[27] Certainly, a scenario of European captives in Ottoman lands was far more plausible in the eighteenth century than the case of a captive Ottoman sultan.

The French Enlightenment, guided by Montesquieu in the *Spirit of the Laws*, was interested in political power in the Islamic world and associated the Orient with despotism, but in the *Persian Letters* Montesquieu also studied Islamic despotism on the domestic level, as exercised in the harem of Usbek in Isfahan. Eighteenth-century drama and opera took up this latter concern, dramatizing the absolute power of Islamic princes over their wives and captives and judging the Turk according to his capacity for magnanimity. Voltaire, who made *Zaïre* into a tragedy of the seraglio, would later conclude his universal history, *Essai sur les Moeurs*, with the observation that "the greatest difference between us and the Orientals is the manner in which we treat women."[28] Operatic scenarios concerning captive women in the seraglio thus put Ottoman masters to the test of European civilization.

Rameau's *Les Indes galantes* in 1735 offered an explicitly non-European spectacle, for the gallant "Indies" of the title referred to the two Indies, East and West, indicating Asia and America. The Turkish act, "Le Turc généreux," was followed by a Peruvian act, and then a Persian act called "Les fleurs"; finally, an Amazonian act entitled "Les sauvages" was added in 1736. The title

Les Indes galantes referred back to Campra's opera-ballet *L'Europe galante* of 1697. Campra had also included a Turkish act but accompanied by three other acts with gallant European scenarios: French, Spanish, and Italian. Rameau removed Turkey from gallant Europe and located it among the lands of the gallant Indies, emphatically non-European. This offered an alternative vision of Turkey's place on the global map, suggesting a more exotic relation to Europe in the spirit of French Turquerie. Rameau's *Les Indes galantes* was often revived until 1761, and Campra's *L'Europe galante* until 1775.[29] This meant that the respective Turkish acts of both operas persisted in the operatic repertory, and during the eighteenth century Turkey appeared simultaneously in European and non-European operatic contexts, depending upon whether the opera-ballet of Campra or Rameau was being performed.

Les Indes galantes affirmed that the power of love was global in its sway, from Persia to Peru, a civilizing influence even among savages. Yet Rameau and his librettist Louis Fuzelier (who had also written *Arlequin Grand Vizir* for the Paris fairs) clearly did not regard the Turkish pasha as a savage. The setting was "the gardens of Osman Pasha, bounded by the sea"—perhaps in tribute to the gardens of the Tulip Period in the reign of Ahmed III. According to Fuzelier's preface to the libretto, the figure of Osman Pasha was based on a true Turkish character, the Ottoman Grand Vizier of 1731–32, Topal Osman Pasha, who had recently died in battle against the Persians:

> I hope it will be agreed that the respectable model I have chosen for my virtuous pasha authorizes the traits I have given to the copy: a Turk like Topal Osman is not an imaginary hero, and when he loves he is susceptible to a nobler and more delicate tenderness than that of the Orientals.[30]

The librettist thus explicitly declared that his exotic Oriental pasha ceased to be both exotic and Oriental under the influence of love, as demonstrated in the opera. Either love made him European, or perhaps, from the perspective of the Enlightenment, he was really European all along.

Osman Pasha loves his French captive Emilie, who has been kidnapped by Mediterranean pirates. The pasha urges her to forget the man she loves and enjoy a life of endless pleasures. She replies, in the spirit of Montesquieu, "I suffer, under your laws, a second slavery." The only "laws" of despotism are those of absolute submission to the despot, but this Turkish despot is full of tender sensibility, rendered with great pathos by Rameau's rococo lyricism.

Osman Pasha cannot bear to see his captive weep:

> C'est trop m'accabler par vos pleurs!
> Cessez d'entretenir d'inutiles ardeurs!
>
> You overwhelm me too much by your tears!
> Stop preserving useless ardors![31]

The music suggested that his sympathy was deeply felt—and also deeply sung, since the part of Osman Pasha was written for a basso, the lowest male voice, and the voice that would hereafter become almost obligatory for the casting of Turks in European opera.

Emilie denounces Osman Pasha as a barbarian—"*barbare!*"—but when the next tempest brings her own European beloved to the scene, the pasha proves that he is not at all a barbarian.[32] He gives the Europeans their liberty and many precious gifts besides, demonstrating his magnanimity and generosity as the "generous Turk." He momentarily abdicates his despotism and surrenders his power over his captives, who salute his virtue: "*O sublime vertu!*"[33] Virtue was presumed to be neither Christian nor Muslim but universal in the spirit of the early Enlightenment, and governed by profound sensibility of the heart.

The sailors dance the "*tambourin*," the rhythmic structure set by Rameau in "gay" semiquavers.[34] The mood of gaiety is then interrupted by Osman himself, declaiming "with grief" (*avec douleur*).[35] In six bars, he sends the reunited lovers on their way, and his musical line is one of gently poignant resignation:

J'entends vos matelots;	I hear your sailors;
Allez sur vos rivages,	Go to your shores,
Mes ordres sont donnés . . .	My orders have been given . . .
Allez, vivez contents.	Go and live content.
Souvenez-vous d'Osman . . .	Remember Osman . . .[36]

The final musical phrase descends a delicate half step, as if he doubts that Emilie will really remember his name. The Paris Opéra, however, would certainly remember Osman, for the piece continued to be performed until 1761, while in Vienna, in 1758, the choreographer Franz Hilverding created a ballet called *Le Turc généreux* that was loosely related to the story from *Les Indes galantes*.[37] It was in Vienna, in 1782, that Mozart would create another magnanimous

"*J'entends vos matelots . . . Souvenez vous d'Osman*"—the sentimental farewell of
Osman Pasha, the generous Turk emancipating his Christian captives, in the act titled
"Le Turc généreux" from Rameau's *Les Indes galantes* of 1735. "I hear your sailors; go
to your shores; my orders have been given; go and live content. Remember Osman."
With the descending half step in the final phrase, Osman effaces himself musically and
dramatically before withdrawing from the stage altogether and removing himself from
the conclusion of the act that was actually named for him, the generous Turk.

Ottoman pasha, who would likewise liberate his European captives at the
conclusion of *The Abduction from the Seraglio*.

Rameau's Osman Pasha is so exquisitely sensitive to the romance of his
former captives that he finally effaces himself completely and exits the stage,
lest his unhappiness dampen the high spirits of their happy ending, and perhaps also to protect his own pride:

> C'est trop à vos regards offrir mon trouble extrême,
> Je vous dois mon absence, et la dois à moi-même.

> It is too much to offer my extreme distress to your gazes,
> I owe you my absence, and owe it to myself.[38]

Like Bajazet, subtracted from the joyous finale by his suicide, so Osman Pasha also withdraws from the scene and from the vocal ensemble. There is a loving duet for the soprano and tenor lovers, a chorus for the Provençal company that will sail with them, and a happy melody labeled "tune for the African slaves."[39]

These slaves of Osman Pasha remain behind with him, still subject to his despotism, but they nevertheless celebrate the departure of the Europeans and presumably wish them well. Since the melody has no words in the libretto or score, the slaves now only dance their enthusiasm as ballet.[40] Led by the departing soprano Emilie, the chorus of African slaves then sings a final farewell:

Partez! On languit sur le rivage, partez,
Tendres coeurs embarquez-vous!

Depart! people languish on the shore, depart,
Tender hearts, embark![41]

The lovers embark, but the slaves remain to languish on the pasha's shores. At the conclusion of the slaves' chorus there is a final rhythmic "*tambourin*," presumably danced by the slaves, since everyone else has departed. One tender heart remains, of course—Osman Pasha, who so discreetly withdraws to spare the lovers the sight of his grief—but there is no suggestion in the opera that the tender sensibility of the "generous Turk" will extend to the emancipation of his other slaves.

The actual historical redemption of captive slaves from Ottoman masters was rarely a manifestation of Turkish generosity, but rather a strictly financial matter of ransom payments. The Church of England sponsored "charity briefs" to raise money through individual contributions for the ransom of captives.[42] In Catholic Europe, religious orders and confraternities played a large role in raising ransom money; the Mercedarians and Trinitarians were active in this regard, and in Rome the Vatican encouraged the role of the confraternity of Santa Maria del Gonfalone. In Denmark, on the Baltic, the crown established a "Slave Fund" in 1715 to ransom Mediterranean captives. In Venice the republican state played a supervisory role in raising money for ransoms, and in Sicily, separated by only a hundred miles of sea from North Africa, public tax money was designated for redeeming captives. Some samples of statistical evidence suggest that after five years of captivity, as many as

75 percent of captives may have been ransomed, so there were always former captives present in European society to tell (and sometimes even publish) their stories.[43]

After redemption the emancipated captives played a role in celebratory religious processions and services, and historian Linda Colley has outlined the course of the French ceremonies:

> The first took place in the port of re-entry, usually Marseilles. The procession of redeemed captives then followed a traditional route that had evolved over centuries: Toulon, Avignon, Lyon, and so on to the sacred heart of France, Paris itself. At each and every stopping-off place, there were ceremonies in which local elites participated and ordinary folk watched. Bells rang. Soldiers assembled. Strewn flowers were crushed into scent under milling crowds . . . And at the heart of it all were the white-robed captives.[44]

Such spectacles, accompanied by elements of ecclesiastical music, were even incipiently operatic, anticipating in public spaces the celebratory concluding chorus and ballet that Rameau staged at the Paris Opéra in 1735. In Italian redemption processions there were sometimes trumpets and drums, sometimes choral singing, and in one case, in Milan in 1764, a military band playing music in the Turkish or Janissary style.[45] In London in 1751 the display of redeemed captives was made into a theatrical event on the stage of Covent Garden. Recently ransomed from Morocco, the former captives were once again put in rags and chains as part of the show. As recounted by Linda Colley, "In words, song, and mime, the enthralled habitués of Covent Garden were informed that these were the same loathsome irons and gaping rags in which the men had labored for so long in Muslim North Africa."[46] Eighteenth-century operas of Ottoman captivity were partly inspired by such spectacles with their lurid claims to authenticity.

Rameau's operatic account of the generous Turk was followed by a scenario among the Incas of Peru, but after that there was a return to the Islamic Orient for "Les fleurs," set in the gardens of Persia. This Persian story was closely related to the theme of the earlier Turkish story, inasmuch as both concerned love between Muslim masters and their female slaves. In "Les fleurs" the Persian masters are in love, each with the other's slave, so that the happy ending can be achieved by exchanging slaves. In Campra's *L'Europe galante* of 1697, there was no doubt that a slave could love her master, and Zaide sang of her love for Zuliman with melancholy baroque intensity. In 1735 the weighty issue of slavery was aired by Rameau in a duet of lighthearted rococo charm. First, the slave Zaïre (named for Voltaire's heroine) poses the question:

Peut-on aimer dans l'esclavage?	Can one love in slavery?
C'est en augmenter la rigueur.	It increases the harshness.[47]

It was of course a powerfully modern and enlightened question: whether it was possible for real love to subsist where one partner held absolute despotic power over the other who was nothing more than a slave. Yet it was answered, by Prince Tacmas, in the decidedly unmodern spirit that Fuzelier and Rameau seemed to attribute to the Islamic Orient:

On doit aimer dans l'esclavage,	One must love in slavery,
C'est en adoucir la rigueur.	It softens the harshness.[48]

Did it mean that she ought to love, so as to soften the harshness of slavery, or that she was compelled to love, since she was, after all, a slave?

The answer was evaded in the most exquisite rococo lyricism as the two voices, tenor and soprano, repeated their respective verses while harmonizing with one another. Rameau offered a "gallant" perspective on Oriental despotism and slavery, represented in Oriental terms as the principles of supreme erotic pleasure, and celebrated in the end with a ballet of the Persian flowers. Emilie, however, in the Turkish act, is not resigned to romantic enslavement, and her European loyalty to the man she loves compels the Turkish pasha himself to rise to a European standard of civilization, a generous Turk in the context of the gallant Indies.

Scanderbeg and the Sultan:
The Ottoman-Albanian Encounter at the Opéra

While *Les Indes galantes* celebrated Turkey and Persia together for their gallantry in 1735, in fact the Ottomans and Persians were at war with one another in the early 1730s. Topal Osman Pasha (the real-life model for Rameau's Osman Pasha) was killed in that war in 1733, and the fighting ended in 1735 with a Persian victory that brought territorial advances against the Turks in the Caucasus. In that same year war began between the Ottomans and the Russians, who attacked the Crimea, further dramatizing Ottoman vulnerability at the very moment that Vivaldi's Bajazet and Rameau's Osman Pasha held their respective stages in Verona and Paris. *Les Indes galantes* opened in Paris on August 23, 1735, and before the end of the year, on October 27, yet another Ottoman subject was brought to the operatic stage in Paris, a full five-act opera set at the Ottoman court of the fifteenth century: *Scanderberg*, composed jointly by François Francoeur and François Rebel.

The historical Scanderbeg (not Scanderberg) was a Christian Albanian prince, taken hostage by the Ottomans and raised as a Muslim; he served in the Ottoman military before turning against Sultan Murad II in the 1440s and leading the Albanian resistance to Ottoman domination. In the opera of 1735 the figure of Scanderbeg represented the complex relation between Ottoman Turkish sultans and their Ottoman European subjects, inhabitants of the lands that were labeled on eighteenth-century maps as "*Turquie en Europe*."

Vivaldi had composed an earlier opera on the subject, *Scanderbeg*, performed in Florence in 1718, the year of the peace of Passarowitz.[49] The libretto was by the same Antonio Salvi who wrote the text of *Il gran Tamerlano* for Alessandro Scarlatti in 1706. Vivaldi's opera (for which the music has been mostly lost) was set at the Ottoman siege of Croia (Krujë, in Albania today), successfully defended by Scanderbeg against Murad ("Amurat," in the libretto). Scanderbeg was designated in the cast as the "King of Albania," but was also understood to be in some sense "Greek," summoned by destiny, according to the libretto, to liberate Greece from the "tyrant of Asia."[50] Scanderbeg was sung by a castrato, while Murad, his Ottoman nemesis, was sung by a tenor.

Each character holds a captive, Murad holding Scanderbeg's wife and Scanderbeg holding Murad's daughter, and this custody becomes a test of civilization, which the sultan notably fails as he attempts to force himself on his captive. Scanderbeg's virtue is dedicated to the pursuit of love and glory, as expressed in a brilliant aria:

Con palme, ed allori	With palms and laurels
M'invita la Gloria,	Glory invites me,
Con serti di fiori	With garlands of flowers
M'alletta l'amor.	Love attracts me.[51]

The sultan, by contrast, is deceitful, ignoble, and barbarous, vices that he almost extols in song:

| Son Tiranno, son spietato, | I am a tyrant, I am merciless, |
| Cosi fosse sempre stato. | And so I have always been.[52] |

The final Albanian chorus celebrates the defeat of the sultan and the return of peace, which was appropriate for the moment of Passarowitz in 1718 but radically different from the dominant theme of operatic sympathy for the Ottomans, as expressed in Piovene's contemporary libretto about Bajazet.

From Vivaldi's Venetian perspective Albania would not have seemed alien or remote, but would rather have evoked a long history of Venetian-Adriatic relations and imperial rule. The vestigial territory of "Albania Veneta" was still on the map in the eighteenth century, though most of Albania had been long subject to the Ottomans. Albania, however, would have seemed rather more remote from the perspective of Paris, and the French opera *Scanderberg* in 1735 followed a completely different scenario, showing the hero at an earlier stage of his life as a captive and hostage at Murad's Ottoman court. The libretto was partly credited to Antoine Houdar de La Motte, who was also the librettist for Campra's *L'Europe galante* back in 1697. It is notable that La Motte's libretto for *Scanderberg* (still incomplete and unperformed at his death in 1731) dated back to 1711, the same year that Piovene created his libretto for *Tamerlano* in Venice.[53] Francoeur and Rebel, the joint composers of *Scanderberg* in 1735, belonged to a younger generation. Not only musical collaborators—inspired first by Lully and later influenced by Rameau—they also formed a powerful partnership in the administration of the Paris Opéra right up until the 1770s.

The plot of *Scanderberg* in Paris made little sense in terms of the hero's biography, which would have been in any event largely unknown to the French public in 1735. The historical Scanderbeg was kept as a youthful hostage at the Ottoman court of Murad. In the opera they are both in love with the same Serbian princess, punningly named "Servilie" in the libretto, and she too is being held at the Ottoman court. The leading sultana of the sultan's harem, Roxane, is also in love with Scanderbeg, though he prefers Servilie. The court was probably located in Edirne, as Murad's reign preceded the Ottoman conquest of Constantinople by his son Mehmed II in 1453. Scanderbeg's subjection to Murad inverted the drama of Bajazet and Tamerlane, as now the Ottoman sultan played the part of the master instead of the captive. The Ottoman role of Murad ("Amurat" again in the libretto) was sung by the famous French basso Claude-Louis Chassé de Chinais, who had played an Incan role in *Les Indes galantes* and was "arguably the greatest male singing actor of the eighteenth century in Paris."[54]

The role of Scanderbeg was sung by a high tenor (*haute-contre*), Denis-François Tribou, who also played a Persian prince in *Les Indes galantes*. In the opening scene Scanderbeg anticipates his escape from the Ottomans, singing in elegant French verse:

> O Nuit, hâte-toi donc de triompher du jour!
> J'entends la gloire qui m'appelle!
>
> O Night! hasten to triumph over the day!
> I hear glory calling to me![55]

His sentiments are generally noble, though he admits that he is also motivated by an impulse of Albanian "vengeance" against the Turks.

Murad, meanwhile, courts the Serbian princess, while a chorus of Greek women in Servilie's service urges her to surrender herself: "*Cedez à l'Amour.*" Roxane, now jealous of Servilie on two counts (since the Serbian princess is beloved by both Murad and Scanderbeg), plots the murder of the sultan. Scanderbeg refuses to act dishonorably by joining in the plot against the sultan, and instead fights on Murad's behalf against the treacherous Grand Vizier and a chorus of Janissaries.

Roxane finally denounces Scanderbeg and Servilie to the sultan, who becomes furiously jealous in the manner of Voltaire's Sultan Orosmane, from *Zaïre*. Murad sings:

> Regnez Haine, Fureur,   Reign hate and fury,
> Regnez jalouse Rage . . .   Reign jealous rage . . .[56]

The Ottoman sultan Murad thus brought together the most important operatic aspects of the singing Turk, who gave voice to the extremes of absolute power and unrestrained emotion.

In the final act, the scene presented—perhaps for the first time in the history of opera—a great mosque, in which Murad was about to marry Servilie. The set was designed by Giovanni Servandoni, who had also worked on *Les Indes galantes*. The *Mercure de France* described this set for the last act of *Scanderberg* as a great peristyle of classical arcades leading to a domed mosque that was not quite classical: "The peristyle is entirely of the Corinthian order, according to the most precise rules, but there is a departure from those rules in the architecture of the mosque, first, to suggest that in the Orient where the arts are not cultivated as in Europe, one does not build with the same regularity; second, to render the place in some fashion more alien [*plus étranger*]." The doors could also be opened, as the act progressed, to enable the audience to see inside the mosque, where elaborate decoration took priority over architecture: "The whole interior of the mosque is encrusted with precious stones of different colors and different kinds, like lapis lazuli, jasper, agate, alabaster, and others fit to enrich in a striking [*éclatant*] manner a magnificent temple." The interior was lit by hanging lamps decorated with ostrich eggs—"according to the custom of the Orientals." The *Mercure* noted that those who inspected Servandoni's stage designs from up close could see "with astonishment the mechanics of this brilliant piece whose ingenious art makes a space quite restricted in itself appear to be an extremely vast place." The mosque designed for the final act of *Scanderberg* seemed to "surpass" all other stage designs by Servandoni.[57]

At the dramatic climax of the act the mufti steps forward in the mosque in the name of "the irritated Prophet" (*le Prophète irrité*)—perhaps the first musical mufti in Paris since Lully's mock-mufti in the Turkish ceremony of *Le bourgeois gentilhomme*. In *Scanderberg*, the mufti is to be taken entirely seriously, as he objects to the marriage between Muslim and Christian, between Murad and Servilie. "The universe is subject to you," the mufti tells the sultan, "but you are subject to the law." Murad rages against Scanderbeg, his rival for Servilie, but she then kills herself in a gesture intended to reconcile the two men. Scanderbeg is about to follow her by killing himself, too, when the sultan intervenes, seizes the dagger, and sings the final lines of the opera:

> Arrête, es tu content barbare!
> Je ne puis soutenir ce spectacle d'horreur.
> Loin de moi, va pleurer notre commun malheur;
> Que s'il se peut la gloire le répare.
>
> Stop, are you content, barbarian!
> I cannot bear this spectacle of horror.
> Far from me, go weep over our common misfortune;
> That glory, if it can, may repair.[58]

Murad seeks to show himself more civilized than his "barbarian" captive. It is too late for him to play the generous Turk and send the originally Christian lovers off together, but he generously gives Scanderbeg his freedom to pursue a glory that will in fact be achieved at the expense of the Ottomans in defense of Albania. The opera represents Murad as a relatively enlightened figure—like Voltaire's Orosmane—struggling to resist the religious prejudices of his own Janissaries and muftis and to contain the violent impulses of his own jealousy. If, however, *Scanderberg* in 1735 was supposed to comment allusively on the political prospects for Ottoman subjects in southeastern Europe—Serbs and Albanians—the wars of the 1730s, including the Turkish reconquest of Belgrade, showed that the Ottomans were by no means completely debilitated or ready to be expelled from "*Turquie en Europe.*"

Conclusion: Scanderbeg Redux

The *Scanderberg* of Francoeur and Rebel in 1735 was undeniably tragic, with the suicide of Servilie, but after that, Murad proved himself to be, belatedly, a generous Turk in his final intervention to save and emancipate Scanderbeg. Similarly, Handel's *Tamerlano* was a tragedy, with the suicide of Bajazet, but ended in the reconciliation of Tamerlane and Andronico and the return of peace, "crowned with lilies and roses." It was perhaps no surprise that the libretto of *Scanderberg*, conceived by La Motte in 1711 and therefore contemporary with Piovene's libretto for *Tamerlano*, should have been similarly tragic in its musical and dramatic impact. Yet if the happy romance of Rameau's "Le Turc généreux" were to be contrasted with the fatal tragedy of *Scanderberg* as the two operatic alternatives of 1735, there would be no doubt that *Scanderberg* belonged to the operatic past while "Le Turc généreux" pointed toward an operatic future full of comedies of captivity. In fact, *Scanderberg* disappeared from the repertory entirely after 1735, until it was rediscovered for one single performance in 1763. That unique revival only confirmed the triumph of comedy for operas on Ottoman subjects, because the libretto was adapted to eliminate the tragedy and provide a thoroughly happy ending.

The performance of 1763 took place at the Fontainebleau palace in the presence of King Louis XV and Queen Marie Leszczyńska (the daughter of Stanisław Leszczyński). Still denominated as a tragedy, the performance of 1763 managed to reach a happy ending: Murad stops Servilie from killing herself at the last minute and then declines to take Scanderbeg's life. Instead the sultan begs their pardon:

Pardonnez-moi vos maux, que l'hymen les répare.
Je serai malheureux; mais je serois barbare . . .

Pardon me for your harms, which marriage may repair.
I will be unhappy; but otherwise I would be a barbarian . . .[59]

It may not have been altogether comfortable for Louis XV to watch a reigning monarch beg for pardon, but he could have reassured himself in thinking that a Muslim sultan was a case entirely different from his own. In fact, the figure of the generous Turk was intended precisely as a mirror for enlightened European princes, and Servilie explicitly thanks Murad for his "generous heart" (*coeur généreux*). Murad then echoes the melancholy dignity of the generous Turk in *Les Indes galantes*, singing:

Partez, dans vos Etats,	Depart, to your countries,
Ramenez vos sujets . . .	Bring back your subjects . . .[60]

With this gesture of generosity the sultan turns and enters the mosque, resolving to respect his own Islamic law, and he is followed by the Muslim imams and the Turkish people.

The stage is left to Scanderbeg and Servilie with their dancing suites of Albanians and Serbians. Scanderbeg sings, "*Qu'un beau jour renaisse sans nuage*" (May a beautiful day be cloudlessly reborn). The Serbian and Albanian dancers join in a ballet of harmonious celebration, naturally unable to foresee the modern history of Serbian-Albanian enmity. In the original 1735 version the program of dances specified sultanas to dance in act 1, Turkish men and Greek women in act 2, Janissaries and sipahis in act 3, Italians, Asiatics, and Scythians in act 4, and odalisques in act 5. The program for 1763 at Fontainebleau specified, for act 5, Serbians and Albanians (instead of odalisques), thus transforming the opera even more fully into a drama of the Ottoman empire and the subject peoples of southeastern Europe.[61] Those peoples were happily liberated at Fontainebleau in 1763, though the first Serbian uprising against the Ottomans would not come until 1804, and Albanian independence was not achieved until 1912.

Murad sends the Serbians and Albanians at the Ottoman court back to their homelands, thus seeming to suggest an implicit renunciation of Ottoman imperial rule. In this regard, it is worth noting that 1763 represented the imperial nadir of French power in the eighteenth century, and the triumphant British terms of the peace of Paris in February (including the definitive loss of Canada to the British) may have conditioned an imperial reticence in the reviving and revising of *Scanderberg* in October at Fontainebleau. Perhaps there was a lesson to be learned from the Ottomans about maintaining national dignity in the face of imperial recession. In the operatic encounter of Scanderbeg and Murad, as in that of Tamerlane and Bajazet, the humbling of the Ottoman sultan was accompanied by the musical demonstration of Ottoman dignity.

The Triumphant Sultana

Suleiman and His Operatic Harem

Introduction: The Operatic Subversion of Ottoman Despotism

The Paris fairs presented musical comedies of Ottoman captivity from the very beginning of the eighteenth century, featuring the popular figure of Arlequin who could easily distract the sultan by disguising himself as a sultana. At the Académie Royale, in "Le Turc généreux," Rameau created a more dignified operatic work of Ottoman captivity, eliminating Arlequin and his farcical travesties, and emphasizing the Turkish pasha's generosity rather than the European captives' ingenuity. From a popular musical farce at the fairs the opera of captivity now became a rococo comedy of sentiment and emotion, and even Osman Pasha himself was able to sound the note of delicate sensibility: "*Souvenez-vous d'Osman.*" The harlequin antics, banished by Rameau in 1735, would irrepressibly return in 1736 at the Saint-Laurent fair, with a musical farce entitled *Les Français au sérail*, probably intended as a response to Rameau's opera. Arlequin was included in the dramatis personae, and his master, Clitandre, the French hero of the piece, sought to rescue his captive beloved by penetrating a Persian harem in the undignified disguise of a eunuch.[1]

Popular farce and sentimental comedy were different aspects of the musical representation of Ottoman captivity in the 1730s. Whether at the Académie Royale or at the Paris fairs, the plot of the comedy involved the escape or emancipation of the captives, so that they might return to Europe. When the curtain came down, Ottomans and Europeans were decisively directed to go their separate ways, to reside ever after on their own native shores of the Mediterranean. Yet beginning already in the 1730s, another storyline emerged in the musical comedy of Ottoman captivity: the drama of the captive European woman who prefers to remain with her pasha or sultan and, without conceding anything to his despotic authority, sets about comically reforming his manners and customs. Rather than return to Europe, she remains among the Turks, reconceiving her own captivity as an opportunity for mastery, for reforming and even civilizing the Ottoman empire. Carlo Goldoni provided an early libretto for such a comedy, performed at Carnival in Venice in the 1730s under the title *Lugrezia Romana in Costantinopoli.*

This new kind of musical comedy of captivity received its most celebrated incarnation in Paris in 1761: *Les trois sultanes* (The three sultanas), created by Charles-Simon Favart. This work presented Sultan Suleiman the Magnificent as the lovesick plaything of a captive French sultana. The historical Suleiman, who conquered a vast empire from Buda to Baghdad in the sixteenth century and even laid siege to Vienna in 1529, now became a figure of light entertainment on the Paris stage. In 1697 Campra's *L'Europe galante* presented, in the Turkish act, the amorous harem of "Zuliman"—who could have been Suleiman. An Italian libretto by Giovanni Ambrogio Migliavacca, set to music by Johann Adolph Hasse for Dresden in 1753, offered Suleiman in the more earnest context of *opera seria.* It was, however, Favart's comical conception in *The Three Sultanas* which would achieve the greatest theatrical success, traveling all over Europe in the later eighteenth century, translated into various languages, with the triumphant sultana sometimes changing nationality to flatter the particular public before which she appeared. The musical skills of the operatic diva played a part in the seduction of the sultan, but the European cleverness of the sultana along with her absolute confidence in her superior European civilization always confirmed her success. The operatic triumph of the diva on stage thus reflected a European triumph over the Ottoman empire, inflected as the political triumph of European liberty over Oriental despotism.

Goldonian Captivity: Lucretia in Constantinople

In the 1730s, while the Ottomans waged war against the Russians and the Habsburgs, Venice fully enjoyed the luxury of neutrality for the first time, even as the culture of the Enlightenment produced a fashionable Venetian Turcheria, corresponding to French Turquerie.[2] In 1737 the young Carlo Goldoni, only thirty years old and not yet embarked on his great theatrical reform, presented for the Venetian Carnival at the Teatro Grimani di San Samuele the comedy *Lugrezia Romana in Costantinopoli*, with music composed by Giacomo Maccari. "It will seem strange," observed Goldoni in the published preface, "that I want to send to Constantinople Lucretia the Roman, who died so many centuries before the Turkish Empire arose."[3] The legendary Lucretia, a virtuous Roman wife, committed suicide after being raped by the son of Roman king Tarquinius Superbus, which led to the establishment of the Roman Republic. The traditional Venetian animus against Rome, combined with a newly lighthearted Venetian view of the Ottomans, conditioned the humor of the comedy. Goldoni imagined the virtuous Lucretia in the harem of the Ottoman sultan, compelled to defend her virtue from his despotic authority and Oriental lust. In 1735 Vivaldi was still composing sultanic tragedy with *Bajazet* in Verona, using Piovene's libretto, but in 1737 Goldoni was ready for Ottoman comedy in Venice.

Goldoni imagined a sultan—Albumazar—who was so susceptible to his Italian harem captives that he was ready to command his Turkish subjects to speak Italian as a sort of comprehensive linguistic reform:

Benchè sia maomettano, Although you may be Muslim,
Se brama il mio favor, If you want my favor,
parli italiano. speak Italian.[4]

Albumazar's whole program of European reform, which involves shaving moustaches and permitting pork, is denounced by the Ottoman official Maimut, who can speak a kind of Venetian pidgin but cannot keep from lapsing into nonsense phrases that are supposed to be Turkish. He sings, "*Ischinai scialacabalai / uzchimoch iraschimintoch*"—verses which suggest that Goldoni was inspired by the much older precedent of Molière's Turkish ceremony.[5]

There is some suggestion that the work involved a parodic attempt to imitate Turkish music, for after the chorus sings nonsense syllables—"*Uzcha, muzcha, scialla acbe aclà aclà*"—Lucretia wonders, "What angry music could that ever be?" Albumazar commands her to sing along, and though she hesitates for fear that the "Turkish" words might be blasphemous, by the end of the scene she too is singing "*Uzcha, muzcha*."[6] The first act ends with the Roman and Venetian favorites, Lucretia and Mirmicaina, biting and scratching one another while singing a musical duet.[7] The second act concludes with everyone denouncing Albumazar as a tyrant: "*Tiranno, sì sì.*"[8] Yet this supposed tyranny is represented as comedy, since the sultan himself—while issuing occasional threats of impalement—is scarcely able to exercise authority over the Italian women in his harem.

In the third act Lucretia cannot quite decide whether she is ready (once again) to sacrifice her life in order to protect her Roman honor, in this case from the sultan. A little lubrication, however, leads to the happy ending, when her Roman husband, Collatino, has the idea of offering wine to the Muslim Maimut, who eagerly accepts. "*Ti voler amizuzia*" (I want your friendship), sings Maimut drunkenly, anticipating the famous duet between Osmin and Pedrillo in Mozart's *Abduction from the Seraglio*, half a century later. "*Mi no star imbriago*" (I'm not drunk), he sings in his peculiar Venetian pidgin. "*Tu mi vomiti adosso*" (You just threw up on me), observes Collatino. Maimut, however, takes no notice, and is already singing a song of pseudo-Turkish nonsense: "*Sallamica, gnescapà / urchibaica retacan . . .*" His song, furthermore, swerving into pseudo-Venetian, now embraces the Westernizing reforms that he earlier opposed:

Mi voler taggiar mustacchia,	I want to cut off my moustache,
Per parer muso talian.	To have an Italian mug.[9]

Meanwhile, Mirmicaina painfully tears out, hair by hair, the moustache of Ruscamar, the harem guard. In the final scene, all the characters are about to commit heroic suicide, in the style of the Roman Lucretia, but then decide they'd rather just live happily ever after. They sing "*pace, pace, e non più guerra*" (peace, peace, and no more war), a pacifically happy ending that was consistent with Venetian neutrality in a decade of international warfare.[10]

The decade concluded in 1740 with a new Turkish drama in Venice, also performed at the Teatro Grimani di San Samuele: *Osmano Re di Tunisi* (Osman, king of Tunisia). It was characterized as a *tragicommedia*, because it was in part a heroic rescue drama involving Christian captives in Tunisia but also involved elements of commedia dell'arte to create a comic subplot among the servants. A Spanish nobleman is seeking to rescue his niece, but King Osman has fallen in love with her. King Osman's sister Felima loves the king's friend Acmat Aga, but he is in love with another Christian captive. At the same time, the commedia dell'arte characters are having romances and adventures of their own: Brighella and Truffaldino are captive servants of the king, "destined for labor, but bitter enemies of all work." Truffaldino even converts to Islam, and in the end has to "renounce the turban which by his foolishness he let himself be persuaded to adopt." In the case of *Osmano Re di Tunisi*, the text has been lost and only a synopsis survives, so neither the Turkish details nor the possibility of musical numbers can be determined. Scholar Anna Scannapieco, however, has hypothesized that this anonymous work may in fact be a lost drama by Goldoni himself.[11]

French Sultanas and Artistic Turquerie

The 1730s, which brought Rameau's "Le Turc généreux" to the Paris Opéra, also witnessed a display of Turkish costumes and scenes in French rococo painting. Jean-Marc Nattier painted "Mademoiselle de Clermont Dressed as a Sultana," enthroned after her bath and surrounded by slaves (today in the Wallace Collection). This European woman posing as a Turkish sultana closely corresponded to the impersonation of Turkish figures that took place on the stage. Meanwhile, Carle Van Loo emerged as a specialist on Turkish themes with paintings that showed turbaned Turks solemnizing a marriage contract, a pasha having his mistress's portrait painted, and "The Grand Turk Giving a Concert to His Mistress" (also in the Wallace Collection). The music of the concert can be identified from the painting as a Handel aria, so Van Loo's conception was to represent turbaned Turks enjoying European music.

The Swiss painter Jean-Étienne Liotard lived in Constantinople from 1738 to 1742, and on his return to Europe not only wore Turkish clothing himself but also made a specialty of painting portraits of subjects in Turkish costume. Empress Maria Theresa was painted in Turkish dress in the 1740s and Lady Mary Wortley Montagu in the 1750s. In 1746 François Boucher consolidated the relation between rococo art and Turquerie when he provided the illustrations for Jean-Antoine Guer's *Moeurs et usages des Turcs*. The rise of Mme Pompadour to power at Versailles in the later 1740s and 1750s, to preside there as the principal mistress of Louis XV, further encouraged a self-consciously Ottoman representation of the monarch and his "harem" of mistresses. Mme Pompadour created a Turkish room for herself at the Chateau de Bellevue, with paintings by Carle Van Loo that showed a sultana drinking coffee, a sultana playing the lute, and two sultanas doing embroidery. The coffee drinker was recognizably Mme Pompadour herself in Turkish cap and costume, seated on a divan and attended by a slave who poured the coffee. "In the domain of Turquerie," writes Marianne Roland Michel, "while the figures dressed or acted in a fashion characteristic of their countries, their features remained European," and therefore, "despite their clothing and hairstyles, the young women in the paintings are merely keeping up an Oriental fiction."[12] The features remained European in part because Turks were presumed to have European features, and this resemblance also facilitated the representation of Turks on the European stage.

In 1754 Carle Van Loo received the further commission to design a set of Gobelin tapestries on Turkish subjects. These would not be carried out until 1772, after Van Loo's death and that of Mme Pompadour, and therefore the project was inherited by his nephew Amédée Van Loo, working in the last years of the reign of Louis XV, the age of a new principal mistress, Mme du Barry. She herself was satirized as the "French Sultana"—in the anonymous *Mémoires secrets*, for instance, where it was also insinuated that she had the tapestries created to stimulate the lust of the old king with Turkish scenarios: "The French Sultana sought to represent herself, in foreign guise, before the eyes of her august lover, so as to fix his attention by any means." Art historian Perrin Stein has concluded that Mme du Barry was probably not the patroness of the tapestries, but that Van Loo may have nevertheless sought to flatter her by giving the sultana something of her aspect.[13] The scenes showed the sultana at her toilette, the sultana having coffee and smoking a long pipe with eunuchs in attendance, the sultana supervising the embroidery work of the odalisques of the harem, and the odalisques entertaining the sultan and sultana—with the whole ensemble of designs titled as *Le costume turc*. In the reign of Louis XVI, both the queen, Marie Antoinette, and the king's brother, the Comte d'Artois, would create Turkish rooms with appropriate furnishings at Fontainebleau and Versailles.[14] Thus the settings and costumes for Turkish scenarios on the stage were developed in French art and design during the middle decades of the eighteenth century.

The theatrical work which both exploited and harmonized these many facets of French Turquerie was the musical comedy *Les trois sultanes* (The three sultanas), also known as *Soliman Second*, created by Charles-Simon Favart in 1761 with music by Paul-César Gibert. In that very same year Gibert also worked on *La fausse Turque* (The false Turkish woman) for the Paris Saint-Laurent fair. Favart had also begun his career writing works for the Paris fairs, and was certainly familiar with their Turkish entertainments.[15] Already in 1735 Favart was participating in parodies of *Les Indes galantes* at the Saint-Laurent fair, mocking the exoticism of "Le Turc généreux": "Ah, look carefully now, we are being transported by the genius of the opera to the shores of the Indian Ocean in Turkey."[16] In 1741, also at the fair, Favart presented the musical comedy *Le bacha d'Alger*, in which the commedia dell'arte rogue Scapin assists in arranging an escape from the pasha's harem. One song reproduced for the crowd a quick summary of the Oriental observations of Montesquieu and Voltaire:

Je veux fuir ces climats affreux	I want to flee these terrible climates
Ou le beau sexe est malheureux.	Where the fair sex is unhappy.
Ici contrainte, sédentaire,	Here constrained and sedentary,
Une femme pour toute affaire	A woman for every affair
S'occupe du matin au soir	Is occupied morning to evening
A maudire un eunuque noir.	In cursing a black eunuch.
Quelle différence en Europe!	What a difference in Europe![17]

In the context of the commedia dell'arte, and the Saint-Laurent fair, one might suppose that the concluding exclamation was intended ironically.

By 1761 Favart was the director of the Opéra-Comique (with which he was so closely associated that its current theater is known today as the Salle Favart). It was at the Comédie-Italienne, closely associated with the Opéra-Comique, that *The Three Sultanas* was presented in 1761, and it would continue to hold the stage through the ancien régime, the French Revolution, the Napoleonic period, and under the Restoration. The music, as provided by Gibert, also involved borrowing popular melodies and would be revised to suit the musical tastes of later decades.[18]

In 1762 the Comédie-Italienne was merged with the Opéra-Comique, both absorbing some of the style and spirit of the Paris fairs and cultivating the genre of *comédie mêlée d'ariettes* (comedy mixed with songs) as it evolved into the modern form of *opéra comique*.[19] As a cultural product of this particular moment, with spoken dialogue and musical numbers, *The Three Sultanas* would become the principal musical-theatrical representation of one of the most powerful and celebrated Ottoman emperors, Suleiman the

Magnificent. In the sixteenth century, Suleiman achieved the maximal extent of the Ottoman empire by his conquests in North Africa, the Middle East, and southeastern Europe. For the French public of the eighteenth century, however, he would become a subject of frivolous musical farce, along with the most powerful woman in the history of the Ottoman harem, his wife Roxelana, or Hürrem Sultan, now theatrically reconceived as an ambitious Frenchwoman—played and sung by Favart's wife Marie-Justine—exercising her charms to captivate the sultan. Mme Favart was painted in her Turkish costume by Liotard, while another contemporary drawing showed her seated upon an Oriental sofa, and an engraved portrait had her playing the harp as she sang for Suleiman.[20] *The Three Sultanas* in 1761 thus manifested on stage all the interest in Turkish scenes, costumes, and furnishings that had been present in French rococo art under the aegis of Mme Pompadour in the 1750s. It would even be possible to interpret the drama as a satire on the influence of Mme Pompadour over Louis XV, as reflected in the relations of their Turkish analogues, Roxelana and Suleiman.

Favart's comedy was based on the story "Soliman II" by the French *philosophe* Jean-François Marmontel, who showed Suleiman transcending the promiscuity of the harem by concluding a real marriage with a European captive. While Suleiman was actually the first sultan of that name, he was sometimes mislabeled as the second—hence "Soliman II"—because Bajazet had a son named Suleiman whom some supposed to have reigned briefly during the interregnum that followed Bajazet's death in 1403. Marmontel's "moral tale" about Roxelana's civilizing influence on Suleiman was taken up by Favart who made it into a musical comedy. Both Marmontel and Favart were supposed to have enjoyed the favor and protection of Mme Pompadour.

Ottoman historian Leslie Peirce notes the unique significance of Roxelana in Ottoman history: Suleiman married her and made her "the first slave concubine in Ottoman history to be freed and made a legal wife."[21] According to a contemporary report from Istanbul, "There has occurred in this city a most extraordinary event, one absolutely unprecedented in the history of the Sultans. The Grand Signior Suleiman has taken to himself as his Empress a slave-woman from Russia, called Roxelana, and there has been great feasting."[22] After her marriage, Roxelana lived with Suleiman in his palace, apart from the harem, and became, as Peirce has observed, the sultan's "political

Marie-Justine Favart as "La Jeune Sultane" (The young sultana). She was the wife of
Charles-Simon Favart who created *Les trois sultanes* in Paris in 1761. Madame Favart
was celebrated in the starring role of the sultana Roxelana and played the harp herself
while singing to captivate Sultan Suleiman. Engraving by César Corbutt of portrait
by Louis-Pierre Legendre, printed in London, 1761. With kind permission of the
Bibliothèque Nationale de France.

Marie-Justine Favart as Roxelana, in a more exotic Oriental costume, a record of her famous eighteenth-century role as depicted in the early-nineteenth-century *Galerie Théâtrale*. Mme Favart, who died in 1772, was still remembered as the star of the original production. Engraving by Pierre-Paul Prud'hon of drawing by Sébastien Coeuré. With kind permission of the Österreichische Nationalbibliothek.

confidante."[23] Marmontel's tale and Favart's comedy reflected upon Roxelana's unprecedented elevation and her female political influence, a subject of major interest in the eighteenth century.[24]

The Three Sultanas took place in "*Constantinople, dans le Serrail du Grand Seigneur.*" The first scene specified "the interior apartments of the Serrail, ornamented with carpets, incense burners, sofas, and other furnishings according to the custom of the Turks."[25] In short, the staging was intended as an illustration of contemporary Turquerie, with props often described in precise detail as if advertised for sale: "two porcelain cups and a little spoon made from the beak of a very rare bird of the Indies, the beak more red than coral and very precious," or "a round table of solid silver, a foot and a half in height, four feet in diameter, with a thickness of two inches," or "a large chandelier ornamented with crystals of different colors and ostrich eggs."[26] These extravagant theatrical effects probably helped to inspire the furnishing of the Boudoir Turc that Marie Antoinette created at Fontainebleau in the 1770s, including Pierre Gouthière's gilded dromedary andirons for the fireplace.[27] Likewise, it may have been performances of *Les trois sultanes* that inspired Fragonard's painting of a sultana seated on an Ottoman sofa in the 1770s, the costume and the piece of furniture constituting a complete Ottoman ensemble.

Favart claimed that the costumes for *The Three Sultanas* were actually made in Constantinople, "the true clothing of Turkish ladies." He remarked that "nothing is more ridiculous than to see seraglios furnished in French style," and therefore authentic sets and costumes were supposed to enhance the "theatrical illusion" of Turkishness.[28] The costumes of *The Three Sultanas* were so much a part of the work's success that they inspired the costumes for the revival of *Scanderberg* at Fontainebleau in 1763.[29] In fact, the revival of that opera, which had probably not been performed since its creation in 1735, belonged to the new moment of operatic Turkishness established by the success of *The Three Sultanas* in the 1760s.

Roxelana and Suleiman: "The pleasures of equality"

The three sultanas of Favart's title were Roxelana from France, Elmira from Spain, and the Circassian Delia. The plot involves Roxelana captivating the sultan by her refusal of obedience, effectively alienating his affections from the other all-too-compliant sultanas, and thus making herself the master of the Turkish sultan and the Ottoman empire. This represented an explicitly French triumph over Ottoman despotism.

Suleiman's submission is witnessed with comic distress by Osmin, "the kislar-aga or chief of the eunuchs," whose eunuch status was treated comically in the spirit of the Paris fairs. The part was taken in 1761 by Antoine Trial, who specialized in comical servants and whose vocal type, according to theater historian Isabelle Moindrot, was "a high tenor voice with a piercing and nasal tone"—perhaps high enough to suggest castration.[30] When Suleiman complains of his unhappiness in love, Osmin reminds him that "there is a still worse state [*un état pire*]: that's mine [*c'est le mien*]." Osmin becomes the spokesman for traditional Muslim gender relations, reminding the sultan:

> Je vous l'ai déjà dit, toutes femmes sont femmes:
> Croyons en Mahomet notre Législateur;
> La nature prudente imprime dans leur âmes
> La complaisance, la douceur.
>
> I told you already, all women are women:
> Let us believe in Mohammed our lawgiver;
> Prudent nature impresses upon their souls
> Compliance and sweetness.[31]

Roxelana polemicizes against this position in the name of equality and does not hesitate to denounce Osmin to his face as an "amphibious monster."[32] On the European operatic stage, Favart's Osmin in 1761 might be seen as a predecessor of Mozart's Osmin in 1782, the pasha's overseer, though the latter would no longer be specified as a eunuch.

At Suleiman's first encounter with Roxelana she already proposes abolishing the seraglio:

> Let the doors of the seraglio be open,
> So that only happiness prevents departure.
> Treat your slaves as ladies,
> Be gallant with all women
> but tender with one alone . . .[33]

She also establishes the relation between herself and the sultan, assuming the role of his instructor in civilized conduct:

> That is my first lesson:
> Profit by it; and we will see whether it is worth the trouble
> To give you another lesson.[34]

Osmin immediately asks Suleiman, "What do you order for a rebellious slave? How should I punish such insulting contempt?"[35] The sultan, however, is too intrigued to think about punishment.

Suleiman sends Osmin to invite Roxelana to have sherbet with him, and ends up apologizing for having woken her. She sarcastically assures him that she expects such things in Constantinople: "These Turks are so polite!" When Roxelana then brazenly declares that "sultans make me laugh," they begin a dialogue on monarchy and equality:

> SULEIMAN: You forget who you are and who I am.
> ROXELANA: Who you are, and who I am?
>   You are a great lord and I am a pretty woman.
>   We could be equal.
> SULEIMAN: Yes, in your country.
> ROXELANA: Ah! am I not there anymore? how disgusting! what a bore!
>   You'd do well to note the difference
>   Between this cursed country and mine.
>   No slaves among us; in France one breathes only
>   pleasures, liberty, and ease.
>   Every citizen is a king, under a citizen king.[36]

This was bold language for Roxelana to use, the language of liberty and citizenry, and entirely anachronistic for the Istanbul of Suleiman. The Paris premiere of *The Three Sultanas* in 1761, however, was contemporary with the appearance of Rousseau's *Social Contract* in 1762 and incorporated the political values of the European Enlightenment. Roxelana's lessons were not only for the sixteenth-century Turkish sultan but also for the eighteenth-century French public.

"I want to establish a reform in the seraglio," declares Roxelana, as if she were completing the harem revolution provoked by Roxane in Montesquieu's *Persian Letters* in 1721. Roxelana's harem reform begins with a banquet in the European style, including wine that even Osmin is commanded to drink: "Oh Mohammed, close your eyes," he exclaims, anticipating his Mozartean namesake. The spirit of the meal is that of European rococo diversion, with Roxela-

Soliman II ou Les trois sultanes, print from 1825, shows Suleiman being entertained by his sultanas. Favart's musical comedy was still being performed during the Restoration. Engraving by Mauduit Frères. With kind permission of the Bibliothèque Nationale de France.

na leading the other sultanas, Elmira and Delia, in the singing of arias to entertain the sultan, arias in praise of love, pleasure, and *volupté*. (The historical Roxelana was also supposed to have been a talented singer.[37]) In *The Three Sultanas* Roxelana not only sang but also played the harp, and contemporary sheet music offered the aria "that Mme Favart sang, accompanying herself on the harp, in the role of Roxelana." B-flat arpeggios on the harp accompany the first phrase of the seductive lyrics:

> O vous, que Mars rend invincible,
> Voulez-vous être au rang des dieux?
> Défendez-vous, s'il est possible,
> D'être esclave de deux beaux yeux.

You whom Mars makes invincible,
Would you like to reach the level of the gods?
Defend yourself, if possible,
From becoming the slave of two beautiful eyes.[38]

Those beautiful eyes brought Mme Favart back to B-flat, and signaled the rococo political lesson that even great sultans could become slaves of love.

Favart was also interested in authentic Turkish instrumentation, adding a note to the libretto, for this musical interlude, to specify: "The cymbals (or *zilis*, as the Turks call them) are little plates of brass or silver, eight to ten inches in diameter; their concavity is about two inches in depth."[39] The stage image would have perhaps been influenced by Carle Van Loo's Turkish concert painting and might have influenced, in turn, Amédée Van Loo's design of 1772 for the tapestry of odalisques entertaining the sultan and sultana. Favart's comedy was closely attuned to eighteenth-century French Turquerie.

At the sultan's banquet Roxelana proposes a spirit of equality between the sexes, formulating the proposal to Suleiman as one of sexual excitement:

Ah! the unfortunate man who has never tasted
The pleasures of equality [*les plaisirs de l'égalité*] . . .[40]

In the realm of rococo politics, "equality" was simply more fun, more pleasurable, more sexually sophisticated, a sort of European aphrodisiac for an Ottoman libido that remained crudely underdeveloped in the context of domestic despotism.

Suleiman in love shows himself to be a generous Turk and, following operatic convention, refuses to force himself upon his European captive:

Do you think me a barbarian, a tyrant?
Ah! you should know Suleiman better:
He will not abuse his supreme power
To obtain a heart that refuses his wishes.
Go, and fear nothing from my scorned love;
I abandon you to yourself.[41]

In the end, she proposes instead to become his wife and to reign over the Turks alongside him. He objects that this runs counter to Ottoman law, but she dismisses the objection with rhyming contempt:

SULEIMAN: Mais nos loix—	But our laws—
ROXELANA: Je m'en moque.	I mock them.
SULEIMAN: Le Muphti, le Vizir, l'Aga—	The mufti, vizir, and aga—
ROXELANA: Qu'on les révoque.	Dismiss them.[42]

She argues that a marriage between equals would benefit the peoples of his empire by seating "the tender humanity" of a woman alongside the majesty of the sultan, and he concedes completely to her proposal.[43] It was an ending perhaps calculated to gratify Mme Pompadour in 1761. Additionally implicit in the union of Suleiman and Roxelana, however, was the particular advantage of joining the authority not only of male and female but also of a Turkish man and a French woman. From the beginning of the comedy, Roxelana made clear to the French public that she had lessons to teach the Turks, and in the end it was understood that the sultan's Ottoman limitations would now be remedied by her superior French perspective.

Suleiman and His Sons

The real Roxelana did exercise unprecedented influence over Suleiman in the sixteenth century. She was not French, of course, but was probably born in the Slavic territories that today form part of Ukraine. By making her French, Favart could celebrate her influence over Suleiman, but it was not always obvious in eighteenth-century Europe that women were to be celebrated for attaining romantic influence over political men. Mme Pompadour had her enemies, and Mme du Barry was vilified in the underground literary *libelles* of the late ancien régime.[44] Roxelana, in fact, tended to be negatively represented in European culture before being largely redeemed by Favart's hugely successful comedy. The principal issue was her influence over Suleiman and especially the accusation, dating back to her own lifetime in the sixteenth century, that she had influenced the sultan against his eldest son, Mustafa, who was eventually put to death. Mustafa was the son of another woman from the harem, and his death conveniently facilitated the succession of one of Roxelana's own sons as Sultan Selim II. The most influential work exploring this subject was the drama *Il Solimano* by Prospero Bonarelli, performed in Florence in 1619.

One century later in 1719 Suleiman was presented in Florence on the operatic stage in *Il trionfo di Solimano, ovvero il trionfo maggiore è vincere se stesso*

(The triumph of Suleiman; or, The greatest triumph is to conquer oneself), by the Bolognese composer Luca Antonio Predieri.[45] The plot concerns the rise of a Genoese slave to become the sultan's Grand Vizier Ibrahim, sung in travesty by a woman. (Ibrahim, who was historically Greek or Albanian, played an important part in Suleiman's conquest of Egypt and of Hungary.) There is no mention of Roxelana in the opera, but it also celebrates the theme of foreign influence on the Turkish sultan and, after some tension, reconciles the Turkish and Italian principal figures. The year 1719, immediately following the peace of Passarowitz in 1718, was also the year of Gasparini's important revision of *Tamerlano* as *Il Bajazet* for Reggio Emilia.

In 1753 Suleiman returned to the operatic stage in Dresden as the eponymous protagonist of *Solimano*, composed by Johann Adolph Hasse to a libretto by Giovanni Ambrogio Migliavacca. The plot follows Suleiman's suspicions against one of his sons, and though Roxelana did not appear as a singing performer in the dramatis personae, the preface named her as the "famous Roxelana" who tried to incite Suleiman to kill his own heir. In at least one version of the libretto she is textually present, as a letter written by her is intercepted, revealing her intrigues. If Roxelana made her presence felt from offstage, there was also a large cast to fill the stage and amplify the impact of the production. According to one report, there were eight hundred performers in the Dresden *Solimano* of 1753 and a menagerie that included camels and elephants.[46]

Solimano was an *opera seria*, but not a tragedy because at the last minute Suleiman comes to his senses and, instead of having his son executed—as occurred historically in 1553—is counterfactually reconciled to him for a happy ending. Migliavacca, a protégé of Metastasio, was closely associated with the Saxon court of Dresden, but the libretto went on to be restaged in other cities and recomposed by other composers: there were performances in Venice in 1755 (with music by Domenico Fischietti), in Reggio Emilia in 1756 and Verona in 1757 (music by Giovanni Battista Pescetti), in Lisbon in 1757 and 1768 (music by Davide Perez), in London in 1758 (a pasticcio, including some music by Handel), in Palermo in 1763 (music by Giovanni Battista Lampugnani), in Padua in 1760 and 1768 and Verona in 1769 (music by Baldassare Galuppi), in Venice again in 1773 (music by Johann Gottlieb Naumann), in Cádiz in 1778 (music by Perez, again), and as late as 1782 in Turin (music by Giuseppe Curcio).[47]

Two operatic versions of Suleiman thus circulated simultaneously during the middle decades of the eighteenth century. On the one hand, there was Migliavacca's serious treatment of the sultan in which he appeared as a despot dangerously susceptible to his own resentments and jealousies, and therefore to the malign influence of Roxelana. On the other hand, there was Favart's comic conception in which Roxelana was transformed into the comic heroine of the piece, a civilizing influence on her good-natured but unsophisticated master. Neither operatic version acknowledged Suleiman's proverbial "magnificence"—which was supposed to be as much a matter of character as costume and included the *terribilità* that so powerfully intimidated contemporary European envoys. At the opera, he was presented somewhat patronizingly: in one case as a man who needs to learn how to control himself, in the other as a man who needs to be kept in his place by a clever wife. By the middle of the eighteenth century Suleiman was unintimidating to the European public. He could be made to sing songs and learn lessons on the operatic stage.

Though the historical Suleiman did actually have his eldest son, Mustafa, strangled by eunuchs, probably with Roxelana's encouragement, in the Migliavacca libretto Suleiman recognizes his error in judgment and is reconciled to both his sons—Mustafa and his younger brother, Giangir—who are allowed to marry the Persian princesses of their choice for a happy ending. Creating a further confusion in relation to the historical record, the naming of the operatic sons was rather flexible, with a note, for instance, in the Dresden libretto (and the London libretto, and the Palermo libretto) that "it was thought opportune to change the names of Mustafa and Giangir to Selim and Osmino, equally Turkish-sounding [*egualmente turcheschi*] but better fitted to the music."[48]

This operatic scenario was also one of the rare ones in which castrati were assigned to significant Turkish roles: never Suleiman himself but rather his sons, the juvenile roles. Hasse's Suleiman in 1753 was a tenor, but Selim was composed for the castrato Angelo Maria Monticelli. In Venice in 1755 Fischietti's Selim was sung by the castrato Carlo Nicolini, and his brother Osmino was represented by the female voice of Armellina Mattei. In London in 1758 Selim was the castrato Pasquale Potenza and Osmino was sung by a woman. In Palermo in 1763 the role of Selim was sung by the castrato Ferdinando Mazzanti, while that of Osmino was sung by Francesco Mazzanti, possibly two castrati brothers. In Lisbon in 1757 Perez had both brothers sung by castrati, as did Galuppi in Verona in 1769.[49] A whole cohort of castrati singers rose through the operatic ranks in the roles of these Ottoman princes, the sons of Suleiman. In fact, investing the princes with the passionate intensity of castrati voices made these young Ottomans, in some sense, the most fully conventional Turkish roles in eighteenth-century *opera seria*.

Suleiman the Magnificent, in the midcentury scenario exemplified by the Migliavacca libretto, is a figure poised between enlightened reason and jealous animosity. Osmino, the younger son, is at first fully admiring of his father and sings about his complete confidence in the sultan's wisdom. He claims to know all about the cruelties of past Ottoman history:

> But Soliman abhors these ways.
> With him mercy is sure to reign upon the throne,
> And he taught his sons that a sultan also knows how,
> Without being a tyrant, to be a sovereign.[50]

Sultano, tiranno, sovrano, were all rhyming words in the Italian text, and the librettist was certainly aware that they could not be sorted out as neatly as the Ottoman prince imagined in his ideal conception of his father. The menace of tyranny and tragedy was present till the very end of the drama, when Roxelana was exposed as the malign intriguer who influenced the sultan, and Suleiman renounced his jealous resentments to reconcile himself with his sons. By attributing the sultan's irrational passions to Roxelana's negative influence, Migliavacca could reimagine Suleiman, at the final curtain, as an exemplar of enlightened absolutism.

In 1776 the French dramatist Sébastien-Roch Nicolas de Chamfort created a nonmusical verse tragedy, *Mustapha et Zéangir*, about the sons of Suleiman. It was performed at Fontainebleau for Louis XVI and Marie Antoinette in 1776 and then in Paris in 1777. Marie Antoinette's mother, Maria Theresa, had sat for her portrait in Vienna in Turkish costume, and her father Francis Stephen had sung the tenor part of Bajazet at a rehearsal for Handel's *Tamerlano*. Sent to France in 1770 to marry the heir to the French throne, Marie Antoinette brought together diverse traditions of Ottoman interest, became a patroness of Turquerie, and created her own Cabinet Turc at Fontainebleau.

Marie Antoinette permitted Chamfort to dedicate *Mustapha et Zéangir* to her in 1778. There was some irony in the queen's patronage since, undeniably, the villainess of the tragedy was Roxelana, intriguing against Suleiman's eldest son. Suleiman ultimately denounced Roxelana as a "monster" at the conclusion of the tragedy, the sort of denunciation that Marie Antoinette herself would eventually face when mythologized as an evil queen during the French Revolution. From the age of Mme Pompadour to the reign of Marie Antoinette the story of Roxelana served as a parable of female influence in an absolute monarchy.

Suleiman's Sultanas as a European Phenomenon

Migliavacca's Suleiman was represented in the spirit of *opera seria* in the 1750s, but in the 1760s Favart in Paris established both Suleiman and Roxelana within the genre of *opéra comique*, conceived as a matter of historical fantasy and rococo Turquerie. Migliavacca's libretto always remained Italian but was recomposed and performed across Europe from Dresden to Palermo. Favart's comedy was disseminated very differently, constantly translated into other languages and reworked with new text and new songs wherever it traveled.

In 1765 a German version for production in Hamburg was created by Rudolf Erich Raspe (later the author of the tales of Baron Munchausen). Then in 1770, the year that Marie Antoinette traveled from Vienna to Versailles to marry the heir to the French throne, *The Three Sultanas* traveled in the opposite direction, from Paris to Vienna, and the work was presented there with a German text by Karl Starke, titled *Soliman der Zweyte, oder, Die drey Sultaninnen, ein Lustspiel*.[51] Much more than in Paris, it was a notable cultural departure to represent Suleiman himself in the spirit of comedy, *Lustspiel*, in Vienna, the city he had besieged in the sixteenth century with an Ottoman army under his personal command.

In 1777 Prince Nikolaus Esterházy had a performance of *Soliman der Zweyte* staged at the family palace theater at Esterháza in Hungary, even closer than Vienna to the former Ottoman border. The prince was able to order incidental music from the palace composer, Joseph Haydn. The music that Haydn composed to represent Roxelana then became the second movement of his Sixty-third Symphony in C, an *Allegretto* movement constructed as a lighthearted theme and variations. The whole symphony is sometimes called "La Roxelane."[52]

The Three Sultanas moved almost immediately from Paris in 1761 to Copenhagen in 1763, where it was translated as *Soliman den Anden* (Soliman the Second). The Danish text was prepared by a woman of letters, Charlotta Dorothea Biehl, for the work was as much a comedy of the sexes as an encounter between Europe and Turkey. Bent Holm notes that for a 1770 production in Copenhagen, Giuseppe Sarti composed new music in the Janissary style, involving piccolos, cymbals, and triangles—though a Danish review regretted that the pliant sultan did not appear more magnificent.[53] A new French edition appeared in Paris in 1772, and another in Avignon in 1774. By December 1774, the eighteen-year-old Mozart was well aware of the scenario of *The Three Sultanas*, writing from Munich to his sister Nannerl in Salzburg, "Please give my compliments to Roxelana, she is probably going to have tea this evening with the Sultan."[54] That year, 1774, marked the end of six years of Russian-Ottoman warfare, and the young Mozart was playfully imagining his acquaintances in the personae of Roxelana and Suleiman.

In 1775, *Les trois sultanes* triumphantly traveled to London and was translated into English. The English title emphasized, and perhaps also satirized, the fundamental prurience of European Turquerie: *The Sultan, or a Peep into the Seraglio*. The literature of the harem, dating back to Montesquieu's *Persian Letters*, had purposefully titillated the public, and the publication of Lady Mary Wortley Montagu's *Turkish Embassy Letters* in 1763, the year after her death, permitted a peep at the naked Turkish women in the baths of Sofia, "as exactly proportion'd as ever any Goddess was drawn by the pencil of Guido or Titian, and most of their skins shiningly white."[55] In London in 1775 the "peep," inspired by Favart, was given a new libretto by the Irish writer Isaac Bickerstaffe and new music by the English composer Charles Dibdin. Roxelana now became an Englishwoman, as performed in the Drury Lane Theatre by the famous Fanny Abington.

In the London production, Roxelana affirmed Suleiman's absolutism, only asking him to be "despotic sometimes on the side of reason and virtue." He acknowledged the persuasiveness of her arguments: "It is enough—my scruples are at an end—my prejudices, like clouds before the rising sun, vanish before the lights of your superior reason."[56] Interestingly, in this political symposium the Englishwoman's superior reason was employed to offer the sultan (and the public) an enlightened defense of his own absolute authority, properly modulated by the values of the European Enlightenment. In 1775, as the American Revolution was beginning on the other side of the Atlantic, the charge of despotism was already being brought against the British king George III.

The librettist Bickerstaffe was probably not present in London when his work was performed in 1775, as he had fled to France in 1772 to avoid prosecution for homosexuality in the context of contemporary British scandals. Bickerstaffe's name had even been linked with that of the famous actor and producer David Garrick, then the manager of the Drury Lane Theatre. It is possible that Bickerstaffe, in exile in France, took a jaundiced view of British liberty as a model to recommend to the Ottoman sultanate. *The Sultan, or a Peep into the Seraglio* was nevertheless revived in 1787 at Covent Garden with Mrs. Abingdon, now fifty, playing Roxelana as a harem flower perhaps just a bit beyond the first bloom.

In Venice, after Christmas in 1784 and at Carnival in 1785, Favart's formula was detached from the historical Suleiman and applied by librettist Giovanni Bertati to a work he called *Il serraglio di Osmano*. The potentate Osmano was not a sultan but a North African emir, the role composed for tenor voice. With music by Giuseppe Gazzaniga, the plot features three principal slaves of the harem: Rosana the Italian, Dima the Greek, and Zaida the Circassian. The Italian subtitle of the opera was sometimes given as *Le tre sultane*, which indicated the connection to Favart. As in Favart's original version, the three sultanas play Turkish music as part of the entertainment, the specified instruments being flute, mandolin, small cymbals, and triangle. One role, Ali, was labeled as a "eunuch of the seraglio," and he exclaimed upon his own condition: "Ah, why was I not born in Italy! There the eunuchs are created to sing, and at their own will. I'm told they earn a lot of gold."[57] The spirit of comedy here licensed one of the very rare cross-references in eighteenth-century opera between the subject of eunuchs and the subject of castrati. The part of Ali the eunuch was performed by the basso Agostino Grismondi, whose voice would clearly have established that he was not a castrato.

In *Il serraglio di Osmano* Rosana purposefully sets herself to captivate the emir, but unlike her original prototype in Favart, she does finally leave him behind to go off with her Italian husband. Comically confident that her charms will win the day, Rosana is perhaps already related in spirit to Rossini's Isabella in *L'italiana in Algeri* of 1813. Yet Rosana, just by passing through Osmano's seraglio, makes it a happier harem, a scene of musical and sensual delight imbued with Italian style and accompanied by Turkish instruments.

The opera concludes with a rococo celebration of the harem in choral form:

Rimbombi il Serraglio	May the Serraglio resound
Di dolci concenti,	With sweet harmonies,
Risponda pur l'Eco	Let the echo respond
Al suon de Stromenti.	To the sound of the instruments.[58]

Published libretti suggest that after the performances of 1784–85, Rosana worked her magic in revival in Venice in 1788 and 1791, with productions also in Bologna and Prague in 1785 and Vicenza and Leipzig in 1786.[59]

The German composer Joseph Martin Kraus, working at the Swedish court of Gustav III, composed his treatment of *Soliman II* or *De tre sultan-ninorna* for Stockholm in 1789, perhaps the last moment when Europeans could afford to be so frivolous about the institution of monarchy. In fact, a French troupe had brought *Les trois sultanes* to Stockholm as early as 1765, but now Kraus used a Swedish libretto by Johan Gabriel Oxenstierna. Following the examples of German and Austrian composers like Gluck, Haydn, and Mozart—and clearly influenced by Mozart's *Abduction* of 1782—Kraus introduced into his opera "Turkish" percussion in the Janissary style, beginning with the overture. There was a specifically designated "March of the Janissaries," but like Mozart's Pasha Selim, Kraus's Sultan Suleiman in 1789 was not musically composed at all but conceived as a speaking role. Musicologist Bertil van Boer has noted that Oxenstierna's Swedish libretto gave the whole work a less farcical, "more elevated tone," appropriate for the inauguration of the Royal Dramatic Theater and suitable for celebrating King Gustav in the guise of Sultan Suleiman.[60] Kraus composed a final chorus celebrating Suleiman, reminiscent of Mozart's choral celebration of Pasha Selim. In the 1780s Gustav emerged as an enlightened absolute monarch, less inclined to consult the Swedish nobles, and this might have made the implicit Turkish analogy more interesting to him. Furthermore, the celebration on the Stockholm stage of Roxelana's marriage to Suleiman might have acted as an antidote to rumors about Gustav's own unhappy marriage and reputed homosexuality.

Gustav was both a Freemason and the architect of Swedish religious toleration, and in *Soliman II* Kraus composed music for the part of a Turkish mufti singing a solemn religious invocation, "O Mahomet," followed by a full mufti chorus.[61] Though still a comedy, Kraus's *Soliman II* was able to take seriously some aspects of its Turkish Islamic setting, and the priestly musical role of the mufti was very far indeed from the farcical singing mufti created and impersonated by Lully in Paris in 1670.

In 1786 the Swedish embassy in Constantinople, in the Pera district, put on a performance of an Italian opera, possibly the first European opera ever performed in the city. The performers came largely from the Pera diplomatic community, and the opera was *La scuola de' gelosi* (The school of the jealous); it had been given in Venice in 1778 with music by Antonio Salieri, but the libretto (by Caterino Mazzolà) may have been recomposed by the Swedish ambassador to the Porte for the performance of 1786. The ambassador, Gerhard von Heidenstam, commented in a letter that "the spectacle, the first in this genre, caused a great sensation in Pera"—though it is not clear whether the sensation went beyond the European community.[62] Heidenstam remained as ambassador in Constantinople during Sweden's war with Russia from 1788 to 1790, which made Sweden the ally of the Ottoman sultan who was also fighting against Russia on the Black Sea between 1787 and 1791. In this context, 1789 was the ideal moment for presenting *Soliman II* in Stockholm.

Franz Xaver Süssmayr, the composer who completed Mozart's *Requiem*, created a new version of *Soliman der Zweite, oder Die drey Sultaninnen* for Vienna in 1799, and followed Mozart's example in making use of Janissary instrumentation. Suleiman, cast as a basso, is welcomed on stage by a Turkish march with bass drum and cymbals. He is attended by eunuchs and slaves, and the odalisques of his harem greet him in chorus before unveiling themselves for his inspection. In Süssmayr's version for Vienna the heroine who tames the sultan is now a German Marianne instead of a French Roxelane.[63]

Süssmayr's opera quickly traveled from Vienna in 1799 to Berlin, Breslau, and Hamburg in 1800 and 1801, to formerly Ottoman Budapest in 1800 and formerly Ottoman Temesvár (Timişoara) in 1801. The Viennese performances of 1799 inspired the young Beethoven to create a set of piano variations on one of the opera's melodies. In fact, the German diva who sang the role of Marianne in Vienna, Magdalena Willmann Galvani from Bonn, supposedly declined a marriage proposal from Beethoven.[64]

The Three Sultanas would have been peculiarly unsuitable in Russia during the reign of Catherine the Great, who certainly ruled in a spirit of enlightened absolutism but, as tsarina and empress, kept a kind of male harem of lovers who were selected in succession for her sexual companionship. The

Soliman der Zweite oder Die drey Sultaninnen. The Three Sultanas was composed again in 1799 in German for Vienna by Franz Xaver Süssmayr, once the close associate of Mozart. This announcement of a performance in 1800 shows that Favart's original Roxelana, conceived as a Frenchwoman who conquered the sultan in Constantinople, was here patriotically replaced by Süssmayr's Marianne, identified as *eine Deutsche*, a German woman. The role was performed in Vienna by Magdalena Willmann Galvani. With kind permission of the Österreichische Nationalbibliothek.

comedy of the Frenchwoman Roxelana coming to Constantinople to civilize the sultan, as staged in Paris in 1761, would have seemed less funny in the Russian context, where the German-born Catherine came to Russia to marry the grandson of Peter the Great, the future tsar, and then murdered him in 1762 to rule in his place. After Catherine's death in 1796, however, *The Three Sultanas* was almost immediately imported for a production in St. Petersburg in

Turkish March ("Tempo di Marcia"), musical manuscript from Süssmayr's *Soliman der Zweite* of 1799. The Janissary instruments are noted as "Tambouro Grande" and "Piatti" (bass drum and cymbals) on the bottom line. The march is introduced by Osmin (the sultan's chief eunuch) announcing Soliman's entrance to the odalisques of the harem: "*Soliman erscheinet nun / Lasset eure Zungen ruhn*" (Soliman now appears / Let your tongues be silent). Soliman then enters to the music of the march, accompanied by eunuchs and slaves. With kind permission of the Österreichische Nationalbibliothek.

1798, where it was performed in French with music by the Venetian composer Caterino Cavos, who was present in the Russian capital.

Fifteen years later, in 1813, a libretto was published in St. Petersburg in Russian, *Suliman vtoroi, ili tri sultanshi*, probably in association with a theatrical production.[65] Russia had just made peace with Turkey in 1812, and then confronted the Napoleonic invasion. In 1813, Napoleon was driven back across Europe by the Russian army, which prepared to enter Paris in triumph in 1814. A production of *The Three Sultanas* in St. Petersburg in 1813 would have had a particular piquancy, inverting the spirit of the original French comedy, and making a mockery of Favart's Parisian presumption.

Conclusion: Operatic Counterfactual History

The Three Sultanas thus made its way around Europe in the generation that followed its first emergence in 1761. Indeed, half a century later, the work would reemerge in England in 1811 as an Italian composition by Vincenzo Pucitta, *Il trionfo di Rosselane, ossia Le tre sultane*, which would later be performed very successfully in Paris, almost inaugurating the Bourbon Restoration in January 1816. Reconceived by Pucitta in an Italian spirit for the Italian diva Angelica Catalani, Favart's comedy still held the stage, even in competition with Rossini's masterpieces on Turkish themes.

Favart created this very durable work in 1761 in the middle of the Seven Years' War, when all of the powers of Europe were at war with one another—except for the Ottoman empire, which was enjoying what Stanford Shaw has noted as "the longest continuous period of peace in its history," from 1747 to 1768.[66] The diplomatic revolution of 1756, which produced the unprecedented alliance of France with the Habsburg monarchy, effectively canceled the long-standing structural dynamics by which, ever since the sixteenth century, the Ottomans had fought against the Habsburgs in tacit alliance with the French. Now Frederick the Great in Berlin, the enemy of Maria Theresa in Vienna, pursued an Ottoman diplomatic understanding and signed a treaty of friendship and commerce in 1761, the year of *The Three Sultanas* in Paris. Mustafa III, the poet-sultan, presided over a peacetime sultanate until the outbreak of the Russian-Ottoman war in 1768, but he did not neglect to attend to military improvements in cooperation with European advisers, notably the Franco-Hungarian officer and military engineer Baron François de Tott. It was Tott, moving between Constantinople and Paris, whose mediating and advisory role seemed to parallel the fictive harem career of the operatic Roxelana.

Initially conditioned by the decorative exoticism of Turquerie, *The Three Sultanas* also represented on stage the balance of civilization between Europe and the Ottoman empire, and suggested a degree of cultural engagement between Constantinople and Paris (or London, or Vienna, or Stockholm) that reflected an evolving continental integration. In the final scene of Favart's original work, Suleiman announces to all his subjects and officials that he will be marrying Roxelana. She immediately decides to exercise her share in his authority—"if I may be permitted to use some absolute power [*du pouvoir absolu*]"—to liberate all the women of the seraglio. Osmin has the last word, to lament his own irrelevance:

Me voilà cassé.	See, I'm broken.
Ah! qui jamais aurait pu dire	Ah, who could have predicted
Que ce petit nez retroussé	That this little turned-up nose
Changerait les loix d'un empire?	Would change the laws of an empire?[67]

The comedy, at its conclusion, became a kind of counterfactual history—"Who could have predicted?"—as if challenging the public to imagine what would have ensued if, back in the sixteenth century, a Frenchwoman really had seized the reins of power in the Ottoman empire and set about reforming its laws in a European spirit.

Part of the appeal of Turquerie in the eighteenth century involved Europeans dressing in Ottoman costume, as if costume were the only distinction that separated the French from the Turks, the same fantasy that was consummated on the operatic stage when Europeans performed and sang their Turkish parts. The rococo pleasure in the representation of ornamental difference corresponded to an enlightened fantasy of discovering a fundamental common identity. The fictive heir of a French sultana and a Turkish sultan would have presided over a counterfactually alternative European history. In fact, the year of *The Three Sultanas*, 1761, was the year of the birth of Mustafa III's son, the future Sultan Selim III, who would later in the century undertake more profound reform of the Ottoman empire with reference to generally European, but especially French, models.

Osmin's final lines were followed in the libretto by the program of a *divertissement*, in which Suleiman and Roxelana, enthroned, are entertained by their singing and dancing subjects in the spirit of Amédée Van Loo's tapestry designs of 1772, the perfect expression of Turquerie. The mufti sings, "O Mohammed, watch over the destiny of the greatest of sultans"—followed by a dance of the dervishes. The mufti then sings again, saluting Suleiman as "invincible" and Roxelana as the "queen of beauty"—followed by the dances of the odalisques and the slaves. Finally, Roxelana is crowned on stage as part of the *divertissement*, while the chorus chants, "*Vivir, vivir sultana, vivir, vivir Roxelana*"—a celebration of French preeminence on the French operatic stage.

At the conclusion of the opera the chorus of Turks sing their tribute to Suleiman in operatically approximate stage-Turkish: "*Salem alekim, Sultan Zilullah, Soliman Padichaïm, Eyuvallah, Eyuvallah.*" A French translation suggested that they were singing of the glory of Suleiman, but this was a Suleiman who had embarked upon a hypothetically divergent historical path, joined to a French sultana and under a civilizing French influence. It was thus that French musical theater in the age of Louis XV—which began with Harlequin disguising himself as a sultana in 1715 at the Paris fairs—now culminated in the enlightened musical celebration of Suleiman the Magnificent. He was invested with the very particular eighteenth-century magnificence of "civilization," which was supplied by Mme Favart in the Turkish costume of a French sultana.

4

THE TURKISH SUBJECTS OF
GLUCK AND HAYDN
Comic Opera in War and Peace

Introduction: "If ever the Turks should be chased from Europe"

Voltaire, in a letter of 1768 to Catherine the Great, commented on the imminent war between Russia and Turkey, and enthusiastically endorsed her foreign policy and military ambitions against the Ottomans. The Russian-Ottoman war of 1768 to 1774 ended with a decisive Ottoman defeat and encouraged the crystallization of Catherine's Greek Project, to conquer Constantinople and reestablish a Greek Orthodox empire. The idea of the Greek Project, which evolved in the 1770s in consultation between Catherine and Grigory Potemkin, was partly already present in Voltaire's letter of 1768. At the same time, his letter suggested that he envisioned the Russian-Ottoman confrontation as a sort of stage comedy about Turks with Catherine as the European heroine:

> If they make war on you, madame, there could well come about that which Peter the Great once had in view, which was to make Constantinople the capital of the Russian empire. These barbarians deserve to be punished by a heroine, for the lack of consideration they have shown till now for ladies. It is clear that people who neglect all the fine arts, and who shut up women, deserve to be exterminated [*méritent d'être exterminés*] . . . I ask your majesty for permission to come and place myself at her feet, and to pass some days at her court, as soon as it shall be established at Constantinople; for I think very seriously that if ever the Turks should be chased from Europe [*chassés de l'Europe*], it will be by the Russians.[1]

Catherine's military antagonist, Sultan Mustafa III, was usually named derisively in Voltaire's letters as simply "Moustapha," as if the sultan himself were a stage figure, shutting up ladies in his harem and thus inviting the intervention of a heroine like Catherine. Foreign intervention in the Turkish harem was in fact one of the principal subjects of operatic comedies of captivity set in the Ottoman empire.

Voltaire's correspondence concerning the Russian-Ottoman war, while "very seriously" advocating the elimination of Ottoman rule in Europe, also considered the campaign in a comical spirit of mockery. This latter spirit also presided on the operatic stages of Europe in the 1760s and 1770s, where Turkish sultans and pashas became the objects of comic redress, thwarted in their sexual and romantic intentions toward enslaved sopranos, who sang beautifully in captivity but steadfastly rejected their Turkish masters. Voltaire, who had created the model of dramatic sultanic tragedy with *Zaïre* in the 1730s, was ready to embrace the formula of comedy in his letter to Catherine in the 1760s. On the operatic stage, the conventions of comedy meant that barbarous sultans would usually turn out to be generous Turks in the end. The possibility of "extermination" would not have provided a satisfying conclusion to the musical comedy.

While Paris produced in 1761 the outrageous comical fantasy of Suleiman submitting to the civilizing influence of a French sultana, and that fantasy flourished in translated productions in both Vienna and Venice, there was also a more intimate operatic perspective evolving in those capitals of the Triplex Confinium, with their extended, precarious, and sometimes permeable Ottoman borders. This intimacy was all the more evident from Joseph Haydn's musical perspective at Esterháza at Fertöd in Hungary, very close to the former Habsburg-Ottoman frontier. One striking feature of this intimacy was the deployment of "Janissary instruments" in operatic scores, inspired by the Janissary bands which were already playing Turkish military music in Vienna and at the German courts during the earlier decades of the century. Now Janissary instruments—bells, cymbals, bass drums—were supposed to establish a degree of musical authenticity in the operatic representation of Turkish scenarios. While this local coloring had a musically exotic effect for European ears, by the middle of the century the intellectual values of the Enlightenment permitted comedies of Turkishness to be understood as comedies of the universal human condition.

The operatic subject of Turkish captivity was treated as comedy by both Gluck and Haydn in and around Vienna during the 1760s and 1770s, before Mozart gave the theme its most famous formulation in the early 1780s with *The Abduction from the Seraglio*. In fact, Gluck and Haydn set to music the same story: Gluck's French comic opera *La rencontre imprévue, ou Les pèlerins de la Mecque* (The unexpected encounter; or, The pilgrims of Mecca), performed at the Burgtheater in Vienna in 1764, and Haydn's Italian comedy *L'incontro improvviso* (The unexpected encounter), performed at Esterháza in 1775. Both were based on the same musical comedy from the Paris fairs in the 1720s. In both, the plot concerns Prince Ali rescuing Princess Rezia from the harem of the sultan in Cairo, where the two lovers have their "unexpected encounter" and try to escape together disguised as pilgrims to Mecca. Egypt was an Ottoman land in the eighteenth century, and the sultanate was an Ottoman institution, so these were clearly intended as operas of Turkish captivity. (Though similarly titled, with corresponding French and Italian libretti, Gluck's opera will be designated here as *Les pèlerins* and Haydn's as *L'incontro* in order to distinguish them clearly.)

Another Haydn opera, *Lo speziale* (The apothecary), performed at Esterháza in 1768, also involved elements of Turkish comedy, and was composed to a Venetian libretto by Goldoni originally written for Venice in 1755. Along with numerous other Turkish-themed comedies of the 1760s and 1770s, such works belonged to a particular period of European interest in Ottoman affairs. Russian military successes—accompanied by a Greek uprising against the Turks in 1770—made it possible for the first time to imagine that Russia might actually conquer Constantinople, as envisioned by Voltaire, and that the Ottoman empire might be toppled altogether. A new sense of the precariousness of Ottoman power attended the development of operatic comedy during these years.[2] In 1770, at the court of Empress Maria Theresa in Vienna, the inventor Wolfgang von Kempelen presented his mechanical chess-playing Turk, a robed and turbaned automaton who dazzled observers for the next half-century—though the apparatus actually concealed a human chess-player.[3] A new age had begun in which the former invincibility of the Ottomans could be transposed to the chessboard, and Europeans could admire Turkish performance in the spirit of entertainment, whether at chess or at the opera.

The Habsburgs did not participate in the Russian-Ottoman war of 1768–74, and from the perspective of Vienna, Russian military success against the

Ottomans was not an altogether welcome outcome. If indeed the end of the Ottoman empire was suddenly imaginable, the Habsburgs were not eager to see Russian power exclusively displacing the Turks in southeastern Europe. In fact, there now emerged a tense balance of power and influence between the Habsburgs and the Romanovs over the course of the next century and a half, as both dynasties carefully attended to the decline and fall of the Ottoman empire. In the 1760s and the 1770s, Vienna for the first time contemplated the possibility of Ottoman defeat with a measure of ambivalence, which was also reflected in the balance of sympathy and mockery in contemporary operatic comedies about the Turks.

Ottoman Diplomatic Envoys and Ottoman Theatrical Roles in Vienna

Gluck's *Les pèlerins* of 1764, Haydn's *Lo speziale* of 1768, and Haydn's *L'incontro* of 1775 all originated in the Habsburg monarchy during the long reign of Empress Maria Theresa, from 1740 to 1780, a time when the Habsburgs were never at war with the Turks. In 1748 Maria Theresa welcomed to Vienna a Turkish envoy, Mustafa Hatti Efendi, in the spirit of Habsburg-Ottoman "friendship."[4] He was taken to the opera in Vienna, and was conducted to the Kahlenberg heights for the view of the city, but perhaps more pointedly to visit the site from which the relieving Christian army descended upon the Ottoman besiegers in 1683. He presented Holy Roman Emperor Francis Stephen with a Turkish sword as a present from the sultan, a gift with some family significance since the emperor's grandfather, Charles of Lorraine, had been one of the generals who helped to defeat the Turks at Vienna in 1683.[5]

In February 1748, a few months before Mustafa Hatti Efendi's visit to Vienna in June, theatrical Turkishness took the forms of both operatic tragedy and musical comedy, as noted by musicologist Thomas Betzwieser: a performance of an opera on the subject of Bajazet (perhaps a pasticcio rather than the work of a particular composer), followed the very next evening by a performance of *Le bourgeois gentilhomme* (probably with new music for the Turkish ceremony rather than that of Lully from 1670). Betzwieser has further noted the existence of a Viennese manuscript, dating to the 1740s or 1750s, containing pieces of generic "Turkish" incidental music, correlated with French descriptions of Ottoman scenes as related in travel literature: a

Turkish meal, an audience with the Grand Vizier, Muslim prayer, and dervish dancing. This musical and literary manuscript suggests some importation of French Turquerie into Viennese cultural life.[6]

When Maria Theresa and Francis Stephen welcomed Mustafa Hatti Efendi to Vienna in 1748 and sent him to the opera, the Habsburgs had only been at peace with the Ottomans since 1739, not even for an entire decade. Yet the somewhat casual entertainment of the Turkish guest suggests that the Ottomans had already ceased to be the Habsburg *Erbfeind*, the hereditary enemy, as they were designated back in 1683 in the age of the grandfathers of Maria Theresa and Francis Stephen. Rather, in 1748, Vienna was concluding the eight-year War of the Austrian Succession, which began in 1740 when Frederick the Great seized Silesia, demonstrating that the modern archenemy of Habsburg Austria was Hohenzollern Prussia. In 1754 the Oriental Academy was established by Maria Theresa in Vienna for instruction in Oriental languages and, more generally, toward the professionalization of Habsburg-Ottoman relations.[7]

By 1758, when the next Ottoman envoy arrived in Vienna, Ahmed Resmi Efendi, the Habsburgs were already fighting again in the Seven Years' War against Frederick. The embassy marked the accession of Sultan Mustafa III, the same who would later be ridiculed in Voltaire's letters to Catherine. In Vienna this became the occasion for the production of a new ballet, *Le Turc généreux*, with choreography by Franz Hilverding and music by Joseph Starzer. While the title alluded to Rameau's Turkish scenario and the story seemed to include a Turkish pasha and a pair of European lovers, musicologist Bruce Brown has observed that Rameau's work need not have been the precise model, since the theme of the generous Turk "was already widespread in European literature and theater—whether as a form of enlightened ecumenism, or as a means of disarming, in effect, the infidel menace."[8] The ballet was a great success in 1758, and another ballet in Vienna in 1759, *Les Corsaires*, possibly with music by Gluck himself, offered the story of Turkish pirates and European captives, with a happy ending.[9] These ballets on Turkish themes would have prepared the Viennese climate for the creation and reception of Gluck's opera *Les pèlerins de la Mecque*.

In 1758 Ahmed Resmi Efendi was actually present for a ballet performance of *Le Turc généreux*. This confrontation of a Turkish representative with a Turkish representation was recorded in a contemporary European journal which noted that "the envoy was struck by the variety of the spectacle and es-

Ahmed Resmi Efendi, Ottoman envoy to Vienna and Berlin, who saw the ballet *Le Turc généreux* in Vienna in 1758 and admired both the costumes and the music, but in Berlin in 1763 was critical of the sound of Frederick's Janissary band. With kind permission of the Österreichische Nationalbibliothek.

pecially by the truth [*verité*] of the last ballet where the costume was perfectly observed and the music very well characterized." Brown's study of Starzer's score suggests that cymbals and Turkish drums were employed, probably to present a troupe of dancers costumed as Janissaries.[10]

An engraved print from the ballet of *Le Turc généreux*, drawn by Bernardo Bellotto, shows the sultan in the final scene, about to demonstrate his generosity.[11] A Turkish pavilion on the stage is framed by a European proscenium, and there are dancers in Turkish costume on the scene and musicians in European dress in the orchestra. With the Turkish envoy viewing the ballet, and the European public viewing the print, one may note the complexity of the interlocking Turkish and European elements and perspectives at this midcentury moment of cultural rapprochement.

This intimate, reciprocal engagement was very different from the more emphatic spirit of exoticism that prevailed for Chinese musical subjects and contemporary artistic Chinoiserie. At the Schönbrunn palace Maria Theresa created "Chinese" rooms decorated with lacquer panels and Chinese porcelain, and in 1754 Gluck presented the one-act opera *Le cinesi* (The Chinese women) to Maria Theresa at Schloss Hof, forty miles from Vienna. Gluck used bells and triangles in the score, while the stage set featured "the reflected brilliancy of the azure-colored meadows of lacquer, the glitter of the gilded foliage, and, lastly, the rainbow-like colors repeated by hundreds of prisms." Adrienne Ward, in her study of Italian operas about China, has suggested that Gluck's Chinese figures on stage in 1754 paid tribute to "the eminence of Viennese courtly culture."[12] Yet the exotic foreign envoys who actually visited the Viennese court in this period were Ottomans: Mustafa Hatti Efendi in 1748 and Ahmed Resmi Efendi in 1758. Operas on Turkish subjects were performed in the context of ongoing European-Ottoman relations.

Janissary Music in Europe

The most significant development in the representation of Turkishness in Gluck's *Les pèlerins* and in Haydn's *L'incontro* was the use of music in the Turkish Janissary style. This style—which would achieve its most famous European form in Mozart's *Abduction*, beginning with the brilliantly percussive overture—made use of certain rhythms, intervals, and oscillations considered characteristically Turkish, and drew upon distinctive percussion

Cymbals-player—costume design by Johann Matthias Steyreiff, for Mozart's *Abduction*, performed in Koblenz in 1787. The musician would have appeared with his cymbals in costume on stage as part of Pasha Selim's Janissary band, a figure within the opera rather than simply a player in the orchestra. With kind permission of the Familienarchiv Ernst Steireif, Koblenz.

Triangle-player—also from the costume designs of Johann Matthias Steyreiff for the Janissary band in the Koblenz performance of Mozart's *Abduction* in 1787. With kind permission of the Familienarchiv Ernst Steireif, Koblenz.

orchestrations, generally consisting of the bass drum, cymbals, and bells. The "Turkish crescent" had jangling bells hanging from brass crescents, often attached to a pole, forming a treelike instrument which inspired the German name *Schellenbaum*, while in English it was sometimes called the "Jingling Johnny"—and in Turkish *çevgen*.[13] The triangle was closely associated with Turkish music in eighteenth-century Europe, characteristically employed by Mozart in the *Abduction*, though it was probably not authentically Turkish.[14] For the 1787 Koblenz production of Mozart's *Abduction*, surviving costume sketches show the pasha's Janissary band, including the cymbals- and triangle-players, in Turkish costume, for they performed on stage as part of the opera rather than in the orchestra.[15]

Real Ottoman Janissary bands accompanied the sultan's army, and the instruments included the *kös* (kettle drum), the *davul* (a double-headed bass drum), *zil* (cymbals), and *zurna* (a sort of oboe or shawm). Antoine Galland, translator of the *Thousand and One Nights*, heard the Janissary band music—called *mehter* in Turkish—when he was in Edirne in 1672, and he reported that "the roar and echo of fifteen drums created such an illusion of wars and battles that I can not find words to describe it." The music was supposed to inspire the Janissaries and unsettle their enemies, and one Turkish account related the musical effect at the siege of Vienna in 1683: "The Grand Vizier's *mehter* band started to play first . . . then the bands of the governors of provinces." Thus, the sounds of the Janissary percussion "joined from every corner the rumble of cannon, and the whole countryside echoed with these sounds."[16] According to the European account of the siege by Paul Rycaut, "The Turks designing to make a furious Assault, caused all their warlike Musick, such as Flutes, Cymbals, and brass Trumpets which gave a shrill Sound, to play with their highest Notes, to encourage their Soldiers to make the Onset."[17] The presence of the *mehter* bands at Ottoman sieges meant that not only European soldiers but also civilian populations along the Triplex Confinium could become fearfully familiar with this Janissary music.

The rhythms and instrumentation of the Janissary *mehter*, called *alla turca* style as adapted by Europeans, began to play a role in European military music, and then operatic music, over the course of the eighteenth century. Mary Hunter has observed that "in instrumental music the connotation of the *alla turca* topos is always hypermasculine saber-rattling barbarism," and its adaptation to European usage involved some degree of domestication.

Edmund Bowles has noted the particular interest of the Saxon elector and Polish king Augustus II, "the Strong," who succeeded Jan Sobieski in Poland and also participated in the Turkish wars at the very end of the seventeenth century. After the conclusion of the wars the Sultan Mehmed IV gave Augustus a *mehter* band for the Dresden court, and a print of 1697 already showed a turbaned band of Turkish musicians on horseback at Carnival in Dresden. Augustus himself is supposed to have costumed himself as the Janissary chief leading the band.[18]

Augustus, whose Saxon reign witnessed the birth of Meissen porcelain, had a room in his treasury dedicated to Turkish artifacts, accompanied by wax figures of Turks. He also possessed a sort of sultanic harem which made him the near legendary father of more than three hundred illegitimate children. When his single legitimate heir married a Habsburg archduchess in 1719, immediately after the peace of Passarowitz, the wedding was celebrated in Turkish style, with a great tent on the Elbe, Turkish coffee, a troop of mounted Janissaries, and a *mehter* band with a dozen pairs of cymbals. A Turkish bath and harem were constructed for the entertainment of the guests, with the harem including costumed wax figures of women. For the opening of the Dresden court opera house in 1733, according to the court calendar, there was a mounted Janissary band of "completely black Moors," playing "drums, shawms, kettledrums, and brass cymbals."[19] In this case the Turkish music was performed outside the opera house, but *alla turca* style would soon be brought inside the opera house and into the performance.

This Saxon musical interest in Turkishness at the court of Augustus II helped to create the conditions for the operatic production, one generation later, of Hasse's *Solimano* at Dresden in 1753, in the reign of Augustus III. According to the research of musicologist Walter Preibisch, Hasse's *Solimano* was one of the earliest eighteenth-century operas to use some Janissary musical elements, including Turkish percussion and wind instruments in the score, typical "Janissary" oscillations in the chorus, and even the presence of a Janissary band on stage. With the vindication of Prince Selim in the end, a Janissary chorus sings "*Viva il magnanimo figlio fidel*" (Long live the magnanimous loyal son).[20] Ottoman dynasticism could be theatrically appreciated in relation to European dynasticism, and in Dresden, for instance, the Wettin princes could be allusively saluted along with Prince Selim by the Janissary chorus.

In the 1730s, Janissary music was also present at the Russian court, even as Russia emerged as the principal military opponent of the Ottomans. The mastery of Ottoman music functioned as the expression of a more general mastery in matters of Turkishness. According to the account of Jacob von Staehlin, a German scholar in St. Petersburg in the 1730s, "on the occasion of the Turkish peace of Belgrade in 1739, a fair imitation [*Nachahmung*] of Turkish music was made fashionable by an ensemble of German court musicians," though the music, according to Staehlin, was "too melodious and not irregular enough." Later, in the reign of Empress Elisabeth, there would be "really wild Turkish music," according to Staehlin, who recorded the presence of a band of genuine Turks in St. Petersburg: "One [musician] played on a shrill transverse flute, one beat a small pair of kettle drums, while another played the bass [part] on an enormous drum . . . Two more [musicians] performed on steel triangles."[21] Wildness was, for Staehlin, the mark of authenticity.

Europeans who experienced the authentic *mehter* music in the Ottoman empire were often critical. The French diplomat Charles Fonton, who spent time in Istanbul, wrote an essay comparing Oriental and European music and ended up censuring the Turks for their excessive use of unison and lack of composition in musical parts. The Italian ex-Jesuit Giambattista Toderini, who was in Istanbul in the 1780s, published in Venice an account of Turkish culture that included a description of Janissary instruments and the observation that they played in unison: "*tutti suonano all'unisono*."[22] Franz Joseph Sulzer wrote a German account of the Romanian principalities, then under the sovereignty of the sultan, and described the sound of Ottoman music as *Katzengeschrey*, the shrieking of cats. He published his book in Vienna in 1781–82, exactly when Mozart was composing the *Abduction*.[23]

On the other hand, the eighteenth-century German writer and musician Christian Friedrich Daniel Schubart wrote with positive interest about the military significance of Turkish music in the 1780s: "No other type of music offers such a firm, definite, and energetically penetrating beat. Each beat is so strongly outlined by its powerful stroke that it is almost impossible to march out of step." He further noted the issue of authenticity, affirming that "whoever has . . . the good fortune to hear the Janissaries themselves—whose musical bands are commonly eighty to a hundred strong—must laugh pitifully at the aping with which we mostly disfigure Turkish music." Schubart reported that the Prussian king Frederick the Great, who signed a friendly treaty with the Turks in 1761, had been wounded to learn from the Turkish ambassador Ahmed Resmi Efendi in 1763 that the Berlin "Turkish" band sounded inauthentic: "Subsequently the King of Prussia has taken actual Turks into service and introduced true Turkish music into several of his regiments."[24] Schubart's (and Frederick's) concern with Turkish authenticity suggests that European interest was not merely a matter of exoticism.

Musicologist Eric Rice has observed that "in the whole of Europe, the Viennese were perhaps most familiar with the sound of *mehter*," dating back to the Ottoman siege when the Viennese would have heard the Janissary bands outside the walls of the city.[25] More than half a century later, in 1741, at the beginning of the War of the Austrian Succession (and only two years after the recent peace with the Ottomans in 1739), a band of Turkish musicians was brought to Vienna to accompany the Habsburg troops and inspire patriotic support for Maria Theresa. It was a particular Austrian officer, Franz von der Trenck, who summoned the Turkish band, and Trenck had spent part of his childhood on Croatian estates along the Triplex Confinium, even participating in campaigns against the Ottomans in the 1730s.[26]

If Janissary music was traumatic for the Viennese in 1683, by the middle of the eighteenth century it was becoming familiar. The Viennese were able to listen to *mehter* as entertainment, and Gluck, Haydn, and Mozart would all employ the Janissary style to dramatize the Turkish themes of their operas created in and around Vienna. Janissary percussion, increasingly recognized as such, became an instrumental part of European regimental music over the course of the century, and a report from Vienna in 1796 specified the instruments necessary for making Turkish music in military bands: "two clarinets, a trumpet, a triangle, a piccolo and a bass drum, a kettledrum and a pair of cymbals."[27] By the end of the century the domestication of Janissary music had proceeded to the point that it could be brought right into the drawing room, as Viennese pianos were being constructed up until the 1820s with the "Janissary stop," which produced drum and bell effects through the use of pedals. A British patent for such pedals was taken out in 1799.[28]

Starzer made use of Janissary percussion in the ballet music for *Le Turc généreux* in Vienna in 1758, and in 1761 Gluck employed some elements of Turkish style and Janissary percussion—triangle, cymbals, the double-headed Turkish drum (*tamburo turco*)—in a one-act opera, *Le Cadi dupé*, about the duping of a Muslim judge, or Cadi, when he attempts to divorce his wife and marry a younger woman. (The same libretto had already been composed by Pierre-Alexandre Monsigny in Paris in 1761, the year of Favart's *Three Sultanas*.) Gluck's version, with its *alla turca* inflections, circulated both in the original French and in German translation (as *Der betrogene Kadi*) in the German opera houses.[29]

Gluck's *Les pèlerins* in 1764 offered the most important programmatic use of *alla turca* style in opera to date, and the opera immediately began with Janissary music in the overture. Eric Rice notes in the overture the pulsing repetition of pitches and also the repetition of sections, along with punctuation by cymbals, while Mary Hunter mentions Gluck's use of grace notes to add a "jangling" ornament before the regular beat in duple meter.[30] In fact, Gluck could have had the opportunity to hear Janissary band music in Vienna at the very time that he was working on the score of *Les pèlerins*. Count Karl Zinzendorf noted in his diary on July 15, 1763, that "yesterday I heard at Schönbrunn the Turkish music of the Harsch Regiment, which had the most beautiful effect in the world."[31] Zinzendorf clearly had no trouble recognizing this as Turkish music, though it had already been appropriated by a Habsburg military band. It might also be noted that in the previous year, 1762, the program of entertainment at Schönbrunn included the six-year-old Mozart, who played the piano—as also noted by Zinzendorf—and sat in the lap of the Empress Maria Theresa. Mozart might thus have had the chance to hear Janissary music in Vienna even in his childhood, though certainly Mozart, like Haydn, would also become familiar with Janissary style from precedents established by Gluck.

The Nonsensical Kalender and the Musical Comedy of Islam

The prototype for Gluck's opera of 1764 was a musical comedy from the Paris fair of Saint-Laurent, dating back to 1726: *Les pèlerins de la Mecque*, with a text by Alain-René Le Sage and Jacques-Philippe d'Orneval. The hero of the show was always Prince Ali, seeking to rescue Princess Rezia, but in the original Paris piece the prince was accompanied by his loyal valet, none other than Arlequin—who would disappear from the dramatis personae to be replaced by the servant Osmin when Louis Dancourt wrote the new libretto for Gluck.[32] Nevertheless, Arlequin would leave behind an intimation of his mischievous character even in works where the overt markers of commedia dell'arte had been purposefully effaced.

Both Gluck's and Haydn's treatments of the story were comedies by virtue of their happy endings, achieved through the magnanimity of the sultan. The unlucky lovers themselves—Prince Ali of Balsora (Basra, on the Persian Gulf) and Princess Rezia of Persia—were treated seriously in the music and the drama. The principal comedy of the opera belonged to the Kalender (or Qalandar), a mendicant Muslim dervish encountered in the first scene by Prince Ali's servant Osmin. The Kalender, a basso, introduced himself to Osmin and the audience in an aria of pseudo-Oriental nonsense that made use of musically "Turkish" intervals. The *alla turca* style was generally used to characterize the music of the Kalender, identified simply by his Islamic title—there was a real order of Qalandar dervishes—and Bruce Brown notes that Gluck seemed particularly interested in building up this role within the opera.[33] Haydn also relished the Turkishness of the Kalender, and in the judgment of Daniel Heartz, "Haydn, in his exotic Turkish music, met Gluck head-on and bested him."[34]

It was in Vienna in 1762 that Gluck inaugurated the revolution of noble simplicity in opera with his deeply serious treatment of *Orfeo ed Euridice*. In 1764 *Les pèlerins* also presented a young man determined to recover his lost beloved, but the comic context was far from the spirit of noble simplicity. The Kalender's opening aria was composed to lines of gibberish, beginning with *castagno*, chestnut, but quickly becoming incomprehensible:

Castagno, castagna, pista-fanache.
Rimagno, rimagna, mousti-limache.
Quic, billic, loulougagne.[35]

The marching military repetitions and oscillations were clearly intended to make this nonsense musically "Turkish," but it was also an expression of the Kalender's charlatanism, a sort of incantatory mystification. Asked about the meaning of his song, the Kalender simply explains that it is how he and his Muslim brothers beg for charity.

The Kalender offers his explanation in the form of an aria, singing in perfectly comprehensible French that the dervishes do not languish in pious poverty and hunger, but enjoy lots of food and the best wines: "*C'est la douce vie des bons Calenders*" (That's the sweet life of the good Kalenders).[36] Osmin immediately declares that he wants to be a mendicant too, and the Kalender sings still a third aria to instruct him in the art of begging. A mendicant, he explains, must ring a bell, and the Kalender himself becomes an instrument of Janissary percussion, singing the bell sound—"*din, din, din, din, din*"—in the Janissary style of oscillating thirds. He then prescribes the words to accompany the ringing bell, again in oscillating thirds: "*illah! illah! illah!*"[37] This was clearly meant to simulate the Muslim Arabic religious affirmation of God. Such cynical lessons in attracting alms were perhaps comparable to John Gay's British irreverence in the eighteenth-century *Beggar's Opera*, but adapted here in a comically blasphemous spirit to the Islamic scenario.

In fact, the *Beggar's Opera*, performed in London in 1728, was roughly contemporary with the original Parisian version of *Les pèlerins de la Mecque* at the fair of Saint-Laurent in 1726. Back in 1726 it was not Osmin but Arlequin who confronted the Kalender. The farcical character of the Kalender, however, was already fully present in the original version for the Paris fair of 1726, and he sang his nonsense song "Castagno, castagna, pistafanache" vaudeville style, to the tune of "Les amours triomphants." The Kalender then explains—in the original libretto of 1726—"it is an old song composed by Mohammed in the obscure style of the Koran."[38] When Arlequin inquires about "the science of being a Kalender," the mendicant replies, "Oh, the science of a Kalender consists of knowing nothing." While the Kalender then sings "*Illah, illah ha!*"—in travesty of Islamic prayer—Arlequin makes his own cheerful noises, "*Talaleri, talaleri, talalerire!*"[39] The evolution of Prince Ali's servant Arlequin in 1726 into the servant Osmin in 1764 led eventually in 1782 to the servant Pedrillo, in Mozart's *Abduction*, a comical character who still reflected some of the original aspects of Arlequin.

In Gluck's opera, when Osmin has received his lesson in how to be a mendicant, he then tries to imitate his mentor's nonsense patter. "*Castagno, castagna,*" sings the basso Kalender. "*Castrato, castrata,*" responds the tenor Osmin in some (though not all) productions and thus, under the pretext of speaking nonsense, enunciates the suppressed relation between Muslim servants (who were sometimes eunuchs) and European singers (who were sometimes castrati).[40] At this point Prince Ali makes his entrance and Gluck's opera changes its tone, but until then the whole opening section of the opera is dominated by the comical hypocrisy of the Kalender as expressed in aria after aria after aria.

While the second act highlights the unexpected romantic reunion of Ali and Rezia, the third act begins with the Kalender again, now joining the caravan of pilgrims to Mecca and sampling the wine that has been provisioned for the journey. The basso leader of the caravan offers an aria about Islam and alcohol, set to the rhythmic patter of Janissary percussion:

Mahomet notre grand Prophète	Mohammed our great Prophet
n'avait pas la cervelle nette	was not in his right mind
quand il a défendu le vin.	when he forbade wine.
Cette liqueur enchanteresse,	This enchanting liqueur,
qu'il crut contraire à la sagesse,	that he thought contrary to wisdom,
est l'antidote du chagrin.	is the antidote to sorrow.[41]

The blasphemy could hardly have been more explicit or more jovial, as Mohammed himself is mocked for his sobriety, and wine is celebrated as an essential and consoling item of the human condition. Religious pilgrims are revealed as dedicated drinkers, and the aria ends with a happy rhyming couplet of intoxication:

C'est là le plus heureux destin.	That is the happiest destiny.
Du vin, du vin, buvons du vin.	Wine, wine, let's drink wine.[42]

Gluck introduced a Janissary oscillation—"*du vin du vin du vin*"—to mark the Turkish character of this blasphemous exhortation.

The particular emphasis on alcoholic hypocrisy was even more prominent in Haydn's treatment of *L'incontro improvviso*, which after an overture punctuated by Janissary percussion, begins with the Kalender leading a trio of subordinate Kalenders, all singing chorally in praise of wine. The operatic forces of a tiny company like that of Esterháza were necessarily small in number, but the Kalenders, designated in the libretto as "*tutti i calandri*," were clearly supposed to represent a collective choral presence of many mendicants, all equally remote from a spirit of true piety. With a hammering Janissary rhythm these Muslims offer an alcoholic salute to Bacchus: "*Evvivo Bacco!*"[43] This would be the inebriated refrain of Osmin and Pedrillo in Mozart's *Abduction*, seven years later.

Haydn's libretto—by Karl Friberth, the Esterháza tenor, director, and librettist, who sang the part of Prince Ali—was in most regards an Italian translation from Dancourt's French libretto for Gluck. In the Kalender's nonsense aria "Castagno, castagna," not only did Friberth preserve most of Dancourt's gibberish but Haydn, interestingly, also preserved much of Gluck's music and Janissary rhythms, as if the song were an authentic piece of Muslim musical expression that could not be freely recomposed. Indeed, Haydn liked the musical setting so much that he brought it back a second time as a full duet for the Kalender and Osmin. In another aria, the Kalender received a set of brand-new Italian lyrics for Haydn to compose in a fully comical spirit:

Noi pariamo santarelli,	We appear to be saints,
e truffiamo quest'e quelli,	and we trick everyone,
dimostrando povertà.	demonstrating poverty.
Ma la borsa intanto avanza,	But the purse meanwhile advances,
e mangiamo in abbondanza,	and we eat in abundance,
e beviamo, come va.	and we drink, as it goes.[44]

Haydn's Kalender (Calandro) made of this aria a rather grand comical statement of self-affirmation, for he was a figure not of sly cunning but rather of broad Falstaffian energy and confidence. While the actual lyrics of Friberth's libretto produced a damning moral indictment of the Kalender, Haydn's music gave him a real bravado that might let him win over a susceptible audience by the richness of his voice and the courage of his non-convictions.

The hypocrisy of mendicant Muslim dervishes thus formed an essential part of the comedy of Gluck and Haydn, all the more evident with reference to the titular "pilgrims" of Mecca. Yet this mocking animus cannot be understood simply as anti-Islamic bigotry. Just as Voltaire's drama *Mahomet* in the 1740s had satirized the dissembling of the Muslim Prophet in order to criticize covertly the hypocrisy of Christianity, so the operatic figure of the Kalender, as treated by Gluck and Haydn in the 1760s and 1770s, satirized the spiritual insincerity of Muslim dervishes in order to make the very same point about Christian monks and religious orders. The Habsburg official Karl Zinzendorf did not fail to notice in 1764 and record in his diary that *Les pèlerins* offered a "biting satire against the monks."[45]

Dating back to the 1720s, Montesquieu in the *Persian Letters* had Usbek recognize Christian monks as "dervishes" and deplore their greed for gain: "The dervishes have almost all the wealth of the nation in their hands. They form a society of misers, constantly acquiring and never giving back." Voltaire, in the *Philosophical Dictionary* in the 1760s, had issued a warning to the religious orders: "You have profited from the times of ignorance, of superstition, of folly, to despoil us of our heritage and to trample us underfoot in order to fatten yourselves on the substance of the wretched: tremble lest the day of reason arrive."[46]

In the Habsburg monarchy the day of reason was already dawning in the 1760s with the coronation of Joseph as emperor in 1765, to reign alongside his mother, Maria Theresa, after the death of his father, Francis Stephen. Joseph held the enlightened conviction that the religious orders were useless and pernicious, and when he finally ruled alone in the 1780s, after the death of Maria Theresa, he would take radical measures, dissolving monasteries and appropriating their properties. Already in the 1770s, however, Joseph and Maria Theresa together sponsored a commission for ecclesiastical reform that limited the prerogatives of the orders and raised the ages at which young men and women could take religious vows. Johann Pezzl, in his account of Vienna in the 1780s, celebrated the closing of so many monasteries by Joseph and deplored "monastic life in all its degeneracy."[47] For Gluck and Haydn, the comedy of Turkishness was also, casually, a satire on European morals and institutions.

Joseph was notably associated with Gluck's *Les pèlerins* from the beginning, when he was still the Habsburg heir in 1764. Prince Ali was so closely identified with Joseph that the death in 1763 of Joseph's young wife, Princess Isabella of Parma, meant that Gluck and Dancourt had to revise their libretto, so that there would be no awkward references to the possible death of the missing Princess Rezia.[48] The absence of Christian Europeans within the opera—the characters came from the Persian Gulf and from Ottoman Egypt—meant that there was no European-Ottoman encounter on stage, and made it that much easier to imagine correspondences and resemblances across the proscenium.

Gluck's opera traveled around Europe, including stagings in Munich in 1767 and the Hague in 1768, returning to Vienna in German in 1780 (*Die Pilgrimme von Mekka*) as part of Joseph's German national theater project. In Vienna the role of Princess Rezia would be taken by Aloysia Weber, with whom Mozart had once been infatuated and whose sister Constanze he would later marry. The role of the Kalender was sung by Ludwig Fischer, for whom Mozart would later create the role of Osmin in the *Abduction*.[49] By 1780 Joseph, as the reigning emperor, would have been identified with the operatic figure of the sultan, not the prince.

In the last act of Gluck's opera the tenor sultan sings in rapid tempo to express his outrage—"*mes transports furieux*"—while Ali and Rezia sing nobly of their readiness to face torture and death together. When the sultan hears that they are royalty, however, he immediately reins in his musical rage and shifts to spoken dialogue in order to pardon the lovers and express his magnanimity.[50] Ali and Rezia together salute him as "prince the model of sultans," wishing him "eternal glory."[51]

As a prince the model of sultans, he was also a sultan the model of princes, and there was no doubt that Gluck and his librettist Dancourt intended the "sultan" to be a model of magnanimous monarchy applicable also to European thrones. Bent Holm has noted the particular relevance of this conception in Denmark, where the young King Christian VII identified with sultanic grandeur at a time when Favart's singing sultanas and Gluck's operatic pilgrims came to Copenhagen in both French and Danish versions in the 1760s and 1770s. The Danish king himself actually performed the role of Voltaire's Sultan Orosmane in *Zaïre*.[52]

In Haydn's *L'incontro* at Esterháza the sultan's angry threats were communicated by message from offstage, so that when he finally came on stage in the final scene he was immediately appearing in the persona of the generous Turk. With noble sonority his first phrases establish him as a paternal presence:

Levatevi,	Arise,
al mio petto ambi venite,	both of you come to my breast,
cari figliuoli miei.	my dear children.[53]

The final celebratory ensemble was punctuated with Janissary percussion in the Turkish style, a triumph of enlightened absolutism that could have been either Ottoman or Habsburg. In fact, Maria Theresa's son and Joseph's brother, Archduke Ferdinand, the governor of Milan, was present at Esterháza for the first (and perhaps only) performance of *L'incontro*. Ferdinand had received the dedication of Mysliveček's *Il gran Tamerlano* in Milan in 1771 and now, four years later, Haydn's comedy of Turkishness was composed especially for the archduke's visit to Esterháza—and produced with notably expensive Oriental costumes. The magnificence and magnanimity of the sultan on stage thus became a tribute to the archduke's own enlightened Habsburg political presence.[54] Mozart would similarly make Pasha Selim into a mirror for the enlightened absolutism of Joseph II in Vienna ten years later.

Esterháza was some 60 miles from Vienna, the Habsburg capital, but also about 120 miles from Budapest which had once been an Ottoman city. The Esterházy family, who employed Haydn as Kapellmeister, had achieved particular power and prominence among the Habsburg Hungarian aristocracy on account of their contributions to relieving the siege of Vienna and driving the Turks from Hungary in the late seventeenth century.[55] Though the Habsburgs had not participated in the Russian-Ottoman war between 1768 and 1774, in 1775, the year of Haydn's *L'incontro*, Joseph and Maria Theresa annexed the province of Bukovina—in northern Moldavia—from the Ottoman empire. In the immediate aftermath of the Russian war, the sultan could not prevent this depredation, which was partly intended to balance the newly expansive power of Russia at Ottoman expense. In this case Turkish "generosity" was the compulsory outcome of Habsburg statecraft. Yet Joseph surely felt that his own magnanimity was being celebrated along with the sultan's in Gluck's *Die Pilgrimme von Mekka* in 1780 at the Burgtheater in Vienna. Gluck's comedy of the Kalender had come to reflect, perhaps had even influenced, Joseph's ecclesiastical reforms, while the happy ending that glorified the sultan with "Turkish" music became a tribute to Joseph's own brand of enlightened absolutism.

Haydn's Curious Apothecary and the Outbreak of War

By the time Haydn came to compose *L'incontro* in 1775 he had already had one earlier experience with Turkish comedy of a very different kind: *Lo speziale* (The apothecary), composed for the inauguration of the new Esterháza theater in 1768. Although the opera presented no Turkish characters, it involved a certain awareness of things Turkish, and the plot culminated in the appearance of one of the characters in Turkish disguise. This sort of comic Turkish travesty was a device that dated back to *Le bourgeois gentilhomme* and involved not only exotic costume but also the comedy of nonsense lyrics, awkward music, and sometimes distorted vocalism. In a certain sense, such travesties highlighted the very essence of all Turkish opera, which really always concerned Turkish figures who were being impersonated by European performers on the stage. The device of Turkish disguise simply inserted that convention of impersonation into the plot of the opera itself. At the same time, the success of the disguise emphasized the balance of difference and resemblance between Europeans and Turks. They might be sufficiently different to require disguises in order to pass for one another, but they were also sufficiently similar for such passing to be comically possible on the operatic stage.

The libretto for *Lo speziale* was originally written by Carlo Goldoni for performance at Carnival in Venice in 1755, set to music by Vincenzo Pallavicini and Domenico Fischietti—the same year that Fischietti composed for Venice his *Solimano*, based on Migliavacca's libretto. Goldoni had created his first musical comedy about Turkey back in 1737, *Lugrezia Romana in Costantinopoli*. In the 1750s, however, Goldoni showed himself to be particularly interested in dramas with Oriental themes, such as *La sposa persiana* (The Persian wife) of 1753 and its two Persian sequels (*Ircana in Julfa* and *Ircana in Ispahan*), and *La Dalmatina* of 1758, which concerned a Dalmatian woman held in Turkish captivity in Morocco.[56] His opera libretto *Lo speziale* was set in Italy, but the apothecary Sempronio took a natural interest in the Orient because of the herbs and spices required for his pharmacopeia. It was probably Karl Friberth who adapted Goldoni's libretto for Haydn, and it was also Friberth who sang the starring role of Sempronio.

In Goldoni's libretto, Sempronio is obsessively curious about the wider world beyond Italy, always reading the gazettes for news of remote eastern locales, such as China and the Moluccas. Much of his news is nonsense, but some reports, especially from less remote eastern sites, are more plausible:

Le navi caricate verso Ceffalonia	The cargo ships for Kefalonia
Han fatto vela e son andate via . . .	Have made sail and departed . . .
La peste ha fatto strage in la Turchia.	The plague has ravaged Turkey.[57]

The Ionian island of Kefalonia belonged to Venice and would have been more meaningful to Goldoni than to Haydn, but the news of plague in Turkey would have been of real concern in both Venice and Hungary with their Ottoman borders, and such reports were not infrequent. The Triplex Confinium remained the region of maximal transcultural contact—both tension and intimacy—between the Muslim and Christian worlds in Europe. Goldoni's Venice and Haydn's Esterháza were natural sites both for receiving Turkish news and for staging operas with Turkish themes.

Beginning in 1768, the apothecary Sempronio might also have expected to read regular reports about the progress of the Russian-Ottoman war in Turkish lands. The Venetian journalist Domenico Caminer, for instance, followed the war closely in his ongoing work of instant history, *Storia della guerra presente*.[58] In *Lo speziale* Sempronio imagines dividing the world imperially among the great powers:

| Tra i signori che adesso son in guerra, | Among the lords who are now at war, |
| La division del mare e della terra. | The division of the sea and the earth.[59] |

The allusion to a current war would have been more meaningful when Haydn composed the music in 1768 than when Goldoni originally wrote the words in 1755. Sempronio imagines himself assigning the spoils of war to the king of the Tartars, the king of the Indies, and the Mogul emperor—while admitting to geographical confusion: "*Ma senza il mappamondo / Mi perdo e mi confondo*" (But without a globe, I become lost and confused).[60] The confusion of international affairs would finally contribute to the travesty of Turkish disguise in the final act.

The production of Haydn's opera at Esterháza in the autumn of 1768 coincided with the outbreak of war between Russia and the Ottomans, which would keep Turkey at the center of European discussion during the ensuing years. There were six performances of *Lo speziale* in 1768 at Esterháza, two more by the Esterháza troupe performing in Vienna in 1770, and perhaps a few more at Esterháza in 1772, all during the course of the Russian-Ottoman war. The original musical setting by Pallavicini and Fischietti, performed in Venice in 1755, was also given in London in 1769 at the King's Theatre in the Haymarket.[61] Haydn's opera should be considered as part of a whole European cohort of operas that dated from this period of special interest in the Ottoman empire and the Islamic Orient and culminated, as Thomas Bauman has suggested, in Mozart's *Abduction* in 1782, after the war was over.[62] Even before the war, Ahmed Resmi Efendi's embassies to Vienna in 1758 and Berlin in 1763 had stimulated German interest in the Ottoman empire, and during the war years of 1768 to 1774 there was a cluster of largely comic operas on Ottoman themes, especially concerning Turkish captivity. Ahmed Resmi Efendi himself participated in the Turkish negotiations at the treaty of Küçük Kaynarca in 1774.

In addition to Haydn's *Lo speziale* at Esterháza, there was *La schiava liberata* at Ludwigsburg in 1768, composed by Niccolò Jommelli, and later revived in Lisbon in 1770; *Der Kaufmann von Smyrna* at Mannheim in 1771, composed by Georg Joseph Vogler; *Der Bassa von Tunis* in Berlin in 1774, with music by Franz Andreas Holly; and Haydn's *L'incontro* at Esterháza in 1775. At the same time, treatments of Favart's *Three Sultanas*, originating in Paris in 1761, continued to circulate in Europe, coming to Vienna in 1770 in German and to London in English in 1775. Migliavacca's *opera seria* libretto for *Solimano* was also in circulation during these years: the setting by Perez was revived in Lisbon in 1768; Galuppi's setting was performed in Padua in 1768 and Verona in 1769; while Naumann's setting was heard in Venice in 1773. Even Piovene's venerable libretto for *Tamerlano*, the operatic tragedy of Bajazet, was set once again by Josef Mysliveček for Milan in 1771. On the whole, however, the Ottoman reversals of fortune in war were accompanied by a veritable festival of musical comedies about Turks on European operatic stages.

Salamelica Constantinupola

The apothecary Sempronio wants to marry his young ward Grilletta, but she is in love with the apothecary's assistant Mengone and is also pursued by another young man, Volpino—so young that the role was performed by a female singer dressed as a boy. Haydn scholar Karl Geiringer has noted the connection between the travesty role of Volpino (composed for a woman, not a castrato) and Mozart's Cherubino two decades later, for both are comically impassioned youths. Grilletta finds him entertaining but thinks he is crazy:

Caro Volpino amabile,	Dear lovable Volpino,
Siete de' pazzi il re . . .	You are the king of the crazies . . .[63]

His craziness takes the form of a Turkish disguise in the final act, as he pretends to be an emissary from Constantinople who has come to do business with Sempronio, while also trying somehow to win the apothecary's ward. Almost all of the music for the third act of *Lo speziale* has been lost, leaving only Volpino's "Turkish" musical monologue and the quartet finale of the opera. The "king of the crazies" presents himself in Turkish costume, singing mispronounced Italian and Italianized Arabic, with mock-Oriental marching rhythms composed for the wind section of the Esterháza princely orchestra.

Volpino begins by singing each phrase on a single note, so that his music is characterized only by "Turkish" rhythm, without any element of "Italian" melody. The single surviving aria of act 3 is therefore scarcely an aria at all:

Salamelica, Semprugna cara.	Salam alaikum, Sempronio dear.
Constantinupola,	Constantinople,
Sempre cantara, sempre ballara,	Always sing, always dance,
Dadl dadl dadl dadl dara,	Dadl dadl dadl dadl dara,
Dei didl dum,	Dei didl dum,
Da didl didl dum.	Da didl didl dum.[64]

"*Salamelica*," from Haydn's *Lo speziale* (The apothecary) of 1768. Volpino appears in Turkish disguise as an envoy from Constantinople with a Muslim greeting ("*salam-aleykum*"). The name "Constantinupola" with the comic repetition *nupola-nupola-nupola* is chanted on a single note, the repeated G. The orchestral accompaniment makes use of a *staccato* "Turkish" oscillating figure on a G chord. The concluding line of "*dadl dadl dadl*" may be intended to suggest a Jewish or Gypsy musical character.

"Sempronio" became "Semprugna," and "Constantinupola" was emphasized with the nonsensical repetition of the final syllables, "*nupola-nupola-nupola.*" In Goldoni's libretto the aria concluded conventionally with "*la la la la,*" but for Esterháza the introduction of "*dadl dadl*" and "*didl dum*" suggested that mock-Turkishness might have Central European inflections, with musical and rhythmic hints of Hungarian, Gypsy, or even Jewish character. Musicologist Caryl Clark observes that "Volpino's mixed alterity and gender confusion is further complicated by interjections of the repeated 'dadl dadl' refrain," such that "the blending of ethnic otherness embraces Jewish vocality." The rhythm was also possibly related to that of the Törökös, the "Turkish" folk idiom that could be traced back to Ottoman Hungary in the previous century.[65]

Although so much of Haydn's third-act music has been lost, the dramatic context of Volpino's aria can still be explicated from Goldoni's original libretto. In the first act Sempronio was studying the news from the Moluccas and reports of plague in Turkey; now, in the third act, he is presented with a message "from Turkey and Persia," announcing the search for an Italian apothecary to deliver medicines against the plague. The credulous Sempronio's only hesitation concerns the alleged recalcitrance of the Turks to embrace modern European medical science: "But the Turks do not use medicines." The report, however, explains that the Turks are prepared to undertake a program of medical modernization under the guidance of a European apothecary. They propose to counter the plague "by introducing medicines" (*con introdurre dei medicamenti*)—at which the apothecary exclaims that he has a "cordial" that will do wonders against the plague ("*per la peste ho un cordial che fa portenti*").[66] The rhyming of *medicamenti* and *portenti* suggests that Goldoni was enjoying the complex ironies of the comedy, inasmuch as the presumption of Turkish backwardness and the program of Turkish modernization could excite no better European response than the cordials and potions of a rather ridiculous apothecary. Indeed, eighteenth-century European medicine was no better equipped than Ottoman medicine to deal with the plague, or any infectious disease, and the fantasy of bringing enlightenment to Turkey was therefore a fit subject for operatic comedy.

The apothecary Sempronio declares himself ready to depart for Turkey immediately:

Questa volta lascio la patria mia,	This time I am leaving my homeland,
a fare lo spezial vado in Turchia.	to be an apothecary I am going to Turkey.[67]

Goldoni certainly knew that for centuries many Venetians had traveled to, and even lived in, the Ottoman empire for commercial purposes. Ottoman Istanbul, like Byzantine Constantinople, had always had a Venetian expatriate community, and Sempronio's resolution was therefore perfectly plausible. In the 1740s Casanova traveled from Venice to Istanbul and claimed to have seriously considered the possibility of settling in the Ottoman capital, marrying a Turkish girl, and even converting to Islam.[68] In the 1750s Goldoni comically outlined a similar scenario for his apothecary: Sempronio packs up his unguents, spirits, drugs, and essences, and a great quantity of "the most perfect pumpkin oil" (*oglio perfettissimo di zucca*), preparing to travel to Constantinople.[69]

Volpino then appears in his Turkish disguise, accompanied by a whole party of fake Turks ("*con seguito di finti turchi*"), and now asks Sempronio to marry him to Grilletta.[70] This was also precisely the point of the Turkish disguise in Molière's *Le bourgeois gentilhomme*: the young man in love disguises himself as a Turkish prince, and Monsieur Jourdain then enthusiastically hands over his daughter in marriage. Similarly, Haydn's Sempronio is happy to agree to the marriage of Grilletta, while he himself thinks only about hurrying off to Turkey to get rich. Volpino then delivers his "Salamelica" nonsense aria, which makes a very favorable impression on Sempronio:

Che bel parlar grazioso,	What beautiful gracious speaking,
Che gente spiritosa e d'allegria!	What a spirited and happy people!
Che paese gentile è la Turchia!	What a nice country is Turkey![71]

The word *gentile* might be translated with a range of more subtle meanings: nice, polite, well-mannered, genteel, civil, even civilized. Unfortunately, Sempronio cannot tell one "Turk" from another, and when Mengone appears in Turkish costume he looks just like Volpino in Turkish costume, and the apothecary therefore lets Mengone marry Grilletta. Volpino learns to his chagrin that Grilletta has already married someone else, and Sempronio explains, "*Con quel bel turco si è sposata*" (She is married to that handsome Turk).[72]

Thus the Turkish disguise succeeds all too well, and Volpino can do nothing but furiously reveal himself: "*E tai baffi e vestiti mando al diavolo*" (These moustaches and clothes I send to the devil).[73] The elements of the Turkish disguise were here described, moustaches as well as clothing, and they could be removed in a moment on stage. The transformation was entirely simple because the general difference in appearance between Turks and Europeans was presumed to be negligible. In 1785 there was presented in London a related musical comedy of disguise and identity, *Turk and No Turk*, composed by Samuel Arnold (who was known for his compilation of Handel's complete works). The comedy concerns an Englishman who disguises himself as a rich Turk to overcome the objections of the parents of the English girl he loves.[74] In 1790 Mozart and Da Ponte would also present a comedy of disguise, false moustaches, and Ottoman costumes in *Così fan tutte* with its mock-Albanians, presumably Ottoman subjects. The device of pseudo-Ottoman disguise advances the courtship of the two sisters, who cannot recognize their own lovers with moustaches in Albanian costume.[75]

The music for the finale of Haydn's opera has survived, and features a refrain informing Sempronio that there is no need for him to go to Turkey after all: "*Constantinupola più non si va*" (No one is going to Constantinople anymore). Sempronio and Volpino both have to resign themselves to having been tricked, but the apothecary's principal disappointment is perhaps not the loss of his ward but rather the evaporation of his fantasy of traveling to Turkey. For it is Sempronio's fascination with Turkey and eagerness to make the journey that dominates the entire last act. Goldoni would have seen this as part of the apothecary's foolishness, but the dramatist was also probably satirizing a real fascination with Turkey that flourished in midcentury Venice, which as historian Paolo Preto has shown, certainly entertained a powerful cultural interest in Turkishness.[76] In the years of the Russian-Ottoman war between 1768 and 1774, however, cultural interest in Turkey was intensified by a sense of its current political importance, more widely registered than ever before in the journals of the public sphere, and more densely apparent on the operatic stages of Europe.

Twenty years later, in 1794, Haydn went on tour to London and presented there his Hundredth Symphony, in G major, called the "Military Symphony" because of the thundering percussion of bass drum and cymbals in the second movement, evoking a battle scene by using elements of *alla turca* style without any particular Turkish reference.[77] Haydn might have been remembering his Turkish-themed compositions during the Russian-Ottoman war of 1768 to 1774, memories perhaps awakened by the more recent Habsburg-Ottoman war of 1787 to 1791. In the 1790s this sort of heavy percussion was already beginning to have general military associations without necessarily recalling Janissary bands or Turkish travels.

Wartime Comedies of Turkishness: Jommelli and Vogler

Jommelli's comic opera *La schiava liberata* (The liberated slave), with a libretto by Gaetano Martinelli, was performed at the Württemberg ducal court in Ludwigsburg in 1768, the same year as Haydn's *Lo speziale* at Esterháza. Jommelli musically juxtaposed a tenor Turk, Solimano the Bey of Algiers, and his son, the naval leader Selim, sung by a castrato. This use of the castrato voice for a heroic Turkish operatic figure in the middle of the eighteenth century was quite rare; that register was generally reserved for juvenile filial roles, like the sons of Suleiman in the midcentury *opera seria* settings of Migliavacca's *Solimano* libretto, beginning with Hasse in 1753. These castrati roles for Turkish princes in Hasse and Jommelli were exceptions to the general downward trend of the Turkish tessitura in European opera. Other exceptions were sometimes comically notable, such as Holly's pasha of Tunis: actually a female European captive disguised as a male Turk and presiding as a pasha over a harem of her own. Haydn's travesty in *Lo speziale* also involved a female voice (not a castrato) cast in a male European role, Volpino, and then pretending to be Turkish.

La schiava liberata employed, at the opposite end of the vocal spectrum, a comic basso in a Turkish role, that of the court dignitary Albumazar, actually specified as Turco Circasso, a Circassian Turk, playing the comical role that Mozart would later definitively compose for Osmin. Albumazar, like Osmin in love with Blonde, is in love with one of the captive European servants, and like Osmin easily jealous and expressively violent. Albumazar sometimes assumes a comic disguise, cross-dressing first as a woman and then as a Frenchman. "I am the great Albumazar!" he sings, farcically full of himself, with a comical octave leap on the penultimate syllable of his name:

Sono il grande Albumazar!	I am the great Albumazar!
Son circasso di nazione!	I am Circassian by nation!
Fiamme, stragi, e confusione,	Flames, massacre, and confusion,
Qui, fra poco, à da regnar.	Will reign here in a little while.[78]

Mozart's Osmin, likewise a comic basso, would participate in the same spirit of hyperbolic and farcical Ottoman threats of violence.

Jommelli combined aspects of *opera seria* and *opera buffa* in rendering the Ottoman circumstances of captivity. In *La schiava liberata*, the castrato hero

Selim falls seriously in love with one of his father's European captives, but the ensuing complications involve men comically cross-dressing as women to enter the harem. Jommelli had composed an *opera seria*, *Bajazette*, for Turin in 1753, using Piovene's libretto. *La schiava liberata*, however, was designated as a *dramma serio-comico per musica*, which suggested the whole range of possible European perspectives on Ottoman affairs.[79]

La schiava liberata was created in 1768 at the moment of the outbreak of the Russian-Ottoman war, and Jommelli was able to mock the Ottoman menace of Albumazar while also celebrating the valor of the castrato hero Selim. Not only a prince but also a naval commander, Selim returns to Algiers—at the opening of the opera—bringing treasure and European captives who will ultimately be liberated to return to Europe. Musicologist Marita McClymonds notes: "Jommelli wrote some of the most beautiful music in the opera for this character, played by [Giuseppe] Aprile, his good friend and supreme interpreter of his music. As *primo soprano* Aprile would have demanded more arias than the others." McClymonds has observed that Selim's first aria was "lavishly tinted with the colors of the oboes and flutes, that allowed Aprile ample opportunity to show off his beautiful voice."[80] At Ludwigsburg the castrato Aprile thus performed Selim, the Turkish prince, as the starring role and romantic hero of the opera. The same part was taken in Lisbon in 1770 by Carlo Reina (or Reyna), the castrato who two years earlier in Padua had also sung the part of another Ottoman Selim, the son of Suleiman the Magnificent, in Galuppi's setting of Migliavacca's *Solimano*.[81]

Jommelli did not neglect the military virtues of his Turkish hero and had the chorus celebrate Selim in the opening scene of *La schiava liberata*:

Del tuo valor sublime	Of your sublime valor
Si cantino le glorie;	May the glories be sung;
Le imprese, e le vittorie	The undertakings, the victories
Son degne del tuo cor.	Are worthy of your heart.[82]

The Lisbon performance took place in the spring of 1770—though the celebration of Ottoman naval victory might have seemed ironic after July, when the Ottoman fleet was destroyed by the Russians at Chesme in the eastern Mediterranean. The libretto of *La schiava liberata* was recomposed in a new postwar version by Joseph Schuster for Dresden in 1777.

In 1771, still in wartime, Georg Joseph Vogler's Singspiel *Der Kaufmann von Smyrna* (The merchant of Smyrna) was presented at Mannheim, just six-ty miles from Ludwigsburg. In Mannheim, at the court of the elector of the Rhineland Palatinate, there was a notable eighteenth-century musical culture of composition and performance, especially in German.[83] The proprietor of the court bookstore, Christian Friedrich Schwan, a central figure in the liter-ary and dramatic life of Mannheim, created the libretto for *Der Kaufmann von Smyrna*, based on a nonmusical French drama of 1770, *Le marchand de Smyrne*, by Sébastien-Roch Nicolas de Chamfort. It was Chamfort who later in the 1770s wrote *Mustapha et Zéangir* and dedicated the Ottoman drama to Marie Antoinette. Later still, after 1789, he became a Jacobin in the French Revolution, and *Le marchand de Smyrne* already suggested some of his revo-lutionary ideals.

The title of *Der Kaufmann von Smyrna* may have been intended as an al-lusion to Shakespeare's *Merchant of Venice*, as both works dramatized the haz-ards and uncertainties of Mediterranean trade, both ambiguously designat-ing two merchants within the same play. Just as Shakespeare's title, intended to designate the virtuous Antonio, has been more often associated with the Jewish moneylender Shylock, so in Chamfort's drama and Schwan's libretto there are two neighboring merchants: the virtuous Hassan and the Armenian slave dealer Kaled. Before the curtain goes up, Hassan has recently returned to Smyrna (today Izmir, on the Mediterranean coast of Turkey) from captivity in Marseille—where he, a Muslim, was magnanimously emancipated by a Chris-tian Frenchman. In gratitude to his personal liberator Hassan has therefore taken an enlightened vow to use his wealth to free one Christian from Otto-man slavery every year. His experience in France has further altered his view of marriage, and following the French example, he has renounced polygamy and lives in happy monogamy with his beloved Zayde. Both Hassan and Zayde, in the spirit of the Enlightenment, renounce any hatred of Christians, and affirm their monogamous love for one another in an operatic duet: "*Dein Hassan liebt nur dich! / Zayde liebt nur dich!*" (Hassan loves only you! / Zayde loves only you!). Just as Hassan is committed to freedom for slaves, he also believes in greater freedom for women, imagining Turkey more like France, so that "*Freiheit*" becomes the unifying enlightened theme of the opera.[84]

The negative example of unenlightened inhumanity is Hassan's neighbor Kaled the slave dealer, whose proximity is unwelcome except for the fact that it allows Hassan regular opportunities to fulfill his emancipatory commitment. Interestingly, the opera did not crudely contrast Ottoman slavery with French freedom, inasmuch as Hassan himself had been the slave of Christians in Marseille. While the libretto was frankly opposed to the slave trade, it clearly acknowledged that slavery transcended religious and cultural boundaries on the Mediterranean. Furthermore, Kaled the slave trader was specified as Armenian and might therefore be presumed to be Christian. Vogler, the composer, was actually a Catholic priest—"Abbé Vogler"—though his Christianity was probably open-minded in the spirit of the Enlightenment.

Vogler presented Kaled the slave dealer as exuberantly evil in his introductory aria, which was also accompanied by Janissary percussion.[85] Despite the violent sentiments, the aria must have been comically conceived by the composer:

> Ich hasse den Frieden, und liebe den Krieg,
> Und wünsche Corsaren beständig den Sieg!
> Dann wimmelt der Haven,
> Von christlichen Sclaven:
> Dann treib ich sie Heerdenweis vor mir daher,
> Und tanze vor Freuden am schäumenden Meer!

> I hate peace, and love war,
> And I wish for victory always for the corsairs!
> Then the harbors would swarm,
> With Christian slaves:
> Then I would drive them in a herd before me,
> And dance with joy by the foaming sea![86]

It would be hard not to recognize here in Vogler's slave trader the same perversely gleeful spirit as Mozart's Osmin, the palace guard, singing "*Ha! wie will ich triumphieren!*" Osmin too would dance for joy:

Hüpfen will ich, lachen, springen,	I want to hop, laugh, and leap,
Und ein Freudenliedchen singen.	And sing a little song of joy.[87]

Vogler's opera in 1771 was more than a decade older than Mozart's *Abduction* of 1782, but the former was revived in Mannheim in February 1778 when Mozart was actually there, hoping to obtain a position at the court of the Palatinate.

The twenty-two-year-old Mozart despised Vogler and mocked him in letters to Leopold Mozart in Salzburg. On the subject of one of Vogler's masses performed in Mannheim in November 1777, Mozart wrote to his father: "He attacks the music in such a way that one must fear he wants to drag you in by your hair; not that he makes it all worthwhile in some interesting way, no, it's all so clumsy." Of course Mozart must have resented an older rival so triply well-established as chaplain, music teacher, and composer in Mannheim, and the letters to Leopold made no mention of *Der Kaufmann von Smyrna*. The revival took place on February 20, 1778, and Mozart's letter of February 22 conveniently offered what might have been his medical excuses for missing the performance: "I have been at home for two days now and have been taking anti-spasmodics and black powder and elderberry tea to make me sweat, because I've been suffering from catarrh, a runny nose, headaches, a sore throat, eye aches, and ear aches."[88] Yet it seems likely that Mozart must have encountered *Der Kaufmann*, either in rehearsal or in performance, simply because one of the stars was none other than Aloysia Weber, with whom he was then completely infatuated.

Even if Mozart somehow, by an overdetermined accumulation of symptoms of eye, ear, nose, and throat somehow managed to avoid seeing or hearing Vogler's opera, the connection to the *Abduction* is nevertheless absolutely clear and undeniable. For in Mannheim in 1778, starring in the comic role of the evil slave dealer Kaled was none other than Ludwig Fischer, for whom Mozart would very specifically compose the role of Osmin in Vienna three years later.[89] Whether or not Mozart thought that Vogler's "clumsy" music suited the morally awkward figure of a comical slave dealer, Fischer himself would have preserved the musical memory from the performance of one comical Ottoman villain to the next.

When Kaled's European captive remonstrates with him, the slave dealer merely replies, "Don't you sell blacks? Now I am going to sell you. Isn't it all the same?" Chamfort had made the same point in his French drama: "*Ne vendez-vous pas des Nègres?*"[90] Schwan and Vogler thus purposefully created a German opera that could have functioned as an abolitionist manifesto of the Enlightenment. Indeed, *Der Kaufmann von Smyrna* almost undermined the premise of Turkish captivity as an operatic theme by pointing out that Europeans really had no legitimate moral grounds for protesting their own captivity, as long as other Europeans were profiting from the slave trade. Kaled's European captive, however, is none other than Hassan's liberator from Marseille, so a happy ending emerges when Hassan and Zayde purchase the freedom of the French lovers Dornal and Amalie (the role of Aloysia Weber). The opera concludes with a "vaudeville" quartet, one verse for each of the four lovers, not unlike the "vaudeville" conclusion to Mozart's *Abduction*.

The quartet in *Der Kaufmann von Smyrna* sings the slogans of the Enlightenment, representing both French and Turkish perspectives, harmonized in German. Dornal sings, "*Wie schön ist es, der Menschheit Pflichten üben*" (How beautiful it is to practice the duties of humanity). Amalie goes further: "*So werden Türken unsre Brüder, / So bald die Tugend uns vereint*" (The Turks will become our brothers, / As soon as Virtue unites us). Finally, the quartet joins together, seemingly singing to a fictive European and Turkish public:

> Seid ihr nicht alle Kinder eines Blutes?
> Habt ihr nicht einen Vater nur?
> Ihr Sterbliche! . . .Drum thut euch Gutes!
> Dies ist die Stimme der Natur.

> Are you not all children of one blood?
> Don't you have only one father?
> You mortals! . . . Be good to one another!
> This is the voice of nature.[91]

This was the voice of the Enlightenment, celebrating the unity of humanity, in the full conviction that Turks and Europeans were all people of "one blood," that Muslims and Christians were all children of the same divine father, that is, worshippers of the same paternal God. The work may have been clumsy in construction, but in 1771 it anticipated by almost a decade the ideology of religious brotherhood represented in Gotthold Ephraim Lessing's celebrated drama *Nathan the Wise* in 1779. Furthermore, the musical setting by the Abbé Vogler (a Roman Catholic priest embracing the brotherhood of Christians and Muslims) permitted an expression of religious harmony through musical harmony.

La schiava liberata in 1768 at Ludwigsburg and *Der Kaufmann von Smyrna* in 1771 at Mannheim presented menacing but comical Ottoman bass roles, Kaled and Albumazar, anticipating Mozart's Osmin. Both operas also involved European captives and happy endings brought about through Turkish magnanimity, later the formula for Mozart's *Abduction*. *Der Kaufmann von Smyrna* was recomposed by Carl David Stegmann in 1773 for Königsberg—where it could have been seen by Kant. Stegmann's version of *Der Kaufmann* was given in Danish in Copenhagen in 1776, as was Gluck's treatment of *Les pèlerins*. Franz Andreas Holly (who came from Bohemia as František Ondřej Holý) created yet another German version of *Der Kaufmann von Smyrna* for the enlightened Berlin of Frederick the Great in 1773, before composing *Der Bassa von Tunis* for Berlin in 1774, the year of the peace of Küçük Kaynarca.

There was further interest in Turkishness in Vienna in 1774, stimulated by the arrival of the grand Ottoman embassy of Suleiman Efendi, to announce the accession of Sultan Abdülhamid after the death of his brother Mustafa III. Holly's setting of *Der Kaufmann von Smyrna* was given Viennese performances in 1776 and 1781, and 1781 was also the year of Emperor Joseph's Patent of Toleration, to some extent reflecting the ecumenical religious spirit of *Der Kaufmann*. In fact, the opera was now renamed to further emphasize its enlightened opposition to slavery: *Der Sklavenhändler von Smyrna* (The slave dealer of Smyrna), performed on February 13, 1781. At this performance the role of Kaled (now in Holly's version) was again taken by Ludwig Fischer, soon to become Mozart's Osmin.[92] Mozart, however, arrived in Vienna on March 16, 1781, and thus missed the performance by a month.

Conclusion: The Grand Turk of Parma and the Peace of Küçük Kaynarca

If Haydn's *Lo speziale* at Esterháza and Jommelli's *La schiava liberata* at Ludwigsburg marked the year of the outbreak of war in 1768, the achievement of peace in 1774 coincided with the production at the ducal palace of Colorno, for Ferdinando the duke of Parma, of a musical comedy entitled *Il figlio del Gran Turco* (The son of the Grand Turk). With music by Antonio Rugarli, this *dramma giocoso per musica* was actually an Italian treatment and translation of Molière's *Le bourgeois gentilhomme*, with the Turkish travesty of the final act now usurping the title of the whole work.[93] The treaty of Küçük Kaynarca was signed in July 1774, humbling the Ottoman empire by enhancing Russia's position on the Black Sea and also giving Russia the right to interfere in Ottoman internal affairs as the protector of Orthodox Christian Ottoman subjects. *Il figlio del Gran Turco* was performed at Colorno in the autumn, coinciding with the arrival of the news of the peace treaty.

The author of the libretto was probably none other than the reigning duke of Parma, Duke Ferdinando, the grandson of the French king Louis XV on one side and of the Spanish king Philip V on the other.[94] The duke would have applied his doubly Bourbon head and hands to the translation of Molière and would probably have selected the title *Il figlio del Gran Turco*, interested as he must have been in issues of royal descent. He would have watched the performance of his libretto together with his wife, Duchess Maria Amalia, the Habsburg daughter of Maria Theresa. In Molière's comedy the suitor Cléonte was presented to Monsieur Jourdain as the son of the Ottoman sultan, and the *bourgeois gentilhomme* was credulous enough to believe in the costumed pretender. In Duke Ferdinando's world everyone really was the son or daughter, grandson or granddaughter, of an important king or queen, emperor or empress. Not for another quarter century would he actually be faced with a real pretender, when he had to turn his duchy over to Napoleon in 1801, before dying under mysterious circumstances in the following year.

Il figlio del Gran Turco is set in Naples, where Turks might plausibly arrive by sea, and opens with a trio performed by singers in the house of Monsieur Giordano (Jourdain). The music master is seated, "leaning on the cymbals," as if to hint at the possibility of Janissary percussion in the final act. While Lully had composed incidental music for Molière's comedy, *Il figlio del Gran Turco* was more fully musical; Rugarli was now working within a tradition that did not yet exist in Lully's time, the genre of the "Turkish" opera. In fact, apart from the presence of the cymbals, there is no Turkishness until the third act, when the servant Coviello appears, *travestito alla Turca*, to announce that the son of the Grand Turk is present in Naples and wants to marry the daughter of Monsieur Giordano.[95]

Cléonte himself appears in Turkish costume and recites a nonsensical "Turkish" greeting, as "translated" by Duke Ferdinando from the original nonsense of Molière:

> Arabcab babedina bulefa
> Giordanu bambecchir salamalica.[96]

When Monsieur Giordano hears that he is to be honored as a Turkish "paladino," he sings an aria of delight:

Giordan fortunatissimo	Most fortunate Giordano
Giordano Paladino	Giordano Paladino
Ogni Turchesco inchino	Every Turk I will see
Vedrò far nanti a me.	Bowing before me.

Signor dell'Arcipelago	As Lord of the Archipelago
Marchese dell'Egitto	And Marquis of Egypt
Presto mi vedrò scritto	I'll soon be inscribed
Se scritto già non è.	If not inscribed already.[97]

The "archipelago" of the Aegean Islands belonged precisely to the news of the recent war, as the Russian fleet asserted its naval domination of the archipelago with the victory at Chesme in 1770; there was an Egyptian rebellion against the sultan as well. Monsieur Giordano's fantasy of bowing Turks and subjugated lands was an original creation of Ferdinando and Rugarli, as Monsieur Jourdain sang no such aria for Molière and Lully. In this regard Monsieur Giordano stood closer to Goldoni's and Haydn's apothecary, with his fantasy of Constantinupola made all the more vivid by the war which ended in Ottoman military defeat. In 1774 even a little princeling like the duke of Parma would not have wanted to trade places with the Ottoman sultan, and the fantasy of Ottoman rule was reserved for the foolish Monsieur Giordano. Napoleon Bonaparte, who was born in 1769 during the Russian-Ottoman war, would one day try to make himself the master of Egypt but would end up coming back to Europe to seize the duchy of Parma from Ferdinando.

Monsieur Giordano is initiated with a beating administered by a team of six singing pashas, in a musical ritual borrowed from Molière and Lully. Once again, however, Ferdinando and Rugarli enhanced the nonsensical Turkish chanting by the cross-dressed European Turks:

CLÉONTE: Clecaricca
    Maccarona
    Bellarona
    Chicchidar.
COVIELLO: Mellaranca
    Ciacciarella
    Billa Bella
    Diventar.[98]

There were perhaps a few favorite foods, like oranges and macaroni, mingled with the extravagant aural play. If Molière made use of a kind of Levantine pidgin for his Turkish ceremonial, Ferdinando took the game to the next level of multisyllabic Italian absurdity. The Ottoman empire itself had receded very significantly in power and importance since Molière's play was first performed in Paris in 1670, and Duke Ferdinando, as the anonymous librettist working in the year of Küçük Kaynarca, revived and perhaps amplified in "translation" the silliness of the Turkish travesty performed in the reign of his great-great-great-grandfather, Louis XIV.

When the Turkishness is ultimately revealed as a deception, with Monsieur Giordano as its victim, he accepts the marriage of his daughter and the trick played upon himself with good grace. In a line not to be found in Molière but very true to the spirit of Goldoni's apothecary, Monsieur Giordano seems to regret most of all that he will not become a powerful Ottoman dignitary: "*Più dell'Egitto / Non son Padron*" (I am no longer the master of Egypt).[99] In comic opera the performance of Turkishness continued to allow Europeans of every rank and role, both on the stage and in the public, to participate in musical claims to the Ottoman empire—even as the European powers began to exercise intrusive arbitration over Turkish subjects and territories, addressing the future of the empire as an international problem that would come to be known as the Eastern Question. Thus the Russian-Ottoman war ended in 1774 not only with a harshly domineering peace treaty at Küçük Kaynarca, just west of the Black Sea, but also with a gently farcical opera, *Il figlio del Gran Turco*, at the Parmesan palace of Colorno.

OSMIN IN VIENNA

Mozart's 'Abduction' and the

Centennial of the Ottoman Siege

Introduction: "The cowards of Istanbul"

On Sunday, September 12, 1783, Vienna celebrated the precise centennial of the defeat of the besieging Turkish army in 1683. On that day in 1683 an army under the supreme leadership of the Polish king Jan Sobieski, joined by Habsburg troops led by Charles of Lorraine, had descended from the Kahlenberg hill to defeat the Turkish army of Grand Vizier Kara Mustafa Pasha before the walls of Vienna. The commemoration of the centennial was observed by the journalist Johann Pezzl:

> What a day that was in the year 1683! It was also a Sunday—the most
> remarkable, the happiest Sunday in the annals of Vienna. As soon as the dawn
> illuminated the peak of the Kahlenberg, one saw the army of the Christian
> allies on the move. They advanced down the mountainside; the Turks were
> beaten, and Vienna was freed forever from their attacks. I saw in 1783 the last
> celebration commemorating that perilous day. They were concluded with the
> hundredth year. In fact the cowards of Istanbul [*die Hasenfüsse zu Stambul*] are
> no longer worthy of the gunpowder exploded in their memory.[1]

The commemoration of 1783 was to be the last, not just because the Ottomans had ceased to be menacing, but more importantly because Emperor Joseph II regarded all such ceremonials—especially ecclesiastical processions—as wasteful ostentation in the age of Enlightenment.

According to Pezzl, "for the perpetual remembrance of the fortunate liberation of Vienna, Emperor Leopold [in 1683] ordered that annually, on September 12, a solemn procession be undertaken from St. Peter's to the Trinity

Column in the Graben, and there a public prayer of thanks should be given for the saving of the capital."[2] The secular commemoration was also attached to a religious occasion, the festival of the Holy Name of the Virgin Mary on September 12, which happened to coincide with the liberation of Vienna and was therefore associated with the Turkish defeat. Pezzl's noting of the centennial suggests that there must have been some anticipation of it, some counting off of the years, and the ninety-eighth and ninety-ninth years in 1781 and 1782 were those of Mozart's arrival in Vienna and his composition of *Die Entführung aus dem Serail* (*The Abduction from the Seraglio*).

Pezzl's comment that "the cowards of Istanbul are no longer worthy of the gunpowder exploded in their memory" would have referred not only to the defeat of Kara Mustafa Pasha in 1683 but also to the much more recent Russian-Ottoman war and the peace of Küçük Kaynarca in 1774, which was so unfavorable to the Turkish "cowards"—*Hasenfüsse*, literally "rabbit-feet." The phrase almost conjured the spirit of *opera buffa* that prevailed in and around Vienna when Turkish figures took the stage during the wartime years. Mozart's *Abduction* would be produced in a similar spirit, anticipating the centennial by just one year and offering a sort of commemoration of the humbling of the Turks.

The *Abduction* was originally commissioned to be performed on the occasion of the visit to Vienna in 1781 of the Russian Grand Duke Paul, the son of Catherine the Great, fully two years before the centennial. In 1781 Russia and Austria also formed an alliance, directed against the Ottoman empire. The opera, which was not finished in time to present to the Grand Duke in 1781, was eventually performed in July 1782, and with its many comical elements represented an Ottoman empire that did not appear as a menace, nor even as an enemy.

The crucially farcical figure at the center of the *Abduction* was the basso role of the pasha's overseer Osmin, whose furious emotional outbursts invited the laughter of the audience in 1782—and today the critical attention of scholars. Peter Kivy has taken "Osmin's Rage" as the title of his book about opera and the musical representation of emotions. The title references Mozart's letter about Osmin's wrathful first-act aria of resentment, "*Solche hergelaufne Laffen*" (Such vagabond dandies). Mary Hunter sees Osmin's musical "incoherence" as an aspect of attributed barbarism, as in his third-act aria, "*Ha! wie will ich triumphieren*" (Ha! how I will triumph), with "its sudden

Die Entführung aus dem Serail—announcement of the first performance in Vienna on July 16, 1782, created as a "new Singspiel" for the Nationalhoftheater (the National Court Theater) of Joseph II and "set to music by Herr Kapellmeister Mozart." The Habsburg double-headed eagle dominates the decorative proscenium frame for the announcement. With kind permission of the Österreichische Nationalbibliothek.

changes of topos, from patter to menacing half notes, to mock-heroic octave leaps, to triplet coloratura, each one illustrating a particular point in the text, but none growing inevitably or predictably out of another." Matthew Head, writing about Mozart and Orientalism, also analyzes the pivotal function of the overseer: "Osmin is a figure who polices boundaries—the entrance to the harem, the limits of musical beauty, the sphere of rational and moral conduct." Osmin's role in the comedy as "the apparent butt of Orientalist degradation and satire," Head observes, has the implicit effect of "producing (through the rhetorical figure of antithesis) the very notion of the European

Self." Mozart scholar Alfred Einstein recognizes Osmin as "Mozart's greatest creation" within the *Abduction*: "no caricature, but as realistic a rogue as Falstaff: coarse, irascible, infinitely comical as a spiteful friend of women and wine, but infinitely dangerous."[3] Osmin may be considered as the culminating figure of the eighteenth-century singing Turk, whose raging emotions, violent comedy, liminal Orientalism, musical Turkish style, and extravagantly masculine basso register pose in all their complexity the issues, questions, contradictions, and dilemmas of operatic Turkishness.

Osmin emerged from a tradition of antecedent operatic characters, and the *Abduction* as a whole was shaped by the body of comical operas about Turks that had flourished in the Habsburg and German lands during the previous decades.[4] The flurry of operatic Ottoman scenarios attending the Russian-Ottoman war of 1768–74 now reached its postwar climax in Vienna in the early 1780s with the approach of the centennial of the Turkish siege of 1683. Mozart's *Abduction*, and especially the conception and composition of the outrageous Osmin, may be considered alongside Pezzl's cultural commentary on the Turks being "no longer worthy of the gunpowder exploded in their memory." Operas on Turkish subjects, including Mozart's *Abduction*, offered another genre of explosive commemoration.

"Here they prefer comedies": From *Zaide* to the *Abduction*

The *Abduction* was Mozart's most successful opera during his lifetime, frequently revived and performed in the Habsburg monarchy and the German states of the Holy Roman Empire during the 1780s.[5] It was not, however, Mozart's first operatic attempt to treat a Turkish subject. Even before *Zaide*, Mozart had contemplated a Turkish entertainment back in 1772, when he was only sixteen, during the Russian-Ottoman war. He made some musical sketches for a ballet about harem jealousies: *Le gelosie del serraglio*, intended as an entr'acte for his opera *Lucio Silla* in Milan. A ballet under the same title, possibly dating back to the 1750s in Vienna, was supposed to have involved the jealous rivalry of two sultanas for the sultan's affections, ending in a happy reconciliation expressed in a *pas de trois*. The final tableau included formations of black and white eunuchs, Janissaries, and dwarves.[6]

In 1778, while in Mannheim, Mozart heard that Joseph II was establishing the German National Singspiel company in Vienna—to perform Singspiel operas that included both music and dialogue, usually with comic elements, and often with some relation to popular theater. By 1779, possibly after having heard Vogler's *Der Kaufmann von Smyrna* in its 1778 revival in Mannheim, Mozart in Salzburg was already at work on the German Singspiel *Zaide* with the intention of presenting it in Vienna. He never finished the opera, as his work was interrupted by the Munich commission for *Idomeneo* in 1780. The fragments of *Zaide* were only discovered by Constanze Mozart in 1799, after the composer's death, and she placed a public advertisement to inquire "if anybody knows the title of this Singspiel."[7]

The name of the heroine Zaide (which was eventually assigned to the opera as a whole) suggested some allusion to Zaïre, the most famous Christian captive of eighteenth-century drama. There was a performance of Voltaire's *Zaïre* in German translation, in Salzburg in 1777, with musical accompaniment by Joseph Haydn's brother Michael whom Mozart knew well. In 1779 Mozart worked on *Zaide* with a Salzburg librettist, the trumpeter Johann Andreas Schachtner. His libretto for *Zaide* may have been modeled on an earlier Singspiel, *Das Serail, oder Die unvermuthete Zusammenkunft in der Sclaverey zwischen Vater, Tochter und Sohn* (The unexpected reunion in slavery of father, daughter, and son), with a heroine of that name, performed in 1777 at Wels (fifty miles from Salzburg); that libretto was by Franz Joseph Sebastiani and the music by Joseph Friberth (the brother of Karl Friberth who sang the role of the apothecary Sempronio for Haydn at Esterháza).[8] The dialogue of Schachtner's libretto for *Zaide* has not survived, but the musical numbers that Mozart completed do suggest the outline of the story: two of Sultan Soliman's European captives, Zaide and Gomatz, fall in love with each other, escape together, and are recaptured by the sultan's overseer Osmin. Though the sultan rages in the surviving excerpts, the earlier precedent of *Das Serail*, as well as the later example of Mozart's own *Abduction*, strongly suggest that Sultan Soliman would have proved himself to be, in the end, a magnanimous Turk—if Mozart had finished the opera.

Vogler and Schwan had made *Der Kaufmann von Smyrna* into a manifesto against slavery, but Mozart and Schachtner in *Zaide* presented an opening chorus of happy slaves who accept their slavery in the spirit of fatalism that the Enlightenment often associated with the Islamic Orient:

> Lasst uns singen, lasst uns lachen,   Let us sing, let us dance,
> kann man's doch nicht anders machen!   if we can't do anything else![9]

Gomatz, the European captive, resists this spirit of cheerful resignation, and Mozart composed the scene in the unusual musical form called *melologo* in Italian, and *Melodram* in German. Instead of singing, Gomatz simply recites, but his recitation is accompanied by the orchestra. He rails against his fate, refusing to resign himself like the other slaves:

> Fühllos bei der strengsten Arbeit jauchzen sie noch laut ihren Unsinn . . .
> Jeder Balsam ist unwirksam für die Wunden meiner Seele . . .
>
> Without feeling at hard labor they rejoice loudly in their nonsense . . .
> Every balsam is useless for the wounds of my soul . . .[10]

His recitation thus expresses his alienation from the fatalism of the Orient, articulating a restless spirit of European resistance. Music historian Nicholas Till, in his book on Mozart and the Enlightenment, has argued that the incomplete *Zaide* was "Mozart's most personal, even autobiographical, work," expressing the frustration of his own conditions of service in Salzburg, experienced as a kind of slavery. Till even suggests that "Gomatz" may have been an anagram for "G. Mozart," with the *G* representing Gottlieb, that is, Amadeus.[11]

As soon as Gomatz encounters Zaide in slavery, they sing a love duet together, and plan their escape—"in Muslim clothes," as if to confirm that the difference between European Christians and Turkish Muslims was merely a matter of costume.[12] The character intent upon their capture was the captain of the sultan's bodyguard, Osmin, who thus established the Mozartean presence which would soon be transposed by name to the *Abduction*, to become the most famous Turkish figure in European operatic history.

The Osmin of *Zaide*—as far as he can be known from his single aria in the unfinished score—is a simple and good-natured servant who sings about the importance of food and drink when hungry and thirsty. His character owes something to the Arlequin of the Paris fairs but also to Osmin, "the kislar-aga or chief of the eunuchs," in Favart's *Three Sultanas*, and to Osmin who serves Prince Ali in Gluck's *Les pèlerins*. All these predecessors, taken together with the Albumazar of *La schiava liberata* who comically invokes "flames, massacres, and confusion," and the comical slave dealer Kaled in *Der Kaufmann von Smyrna*, contributed to the shaping of the Osmin of the *Abduction*, the definitively comical Ottoman underling whose raging menace was itself laughably unmenacing.

Mozart's considerations concerning the composition of *Zaide* in Salzburg were always connected to making an impression in Vienna. Daniel Heartz has suggested that one motivating circumstance may have been the performance of Gluck's *Die Pilgrimme von Mekka*, produced in German in Vienna in July 1780, starring Aloysia Weber, Mozart's former love and future sister-in-law.[13] The death of Empress Maria Theresa in November 1780 was noted in a December letter from Mozart's father in Salzburg, and Leopold sent a black suit to Munich so that Mozart would have proper mourning clothes. According to Leopold, the period of prescribed mourning was one reason to postpone work on *Zaide* for some future occasion in Vienna:

> As for Schachtner's drama it is impossible to do anything at the moment, for the theaters are closed . . . It is better to let things be, as the music is not finished. Besides, who knows but that this opera may later give you an opportunity of getting to Vienna?[14]

In Vienna, however, on April 18, 1781, Mozart announced to his father the definitive end of his work on *Zaide*, after discussions with Johann Gottlieb Stephanie about writing a new libretto for another opera, also on a Turkish subject. It was all a matter of Viennese taste, according to Mozart:

> There's nothing to be done with Schachtner's operetta right now. The reason is—well, it's the same reason that I mentioned to you many times. Stephanie the Younger will provide me with a new piece, and, as he says, a good piece; if I should no longer be here, he'll forward it to me. Also, I couldn't disagree with his assessment. I told him that the work, with the exception of the long dialogues (which can easily be altered) is really very good; but it's not suitable for Vienna; here they prefer comedies.[15]

Indeed, the Viennese preference for comedy was evident from the contemporary repertory, and the most popular opera at the National Singspiel during 1780 and 1781 was Gluck's *Die Pilgrimme von Mekka*.[16]

For Mozart, who was still in the service of the archbishop of Salzburg in April 1781, the plan to collaborate on an opera with Stephanie in Vienna was closely tied to his intention of emancipating himself from the archbishop. On April 28 he wrote to his father:

> One thing I beg of you, dearest father, you must give me permission to return to Vienna during next Lent at the end of the Carnival season—and this depends on you alone, not on the archbishop—because if he doesn't give

me permission I'll go anyway, and it won't be my misfortune, certainly not! Oh, if he could only read this! I would not mind at all. But you must give me your promise in your next letter, for I shall return to Salzburg only under that condition; but it will be a definite promise, so I can give the ladies here my word. Stephanie will give me a German opera to compose.[17]

If Mozart, in *Zaide*, was already interested in the politics of despotism and slavery, his composition of the *Abduction* would be exactly contemporary and closely connected to his own struggle for personal emancipation.

Stephanie in 1781 was not just any librettist but the director of Joseph's National Singspiel company. In constructing a comic Turkish piece for Mozart, Stephanie adapted the very recent German libretto of Christoph Friedrich Bretzner, *Belmont und Constanze, oder Die Entführung aus dem Serail*, which was performed in the Berlin of Frederick the Great in 1781 with music by Johann André. Also created at the same time and notably similar in plot was the Singspiel opera *Adelheit von Veltheim*, composed by Christian Gottlob Neefe to a libretto by Gustav Friedrich Grossmann, performed in Frankfurt in 1780—and then Vienna in 1781 with new music, possibly by Giuseppe Sarti.[18]

The German captive Adelheit (Adelheid) is loved by the pasha of Tunis, but she has a proper German betrothed who is disguised as a Muslim gardener in Tunis. Adelheit resides in a multinational seraglio with her fellow French, English, Spanish, and Italian captives, providing a harem comedy of national caricatures, under the guardianship of a Muslim overseer, Mehmed, whose principal interest is violating Islamic law in order to get drunk. Unlike Mozart's Osmin, Neefe's Mehmed was a tenor, as was the pasha himself, and the chorus included slaves, blacks, eunuchs (*Verschnittene*), and Janissaries. Neefe's pasha makes his entrance accompanied by a Janissary march, orchestrated with Janissary percussion. A surviving copy of Neefe's score has the notation: "Among the instruments of the theater orchestra will be required a complete Janissary ensemble, i.e. a bass drum, together with kettledrums, fifes, cymbals, triangle."[19] The elements of the plot further suggest a scrambled correspondence to Bretzner's and Stephanie's librettos for the *Abduction*, indicating a constellation of closely related operas in the early 1780s.[20]

Mozart acknowledged his own attempt at a serious Turkish opera *Zaide* to be a misjudgment of public expectations, and in the *Abduction*, working with Stephanie, he enthusiastically cultivated the comic aspects of the captive drama. Though the European lovers of the *Abduction*, Belmonte and Konstanze, were fundamentally as serious as the romantic captives in *Zaide*, and Pasha Selim was taken totally seriously—both in his despotic mastery and in his ultimate magnanimity—the servant roles provided all the necessary comedy: the European servants Blonde and Pedrillo, and especially the Turkish overseer Osmin. In the case of Osmin, Mozart and Stephanie purposefully expanded what had been a smaller role in Bretzner's libretto, making the Turkish overseer arguably the dominant character of the opera, the singing Turk whose musical and dramatic Turkishness has remained both comically and charismatically compelling for the operatic public ever since the 1780s.

Mozart's "Turkish Music"

Following the precedents of Gluck and Haydn in their treatment of Ottoman themes, Mozart systematically and with great relish undertook to apply the principles of supposedly Turkish musical style—*alla turca*—to dramatize the Turkishness of his operatic scenario. European and Turkish characters, encountering one another in a Turkish harem and palace, were animated by a European score of music in the classical style, punctuated in certain numbers by elements of supposedly Turkish instrumentation, intervals, and rhythms. While this formula involved cultivating an exotic musical language, European composers, including Mozart, also drew upon a limited but real knowledge of Turkish music as publicized by the presence of Janissary bands in European cities during the eighteenth century.

By 1782, approaching the centennial of the Turkish siege, no one survived in Vienna who could actually remember the frightening sound of Janissary bands outside the walls of Vienna in 1683. Music in the Janissary style, however, had become fashionable. In the autumn of 1775 a regimental band played "Turkish music" in the Schönbrunn gardens to mark the seasonal harvesting of grapes for wine, and in 1781, the year that Mozart came to Vienna and began writing the *Abduction*, "Turkish music" was being played in the Prater.[21] Mozart, with his perfect ear for remembering music, would only have to have heard them playing once to be able to imitate the sound in the score of the *Abduction*. Furthermore, Michael Pirker has found evidence in the records of the Viennese Hoftheater that a payment was made to an artillery band to play in performances of Mozart's *Abduction* during the 1782–83 season, presumably including the Janissary instruments then in use among such European military ensembles.[22]

Hungary, which had actually been ruled by the Ottomans from the 1520s to the 1680s, still preserved some folk remains of Turkish music within the Habsburg monarchy in the eighteenth century. Bence Szabolcsi has found traces of Turkish rhythms and melodies in Hungarian folk music, and he has noted the possibility of a Hungarian-Turkish influence on the *alla turca* music of Gluck, Neefe, Mozart, and both Joseph and Michael Haydn. Furthermore, Szabolcsi has observed that Michael Haydn's specifically Transylvanian experience at Grosswardein (Nagyvárad in Hungarian, Oradea in Romanian), before moving to Salzburg, may have conditioned his compositions in *alla turca* style—his Turkish march and the incidental music for Voltaire's *Zaïre*—and may have influenced the young Mozart in matters of musical Turkishness.[23]

From the opening page of the overture to the *Abduction*—the bass drum, the triangle, and the cymbals enter in the ninth measure—the Viennese public was presented with the sounds and rhythms that would have been immediately recognizable as Turkish Janissary music. Thomas Bauman and Miriam Whaples have noted the several particular melodic and rhythmic strategies for representing Turkishness in the *Abduction*: repeated notes, oscillating intervals of a third, and long sustained notes followed for contrast by a cluster of much shorter ones.[24] Mozart had already made use of some of these qualities in his "Turkish" violin concerto in A major (K.219) composed in Salzburg in 1775, and some years later his piano sonata in A major (K.331) concluded with a rondo that Mozart called "*alla turca*" because of its Janissary rhythms. Daniel Heartz notes in the violin concerto the playing of "cellos and basses *col legno* [with the wood of the bow] to achieve a proper percussive effect," and imagines "Mozart's delight in creating his own harem scene." The "rondo *alla turca*" in the piano sonata—probably composed in 1783, and possibly with reference to the centennial of the siege—was later sometimes performed on a piano with the special "Janissary" pedal to provide percussive accompaniment.[25] In October 1777, Mozart in Munich received a letter from his father in Salzburg, reporting on the performance of Michael Haydn's incidental music for Voltaire's *Zaïre*: "Turkish music, which was so sudden and unexpected that all the women were terrified, and there was laughter."[26] Mozart was thus fully aware of both the dramatic and the comical potential of employing such musical devices, though *Zaide*, judging from what was completed, does not seem to have involved Janissary music or *alla turca* style. The turning from *Zaide* to the *Abduction* brought about a new level of engagement with Turkish music.

Mozart wrote to his father in April 1781 that he was beginning the new operatic project with Stephanie. The following months were immensely important in the composer's life, as they brought Mozart's definitive break with Salzburg, his consequent determination to remain in Vienna, his renting of a room with the Weber family, and the beginning of his romance with Constanze Weber. On August 1 Mozart reported to his father that he had received the new libretto:

> The day before yesterday Stephanie the Younger gave me a libretto to compose ... The libretto is very good. The subject is Turkish ... I am going to write the overture, the first-act chorus, and the final chorus with Turkish music.[27]

It was thus one of Mozart's very first strategic decisions about the composition of the new opera: which of the pieces would be composed as "Turkish music," in order to represent the Turkish subject.

Though Mozart had received the libretto only "the day before yesterday" (*vorgestern*), he had already begun to compose, and felt that he was working under the pressure of a deadline:

> I am so happy to be working on this libretto that I have already finished the first aria for Cavalieri [Konstanze] and one for Adamberger [Belmonte] as well as the trio that will conclude the First Act. Time is short, that's true; the work is supposed to be performed already in mid-September; but the circumstances connected with its performance and, generally, all the other prospects have lifted my spirit so much that I am now hurrying to my writing desk with the greatest eagerness and remain seated there with the greatest joy. The Grand Duke of Russia will be coming here; and that's why Stephanie asked me, if possible, to compose the opera in so short a time. Because the Emperor and Count Rosenberg will soon return to Vienna and it will be asked whether anything new is in preparation.[28]

Mozart thus learned, and reported to his father under strict secrecy, both the Turkish subject of the opera and the political conjuncture that compelled its timely composition: "nobody knows anything about this, except Adamberger and Fischer."[29] If the basso Ludwig Fischer was one of the select few who knew the secret of the intended opera, then Mozart had surely already begun to envision the importance of the role of the pasha's overseer Osmin.

The arrival in Vienna in late 1781 of the Russian Grand Duke Paul and his wife the Grand Duchess Maria Feodorovna could be made into an occasion for Turkish musical comedy, recalling the successful Russian war against the Ottomans in the previous decade. It was a piece of political programming that would require some consultation by the emperor himself with Count Franz Xaver Orsini-Rosenberg, the court official with principal responsibility for opera. In fact, the visit of the Grand Duke became the occasion for Gluck to present his opera *Iphigenie en Tauride*, reworked in German as *Iphigenia in Tauris*, and now subtly intended to celebrate the Russian occupation of the Tauride, that is, the Crimea. The Scythian choruses and dances in *Iphigenie* even made use of some percussive and rhythmic elements of Janissary music. The role of the Scythian king Thoas, Iphigenia's captor, was performed in 1781 by Ludwig Fischer, who would have been already preparing the role of Mozart's Osmin.[30] Cesare Questa has suggested that the Greek legend of Iphigenia in Tauris, as presented by Euripides, was understood as a drama of captivity—Iphigenia as captive of the Scythians, rescued by Orestes and Pylades—and therefore provided the classical model for modern dramas of Ottoman captivity, like Mozart's *Abduction*.[31]

"The Grand Duke is to remain here until the New Year," wrote Mozart to his father in December 1781, "and the Emperor is wondering how he is going to entertain him for such a long time."[32] Haydn presented the string quartets that would become known as the "Russian" quartets, and Mozart and Muzio Clementi performed in a piano competition as rival virtuosos. The mechanical chess-playing Turk was brought forth for Paul's entertainment.[33] Mozart's *Abduction*, however, was not finished in time for the royal visit of 1781 and would have its premiere without Russian royalty in July 1782. The opera would eventually be performed for the Grand Duke when, having completed his Grand Tour of Europe, he passed through Vienna again in October 1782 on his way back to Russia. Mozart wrote to his father on October 19:

> The Russian Court left today. My opera was performed for them not so long ago; on that occasion I thought it advisable to resume my place at the clavier and do my conducting from there, partly to wake up the orchestra, which had fallen into a slight slumber, partly (as I happened to be in Vienna anyway) to show myself to the royal guests as the father of my child.[34]

Mozart's composition of the *Abduction* in 1781 and 1782 was conditioned by contemporary international affairs, involving Russia, Austria, and the Ottomans, even as Vienna was approaching the centennial moment for the commemoration of the Ottoman siege of 1683.

"An arch-enemy of all foreigners"

In September 1781 Mozart sent to his father in Salzburg some first samples of the music, including the Turkish opening of the overture, a part of Osmin's comically furious first-act aria "*Solche hergelaufne Laffen*," and a portion of the text of the heroine Konstanze's aria "*Ach, ich liebte*" (Ach, I loved) copied out by Constanze Weber, Mozart's own new romantic interest. "I am sending you a little Praegusto of the opera, because there's nothing new or important to write at the moment," wrote Mozart to his father—though the new and important item of personal news was actually suggested by the association of Constanze with Konstanze. Mozart also listed the presumed cast of the *Abduction*, with important details concerning the Turkish characters. Osmin, the overseer (*Aufseher*) of the pasha's estate, was characterized as "a rude fellow" (*ein grober Kerl*) to be sung by the basso Fischer. The part of Pasha Selim, however, was assigned to Dominik Joseph Jautz—"an actor, has nothing to sing." In fact, the pasha was conceived as a speaking role already in Bretzner's original libretto that Stephanie adapted, and the casting of the pasha as a nonsinging actor had particular implications for the Turkishness of the whole work.[35] The pasha's despotic Ottoman authority remained aloof from the whole musical scoring of the opera, including the "Turkish" music, which was, however, featured in the choruses that saluted and celebrated the pasha. As the incarnation of absolutism the pasha functioned on a different dramatic plane, while the musically charismatic starring Ottoman role was reserved for the comic basso Osmin.

Mozart's letter to his father of September 26, 1781, offered one of the composer's most detailed accounts of his approach to composing opera, and in particular composing Turkishness in opera:

> I sent you only 14 measures of the overture—which is fairly short—and alternates between forte and piano; each forte produces some Turkish music and keeps modulating in this manner throughout—I venture to say you can not fall asleep while it plays, even if you haven't slept all night.[36]

Turkish music with its special percussion effects was thus considered, almost by definition, to be loud music, best used for emphatic dynamic contrast and deployed in order to grab and hold the attention of the audience. For Mozart, presumably composing at the piano without the Turkish percussion instruments at hand, this was Turkish music that he could already hear emphatically in his mind, music that was already keeping him awake as he threw himself into the frenzied activity of composition. He could also hear in his mind the Turkishness of the choral music which he composed by the end of September: "The Janissary Chorus has everything you can desire from a Janissary Chorus, it's short and lively—written entirely for the Viennese."[37] The overture and chorus offered Turkish music, comically conceived by its liveliness and its contrasts, but the essence of Mozart's comic Turkish intention was expressed in his detailed comments on the music for Osmin.

In the letter of September 26 Mozart explained the character of Osmin to Leopold in Salzburg: "He is also rude and boorish and an arch-enemy [*Erzfeind*] of all foreigners."[38] While Osmin's boorishness could be simply comical, his deep hostility to foreigners gave him a nastier edge which Mozart and Stephanie built into a complete operatic conception of Turkish hostility to the West. In 1781 this conception did in fact roughly coincide with a new awareness of the West within the Ottoman empire, in the aftermath of the peace of Küçük Kaynarca. Indeed, dating from this period, the actual Ottoman perspective on Europe would combine in varying admixtures the interest, ambivalence, suspicion, and frank hostility that Mozart creatively imagined when he made Osmin the "arch-enemy of all foreigners." No longer a fearsome military danger, as in the age of Suleiman, the "cowards of Istanbul" might nevertheless be envisioned as harboring fierce resentments against foreigners they could no longer hope to conquer—except for individual captives by piracy, as in the scenario of the *Abduction*. Within the opera's complex play of perspectives, Mozart's creation of an anti-European Turkish character, Osmin as *Erzfeind*, could be construed in itself as culturally hostile to the Ottomans—though the composer would also go a considerable way toward bridging the mutual animosities that formed the premise of his operatic scenario.

In the libretto for *Zaide* it is Sultan Soliman who uses the term "*Christenhund*" (Christian dog), as he rages in Mozartean *melologo* against Gomatz for abducting Zaide, and the epithet was intended in all seriousness as evidence of his anger and arrogance.[39] In the finale of the *Abduction* it is Osmin who rages against the Christian foreigners as dogs:

| Verbrennen sollte man die Hunde | One should burn the dogs |
| die uns so schändlich hintergehen. | who have so shamefully tricked us.[40] |

He then leaves the stage to his enemies, who join in a celebratory happy ending that makes his own ranting appear as merely comical.

The Osmin of *Zaide*, who assists Sultan Soliman in pursuing the "Christian dog," has an entirely different temperament and does not manifest such emotionally excessive resentments: "I expect confidently at any moment the capture of the fugitives," he reports dispassionately to the sultan, acknowledging responsibility for the recapture.[41] By implication, this Osmin is perhaps also responsible for Zaide's escape, and his role as captain of the sultan's guard can be conflated with another role as guardian of the harem. In these functional aspects this Osmin of *Zaide* already resembles his namesake, the Osmin of the *Abduction*, for they both act as the agents of despotic Turkish power, and both sing in the basso register. Yet when Osmin in *Zaide* sings his aria—the only piece of his music that Mozart completed for him—there is little trace of rage in the musical character of the piece. It is a laughing aria which ends in a refrain of the reiterated syllable *ha ha ha!*

The verses expressed the mundane and material sensibility that characterized popular characters of lower station, generally appearing as servants on the operatic stage in comic counterpoint to their noble and serious masters. Osmin in *Zaide* implicitly justifies his servile complicity in the sultan's despotism by pleading the necessities of human survival. Accompanied by rolling triplets, *allegro assai*, this Osmin sings out his simple philosophy of life:

Wer hungrig bei der Tafel sitzt
und schmachtend Speis' und Trank nicht nützt,
mag selbst sein Glück nicht machen.
Er is fürwahr ein ganzer Narr.
Wer soll nicht drüber lachen, ha ha ha!

Whoever sits hungry at the table
and, languishing, doesn't take food or drink,
does not want to make his own fortune.
He is truly a complete fool.
Who would not laugh about that? ha ha ha![42]

Such wisdom was closely related to the amiable common sense of Harlequin at the Paris fairs or, later, Papageno in Mozart's *Magic Flute*. In *Zaide*, intended as an opera of noble passions—the love of the fugitive captives, the jealousy of the volatile sultan—Osmin provides the comic perspective of an ordinary man who understands that life is about eating when you are hungry and drinking when you are thirsty.

The final verse makes clear that the grander operatic passions are themselves the objects of Osmin's laughter:

> Wer winselt, jammert, schreit und flucht,
> und was er hat, erst ängstlich sucht . . .
> Er ist fürwahr ein ganzer Narr.

> Whoever whimpers, moans, shouts, and curses,
> and seeks anxiously for what he already has . . .
> He is truly a complete fool.[43]

This Osmin, like Mozart's later Osmin in the *Abduction*, provided the comic counterpoint to more serious operatic characters, but in this case remained generally amiable in his single aria. If Mozart suggested a possible undertone of harshness in the reiterated laughing syllables, there was certainly none of the raging resentment that made the later Osmin the object of the audience's laughter. The Osmin of the *Abduction* shouts and curses, especially at foreigners, and is therefore by the standards of the earlier Osmin nothing but a fool— but Mozart made something more complicated out of his foolish raging.

Osmin and Mozart: The Humiliations of Service

The long letter of September 26 suggested that Mozart put quite a lot of musical thought into the nature of Osmin's foolishness and the expression of both his coarseness and his animosity. In *Zaide* Osmin was meant to be only a minor character, and the Bretzner libretto of *Belmont und Constanze* also gave Osmin a much smaller musical role than he would come to hold in the *Abduction*. Mozart's letter to his father clearly suggested that it was the composer himself—more than the librettist Stephanie—who remade the role of Osmin:

> Since we assigned the role of Osmin to Herr Fischer—who has an excellent bass voice—though the Archbishop said to me that he sang too low for a bass

and I assured him that he would sing higher next time—we had to make use of such a man, especially since he is a favorite with the public here. In the original text Osmin has only this one little song to sing, and nothing else, except the trio and the finale. So he has been given an aria in the first act and will be given another in the second act as well. I described the aria fully to Herr Stephanie—in fact, I had finished most of the music already before he even knew anything about it.[44]

Mozart thus seemed to have such a clear sense of Osmin's musical characterization that he needed no text from Stephanie in order to write the aria, and at the same time Mozart suggested that it was his own strategic magnanimity toward Fischer—and by extension toward Osmin—that led to the expansion and development of the role. Fischer, originally from Mainz, sang in Schwetzingen, Mannheim, and Munich before coming to Vienna in 1780. In that year a contemporary praised him for singing "the deepest tones with a fullness, lightness, and pleasantness that is usually found only in good tenors." A later commentary noted that his basso voice offered "what might almost be called the bottomless deep with a certainty and fullness of intonation that astonishes." Fischer was also notably experienced as a comical singing Turk, since he had performed the role of the slave dealer Kaled in Vogler's *Der Kaufmann von Smyrna* in Mannheim in 1778 and the role of the Kalender in Gluck's *Die Pilgrimme von Mekka*, as presented in German in Vienna in 1780.[45] Singing the roles of Vogler's Kaled, Gluck's Kalender, and Mozart's Osmin, Fischer would come to define the comical basso Turk in the late eighteenth century much as Borosini had defined the tragic tenor Turk in the early eighteenth century.

Mozart's reference to the archbishop of Salzburg in the letter of September 26 suggests some of the implicit issues of power and service in Osmin's circumstances, which were in fact closely related to the issues of power and service in Mozart's own life. In September 1781 Mozart had recently left the service of the archbishop Hieronymus Colloredo—and claimed to regard him with complete contempt. "The Archbishop said to me that he [Fischer] sang too low for a bass," wrote Mozart sarcastically, "and I assured him that he would sing higher next time." The foolishness was implicit in the question—for how could you sing too low for a bass?—and was further affirmed in Mozart's reply, for only a perversely autocratic patron would demand that a low voice be made to sing higher. In fact, the score of the *Abduction* shows that Mozart went in precisely the opposite direction. He let Fischer as Osmin

LUDWIG FISCHER

Ludwig Fischer, the basso for whom Mozart developed and expanded the role of Osmin in the *Abduction*. "Since we assigned the role of Osmin to Herr Fischer—who has an excellent bass voice . . . we had to make use of such a man, especially since he is a favorite with the public here." Fischer had already performed the "Turkish" roles of Kaled the slave dealer in Vogler's *Der Kaufmann von Smyrna* and the Kalender in Gluck's *Die Pilgrimme von Mekka*. With kind permission of the Österreichische Nationalbibliothek.

sing as low as he could possibly go, almost freakishly low—perhaps to spite the archbishop—and lower than many basses are able to sing.

Mozart was finished with the archbishop and from now on would seek instead the patronage of the emperor—as intended with the *Abduction*—but also, in a new and more modern gambit for a musician, would court the public of Vienna. If Fischer was "a favorite with the public here [*das hiesige Publikum*]," then it was essential "to make use of such a man [*so einem Mann nutzen*]."⁴⁶ In the emerging public of the eighteenth century, the possibility of a musical public exercising its tastes and preferences suggested a radically modern alternative to traditional patronage. For Mozart this meant not just taking advantage of—using, deploying, exploiting—the singer's popularity, but also making use of a general theme or style, in this case Turkish comedy with Turkish music; hence, the Janissary chorus, "written entirely for the Viennese" (*ganz für die Wiener geschrieben*).⁴⁷ The creation of Osmin was intended to satisfy the public.

The problem, as Mozart explained it to his father, was how to make musically palatable to the public a character full of anger, full of hatred of foreigners, especially as the public itself—Viennese and not Turkish—would be implicitly targeted by that hatred. Thus he explained the first-act aria "*Solche hergelaufne Laffen*" in which Osmin would be angry within the opera but funny to the public:

> The rage of Osmin will be thus rendered comical [*der Zorn des Osmin wird dadurch in das komische gebracht*], because Turkish music will be used for it. In the composition of the aria I have let Fischer's beautiful deep tones really glisten, in spite of that Salzburger Midas. The passage, "Therefore by the Beard of the Prophet" is, to be sure, in the same tempo, but with quick notes—and as his rage increases more and more, the *allegro assai*—which comes just when one thinks the aria is over—will produce the best effect, because it is in a different tempo and in a different key. A person who gets into such a violent rage oversteps all order, measure, and object [*überschreitet alle Ordnung, Maas, und Ziel*]; he no longer knows himself. In the same way the music must no longer know itself—but because passions [*die Leidenschaften*], violent or not, must never be expressed to the point of disgust, and music must never offend the ear, even in the most horrendous situations, but must always be pleasing, in other words always remain music, I have not chosen a tone foreign to F, the key of the aria, but one that is friendly to it, not however its nearest relative in D minor, but the more remote A minor.⁴⁸

Thus, it was precisely Osmin's Turkishness, conveyed in part by "Turkish music"—particular rhythms, intervals, repetitions, and percussion effects—that would make him both angry and funny at the same time. Turkish rage could be musically expressed in such a fashion that a Viennese public would find it comical.

Baron François de Tott, who helped to improve Ottoman weaponry and fortifications in the 1770s, wrote in the 1780s about what he perceived as the relation between Ottoman political despotism and Turkish extreme emotions. "If the climate that the Turks inhabit relaxes their fibers," observed Tott, "the despotism to which they are subject brings them to violence; they are sometimes ferocious."[49] Reasoning from the principles of Montesquieu, Tott thus offered an emotional calculus that Mozart would have recognized as relevant to the operatic challenge. While opera conventionally served as a vehicle for expressing extreme emotions, Turkishness posed the particular challenge of a ferocity that might "offend the ear," and even the sensibility, of the European public.

Here Mozart pressed up against the boundaries of what he understood to be the rules of classical music. Osmin's rage would take music in the disorderly direction of the unmusical, and it was up to the composer to contain the emotions by strategically deployed transitions of tempo and harmony, so that the orderly and aurally satisfying conventions of classical music might be maintained. In a letter from two weeks later, on October 13, Mozart wrote to his father about Osmin's character in the libretto:

> As far as Stephanie's work is concerned, you are quite right, indeed. Yet, the Poesie is totally in tune with the character of this stupid, coarse, and malicious Osmin [*des dummen, groben, und boshaften Osmin*]. And I am well aware that the kind of verse used here is not the best—but it agrees so completely with the musical ideas that had been wandering around my head, even before I had seen the text, so I couldn't help liking it.[50]

The verses might be coarse, like Osmin's character, but the music would not allow them to be offensive to the ear. Osmin's Turkish fury tested the emotional limits of the operatic stage, unleashing extreme emotions that would be frankly ugly if they were not allowed to be comically Turkish. The history of the emotions, as suggested in the work of Norbert Elias, was one of evolving restraint in the early modern centuries, intersecting with the history of

Osmin, turbaned and bearded, in the costume design for the Koblenz production of 1787, with an impressive curved sword. Mozart wrote of "this stupid, coarse, and malicious Osmin," but the designer obviously intended for him to possess a certain confidence and charisma. As Osmin himself declares, "*Ich hab' auch Verstand*." With kind permission of the Familienarchiv Ernst Steireif, Koblenz.

manners in the context of a "civilizing process." By the 1770s the German literary movement of Sturm und Drang (alongside French sentimentalism) encouraged a higher degree of emotional intensity, and made the emotions all the more a matter of cultural concern.[51] The sculptor Franz Xaver Messer-schmidt, who enjoyed Maria Theresa's patronage in Vienna in the 1760s, began in the 1770s to work on his series of intensely emotional "character heads," an ongoing study of the extreme emotions, which concluded with the sculptor's death in Bratislava in 1783.[52] Opera also continued to provide a cultural site for the expression of strong emotions, but generally, as Mozart recognized in the early 1780s, within the ordered framework of musical form.

The opening phrase of Osmin's aria refers to the Europeans as "Laffen," dandies or showoffs, thus seeming to underline their presumption of supe-riority which Osmin so tremendously resents. The word itself has its two syllables extended over five measures, including trills and chromatic runs, by which Osmin expresses his contempt—while showing off his own vocal prowess. His anger finds even more emphatic expression when he denounces the foreigners for their deceits and schemes (*"eure Tücken, eure Ränke"*), but he confidently affirms that these tricks are already well known to him (*"sind mir ganz bekannt"*), that he cannot be fooled by European stratagems. In his letter Mozart casually dismissed Osmin as stupid (*dumm*), but the first part of the aria concluded with Osmin affirming his own human reason, *"Ich hab' auch Verstand"*—I also have a mind—over and over with increasing empha-sis. Mozart thus showed Osmin's mind under fierce assault from his emo-tions, his fury and hatred. The composer, however, permitted this comical Turk, in spite of his barely controllable rage, to affirm his sense, his reason, his mind, in such a manner as to stabilize the music and bring the first part of the aria to a secure conclusion on a very low F, the key of the aria as a whole. The affirmation—*"Ich hab' auch Verstand"*—also constitutes Osmin's defi-ant response to his own emotional excesses, which were actually attributed to him by the librettist and composer. Osmin not only defies the presumed superiority of the European foreigners within the opera but also, from with-in the opera, seems to resist the condescending perspective of the European public for whom he was created. If the restraining of emotions was a part of the European civilizing process, Mozart's music showed Osmin struggling to achieve that restraint.[53]

After Osmin's affirmation of *"Verstand"* on the sustained low F, there

"*Ich hab' auch Verstand*" (I also have a mind), sings Osmin over and over again in Mozart's *Abduction*. The basso finally descends to a low F on the last line—affirming also his testosterone-based masculinity—followed by a *fermata*. The longer notes then shift to "quick notes". (mostly eighth notes)—"as his rage increases more and more," Mozart comments—with the phrase "*Drum beim Barte des Propheten!*" (By the beard of the Prophet!) hammering largely on the same F note.

then follows the gunfire rapidity of the "quick notes," as Osmin swears by the beard of the Prophet. The aria actually seems to be complete when the music stops, and Pedrillo, the European servant, begins to speak: "*Was bist du für ein grausamer Kerl*" (what a horrible fellow you are). Osmin's emotions and his music, however, cannot yet be contained, and both erupt immediately again. Now comes the shift in tempo and harmony, to *allegro assai* and A minor, while the orchestration also changes, introducing both a piccolo at the top of the orchestral ensemble and the Turkish percussion of drums and cymbals: all this so that Osmin can comically enumerate the terrible ways that he hopes to see his European enemies die in horrible torment:

Erst geköpft, dann gehangen,	First beheaded, then hung,
dann gespiesst, auf heisse[n] Stangen,	then impaled on hot stakes,
dann verbrannt, dann gebunden,	then burned, then bound,
und getaucht, zuletzt geschunden.	then drowned, then flayed.[54]

Mozart presumably relished the grisly comedy of planning to cut off the head before hanging the body: by what would it hang? If this was the text that Mozart, in his letter to his father, thought "not the best," the music certainly made the best possible case for it. The celebration of torture and execution received a frenzied setting as Mozart sought to find musical expression for Osmin's litany of graphic violence, the tempo almost outpacing his horrific fantasies.

Osmin's verse seems almost to parody the poetry of the early sixteenth century, responding to the first Turkish siege of Vienna in 1529. Hans Sachs the Meistersinger of Nuremberg wrote a poem "Against the Bloodthirsty Turks" (1532) and in another verse enumerated Ottoman atrocities against Christians:

Zertreten und entzwey gerissen	Crushed underfoot and torn in two
An spitzig pfäl thet er sie spissen.	He has them impaled on sharp stakes.[55]

Osmin's verse echoed the spirit of this earlier epoch but now transposed it into a comic register, and this transposition constituted Mozart's challenge and dilemma. On the one hand, from the moment he began working on the opera, Mozart described Osmin as "rude and boorish and an arch-enemy of all foreigners." On the other hand, as Mozart also insisted, Osmin's music must remain musical, and his character comical—"because passions, violent or not, must never be expressed to the point of disgust, and music must nev-

Pedrillo. Was bist du für ein grausamer Kerl, und ich hab' dir nichts gethan.

Osmin. Du hast ein Galgengesicht, das ist genug.

"*Erst geköpft, dann gehangen, dann gespiesst auf heisse Stangen*" (First beheaded, then hung, then impaled on hot stakes)—Mozart's *Abduction*. The explosion of Osmin's rage comes with the change of tempo to *allegro assai*, the change of key to A minor, the orchestral entrance of the Janissary percussion (*Schlagzeug*), and the pounding *forte* emphasis on the first note of each measure. Mozart: "And as his rage increases more and more, the *allegro assai*—which comes just when one thinks the aria is over—will produce the best effect, because it is in a different tempo and in a different key. A person who gets into such a violent rage oversteps all order, measure, and object; he no longer knows himself. In the same way the music must no longer know itself . . . [but] passions, violent or not, must never be expressed to the point of disgust, and music must never offend the ear."

er offend the ear." With Osmin's musical outburst—"*Erst geköpft*"—Mozart tested the limits of this artistic calculus.

Eunuchs and Castrati

Mozart had Osmin sing all the way down to low F in the aria of the first act—"*Solche hergelaufne Laffen*"—and then in the great aria of the third act—"*Ha! wie will ich triumphieren*"—Fischer was supposed to sing all the way down to the D below F. Mozart's letter of September 26 suggested that he might regard the very low notes of Osmin's music as pointed mockery of the musical stupidity of the archbishop who thought Fischer sang "too low for a bass." That, of course, would not have been the only significance the composer found in the basso register. On the most obvious level, Osmin's "lowness"—his coarseness and vulgarity (like Gluck's Kalender), but also the moral turpitude of his bloodthirsty fantasies (like Jommelli's Albumazar)—was underlined by his low vocal register. Indeed, he stood in obvious contrast to Konstanze whose moral virtue and high European refinement were expressed by musical notes as extravagantly high as Osmin's were low. Osmin's basso singing also emphasized his Turkish masculinity, which was further musically enhanced by the *alla turca* style with its Janissary instrumentation and military associations. Mary Hunter has suggested that this style represented a specifically gendered "hypermasculine saber-rattling barbarism."[56]

Dating back to the conception of Bajazet as a tenor by Gasparini and then Handel—a tenor singing between two castrati in the roles of Tamerlano and Andronico—the Turkish protagonist in European opera, from the beginning of the eighteenth century, was almost always cast in the masculine register. The role of Bajazet was created by the tenor Borosini for both Gasparini and Handel in performances that actually pioneered a new dramatic importance for tenors in opera. There were, unusually, castrati and female travesty roles for the sons of Suleiman in the operas composed to Migliavacca's libretto *Solimano*, beginning with Hasse in the 1750s. This casting of castrati as the young Ottoman princes, almost juvenile roles, followed the convention of *opera seria*. In Jommelli's *La schiava liberata* of the 1760s the Bey of Algiers was sung by a tenor, while his son Selim, the heroic naval commander, was sung by a castrato, perhaps the most significant Ottoman role composed for castrato in the eighteenth century.

Yet castrato parts were relatively rare for singing Turks, as these roles were generally composed in the masculine registers. Walter Preibisch argued that Jommelli's *La schiava liberata* might have served as a model for Mozart's *Abduction*, and that each role in the former opera could be correlated with a parallel role in the latter—except for Jommelli's castrato Selim.[57] Mozart and Stephanie made a purposeful statement about the voice of Turkish authority when, following André and Bretzner, they removed Pasha Selim from the musical staff altogether, casting him as a speaking actor. At the same time, Fischer as Osmin was encouraged to explore the very lowest notes of his basso register. The basso Turk would thereafter become the dominant convention, as Rossini went on to create starring bass roles for his great Turkish operas in the next generation: *L'italiana in Algeri*, *Il turco in Italia*, and *Maometto Secondo*.

The association of Osmin's basso register with his Ottoman masculinity was also related to the question of whether he could be supposed to be a eunuch. In fact, the role of overseer or guardian of the harem might plausibly have been considered appropriate to a eunuch—in accordance with the actual staffing of Ottoman harems. By casting the role as a basso, and letting him sing his way down to the lowest possible notes of the operatic voice, Mozart implicitly insisted that Osmin was not a eunuch.

Dating back to the early Enlightenment, there was a tremendous interest in the eunuchs of the Orient, and they played starring roles in Montesquieu's *Persian Letters* of 1721. The jealously protective and cruelly vindictive chief eunuch who guards the harem of Usbek in Isfahan expresses himself in the epistolary novel with an intensity of resentment and outrage worthy of the arias of Osmin: "The seraglio for me is like a little empire, and my desire for power, the only emotion which remains to me, is to some extent satisfied." In 1731, in the *History of Charles XII*, Voltaire described the Ottoman empire with "the Sultan shut up in his seraglio among his women and eunuchs"—and eunuchs would recur in Voltaire's fictions, historical reflections, and philosophical parables, especially associated with the Orient.[58] The literary and historical interest in eunuchs in the early Enlightenment happened to coincide with the musical mania in European opera for the voices of the great castrati—including Nicolini, Senesino, and Farinelli—in the first several decades of the eighteenth century. It was Senesino who starred in Handel's *Tamerlano* in 1724, taking the part of the Byzantine Andronico, before going on to create the title role of *Giulio Cesare* and that of Bertarido in *Rodelinda*. The sensational career of Farinelli on the operatic stages of Europe belonged to the 1720s and 1730s, exactly when Montesquieu and Voltaire were paying literary attention to eunuchs. The question then arises of how these simultaneous cultural interests—in Oriental eunuchs, in operatic castrati—might have overlapped, and whether it would have been conceivable for a castrato actually to perform the role of a eunuch on the operatic stage, thus offering the highest degree of vocal and physiological verisimilitude. The quality of the voice would have stunningly demonstrated the absence of testosterone—but it is not clear that this ever actually happened.

The castrati performed the parts of romantic heroes on the operatic stage and were passionately appreciated as such. There was an enraptured female public for the great Farinelli when he performed in London from 1734 to 1737, and the paradoxical aspect of this fascination was underlined by explicit references to the castrati as eunuchs, as in the verse of Lady Mary Wortley Montagu:

> Now softening eunuchs sing Italian airs,
> The dancing dame to midnight ball repairs.[59]

Voltaire was similarly casual in *Candide* in the 1750s, when he conflated the categories of eunuch and castrato: "I was born in Naples," reports the eunuch (designated as such in the text). "There they castrate two or three thousand children each year. Some die of it, others acquire a voice more beautiful than that of women, and still others go on to govern states. They performed this operation on me with great success, and I have been a musician of the chapel of the Princess of Palestrina."[60] The eunuch and the castrato were, in literature, sometimes the same character, and both were regularly present in the major writings of the Enlightenment.

European operas about the Ottoman empire did sometimes allude to eunuchs. At the Paris fairs it was a matter of comedy when Pierrot proposed that Harlequin assume the office of the "black eunuch." In *Les trois sultanes*, Sultan Suleiman is attended by Osmin, "the kislar-aga or chief of the eunuchs," mocked by Roxelana as an "amphibious monster." In the Venetian version of 1784, with a libretto by Giovanni Bertati, the eunuch of the harem actually wishes that he could have been a castrato: "Ah, why was I not born in Italy! There the eunuchs are created to sing . . . I'm told they earn a lot of gold."[61]

By the 1780s it was not difficult to make the connection between eunuchs and castrati.

Yet the casting of castrati in Turkish roles was generally avoided, and all the more so for the roles of underlings who might plausibly have been eunuchs in the Ottoman empire. To have a real physiological castrato sing the part of a fictive theatrical eunuch, that is, to have a eunuch sing the part of a eunuch, would have undermined the dramatic liberty and romantic mystique of castrato performance. At the same time, such casting would have risked provoking disturbing thoughts about testosterone, castration, and eunuchs as features of the Ottoman scenario. It could have been culturally uncomfortable if these two eighteenth-century literary and artistic preoccupations—the interest in Oriental eunuchs and the appreciation of Italian castrati—had been permitted to intersect on the stage in European operas on Turkish themes. Sultans and pashas could hardly be eunuchs, but overseers, guardians of the harem like Osmin, were quite likely to be eunuchs, and Osmin's basso singing was therefore a reassuring guarantee of physiological completeness. It was not just that he was not a castrato—which he would not have been anyway by the conventions of the Viennese Singspiel—but that as a basso he was as far as he could possibly be from seeming to be a castrato. When he sang "*Ich hab' auch Verstand*," ending on the low F, he not only emphatically affirmed in the text that he had a mind but also affirmed, in the music, that he had kept his testicles.

The Pasha's Overseer and the Archbishop's Steward

Osmin's position as the pasha's overseer was crucial to his whole role and character in the *Abduction*. Just as Montesquieu's eunuchs of the Persian harem exercised power over their female charges with purposeful psychological cruelty that stemmed from their own castrated condition of service, so in the *Abduction* Osmin's sadistic ecstasies about hanging, beheading, and other grisly forms of execution followed from his own condition as an underling who cherished what little power he had over others. In Bretzner's original libretto, Osmin actually speaks contemptuously of his master's softness—"The pasha is soft as butter!"—and, addressing Belmonte and Pedrillo, imagines himself in the pasha's role: "If I were the pasha [*wär ich Bassa*], you would have been impaled long ago."[62] Mozart's perfect appreciation of this subjunctive relation to power indubitably derived from his own very recent experience in the service of the archbishop of Salzburg, and in particular at the hands of the archbishop's chamberlain Count Karl Joseph Arco. It was he who was authorized to exercise the power of the archbishop over the entire household and entourage, including Mozart, and he who gave Mozart the physical kick that ended the whole relationship with the archbishop. Count Arco, standing between Colloredo and Mozart, thus paralleled Osmin, standing between the pasha and Pedrillo in the first act of the *Abduction*, and Mozart must often have thought about Count Arco, as Pedrillo did about Osmin, "*Was bist du für ein grausamer Kerl!*" Arco and Osmin were both overseers and underlings, exercising intermediary power in the service of despotic masters.

Mozart came to Vienna in March 1781 as part of the traveling entourage of the archbishop of Salzburg. The young composer, age twenty-five, was deeply resentful of what he saw as his insultingly low status within the household. On March 17 Mozart complained to his father bitterly about the seating for lunch:

> We go to the table at 12 o'clock noon—unfortunately a little too early for me—dining there are the two valets who are the archbishop's body-and-soul attendants, the Herr Comptroller, Herr Zetti, the pastry chef, the 2 cooks, Ceccarelli, Brunetti, and—little me [*meine Wenigkeit*].[63]

Antonio Brunetti was a violinist, but Francesco Ceccarelli was the archbishop's castrato, someone Mozart regarded as something of a friend, and for whom Mozart had composed church music back in Salzburg. To have lunch with Ceccarelli, however, was clearly something that Mozart regarded as no honor. On March 24 Mozart elaborated further on the indignities of mealtimes, and noted the special place of Count Arco:

> What you are telling me about the Archbishop—that it tickles his pride to have me around—is pretty much true; but of what use is all that to me?—one can not live on that—and believe me, here he will not let my light shine— what distinction is he really giving me?—Herr von Kleinmayer and Benecke sit at a separate table together with the illustrious Count Arco; if I were at that table, that would be a distinction; but there is no distinction in sitting with the valets.[64]

The sarcasm about the supposed illustriousness of Count Arco was all too evident, and seemed to hint at the count's own inflated self-opinion.

Mozart's chief resentment against Count Arco was the latter's intermediary exercise of the power of the archbishop, as was evident in the composer's letter of early April. Colloredo was already set to depart from Vienna, but Mozart was not:

> Now listen to this: Brunetti said at the table today that Arco told him, from the archbishop, that he should tell us that we will be receiving money for the coach and should depart by Sunday; but whoever wanted to stay—O Reason!—could stay, but would have to live at his own expense, because food and lodging would no longer be provided.[65]

Clearly, Mozart understood very well how the dynamics of power might work in a princely household like that of Pasha Selim—the interplay of insults, distinctions, and resentments among masters, intermediaries, and underlings.

On April 11, facing the deadline of the order to return from Vienna to Salzburg, Mozart was drawing closer to the castrato Ceccarelli, his fellow musician, fellow underling, and mealtime companion at the lesser table:

> Te Laudamus, that rude and filthy Brunetti is finally gone; he is a disgrace to his master, to himself, and to the whole orchestra—that's what Ceccarelli and I are saying—the messages you got from Vienna are all lies, except that Ceccarelli will sing at the opera in Venice during the coming carnival season . . . Tomorrow, that's on Thursday before Easter, the Archbishop, himself, in his own Exalted Persona, will give communion to the entire court . . . Now briefly: a week from next Sunday, that's on the 22nd, Ceccarelli and I are supposed to return to Salzburg . . . But what's driving me to despair is that on the same evening when we had our stinky concert, I had also been invited to the Countess Thun—but wasn't permitted to go; and who was there?—the emperor![66]

As the imminent return to Salzburg drew near, Mozart's resentment was growing, crescendo, and his sense of the musical opportunities in Vienna became all the more tantalizing. Even as he suffered the frustration of his subordinate status, he also drew closer to the similarly subordinate figure of the castrato Ceccarelli, Mozart's momentary comrade in resentment.

On April 18, Mozart reported that Stephanie thought *Zaide* inappropriate for Vienna, that a comedy was needed, and that he would "provide me with a new piece, and, as he says, a good piece"—the first intimation of the *Abduction*. By May 9, the deadline for returning to Salzburg had passed, Mozart was still in Vienna, and had definitively broken with the archbishop of Salzburg. He wrote to his father:

> I am still full of bitterness! [*Ich bin noch ganz voll der Galle!*]—and I am sure that you, as my best and dearest father, certainly feel it with me—my patience has been tested for such a long time—but finally it broke down. I am no longer so unfortunate as to be in Salzburg service—today was that happy day for me.[67]

The archbishop had berated him to his face, and Mozart's service was terminated in a spirit of mutual rage: "I hate the archbishop to the point of madness [*zur Raserey*]."[68] Mozart was now independent, free of the archbishop; he had achieved his own escape from the seraglio.

The formalities of concluding Mozart's relationship with Salzburg involved meetings with Count Arco, with increasing animosity between the parties. On June 2, Mozart reported somewhat sympathetically: "Among other things he asked me whether I realized that he, too, had to swallow some harsh words now and then?—I shrugged my shoulders and replied: I'm sure you have your reasons for putting up with it, just as I have mine for not putting up with it."[69] This was Osmin's position precisely, the underling as overseer, subordinate to an autocratic master but vested with authority over others in his master's service, those eating at the lesser table. Count Arco then showed himself capable of Osmin's sort of abusive hostility, as Mozart sarcastically testified in his letter of June 9: "Now Count Arco has really done it alright!" The mode of mistreatment was to "throw around words such as lout and boy [*Flegel und Pursche*] and then throw one out the door with a kick in the ass [*durch einen Tritt im Arsch*]; but I am forgetting that maybe it all happened on high princely orders."[70] Mozart was furious, and Count Arco was presumably furious, but the whole scene—punctuated by the kick in the ass—played out in the Viennese spirit of comic opera.

The issues were closely related to those that Mozart would reflect upon in September when he considered how Osmin's coarse authority and brutal animosity could be contained within the bounds of comedy and music. Osmin was Turkish in his name, in his situation, and in some aspects of his percussion accompaniment, but his character as an overseer who worked for a princely master and exercised abusive authority on behalf of his master was quite familiar in a European context. Mozart surely drew upon his own recent experience of overseers and underlings when he dramatized the psychology of authority and subordination; the Ottoman scenario would simply have permitted him to formulate the situation in its most extreme form on the supposition that Oriental authority was more absolutely despotic than elsewhere. Montesquieu, in the *Spirit of the Laws*, saw Asia, including the Ottoman empire, as the domain of despotism, where subjects were reduced to the condition of slavery. In the *Abduction* Mozart considered what happened when a slave like Osmin was invested with authority over others. In short, for all his musical and emotional Turkishness, the character of Osmin was not absolutely alien to European circumstances, as Mozart understood and experienced in his own professional life. The question of Osmin's rage was, as Maynard Solomon has suggested, also a question of Mozart's rage.[71]

Ottoman Masters and European Captives

While the pasha becomes increasingly determined to make Konstanze submit to him sexually as a captive in his harem, Osmin regards Konstanze's servant Blonde as his own proprietary sexual interest. Blonde's aria, which opens the second act, *andante grazioso*, is a European tutorial on love in the spirit of Favart's Roxelana, explaining that "tenderness and flattery" (*Zärtlichkeit und Schmeicheln*) win girls' hearts and that "surly commands" (*mürrisches Befehlen*) have the opposite effect. Osmin replies unmusically in spoken dialogue, as if quoting Montesquieu on slavery and despotism in Asia:

> OSMIN: Tenderness? Flattery? . . . We are in Turkey here, and the tone is different. I am your master and you are my slave. I command, and you must obey.
>
> BLONDE: Your slave? Me, your slave! Ha, a girl a slave! Say that to me once more. Once more![72]

In Vogler's *Der Kaufmann von Smyrna*, the presence of the slave dealer Kaled, even as a comical character, helped to make the opera into a sort of enlightened symposium about Mediterranean slavery. Osmin in the *Abduction*, like Kaled a comical basso villain—though an overseer of slaves rather than a trader—also became the polemical focus for discussing slavery as a contemporary social and moral issue. "We are in Turkey here," declares Osmin, but in fact they were on the stage in Vienna, and the lessons concerning slavery, drawn from the Enlightenment's political principles concerning Oriental despotism, were presumably intended for a European public.

The singer Therese Teyber, Mozart's Blonde, was an experienced captive, having previously sung the role of Balkis, Rezia's maid in captivity in Gluck's *Die Pilgrimme von Mekka*.[73] While Fischer's Osmin harmonized in the basso range, Teyber's Blonde sang charming soprano runs up and down the E-flat scale, declaiming:

> Ein Herz, so in Freiheit geboren,
> lässt niemals sich sklavisch behandlen.

> A heart born in freedom
> never allows itself to be treated as slavish.[74]

There was nothing musically sinister about the scene, and the audience could not have felt that Blonde was in any sexual danger from her Turkish master. In the Josephine decade of the late Habsburg Enlightenment slavery was something to be censured, but within the cultural context of the Viennese Singspiel it could be censured in the spirit of comic banter and lyrical song. In 1783, when Joseph was carrying out his church reforms and the dissolution of Habsburg monasteries, he actually suppressed the Trinitarians, the very order responsible for redeeming Christian captives held in the Ottoman empire.[75] For Joseph it did not appear as a sufficiently urgent issue to justify the usefulness of the religious order, and Mozart's operatic captives of 1782 seemed to anticipate this ruling by attempting to manage their own escape.

Mozart imagined that a captive Englishwoman like Blonde would be fully in control of her situation. In fact, a real eighteenth-century Englishwoman, Elizabeth Marsh, was taken captive in Morocco in 1756 (the year of Mozart's birth) and then in 1769 published an account, *The Female Captive*, stressing the sexual danger to herself. Linda Colley observes that within British culture this publication reflected a notable shift in the representation of captivity, since earlier narratives, mostly written by men, had emphasized the sexual danger to men from sodomy in the Muslim Mediterranean world. Actually, most captives really were men, just because, as Robert Davis has noted, "women made up only a miniscule proportion of the passengers or crews captured on merchant ships."[76]

A seventeenth-century Italian priest worried that young male captives were "purchased at great price by the Turks to serve them in their abominable sins," and that sodomy was the first step toward Islamic conversion, since "by dressing them up and caressing them, they persuade them to make themselves Turks." In 1670 the British House of Commons was petitioned on behalf of Englishmen in Algerian captivity, whose masters "do frequently bugger the said captives . . . run iron into their fundaments, rip open their bellies with knives, cut their britches across, and washing them with vinegar and salt, and hot oil, draw them in carts like horses."[77] This litany of cruelties bore some relation to Osmin's later operatic exclamations:

Erst geköpft, dann gehangen,	First beheaded, then hung,
dann gespiesst, auf heisse Stangen . . .	then impaled on hot stakes . . .

If Osmin's sadistic imagination—initially focused on Belmonte and Pedrillo—was not explicitly sexual in character, one might nevertheless note that the impalement of captives on hot stakes bore some resemblance to inserting "iron into their fundaments," that is, their buttocks, in the British petition. On the whole, however, operas of captivity like the *Abduction* displaced this element of male sexual endangerment by emphasizing the precarious chastity of captive Christian women, which also corresponded to the spirit of Elizabeth Marsh's authentic memoir of 1769. Though the sexual menace of Osmin was presented comically—as more of a nuisance than a danger to Blonde— the power of Pasha Selim over the captive Konstanze was treated with greater seriousness within the opera.

Just as Blonde can manage the obstreperousness of Osmin at the opening of the second act, so her male counterpart in service, Pedrillo, shows himself equally able to disarm the pretensions to authority of the Turkish overseer. A little later in the second act Osmin and Pedrillo encounter one another in what Mozart had called, in the letter of September 26, "the drinking duet [*Saufduet*], for the Viennese Signori, which is a sort of Turkish tattoo [*Zapfenstreich*]."[78] *Saufen* is a stronger verb than *trinken* and suggests getting drunk more than just drinking—hence a duet for the boys: Pedrillo and Osmin within the opera and the male public of Viennese gentlemen in the audience. By the word *Zapfenstreich*, the Turkish tattoo, Mozart conveyed the military rhythm of the male bonding that ensued, and that rhythm was given further emphasis by the use of Turkish Janissary percussion. The drinking duet begins with a very specific point of Islamic law—the prohibition on alcohol—but once that issue is set aside, Pedrillo and Osmin discover in wine the possibility for musical and sentimental harmonizing that finally breaks down the barrier between the European and the Turk.

While the condition of enslaved captivity in Ottoman lands could be brutal, there were some redeemed captives who later wrote about their experience without extreme bitterness toward their Muslim masters. Linda Colley cites the instance of William Okeley in the seventeenth century, with a master in Algeria who offered "not only pity and compassion, but love and friendship," such that Okeley hesitated to try to escape: "For where could I hope to mend myself? Or better my condition? I might possibly find worse quarter in England." Joseph Pitts in the later seventeenth century came away from his captivity with a favorable view of Islam and appealed to God ecumenically to "have mercy upon all Jews, Turks, infidels, and heretics."[79] In the eighteenth century, the Enlightenment encouraged such ecumenical outlooks, and Mozart was very well able to imagine the hostility between Pedrillo and Osmin dissolving into some sort of sense of fellowship.

The drinking duet is introduced by spoken dialogue, in which Pedrillo expresses the opinion that "merriment and wine sweetens the hardest slavery," thus continuing the polemical discussion of enslavement. He seems to be aware that he and Osmin are both slaves in the common context of Ottoman despotism, and equally in need of alcoholic consolation. Pedrillo, in the spirit of Harlequin, regrets that Mohammed forbade wine to Muslims— and then cheerfully lures Osmin into insobriety so that Belmonte and Konstanze can get together and plan their escape from the seraglio. Pedrillo assures the anxious Muslim that Mohammed had "more urgent things to do" (*hat nöthiger zu thun*) than worry about men drinking wine.[80] Mozart and Stephanie clearly felt no need to be respectful of the Islamic Prophet, while Osmin's comical attraction to the forbidden wine actually showed him to be no different from his Christian counterpart Pedrillo. Furthermore, Mozart's music, carrying on the dialogue, made perfectly clear that the composer's sympathies were entirely on the side of the bottle, that Osmin and Pedrillo really are brothers—or rather companions in service—once they begin to drink.

The duet was introduced by flute and piccolo playing lively runs up and down the C major scale in very rhythmic, almost military, two-fourths time, with a strong emphasis on the first beat of the measure. Pedrillo leads the drinking toast to Bacchus, a pagan deity neither Christian nor Islamic: "*Vivat*

Mozart (probably 5 feet 4 inches tall) at a performance of the *Abduction* in Berlin in 1789, watching a scene between Osmin and Pedrillo. Artist unknown, Wikimedia Commons.

Bacchus! Bacchus lebe!" (Long live Bacchus!). Osmin hesitates, slowing the rhythm, wondering "whether I dare? whether I should drink? whether Allah can see it?" Mozart placed a fermata over the C-sharp of the first syllable off Al-lah, thus sustaining the note and dramatizing not only Osmin's hesitation but Mozart's own comical blasphemy.

"*Vivat Bacchus*" (Long live Bacchus)—Mozart's *Abduction*. Osmin and Pedrillo sing together after drinking together; the orchestra underlines the Turkish aspect of their solidarity with the entrance of the Janissary percussion (*Schlagzeug*). They then move on to celebrate women together: "*Es leben die Mädchen, die Blonden, die Braunen.*" Though Osmin sometimes appears both bloodthirsty and ridiculous within the comedy, Mozart here affirms in C major in a 2/4 marching rhythm the common humanity of the Turk and the European, singing in unison about wine and women. Pedrillo's role here is reminiscent of that of Harlequin at the Paris fairs.

After Osmin finally does drink—written into the music as a rest with a fermata—the men simultaneously break into a celebratory toast, not to Bacchus but to girls: "*Es leben die Mädchen, die Blonden, die Braunen*" (Long live girls, the blonde ones, the dark ones). In fact, they both like the same girl—Blonde—but in Mozart's *Saufduet* this ceases to be a point of antagonism and becomes another aspect of their common humanity: they love wine, they love girls, and can now at last express their masculine harmony, tenor and bass. The singular Blonde is really just one of many—*die Blonden*—and can hardly provoke angry rivalry in men under the influence of alcohol. When they next take up the toast to Bacchus, Osmin now joining Pedrillo in comradely inebriation, the Turkish percussion instruments also join the orchestral accompaniment as if to underline the newly established drunken harmony between Turkish and European spirits.[81]

Conclusion: Harlequin the Turkish Slave

Matthew Head has observed of Mozart that "his favorite Carnival persona was Harlequin."[82] In January 1783, planning to take the role of Harlequin at a Carnival ball, Mozart wrote to his father in Salzburg: "I would like to ask you to send me your Harlequin costume." In March Mozart reported wearing the costume as part of a Carnival performance: "The idea for the pantomime, and the music for it, both came from me."[83] The music and plot of the pantomime (K.446) survive only in fragmentary form, but Head believes that the story may have echoed that of the *Abduction*, as one of the characters was designated as a Turk—which would have been appropriate for the centennial year of the Turkish siege.[84] In fact, there was also a centennial performance on September 11, 1783, at the Kärntnertor Theater in the commedia dell'arte tradition: *Arlekin der Türkensklave* (Harlequin the Turkish slave).[85] Mozart could have been present.

The figure of Harlequin had played an important part in introducing Ottoman scenarios for European musical comedies at the Paris fairs of the early eighteenth century, and he remained a lively presence in Mozart's Vienna in the 1780s. The lighthearted role of Mozart's Pedrillo could clearly be traced back to a theatrical ancestry in Harlequin's commedia dell'arte, with Blonde as his Columbine. They were both well able to confront the condition of Turkish slavery in the spirit of musical comedy, and Osmin, though he might dominate the opera, could not intimidate them. For Mozart the centennial moment was unquestionably a moment for Turkish comedy, and that was the principal reason for putting aside *Zaide* and beginning to work on the *Abduction*. There were also noble and beautiful emotions that Mozart meant to convey through the Turkish captivity of Konstanze and the distress of her beloved Belmonte, but the Turkishness of the scenario was most vividly conveyed as the Europeans provoked, evaded, and ultimately disarmed the comical rage of Osmin.

The strategic triumph over the Turks in 1683 was comically recapitulated in the *Abduction* through the intoxication of Osmin, who could not resist the bottle. The centennial celebration of 1783 did actually include as a piece of popular entertainment a travesty procession at Hernals, near Vienna, involving the figure of a drunken pasha riding a donkey. This was a recurring annual ritual that supposedly concluded in 1783 when Joseph II put an end to commemorations of the siege. The drunken pasha at Hernals bore some relation in popular entertainment to the drunken overseer in Mozart's *Abduction*, and the spectators at Hernals actually participated in the event by passing the pasha the bottle, so that the comedy was not just seeing him drunk but actually getting him drunk.[86] Mozart could have been aware of, and certainly would have relished, this carnivalesque commemoration of the defeat of Kara Mustafa Pasha in 1683.

The centennial of 1783, the last celebration of the victorious anniversary, concluded in the Prater on September 14 with a display of fireworks representing "The Siege and Relief of Vienna." The display was created and presented by Johann Georg Stuwer, who commented, "I have spared neither cost nor effort, and used all of my art to present this remarkable scene as vividly [*lebhaft*] as possible, so that one could almost believe one was actually displaced [*wirklich versetzt*] into the situation of that time."[87] Scholars Johann Heiss and Matthias Pernerstorfer have also described the dramas that accompanied the centennial, including the play *Das befreite Wien* (Liberated Vienna) by Paul Weidmann, originally written in 1775 but revived in September 1783, and *Die belohnte Treue der Wiener-Bürger, oder der 12te September 1683* (The rewarded loyalty of the Viennese citizens, or the 12th of September 1683), performed on Sunday, September 21, 1783, at the Kärntnertor Theater. This latter play included songs and choruses, and there were scenes set in the Turkish camp with Janissary soldiers and "Turkish music" for the changing of the guard.[88] Such music, as in Mozart's *Abduction*, would have had the aural effect of making the theatrical occasion so vivid that the public might feel "actually displaced" to the besieged Vienna of 1683.

Yet Mozart's *Abduction* also produced the reciprocal displacement, removing the triumph of 1683 from its seventeenth-century context of baroque religious and imperial solemnity and staging a modern triumph in the secular and comical spirit of the eighteenth-century Enlightenment. Osmin and Pedrillo drink together and discover that they not only share a common humanity but are also, in another sense of the word, common men, members of the serving class within their respective societies.[89] Theirs could be the same sort of fellowship that Mozart the composer and Ceccarelli the castrato enjoyed at the lesser table of the archbishop's entourage. Osmin, when he surrenders to alcohol, is clearly related to the earlier Osmin of *Zaide*, who felt that anyone sitting at the table without eating and drinking was certainly a fool. Osmin and Pedrillo in the *Abduction* demonstrate the same coarse and ordinary values—wine and women—that would likewise motivate Papageno, ten years later, in the *Magic Flute*.

In 1956, on the occasion of the Mozart bicentennial, Turkish musicologist Cevad Memduh Altar argued that even in the *Abduction* it was possible to discern a Mozartean ideological commitment to international understanding and the reconciliation of peoples.[90] Hungarian musicologist Bence Szabolcsi, also writing in 1956, saw Mozart's "exoticisms" as "part of his all-embracing understanding of life," as "a clue to his knowledge and his delineation of mankind."[91] While one might certainly also note aspects of disparagement and mockery of Turkishness in the *Abduction*, especially with regard to the character of Osmin, the *Saufduet* seemed to bridge the cultural distance between Europe and the Ottomans. As surely as Shakespeare made Caliban, the indigenous "monster" of the New World, fully human, getting drunk in plebeian fellowship with Stephano and Trinculo—"kiss the bottle!"—so Mozart initially made Osmin into an Ottoman monster only to humanize him entirely as the musical comedy proceeded to a state of intoxication.

The plot of the *Abduction* suggested that Pedrillo was playing a harlequin trick on Osmin, seducing him from his religious principles and distracting him from his watchful duty, but Mozart's music permitted the composer to seduce the public, distracting them from Osmin's Turkishness and from the supposed difference between Turks and Europeans. The fellowship and harmony of Osmin and Pedrillo, judged only from its musical manifestation in the *Saufduet*, sounded entirely sincere: the triumph of Bacchus over the clash of Islamic and Christian civilizations. Mozart thus envisioned an alternative and enlightened perspective on the centennial of the Christian triumph of 1683. In 1783 the Viennese male public—the Viennese Signori—would take note of Osmin's comic Turkish rages but would also recognize him as a man like themselves, singing about the common frustrations of service and subordination and the common satisfactions of wine and women. In the *Abduction* Mozart was able to find comedy in Osmin's rage, in the caricatured violence of his Turkish hostility to foreigners, but for Mozart there was no doubt at the end of the day that Osmin, with his spitefulness, his bullying, his rages, his lusts, was merely and fully human.

Ludwig Fischer left Vienna in 1783 with the collapse of the National Singspiel company, and he traveled to France and Italy where he actually encountered Emperor Joseph who was visiting Rome. Nearby, on the Italian coast at Civitavecchia, Fischer reported an unusual sighting: "We saw two Roman galleys put out to sea in pursuit of Turkish pirates, with several Neapolitan feluccas following. In the galley's yard I saw over a hundred captured Turks."[92] After performing Osmin in Vienna, Fischer now came into contact with the reality of the European-Ottoman encounter on the Mediterranean. In this case it was the Turks, not the Europeans, who were the captives. Four years later in 1787, when the Habsburgs went to war against the Ottomans, Fischer returned to Vienna for a concert and sang an aria composed for him by Mozart, an aria (K.512) of introspective romantic emotion, "*Non so d'onde viene quel tenero affetto*" (I don't know where it comes from that tender affection). Fischer reciprocated with a verse that he penned in Mozart's personal album, including the lines:

> Wirst du mich im Grund recht kennen   If you know me well deep down
> Willst mich dann dein' Freund noch nennen. You'll still call me your friend.[93]

Perhaps, as Fischer expressed his friendship for Mozart and invited his friend to know him fully and truly, the basso may have recalled Osmin's alcoholic moment of operatic friendship for his light-hearted captive and companion.

6

"To honor the Emperor"
Pasha Selim and Emperor Joseph
in the Age of Enlightened Absolutism

Introduction: Oriental Despotism and European Absolutism

Ever since the operatic imaginings of Sultan Bajazet in the early eighteenth century, European composers—like Gasparini, and Handel, and Vivaldi—had to address the musical question of how to portray the sultanic figure of Turkish authority. The tenor Borosini, working with both Gasparini and Handel, made the Ottoman sultan into a distinctively masculine vocal presence flanked by brilliant castrati in the other male roles. Bajazet was a sultan in captivity, but throughout the eighteenth century the operatic casting of Ottoman figures of authority intersected with contemporary discussion about the character of Oriental despotism. Mozart inevitably gave this matter some thought when he created the tenor part of Sultan Soliman in *Zaide*, using the distinctive form of *melologo* to characterize him, and later in the *Abduction*, envisioned Pasha Selim as a nonsinging role for a stage actor.

Pasha Selim was set radically apart from every other character in the opera by his strictly spoken dialogue—suggesting "the immensity of his power by excusing him from the aesthetic rules of the genre," as Mary Hunter has observed.[1] The Turkish chorus and the Turkish overseer would be musically differentiated from the Europeans by Mozart's use of *alla turca* style and Janissary instrumental accompaniment, while Osmin was further distinguished as a deep basso, flanked by tenors in both of the European male roles. The speaking role of the pasha, however, made him seem all the more like an illustration from a treatise on political theory. Ultimately magnanimous, standing aloof from the musical comedy, and speaking in prosaic German on the stage in Vienna, Pasha Selim became a theatrical mirror for the Habsburg emperor Joseph II in the audience at the first performance in 1782.

Historian Lucettte Valensi has argued that early modern Venetian writings about Ottoman government were closely attuned to European concerns about despotism, while Joan-Pau Rubiés has suggested that early modern European political theory found in the Ottoman empire not an Oriental Other but rather a lesson in the nature and degrees of despotism, a lesson that could be learned at the intellectual intersection of travel writing and philosophy.[2] The history of opera also has something important to contribute to understanding the discourse of Oriental despotism in the eighteenth century, with operas on Turkish subjects illuminating European ambivalence not just about Turkey but about issues of power and authority in Europe itself. There was both debate and ambivalence in Europe over the desirable degrees of royal power, and philosophes of the Enlightenment were often ready to acknowledge the merits of absolute power when it was wielded by an enlightened prince, such as Frederick the Great after 1740, Catherine the Great after 1762, and finally Joseph II when he became sole ruler upon his mother's death in 1780.

By 1782, when Mozart presented the *Abduction*, Joseph had given very clear signs of his commitment to using his monarchical power to introduce enlightened reforms, including the edict of religious toleration and the reform of serfdom in 1781. Joseph's absolute power was directed against the inveterate privileges of the Catholic Church and the feudal nobility. In 1782 his church commission was already looking toward the dissolution of the monasteries, the establishment of state seminaries, and the detailed state regulation of religious worship. It was in 1782 that Pope Pius VI made an unprecedented papal voyage to Vienna in order to express his dissatisfaction with Joseph, who refused to back down in the confrontation between church and state.

The early reign of Joseph—before the rise of serious opposition in the later 1780s—offered perhaps the most inspirational moment for enlightened absolutism in the whole history of Europe, and Mozart's contribution to that moment was the *Abduction* with its musical celebration of a magnanimous Turkish pasha. Indeed, even the German language of the Singspiel, encouraged by Joseph, was a token of his intention to impose German upon the multilingual Habsburg monarchy as the unified language of enlightened administration. Mozart therefore had every reason to endorse absolutism in its

Turkish operatic guise, both to satisfy the Viennese public and to attract for himself the benevolent patronage of the Viennese emperor. Mozart's musical perspective on Turkishness, and especially his conception of Pasha Selim in the *Abduction*, must be understood in the political context of the Habsburg Josephine moment.[3]

The Proud Lion: Sultan Soliman in Zaide

In January 1778 Mozart, then in Mannheim, was excited to learn that Joseph II was creating a German opera company in Vienna, the National Singspiel, and the young composer immediately began to contemplate creating a German opera. Mozart, twenty-two years old, already imagined himself as the Kapellmeister in Vienna as he wrote to his father in Salzburg:

> I know, very definitely, that the Emperor has in mind to set up in Vienna
> a German opera company and that he is seeking very seriously a young
> Kapellmeister who understands the German language . . . If the Emperor will
> give me a thousand gulden, I will write a German opera for him . . . Please
> write to all our good friends in Vienna you can think of and tell them that I
> am in a position to honor the Emperor [*dass ich in Stande bin, dem Kaiser Ehre
> zu machen*].[4]

All references to the emperor in this letter were written in coded cipher, as if to conceal the very particular nature of Mozart's Viennese ambition from possibly resentful Salzburgers. The following year, in 1779, Mozart would begin to compose the indicated German opera, *Zaide*, which was intended to do honor to the emperor. The libretto concerned the Turkish sultan Soliman, who was addressed as "Grossmächtigster Kaiser" (Most Powerful Emperor). Mozart's work on *Zaide*, never completed, would eventually lead into the project for the *Abduction*, when Mozart definitively moved to Vienna in 1781. The figure of Sultan Soliman would evolve into Pasha Selim, whose unexpectedly enlightened magnanimity would be enacted and celebrated for the emperor in person, to do him honor at the premiere in 1782—and just in time, since Joseph's National Singspiel project collapsed the following year, in 1783.

Sultan Soliman, in *Zaide*, was dramatically and musically unusual, even in the fragmentary form of the incomplete opera, inasmuch as his tenor arias were extensively supplemented with composition in the *melologo* form. Mozart wrote enthusiastically to his father in November 1778 about seeing an opera in Mannheim composed entirely in *melologo* form, *Medea*, by the Bohemian composer Georg Anton (Jiří Antonin) Benda:

> In fact, nothing ever surprised me so much!—I had always imagined that something like this would have no effect on stage!—You know that nothing is sung, but only declaimed—and the music is like an obbligato recitative—occasionally the words are recited with the music and then the effect is most superb . . . you know what my opinion would be?—one should treat most operatic recitatives in this manner.[5]

In spite of this sweeping judgment Mozart seems to have made use of the form very rarely—and most notably in *Zaide*. The rage of Medea inspired the rage of Sultan Soliman, but Mozart, unlike Benda, did not restrict himself only to orchestra and recitation. Just as Handel's Sultan Bajazet sang a dramatic death scene that distinctively varied aria form with accompanied recitative in unprecedented fashion, so half a century later Mozart sought to dramatize the emotions of Sultan Soliman in an extended tenor scene by combining aria form with *melologo*.

Sultan Soliman's dramatic scene follows upon the discovery of the escape of the Christian lovers: "*Zaide entflohen!*" There could be no analogous scene for Pasha Selim in the *Abduction*, not only because he cannot sing but also because the lovers are prevented from escaping by Osmin's intervention. Pasha Selim threatens a terrible judgment upon the lovers and then leaves the stage so that they can sing their love duet about the bliss of dying together: "*O welche Seligkeit!*" When Pasha Selim returns to announce his verdict, he is already transformed into the generous Turk and demonstrates his magnanimity by setting the lovers free. What is missing from the *Abduction* is any musical account of the pasha's inner conflict, wounded pride, and ambivalent emotion. That was precisely what Mozart had already composed for Sultan Soliman in *Zaide*, and it is perhaps worth noting that the sultan's scene in *Zaide* is just the same length—about nine minutes—as the love duet of Konstanze and Belmonte in the *Abduction*, that is, the time that Pasha Selim spends offstage, with his emotions completely unknown to the other characters or the audience.

Sultan Soliman, in contrast to Pasha Selim, is entirely emotionally transparent in his great scene, speaking dramatically while the orchestra expresses his inner life in even greater depth and subtlety:

Zaide entflohen!—
Kann ich den entsetzlichen Schimpf überleben?
Von einem Christenhund, von einem Sklaven lässt sie sich verführen!

Zaide escaped!—
Can I survive the terrible disgrace?
She has let herself be seduced by a Christian dog, by a slave![6]

The *melologo* is introduced with a phrase of brassy pomp, but the lines are then punctuated with swirling musical expressions of the sultan's emotional turmoil. He is at first determined to have Zaide "hacked to pieces" as soon as she is in his power again, but the *melologo* form permits him to turn inward and explore the emotional dimensions of his own rage. Now he curses love itself—*"Verfluchte Liebe!"*—because his love for Zaide reduces him, the sultan, to slavish subjection.[7] Initially furious at being humiliated by one of his own slaves, Sultan Soliman then rages against himself in *melologo* form.

The *melologo* leads into an aria which permits Soliman to further explore his own emotional state, now in rhymed German verse and making use of the metaphor of the lion, king of the beasts:

Der stolze Löw' lässt sich zwar zähmen,
er nimmt von Schmeichler Fessel an.
Doch will man sklavisch ihn beschämen,
steigt seine Wut bis zum Tyrann.

The proud lion lets himself be tamed,
he accepts the chain from the flatterer.
But if someone wants to humiliate him as a slave,
his fury rises to the point of making him a tyrant.[8]

The language of slavery and tyranny belonged to the political vocabulary of early modern European political theory, and was considered especially relevant to the governments of Asia, including the Ottoman empire. Schachtner's verse and Mozart's music, however, combined to suggest that tyranny was not the essential and inevitable political status of an Ottoman sultan, but rather something psychologically conditioned.

Mozart caressingly ornamented the phrase of flattery that tamed the beast, then sharply altered the musical tone for the humiliation that followed, and made use of ascending notes to convey the rising rage that transformed the lion into a tyrant. Soliman's lengthy and expressive scene, *melologo* followed by aria, conveys the suffering of his wounded tenor pride and honor, not altogether unlike Handel's Bajazet, so that Soliman becomes a troubled tenor tyrant, not altogether unlike Mozart's Idomeneo. Furthermore, the metaphor of the proud lion, subject to humiliation, was also relevant to international relations in Mozart's lifetime, with the humiliation of the Ottoman empire by Russia at the peace of Küçük Kaynarca in 1774.

In *Zaide*, Oriental despotism was interpreted operatically in terms of universal human psychology; as the sultan himself declares in his next aria, "*Ich bin so bös' als gut*" (I am as much bad as good).[9] Judging from the model for *Zaide*—that is, Joseph Friberth's 1777 Singspiel *Das Serail*—one might reasonably suppose that Sultan Soliman in *Zaide* would very probably have turned out to be magnanimous in the end, as much good as bad. When Friberth's sultan announces that he is setting Gomatz and Zaide free (after discovering they are brother and sister), he points to the geopolitical moral, as if commenting on Montesquieu: "Not only Europe but also Asia can produce virtuous souls."[10] The concluding chorus of *Das Serail* celebrates the sultan:

Grossmuth und Tugend	Generosity and virtue
Stammet von Göttern.	Come from the gods.
Götter die krönen	The gods who crown
Die Fürsten auf Erden.	Princes on earth.[11]

The plurality of princes (*Fürsten*) suggested that this axiom pertained not only to Sultan Soliman but also to other princes—presumably Christian European princes—and the plurality of gods (*Götter*) indicated perhaps that the moral conduct of princes was comparable across religious boundaries. Since Mozart never finished *Zaide*, it is impossible to be certain that the opera would have ended the same way, but the parts that were composed suggest that the dramatic conception of Turkishness did not rest on an assumption of essential cruelty. A Turkish sultan, like any other ruler, could be either good or bad—"*so bös' als gut*"—vindictive or magnanimous, barbarous or enlightened, depending on the circumstances of his reign.

A Pasha with a Heart

In the *Abduction*, composed as a Singspiel, Mozart's intentions were fundamentally comic, but the opera preserved an admixture of gravity and musical elements of *opera seria*, which were most readily evident in the figure of Konstanze and the tragedy of her captivity under the absolute power of the pasha. If his power were represented comically then her situation would also become comical, like that of her servant Blonde, and Mozart preferred to take Konstanze seriously. Pasha Selim and Konstanze were thus linked to one another in the seriousness of their respective circumstances, he as ruler and she as captive, but barely able to connect with one another across the gap that separated them in their European-Turkish encounter: her singing musicality and his dramatic dialogue.

Though the pasha himself stood outside the musical domain of the work, operatic Turkishness was deployed to celebrate his power and importance. At his first appearance he was greeted by a "Janissary chorus" composed in the *alla turca* style. The 2/4 *allegro* marching rhythm was "Turkish" as was the instrumental intensity of piccolo, triangle, cymbals, kettledrums, and bass drum. The musicians who played Janissary instruments probably stood on stage in Turkish costume in Vienna, as they certainly did in the Koblenz production of 1787. In fact, the Janissary band for the *Abduction* in Vienna may have been supplied by the Habsburg army. The chorus members were in Turkish costume and seemed to urge one another to join in the political acclamation: "*Singt dem grossen Bassa Lieder*" (Sing songs to the great pasha).[12]

Later in the 1780s Mozart would compose Masonic songs to celebrate Joseph: "*Vereineter Herzen und Zungen / sei Joseph dies Loblied gesungen*" (With united hearts and tongues, sing this song of praise to Joseph).[13] Like the Turkish chorus members in the *Abduction* who sang songs to "the great pasha," Mozart himself was the enthusiastic subject of an absolute monarch, Emperor Joseph. Indeed, what Mozart sought above all in Vienna, after breaking with the archbishop of Salzburg in 1781, was the supreme patronage of the emperor, and the composer's enthusiasm was therefore not only ideologically sympathetic, in the spirit of the Enlightenment, but also politically opportune. "The emperor had another attack of fever—I fear—he will not live much longer," wrote Mozart to his father in November 1782. "I so wish to be wrong."[14] The *Abduction*, with its premiere in July, was Mozart's most ambitious effort to impress himself upon Joseph, and it is natural to look within the opera for intimations of that purpose, and therefore to consider the Josephine significance of the pasha's magnanimity.

While the *Abduction* was a great success in Vienna, frequently revived

"*Singt dem grossen Bassa Lieder*" (Sing songs to the great Pasha)—Mozart's *Abduction*. The 2/4 marching rhythm, the Janissary percussion (*Schlagzeug*), and the unison of the choral parts in C major all made this a "Turkish" celebration of the pasha on stage, which also allusively celebrated the absolutism of Habsburg emperor Joseph II who was in the audience for the first performance in 1782.

and also performed all over Europe, Joseph himself was supposed to have responded to the opera with the peculiar criticism of Mozart's elaborate composition, "Too many notes!" In this regard the political figure of the pasha would have ideally suited Joseph's spirit of austerity inasmuch as there was not one single note to sing. The pasha's gravity was guaranteed by his dramatic isolation upon the pedestal of absolute prose. Within that separate sphere, his character demonstrated its development across the three acts of the opera. With the conclusion of the first Turkish chorus, which announces the advent of the pasha, the music completely ceases and he reveals his sympathetic character in the spoken question, "*Immer noch traurig, geliebte Konstanze?*" (Still always sad, beloved Konstanze?). He reminds her that he has not forced himself upon her sexually, even though he could have done so. Instead, he declares his love for her and his determination to have her love him freely, according to her own heart.[15] Yet the one thing he cannot offer her is music. Mozart would not permit him to sing to Konstanze of his love, as if it were unworthy of the pasha's political dignity to try to compete with Belmonte's tenor ardor.

As soon as Konstanze leaves the stage, Selim reflects on his own reluctance to force her submission: "*Auch Selim hat ein Herz*" (Selim also has a heart).[16] His prosaic affirmation that he also possesses a heart echoes Osmin's musical

Pasha Selim, according to the costume design by Johann Matthias Steyreiff, for the Koblenz production of the *Abduction* in 1787. The elaborate decoration of the pasha's befeathered and bejeweled turban underlines the magnificence of his authority. With kind permission of the Familienarchiv Ernst Steireif, Koblenz.

declaration that he possesses a mind: "*Ich hab' auch Verstand.*" In both cases the *Abduction* eschewed an Orientalism of absolute Otherness and insisted upon the human and humane qualities of its Turkish characters. Timothy Taylor has suggested that one might view Pasha Selim as a sort of "noble savage" in the fashionable style of the Enlightenment, but there was very little that was "savage" in his Ottoman circumstances. Rather, he was a noble despot, a pasha with a heart. This operatic representation of an absolute ruler who listened to his own heart possessed a political meaning for the Habsburg monarchy in the 1780s.[17]

In the second act, however, the pasha is also wrestling with his own dark side—perhaps his Turkish side, or perhaps simply his sense of his own absolute power. He is ready to give his captive an ultimatum:

PASHA: Now Konstanze, are you thinking about my desire? The day is almost over. Tomorrow you must love me, or—
KONSTANZE: Must? What a foolish desire! As if one could command love.[18]

He then threatens her in prosaic speech with "*Martern aller Arten*" (tortures of all kinds), a phrase which she takes up musically in the famous display aria of that name. His barbarous threat becomes the point of departure for her dazzling musical acrobatics, a triumph of vocal ornamentation that anticipates the certain triumph of her European virtue. He possesses absolute power over her, but she demonstrates her defiance by showing in the extraordinary range, length, and ornamentation of the aria that she can do something that he can never do: she can sing! Her spectacular musicality becomes the emblem of her sentimental independence in the key of C major. While Blonde resists Osmin's advances in the comical spirit of the Singspiel, Konstanze sings her aria in the style of *opera seria*, treating the pasha's sexual menace with all seriousness. The clash of civilization between Turkey and Europe here appeared in its starkest outlines, represented as an inseparable chasm between barbarous menace and brilliant civilization, the latter expressed in a vocal display of operatic mastery.

While the threat of torture or torment might seem to signal Oriental barbarism, Mozart and Stephanie would probably have been aware that judicial torture (*Folter*) in the Habsburg monarchy had been abolished by Joseph together with his mother, Maria Theresa, as recently as 1776. In 1782 the threat of tortures (*Martern*) by the pasha in the *Abduction*, which was further detailed in the rages of Osmin ("*Erst geköpft, dann gehangen, dann gespiesst auf heisse Stangen*"), suggested a barbarous Turkishness but also perhaps referred more generally to the unenlightened exercise of power and justice under the ancien régime in Europe. Joseph himself may have noted this point while watching the opera, for it was in the elaborate ornamentation of Konstanze's aria, her defiance of torture, that Mozart most lavishly made use of what the emperor called "too many notes."

"Long live Pasha Selim"

In the first act the pasha shows himself to be sympathetic and loving ("*Immer noch traurig, geliebte Konstanze?*") and in the second act menacing and cruel ("*Martern aller Arten*"), alternative expressions of his absolute power. In the third act he appears twice, recapitulating the same emotional course in reverse, first angry and vindictive and then finally merciful and magnanimous. When Osmin recaptures the Christians trying to escape, he celebrates with exultant and frenzied cruelty in his own display aria:

> Ha! [O!] wie will ich triumphieren,
> wenn sie euch zum Richtplatz führen . . .

> Ha! how I will triumph,
> when they lead you to the place of execution . . .[19]

Here Osmin identifies his own vengeful frenzy entirely with the pasha's despotic justice. The likelihood of execution becomes even greater when Pasha Selim learns that Belmonte is the son of his own political enemy, the Spanish commander of Oran in Algeria. "To have the son of my worst enemy in my power!" the pasha exults. "Your father, that barbarian, is responsible for the fact that I had to leave my fatherland."[20]

The identification of Belmonte's father as the pasha's worst enemy was of course a dramatic coincidence of the stage, but it also accurately conveyed the Braudelian intimacy of Mediterranean rivalries between Christians and Muslims. The city of Oran was actually ruled by Spain from the sixteenth to the eighteenth century, though briefly occupied by the Ottomans from 1708 to 1732 when it was retaken by Spain, the moment when an Ottoman official like Pasha Selim might have been displaced by a Spanish commander. (Ultimately, the Spanish crown would cede Oran to the Ottomans in 1792, ten years after Mozart composed the *Abduction*.) Belmonte, when caught trying to escape, initially proposed to the pasha a generous ransom to be raised by his family—which was a historically common procedure in the early modern Mediterranean region.[21] On the Mediterranean, and also across the Triplex Confinium, enemies were not necessarily strangers to one another, and they reciprocally recognized one another's codes of conduct. "Tell me, what would he do in my place?" the pasha asks Belmonte about his father, and Belmonte acknowledges that his own father would not be merciful if the places were reversed.[22] Mozart and Stephanie were sufficiently men of the Enlightenment to recognize that while Turks might seem barbarous to Christian Europeans, the Christians might likewise appear barbarous from the perspective of the Turks: "Your father, that barbarian!"

In Bretzner's original text for *Belmont und Konstanze* the pasha is a renegade Christian, converted to Islam and assimilated to Turkishness, and he then discovers in the denouement that Belmonte is his long-lost son: "*Mein Sohn, mein Sohn!*"[23] Stephanie and Mozart altered the story to make Belmonte the son of the pasha's worst enemy, thus magnifying the magnanimity of the final pardoning. Pasha Selim appears as a humane Muslim, more humane, indeed more Christian, than his enemy, Belmonte's Christian father:

> I detested your father far too much to ever be able to follow in his footsteps. Take your freedom. Take Konstanze, sail to your fatherland, and tell your father that you were in my power, and that I set you free.[24]

Osmin protests in Allah's name, but the pasha is determined to be merciful.[25] The opera thus concludes with an Ottoman pasha teaching lessons in moral virtue to his Christian captives—at the same historical moment that Joseph was proclaiming Habsburg religious toleration. On the stage an absolute monarch offers the gift of "freedom" to those he holds in his power—at the same historical moment that Joseph gave some measure of freedom to peasant serfs by limiting the powers and prerogatives of their noble masters. The magnanimity on stage thus reflected the spirit of enlightened reform in Josephine Vienna.

The pasha, having spoken and shown himself to be a generous Turk, is then silenced by the musical finale which is entirely a celebration of himself. He cannot participate, or even respond, since he cannot sing. "Stephanie expanded Bretzner's Pasha into a more complex and interesting character,"

"*Nie werd' ich deine Huld verkennen*" (I will never fail to recognize your benevolence), sings Belmonte as he opens the concluding "vaudeville" number of Mozart's *Abduction*. At the refrain, all four of the Europeans, the two sopranos and the two tenors, will harmonize to sing, "*Wer so viel Huld vergessen kann, den seh' man mit Verachtung an*" (Whoever can forget such benevolence, let him be regarded with contempt). At first Osmin harmonizes with them on the basso line, but when he finally breaks with their musical harmony and denounces them as dogs, the Europeans must reconstitute the harmony of the refrain among themselves. The operatic exploration of the magnanimity of a generous Turk, in this case Pasha Selim, became one cultural means for delineating, analyzing, evaluating, and affirming enlightened absolutism as a principle of European political theory in the eighteenth century.

observes musicologist Thomas Bauman.[26] Yet by the end of the opera, the pasha seems to have become the embodiment of an abstract political principle, the virtuous incarnation of enlightened absolutism. It is therefore entirely appropriate for him to remain silent in the finale, while the other characters are singing to him and about him.

The finale was designated as a "vaudeville," meaning in this case that each of the characters sings a verse, but then all join together in the refrain which also sums up the moral of the piece—"*Huld*" and "*Dank*," the benevolence of the pasha and the gratitude of the others, beginning with the verse of Belmonte:

Nie werd' ich deine Huld verkennen,
mein Dank bleibt ewig dir geweiht . . .

I will never fail to recognize your benevolence,
my gratitude remains ever yours . . .

The others join in the refrain:

Wer so viel Huld vergessen kann,
den seh' man mit Verachtung an.

Whoever can forget such benevolence,
let him be regarded with contempt.[27]

The refrain thus invokes a compulsory unanimity, an acclamation in favor of the benevolent prince, who is none other than the Turkish Muslim pasha Selim. Yet as they sing, he only passively and silently receives their tribute and might as well be a stone monument to enlightened rule.

The living, breathing enlightened monarch would have been present in the audience at the premiere on July 16, 1782, and it is not hard to imagine that this concluding musical number, sung to the pasha on the stage, was also being sung to the emperor in the audience. In 1778 the aged Voltaire came to Paris to die, and visited the Comédie-Française to witness "the coronation of Voltaire"—his marble bust crowned with laurels on the stage while he himself looked on, in the flesh, from a box in the audience. Mozart was in Paris at that time, a struggling young musician of twenty-two, and he may well have seen copies of the famous print that represented the scene in the theater. Just so did the living emperor look on silently at the musical celebration of his theatrical counterpart, the silent pasha on the stage, the emblem of benevolence and object of eternal gratitude.

Perhaps never in European history did a prince engage himself so completely in seeking to revolutionize, enlighten, and ameliorate the lives of his subjects, but despite Joseph's enlightened intentions his reforms provoked widespread hostile reaction. A pamphlet of 1787 summed up the situation: *"Warum wird Kaiser Joseph von seinem Volke nicht geliebt?"* (Why is Emperor Joseph not loved by his people?). Already in 1782 there was some grumbling and discontent, and after all, the pope made an unprecedented voyage to Vienna in that year to register his dissatisfaction with Joseph and mobilize the sentiments of devout Roman Catholics. The vaudeville that promised eternal gratitude for enlightened benevolence already anticipated that some would refuse their tribute, would remain outside the circle of the grateful, would be condemned to the eternal contempt of the enlightened. In fact, Mozart inscribed that political dissent within the vaudeville itself, as Osmin separates himself from the universal acclaim of the pasha. Osmin actually joins three times in the refrain—"Whoever can forget such benevolence"—but then the fourth verse is sung by Blonde and contains a gratuitous insult aimed in his direction, sung to the tune of the refrain:

| Denn seh' er nur das Tier dort an, | Just look at that beast over there, |
| ob man sowas ertragen kann. | if something like that can be endured.[28] |

Now Osmin takes up the verse in a very different spirit, without even waiting for Blonde to finish: "We should burn these dogs, who have tricked us." As the tempo picks up and the key shifts from F to A minor once again, suddenly the Janissary instruments join in—piccolo and percussion—and Osmin is once again in the same rage that Mozart created for him so meticulously in the first act: *"Erst geköpft, dann gehangen / dann gespiesst, auf heisse Stangen."*[29] With the invocation of beheading, hanging, and impalement, unenlightened Turkish fury thus rears its head one last time, and after building through a tremendous crescendo, ends with Osmin running off the stage, still raging and unreconciled.

The tempo then slows to *andante sostenuto*, the percussion falls silent, the key modulates back toward F, and the four Christians sing together in hushed tones, marked *sotto voce*: "Nothing is so ugly as revenge." It is the lesson that they have learned from Pasha Selim, who refused to take his just revenge, and that lesson is now reinforced in watching Osmin reject the moral. Yet in the vanquishing of Osmin it is not Turkishness that has been silenced, for the Turkish instruments, march tempo, and oscillating intervals all return in their clamorous brilliance for the concluding Janissary chorus celebrating the Pasha: "*Bassa Selim lebe lange*" (Long live Pasha Selim).[30]

The sultan Bajazet was the sympathetic hero of Handel's *Tamerlano* in London in 1724, but died tragically on stage as a captive suicide. The "generous Turk" of Rameau's *Les Indes galantes* in Paris in 1735 was saluted for his "sublime virtue," but was left sadly lamenting his lost love. In Favart's *Les trois sultanes* of 1761 Suleiman the Magnificent was comically captivated, dominated, and civilized by the captive Frenchwoman in his harem. Favart's representation of Ottoman authority was still circulating in Europe in the 1780s, with Bertati's libretto for Venice in 1784 and Kraus's music for Stockholm in 1789—but Mozart in Vienna offered something very different. In the final scene of Mozart's *Abduction* Pasha Selim stands alone, absolute, magnanimous, magnificent, and enlightened in a triumphant tableau of Turkishness, set to music in the *alla turca* style. The departing Europeans vow never to forget his benevolence, while his Turkish subjects wish him glory and long life. The Turkish figure on the European stage surrenders his European captives but wins his moral victory over them and proudly offers a lesson in political virtue to the enlightened European public. Mozart, new in Vienna, seeking to obtain the favor of Emperor Joseph, took a circuitous route through the Ottoman world and presented himself to the Habsburg emperor by celebrating the benevolence of the Turkish pasha. One hundred years after the Grand Vizier Kara Mustafa Pasha failed in his siege of Vienna, in 1683, Pasha Selim conquered the city in 1782 from the operatic stage.

"The good reception of my opera"

Mozart himself recorded the triumph of the *Abduction* in his letters to his father. Just as the rage of Osmin, representing the enemies of enlightened rule, had to be voiced and then silenced in the finale of the opera, so Mozart's own enemies apparently made themselves known at the first performances and were vanquished by those who appreciated the opera:

> Yesterday it was given for the second time; would you have guessed that there was an even stronger cabal against it than on the first evening? Throughout the whole first act there was hissing, but this couldn't prevent the loud shouts of Bravo during the arias . . . The theater was even more full than the first night.[31]

Mozart's reaction suggested how studiously he was attending to the reception of the opera in Vienna, not only with the emperor but also with the public. Operatic and theatrical audiences in Vienna in the Josephine 1780s, as in contemporary Paris and London, were beginning to take on some of the features of a modern public sphere. Mozart's whole career in Vienna in the 1780s would be balanced between the parallel priorities of imperial favor and public opinion.[32]

Mozart therefore could not remain unperturbed when at the second performance Fischer, in the role of Osmin, made some musical mistakes and ruined the concluding trio of the first act:

> Unfortunately Fischer was off . . . so the whole effect of the trio was lost, and this time there was no encore. I was in such a rage that I didn't recognize myself [*Ich war so in Wuth dass ich mich nicht kannte*], and so was Adamberger [Belmonte]—and I said immediately that I would not allow another performance until we had a short rehearsal for the singers.[33]

Writing about Osmin one year before, Mozart had used the same language to explain that a person in a rage "no longer knows himself" (*er kennt sich nicht*).[34] Now it was Mozart himself, not only Osmin, who fell into a rage, making himself into the angry overseer of the singers.

Mozart sought the favor of the public, but he also craved the musical approval of his father, and therefore sent the score of the *Abduction* to Salzburg. The "Turkish music," however, was not fully included:

> As you receive it, that's the way it was performed. Here and there the trumpets and drums, flutes, clarinets, and the Turkish music are missing, because I couldn't get music paper with so many lines; those parts are written on separate sheets of paper; the copyist probably lost them, and then he couldn't find them. Unfortunately, the first act fell into the mud; that's why it is so dirty . . . By a week from Sunday my opera must be arranged for wind instruments; otherwise someone else will do it before me—and will have the profits instead of me.[35]

In the standard score, the Turkish music, when it occurs, requires the addition of a line at the top for the piccolo and four lines at the bottom for triangle, cymbals, kettledrums, and bass drum. Mozart's use of extra sheets of paper emphasized the unusual nature of the additions, and also the more general issue of "too many notes." In the arrangement that Mozart made for wind instruments the Turkishness of the music largely disappeared, preserved only in some of the oscillations and march rhythms, since the wind instruments (without piccolo, without percussion) did not provide any of the Turkish coloring. Wind bands were popular in Vienna in the 1780s, and the reconstruction of Mozart's wind instrumentation for the melodies from the *Abduction* suggests that the scoring involved two clarinets, two oboes, two bassoons, and two horns.[36] There would have been no crashing of the cymbals, Janissary style. It was, however, a mark of the opera's success that its music would enjoy a wider circulation performed by serenading Viennese wind bands.

On July 27 Mozart wrote to Salzburg about the performance the day before, on St. Anne's day, the name day of his sister Nannerl:

> My opera was given yesterday for the third time with all applause in honor of all Nannerls—and in spite of the terrible summer heat the theater was packed full. It was supposed to be given again next Friday, but I protested, because I don't want it to be whipped to death. I can say that people are quite crazy about this opera [*recht närrisch auf diese Oper*]. It really feels good to have such applause. I do hope you have received by now the original score of the opera. Dearest and best of all fathers! I must implore you, implore you for all you hold dear in the world: please give me your consent so that I can marry my dear Constanze.[37]

The success of the opera was obviously exciting for Mozart, who emphasized it powerfully in writing to his father, not only because his father was his musical mentor but also because the young composer, age twenty-six, hoped to marry the woman he loved on the strength of this professional success. In the opera Belmonte must rescue Konstanze from the pasha, but in real life Mozart had to plead with his own father for permission to marry Constanze. Leopold had been his music teacher and impresario from early childhood, but as a figure of authority was not always sympathetic and magnanimous toward his brilliant son.

With the triumph of the *Abduction* Mozart claimed to have obtained the emperor's favorable opinion, even as he appealed for his father's approval: "I know what Prince Kaunitz said about me to the emperor and Archduke Maximilian. I am waiting eagerly for your consent, my beloved father."[38] Mozart infused into the drama of the *Abduction* some of his own frustrations with Salzburg—with the domineering archbishop, with the abusive overseer Count Arco—and in this regard the opera also celebrated Mozart's own emergence from professional captivity. His filial obligations to his father in Salzburg still weighed heavily on him as he tried to identify the path to independence, and paradoxically the favor of Emperor Joseph, the supreme absolute monarch, seemed to promise a kind of emancipation from all intermediary authorities.

In Salzburg, however, on July 26, St. Anne's day, Leopold wrote to his son a letter that showed the father to be still unimpressed by the success of the *Abduction* and unenthusiastic about the proposed marriage. Mozart responded in a letter of July 31, claiming the support of the Viennese public:

> Today I received your letter of July 26, but I could never have imagined such an indifferent, cold reply to the report I sent you concerning the good reception of my opera. I believed . . . that in your eagerness you would scarcely be able to open the packet, just to see your son's work, which is not only pleasing the Viennese audiences but makes such a din [*so Lärm macht*] that they don't want to hear anything else, and the theater is always teeming with people [*von Menschen wimmelt*]. Yesterday the opera was given for the 4th time and will be given again this Friday. But—you didn't have enough time.[39]

In Leopold's letter of July 26 (now lost) he must have mentioned that he had not hurried to read the score of the *Abduction*, and Mozart, in response, reminded his father over and over again what a tremendous success the opera was in Vienna. Then, in a letter of August 7, Mozart announced that he had married Constanze without waiting for his father's permission, and also mentioned, as if to vindicate himself, the ongoing triumph of the *Abduction*: "My opera was given again yesterday—at Gluck's request. Gluck has given me many compliments about it. Tomorrow I will lunch with him."[40] Gluck, the great operatic composer, who belonged to Leopold Mozart's generation, provided the validation that was not immediately forthcoming from Salzburg. Gluck in fact had helped to establish the interest in Ottoman operatic subjects and *alla turca* music in Vienna with *Les pèlerins de la Mecque* in 1764.

The success of the *Abduction* during the summer of 1782 was extended into the fall, when Mozart was finally able to present his opera to the Russian Grand Duke Paul in Vienna, and there was also an autumn production in Prague. In 1783 the opera was performed in Warsaw, Bonn, Frankfurt, and Leipzig.[41] In Vienna, on September 12, 1783, there were particular commemorations to mark the centennial of the failed Turkish siege of 1683, while the *Abduction* circulated around Germany and Poland as a Viennese musical reformulation of the former Turkish menace. It was the Polish king Jan Sobieski who saved Vienna in 1683, and the Warsaw production of the *Abduction* in 1783 may also have had some centennial associations. The Ottoman empire was in the European news in 1783, as that was the year that Russia dramatically annexed the Crimea, displacing its Muslim ruler, the Tatar khan Şahin Giray. At the conclusion of war in 1774, Catherine had already removed the khan from Ottoman political suzerainty, and placed the khanate unofficially under Russian protection, but the annexation of 1783 was a further blow to Ottoman prestige.

Though Mozart's *Abduction* was originally intended for a Russian occasion, the visit to Vienna of the Russian Grand Duke, the far-flung performances of the opera following its Viennese premiere do not seem to have included a production in St. Petersburg or Moscow. In Russia in 1782 a parallel work was produced, *Pasha tunisskiy* (The pasha of Tunis), composed by Vasily Pashkevich to a libretto by Mikhail Matinsky and produced at the Karl Knipper Theater in St. Petersburg.[42] Several of Pashkevich's other operas were composed to libretti written by Catherine the Great herself, so his career did not lack official patronage, and *The Pasha of Tunis* in 1782 probably enjoyed some imperial sponsorship.

In 1783 Joseph had the opportunity to display Christian hospitality to visiting Muslim guests in Vienna, the Moroccan embassy from Sultan Mohammed III of the Alaouite dynasty, reigning just beyond the Ottoman frontier in North Africa. The visitors remained in Vienna from mid-February till early May and excited considerable interest that encompassed some of the same Oriental aspects dramatized in the *Abduction* in 1782. For instance, a Viennese pamphlet of 1783 explained that in Morocco "the government is despotic, and there are no limits to the power of the king." Johann Pezzl published in 1784 a work of *Marokkanische Briefe* (Moroccan letters), modeled on Montesquieu's *Persian Letters*, purporting to describe the Viennese reception as experienced by the Moroccans: "Since our coming people have in a hundred ways etched, painted, chiseled and molded us. On wood, stone, plaster, porcelain, ivory, glass, fabric, wax, sugar, and paper, people have our images for sale. Clocks, tins, and fans will perpetuate [*verewigen*] the fact that there were Moroccans in Vienna."[43] The premiere of Mozart's *Abduction* actually preceded this Moroccan visit, but the ongoing productions of the opera overlapped with the visit and its potent impact. Opera was one of the many varied forms and commodities for representing and perpetuating foreign, Muslim, and Oriental images that were not altogether alien to Viennese life in the age of Josephine absolutism.

Pashas and Harems in Grétry and Mozart

While Mozart's *Abduction* continued to be staged and appreciated in 1783, and the Viennese celebrated the centennial of their liberation from the Ottoman siege, there was performed in France at Fontainebleau André Grétry's comic opera *La caravane du Caire* (The caravan of Cairo). This would become the most popular French opera on a Turkish subject of the later eighteenth century, building on the earlier French precedents of the Paris fairs, Rameau's generous Turk, and Favart's three sultanas. In the audience at Fontainebleau in 1783 were King Louis XVI and Queen Marie Antoinette, the Habsburg sister of Joseph II. The libretto was written by Étienne Morel de Chédeville, possibly with the collaboration of the French king's brother, the Comte de Provence (who thirty years later would reign as King Louis XVIII). The opera was set in Egypt, by the banks of the Nile, and then in the palace of the pasha of Cairo, with the title of pasha clearly suggesting that this was Ottoman Egypt and therefore a Turkish scenario. *La caravane du Caire* went straight from Fontainebleau in 1783 to the Paris Opéra in 1784, and its success thus belonged to the same operatic Turkish moment as that of Mozart's *Abduction*.

In the previous decade Grétry had captivated France, and then Europe, with *Zémire et Azor*, an Oriental fairy tale with a story that resembled "Beauty and the Beast." The Persian maiden Zémire becomes the prisoner of the monstrous Azor, thus partly mirroring the plot structure of a Turkish captivity opera. By the end of the opera they are in love with one another, and Azor is able to recover the handsome countenance of a Persian prince. The work was performed in Fontainebleau and Paris in 1771, in Berlin in 1773, in Frankfurt in 1775, and in London and Vienna in 1779.[44] It was this exotically Oriental fairy-tale opera of the 1770s that paved the way for Grétry's even greater success in the 1780s with the specifically Ottoman scenario of *La caravane*.

The first act presents a caravan en route to Cairo with slaves to sell, including Zélime, the daughter of a "nabob"—and therefore perhaps originally from India. Zélime, presumably Muslim from her name, is married to a Frenchman, Saint-Phar, who rightly fears that she will be sold to the pasha when the caravan arrives in Cairo. The chorus of slaves sings a lament on the misfortunes of slavery. The opera, however, is not quite a solemn manifesto of abolitionism, for one unnamed French slave sings with rococo charm from her own individual French perspective:

Ne suis-je pas aussi captive?	Am I not also a captive?
Je devrais gémir comme vous;	I ought to groan like you;
Mais, Française, ma gaité vive,	But, being French, my lively gaiety,
Du sort me fait braver les coups.	Helps me bear the blows of fate.[45]

She is confident that her beautiful eyes (*beaux yeux*) will save her situation, and that a mere pasha will be no problem for her to manage:

Je soumettrais un sultan même,	I would conquer even a sultan,
Les femmes règnent en tous lieux.	Women rule everywhere.[46]

While Blonde in the *Abduction* celebrates her freedom as an Englishwoman and refuses to be treated as a slave, the anonymous French slave of Grétry's *Caravan* is quite comfortable with the title of slave, confident that even as a slave a woman is sure to dominate the man who loves her. This had been emphatically the perspective of Favart in *The Three Sultanas*, when he imagined the harem slave Roxelana as a Frenchwoman capable of conquering a sultan.

The second act is set in the pasha's apartments in Cairo, where the head of the caravan, the slave trader Husca, is conferring with the pasha's eunuch Tamorin. In the tradition of the Paris fairs, and Favart's *Three Sultanas*, French operatic comedies could be uninhibited about eunuch humor, and the part of Tamorin was even assigned by Grétry to the high tenor voice known as *haute-contre*, related to the modern countertenor: not a castrato, to be sure, but producing as high a vocal register as would be possible for an uncastrated male singer. Grétry took the comedy of the eunuch figure on stage almost to the point of vocal verisimilitude. Furthermore, Grétry, together with his librettist, Morel de Chédeville, assumed that the public would enjoy the humor of slave trading. Husca sings a cheerfully rhythmic song about his girls: "*J'ai des beautés piquantes*" (I have piquant beauties). He promises that his girls—including French and African girls—will be able to satisfy all the pasha's tastes: "*contenter tous les goûts*." This becomes a lighthearted duet between Husca the trader and Tamorin the eunuch, who also considers himself to be a connoisseur of female flesh. The two men, baritone and high tenor, harmonize as they repeat together the refrain: "*contenter tous les goûts*."[47] There is perhaps even a musical suggestion that such different male registers, in pursuit of piquancy, might seek to gratify perversely diverse sexual tastes.

The eunuch and the pasha provide the same vocal harmony between high tenor and low bass, with the eunuch comically playing the role of the pasha's sexual counselor—or even therapist. The pasha is bored with his harem and has lost interest in his recent harem favorite, Almaide. The eunuch Tamorin explains in an aria that "it is sad monotony that extinguishes the desires of the heart," set to a musical line suggestive of sad monotony. The music then changes completely as Tamorin celebrates the inconstancy of the butterfly who flits from flower to flower. Grétry provides brilliant tenor ornamentation as the eunuch attempts to titillate the pasha with the butterfly's promiscuity. The pasha, however, sings a sad little aria, noting paradoxically that it is precisely inconstancy and infidelity that have produced his current state of "indifference and languor"—the presumed consequences of Oriental sensuality. The pasha declares himself to be in search of a new kind of sexual relation: "I seek a companion, not slaves."[48] If, as Voltaire had observed, the great difference between Orientals and Europeans lay in their different treatments of women, then Grétry's Oriental pasha showed himself to be an aspiring European in search of romantic companionship.

In the trio that follows, for pasha, slave trader, and eunuch—basso, baritone, and high tenor—they cheerfully celebrate the charms of women in the same spirit as Osmin and Pedrillo. Tamorin takes turns harmonizing his tenor with the slave trader, who extols the charms of the girls, and with the pasha, who is excited at the prospect. "*Piquant!*" sings the pasha. "*Charmant*," agrees the trader. The eunuch and the trader assure the pasha, "*Chaque jour plus séduisantes*" (Every day more seductive). The pasha and the eunuch are gratified together: "*Et toujours intéressantes*" (And always interesting).[49] The musical spirit is altogether lighthearted as the approaching sale seems to promise satisfaction to the pasha's jaded palate.

It should be noted that this was a pasha with none of the gravity or dignity of Mozart's Pasha Selim in the *Abduction*, but rather more resemblance to Favart's unintimidating Soliman—or even the ridiculous Mustafa the Bey of Algiers, whom Rossini would create thirty years later in *L'italiana in Algeri*. If Mozart intended his pasha to serve as a flattering mirror for Joseph II, Grétry could hardly have intended his pasha as tribute to Louis XVI at Fontainebleau. Louis XVI was certainly not a polygamous pasha, and his sexual dysfunction meant that his marriage to Marie Antoinette in 1770 was for a long time unconsummated; their first child was not born until 1778. The court at Fontainebleau might have understood Grétry's pasha as a kind of comical tribute to the celebrated promiscuity of the late Louis XV, who very nearly kept a harem at

Six costumes for Grétry's *La caravane du Caire*, designed by the painter Jean-Simon Berthélemy for a Paris production in 1790 during the French Revolution. The opera remained extremely popular from the 1780s to the 1820s. The lower row shows the particularly elaborate costumes for the male protagonists: Husca the slave trader, Osman the pasha, and Tamorin the eunuch. In the opera they sing a comic trio together in tribute to the charms of women. With kind permission of the Bibliothèque Nationale de France.

Versailles, and whose last principal mistress, Mme du Barry, might even have been present at the performance of *La caravane du Caire* in 1783.

The second scene of the second act takes place in the Cairo bazaar, with the pasha's entrance accompanied by a march that includes elements of Janissary percussion. The pasha purchases Zélime for ten thousand ducats, leaving a despairing Saint-Phar to contemplate the rescue of his bride. The first two acts of Grétry's *Caravan* thus took the plot to the point where Mozart's *Abduction* actually began. The presumption of most Turkish captivity operas was a background story involving pirates and slave traders, setting up the circumstances of captivity before the curtain went up. Mozart never composed the buying and selling of Konstanze, and when the curtain rose she was already established in the seraglio, in tragic captivity awaiting comic abduction. *La caravane du Caire*, however, was unembarrassed about the commercial details of the slave trade that ultimately led to the pasha's harem, and was even sometimes given the secondary title *L'heureux esclavage* (The happy slavery). Ottoman slavery could still be conceived as operatic comedy, though by the 1780s there would certainly have been some enlightened figures in the French public who would have found joking about slavery to be unfunny. The political society *Amis des Noirs* (Friends of the Blacks), was founded in 1788 to oppose slavery, and in 1794, at the height of the French Revolution, slavery was actually abolished.

In Grétry's opera the pasha was blessed with a French military adviser, a theatrical detail which was plausibly related to the historical record of eighteenth-century French officers and Ottoman military reform: from the Comte de Bonneval, who developed Ottoman artillery in the 1730s (and became a pasha himself), to the Baron de Tott, who played a major military advisory role in the 1770s.[50] In Grétry's *Caravan* the military adviser is also a Frenchman, Florestan by name, and the pasha is preparing to welcome him to Cairo. The eunuch Tamorin is looking forward to preparing the feast: "How surprised Florestan will be to find in Cairo the talents and arts that one admires in Paris!" While the court at Fontainebleau would certainly have laughed at such naïve presumption, they would probably have been flattered by the pasha's *ariette*: "*Oui, oui, toujours j'aimai la France*" (Yes, yes, I have always loved France). The French character was praised as joyous, sensitive, generous, and noble: an enthusiastic tribute to France and the French from a fictive Ottoman-Egyptian perspective. *La caravane du Caire* would hold the French stage for almost half a century with about five hundred performances from the

Printed textile, called "La Caravane du Caire" with scenes from the opera, made in France, possibly in Nantes, probably from the early nineteenth century. The manufacture of such a fabric, named for an opera and designed with reference to that opera, testifies to the enormous popularity of *La caravane du Caire* from the 1780s to the 1820s. Another surviving fabric sample, also named for the same opera, dates back to the 1780s. With kind permission of the Metropolitan Museum of Art, New York.

1780s to the 1820s.[51] Its popularity was such that during this period French fabrics were printed with Ottoman-Egyptian scenes from the opera and sold commercially under the name "La Caravane du Caire"—as if alluding to the more dubious commerce of the caravan within the opera.[52]

When it turns out that the French military adviser Florestan is actually the father of Saint-Phar, the pasha shows himself to be a generous Turk and liberates Saint-Phar together with Zélime.[53] Their liberation thus becomes a token of French-Ottoman understanding, and the pasha expresses the hope that "this day may tighten our bonds." If the pasha is initially represented as ridiculous in his sexual boredom and his search for titillation, he rises above that representation to achieve an emancipatory magnanimity in the closing scene of the opera. It was the same magnanimity that Mozart attributed to Pasha Selim the previous year, suggesting the enlightened virtues of Joseph. The Swedish treatment of Favart's Suleiman played a similar role in celebrating Gustav III in Stockholm, while the Danish version of Gluck's *Les pèlerins* was repeatedly performed after 1776 in the Copenhagen of Christian VII.[54] In Stockholm and Copenhagen, as in Paris and Vienna, operatic comedy illuminated the relevance of Ottoman subjects for considering European issues of authority and enlightenment.

Mozart in Wartime

Mozart in Vienna in 1783 continued his professional ascent and continued to conciliate the good opinion of Joseph. Mozart wrote to his father on March 29 about a recent concert:

> I think it will not be necessary to tell you much about the success of my concert; you may already have heard about it. Enough; the theater could not have been fuller, and all the loges were occupied. But what pleased me most was that His Majesty, the Emperor, was also there, how delighted he was, and the loud applause he gave me.[55]

If Mozart had made his characters salute the enlightened emperor in the *Abduction*, now it was time for the emperor to return the favor with his patronage and applause. The concert included a symphony, two piano concertos, and Mozartean piano variations (K.455) on one of the Kalender's comical arias from Gluck's *Les pèlerins*; there were also vocal pieces, though nothing from the *Abduction*. With the lapsing of the German Singspiel company and the arrival of an Italian opera company in 1783, Mozart would not have an immediate opportunity to follow up on his operatic triumph. The piano would offer him an alternative means of reaching the public, and on April 12 he reported on another concert: "They didn't just applaud but shouted Bravo and Bravissimo! The emperor stayed and listened until I had finished playing—and when I left the clavier, he left his loge. He stayed just to hear me."[56] Joseph's reign and Mozart's career progressed apace.

In 1784 Joseph established the Allgemeine Krankenhaus, Vienna's modern general hospital, while Mozart, perfectly healthy, ran a successful series of subscription concerts with himself as the star, playing the piano. In December he was initiated into one of Vienna's Masonic lodges, and freemasonry with its Egyptian rituals and ecumenical spiritual values would remain important to him for the rest of his life. Some of his Masonic music would celebrate Joseph by name, and all of it reflected the enlightened values of Josephine Vienna. In 1784 the Ottoman Grand Vizier in Istanbul inaugurated a program of military modernization under French tutelage. He was reacting to the Russian annexation of the Crimea and preparing for the possibility of war.[57] Nevertheless, Turkish comedy still flourished in Europe, and in 1784 Mozart's *Abduction* was performed in Vienna, Mannheim, Karlsruhe, Cologne, and Salzburg. In 1785 it played in Vienna, Dresden, Riga, Munich, Weimar, Aachen, Kassel, Nuremberg, Augsburg, Mainz, and Bratislava.[58]

In 1786 Mozart produced another operatic masterpiece, *Le nozze di Figaro*, his first *opera buffa* collaboration with the Venetian writer Lorenzo Da Ponte. They would collaborate together on two more of the greatest works in the operatic repertory, *Don Giovanni* in 1787 and *Così fan tutte* in 1790. None of these three masterpieces offered a Turkish theme, but in *Così fan tutte* the tenor Ferrando and baritone Guglielmo disguise themselves as Albanians to test their lovers' fidelity.

Whether or not Ferrando and Guglielmo were supposed to appear as Muslim Ottoman Albanians was not explicitly specified in the libretto. Most Albanians were Muslim Ottoman subjects in the eighteenth century, though some were Christians and some inhabited "Venetian Albania" in the vicinity of modern Montenegro. Mozart and Da Ponte, taking the Viennese and Venetian perspectives on the Ottoman empire and the Triplex Confinium, clearly relished the mock-Albanian comedy of southeastern Europe. At the first appearance of the mock-Albanians, the maid Despina, greatly entertained, sings appreciatively about their exotic appearance, seeing through but not quite identifying their disguise:

Che sembianze! Che vestiti!	What appearances! What costumes!
Che figure! Che mustacchi!	What figures! What moustaches!
Io non so se son Valacchi	I don't know if they are Wallachians
o se Turchi son costor!	or if they are Turks![59]

The Romanian principalities of Wallachia and Moldavia were politically autonomous in the eighteenth century, ruled by their Greek Phanariot hospodars, who were nevertheless still subject to ultimate Ottoman sovereignty.

For Mozart and Da Ponte, creating operatic entertainment in the 1780s, the miscellaneous attributes of the Ottoman lands and peoples might be promiscuously deployed in Vienna to notable theatrical effect. The *Sketch of Vienna* in the 1780s, by Johann Pezzl, observed that Ottoman subject populations were in fact a recognizable presence in the streets of the Habsburg capital:

Armenians, Wallachians and Moldavians, with their half-Oriental costumes, are not uncommon. The Serbians with their twisted moustaches occupy a whole street. The Greeks in their wide heavy dress can be seen in hordes, smoking their long-stemmed pipes in the coffee-houses on the Leopoldstädter Bridge. And the bearded Muslims in yellow mules, with their broad, murderous knives in their belts, lurch heavily through the muddy streets.[60]

The knives seemed to make the Muslims in Vienna somewhat fearsome, but their appearance, like that of the other Ottoman subject populations, was also highly theatrical, described by Pezzl with reference to costumes and props that could easily be imagined on the stage. The Serbians in the streets of Vienna had the same moustaches that were assigned to the mock-Albanians in *Così fan tutte*.

In *The Marriage of Figaro* the amorous adolescent Cherubino is humorously sent off to war by Figaro with an aria ("*Non più andrai*") that envisions the young soldier in a turban:

Tra guerrieri, poffarbacco!	Among soldiers, by Bacchus!
Gran mustacchi, stretto sacco.	Big moustaches, a narrow sack.
Schioppo in spalla, sciabla al fianco	Gun on shoulder, saber at the side
collo dritto, muso franco,	neck straight, face frank,
un gran casco, o un gran turbante,	a great helmet, or a great turban,
molto onor, poco contante!	much honor, little money![61]

Figaro seems to find it almost as easy to imagine Cherubino fighting among Turks as among Europeans, for moustaches, sabers, and especially turbans would have conjured a Turkish Janissary regiment in the minds of the Viennese public for *Figaro* in 1786.

The decisive years for Ottoman military matters, however, were those that followed, when the Habsburgs, in alliance with Russia, went to war against the Turks from 1787 to 1791. The war was fateful for Joseph, because the strains of war added to the tensions of the political resistance to his revolutionary program of enlightened reforms: 1787 was the year of the pamphlet "Why is Emperor Joseph not loved by his people?" Furthermore, it may have been at the military front that he contracted the illness that led to his early death in 1790 at the age of fifty. The war was also probably fateful for Mozart inasmuch as it drained some of the wealth from the Viennese urban economy, wealth that might otherwise have been spent on musical patronage, and in this sense the Turkish war may have contributed to bringing about Mozart's own economic downturn during the last years of his life.[62] In 1790, when Mozart composed *Così fan tutte*, the plot required that Ferrando and Guglielmo pretend to be going off to war, so they could return disguised as Albanians; in fact, the Viennese public, like Mozart and Da Ponte themselves, would have been well aware that there was a real war going on in 1790, that turbans and helmets were not merely matters of comedy as they had been for Figaro in 1786.

In the spring of 1787, before the outbreak of war, Joseph traveled abroad to join Catherine the Great on her celebrated tour of her newly annexed province of the Crimea—now decisively detached from the Ottoman empire. The Crimea offered the travelers an Oriental fantasy which they experienced as scenes from the *Thousand and One Nights* of Scheherazade. Catherine actually ruled over the Crimea, but her guests—including the Habsburg emperor Joseph, his close associate Charles-Joseph Lamoral, prince de Ligne, and the French diplomat Louis-Philippe, comte de Ségur—all experienced the Crimea as an Oriental Islamic land which lay entirely at their disposal, presented for their entertainment, subject to their Western whims. The prince de Ligne fantasized about the whole party being taken captive by Tartars and delivered to the sultan in Constantinople—an operatic fantasy, especially titillating just because it could not actually happen in a land under Russian rule.[63]

The comte de Ségur, at Bakhchisaray, noted that "we could believe ourselves veritably transported to a town in Turkey or Persia, with the only difference that we had the leisure to examine everything without having to fear any of those humiliations to which Christians are forced to submit in the Orient." Ségur dreamed that he himself was a "true pasha," especially when he was being served by the local Crimeans: "I could believe for some moments that I was a veritable Muslim prince, whose aga or bostangi came to take his sacred orders." The prince de Ligne described himself similarly, "surrounded by Tartars who watch me write, and raise their eyes in admiration, as if I were another Mohammed." He was eager to see Muslim women without their veils, enjoyed the thought that he might "convert the Muslim Tartars by making them drink wine," but also sometimes fantasized, with perverse pleasure, that he was in their power: "Am I a Turkish prisoner? Have I been thrown upon this shore by a shipwreck?"[64] In short, the travelers—with the Habsburg emperor Joseph among them—could not resist trying out the various fantasy scenarios that were also part of the *Abduction from the Seraglio*: shipwrecked in Turkey, captive in Istanbul, becoming themselves true pashas, violating Muslim laws and customs, converting the Muslims by making them drink wine. Mozart relished that same scenario in the drinking duet between Pedrillo and Osmin.

The outbreak of war between Russia and Turkey in 1787 gave the Ottomans an opportunity to try to retake the Crimea, while Catherine aimed to capture Constantinople itself. The Russians conquered the Ottoman fortress at Ochakov on the Black Sea in 1788, and in that year the Austrians joined in the military effort in accordance with Joseph's alliance with Catherine. Pezzl recorded the momentous declaration:

> After a fifty-year truce, Austria has recently begun fresh hostilities with the Ottoman Empire. On 9 February 1788 the Austrian declaration of war was made formally known to the Divan in Istanbul, the Pasha of Belgrade, and the various Turkish border officials in Bosnia, Serbia, Wallachia, Moldavia . . . Next day fighting broke out in several places. The whole of Europe has turned its attention to this spectacle, in which parts of Asia and Africa are also involved. Vienna more than anywhere else is closely involved in this affair. The activities of the Austrian army, and its fate, on the Turkish borders, are the leading topics of interest among the public.[65]

Turkey was no longer simply a subject for comic entertainment but the crucial subject—indeed spectacle—of international affairs, and the Viennese became newly aware of the long border between the Habsburg monarchy and the Ottoman empire in southeastern Europe.

Pezzl claimed to be optimistic about the outcome of the war, but his optimism did not involve complete contempt for the Turkish enemy:

> The Turks are in no sense an enemy to be despised. They have a high opinion
> of themselves; their patriotism, fanaticism, greed for money, lend them
> a high degree of personal courage. Considered individually, they may be
> counted the equals of soldiers of any army. They also have the advantage of
> an inexhaustible supply of manpower which their despotic rulers can draw
> on from Asia and Africa; on account of their modest and poor nutrition
> the cost of feeding them is only about half of what our troops require. It is
> to be presumed that superior strategy and good artillery, which habitually
> decide the outcome of wars nowadays, and in which the Turkish armies are
> particularly wanting, will be decisive here as well, and will prevail over wild
> and disorderly fighting.[66]

Pezzl showed some respect both for the courage of ordinary Turkish soldiers and for the "despotic" power of the sultan. He failed to appreciate the advances in military organization and artillery achieved by the Turks with French guidance in the 1770s and 1780s. In fact, it was the Austrian army in 1788 which suffered a disaster at Karansebesch (Caransebeş in Romania today)—where drunken soldiers mistakenly thought they were being attacked by the Ottomans and, supposedly, ended up firing on one another before retreating in disarray.

Mozart composed his three last symphonies in 1788, culminating in the Jupiter Symphony in C major, all intended for concerts, but in the wartime circumstances it remains uncertain whether those concerts ever took place. Short of income, Mozart wrote letters to plead for loans from his Masonic brother Michael Puchberg. Maynard Solomon, in his biography of Mozart, has observed that "Mozart's career difficulties and financial embarrassments could not be readily solved as long as Austrian cultural life itself was suffering the consequences of a debilitating and unpopular war against Turkey."[67] The advent of the Turkish war, however, did not mean any decline of interest in the *Abduction from the Seraglio*, which was performed in Koblenz in 1787 for the court of the archbishop-elector of Trier—a production of considerable lavishness to judge from the surviving costume designs.[68] The opera was staged in 1788 in Graz and Budapest, within the Habsburg monarchy, and outside the monarchy in Berlin, Brunswick, Hildesheim, and Königsberg. In January 1788 Mozart, who succeeded Gluck in 1787 as the court *Kammermu-*

sicus, or chamber composer, wrote dances for the Viennese Carnival balls, and one of them, "La bataille" (K.535), included elements of a Turkish march.[69]

Mozart however was also applying himself to a very different sort of Turkish music in 1788. Historian Derek Beales has noted that as soon as Austria went to war in 1788, Mozart composed a patriotic song (K.539), making use of an older set of lyrics, *"Ich möchte wohl der Kaiser sein"* (I wish I were the emperor). "The Muslims would tremble," the song continued. "Constantinople would be mine!"[70] Here Mozart musically imagined himself as Joseph, the conqueror of Constantinople—and, strangely, he made use of Turkish percussion to emphasize the bellicose braggadocio of the music and lyrics.

Beales further notes that Mozart composed later in 1788, indeed the day after finishing the Jupiter Symphony, another patriotic song (K.552) for the war against the Turks, "Beim Auszug in das Feld" (On leaving for the front).[71] Patriotism once again meant a celebration of Joseph—this time as a hero of the Enlightenment. In the spirit of Lessing's *Nathan the Wise*, the lyrics affirmed a spirit of perfect ecumenism:

> For human beings everywhere
> Are God Almighty's creatures;
> Heathen and Turk, Christian and Jew
> Are all alike his children.[72]

According to the lyrics it was Joseph who translated this enlightened wisdom into state policy through his edict of toleration in 1781 for Protestants and Orthodox, extended to Jews by a further edict of 1782:

> Thus Joseph, like a God on earth,
> Showed Turks and Jews toleration,
> And shielded them from oppression and hurt
> And sought peace for every nation.[73]

The Turks, however, allegedly refused to accept this prescription for universal peace:

> This one believes itself the only chosen race
> And knows no other brothers;
> And knows no right but its own hand
> And no duty but murder,
> So that many a lovely land
> Has sunk in waste and horror.[74]

If Mozart was capable of infusing the *Abduction* with a good-natured spirit of qualified sympathy for the Turks, he was in wartime also quite able to compose something more hostile for the occasion. In "Beim Auszug in das Feld" the moral model of enlightened absolutism was Joseph, and the Turks were the one people more than any other who needed to be taught, by military force, the lessons of the Enlightenment.

The Habsburg army under Field Marshal Ernst von Laudon conquered Belgrade from the Turks in 1789, a proud victory recalling the previous conquest of Belgrade in 1717 by the legendary Habsburg general Prince Eugene of Savoy. Belgrade had been restored to Ottoman rule after the Habsburg-Ottoman war of 1737–39, and would be returned to the Turks again with the peace of Sistova in 1791. Emperor Leopold II, Joseph's brother and successor, would find it necessary to conclude Joseph's war with Turkey in a negotiated peace based on the *status quo ante*.

In 1789, however, just after the conquest of Belgrade, a spirit of patriotic triumph briefly prevailed in Vienna. According to Pezzl, the news of the victory arrived in the capital on October 12, and marked the beginning of a three-day celebration:

> On October 14, a grand Te Deum was performed in St. Stephen's Cathedral, attended by the Emperor, who rode there in full dress, escorted by his entire official retinue and by the noble guards. Every window and side street en route was crowded with spectators, and when he arrived in the Kohlmarkt, a hundred thousand hands applauded, and in the Graben he was greeted with deafening cheers. A cavalry regiment paraded before the church, and a battalion of grenadiers with green battle insignia on their caps fired a triple salvo during the singing of the Te Deum. With each salvo of the grenadiers, fifty cannon all around the city walls thundered out the victory signal.[75]

In 1782 Mozart had staged the celebration of Pasha Selim at the Hoftheater as a bid for Joseph's favor. Now, in 1789, the whole city of Vienna—from the Kohlmarkt to the Graben to St. Stephen's—became a theatrical site for staging the celebration of Joseph as the conqueror of the Turks.

At the beginning of Joseph's reign he could be celebrated as a pasha under the sign of magnanimity. By the end of his reign, with his authority in crisis, his reforms under assault, with rebellions in Hungary and the Austrian Netherlands, and his health past recovery, the moment for magnanimity was past. In 1789 Joseph resorted to the rituals of pomp and power, while the Viennese celebrated the taking of Belgrade in their own urban fashion, as recounted by Pezzl:

> In the evening entrance to the theaters was free, and as night fell there began a spectacle I shall remember with pleasure all my life. The night was fine, dry and clear, the air mild. Within an hour the whole of Vienna was lit up from the first-floor windows to the attics. . . . Some of the great houses handed out free wine and beer; from others money was thrown among the crowd. . . . The celebrations continued all night long: at 6 o'clock in the morning bands of musicians were still wending their way through the most crowded streets.[76]

For Mozart the most notable aspects of the occasion might have been the opening of the theaters and the presence of the musical bands, which suggested opportunities for a composer. In fact, Mozart composed two dances to mark the Habsburg military campaigns (one of them even called "The Siege of Belgrade") and a piece for mechanical organ to commemorate Field Marshal Laudon, the conqueror of Belgrade, after his death in 1790.[77] War against the Turks offered such limited musical opportunities as these for Mozart, even as it created difficulties for the performance of his symphonies and contributed to his financial hardship.

Suna Suner has discovered that in Belgrade itself in 1791, during the brief period of Habsburg occupation, the traveling theater company of Johann Christian Kuntz performed a German version of Favart's *Three Sultanas* in a Turkish mosque, which was blasphemously adapted as a theater for musical comedy. Mozart's *Abduction* was also in the repertory of the Kuntz company, and may also have been considered for possible performance in the Belgrade mosque.[78]

In London, on New Year's Day 1791, an English comic opera titled *The Siege of Belgrade* commented allusively on the current war, though the plot actually concerned the fifteenth-century Ottoman siege of the city. The composer Stephen Storace borrowed elements of the plot and much of the music from Vicente Martín y Soler's *Una cosa rara*, created in Vienna in 1786 with a Spanish rather than Turkish scenario. In London the Irish tenor Michael Kelly (Mozart's friend in Vienna) sang the role of the Turkish commander, the Seraskier, and Storace's sister Nancy (Mozart's original Susanna in the *Marriage of Figaro*) took the part of the Seraskier's captive. The melody of Mozart's "Rondo alla turca" was used in the opera to set a Turkish tone, thus linking Mozart to Ottoman warfare at the very beginning of the year, 1791, when Vienna would have to return Belgrade to the Turks—the year which would end in December with Mozart's death.[79]

Conclusion: The Catalogue of Turkish Conquests

In 1789, the year of the fall of Belgrade, the last triumph of Joseph's reign, the Ottoman sultan Abdülhamid I died in Istanbul and was succeeded by his nephew Selim III. While the viziers of Abdülhamid had undertaken the modernization of the Ottoman military force, the young Selim, not yet twenty-eight at his accession, was open to more generally modernizing, even Westernizing, reforms. Though his reign overlapped with that of Joseph by only a year, and Selim belonged to another generation, the young Turkish sultan ruled in a spirit somewhat related to that of Josephine enlightened absolutism, with bold reforms of the Ottoman army, the feudal structure, and the state administration.[80] Like Joseph, Selim called forth much animosity among his less enlightened subjects, especially in the Janissary corps, and unlike Joseph, he was actually killed by his enemies in a palace coup, murdered in the harem in 1808. The conspiracy was supposed to have involved one of the chief eunuchs. In the *Abduction* Mozart uncannily anticipated the tensions of Selim's reign, between enlightened and unenlightened forces within the Ottoman empire: imagine the *Abduction from the Seraglio* concluding with Osmin conspiring to murder Pasha Selim.

Sultan Selim III was just five years younger than Mozart, and though Mozart would not live long enough to appreciate the new sultan's qualities, there is no doubt that Selim would have been his ideal exemplar of an Ottoman despot. For above and beyond Selim's enlightened perspective and openness to Europe, the new sultan was also a musician and composer of considerable distinction, as well as a generous patron of musicians. Selim's compositions are still performed today as Turkish classical music, and in his own time he was an instrumental performer on the *tanbur*, an Ottoman lute, and the *ney*, an Ottoman flute. This latter talent would have made him the perfect model for Mozart's last opera, *The Magic Flute*, in 1791, about a young prince who plays the flute and searches for the path to enlightenment. In 1797 Selim actually sponsored a European opera performance in the Topkapi palace. According to the French consul it was the sultan who took the initiative: "The sultan wanted to enjoy the spectacle of a comedy. He summoned some Italians who were in Pera, and staged a piece. The sweetness and charm of the Italian music appeared not to touch Selim." The opera itself remains unknown, but the Turkish court chronicle was unfavorable: "An elaborate Frankish play known as Opera was performed in which a sort of shabby playing, reminiscent of our male impersonator performances . . . is watched by the Franks displaying Frankish behavior." The negative judgment suggests some tension surrounding the introduction of this European (or "Frankish") entertainment into Topkapi.[81]

The death of Joseph in February 1790, at the nadir of his popularity, signaled the end of the Enlightenment's greatest experiment in philosophical absolutism, and indeed the French Revolution of 1789 already marked the beginning of a very different approach to enlightened politics. Mozart's decade in Vienna coincided almost precisely with Joseph's reign, and the composer's initial hopes of winning the emperor's favor had been only partly satisfied by obtaining the post of court chamber composer in 1787. With Leopold's succession, Mozart, notably in debt, had no time to be sentimental about Joseph but turned immediately to seeking the new emperor's favor, putting himself forward unsuccessfully for positions as Kapellmeister and as music teacher to the Habsburg family. He traveled to Frankfurt at his own expense to be present for Leopold's imperial coronation, hoping to find musical opportunities, and was present for a performance there of the *Abduction from the Seraglio*.[82] The time for Turkish political parables was past, however, as Leopold sought to disengage from Joseph's war. When Mozart attended Leopold's royal coronation as king of Bohemia in Prague in 1791, the composer had a new operatic commission and presented *La clemenza di Tito*. The model of magnanimous absolutism was no longer a Turkish pasha but a Roman emperor. Benjamin Perl has raised the question of whether Mozart's final opera, *The Magic Flute*, with its elaborate Egyptianisms, might be considered as a sort of Masonic transformation of the "Turkish" structure of the *Abduction*: the basso Sarastro taking Pamina captive in his temple, guarded by the Moor Monostatos, with Tamino as the tenor intruder come to abduct the captive. The formerly magnanimous Ottoman pasha could thus have been reconceived as a magnanimous Masonic grand master.[83]

While Mozart was in Prague for Emperor Leopold's Bohemian coronation in 1791, there was also a Prague performance of *Don Giovanni*, which was attended by Leopold himself.[84] *Don Giovanni* had been originally composed for Prague in 1787, at a time when the Prague public seemed more interested than the Vienna public in Mozart's music. Emperor Joseph attended a performance of *Don Giovanni* in Vienna in December 1788. According to Volkmar Braunbehrens, "It was his [Joseph's] first public appearance since returning from the [Ottoman] war, and the audience gave him such an insultingly cold and indifferent reception that he left long before the end of the opera."[85] By 1788 Joseph no longer appeared at the opera as a brilliant beacon of enlightened absolutism, as he had at the premiere of the *Abduction* in July 1782, back when both emperor and composer had such high hopes of the decade before them—and when the Turkish subject of the opera seemed both entertaining, edifying, and reassuringly remote.

Though Joseph walked out of *Don Giovanni* he probably stayed long enough to witness its celebrated reference to Turkey. Early in the first act Don Giovanni's servant Leporello enumerates his master's sexual conquests in the "catalogue" aria, "*Madamina*," and the aria includes a breakdown by country of origin:

In Italia seicento e quaranta,	In Italy 640,
In Lamagna duecento e trentuna,	In Germany 231,
Cento in Francia,	100 in France,
in Turchia novantuna,	91 in Turkey,
Ma ma ma in Ispagna,	But, but, but in Spain,
Ma in Ispagna son gia mille e tre.	But in Spain already 1003.[86]

Da Ponte the Venetian librettist, collaborating in Vienna with Mozart, thus offered a catalogue of Don Giovanni's women in which Turkey was fully, and casually, integrated into Europe, alongside Italy, Germany, France, and Spain. There was nothing exceptional or exotic about Turkey in this presentation, and in spite of its relative cultural remoteness within the Islamic world, the count of ninety-one was only a little behind that of Christian France. In the *Abduction* the Turkish pasha Selim loves one Christian woman in his harem, and that circumstance constitutes the central drama of the entire opera. In *Don Giovanni* the great European seducer has made love to ninety-one Turkish women before the opera even begins. Mozart and Da Ponte in some sense registered Turkey as an unexceptional European country when they included it on Don Giovanni's list in casual conjunction with Italy, Germany, France, and Spain.

At the same time, Don Giovanni's sensational libertinism seemed to bear some relation to conventions of Turkishness on the operatic stage. The comical pasha in *La caravane du Caire* is bored with his harem, and commiserates with his faithful eunuch, while the pasha in the *Abduction* seems only able to love the one captive woman who absolutely refuses his marks of favor. The romantic rewards of Ottoman polygamy appeared very poor indeed in the comic operas of the eighteenth century, but *Don Giovanni*, in 1787, demonstrated a libertine life of serial European polygamy, the protagonist taking pleasure in his seductions right up to the moment when he was dragged down to hell. Benjamin Perl has observed that some of Don Giovanni's music—such as the "champagne" aria, "*Fin ch'han dal vino*"—may have Turkish aspects, and that Leporello's catalogue could be considered "a harem in book form."[87] The sexual prerogatives of Turkish masculinity achieved their most compelling incarnation in the form of the European libertine, just as the political prerogatives of Turkish despotism served as a dramatic foil for the better appreciation of European figures and institutions of authority.

In the finale of the *Abduction* a Janissary chorus sings in the *alla turca* style to celebrate Pasha Selim and the beneficent exercise of enlightened absolutism. The cymbals crash and the bass drum pounds as the chorus sings, "*Bassa Selim lebe lange, Ehre sei sein Eigenthum*" (Long live Pasha Selim, may honor be his portion). In 1778, when Mozart first contemplated writing a German opera for Vienna, for Joseph's National Singspiel, the composer was determined to create a work "to honor the Emperor" (*dem Kaiser Ehre zu machen*).[88] From the beginning Mozart envisioned an Ottoman subject, initially *Zaide* and eventually the *Abduction*, for his German opera. With the concluding Janissary chorus of the *Abduction*, Mozart was able to affirm the honor of both Pasha Selim and Emperor Joseph in an age of enlightened absolutism.

THE OTTOMAN ADVENTURES OF
ROSSINI AND NAPOLEON
Kaimacacchi and Missipipi at La Scala

Introduction: The Composer as Conqueror

"Since the death of Napoleon," declared Stendhal, "there has been another man spoken of every day in Moscow and Naples, London and Vienna, Paris and Calcutta." Stendhal, with his characteristic sense of irony, was writing about the composer Gioachino Rossini, implicitly making him the successor to Napoleon, a new world conqueror whose empire had been achieved at a precociously young age. Stendhal published his *Vie de Rossini* in 1824, when Rossini triumphantly arrived to establish himself in Paris, three years after Napoleon's death on Saint Helena in 1821. Rossini was already the most celebrated operatic composer in Restoration Europe: "The glory of this man knows no other limits than those of civilization itself," according to Stendhal.[1]

Rossini had established his celebrity in Italy a decade earlier, while Napoleon still ruled over all of Europe. Born on the Adriatic Sea at Pesaro in 1792, Rossini was a teenager when his earliest operatic works were performed in Venice, then part of the Napoleonic Kingdom of Italy. In 1812, the year of the fateful invasion of Russia, the twenty-year-old Rossini conquered La Scala in Milan, the capital of the kingdom, with *La pietra del paragone*. It was also a Turkish triumph inasmuch as one of the most celebrated scenes brought the principal character on stage in Turkish disguise. This comic device—recalling the musical Turkishness in *Le bourgeois gentilhomme* from the seventeenth century—was notably used in the eighteenth century by Goldoni and Haydn to deceive the apothecary Sempronio and by Da Ponte and Mozart in *Così fan tutte* with its Ottoman Albanian disguises.

In 1813 Rossini had a huge triumph in Venice with *L'italiana in Algeri*, the same year that Napoleon was disastrously defeated at the battle of Leipzig. *L'italiana* was a comedy of Turkish captivity that followed and transcended the precedent of Mozart's *Abduction* thirty years before. If Rossini was a conqueror of European opera houses from Vienna to Naples, his heroine Isabella, the Italian girl in Algiers, was herself a conqueror who utterly vanquished her besotted Turkish admirer, Mustafa the Bey of Algiers.

Following the travesty of Turkishness in *La pietra del paragone* in 1812, *L'italiana in Algeri* in 1813 inaugurated a Turkish operatic program that Rossini would pursue in the comedy of *Il turco in Italia* in 1814 and in the tragedy of *Maometto Secondo* in 1820, when the musical conqueror Rossini would encounter the Ottoman sultan Mohammed the Conqueror. With these works of the early nineteenth century Rossini produced a final flourishing of Turkish figures on the European operatic stage. For more than a hundred years, musical and dramatic representations intersected with military and diplomatic projects concerning the Ottoman empire; operatic productions punctuated the ongoing encounters of warfare and coexistence, shaped by contemporary values of religious difference and vectors of cultural influence. At the very end of the eighteenth century, in 1798, the young Napoleon, not yet thirty, brought about one of his most spectacular short-term military accomplishments by leading the French invasion of Ottoman Egypt. Rossini was only six years old in 1798, but he participated in the musical band of the civil guard in Pesaro, probably playing the triangle—an instrument that could also be used for "Turkish" percussion.[2] It was certainly no coincidence that in Paris in 1798 there took place the first French performance of Mozart's *Abduction from the Seraglio*, as *L'enlèvement du sérail*.

Napoleon's Invasion of Egypt and Mozart's *Abduction* in Paris

In 1782, the year of Mozart's *Abduction*, Mozart's French contemporary Constantin-François de Chasseboeuf, comte de Volney, set out on a voyage to the Ottoman empire, beginning in Egypt. Volney published in 1785 the account of his *Voyage en Égypte et en Syrie*, and then, in 1791, *Les ruines*, his reflections on the fate of empires. Volney prophesied the downfall of the Ottomans: "The day approaches when this broken colossus of power will collapse under its own weight; yes, I swear it by the ruins of so many destroyed empires." Historian Henry Laurens has suggested that such reflections on Ottoman collapse were influential on the young Napoleon and his contemporaries.[3]

Napoleon, seizing Egypt from the Mameluke government that ruled on behalf of the Ottomans, was actually aiming his blow at British interests and concerns, and the French campaign of 1798 transformed the constellation of European interests in Ottoman affairs. In the nineteenth century the geopolitical problem posed by the Ottoman empire would engage all the principal powers of the continent, and would come to be known as the Eastern Question. England and France, as much as Austria and Russia, would dedicate themselves to this question of whose interests would prevail as the Ottoman empire—"this broken colossus"—became relatively weaker, losing control and eventually sovereignty over its far-flung territories in southeastern Europe, the Middle East, and North Africa.

Napoleon's expedition of 1798 was also a landmark for the study of the Ottoman Orient, as his fighting contingents were accompanied by some 150 scholars with the assignment to study Egypt as a prize of war for European knowledge and culture. The fruits of this intellectual campaign included the discovery of the Rosetta stone, eventually the linguistic key to deciphering hieroglyphics and the founding of modern Egyptology. Edward Said has suggested that this campaign of 1798 was the starting point for modern European Orientalism, the cultivation of comprehensive knowledge of the Other that would ultimately enhance European imperial mastery over the Orient.[4]

Yet the French invaders did not explicitly insist on the absolute difference or "otherness" of Ottoman Egypt. Napoleon's proclamation to the Egyptians in 1798 announced his respect for the Prophet and the Koran, even affirming that "the French are also sincere Muslims" (as enemies of the pope) and "sincere friends of His Excellency the Ottoman Sultan." Indeed, Napoleon encouraged the rumor that he himself was actually contemplating conversion to Islam. He wrote to one of the Egyptian sheiks: "There are two great difficulties preventing my army and me from becoming Muslims. The first is circumcision, the second is wine."[5] It was a lighthearted reflection, somewhat in the spirit of Arlequin in the musical comedies of the Paris fairs of the early eighteenth century.

Napoleon only jested about the possibility of being circumcised, but the Cairo muftis took the trouble to issue a ruling that French Muslims might go to heaven even without circumcision and without abstaining from wine, and there actually were some French conversions in Egypt. Napoleon himself participated in Islamic ritual occasions, such as the birthday of Mohammed, when the French commander "dressed in Oriental costume and declared himself protector of all the religions," permitting himself to be called "Ali Bonaparte."[6] He even made himself the patron of the pilgrimage to Mecca. According to historian Juan Cole, "Bonaparte was playing the role of a Muslim sultan" and encouraged the Egyptian imams to substitute his own name for that of Sultan Selim III in Istanbul.[7] Napoleon thus promoted the semblance of some sort of convergence between the French and the Egyptians, and he preferred not to seem to rule as a Christian conqueror over Muslim subjects. Historian Maya Jasanoff writes about "Napoleon's chameleon approach" during the Egyptian expedition. It was "by making myself Muslim that I established myself in Egypt," he later explained.[8] Orientalism was deployed to bring him closer to the Muslim Egyptians rather than to emphasize the difference between Christian Europe and the Islamic Middle East.

Sultan Selim III, reciprocally, was interested in reforms that would bring some Ottoman institutions closer to European models. After becoming sultan in 1789, Selim set about purposefully creating a "new order," the Nizam-i Cedid, the same name that the Ottomans also applied to the contemporaneous French Revolution. The Ottoman Nizam-i Cedid of the 1790s undertook a modernizing reform of administration, finance, and economy as well as military organization, and Selim III took the unprecedented step of establishing permanent Ottoman embassies in the capitals of Europe: London, Paris, Vienna, and Berlin. Historian Bernard Lewis has noted that such embassies reflected a new Ottoman concern with "securing more direct and reliable information on European countries and affairs, as well as bringing Turkey into line with the normal practice of Western states." Lewis further notes the preponderance of French influence in Selim's reforms, which were advanced by French officers and teachers, French language instruction in Istanbul, and the Ottoman acquisition of French books, including the principal intellectual monument of the Enlightenment, the *Encyclopédie* of Diderot and d'Alembert.[9] Napoleon's attempted conquest of Ottoman Egypt in 1798 thus concluded a decade of reciprocal engagement between France and the Ottoman empire.

Napoleon's fleet reached Alexandria on July 1, 1798, and he won the battle of the Pyramids on July 21. On September 26, in Paris at the Lycée des Arts, there took place the first French performance of Mozart's *Abduction*, with a French libretto by Pierre-Louis Moline under the title *L'enlèvement du sérail*. The performance was apparently not a lavish one, taking place at the Lycée (founded during the Revolution) with only a harpsichord reduction of Mozart's score as prepared by Christian Gottlob Neefe (the composer of *Adelheit von Veltheim*).[10] By 1798, sixteen years after the Vienna premiere, the *Abduction* had already been performed in Amsterdam, Berlin, Budapest, Dresden, Munich, Prague, Riga, Warsaw, and many other German cities—but not in Paris. The arrival of Mozart's Turkish opera in Paris now meaningfully coincided with the arrival of Napoleon's French army in Ottoman Egypt.

Earlier in his career Moline had worked as a librettist with Gluck, and wrote the French version of Gluck's *Orphée et Eurydice* for Paris in 1774. Now Moline's French version of Mozart's *Abduction* seemed to smooth over some of the more violent excesses of Osmin's Turkish rage: "*Erst geköpft, dann gehangen, dann gespiesst auf heisse Stangen*" (First beheaded, then hung, then impaled, on hot stakes) became "*Envieux, entreprenant, ayant l'air, fort insolent*" (Envious, enterprising, having an air, quite insolent).[11] Osmin's "*Ha! wie will ich triumphieren / wenn sie euch zum Richtplatz führen*" (How I will triumph when they lead you to the place of execution) became less excessively vindictive in French, indeed almost reasonable: "*Les, voilà pris ces infâmes / qui voulaient ravir nos femmes*" (Here they are, captured, these infamous men, who wanted to carry off our women).[12] This Ottoman resentment might have seemed plausible enough at a moment when French soldiers were looking for sex in Ottoman Egypt.

Eugène de Beauharnais, the son of Josephine, left an account of French soldiers in a harem in Cairo: "We found in that harem soldiers of different regiments giving themselves over to all the excess and brutality that a long privation could, while not excusing it, at least allow us to understand."[13] The adventure was interrupted and discipline was imposed on the soldiers, but the indulgent inclination of Beauharnais in Cairo—to understand, if not to excuse—would have been echoed by the humor of the French public in Paris, enjoying Osmin's resentment against the Europeans "who wanted to carry off our women." In a similar spirit, Parisians might have imagined participating in Osmin's duet with Pedrillo, as rendered by Moline: "*goûtons de ce vin char-mant*" (let's taste this charming wine).[14]

The concluding vaudeville, which Mozart and Stephanie had created to celebrate Pasha Selim on stage, and by refraction Joseph II in the audience, became in Paris in 1798 a more general rococo celebration of pleasure. The vaudeville refrain—"*Wer so viel Huld vergessen kann / den seh' man mit Ver-achtung an*" (Whoever can forget such benevolence / let him be regarded with contempt)—became "*Il faut répandre des bienfaits / pour goûter des plaisirs parfaits*" (It is necessary to spread around good deeds / in order to enjoy perfect pleasures).[15] The notion of spreading around *bienfaits*—good deeds or benefits—was vaguely consistent with a Napoleonic imperial message, as if encouraging Europe and Turkey (or France and Egypt in 1798) to develop reciprocally beneficial relations. Napoleon would have seen himself as bring-ing *bienfaits* to all the lands that he conquered. Yet the reward of "perfect pleasures," as proposed by Moline, was entirely rococo and would have fit nicely into the libretto of Rameau's *Les Indes galantes*; certainly it was very far from the pointed moral and political message of Mozart and Stephanie in Vienna in 1782.

Within Moline's concluding vaudeville verses, Pasha Selim was also cele-brated by name, which would have acquired a new relevance in 1798 when Se-lim was the name of the actual reigning Ottoman sultan, Selim III. Looking to Europe and especially to France for advisers and examples as he pursued his regime of reform, Selim established regular diplomatic relations with revolu-tionary France in the 1790s, exchanging ambassadors: General Jean-Baptiste Aubert-Dubayet to Istanbul, Seyyid Ali Efendi to Paris. Under these circum-stances the celebration of Pasha Selim on the stage in Paris could have been construed as a contemporary allusion. Indeed, Napoleon originally claimed that he was coming to Egypt on behalf of Selim III and Ottoman authority, in order to discipline the insubordinate Egyptians.

The performance of *L'enlèvement du sérail* in Paris in 1798 celebrated a comical triumph over the Turks, consistent with the Napoleonic invasion of Egypt, and also held out the hopeful prospect for a future of Franco-Otto-man cooperation. Ottoman magnanimity at the end of the opera even sug-gested a sort of theatrical reconciliation with the forces of French imperial-ism in 1798. In the same year, 1798, François-Adrien Boieldieu, composing in a somewhat Mozartean style, presented his opera *Zoraïme et Zulnar*, set in Moorish Granada, performed at the Salle Favart of the Opéra-Comique. Like Mozart in the *Abduction*, Boieldieu made use of Janissary triangles for a sort of Turkish march (albeit in Muslim Spain), and he used Janissary instrumentation again for *Le calife de Bagdad* at the Opéra-Comique in 1800.[16] In Napoleonic Milan, in February 1799, the Egyptian adventure was celebrated explicitly with a ballet at La Scala entitled *I francesi in Egitto* (The French in Egypt), choreographed by Urbano Garzia.[17] The ballet presented a cruel pasha of Alexandria and an unhappy female captive, to be liberated in this case by Napoleon himself.[18]

In September 1798 Haydn's "Missa in Angustiis," a mass for troubled times, was composed and performed for the Esterházy family in honor of the name day of Princess Maria Esterházy. The designation of "*angustiis*" probably referred to the troubled times of war with revolutionary France, and the composition of the mass actually coincided with Napoleon's invasion of Egypt; the mass would later be designated as the "Nelson Mass," recalling Horatio Nelson's naval victory over the French at the Battle of the Nile in August 1798. The research of musicologist Jeremiah McGrann has shown that the name day of the princess would have also coincided with the festival of the Holy Name of the Virgin Mary, which ever since September 12, 1683, had been particularly associated with the victory over the Turks at the siege of Vienna. The Esterházy princes sometimes celebrated the annual occasion with "Turkish music"—and in 1798 Haydn's mass "*in angustiis*" created an implicit connection between the once momentous Habsburg wars against the Ottomans and the current Habsburg engagement against the French.[19]

In Vienna in 1800 Napoleon's expedition to Egypt was also dramatized in musical theater with a work entitled *Heroine, oder die schöne Griechin in Alexandria* (Heroine, or the beautiful Greek girl of Alexandria), written by Karl Friedrich Hensler with music by Wenzel Müller. In this work it was not a despotic Turk who tried to use his arbitrary power to victimize the Greek girl—but rather a lustful French officer. The drama, *Heroine*, created from the Viennese perspective, was anti-French and therefore pro-Turkish. The French were mockingly shown as they attempted to decipher Egyptian hieroglyphics in order to discover the secret treasures of the land. In the final scene, the French defense of Alexandria was compromised by a Jewish agent, acting for the Turks, who laced the French wine with opium so that the Muslim army could reconquer the city. Mozart's joke in the *Abduction* involved overcoming the Turkish resistance to alcohol, thus intoxicating Osmin, but in *Heroine* Viennese humor contemplated the drugging of the oenophile French army.[20]

Napoleon returned from Egypt to France in 1799 after defeating the Ottoman army at Aboukir, but thereafter the French army, facing Egyptian resistance as well as Ottoman and British forces, had to withdraw from Egypt in 1801. The peace treaty of Paris in 1802 ended the war between France and the Ottoman empire, and soon led to the resumption of French influence in Ottoman reform and Selim's recognition of Napoleon as emperor of France. The French officer Horace Sébastiani participated in Turkish resistance to the British naval assault on Constantinople in 1807.[21] It was in part Turkish resentment of French influence that led to Selim's deposition in 1807, following a rebellion of soldiers who refused to wear modern uniforms in the European style. Selim was succeeded very briefly by his cousin Mustafa IV and then, in 1808, by Mahmud II. One Ottoman chronicler, writing from a traditional perspective, noted the supposedly sinister influence of the French at that time:

> Certain [Ottoman] sensualists, naked of the garment of loyalty, from time to time learned politics from them [the French] . . . [and] desirous of learning their language, took French teachers, acquired their idiom, and prided themselves . . . on their uncouth talk. In this way they were able to insinuate Frankish customs in the hearts and endear their modes of thought to the minds of some people of weak mind and shallow faith.[22]

One of the bastions of traditional resistance to reform and foreign influence was the Janissary corps of soldiers, whose military bands had signified musical Turkishness to the European public dating back to the early eighteenth century. In 1808, when Selim was murdered in the harem, the Janissaries were triumphant.

In 1809 Napoleon defeated the Austrians and occupied Vienna, imposing the Treaty of Schönbrunn; he also found time to play chess against the mechanical Turk in Vienna and could not win a game, even though he tried to unsettle the automaton by making incorrect moves.[23] In 1810 the Oriental Academy in Vienna presented a drama in Ottoman Turkish composed by the students of the school: *Hadji Bektash or The Creation of the Janissaries.* The school was originally founded in 1754 under Maria Theresa to encourage the study of Oriental languages for diplomatic purposes, and the great nine-teenth-century Ottoman historian Joseph von Hammer-Purgstall received his early linguistic training there in the late eighteenth century, before being dispatched to Istanbul. The 1810 drama suggested a real seriousness of inter-est in Ottoman language, Ottoman history, and the Janissaries in particular. Thomas Chabert, who came from an originally French family of Istanbul dragomans, was a teacher at the Oriental Academy in Vienna and was named as the author when *Hadji Bektash* was published.[24]

The French introduction to the Ottoman text, probably written by Chabert, noted that "the principal purpose was to exercise the students of the Academy," furthering their knowledge of the Ottoman language, but also "to amuse the spectators" with details of Islamic religion and Ottoman history. The story concerned Sultan Murad I, representing his founding of the Janis-saries and his public commitment to Islam, under the influence of the Bek-tashi dervishes. The drama was to demonstrate "the initiation of the dervish-es, their different dances, their religious exercises, and their music"—so this was, at least in part, a work of musical theater, possibly including the musical style that was already well known in Vienna as Janissary music. The drama of 1810 was intended to represent "everything that characterizes this famous corps of Janissaries who, since their creation, have dethroned so many sover-eigns, and in recent times have incited two terrible revolutions of which Selim III and Mustafa IV have been the victims."[25] In Vienna, at least, there was no doubt that theatrical representations of Ottoman history reflected an interest in contemporary Ottoman affairs.

Napoleonic Personae and Operatic Ottomans in Paris

In 1802, the year that Napoleon was confirmed as First Consul for Life, and in 1803, with the beginning of the war of the Third Coalition, the themes of war, conquest, and world domination were also pursued upon the operatic stage in Paris. The German composer Peter Winter had his French opera *Ta-merlan* presented in Paris in 1802, composed to the libretto created (though not performed) back in the 1780s by Étienne Morel de Chédeville.[26] Also the author of the libretto for Grétry's *Caravan* in the 1780s, Morel de Chédeville envisioned his *Tamerlan* as a transposition of Voltaire's drama *L'orphelin de la Chine*, retelling the story of Genghis Khan as that of Tamerlane. Capitalizing on the huge eighteenth-century success of the operatic tragedy of Bajazet, Morel de Chédeville (now "Citoyen Morel") began where Piovene left off. The curtain rises on the interior of a mosque in Adrianople with a mufti exclaiming, "*Bajazet et mort!*" (Bajazet is dead!). A chorus of Turks then responds:

O perte irréparable!	Oh irreparable loss!
O malheur effroyable!	Oh horrifying misfortune![27]

Thus Bajazet's death, one of the recurrent sensations of eighteenth-century opera, was further dramatically appreciated as tragedy within the context of its operatic sequel.

In 1802 the public would already have recognized in the great conqueror Tamerlane a historical counterpart to the great conqueror Napoleon. Winter composed a chorus in celebration of Tamerlane:

Honneur au héros vaillant;	Honor to the valiant hero;
Qu'il règne, qu'il soit puissant:	May he reign, and be powerful:
Du monde il brise les chaînes.	He breaks the chains of the world.[28]

There were seventeen performances of *Tamerlan* in 1802 and 1803 and a brief revival of four performances in 1815, as if to mark Napoleon's downfall with a nostalgic last sounding of imperial pride. England went to war against Napoleon in 1803, and a British cartoon of that year showed a miniature Napoleon imprisoned in a cage and on display; the cartoon was titled "The Corsican Bajazet in London."[29] The Turkishness of the Napoleonic phenomenon was recognized on both sides of the Channel.

It was in London in 1805 that the celebrated Italian diva Giuseppina Grassini triumphed as the heroine of Peter Winter's opera *Zaira*, based on Voltaire's play, with a libretto sometimes attributed to Lorenzo Da Ponte.[30] Grassini was supposed to have been Napoleon's lover (and later the lover of the duke of Wellington), but London was one of the few great European opera cities where Napoleon absolutely could not have gone to see her performance in 1805. She was, however, painted as Zaira in her Oriental-Turkish costume, so that Napoleon himself, or any other male viewer of the painting (by Elisabeth Vigée-Lebrun), could imagine himself as the sultan who loved her with extreme passion and fatal jealousy.[31]

In Paris in 1803 at the Opéra-Comique there appeared a one-act comedy,

Le médecin Turc, about a Turkish doctor in Constantinople with an amorous eye for his French slave, set to music by Nicolas Isouard, including Janissary instruments.[32] In the same year, 1803, Louis Jadin's *Mahomet II* was presented at the Paris Opéra, offering the scenario of the most unambivalently triumphant Ottoman sultan, Mehmed (or Mohammed) the Conqueror, the man who breached the walls of Constantinople in 1453. Jadin's treatment of 1803 was certainly inspired by the Napoleonic moment, reflecting some sense that the French public was ready to appreciate a maximally ambitious conqueror, even in Turkish costume—though the opera sputtered and failed after only three performances. The date of the first performance, 21 Thermidor, or August 9, suggests that if it had been more successful, the run would have culminated in a birthday performance for Napoleon on August 15.

The role of Mahomet II—performed by Martin-Joseph Adrien, a leading bass of the Paris Opéra—would have been pointedly received by the French public in the context of contemporary events, as if the Ottoman conqueror were now expressing the Napoleonic perspective:

J'ai laissé trop longtemps reposer mon tonnerre;
Mais bientôt du croissant les glorieux drapeaux,
Vont, en se déployant, épouvanter la terre . . .

I have too long left my thunder at rest;
But soon the glorious flags of the crescent,
Will be unfurled to go forth and terrify the earth . . .[33]

In the end, the chorus celebrates the sultan's prospective universal dominion with lyrics reflecting the hyperbolic scale of Napoleonic ambition:

Nous voulons, sous votre puissance,	We want, under your power,
Ranger et la terre et les mers,	To range over the earth and the seas,
Et que du trône de Byzance,	And from the throne of Byzantium,
Vous commandiez à l'univers.	You may command the universe.[34]

The French public was thus treated to a celebration of Ottoman power at the very moment when the Turks had actually fought off the French invasion of Egypt and Syria and achieved a decorous peace in 1802. In fact, Mehmed the Conqueror had been made into a mirror for Napoleon himself, whose aspirations to universal empire could be confirmed in song by the chorus.

The sultan, who loves a Christian captive within the plot of the opera, finally renounces romance in the name of military glory:

> Mahomet, pour jamais, vient de vaincre l'amour,
> Et son coeur sans retour
> S'abandonne a la gloire.
> A l'ivresse, au plaisir, consacrez le grand jour;
> Demain je vous conduis aux champs de la victoire.

> Mehmet forever has conquered love,
> And his heart irrevocably
> Abandons itself to glory.
> You may dedicate today to inebriation and pleasure;
> Tomorrow I will conduct you to the fields of victory.[35]

Abandonment to glory and dedication to victory were the Napoleonic motifs that made Mehmed the Conqueror into an operatic model for Bonaparte. The pleasures of the day (preceding the battles of the morrow) were represented in a concluding ballet, with the dancers specified as Indians, Syrians, Africans, and women of the seraglio, including a troupe of Jeunes Odalisques.

Napoleon would be crowned as emperor alongside his wife, Josephine, the next year in 1804. In 1805 he would go on to his greatest victory over the Russians and Austrians at Austerlitz, a victory that would also be celebrated by Jadin with the piano piece entitled "La grande bataille d'Austerlitz." The opera *Mahomet II*, with its happy ending, seemed to point toward a brilliant future for the Napoleonic empire, and though the opera itself was a failure, the same story was staged again in 1811 as a straight play without music at the Comédie-Française. One performance took place at the Tuileries Palace in the presence of Napoleon himself and his empress (no longer Josephine, but now Marie Louise). In an introduction to the published play, the author Pierre Baour de Lormian noted that he had been accused of pilfering his plot from Jadin's opera ("performed without success some years ago"), but explained that he had simply mined the same literary source, *Histoire des amours du fameux empereur des Turcs Mahomet II,* dating back to the eighteenth century.[36] The Napoleonic moment seemed apt for the rediscovery of Mehmed and his vision of universal conquest. After the Napoleonic collapse Rossini would take up again the Ottoman subject of *Maometto Secondo*.

Jadin's *Mahomet II* at the Opéra in 1803, with its ballet of Jeunes Odalisques, was preceded by *Arlequin Odalisque* in 1800 (Messidor, *an 8*) at the Théâtre des Troubadours, and followed by *Arlequin à Maroc* in 1804 (Thermidor, *an* 12) at the Théâtre des Jeunes Artistes.[37] These adventures of Arlequin explored Ottoman and Islamic themes in the comical spirit of the popular theater where Turkishness also abounded in the Napoleonic period. In 1800 there was performed in Paris a popular drama by Joseph Aude at the Théâtre de l'Ambigu, *Madame Angot au sérail de Constantinople*. Madame Angot was a Paris fishwife, *poissarde*, of comical vulgarity; usually performed by a man in drag, she was in this case doubly cross-dressed in a Turkish female costume, and mockingly made to believe that she had been chosen by the sultan to become—like Arlequin—a sultana.[38]

In March 1811 there was a one-act comedy performed at the Théâtre des Variétés in Montmartre: *Mahomet Barbe-Bleue, ou La terreur des Ottomanes* (Mahomet Bluebeard, or The terror of the Ottomans). The piece was described as a "burlesque"—presumably a satire on the drama of *Mahomet II* (by Baour de Lormian), which was performed at the Comédie-Française a few weeks before. The premise of the burlesque—which included songs— was that Bluebeard had come from France to Turkey and taken the name of Mahomet. He amorously courts the Greek captive in his Turkish harem by offering to entertain her with comical cruelties that might have been borrowed from the works of the Marquis de Sade:

Faut-il faire fouetter un page,	Must I have a page whipped,
Ou faut-il le faire étrangler?	Or must I have him strangled?
D'un esclave, acceptant l'hommage,	Accepting the homage of a slave,
Voulez-vous le voir empaler?	Would you like to see him impaled?[39]

Though Mahomet Bluebeard has murdered several wives in France ("reading the *Thousand and One Nights* had excited my imagination"), he is better behaved in Turkey. "Since you came to this barbarous country," observes his secretary, "your customs have become milder." Mahomet replies, "That is because in Turkey a man is not obliged to kill his wife in order to take another."[40] Indeed, the same was now true for France, where Napoleon had divorced Josephine and married the Habsburg archduchess Marie Louise in 1810. *Mahomet Barbe-Bleue* was performed at the Théâtre des Variétés on March 30, 1811, ten days after Empress Marie Louise gave birth to Napoleon's heir, the infant King of Rome, born on March 20.

In 1811 the *Thousand and One Nights* also excited the imagination of the young German composer Carl Maria von Weber, whose one-act Singspiel *Abu Hassan* was set in the Baghdad of Caliph Harun al-Rashid and performed in

Munich. With Mozart in mind, Weber made use of Janissary style to celebrate the wisdom of the caliph, whose beneficent justice resolved the comical plot.[41] Conceived as a speaking role, the figure of the caliph offered some allusion to the operatic precedent of Pasha Selim, but probably also some reflection of the mystique of Napoleon and the judicial enlightenment of the Napoleonic Code. Weber would return to the Baghdad of Harun al-Rashid in London in 1826 when the composer presented his last opera, *Oberon*.

In Paris in 1811 another work of popular musical theater explored the theme of Turkish pashas and their harems at the Théâtre du Vaudeville: *Les pages au sérail* (The pages in the seraglio). This work concerns a geographically specific Ottoman dignitary, the pasha of Smyrna, who has two captive French girls in his seraglio, Zoe and Julie. They have, so far, resisted his amorous advances, and he has, so far, not forced himself upon them. As Julie remarks, "In fact, for a Turk, he has extremely polite manners," and these polite manners are supposed to have been formed during a voyage to France. Zoe sings a song in tribute to Paris:

Paris est la brillante école	Paris is the brilliant school
Ou l'Europe entière s'instruit	Where all Europe learns
L'art d'être leger et frivole . . .	The art of being light and frivolous . . .[42]

Zoe and Julie have also learned those arts, such that their enslavement to the pasha becomes a kind of extended flirtation. Eventually, a French count comes to visit Smyrna, accompanied by two pages who turn out to be the girls' French lovers. After a frivolous cross-dressing episode—the pages dressed as harem girls, the girls dressed as pages—the lovers are reunited, and the pasha lives up to his French manners by showing that he conforms to the French model of a generous Turk.

Musical historian David Chaillou has studied Napoleon and the Paris Opéra, and has concluded that opera played a significant role in amplifying the glory of the emperor, who therefore naturally took an interest in the repertory and its political implications.[43] Chaillou further suggests that opera performances became a kind of "political ritual" with Napoleon as the "principal protagonist" of the occasion: "He dominated the public physically by his place in the hall and symbolically through the gods, kings, and heroes represented on the stage." Napoleon at the opera thus created "a connection between contemporary political events and fiction, between reality and myth."[44]

In this regard, it is interesting to note that according to Chaillou's count, the most frequently performed opera at the Académie Imperiale (that is, the Paris Opéra) between 1810 and 1815 was Grétry's *Caravan of Cairo*, dating back to 1783 and still holding the stage.[45] The political hero of the opera, in the end, was the magnanimous pasha of Cairo, ironically serving as a mirror for Napoleon, who had himself tried to conquer Egypt in 1798.

Kaimacacchi and Missipipi at La Scala

Napoleon Bonaparte was the French general who took Milan from the Habsburgs in 1796, two years before the Egyptian campaign. In 1799 La Scala presented the ballet *I francesi in Egitto* to celebrate Bonaparte. Following Napoleon's formal coronation as king of Italy on May 16, 1805, a cantata was performed on June 1 at La Scala in his honor and in his actual presence. The composer was Vincenzo Federici, who would then compose another cantata for La Scala in 1806 to celebrate Napoleon's triumphant peace settlement at Pressburg after the battle of Austerlitz in 1805 (*Il trionfo della pace di Pressburgo*). On August 15, 1807, Napoleon's birthday was celebrated at La Scala with a stage setting that represented an Egyptian temple, and on August 16 a cantata by Johann Simon Mayr was performed in honor of Saint Napoleon. Bonaparte's birthday was celebrated during the years of his imperial reign as the festival of Saint Napoleon—a saint of very dubious authenticity who was endowed with Egyptian associations by his supposed martyrdom in Alexandria in the third century. On August 16, 1809, the day after Napoleon's fortieth birthday, there was a ballet performed, *Cesare in Egitto* (Caesar in Egypt), as part of a festival dedicated to the emperor.[46] The celebration of the Egyptian adventure (long after its evident failure) thus made Ottoman scenarios an implicit part of Napoleonic culture in Milan.

Luigi Mosca's opera *L'italiana in Algeri* was performed at La Scala on August 16, 1808, suggesting some association with Napoleon's birthday. The libretto—which Rossini would make famous when he recomposed it five years later—was by Angelo Anelli, the Lombard writer who had created the libretto for the Mayr cantata in honor of Saint Napoleon the previous year.[47] In 1808, the year of Mosca's *L'italiana*, Rossini was still a sixteen-year-old composition student in Bologna, working on a mass, a cantata, and a symphony. Since Selim III was murdered in Istanbul at the end of July, the comic humiliation of Mustafa on the stage of La Scala in August would have roughly coincided with the news of the sultan's demise in Istanbul.

The ghost of a different sultan haunted La Scala in 1812, the year that Mayr composed his *Tamerlano*, an Italian treatment that followed the same story as Winter's French *Tamerlan* in Paris in 1802. Since this was the sequel to the story of Bajazet's captivity, the opera began with Bajazet already dead, and the libretto, by Luigi Romanelli, suggested that the teetering Ottoman empire was haunted by the "unavenged spirit of Bajazet."[48] The orphaned Ottoman heir Solimano was a silent role in the opera, while Bajazet, the tragic hero who sang his pride and rage in so many eighteenth-century operas, was now no more than a memory and a ghost in the operatic sequel. The glory of the Ottomans was effaced by Tamerlane on stage and by Napoleon in the actual historical moment—though by 1812 the Napoleonic enterprise was already at the limit of its glory and on the brink of its collapse.

While the great international event of 1812 was Napoleon's invasion of Russia, it was immediately preceded that year by the end of the Russian-Ottoman war with the Treaty of Bucharest between Tsar Alexander I and Sultan Mahmud II. The war, ongoing since 1806, culminated in a victory by General Mikhail Kutuzov on the Danube in 1811. The treaty of 1812 then compelled the Ottomans to cede Bessarabia to Russia—which left the Russians, and Kutuzov in particular, free to focus on the Napoleonic invasion. The new concessions by the Ottomans in 1812, coinciding with Napoleon's most audacious military adventure, formed the international context for the performance of Rossini's *La pietra del paragone* and Mayr's *Tamerlano* at La Scala.

Tamerlano, opening in December 1812, was moderately successful with twenty-four performances at La Scala, but it followed the even greater success of *La pietra del paragone* which had already opened in September and ran for fifty-three performances.[49] The veteran Romanelli, born in Rome in 1751, was the librettist for both works, conjuring the tragic Ottoman ghost of Bajazet from an earlier operatic tradition, but only after participating in the creation of Rossini's brand-new operatic comedy with its brilliantly successful farcical deployment of Turkish disguise.

La pietra del paragone (The touchstone) is set in a country house in Italy, and the plot involves the wealthy Count Asdrubale testing the affections and loyalties of his friends by the "touchstone" of a disguise: "I'll dress as an African [*all'africana*]." His friends, however, do not recognize the disguise as

African, and they, after hearing him speak nonsense, suppose that he might be speaking "Etruscan."[50] Stendhal, who was living in Milan two years later, in 1814, had no doubt that the public recognized the disguise as indisputably Turkish: "The count vanishes out of sight, only to reappear a moment later disguised as a Turk."[51] Rossini even offered a few bars of something like Janissary music as the guests begin to speculate on the identity of the visiting stranger who is about to appear before them. Rossini scholar Herbert Weinstock notes that the farcical libretto encouraged Rossini "to echo some of the eighteenth century's 'Turkish' or 'Janissary' sound effects, which Mozart had used so entertainingly in *Die Entführung aus dem Serail*."[52] Already in *La pietra del paragone* Rossini was self-consciously working with reference to an eighteenth-century tradition of Ottoman operatic subjects and styles.

The setting of *La pietra del paragone* at the country villa of Count Asdrubale, "not far from one of the principal cities of Italy," may have recalled to some members of the public an occasion that took place two years earlier, in 1810. In that year, in a private villa somewhere in the vicinity of Milan, there took place a special performance of a comic opera entitled *Il serraglio*, about the rescue of European captives held in the harem of the pasha of Smyrna. It was staged at the villa in honor of the host's daughter after her recent marriage. The music was unashamedly borrowed from François Devienne's *Les visitandines*, a revolutionary opera that had been performed in Paris in 1792 about the rescue-abduction of reluctant nuns from an oppressive convent— clearly modeled on earlier operas about the rescue-abduction of Christian captives in Ottoman harems. Now, in 1810, Devienne's convent opera was musically dismantled and fittingly refashioned as a harem opera, *Il serraglio*, for the private Italian villa celebration.[53] Thus, the notion of Turkish farce in an Italian country house was actually played out in reality in 1810 before Rossini staged *La pietra del paragone* at La Scala in 1812.

In *La pietra del paragone* the supposed Turk comically presents a bill to show that he has an enormous claim upon the estate of Count Asdrubale, and the count, in his Turkish disguise, can thus determine which of his friends would still remain his friends if he were poor. The comedy is enhanced by the Turk's peculiar way of articulating his business claim, alternating nonsensical phrases with a sort of preposterous attempt at legal Italian formality. At first, he barely sings at all but recites awkwardly and unmelodically in a disguised voice, supposedly struggling to communicate in Italian. Then, however, he musically expresses his own comical Turkishness, singing melodically in his natural basso register, as if finally comfortable in his own language: "*Baccalà. Tambelloni Kaimacacchi.*" The first word is "codfish"; the second might suggest some sort of drum or Janissary percussion; and the third might reference Turkish "*Kaymak*"—thick cream—though the word is rendered scatological by its ending. When the guests thank him, "*Mille grazie,*" the Turk simply replies, "*Baccalà,*" codfish, again.[54]

For Stendhal, however, the great humor of the scene lay in the Turk's repetition of a pseudo-Latinate legalism as he pretended to confiscate the property by putting a "seal" upon it: "*Sigillara.*" Stendhal described this particular scene with the greatest enthusiasm for the Turkish impersonation:

> *Sigillara* is the barbarous and semi-Italian word with which [Filippo] Galli, disguised as a Turk, responds to all objections that are made to him. He wants to put the seal everywhere. This baroque word, ceaselessly repeated by the Turk, and in every tone, since it is his response to everything one can say to him, made such an impression in Milan . . . that the name of the piece was changed. If you speak of *La pietra del paragone* in Lombardy, nobody understands you: you have to say *Il Sigillara.*[55]

Thus Stendhal, writing a decade later, in the 1820s, felt that the "Turk" (with one single scene) was so central to the opera that he had displaced the actual title of the work with his own signature expression: *Sigillara.* Indeed, the automatic repetition of the same term gave the false operatic Turk some resemblance to the famous mechanical Turk. Somehow, Stendhal implied, this word *Sigillara* was even funnier for the public than *Baccalà* and *Kaimacacchi*, perhaps because the humor involved the Turk trying to function as a European and dealing with European business. Just as Rossini made his Italian count into a Turk, so he made his Turk into a "semi-Italian" barbarian, the farcical mingling of the cultural aspects providing the essence of the comedy.

As for the Roman basso Filippo Galli, whom Stendhal noted in the role, he was identified not only with the travestied Turk in *La pietra del paragone* in 1812 but with every other Turkish role that Rossini created over the course of the next decade: Mustafa in *L'italiana in Algeri* in 1813, Selim in *Il turco in Italia* in 1814, and finally Sultan Mehmed the Conqueror in *Maometto Secondo* in 1820.[56] Like the tenor Francesco Borosini who specialized in the role of Sultan Bajazet for Gasparini and Handel in the early eighteenth century, so the basso Galli in the early nineteenth century defined what it meant to be a Turk on the European operatic stage.

The French artist Antoine-Laurent Castellan, who had traveled in Turkey, published in Paris in 1812 an account of *Moeurs, usages, costumes des Othomanes,* presenting both Turkish customs and costumes to the European public. Consistent with the spirit of disguise in *La pietra del paragone,* Castellan argued for the resemblance of Turks and Europeans:

> The wide and flowing garments of the Turks form a striking contrast with those of the other nations of Europe and constitute in some respect the most prominent feature in the physiognomy: for if you take away from a Turk his beard, his long moustaches, and his turban, and put on him our dress and hat, he will entirely lose his Oriental character.[57]

From an artist's perspective, recognizable Turkishness was merely a matter of costume and facial hair. Otherwise a Turk could always be mistaken for a European and, as in *La pietra del paragone,* vice versa. This was one of the fundamental axioms of operatic Turkishness, permitting the European public to recognize itself in the figure of the singing Turk.

La pietra del paragone was a huge success, attracting a broad public, and according to Stendhal, "crowds rushed to Milan from Parma, from Piacenza, from Bergamo, from Brescia." Rossini became an Italian phenomenon, "the first personage of the country."[58] Stendhal himself was not present for this first season of performances, since he was participating in the invasion of Russia. Later, when he wrote his life of Rossini in the 1820s, he suggested that the Russian campaign must have cast its shadow over the comedy at La Scala:

> This happiness of Lombardy in 1813 was all the more touching as it was about to end. I do not know what vague presentiment made people already listen for the sound of cannons in the North. During the mad success of *La pietra del paragone,* our armies were in retreat along the Dnieper.[59]

Habsburg restoration in Lombardy was coming, and the glory of Rossini would continue to flourish in the post-Napoleonic era of the Restoration.

Though the staging of *La pietra del paragone* coincided with the invasion of Russia, the opera's Napoleonic associations extended back to the time of the French campaign in Ottoman Egypt. Stendhal noted the fact that one of the singers in the premiere in 1812 was a Napoleonic veteran of the invasion of Egypt in 1798: "The generosity of the public even extended to poor [Pietro]

Vasoli, a former grenadier from the Army of Egypt, now almost blind, and a third-rate singer who made his reputation with the aria about the Missipipi."[60] The mispronunciation of the exotic Mississippi as the urological Missipipi, with the farcical repetition of the last two syllables, was perhaps an irreverent allusion to the fact that Napoleon had sold the European stake in the Mississippi region to the United States with the Louisiana Purchase of 1803. For the American president Thomas Jefferson it was well worth the price, but the Napoleonic regime perhaps undervalued the Mississippi, and it was humorously appropriate to put this disparaging little number into the mouth of a Napoleonic veteran of the Egyptian campaign. The opera thus comically celebrated both the Orient of the Kaimacacchi and the America of the Missipipi, while the presence of Vasoli enabled the public to make the connection between Napoleon's assault on the Ottoman empire in Egypt in 1798 and Rossini's comedy of Turkishness in 1812.

A more critical view of the Ottoman empire emerged in formerly Ottoman Budapest in 1812, with August von Kotzebue's philhellenic German drama, *Die Ruinen von Athen* (The ruins of Athens), an indictment of Turkish rule in Greece.[61] Yet the incidental music—composed by none other than Beethoven—offered a Turkish march that was somehow more exuberant than oppressive and a chorus of dervishes that was full of lively, rhythmic, even comical chanting: *Kaaba! Kaaba! Kaaba!* In 1812 Beethoven seemed to enjoy his Kaaba Turks as much as Rossini enjoyed his Sigillara Turk.

In Mozart's *Abduction* it is the Turkish pasha who is tested in the final scene, and proves his magnanimity as a generous Turk. *La pietra del paragone* reverses this formula, inasmuch as it is the count's Turkish persona that enables him to test his European friends and acquaintances, "the crowd of parasites and flatterers of all sorts who are numerous at the chateau of the count," in Stendhal's words.[62] Turkishness was the touchstone that served to test the sincerity of European values, and interestingly, the values of friendship and loyalty were precisely those that were being tested within the Napoleonic imperium, as diverse European contingents joined with the Grande Armée for the invasion of Russia—and then eventually deserted the Napoleonic cause in retreat and disarray. Napoleon was also about to learn about false friends and fickle allies in France, in Italy, in Germany, and all over Europe.

Conclusion: Napoleonic Collapse and Rossinian Comedy

Stendhal, in the opening pages of his novel *The Charterhouse of Parma*, celebrated Napoleon's arrival in Milan in 1796 as a moment of national awakening for "a sleeping people," the Italians, roused by Napoleonic inspiration. Habsburg rule was abolished, losing all at once its legitimacy and credibility: "a whole nation became aware, on 15 May 1796, that everything it had respected until then was supremely ridiculous and sometimes odious."[63] In 1812 that transformative revolution was about to be overturned by a new reversal of political values, and the imminence of a new international order. Certainly, as Rossini composed his opera in 1812, the Napoleonic invasion of Russia might still have seemed imminently triumphant, as late as the French victory at Smolensk in the middle of August. The ominously costly Battle of Borodino took place on September 7, and the initially encouraging French entry into Moscow one week later on September 14, so that mixed reports might have been arriving in Milan as *La pietra del paragone* opened on September 26 at La Scala. The fifty-three performances of the successful run would have overlapped with the French retreat from Moscow which began already in the middle of October. Thus the high spirits of the premiere of the opera in September would have accompanied the boldest Napoleonic enterprise, while the ongoing triumph of the opera must have accompanied the first reports and continuing intimations of disaster.

Conscripted Italian soldiers were a very large presence in Napoleon's campaigns, including the invasion of Russia, and historian David Laven has noted the unpopularity of Italian military service:

> Probably the most hated of all Napoleon's policies was the imposition of conscription, hitherto unknown in Lombardy or Venetia. The raising of troops in the Kingdom of Italy caused widespread popular resistance. Draft-dodging was endemic, as was the constant haemorrhage of desertion.[64]

One of the Italians who definitely preferred not to serve in the Napoleonic army was Gioachino Rossini, and, according to Herbert Weinstock, it was *La pietra del paragone* which "helped to win for him exemption from military service to which his age now made him liable." Rossini turned twenty in 1812, but according to his later account, "the success of that opera [*La pietra del paragone*] disposed the commanding general kindly toward me. He appealed to the Viceroy Eugène [de Beauharnais] . . . and I was permitted to go on with more peaceful occupations." The composer is supposed to have remarked, "I would have been a terrible soldier."[65] The opera's comic remoteness from the great military encounter of the moment thus confirmed Rossini's personal remoteness from the final mobilizations that could not prevent Napoleon's ultimate defeat. In 1811 Eugène de Beauharnais had purchased the Austrian mechanical Turk, who first played chess at the court of Maria Theresa in 1770; thus, the mechanical Turk was actually present in Milan in 1812 when Rossini's Sigillara Turk appeared at La Scala.[66]

From 1798, when Napoleon invaded Egypt, announcing the advent of a broader French imperial agenda, until 1812, when he invaded Russia, leading to the downfall of his empire, the Napoleonic progress served as the background to Rossini's coming of age, from the six-year-old triangle-player in Pesaro to the twenty-year-old composer of *La pietra del paragone* at La Scala. European-Turkish relations influenced the respective political contexts of the Napoleonic and Ottoman empires, accompanied by the continued production of operatic events on Ottoman themes. The invasion of Egypt was immediately followed by the premiere of a French version of Mozart's *Abduction* in Paris in 1798. The peace treaty between France and the Ottoman empire concluded in June 1802—affirming mutual commercial prerogatives and a joint policy against pirates—was followed by the production of Winter's *Tamerlan* at the Paris Opéra in September, and then by Jadin's *Mehmet II* the next year. The murder of Sultan Selim in 1808 coincided with the outbreak of the Peninsular War against Napoleon in Spain and the performance of Mosca's *L'italiana in Algeri* at La Scala in Milan. When Lord Byron went to Constantinople in 1810—with the Ottomans at war—his impressions were explicitly theatrical, for he would later, in *Don Juan*, describe the villas of the Bosphorus as forming "a pretty opera scene."[67]

In 1812 *La pietra del paragone* became Rossini's triumph at La Scala, even as victory eluded Napoleon in Russia. Rossini provided a comical "Turk," who ended up serving as a convenient and conventional object of comedy for this transitional moment when the Milanese public was supremely unsure about the social and political future. In the spirit of Turkish travesty—dating back to Molière and Lully—the "Turk" rendered himself comical by singing nonsense for the entertainment of the public. The supreme crisis of Napoleonic Europe could be obliquely and conveniently evaded in the spirit of Rossinian comedy. The "Missipipi" was a long way from the Dnieper; the Sigillara Turk bore no relation to the Russian enemy; and "Tambelloni Kaimacacchi" was not a politically compromising formula at the moment when the Napoleonic regime no longer seemed invincible. Rossinian farce affirmed an operatic mastery of the world map, and at the same time offered a sort of camouflage for some aspects of political complexity and ambivalence in the circumstances of 1812. The very next year, in 1813, as the Napoleonic collapse continued, Rossini would make farcical Turkishness into an even more important aspect of *L'italiana in Algeri*.

8 Pappataci and Kaimakan

Reflections in a Mediterranean Mirror

Introduction: Rossini's Venetian Triumph

Considering the premiere of Rossini's *L'italiana in Algeri* in May 1813, Stendhal felt that it was as important to evaluate the Venetian public as the opera itself: "They want above all, in music, agreeable songs, lighter rather than passionate. They were served to perfection by *L'italiana*; never has a people enjoyed a spectacle that better fit its character; and of all the operas that have ever existed, it is this which must have most pleased the Venetians."[1] The Islamic Mediterranean scenario of *L'italiana in Algeri* (usually translated as *The Italian Girl in Algiers*) was particularly appropriate for Venice, inasmuch as the Serenissima Repubblica, abolished by Napoleon in 1797, had enjoyed over the course of the eighteenth century, more than any other state in Europe, a highly complex commercial and cultural relationship with the Ottoman world. After the wars of the late seventeenth and early eighteenth centuries, the delicately preserved Venetian neutrality, lasting from the peace of Passarowitz in 1718 till the end of the republic in 1797, allowed Venice to experience an unprecedented intimacy with the Ottoman empire and its Islamic dependencies along the coast of North Africa, with multiple points of contact from Istanbul to Algiers.

In 1813 the organ of Napoleonic Venice, *Giornale Dipartimentale dell'Adriatico*, was sufficiently confident of its Mediterranean expertise to begin its review of *L'italiana* by doubting the fidelity of "customs and costumes" in the operatic representation of Algiers on the stage of the Teatro San Benedetto. Yet that said, there was no denying the "fervid genius" of Rossini at age twenty-one, already to be ranked among "the most sublime masters of the art." The reviewer noted that the Venetian public was "transported" by its enthusiasm at the premiere of *L'italiana*, and that the applause at the end was tremendous: "We conclude with the fury of the most widespread applause, which deafened without respite."[2] Rossini himself remarked, "I thought that having heard my opera, the Venetians would treat me as a crazy man; they have showed themselves to be crazier than I am."[3] The subject of his opera, and notably its comic treatment of an Ottoman scenario, was perfectly pitched for the contemporary Venetian public, just as Mozart composed the *Abduction* for the taste of the "Viennese Signori" in the 1780s.

Rossini's libretto was by Angelo Anelli, born in 1761 on Lake Garda in Lombardy, a man of Mozart's own generation, and this libretto had already been set to music once by the Neapolitan composer Luigi Mosca, for La Scala in 1808. Anelli modeled his title, and some of the structure of the drama, on the work of Pietro Chiari, *La veneziana in Algeri*, dating back to 1760.[4] Rossini's opera may be seen as the culmination, and even conclusion, of a long tradition of dramatizing the fate of Christian women escaping amorous Turkish masters: from Rameau's generous Turk in 1735, to Mozart's Pasha Selim in 1782, to Rossini's Bey Mustafa in 1813. Since the *Abduction* was not actually performed in Italy, Rossini's *L'italiana* became in some sense the Italian reconception of Mozart's opera of Turkish captivity.[5] *L'italiana* was arguably the last important operatic comedy of Ottoman captivity, and the role of Mustafa, Bey of Algiers, represented a comical pinnacle in the succession of operatic Turkish dignitaries. Filippo Galli created the role for Rossini, after starring in *La pietra del paragone* the previous year, impersonating the "Sigillara" Turk.

Stendhal's notion of Rossini as a sort of successor to Napoleon, a new conqueror of Europe, is particularly interesting with regard to *L'italiana*, inasmuch as the opera's huge triumph in Venice coincided precisely with Napoleon's disastrous collapse in 1813 following the retreat from Russia. Rossini purposefully made the opera into a study of musical conquest, in which the vocal character of the Italian heroine Isabella was musically essential to her conquest of the Bey of Algiers. Every time the opera was performed, the European "conquest" of North Africa was consummated, thus performing on stage what Napoleon had set out to achieve in Egypt in 1798 and what would ultimately be accomplished in an enterprise of modern military imperialism when the French occupied Algeria in 1830.

Mediterranean Pirates and Captives in the Age of Napoleon

In early 1813 Rossini actually created two masterpieces, both performed in Venice: first *Tancredi*, an *opera seria*, at La Fenice in February, then *L'italiana in Algeri*, an *opera buffa*, at the Teatro San Benedetto in May. "Had the King-Emperor Napoleon himself thought to honor Venice with his presence," wrote Stendhal about the triumphant premiere of *Tancredi*, "his arrival would not have distracted from Rossini. It was madness [*folie*]."[6] *Tancredi*, based on a drama by Voltaire, is set in medieval Sicily, and features a great crusading struggle between the Christian Syracusans and the Muslim Saracens. The Saracens appear in the opera as a militant chorus threatening "terror" in the city of Syracuse. The Syracusan heroine Amenaide loves the Christian knight Tancredi, and her love letter to him is intercepted and misinterpreted as a treasonously amorous message to the Saracen leader Solamir (who does not appear in the opera). All her compatriots, including her father, now regard Amenaide with horror, and it is only when Tancredi slays Solamir in combat (offstage) and Solamir reveals with his last breath (offstage) Amenaide's innocence that the girl is vindicated.

Tancredi offered a very limited musical treatment of the Muslim enemy on the operatic stage. It did, however, contemplate the possibility of love between Christians and Muslims (as construed from the intercepted letter) and represented that possibility with utter horror in the completely earnest spirit of *opera seria*. In contrast to *Tancredi*, *L'italiana in Algeri* would put the Muslim world and Muslim characters at the very center of the operatic stage, and would represent the possibility of love between Christians and Muslims as a subject of pure comedy.

Following the Venetian production of *Tancredi* in February (and before the advent of *L'italiana* in May), the Paris Opéra presented in April 1813 another *opera seria* with a crusading scenario. Luigi Cherubini, a generation older than Rossini, had been celebrated for his operas in revolutionary France in the 1790s, and now composed *Les Abencérages* for Paris. The work is set in the Alhambra, in late Moorish Granada, under siege from the Castilians and riven by internecine tensions among the Muslim Moors. The plot concerns a Moorish conspiracy against Almansor, the heroic Muslim ruler of the Abencerraje dynasty. The Oriental associations of Islamic Spain were suggested not by musical effects but by stage settings that represented the architectural spaces of the Alhambra, for instance the famous Court of the Lions—reconstructed on the stage with some degree of stylistic fidelity to the original.[7]

Napoleon himself was present for the premiere of *Les Abencérages* in Paris in April 1813, after his disastrous winter retreat from Moscow but before the decisive military defeat at Leipzig in October. Though Napoleon did not greatly esteem Cherubini as a composer, both the emperor and empress arrived in time for the first act and stayed for the whole opera, an unusual instance of imperial punctuality and persistence. With the first appearance in the theater of Napoleon and Marie Louise, "the public burst into the most lively transports"—at a moment when the whole Napoleonic performance desperately needed approval and applause.[8] Yet in spite of this enthusiasm for the imperial couple it was arguably the wrong moment for a celebration of the doomed Muslim defenders of Granada facing the Spanish reconquest, for in the spring of 1813 the Spanish Peninsular War was turning decisively against Napoleon. Spanish guerillas and British troops under the duke of Wellington were carrying out their own relentless reconquest of Bonapartist Spain. The research of David Chaillou demonstrates that the libretto was in fact attentively reviewed by the Napoleonic censors for precisely this reason. One censor commented, "Although the subject of the *Abencérages* offers no allusion to the current events of Spain, we have nevertheless removed most of the expressions that could suggest the thought."[9] Such a comment confirms that the public was expected to make some connection between a performance on the operatic stage and the fortunes of the Napoleonic enterprise.

While the representation of Granada at the Paris Opéra was intended to evoke the vanished Muslim domain of Andalucía, the stipulation of Algiers in the title of Anelli's libretto pointed to a well-publicized problem of the contemporary Mediterranean: the importance of piracy, which was especially associated with Algiers. In fact, piracy was implicitly essential to the prehistory of most captivity operas. In the *Abduction* Pedrillo explains his situation thus to Belmonte: "Our ship was taken by the pirates [*von den Seeräubern*] . . . Luckily, it turned out that Pasha Selim bought all three of us: your Konstanze, my Blonde, and myself."[10] This backstory, which set up the whole opera, was founded on the social and economic reality of piracy and slave trade in the early modern Mediterranean world. In 1783, one year after the premiere of the *Abduction* in Vienna, Ludwig Fischer, the original Osmin, witnessed from Civitavecchia the pursuit of Turkish offshore pirates by Roman and Neapolitan vessels and the taking of Turkish captives.[11]

In the sixteenth century the celebrated Turkish naval figure "Barbarossa" began as a pirate, then became an Ottoman admiral and additionally the pasha of Algiers. North Africa remained a base for Muslim pirates—the famous Barbary pirates—right up until Rossini's time, and the business of piracy involved the capture of Christian men and women who were either sold into slavery or ransomed to their families.[12] The violence of piracy was usually relegated to the prehistory of comic operas about captivity, but the specific setting of *L'italiana* emphasized the importance of piratical practice within the opera itself. In fact, the leading basso Mustafa was accompanied by a secondary basso, Haly (or Ali), "captain of the Algerian corsairs," specifically commissioned by the bey to supply an Italian woman.[13]

Mustafa was characterized by Anelli as the "Bey or Dey of Algiers," and the title of "dey" was actually correct for the contemporary Ottoman Regency of Algiers, though "bey" was favored in the Italian libretto. The Barbary pirates did not necessarily take orders from the beys or deys of North Africa, and those rulers in turn were not necessarily obedient officials of the Ottoman empire even if they acknowledged its ultimate, and remote, sovereignty. Yet the serial roles of Barbarossa in the sixteenth century—independent pirate, Ottoman admiral, pasha of Algiers—suggest the inevitably symbiotic and related spheres of Ottoman government, North African authority, and Barbary piracy. From the European operatic perspective they might all have been imaginatively confused and commingled, related aspects of the Ottoman Islamic Mediterranean, denominated generally as "Turkish" even if its North African extension was more likely to involve ethnographically Arabic and Berber populations.

By the seventeenth century, according to historian Robert Davis, the Barbary corsairs operated "with the tacit protection of their local pashas—and, at another remove, with the benign and neglectful tolerance of the sultans in Constantinople."[14] Venice maintained complex commercial and diplomatic ties with Constantinople but also engaged in major naval campaigns against the Barbary pirates, who harassed Venetian shipping. There were tensions with the Bey of Tripoli in the 1760s, and naval expeditions against the Bey of Tunis during the 1780s; the beys were presumed to be encouraging if not actually ordering pirates to raid European ships in the Mediterranean. In Venice Carlo Goldoni's drama of 1758, *La dalmatina*, presented a Dalmatian girl taken captive by Barbary pirates and held in Morocco.[15] In Vienna in 1782 the libretto of Mozart's *Abduction* presupposed the activity of Muslim pirates in the Mediterranean. In Venice in 1813 Rossini's *L'italiana* gave this scenario its fully farcical formulation.

In fact, the age of Mediterranean piracy was drawing to a close in the early nineteenth century, as British and French fleets struggled for mastery of the sea in the Napoleonic wars, and Thomas Jefferson, the American president, undertook a Mediterranean campaign against the Barbary pirates. Refusing to continue the payment of tribute to the Barbary states of Tripoli, Tunis, Algiers, and Morocco for the protection of American shipping, Jefferson went to war—American's first war after independence—between 1801 and 1805, culminating in the taking of Tripoli.[16] (The Unites States Marines hymn—"From the halls of Montezuma to the shores of Tripoli"—commemorates the encounter.) Thus, Anelli's libretto for Mosca in 1808, the first version of *L'italiana in Algeri*, would have followed immediately upon the conclusion of the American war against the Barbary pirates. Rossini's definitive version in 1813 was in turn followed by the second American war against the pirates in 1815, when the American navy imposed terms upon the ruler of Algiers, Dey Omar, and brought about the liberation of a cohort of Christian captives. In 1816 the British navy bombarded Algiers with similar intent.

Rossini's comedy of Turkish captivity was thus presented not only in the context of Ottoman defeat in the Russian-Ottoman war that ended in 1812, but also in the waning age of Barbary piracy when European and American naval campaigns were about to put an end to three centuries of Muslim piracy and Christian captivity on the Ottoman Mediterranean. There was a noted case in 1805 involving a young woman from Milan taken captive by Algerian pirates and sold into a harem—still recent when Anelli wrote his libretto for Mosca in 1808. Lord Byron further claimed that he saw a performance of Rossini's *L'italiana* in Venice with the cast including a female singer who had herself been recently liberated from captivity in Algiers.[17]

Luigi Mosca's original setting of Anelli's libretto was performed at La Scala in Milan in 1808 for a successful run of thirty-five performances. Milan was the capital of the Napoleonic Kingdom of Italy, and Mosca's *L'italiana* opened on August 16, the day after Napoleon's birthday. In 1808 it was Mosca, five years before Rossini, who decided that Mustafa had to be a basso,

IOANNI LA VALETTE
ORDINIS·HIEROSOLYMITANI·SANCTI·IOANNIS
MAGNO·MAGISTRO
QVI·PERICLITANTI·EVROPAE
DIFFICILLIMO·TEMPORE·SVBVENIENS
IN·PLVRIBVS·CONTRA·TVRCAS·PRAELIIS
CAPTIS·L·NAVIBVS
MELITE·OBSIDIONE·LIBERATA
ET·NOVA·VRBE·A·SVO·NOMINE·DICTA
FIRMISSIMIS·INSTRVCTA·MVNIMENTIS
SOLIMANVM·MVLTIS·VICTORIIS·FEROCEM·COERCVIT
AMPLIATORI·ORDINIS·SVI
ADSERTORI·LIBERTATIS·POPVLI·CHRISTIANI
FRANCISCVS·S·R·I·COMES·A·COLLOREDO
SACRI·ORDINIS·BAIVLIVVS
AEDI·SVA·CVRA·REFECTAE
TANTI·VIRI·MEMORIA·SPLENDOREM·ADIICIENS
P·C·AN·CIƆIƆCCCVI

Captive Turks, monument in the Malteserkirche (Maltese Church) in Vienna, on the Kärntnerstrasse; in the Napoleonic age it was still possible to commemorate the great struggles against the Turks on the Mediterranean in the sixteenth century, as in this 1806 monument to Jean de la Valette, the defender of Malta in 1565. In fact, piracy and captivity remained issues on the Mediterranean in the early nineteenth century, and Rossini remained interested in the fate of Italians in Algiers, but the monument in the Malteserkirche—theatrically mustachioed Turks in bondage—also suggests that there was artistic interest in the reciprocal fantasy of captive Turks. Photograph by the author.

in this case Andrea Verni who would later create the role of Don Magnifico in Rossini's *La Cenerentola*. Mosca, born in Naples in 1775, belonged to an intermediary generation between Mozart and Rossini, and was stylistically very much aware of Mozart, as was evident from the opening Mozartean chords of the overture to *L'italiana*. Mustafa's rejected harem wife, Elvira, echoed some of the musical distress of Mozart's Donna Elvira. Mustafa himself had little of the farcical musical characterization he would receive from Rossini, but sounded a little more like such libertine low voices as Mozart's Count Almaviva or even Don Giovanni, affirming himself as "*un uomo singolar*," a singular man, at the conclusion of his aria in the first act.[18] Mosca's *L'italiana*, however, involved none of the instrumental coloring or rhythmic emphasis of the "Turkish" music that Mozart employed with such relish in the *Abduction*.

In 1813, by contrast, the Turkishness of Rossini's scenario was quickly signaled with dramatic Janissary percussion in the overture: bass drum, cymbals, triangle. The notation in the score, B.T., for Banda Turca, may even have indicated the use of the "Turkish crescent," a crescent-topped pole with bells—and perhaps a decorative horsetail plume made of actual horsehair, as in the Ottoman Janissary standard.[19] In Rossini's case it seems very likely that he was familiar with Mozart's score, even if he had never heard the *Abduction* performed. Mozart's son Karl was present in Milan after 1805, and after 1810 there was also Karl's friend Peter Lichtenthal, who promoted Mozart's music and who sought (without success) to encourage a production of the *Abduction* at La Scala.[20]

The opening scene of Rossini's *L'italiana* immediately describes an Islamic society of extreme inequality between the sexes, with a male chorus intoning what they see as the self-evident circumstances:

Qua le femmine son nate	Here the women are born
Solamente per soffrir.	Only to suffer.[21]

Singing over the male chorus, Mustafa's favored harem wife Elvira, a soprano, prettily regrets that her husband no longer loves her, while her slave Zulma strategically advises her not to protest.[22] Thus the stage is set for the extravagant comedy of Mustafa's first appearance.

The key shifts dramatically from G major to E major, and with the onset of sharps Mustafa announces his presence in a political statement of relations

Elvira, the "wife" of Mustafa, or leading lady of his harem, whom he proposes to replace with the Italian Isabella in Rossini's *L'italiana in Algeri*. In this costume design for a French production of 1821 the drawing was accompanied by detailed notes about fabrics and ornaments, e.g., "turban of white muslin, bands embroidered with gold leaf, diamond clasp, curved 'esprit' plume." Elvira has a major vocal role in *L'italiana* and is provided with elaborately beautiful costumes, but her submissive spirit as a harem odalisque offers the most emphatic contrast to the unflappable defiance of the Rossinian heroine. With kind permission of the Bibliothèque Nationale de France.

between the sexes, affirming his own masculinity against the "arrogance of women." He is too presumptuous, too self-congratulatory in his ornamentation to be anything but farcical. His preposterousness is underlined in the big ensuing ensemble—undertaken by Rossini five minutes into the first act—with Elvira, Zulma, and Haly the pirate, back in the key of G, all agreeing in the exclamatory text that Mustafa is outrageous:

Oh! che testa stravagante!	What an extravagant head!
Oh! che burbero arrogante!	What an arrogant boor![23]

Mustafa joins with Haly on the bass staff, boasting of the male mistreatment of women, which the women themselves deplore on the treble staff, but with both men and women singing the same words to define the Turkish masculine character: "*delle donne calpestando le lusinghe e la beltà*" (trampling upon women's charms and beauty).[24]

In the 1750s Voltaire had affirmed that Europeans distinguished themselves from Orientals in the treatment of women.[25] In the 1780s Mozart's Blonde had boldly pronounced the same principle to the enamored Osmin who dared to regard himself as her master. In *L'italiana* Mustafa would offer the most hyperbolic and boorish illustration of that principle, and the whole plot of the opera would involve bringing about the proper punishment for his outrageous presumption, his Oriental ignorance of gallantry, his blasphemy against the charm and beauty of women.

Mustafa explains to Haly that he is tired of his current wife, Elvira, and therefore intends to marry her off to his Italian slave Lindoro. Haly objects that Lindoro is not a Turk, thus reminding Mustafa that a Muslim woman is not permitted to marry a non-Muslim man:

HALY: Ma di Maometto la legge non permette un tal pasticcio.
MUSTAFA: Altra legge io non ho che il mio capriccio.

HALY: But the law of Mohammed does not permit such a mess.
MUSTAFA: I recognize no other law but my own caprice.[26]

Mustafa himself casually dismisses Islam in favor of the most extreme expression of capricious Oriental despotism, and the violence of despotism is evident in Mustafa's deadline for Haly: six days for the pirate to obtain and deliver an Italian girl, or face impalement. The pirate's appeal to the uncertainty of the sea (*l'inconstanza del mar*) is promptly rhymed with the despot's threat of impalement (*ti faccio impalar*).[27] Yet the opening scene already puts the audience on notice that in this operatic Oriental despotism of Algiers, the menace of violence was not to be taken too seriously.

Isabella and Mustafa: "Che pezzo da sultano!"

"*Cruda sorte*" (cruel fate), sings Isabella, the titular Italian girl, as she makes her stage entrance on the coast of Algiers after a providential shipwreck. It is providential just because she is searching for her lost lover, Lindoro, who happens to be right there in Algiers as the Italian captive of Mustafa. While Isabella sings of her cruel fate—with the aria marked as "majestic" (*maestoso*)—Haly and the Algerian pirates lie hidden to listen and observe, punctuating her serious lament with the comical choral interjection, "What a mouthful [*boccone*] for Mustafa!"[28] This choral phrase then provides the pivot for a change in tempo and mood, thus concluding the tragic aria with a spirited and comic cabaletta.

In the cabaletta Isabella puts aside fear and takes courage (*corraggio*), now confident that she will be able to control the situation wherever she may find herself. For she possesses the particular feminine understanding of how to tame men: "*so a domar gli uomini—come si fa—sì, sì, sì, sì*" (I know how to tame men—how it's done—yes, yes, yes, yes). Tripping sixteenth notes demonstrate the facility with which she will undertake the taming of the Turk. All men, after all, are alike (*son tutti simili*), as they all desire the same thing from women.[29] Isabella thus presents herself as the perfect female counterpart to Mustafa who has previously proclaimed his own masculine mastery over women. The prima donna at the premiere in Venice was Marietta Marcolini, whom Stendhal saluted "for her delightful contralto voice and for her admirable comic play"; she had already "tamed" Rossini and made him her lover, supposedly preferring him to Napoleon's brother, Prince Lucien Bonaparte.[30]

Isabella's cabaletta clearly demonstrates her kinship to Rosina, the later heroine of Rossini's *The Barber of Seville* in 1816, who in the cabaletta of her aria "*Una voce poco fa*" would declare her confidence in emerging victorious from her difficult situation by deploying a "hundred traps" (*cento trappole*). In fact, *The Barber of Seville*, in which Count Almaviva seeks to rescue Rosina from the captivity of her despotic guardian, the basso Doctor Bartolo, is in some sense a Turkish captive opera without the Turks. The struggle between the sexes could be set as an encounter between Turkish and European customs, according to the conventions of Voltaire, Mozart, and the Enlightenment—but for Rossini such conventions also served to dramatize comic conflicts that also existed entirely within European society. The principle that "all men are alike" (*son tutti simili*) emphasized the convergence between Turks and Europeans rather than any emphatic Orientalist conception of difference.

Haly the corsair learns that Isabella is Italian, from Livorno, and then informs her that she is intended for Mustafa, to be "the star and the splendor of his seraglio." Isabella does not know that she is also about to be reunited with the man she loves, Lindoro, already in captivity. For now, she converses in recitative with another admirer, Taddeo, who has been taken captive along with her and who worries anxiously about her fate in Algiers:

TADDEO: Did you not hear that ugly word?
ISABELLA: What word?
TADDEO: Seraglio.
ISABELLA: And so? [*Ebben?*]
TADDEO: So you will be the prize of a bey? of a Mustafa?
ISABELLA: What will be will be. I don't want to get upset about that.[31]

In fact, "seraglio" had not been an ugly word for quite some time in European opera. Mozart had no qualms about using it in the title of *Die Entführung aus dem Serail*, and *Arlequin au sérail* had an even older pedigree in the Paris fairs.

The duet between Taddeo and Isabella harmonizes his fears about what will happen to her in Mustafa's seraglio ("*ma quel Bey, ma quel Bey*") with her confidence that she can handle the situation: "*Non ci pensar, no no no no no no no, sarà quel che sarà*" (Don't think about it; what will be will be). The rhythmically descending staccato eighth notes of *no no no no no no no* are followed by an ecstatic ornamental display of sixteenth and thirty-second notes on the word *sarà*: what will be will be![32] Thus undaunted, she faces the prospect even of the seraglio, that is, the possibility of sex with Turks.

Meanwhile, Mustafa is already congratulating himself on the advent of the Italian girl whom he will soon welcome to his seraglio. "*Or mi tengo da più del gran Sultano*," he sings in recitative: "Now I consider myself greater than the great Sultan."[33] Here the libretto alluded to the Mediterranean political circumstances in which individual pashas and beys, theoretically subordinated to the great sultan in Constantinople, actually ruled autonomously, while measuring themselves against the power and prestige of the supreme Ottoman sultan. In 1808, the year that Anelli first wrote the libretto for Mosca, the twenty-three-year-old Mahmud II became sultan, the same year that the deposed Selim III was murdered in the seraglio. While Mahmud would rule until 1839 and undertake important reforms to strengthen the Ottoman state, his reign would also see powerful pashas emerge to rival the sultan with their independent power. Muhammad Ali Pasha, who began his career as an Ottoman officer fighting against Napoleon's Egyptian expedition, went on to become the virtually independent ruler of Ottoman Egypt. Ali Pasha of Janina likewise ruled almost independently over Albania and much of Greece in the early nineteenth century, his political reputation entering into English poetry through Lord Byron's *Childe Harold's Pilgrimage* and into German opera through Albert Lortzing's *Ali Pascha von Janina*. For Rossini's imaginary Mustafa, Bey or Dey of Algiers, to measure himself and his harem against the great sultan in Istanbul was consistent with the political circumstances of the contemporary Ottoman empire.

Mustafa summons his seraglio to the great hall where he will receive Isabella. He sings in happy, flowing triplets about "the fire, the transport, the desire" that his heart cannot resist, and about the "new triumph" that he anticipates.[34] In the great hall the women of the seraglio assemble, but it is a male chorus—a chorus of eunuchs according to the libretto, a chorus of tenors and basses according to the score—that hails Mustafa's arrival by celebrating his power over women. The choral line begins with the rising notes of a C major chord, like the heralding call of a trumpet:

> Viva, viva il flagel delle donne,
> Che di tigri le cangia in agnelle.
> Chi non sa soggiogar queste belle
> Venga a scuola dal gran Mustafà.

> Long live the scourge of women,
> Who changes them from tigers to lambs.
> Whoever does not know how to subjugate these beauties
> May come to learn from the great Mustafa.[35]

No longer the "scourge of Christendom," as in early modern rhetoric, the Turks now appear merely as the "scourge of women"—and even that title is attributed facetiously. The tenors of the chorus are divided into two separate parts, singing fanfares of *"viva, viva Mustafà,"* while the basses harmonize in the lower register.[36] The musical harmony, however, does not resolve the paradox of the libretto, as Mustafa, the Oriental despot whose women are his captive slaves, is celebrated as if he were some sort of brilliant libertine seducer, as if he were Don Giovanni or Casanova.

The distinct eighteenth-century categories of the Oriental despot and the European libertine here became confused in this nineteenth-century *opera buffa*, as both concepts were about to be farcically exploded. For as soon as Isabella herself appears, Mustafa's despotic power is revealed to be as feeble as his supposed seductive charm. The mock seriousness of the eunuch chorus singing—*"Viva, viva il flagel delle donne"*—gives way immediately to flagrant mockery in the spirit of Rossinian *opera buffa*.

"Che muso!" (What a mug!), exclaims Isabella at her first sight of Musta-fa, as the music shifts dramatically from C major to E-flat. Rossini gives the leisurely marking *"andantino"* and allows a rest in the vocal line after *"Che muso!"*—perhaps so that the audience can laugh—before Isabella continues, *"che figura!"* (what a figure!). Then she rests again, allowing the audience to laugh again, consolidating the comical European perspective on Mustafa. As Isabella sings, *"Del mio colpo or son sicura"* (Now I am sure of my blow), she arpeggiates the E-flat major chord with perfectly controlled and neatly em-phatic semistaccato sixteenth notes: the rise and fall of laughter, but laughter so precisely articulated as to demonstrate her complete mastery of the come-dy that is about to ensue.[37]

"Che muso, che figura" is actually a duet, and Mustafa follows Isabella at her pace, *andantino*, and in her key, E-flat, but with sentiments all his own. *"Che pezzo da sultano!"* he exclaims: "What a piece for a sultan!" Again he is measuring his masculine glory with reference to the Ottoman sultan, while he also proceeds to declare his infatuation: *"M'incanta, m'innamora"* (She enchants me, I am falling in love). His declaration, however, is only for the benefit of the audience. Just as she declares her mockery to the audience but conceals it from Mustafa, so he reveals his infatuation to the audience but tries to conceal it from Isabella. In fact, he imitates her articulated semistac-cato notes of the E-flat chord to sing, purposefully, *"ma convien dissimular"* (but best to dissimulate). Unfortunately for him, she sees right through his dissimulation, and she opens the concluding section of the duet with a dec-laration of victory:

In gabbia è già il merlotto,	The bird is already in the cage,
Ne più mi puo scappar!	And can no longer escape from me!

He immediately follows her rhythm, her rhyme scheme, and her metaphor, showing himself to be musically as well as sentimentally in her thrall:

Io son già caldo e cotto,	I am already boiled and cooked,
Ne più mi so frenar.	And can no longer control myself.[38]

In fact, he can control himself just well enough to follow Isabella musically through the challenging runs of sixteenth notes that conclude the duet. Mosca in 1808, working with the same phrases, harmonized the two voices in a more balanced, less humorous, and less interesting fashion, while Rossini in 1813 reveled in the musically acrobatic imbalance that structured the ethnographic encounter on the operatic stage.[39]

Isabella proceeds to demonstrate her mastery of the situation by commanding Mustafa not to send his wife Elvira away with Lindoro, as originally planned. Isabella, of course, wants to keep Lindoro close to her, but she formulates her command as a matter of civilized principle. With an authoritative run of sixteenth notes down the A-flat scale, she rhetorically demands to know whether Mustafa hopes to win her own love by sending away his wife. Then, in rollicking triplets, as if to indicate the humor of her civilizing pretense, she declares:

Questi costumi barbari	These barbarous customs
Io vi farò cangiar.	I will make you change.[40]

The civilizing of the Turkish barbarian becomes a purely comical matter here, and the civilizing project of the Enlightenment is dissolved into Isabella's personal project of "taming" Mustafa, as she claims to be able to tame all men: "*so a domar gli uomini—come si fa—sì, sì, sì, sì.*"

At the same time, within the opera, Elvira, Zulma, and Lindoro (*ridendo*, laughing) recognize that what is being "changed" is not Turkish customs but the Turk himself, subjected by Isabella to an undignified metamorphosis:

Ah! di leone in asino	Ah! from a lion into an ass
lo fa costei cangiar.	she makes him change.[41]

The subjects of Mustafa's personal despotism all sing in unison, laughing, about the subversion of his absolute power and the transformation of his role. Ten minutes earlier the chorus saluted him as he whose mastery of women could "change tigers into lambs," but now they relish the fact that a woman

"Questi costumi barbari io vi farò cangiar" (These barbarous customs I will make you change), sings Isabella in Rossini's *L'italiana*, articulating Europe's civilizing mission in cheerful triplets and bringing home the point with brilliant runs of sixteenth notes.

is making him into an ass. What actually transformed Mustafa into an ass, of course, was the spirit of Rossinian comedy as received by the European public. Mozart had made Osmin ridiculous, but Osmin was only the pasha's servant and the pasha's own dignity was scrupulously preserved. Rossini, in his opera, ridiculed the figure of Turkish authority, the bey, while the members of his harem and entourage were not only spared such derisory treatment but actually allowed to appreciate the comedy of their master's humiliation.

The order of the Ottoman court of Algiers was thus, in Rossini's comic vision, completely subverted by the transformative operatic presence of Europeans.

Immediately after Elvira, Zulma, and Lindoro observe Mustafa's asinine metamorphosis, Rossini initiates the *allegro vivace* conclusion to the act 1 finale. The seven Rossini soloists, from Elvira the soprano at the top of the score, down to Mustafa the basso at the bottom, sing about their complete confusion and then, led by Elvira, represent that confusion as an explosive percussion inside their heads. Elvira sings in the soprano range: "*Nella testa ho un campanello*" (In my head I have a bell). Mustafa sings in the basso range: "*Come scoppio di canone*" (Like the explosion of a cannon). The others occupy the intermediary ranges, eventually joined by a chorus of sopranos, tenors, and basses, representing the Barbary pirates of Algiers and the women of the harem.

This mostly Muslim ensemble might have been, in Mozart's hands, the occasion for creating a Janissary chorus of "Turkish" music, as at the conclusion of the *Abduction*. Rossini, instead, both engaged and subverted the Janissary style by assigning its percussive elements to different vocal parts, Elvira becoming the bell at the top of the score, singing "*din din din din*," and Mustafa becoming the bass drum at the bottom, singing "*bum bum bum bum*." This part of the score made use of new text that was not part of Anelli's libretto for Mosca in 1808. Rossini's conception was to present, on the stage, European performers who impersonated Turkish characters impersonating Turkish instruments as deployed in a European composition: the encounter of East and West, Turkey and Europe, Orientalism and Occidentalism.

Rossini's intention to compose Janissary music in vocal parts is perfectly evident in the characteristic oscillation of thirds—as in Mozart—such that Elvira sings "*din din din din*" alternating high E and G, while Zulma harmonizes one third lower, alternating C and E, and Isabella rounds out the C major chord by alternating C and G.[42] The martial and ceremonial quality of Janissary music in Mozart's *Abduction*, celebrating the Ottoman order as reflected in Pasha Selim, was completely subverted in Rossini's conception of chaotic confusion and consternation. The singers became percussion instruments and were played upon, struck, and sounded by some higher power whose purposes they themselves could not fathom. The contemporary sultan in Istanbul, Mahmud II, would himself eventually decide that the Janissary corps was a force of disorder, rebellion, and instability within the Ottoman empire, and in 1826 he would abolish the Janissaries altogether, including their bands. In 1812 the French artist Antoine-Laurent Castellan reported, on the basis of his travel in Turkey, that authentic Janissary music was "of the most barbarous kind" and "the most discordant noise that can be imagined."[43] In 1813, in the act 1 finale of *L'italiana*, Rossini already suggested that the Janissary band had reached the limit of its dramatic and musical significance for European opera.

Kaimakan and Pappataci

At the beginning of the second act, the male chorus was no longer singing of the glory, but rather of the idiocy, of Mustafa: "*Uno stupido, uno stolto diventato è Mustafà*" (Mustafa has become stupid and foolish). The musical setting was entirely casual, as if the sentiment were to be taken quite for granted, as the chorus sang and then repeated the rising notes of an A major chord: "*Uno stupido, uno stolto.*"[44] Coming fifteen years after Napoleon's invasion of Egypt in 1798, *L'italiana* could plausibly be considered to present the scenario of modern imperialism in the Orient. The substance of act 1 was the European invasion, led by an Italian woman; the circumstances of act 2 were already colonial, with the natives now accustomed to regard their former despot as a foolish pawn in the power of the foreign invader. In this case, of course, the Muslim ruler had been subjugated by love, not by war.

Rossini, however, had only just begun to ridicule Mustafa, and the central business of the second act involves the reciprocal assignment of Oriental and Occidental dignities to characters of the other culture. First, Mustafa bestows upon Taddeo (whom the bey believes to be Isabella's uncle) the actual Ottoman title of Kaimakan. Then, returning the favor, the Europeans proceed to initiate Mustafa into the completely fabricated European secret society of the Pappataci, with the initiation ceremony staged as cover for the escape of the Europeans from Algiers.

Kaimakan was an Ottoman administrative title, though it was deployed as mere nonsense syllables in the libretto, and Rossini had used a related form of the word in an even sillier fashion in *La pietra del paragone*: "*Tambelloni, Kaimacacchi!*" Taddeo is stripped of his European clothes and dressed in Turkish costume, complete with turban and saber. Now the chorus bows down before the Kaimakan Taddeo and salutes him in musical phrases that are closely related to Mozart's Turkish choruses:

"*Viva il grande Kaimakan, protettor de' Mussulman*" (Long live the great Kaimakan, protector of the Muslims). The male chorus in Rossini's *L'italiana* thus salutes the travesty transformation of Taddeo into a Muslim dignitary—"Kaimakan"—with tenors and basses singing in unison *fortissimo* to a marching rhythm.

> Viva il grande Kaimakan, Long live the great Kaimakan,
> Protettor de' Mussulman. Protector of the Muslims.[45]

The rhyming of "Kaimakan" with "Mussulman" suggests that Rossini's opera is a comedy not just of Turkishness but also, incidentally, of Islam. Taddeo, with his new Turkish costume and his new Islamic role, is not eager to embrace the role of Kaimakan but fears that he might be impaled if he were to decline the honor.

Later Taddeo and Lindoro together reciprocate by informing Mustafa that Isabella has decided to make him a Pappataci. Already in the first act, Taddeo marveled at the prospect of the Turk becoming a "cicisbeo," the Venetian term for the *cavaliere servente*, who by social custom devotedly attended a respectable woman.[46] This was the first step in Isabella's "taming" of the Turk, making him into an infatuated escort, and with "Pappataci" Rossini took "cicisbeo" to the next level of domestication, assigning Mustafa a role summed up in a word that could be musically set as nonsense syllables. In fact, the word apparently possessed a vernacular compound meaning, etymologically derived from *pappare* (to gobble) and *tacere* (to be silent), the twin principles of the Society of Pappataci as described by Anelli in the libretto. In popular culture the term could be used to describe a variety of cuckold, who went on eating quietly while his wife was unfaithful to him. The term was appropriated by scientific language in 1786 when the natural historian Giovanni Antonio Scopoli named the sandfly *Phlebotomus papatasii*, because it fed (on human blood) silently (unlike the buzzing mosquito). It would later be discovered that this sandfly transmitted what would come to be known as Pappataci fever.[47] Anelli thus took a term with meanings in both popular culture and natural history, and invented the nonsensical Society of Pappataci.

With the word "Pappataci" Mustafa launches a male trio in which he first expresses his delight, then asks what the word means, and finally permits Taddeo and Lindoro to enlighten him. Pappataci, they explain, exists in perfect correspondence to Kaimakan: Taddeo sings "Kaimakan" on three descending

"*Pappataci dee mangiar, dee dormir*" (Pappataci must eat, must sleep), explains Taddeo in Rossini's *L'italiana*, while Mustafa exclaims, "*Bella vita! oh che piacere!*" (Beautiful life! oh what a pleasure!). The vocal lines of the two basses happily complement one another, each picking up where the other leaves off in a lively *staccato* spirit. As in Mozart's drinking duet for Osmin and Pedrillo, here too the ostensible mockery of Mustafa really suggests that European and Turkish men are both well able to relish the Pappataci life.

notes, and then "Pappataci" on a symmetrically ascending phrase. Pappataci is a mysterious honorary order of men whose principal obligations are to eat, drink, and sleep: *"Ber, dormir, e poi mangiar."* Rossini composed a sort of patter trio, in which the singers express over and over again, in staccato eighth notes, the same sentiments: *"Pappataci dee dormir, Pappataci dee mangiar"* (Pappataci must sleep, Pappataci must eat). *"Bella vita!"* exclaims Mustafa.[48] Surely, Rossini must have had in mind Mozart's drinking duet in the *Abduction*, when Pedrillo persuades Osmin to drink the wine. The Rossini trio, like the Mozart duet, gaily celebrates the temptation of the Muslim basso by European tricksters, two against one in the case of Rossini, and Mustafa, like Osmin, immediately succumbs to the false comradery proffered in the name of food, drink, and sleep.

Yet Rossini, like Mozart, could not have failed to note that in fact all men like to eat, drink, and sleep, and that Mustafa, in becoming a Pappataci, merely demonstrates that he is human like everyone else. Even an Oriental despot might like to eat and drink. It is perhaps worth noting that the syllables of Pappataci do call to mind the name of Mozart's Papageno, who also loves to eat and drink, and was always the character in the *Magic Flute* most beloved by the operatic public, even if—or precisely because—he could not live up to the opera's Masonic ideals.

Just as the dignity of Kaimakan means cross-dressing Taddeo as a Turk with a turban, so the ceremonial initiation of Pappataci means that Mustafa has to trade in his turban for a wig and a Pappataci costume. While the staging of the opera might allow for this costume to be designed as something completely ridiculous, Mustafa himself supposes that his Pappataci costume is simply European, and the specification of the wig did indeed suggest some sort of powdered European style of the ancien régime. Napoleon in Egypt ordered that Egyptian officials wear the French revolutionary tricolor, as acknowledgment of the French conquest, and the Pappataci costume functioned similarly as the emblem of the imperial triumph of the Italian girl in Algiers.

In the Pappataci ceremony Mustafa is enjoined not only to eat and drink, but at the same time to see and not see, to hear and not hear—*"di veder, e non veder, di sentir, e non sentir"*—to achieve the most perfect condition of lethargic obliviousness. A chorus sums up for Mustafa his obligations as a Pappataci:

Lascia pur che gli altri facciano:	Let other people act:
Tu qui mangia, bevi e taci.	You eat, drink, and be quiet.
Questo è il rito primo e massimo	This is the first and greatest rite
Della nostra società.	Of our society.[49]

Mustafa finds this initiation irresistible, and it comically distracts him while the European captives make their escape from Algiers. It should be noted, however, that the Pappataci values are presented as European values, that the Society of Pappataci is supposedly a European society to which he is being admitted by Isabella's special dispensation. Anelli, Mosca, and finally Rossini were also satirizing their own Italian society when they staged the ceremonial of the Pappataci in Algiers. One might even wonder whether Rossini, himself a famous gourmand who deeply loved his dinner and gave his name to Tournedos Rossini, might have approached the Pappataci in a spirit of indulgent gastronomic sympathy.

Goethe traveled to Italy in the 1780s, one generation earlier, but his celebrated account of the voyage, *Italienische Reise*, only began to be assembled in 1813, the year of Rossini's *L'italiana in Algeri*. In Verona Goethe observed: "The people shout, throw things, scuffle, laugh and sing all day long. The mild climate and cheap food make life easy for them." In Rome he generalized further: "All I can say about the Italians is this: they are children of Nature, who, for all the pomp and circumstance of their religion and art, are not a whit different from what they would be if they were still living in forests and caves." In Naples he had the impression of "a happy country which amply satisfies all the basic human needs and breeds a people who are happy by nature, people who can wait without concern for tomorrow to bring them what they had today and for that reason lead a happy-go-lucky existence."[50] Goethe's observations would become the basis for long-lasting future generalizations about Italy as a backward but happy land of warm sun, cheap food, and easy satisfaction—forming, in some sense, a society of Pappataci.

In 1806 the French traveler Auguste Creuzé de Lesser published an account of recent Italian travels, claiming to observe in Naples an inordinate interest in eating and a general lack of energy, the perfect profile for the Pappataci. He further noted that "Europe ends at Naples, and ends badly," so that "Calabria, Sicily, all the rest is Africa." The Mediterranean proximity of northern Africa and southern Italy made it possible to envision a common domain, construed as a domain of backwardness. Creuzé de Lesser worried about Barbary pirates when he sailed from Palermo to Naples, but the issue of captivity would have been complicated for him by his conviction that Italian women already lived in "slavery" in southern Italy.[51] In fact, Italians in Algiers might not be geographically, or even culturally, so very far from home, and various Mediterranean values, including those of Pappataci, could have been seen as mutually relevant. By the early nineteenth century there were already strongly conceived notions of Italian character that would have shaped the operatic reception of the Society of Pappataci, first in Milan in 1808 and then in Venice in 1813.

The *Giornale Dipartimentale dell'Adriatico*, reviewing Rossini's Venetian premiere in 1813, did not doubt that Pappataci had some real meaning for Europeans, and that since the opera was anyway unfaithful in rendering "customs and costumes," the story of Mustafa could be told without reference to his Turkishness:

> We see a bully [*spaccone*] who mistreats women and, tired of his wife, stumbles into the nets of a shrewd woman who makes herself into the decoy, deceives him, and flees with her true lover. Therefore the character of Pappataci is not applied to the bully in its true sense, that of a low character who vilely suffers shameful things because he likes to eat and who profits from the dissipation of his wife or lover—but here he's just a silly fool. There is much that is ridiculous, but nothing characteristic.[52]

This passage was so thoroughly stripped of ethnic identifiers that it was impossible to say, by the end, in what way the opera failed to be characteristic: of Turks? of Italians? Certainly, the reviewer, who seemed to claim a certain expertise on the subject of Pappataci, believed that either an Italian or a Turk was capable of bearing the epithet. Already in Venice in 1813 the Society of Pappataci was understood to offer the public some element of satirical mirroring.

Stendhal claimed to believe that the Pappataci in *L'italiana* were intended as a satirical mockery of the Napoleonic Italian Senate, and credited the genius of the librettist Anelli: "Did he not have the boldness under Bonaparte to mock the nullity of the Senate of Italy? That is the whole secret of the long scenes of Pappataci."[53] In fact, the purely consultative senate of the Kingdom of Italy was created in Milan in 1808, the same year that Anelli's libretto was composed by Mosca and performed at La Scala. Anelli, who was politically active in the Cisalpine Republic preceding the creation of the Kingdom of

Italy, may have intended the Pappataci to satirize the political institutions created by Napoleon for Italy, but the satire also clearly extended to the more general character of Italian customs and society.

Rossinian Patriotism in Algiers: "Pensa alla patria"

Italy would continue to be the object of European diplomacy at the Congress of Vienna in 1815, as Metternich designed the political structure of Restoration Europe. In 1848 the political slogan *"L'Italia farà da se"* (Italy will do it alone) reflected the Risorgimento reaction against the passivity of the past, when Italians had "let other people act." In *L'italiana* Anelli and Rossini were already sensitive to the perceived problem of Italian passivity, and the opera included an Italian patriotic anthem that addressed the worrisome implications of Pappataci values, not only among the Turks but among the Italians themselves.

This anthem was composed by Rossini as the musical culmination of the second act, Isabella's rondo aria with a recurring patriotic refrain, to stoke the Italian patriotism of the captives and especially of her beloved Lindoro as she prepares them all for their escape from Algiers and return to Italy. Because they are captives, she has all the more need to rouse their spirits, like Moses preparing to lead the enslaved Hebrews out of Egypt, another subject that Rossini would soon set to music for Naples in 1818. Isabella urges Lindoro to "show you are Italian" (*mostrarti italiano*), embracing the values of fatherland, duty, and honor (*patria, dovere, e onor*).[54] When Taddeo dares to laugh, she dismisses him with contempt. The refrain, *"Pensa alla patria"* (Think of the fatherland), stands in absolute contrast with the obligations of the Pappataci: to eat, drink, and sleep.

With elaborate ornamentation, playing upon all the sharp notes of E major, Isabella proclaims the advent of the Italian Risorgimento:

Vedi per tutta Italia	You see all over Italy
Rinascere gli esempi	Reborn the examples
D'ardir e di valor.	Of daring and of valor.[55]

Yet to proclaim such rebirth implied that these values and examples were lacking in the recent past, that Italians were in fact awakening from the Pappataci past, when they were no better than Turks. Taddeo, by his laughter, shows that he still cannot take seriously these new Risorgimento values, and therefore perhaps deserves to wear the turban of the Kaimakan.

Inasmuch as this aria was the star turn of the second act, the importance of Italian patriotism was meaningfully embedded in the Turkish scenario, and the whole comedy of Turkishness served to hold up a mirror to Mediterranean Pappataci values in Italian society. Italians were accordingly urged to elevate themselves above the level of the Turks whom they risked resembling through similar moral, social, and political values. Rather than affirming a clash of civilizations, the opera acknowledged the human similarities that underlay contrasting cultures, sometimes no more than a matter of costume: the turban of the Kaimakan, the wig of the Pappataci.

In February 1813, a few months before the premiere of *L'italiana*, Rossini had already offered Venice a sample of musical patriotism in *Tancredi*, an *opera seria*. In the first act Tancredi returns to Sicily from exile and his first words are a salute to his *patria*, or fatherland:

O patria! dolce, e ingrata patria!	Oh fatherland, sweet and ungrateful!
Alfine a te ritorno!	At last I return to you!
Io ti saluto, o cara terra	I salute you, o dear earth
degli avi miei: ti bacio.	of my ancestors: I kiss you.[56]

The kiss was presumably performed upon the stage in February, in the solemn spirit of *opera seria*; Isabella would further articulate Rossinian operatic patriotism in May, in the context of *opera buffa*.

The phenomenon of modern nationalism emerged in Europe in the age of the French Revolution, as the Declaration of the Rights of Man declared that sovereignty resided in "the nation," as the *levée en masse* brought all men into the revolutionary army fighting for France, as the Marseillaise musically celebrated the children of the fatherland, *les enfants de la patrie*. The same spirit of modern nationalism spread across Europe along with—and sometimes in reaction against—the French revolutionary army, which conceived of itself as a force of liberation, even as the revolutionary republic gave way to the Napoleonic empire. It was still the age of the republic in 1796 when the young Napoleon Bonaparte led the French army into Italy and drove the Habsburgs from Milan. Stendhal, in *The Charterhouse of Parma*, saw Napoleon's entry into Milan as the crucial moment of Italian national awakening for a people who now recognized "that to be happy after centuries of debilitating sensations, it was necessary to love the fatherland [*aimer la patrie*] with a real love and look for heroic actions."[57] This was also the spirit of Isabella's "*Pensa alla patria*," and likewise of Tancredi's return to Sicily, "*O patria!*"

Stendhal had no doubt that Rossini's patriotism was a matter of Napoleonic inspiration, a patriotism that "no Italian maestro could have imagined before Arcole and Lodi." Arcole and Lodi evoked glorious military moments from Napoleon's campaign in Italy against the Austrians in 1796. "These names were the first that Rossini would have heard pronounced around his cradle, these sublime names from 1796. Rossini was five, and he could see passing through Pesaro those immortal demi-brigades of 1796."[58] Anelli, when he wrote the text for Isabella's aria in 1808, would have been inspired by the Napoleonic awakening of Italy in the 1790s.

As emperor, Napoleon governed Italy through two separate satellite kingdoms, that of Italy in the north and that of Naples in the south, but Napoleonic rule, merging so many formerly distinctive principalities, stimulated Italian nationalism and posed the question of Italian unification more emphatically than ever before. The patriotic values of "*Pensa alla patria*" reflected the French revolutionary values associated with Napoleon's Kingdom of Italy—including even a musical intimation of the Marseillaise—but by 1813 the Russian invasion had failed and the collapse of the Napoleonic order was imminent. Rossini composed his opera at a pivotal moment when it was possible—and perhaps necessary—to preserve some ambiguity over whether the Italian "*patria*" envisioned was to be Napoleonic or post-Napoleonic. The Napoleonic Kingdom of Italy could be considered as a Pappataci example of what happens when Italians "let other people act," and the Napoleonic regime had anyway made itself unpopular in Italy with its heavy taxes and massive conscription. A comedy of Turkishness became the vehicle both for evading the political crossroads of the moment in 1813, and for suggesting at the same time a hopeful vision of Italian rebirth.

In fact, the early performance history of *L'italiana* between 1813 and 1815 suggests a pushpin map of the future unification of Italy: from Turin to Trieste, and as far south as Naples. The original Venice production moved to nearby Vicenza in the summer of 1813, and there was a production in Turin by the fall of 1813 at the Teatro Carignano. In 1814 *L'italiana* came to Milan, Florence, Ancona, and Trieste, followed by Ferrara, Rome, and Naples in 1815.[59] This pan-Italian celebration of Isabella in Algiers would have exercised its maximum effect during the very years when the Napoleonic order was crumbling and the Restoration had not yet arrived to inhibit expressions of Italian national sentiment.

The Venetian *Giornale Dipartimentale dell'Adriatico* of May 24, 1813, the same issue that reviewed the premiere of *L'italiana*, was just receiving the news of Napoleon's victory over the Russians and Prussians at Lützen, near Leipzig, on May 2. Empress Marie Louise, from the French chateau of Saint-Cloud, declared the victory to be "a special act of divine protection" and asked the bishops of the Napoleonic empire and kingdoms to schedule a Te Deum in the churches. The *Giornale* reported that the Te Deum was duly sung in Venice in the basilica of San Marco on May 23—the day after the premiere of *L'italiana*.[60] This may have been the last Te Deum to be sung for a Napoleonic victory.

The favorable review of *L'italiana* in the *Giornale* noted the genius of Rossini on the level of the most sublime masters, and offered approving words about "*il bravo Galli*" as Mustafa. The review, however, was principally enthusiastic about the diva Marietta Marcolini and most excited about her singing of the patriotic rondo "executed with such perfection, with such a masterful handling of her ample and penetrating cords, that it inspired ecstasy." The reviewer emphatically rejected insinuations that she had borrowed her ornamentations from some other singer, and praised her particularly for performing in spite of illness.[61] The Venetian journal made no mention of the political content of Isabella's aria, but it was politically controversial enough so that in a subsequent Roman production the aria had to be rephrased as "*Pensa alla sposa*" (Think of your wife). In Naples in 1815 it would be replaced altogether with a new piece for the prima donna.[62] Such later substitutions confirm the political impact of the original aria in Venice, with the word "*patria*" deployed to powerful effect, indeed to rapturous and ecstatic effect, in an opera more generally concerned with ridiculing Mustafa.

Conclusion: Contented Turks and Italians

Milan had already seen Mosca's *L'italiana* in 1808, but Rossini's treatment arrived in 1814 at the new Teatro Re, and in 1815 the opera claimed the stage of La Scala. The political condition of Europe was completely transformed since the premiere in Venice in 1813, and the return of *L'italiana* to Milan in August

1815, two months after Waterloo, coincided with the arrival of the newly re-stored Habsburg emperor and empress. *Il Corriere Milanese* saluted Emperor Franz, "our most beloved sovereign" (*l'amatissimo nostro sovrano*), and noted according to the news from Genoa that his Italian-born wife, Empress Maria Ludovika, would be arriving by sea and would soon "land upon our shores" (*approderà alle nostre spiaggie*)—a triumphant arrival which was the radical inversion of the shipwreck of Isabella on the shores of Algeria.[63]

The review of *L'italiana* in the *Corriere* welcomed Isabella to Milan as an old friend:

> This noble pilgrim, after having traveled around half the musical world, has come to find her fortune in the great theater of Milan . . . To speak of the merits of this composition would be to repeat that which is already well-known . . . La Marcolini, for whom the music of the Italiana was originally written, is in every respect someone to make every bey lose his head. She is to be admired for the constant courage with which she goes in search of the greatest challenges of art in order to conquer them.[64]

The genius of Rossini, celebrated in Venice, was almost effaced here in Milan as the heroine herself emerged as the new conqueror for the new post-Napo-leonic age, a woman who could dazzle any Turkish bey and any Italian opera audience.

In fact, Marcolini in Milan was dazzling the same old bey she'd first daz-zled in Venice two years before: Filippo Galli, already emerging as the defini-tive Rossinian Turk of the European Restoration. The review of the premiere in Venice had little to say about his Turkishness, regarding him as the general type of the male bully (*spaccone*), who perhaps cut a little too close to aspects of the Italian character. The Milan review of 1815, however, took more plea-sure in Galli's artful Turkishness, already recognized as his trademark:

> On the stage there is no better Turk than Galli. We saw him in *La pietra del paragone* awaken universal applause when he emerged cross-dressed as an Arab or an Ottoman [*travestito da arabo o da ottomano*]; we see him now sustain with great self-possession [*disinvoltura*] and with uncommon intelligence the part of the Bey: wrapped in an ample robe [*zimarra*], with a heavy turban, and with a thick beard, he is a true chief of Barbary. I do not speak of his singing, as it is well known how he surpasses by far so many other virtuosi who call themselves comic singers and are neither the former nor the latter.[65]

Different reviewers might have different perspectives, of course, but this suggests some revaluation of Mustafa, from 1813 to 1815, from Venice to Milan—for the Venice reviewer thought the same performer in the same role was "just a silly fool" who showed "much that is ridiculous, but nothing characteristic." In Milan Galli's Turkishness was taken seriously, and the impersonation of a Turk was treated as a matter of intelligence. Indeed, the Turk himself appeared almost admirable in this reviewer's portrait, as if there were some point of Turkish pride in Galli's virtuoso impersonation.

Following so many eighteenth-century precedents, Rossini composed an operatic perspective on despotism, embodied as a singing Turk and cross-dressed in Ottoman robes. From 1813 to 1815 as the Napoleonic hegemony in Europe tottered and collapsed, it became increasingly plausible for the public to look beneath the robes and identify the despot as he lurched toward his ultimate humiliation. It was possible to laugh at Mustafa, as it was always possible to deride a despot upon whom the tables were turned, to mock a former master and relish his abasement, but Galli also managed to find in the public a note of sympathy for the mighty who had fallen. The Milan review appeared in the *Corriere* on August 11, and four days later, on August 15, the newspaper noted, perhaps without enthusiastic conviction, that "all Europe is now armed in order to secure finally the happiness and repose of the present generation."[66] There was no mention of the fact that August 15 was Napoleon's birthday, the former festival of Saint Napoleon.

In 1815, during the Hundred Days that followed Napoleon's escape from Elba up until his defeat at Waterloo on June 18, Joachim Murat, the Napoleonic king of Naples, issued a national manifesto to the Italians in the hope of unifying Italy behind the Napoleonic cause. Murat, who had served Napoleon in Italy in 1796, and in Egypt in 1798, became his marshal, his brother-in-law, and the king of Naples after 1808. In 1815 Murat spoke the language of Italian nationalism and unification, and Rossini responded by composing an anthem of Italian patriotism, "*Agli italiani*" (To the Italians), also known as the "*Inno dell'indipendenza*" (Anthem of independence), "*Sorgi Italia*" (Arise, Italy), and even the Italian Marseillaise. Rossini conducted a performance of the anthem in Bologna on behalf of Murat, one day before the city was taken by the Habsburgs, and Rossini was thereafter a figure who merited some suspicion in the age of the Habsburg Restoration.[67]

In October 1815, four months after Waterloo, at the premiere of *L'italiana*

in Naples there was an alternative recitative and aria to replace the provocative "*Pensa alla patria*." Without reference to Italian patriotism, Isabella sang
in the recitative about the anticipated Italian escape as an imminent political
reversal for Mustafa:

> ed il briccone qui lasceremo all'inatteso caso
> con tre palmi di orecchie e sei di naso.

> and we'll leave that scoundrel behind, unexpectedly,
> with big ears, three palms, and a big nose, six palms.[68]

The conceited bey would be left behind, humiliated, with ridiculously swol-
len features, the extremely long nose perhaps vulgarly suggesting his priapic
frustration at the escape of his sexual prey. There was, however, another *bric-
cone*, another scoundrel, who just at that time was being left behind by European history, for October 1815 was the very month that marked the beginning
of Napoleon's exile on St. Helena.

Fifty years later in 1864, after the achievement of Italian unification, Rossini would assert his patriotic credentials by citing the aria of Isabella:

> In my artistic adolescence, I set to music with fervor and success the following
> words:

> Vedi per tutta Italia
> Rinascere gli esempi
> D'ardir e di valor . . .

> and later, in 1815, when King Murat came to Bologna with sacred promises,
> I composed the "Inno dell'indipendenza," which was performed under
> my direction at the Teatro Contavalli. In this hymn is found the word
> "indipendenza"—which, though it is not very poetic, aroused lively
> enthusiasm as intoned by me in my then resonant voice and repeated by the
> people, choruses, etc.[69]

In his seventies Rossini could still look back across half a century and remember himself singing of Italian independence in Bologna in 1815, at the
last possible moment for Napoleonic fantasies, and he also cited as evidence
of his own youthful patriotism the aria of the Italian girl in Algiers. On the
stage in Venice in 1813, with the whole Napoleonic enterprise in the throes
of impending disaster, Rossini had encouraged the Italian public to think of
their fatherland and laugh at the Turks.

"Travelling through the province of Venice in the year 1817," wrote Stendhal, "I found *L'italiana* being performed simultaneously in Brescia, in Verona, in Venice itself, in Vicenza, and in Treviso."[70] Venetia was just another Habsburg province in 1817, and it is possible that the original Venetian enthusiasm for the opera, nationally magnified in the context of the Napoleonic Kingdom of Italy, was experienced differently, provincially, under the Restoration in 1817. In that same year, the opera was also performed in Bourbon Paris at the Théâtre-Italien and in Habsburg Vienna at the Kärntnertor Court Theater. Both the Habsburgs and the Bourbons had suffered their own humiliations in the age of Napoleon, and the Habsburg Emperor Franz was even ignobly compelled to send to Paris his own daughter, Marie Louise, to be the bride of Napoleon in a sort of Turkish captivity. The triumph of Isabella over Mustafa, over the outrageous pretensions of a self-important potentate, may have had its reassuring aspects even in the Restoration capitals.

In Venice the excitement over the premiere of *L'italiana* in 1813 may genuinely have fed upon some emancipatory excitement over the imminent Napoleonic collapse, but by 1817, when Stendhal found the opera being performed all over northern Italy, public response would have been tinged with the recognition that Napoleonic rule had been simply displaced by restored Habsburg rule. The Ottoman empire, by then, had clearly survived the Napoleonic interlude—indeed, successfully resisted the Napoleonic assault on Egypt—and had outlived both the Venetian Republic of San Marco and the Napoleonic Kingdom of Italy. Nevertheless, the Venetians, the Bresciani, the Veronesi, the Trevigiani of 1817, provincial Habsburg subjects, still came to the opera to see Mustafa comically subjugated on the operatic stage.

As Lindoro and Taddeo watch Mustafa's happy initiation as a Pappataci, they sing their satisfaction:

Che babbeo! che scimunito!	What an idiot! what a fool!
Me la godo per mia fe.	In faith, I'm enjoying it.[71]

The public enjoyment of Mustafa's foolishness would have echoed that of the Italian characters on the stage, tinged perhaps with some recognition that ridicule and respect were variable perspectives, and that Turks and Italians bore some Mediterranean relation to one another. From the premiere in 1813 to the wide-ranging productions of 1817, one fact that all Europeans would have learned to acknowledge was the changeability of political fortune. Opera audiences would have known very well how to understand the chorus of eunuchs that sang "*Viva viva il flagel delle donne*" in the first act, and then "*Uno stupido, uno stolto diventato è Mustafà*" in the second. The transformation from "scourge" to "fool," from lion to ass, was a historically verifiable fact in 1817, and the Italian public, like the chorus of eunuchs, was singing new anthems. Haydn's Habsburg hymn, "*Gott erhalte, Franz den Kaiser, unsern guten Kaiser Franz!*" became in Italian, "*Serbi Dio, l'austriaco regno, guardi il nostro imperator!*" The figure of the singing Turk on the operatic stage was all the more meaningful for the public of 1817 who could now see, even more clearly than in 1813, that the potentate who sang to celebrate himself—"Now I consider myself greater than the great Sultan"—was failing to notice how vulnerable he actually was to the volatile forces of political destiny.

If laughing at the presumption of Mustafa is undeniably a part of the opera's appeal, *L'italiana* nevertheless ends in a spirit of remarkable cordiality, as well as musical harmony, between the Turks and the Italians. The Pappataci initiation becomes the occasion for the Italian captives to make their escape, and when Mustafa is roused from reciting his Pappataci slogans—"*di veder, e non veder, di sentir, e non sentir*"—and told that the Italians are gone, his rage flames up and then dies away in about twenty measures. Turning to Elvira, he begs her pardon, as if he were Count Almaviva begging pardon of the Countess at the end of Mozart's *Marriage of Figaro*:

Sposa mia: non più italiane,	My wife: no more Italian women,
Torno a te. Deh! mi perdona.	I return to you. Pardon me.[72]

Of course she does, and in the final ensemble the Turks on shore happily harmonize with the Italians now at sea, echoing again the finale of *The Marriage of Figaro*: "*Ah, tutti contenti saremo così.*" In *L'italiana* the Turks sing to the Italians: "*Buon viaggio, stian bene!*" (Bon voyage, be well!). Then all together, the Turks and Italians sing the same verse of contentment with a mere variation in the grammar of the verb: "*possiamo/potete contenti lasciar queste arene*" (we can/you can leave these arenas contented).[73] They conclude in D major, also the concluding key of *The Marriage of Figaro*. Mozart harmonized masters and servants, but Rossini harmonized Turks and Italians. Thus, contentedly reintegrated into their separate cultural spheres, Ottoman and European, Muslim and Christian—blissfully unaware that the French army would come to conquer Algeria in 1830—the two choruses hope to live happily ever after on their different shores of the Mediterranean. In 1813 the conventions of *opera buffa* meant that Turks and Italians could be both culturally separated and also musically harmonized in the finale. After all, the opera had already demonstrated how much they had in common.

9

AN OTTOMAN PRINCE IN
THE ROMANTIC IMAGINATION

The Libertine Adventures of
Rossini's Turkish Traveler

Introduction: "Bella Italia" after Napoleon

The premiere of Rossini's *Il turco in Italia* took place at La Scala on August 14, 1814, the day before Napoleon's birthday, which could not be celebrated now, with Napoleon a prisoner on Elba and the Habsburgs occupying Milan. Bonaparte's passing from the political scene also meant the implosion of the Kingdom of Italy, but the moment seemed as suitable as ever for Turkish entertainment, which could be politically suggestive and at the same time politically uncompromising. The eponymous star of *Il turco in Italia* could have been no one else but Filippo Galli, fresh from his triumph as Mustafa in *L'italiana* in Venice, a role that he would also perform at La Scala in 1815.

Stendhal, who came to live in Milan in 1814, saw *Il turco in Italia* and later recalled the sensation of the Turk's first appearance on stage: "The superb voice of Galli was deployed to great advantage in the salute that the Turk, just disembarked, addresses to beautiful Italy: '*Bella Italia, alfin ti miro.*'"[1] Perhaps Stendhal identified with the Turk's sentimental enthusiasm—"Beautiful Italy, at last I gaze upon you"—as the French writer himself was returning to Italy in 1814 after the terrible rigors of the Russian campaign. Yet for the Italian public, Italy, in its Napoleonic form, had actually just disappeared from the geopolitical map, and Italians would now only be able to recall the Kingdom of Italy in the mind's eye. In this case, they would see it mirrored in the admiring gaze of an alien Turk on the operatic stage, looking out at them, the putative Italian public, the only Italy that remained. "*Vi saluto,*" sings the Turk, I salute you, and with this salutation to Italy Rossini greeted the new era of the Restoration.

Following the success of *L'italiana in Algeri*, he now commenced upon an even more intricate engagement of Italian sentiments and Turkish themes.

Stendhal, who loved *Il turco in Italia*, admitted that it was not a success at the premiere but received a "cold reception"—because the proud Milanese "maintained that Rossini had copied himself" and had not created something entirely original for La Scala.[2] The reviewer for the *Corriere Milanese* began by describing himself sitting in a café on a rainy evening in Milan, and then hurrying over to the theater to be in time for the curtain, full of anticipation.[3] After listening to the opening of the first act, including Galli's entrance as the Turk, the reviewer could not help commenting to his "very discreet" neighbor in the theater, "*C'est du vin de son cru*"—This is wine of its vintage—in other words, disappointingly dated and familiar from earlier Rossini efforts. The reviewer further described a public that was generally disapproving, with some in the audience even expressing disappointment out loud during the performance.[4] Herbert Weinstock, writing Rossini's biography, calls the premiere production a "disaster."[5]

The Milanese women's journal, *Corriere delle dame*, reviewing the premiere of *Il turco in Italia*, was particularly critical of the libretto:

> All the music of this *opera buffa* is as great as the fame of the maestro, since at its center he has assembled the various beauties and jewels dispersed throughout *L'italiana in Algeri*, *La pietra del paragone*, and other operas written by this young and worthy composer. In doing so, perhaps Rossini has taken into account that the poetry of this drama is extracted from a rancid libretto, written in Dresden, whose aim was to ridicule the customs of Italian lovers and husbands . . . *L'italiana in Algeri* needed a husband; and the fecund genius of the poet and composer served as witnesses to her marriage with *Il turco in Italia*. Will children be born of this wedding? Public opinion would prefer that the nuptial bed remain sterile.[6]

The libretto was by Felice Romani, from Genoa, who was almost as young as Rossini, and would go on to collaborate on such masterpieces as *Norma* with Bellini and *L'elisir d'amore* with Donizetti. Yet in the *Corriere delle dame* the libretto of *Il turco in Italia* was considered to be German, since Romani's model was an earlier text composed and performed in Dresden and Vienna in the 1780s. The opera was thus received as a German satire on Italian customs.

The music of *Il turco* was certainly very different from that of *L'italiana*, while the two libretti were in some sense structurally opposite, especially in relation to their central Turkish figures. In *L'italiana* Mustafa is a completely ridiculous Turk, and the Venetian public of 1813 was able to enjoy his humiliation, but Selim, the hero of *Il turco*, is altogether admirable, romantically irresistible, and musically charismatic from the moment he appears upon the stage to salute the land of Italy. As the *Corriere delle dame* pointed out, the overt objects of ridicule in *Il turco* were none other than the Italians themselves—"the customs of Italian lovers and husbands"—and this may not have been an altogether welcome message in Milan in 1814, in the immediate aftermath of the collapse of the Kingdom of Italy. Above all, *Il turco in Italia* radically broke with the conventions of Turkish subjects in European opera by offering the public a fully sympathetic, freely engaged, entirely reciprocal romance between a Turkish man and an Italian woman, set in European Italy without any of the elements of compulsion imposed by pirates or harems.

"A Turkish prince who is traveling"

Some of the substance of Romani's libretto derived from the work of the eighteenth-century Venetian poet Caterino Mazzolà, who had written a libretto for an opera by Franz Seydelmann performed in Dresden in 1788 and in Vienna in 1789. A closely related libretto was set to music for Prague in 1794 by Mozart's close associate Franz Xaver Süssmayr, employing the alternative title *Il musulmano in Napoli* (The Muslim in Naples). Another version was composed by Francesco Bianchi for the Teatro San Moisè in Venice in 1794, and performed under the title *La capricciosa ravveduta* (The capricious woman repentant)—thus focusing less on the Turk and more on the prima donna, the married Italian woman who only at the very end of the opera renounces her romantic intrigue with the Turkish hero.[7] The treatment by Rossini and Romani thus represented the operatic culmination of a thematic development that had already passed through both Vienna and Venice in the late eighteenth century.

The audience at La Scala in 1814 was perhaps not fully prepared to acknowledge the gallantry and charisma of an irresistible Turk on the operatic stage. *Il turco in Italia*, however, would go on to have better and broader reception beyond Milan, including Rome and Florence in 1815, Udine, Ferrara, Venice, Turin, Bologna, and Dresden in 1816, Mantua, Verona, Ravenna, Siena, and Naples in 1817, Livorno, Modena, and Madrid (in Spanish) in 1818,

Munich in 1819, Paris and Vienna (in German) in 1820, London and Moscow in 1821, Madrid in 1822, and Palermo, Prague, and St. Petersburg (in Russian) in 1823.[8] Like *L'italiana in Algeri, Il turco in Italia* was being staged everywhere in the early years of the Restoration.

Romani's libretto in 1814 described Selim as "*Principe turco che viaggia,*" a Turkish prince who is traveling. He seemed to be intended as a grand figure of the Ottoman elite—possibly of the ruling dynasty—though without any specified political role comparable to the despotic enterprises of Pasha Selim or Mustafa, Bey of Algiers. In fact, back in 1788 when the first version of this operatic subject was performed in Dresden, and Prince Selim first appeared in the dramatis personae, the crown prince of the Ottoman empire actually was of that name, the future Selim III, who came to the throne the following year, in 1789, the year of the Vienna production of Seydelmann's *Il turco in Italia*. No Ottoman sultan had ever been so seriously interested in Europe as Selim was, and as sultan he would be a great reformer, but even before coming to the throne he was known to have European interests and actually corresponded with Louis XVI, the king of France. It was thus possible that Mazzolà borrowed the name from the actual Ottoman dynasty, and certainly the name Selim was very apt for a Turk with European interests. By the time of Rossini's opera in 1814, however, Selim was already deposed and deceased.

The traveling Ottoman prince arrived by sea at a locality specified in the libretto as the countryside near Naples. In 1480, late in the reign of Mehmed the Conqueror, an Ottoman fleet landed at Otranto in southern Italy, a fearful moment in the golden age of the Italian Renaissance, but a Neapolitan force dislodged the Turks in 1481. Again in 1537, during the reign of Suleiman the Magnificent, the Ottoman admiral Barbarossa briefly occupied Otranto. An account from the later sixteenth century noted the frequent raids of Barbary corsairs: "They have ravaged and ruined Sardinia, Corsica, Sicily, Calabria, the coasts of Naples, Rome, and Genoa."[9] These pirates, who carried off captives to be sold as slaves, would continue to be a presence on and off the coast of southern Italy, and especially Sicily, in the seventeenth and eighteenth centuries, and the popular Italian expression of fear—"*Mamma li turchi!*"—may date back to this era. Basso Ludwig Fischer noted the presence of Turkish pirates off the coast at Civitavecchia in 1783. Tunisian corsairs carried off nine hundred captives from the island of San Pietro near Sardinia, in 1798, and Robert Davis notes that the period of the Napoleonic wars was actually favorable to Barbary raids on the Italian coast. Indeed, 150 captives were taken from Sant'Antioco off Sardinia, in 1815, even as Rossini's operas *L'italiana* and *Il turco* were making their way around the opera houses of Italy.[10] Selim, however, was no pirate but simply a traveler.

The most dedicated Ottoman traveler of the seventeenth century, Evliya Çelebi, who left behind a ten-volume account of his travels, the *Seyâhatnâme*, explored not only the Ottoman empire itself but, additionally, when he was sent as an envoy to Vienna in the 1660s, Christian European lands. There were also celebrated Ottoman diplomatic missions to Europe, like that of Suleiman Aga to the court of Louis XIV in 1669, and that of Mehmed Efendi early in the reign of Louis XV in 1720–21. In Rossini's opera, however, Selim was clearly traveling not on any sort of diplomatic or government mission but entirely out of his own curiosity and for his own pleasure. In this regard he resembled eighteenth-century European travelers from England, France, or the German lands, who traveled to Italy as tourists on the Grand Tour. Their purely fictional Muslim counterparts might have been the Persians created by Montesquieu in the *Persian Letters*, as observers of European society. "We arrived at Livorno after a voyage of forty days," wrote Montesquieu's Usbek. "The town is new and bears witness to the ability of the dukes of Tuscany, who have created, out of a village in the marshes, the most prosperous town in Italy. The women here enjoy great freedom."[11] One of those women would be Rossini's Italian girl in Algiers, who hailed originally from Livorno and certainly knew how to exercise her freedom, even in supposed captivity. Romani, the librettist, came from Genoa along the same coast as Livorno.

At the moment that Selim, the traveling Turk, first appeared off the coast of Naples, on the operatic stage in Dresden in 1788 and Vienna in 1789, the most celebrated traveler to Naples was none other than Goethe, who had been there in 1787 and remained in Rome for part of 1788, sending news of his Italian journey back to his German correspondents in Weimar. Goethe traveled to visit the classical world, to see the natural beauty of the Mediterranean, and to appreciate the customs of the Italian people as the children of nature. Selim, as conceived for the stages of Dresden and Vienna, surely reflected the same German interest in Italy that also sent Goethe traveling to the Mediterranean, and the operatic Turk was likewise interested in the natural beauty of Italy and the customs of the Italian people, especially Italian women. "We met a company of lively Neapolitans, who were as natural and lighthearted as could be," wrote Goethe of an excursion to Pompeii. "One of the Neapolitans declared that, without a view of the sea, life would not be worth living." A few days later Goethe exclaimed: "Naples is a paradise; everyone lives in a state of intoxicated self-forgetfulness, myself included. I seem to be a completely different person whom I hardly recognize."[12] Rossini, bringing the spirit of the late Enlightenment into the epoch of Romanticism, musically conjured the spirit of supremely lighthearted, totally intoxicated Italian romance, accented by the perspective of an exotic alien, the Turk.

In August 1814, at the time of the opera's premiere at La Scala, the *Giornale Italiano* (which was published in Milan) reported on the ships arriving that month at the port of nearby Genoa: from Livorno with cod, from Palermo with sugar and pistachios, from Barcelona with wine, from Messina with silk and anchovies, from Lisbon with leather and coffee—but no ships from Turkey that might plausibly have carried Prince Selim.[13] In fact, such ships would hardly have been welcome, since the *Giornale* reported a few days later on the presence of plague in the Ottoman empire, at Smyrna in particular, even as Prince Selim was enthusiastically arriving in Italy on stage at La Scala.[14] Another newspaper, the *Corriere Milanese*, reported that the plague was present in Ottoman Belgrade and, it was feared, might spread to Bosnia and reach Christian Europe at the Habsburg border.[15] If Prince Selim had actually appeared in an Italian port in 1814, he would have been placed immediately in quarantine, and the opera would have been over almost before it began.

The first scene of the opera presents a tent camp of Gypsies or Roma (Zingari, for Rossini), singing *fortissimo* in a male chorus of tenors and basses: "*Nostra patria è il mondo intero*" (Our fatherland is the entire world).[16] Yet some of these Gypsies, it seems, have original homelands and identities that are now hidden beneath their Gypsy costumes and customs. The Gypsy girl Zaida is interrogated by a poet who happens to be on the scene, observing the Gypsies and wondering if they might provide human material for a drama. Zaida tells him that she was born in the Caucasus Mountains.[17]

"You must have been in some seraglio," the poet guesses, thus revealing precisely what sort of drama he would like to write: a Turkish drama with captives and harems. In fact, her name had already served Mozart for the heroine and title of his incomplete harem opera of 1779. Rossini's Gypsy Zaida was the perfect subject for such a drama: "I lived in Erzurum as the happy slave [*felice schiava*] of Selim Damelec." Indeed, Zaida and Selim loved one another in Erzurum when he was the master and she was the happy slave, but the malicious rumor of her infidelity made him so jealous that he would have murdered her if she had not escaped with fellow slave Albazar to become a Gypsy in Italy.[18] Originally, Mazzolà had been even more specific than Romani about the Turkish background story, identifying Zaida as a Georgian and Albazar as the sultan's "first eunuch"—perhaps so that there would be no hint of romance between him and Zaida.[19] This anatomical detail from the Viennese libretto of 1789, which remained in the Venetian libretto of 1794, was eliminated in Romani's libretto for Rossini in 1814. The original versions in Venice and Vienna also included a black eunuch (*eunuco nero*), Almanzor, who accompanied Prince Selim on stage but remained mute.[20] He would be altogether eliminated by Rossini and Romani.

The figure of the unnamed poet occupies an unusual place in the opera: while standing outside the drama, he seems to be controlling it, even writing it, as it proceeds. Zaida complains of her "cruel destiny" and the poet tells her, "I have a beautiful idea that could make you happy." Naturally she asks what he is thinking:

POET: Debbe arrivar stasera	This evening there should arrive
Un certo Principe	A certain prince,
Turco, il qual viaggia	Turkish, who is traveling
Per visitar l'Italia, ed osservar	To visit Italy, and observe
I costumi Europei.	European customs.
ZAIDA: Mi sembra strano	It seems strange to me
Che salti in testa a un Turco	That there would occur to a Turk
Questa curiosità.	This curiosity.
POET: Il caso è molto raro in verità.	The case is in truth very rare.[21]

They agree that it is "very rare" for a Turk to be traveling out of curiosity to observe European customs, but in fact the historical emergence and development of such Turkish curiosity—which shaped the course of Ottoman reform following European models—was to become fundamental for the whole modern history of the Ottoman empire and the Islamic world.

The Public Appreciation of Prince Selim: "Che bel turco!"

While the fictional poet claimed to be staging his drama in order to bring Selim back together with Zaida, the real operatic purpose of Romani and Rossini was to represent the dramatic and musical encounter between the Turkish prince and the Italian girl Fiorilla, who would be the prima donna of this opera. Only after the stage has been set by the poet and the Gypsies, however, does Fiorilla herself finally appear on the scene. While the Gypsy Zaida is a former harem slave from the Caucasus, and Fiorilla is a married European woman from Sorrento, there is not actually any unbridgeable divergence in customs and morals between them. The brilliant cavatina by which Fiorilla introduces herself to the audience begins with a declaration of promiscuous character:

Non si da follia maggiore	There is no greater madness
Dell'amare un solo oggetto ...	Than loving one sole object ...[22]

Her foolish husband, Don Geronio, is a kind of Pantalone from the tradition of commedia dell'arte, the predestined cuckold. Fiorilla is therefore already predisposed to take an interest in an exotically masculine stranger when a ship is sighted off shore, preparing to land.

The tenors and basses of the Turkish sailors' chorus are heard singing from their ship, while the orchestra ripples in eighth notes around E minor chords, and Fiorilla punctuates the chorus with her interested observations: "*Un naviglio! Turco pare*" (A ship! Seems Turkish). She recognizes the vessel as Turkish, while the Turkish sailors recognize the coast as Italian, anticipating repose after their labors and revealing that they all harbor deep Italian longings:

E scordare il ciel d'Italia	The sky of Italy
Ogni pena ci farà.	Will make us forget every pain.[23]

Italy is presumed to offer restorative comfort to all Mediterranean men, a haven for weary seamen even of Ottoman origin.

With the repetition of this phrase—"*e scordare il ciel d'Italia*"—the chorus builds toward Selim's entrance, and the key of E minor gives way to a brilliant E major chord, followed by a dramatic pause. Now Selim begins to sing, "*Bella Italia*," and already in his first measure he ornaments with a run of sixteenth notes, while his tribute to Italy's friendly shores, "*amiche sponde*," requires ornamentation in thirty-second notes, and his concluding invocation of "*Italia*" produces an even more dazzling run of 128th notes![24] In a mere eighteen measures Selim establishes himself as the most romantically charismatic Turk in the whole history of European opera. In fact, this entrance was entirely Romani's and Rossini's conception, for in Mazzolà's earlier treatment Selim's arrival in Italy took place off stage and was merely reported as news.

"*Bella Italia, alfin ti miro*" (Beautiful Italy, at last I gaze upon you), sings Prince Selim at his brilliant entrance in Rossini's *Il turco in Italia*, and the prince is soon displaying his vocal prowess with a run of thirty-second notes. "Galli's magnificent voice found full scope for its powers in the paean of greeting which the Turk, scarcely come to land, addresses to the fair realm of Italy," wrote Stendhal. Italy, on the brink of its post-Napoleonic political transformation in 1814, saw itself reflected as a beautiful whole in the gaze of an admiring Rossinian Turk.

"*Che bel turco! Avviciniamoci*" (What a beautiful Turk! Let's get closer), comments Fiorilla immediately after Selim's brilliant self-presentation. Her sentiment is true to her character but also perfectly reflects the reaction that Rossini sought to inspire in his audience with Selim's appearance on stage. The Italian public was encouraged to be all the more receptive to his beauty, inasmuch as he revealed himself to be such a dedicated lover of Italy.

"Galli's magnificent voice found full scope for its powers in the paean of greeting which the Turk, scarcely come to land, addresses to the fair realm of Italy," wrote Stendhal, who reported that the audience cheered for Gal-

Filippo Galli, born in Rome in 1783, made his career as a Rossinian basso, and especially as a Rossinian Turk. He was Count Asdrubale in Turkish disguise in *La pietra del paragone* in 1812, Mustafa in *L'italiana in Algeri* in 1813, Prince Selim in *Il turco in Italia* in 1814, and finally the eponymous star of *Maometto Secondo* in 1820. More than anyone else he was able to express all the aspects and dimensions of the singing Turk—from farcical tyrant to romantic libertine to fierce conqueror—including both comedy and tragedy, as suggested by the classical masks. In this engraving his charismatic basso masculinity is emphasized by the Napoleonic hand-in-jacket pose and the very open collar. The engraver has managed to emphasize Galli's dark Mediterranean complexion while also allowing for just enough contrast to reveal the dark hair on his chest. With kind permission of the Österreichische Nationalbibliothek.

li, even if they did not cheer for Rossini at the premiere. "The librettist had built into his text a special virtuoso scene for Galli, who was worshipped in Milan."[25] Filippo Galli, Rossini's "Turkish" basso, had already disguised himself in Turkish costume as the preposterous "Sigillara" Turk of *La pietra del paragone*, and he had created the farcical Pappataci Turkish role of Mustafa in *L'italiana*. Now, in his third Turkish role for Rossini, he deployed his basso to glamorous effect as the romantic hero of *Il turco in Italia*.

In the fifteenth and sixteenth centuries Ottoman armies actually came to southern Italy with the intention to conquer, but in Rossini's modern Mediterranean scenario Prince Selim's conquests were entirely romantic, carried out without coercion by means of charm, vocal display, and his exotic appeal: *Che bel turco!* His progress might thus be seen as the perfect dramatic counterpart to Rossini's own Napoleonic "conquest" of Europe through purely musical means. Indeed, Stendhal's enthusiastic reaction to Selim's opening declamation, and indeed to the whole opera, suggests that the French writer might have identified himself with the brilliant foreigner arriving in Italy. Stendhal, after all, settled in Milan in 1814, the very same year that Selim first appeared at La Scala.

In August 1814, at the time of the premiere in Milan, the *Corriere Milanese* also reported news from the Ottoman capital at Constantinople, where the defeat of Napoleon had been recently marked with a public ceremonial. According to the *Corriere*, it was the Habsburg representative in Constantinople who sponsored a religious celebration in the Pera quarter, giving thanks to God for "the happy reestablishment of peace, which had been banished for so long from Europe."[26] Pera was the foreign quarter of Constantinople, situated at the extremity of Europe, and the Ottoman perspective on the Napoleonic wars was both marginal and ambivalent. The Ottomans had fought against Napoleon in 1798 when he invaded Egypt, but more recently they had fought against Russia and England in tacit cooperation with Napoleon. Now in 1814, according to the *Corriere Milanese*, the celebratory anti-Napoleonic peace procession passed through the streets of Constantinople, and "the streets and windows were crowded with spectators who blessed with enthusiasm the most high monarchs through whom Providence restored peace to the world."[27]

On stage at La Scala, Prince Selim's intentions were entirely peaceful. As Fiorilla drew closer to him (*avviciniamoci*), they both sang in parentheses, expressing thoughts unheard by one another but showing that they were perfectly attuned, mentally and musically. Each one gazes upon the other and reacts in the spirit of easy-going libertinism: "*E mi voglio divertir*" (And I want to amuse myself). Still in the key of E major, she first sings the line on a syncopated ascent from B to E, while he harmoniously descends on the bass clef from B to G-sharp. They then repeat the phrase with synchronized, harmonized ornamentation in sixteenth notes. They sing their mutual assent—

sì, sì, sì, sì—in perfect affirmative accord before shifting the key together to A major, picking up the tempo with the marking *allegro* and expressing their thoughts of mutual admiration. She in particular observes that he, the Turk, is "so full of civility" (*così pien di civiltà*), a phrase that receives strong emphasis as sung in long half notes.[28] She finds him pleasingly exotic, of course, but she is perhaps surprised to find that Selim is also civilized.

It is one of the striking aspects of the opera that Romani and Rossini conceived of a Turk who was not only supremely attractive but completely civilized. Europe and Turkey had never been so intimate upon the operatic stage as they now appeared in 1814, when Selim and Fiorilla harmonized with tripping rapidity on their reciprocal thoughts:

> FIORILLA: Non è poi così difficile questi Turchi a conquistar.
> SELIM: Non è poi così difficile l'Italiane a conquistar.
>
> FIORILLA: It's not so difficult to conquer these Turkish men.
> SELIM: It's not so difficult to conquer these Italian women.[29]

The military meaning has been completely emptied from the concept of "conquest"—now made entirely romantic and libertine—while the perfect harmony of the duet makes it impossible to determine who is conquering whom. Here Europe and Turkey encounter one another on a footing of perfectly equal and mutual engagement.

"Siete Turchi": Selim, Fiorilla, Stendhal, and the Pope

"*Partono dandosi il braccio*" (They leave arm in arm).[30] This stage direction, coming at the conclusion of the amorous duet of reciprocal conquest, might suggest that Fiorilla and Selim are going off immediately to consummate their newly established relationship. Ostensibly, however, they are only going to have coffee at Fiorilla's house. It is her husband, Don Geronio, who notifies the poet (and the audience) of this development:

In casa mia lo guida	To my house she leads him
A prendere il caffè.	To have coffee.
Sian maledetti	Cursed be
Tutti i Turchi del mondo.	All the Turks in the world.[31]

The curse came too late to be taken seriously, for the audience, like Fiorilla, had already been completely charmed by Selim the Turk.

The scene now changed to show Fiorilla offering Selim coffee at home. In the earlier treatments of *Il turco in Italia*, before Romani and Rossini created Selim's spectacular "*Bella Italia*" entrance, this coffee scene was actually the one that introduced the Turk to the audience.[32] Coffee was known to have come to Europe from the Ottoman empire in the seventeenth century, probably arriving first in Venice, and its qualities as a stimulant were supposed to make coffee a possibly libidinous drug. The disreputable character of coffeehouses was such that women were officially banned from them in eighteenth-century Venice—though the ban was difficult to sustain.[33] Turks, with their predilection for coffee, were perhaps supposed to be particularly susceptible to its arousing effects. In *L'italiana* Isabella dresses in Turkish costume when she invites Mustafa to have coffee with her. Elvira, the previous favorite, well understands what it means to "have coffee" with Mustafa, and she warns Isabella: "The Bey wants to have it with you one on one [*da solo a sola*]." Isabella appreciates perfectly what that signifies, and claims to be shocked: "One on one? and his wife tells me this?"[34]

In *Il turco*, meeting for coffee stimulates flirtatious recitative, and Selim tells Fiorilla that beauty such as hers deserves to reside in a temple, promising her that in Turkey she would have a magnificent one. Her comeback is completely flippant: "*Qualche serraglio forse?*" (Some seraglio perhaps?).[35] The scenario of captivity in the seraglio, which once inspired Mozart's Konstanze to sing about "*Martern aller Arten*," serves merely as a playful allusion for Rossini's Fiorilla. In the recitative over coffee Fiorilla both serves her guest—"*Il zucchero è bastante?*" (Enough sugar?)—and poses coquettish questions about his Turkish harem promiscuity: "*Quante donne amaste? Quante vorreste averne?*" (How many women have you loved? How many would you like to have?). He tells her that he has only loved once in the past (meaning Zaida), and that now he is ready to love again, to love Fiorilla alone.[36]

The recitative conversation over coffee leads to a C major duet in which Fiorilla doubts that Selim could ever be faithful and, in a spirit of further flirtation, imagines his harem:

Siete Turchi: non vi credo:	You are Turks, I don't believe you:
Cento donne intorno avete:	You have a hundred women around:
Le comprate, le vendete	You buy them, you sell them
Quando spento è in voi l'ardor.	When your ardor is spent.[37]

He replies, in the dominant key of G major to her C major, and assures her—with a seductive run of triplets—about his capacity for fidelity: "*Sente un Turco anch'ei l'amor*" (Even a Turk feels love).[38]

Stendhal, in his biography of Rossini, quoted her verse in full, "*Siete Turchi, non vi credo,*" because he loved it so much:

> I have been unable to resist the temptation to copy this quatrain, because every phrase, every word has a new grace in the delightful music of Rossini. Once one has heard it, one never stops repeating the words, so pretty in the mouth of a young woman who uses them as the pretext for not allowing love, and who longs to see the pretext refuted. The response of the Turk is as pretty as a madrigal by Voltaire. Rossini alone in the world could make this music which depicts gallantry passing away and changing into love.[39]

Just as the entrance of Selim with "*Bella Italia*" was intended to seduce the Italians in the audience, to make them respond emotionally to the Turkish hero, so Fiorilla's flirtatiousness was intended to be similarly seductive, and certainly she captivated Stendhal.

Selim, furthermore, seemed to Stendhal not only gallant but somehow even French in the style of Voltaire. The allusion to Voltaire suggests also that one of the things Stendhal cherished in the duet was some element of nostalgia for the eighteenth century with its elegant confection of libertinism and Turquerie. His appreciation of Rossini's transformation of gallantry into love was also a gesture of fondness for the last intimations of the lighthearted rococo style in Europe, even then giving way to the far more serious passions of the age of Romanticism.

Most titillating of all was the rococo formulation of the slave trade, the buying and selling of harem women, invoked by Fiorilla with merely mock disapproval as a form of flirtation. "How to depict the delightful nuance of reproach—'*le comprate, le vendete*'—repeated several times, and always with new sentiment?" wondered Stendhal. "Happy Italy! It is only there that people know love."[40] Stendhal's salute to Italy seemed to echo that of Selim in the opera, and he praised as the great virtue of Italy its national ability to appreciate Ottoman slavery in just the right romantic spirit. When Rossini composed this particular reproach, which was actually a tribute, to Ottoman slavery in 1814, the slave trade (though not the institution of slavery itself) had already been abolished in Britain in 1807; it was further abolished in the Netherlands in 1814, the year of *Il turco*. The slave trade was denounced at the

Congress of Vienna in 1815 and forbidden in France in 1818. Slavery was abolished in some of the Habsburg lands in 1811—according to the *Allgemeines bürgerliches Gesetzbuch* issued by Emperor Franz.[41] In Habsburg Milan, however, on the stage of La Scala in 1814, the buying and selling of slaves was still a subject for flirtatious musical exchange between an Italian woman and a Turkish man. It was almost as if they were too modern to believe in the reality of slave trading, even though there were still European captives being sold by Barbary corsairs, and African captives by European traders.

Many years later, in 1866, the elderly Rossini wanted to arrange for a performance in church of his *Petite Messe Solonnelle*, and wrote to a friend about a possible appeal to the pope:

> I want to write to Pius IX to get him to issue a new Bull that would permit women to sing (promiscuously with men) in the churches. I know that he loves music. I know also that I am not unknown to him, because someone heard him singing "*Siete Turchi, non vi credo*" while walking in the Vatican garden, and approached him to compliment him upon his beautiful voice and beautiful manner of using it, to which His Holiness replied: "My dear, as a young man I always sang the music of Gioachino!"[42]

Giovanni Maria Mastai-Ferretti, Pope Pius IX, was born in 1792, the exact same year as Rossini, and began studying theology in Rome in 1814, the year that Rossini composed *Il turco in Italia* for Milan. Indeed, 1814 was also the year of the restoration of the Papal State under the rule of Pius VII, after the Napoleonic years when Rome had been annexed to France as the Department of the Tiber. In 1815 *Il turco* was presented in Rome, almost an inaugural event of the papal restoration, and the young Mastai-Ferretti could have seen a performance at the Teatro Valle.[43]

That Pius IX should still have been singing "*Siete Turchi*" half a century later in the Vatican was tribute indeed to the irresistible power of Rossini over his contemporaries. Furthermore, the 1860s were not an easy time for Pius IX, who had lost most of the Papal State, excepting Rome itself, after the unification of Italy in 1861. Naturally, in 1866 he would not have been whistling "*Pensa alla patria*," for Italian nationalism had completely undermined his temporal rule over the patrimony of St. Peter.

As Fiorilla's romance with Selim progresses, she advises her husband, Don Geronio, that he should remain deaf (*sordo*) and blind (*cieco*) to what is going on around him.[44] In other words, she invites him to become a Pappataci: "*di veder, e non veder, di sentir, e non sentir."* Selim and Fiorilla are already planning to sail away together, when the poet finally brings together Zaida and the Turk so that they might recognize one another as long-lost lovers from Erzurum. In the first-act finale Fiorilla and Zaida come face to face as romantic rivals—the capricious Italian wife and the Oriental harem slave—for the affections of the same Turkish prince.

The reviewer for the *Corriere Milanese* reported that a "reinforced applause honored the finale of the first act and the appearance of the maestro on the stage."[45] The two acts of *Il turco* were separated by a ballet performance of *Ifigenia in Tauride* created by Urbano Garzia, who had choreographed *I francesi in Egitto* for La Scala in 1799 to celebrate Napoleon's invasion of Egypt. The *Corriere* reviewer of 1814 took a nap during the ballet, but with the resumption of the opera he remained offended in his Italian national pride:

> A woman, vain, capricious, unfaithful, who has a secret lover, a special friend,
> an imbecile husband, is at the core of this most highly moral drama; and
> do you think perchance that this woman and these men might be Tartars or
> Chinese? No, sirs, they are Italian. And foreigners will at least recognize that we
> do not flatter ourselves.[46]

It might have been perfectly acceptable to project negative qualities of character on peoples of the Orient, perhaps even including the Turks, but the charming Turkish protagonist of Rossini's opera served only to dramatize the ridiculous foibles of the Italian dramatis personae. The more musically irresistible Rossini made his Turkish prince, the more the *Corriere Milanese* attempted to resist submitting to his Ottoman charisma.

Making Love in Italy and in Turkey

In the second act of *Il turco* there is a comic duet for the two basses, the noble Turkish lover and the ridiculous Italian husband, as they anthropologically compare the respective customs of Turkey and Italy. Selim proposes to purchase Fiorilla from Don Geronio, allegedly according to Turkish custom:

D'un bell'uso di Turchia	There's a fine Turkish custom
Forse avrai novella intesa,	Of which you may have heard,
Della moglie che gli pesa	When a wife is a burden
Il marito è venditor.	Her husband becomes a seller.[47]

Don Geronio's verse, in reply, explains that it is an Italian custom, when someone tries to buy your wife, you have to punch him in the face. They then harmonize energetically, each thinking that the other has a "strange brain," but Rossini and Romani seemed to make no judgment about which nation had the stranger customs.

Stendhal particularly loved this duet, citing especially the lightness of tone (*ton de légèreté*), but he also expressed no judgment about the relative merits of the Turkish and Italian customs in question: "It is impossible to bring together more lightness [*légèreté*], more gaiety and more brilliant grace, which no one has known how to render like the swan of Pesaro. This duet can boldly challenge all the arias of Cimarosa and of Mozart."[48] Lightness, delicacy, decoration, grace, and charm in the rococo spirit of the eighteenth century: these were the Rossinian virtues that Stendhal so much admired. The music completely leveled the cultural difference and personal antagonism between the Turk and the Italian. The sale of a wife—like the buying and selling of slaves—was all very well if treated with a suitable lightness of touch.

Similarly anthropological is the brilliant second-act duet for Selim and Fiorilla, who becomes jealous over his encounter with Zaida. The duet begins *andante* with staccato emphasis and ornamental triplets as Selim sings, "*Credete alle femmine*" (Can you believe women). Fiorilla replies, "*Credete a quest'uomini*" (Can you believe these men), and of course she competitively matches his ornamentation.[49] Thus far, their antagonism is framed in terms of the universal struggle between the sexes. As the *andante* gives way to the *allegro*, however, this becomes a matter of Turkish-Italian disputation, with Fiorilla this time taking the lead: "*In Italia certamente, non si fa l'amor così, no no!*" (In Italy certainly, one does not make love like that, no, no!). "*In Italia*," she sings, with a flourish of thirty-second notes on the first syllable of "*Italia*." Then, for emphasis, she repeats the phrase, singing staccato on the descending B-flat scale: "*in Italia certamente . . .*" The last syllable of *così* falls on a B-flat and intersects with the much lower B-flat that the Turk sings as he begins his reply: "*In Turchia sicuramente, non si fa l'amor così*" (In Turkey definitely, one does not make love like that). They vocalize on these two closely related lines for several pages, trading off their ornamentations in alternating measures, Fiorilla reaching all the way up to the B-flat just below high C, and Selim reaching all the way down to the B-flat below low C.[50] They are notably not singing together in any sort of unison but trading vocal lines in

"*In Italia certamente, non si fa l'amor così*" (In Italy certainly, one does not make love like that), sings Fiorilla—"*con dispetto*" (with scorn)—in Rossini's *Il turco*; and Selim matches her in both style and sentiment when he sings, "*In Turchia sicuramente non si fa l'amor così*" (In Turkey definitely, one does not make love like that). With dazzling runs of thirty-second notes they trade phrases back and forth in an explosion of musical sexuality that proves, beyond any possible doubt, that they make love in exactly the same way.

competitively opposed registers; but at the same time, they are so closely related in their musical styles, emphases, and flourishes as to refute completely the declaration of the libretto. There can be no doubt: these are two people who make love in exactly the same way.

Indeed, the very assertion that their cultures do not make love the same way becomes, in their vocal arrangements, a new way for them to make love musically to one another in perfect counterpoint. To "make love" (*fare l'amore*), of course, had a wide variety of implications from courtship to seduction to sex, and Rossini's spectacular flights of ornamentation in the vocal lines gave the phrase a maximally sensual character. Ultimately, the highly charged tension between them, as man and woman, Turk and Italian, leads to a musical reconciliation in the conclusion of the duet, as they finally sing the same text in close harmony: "*Tu m'ami, lo vedo*" (You love me, I see it). All the conventions of operas about Turks dating back to the middle of the eighteenth century, from Rameau's generous Turk, to Mozart's Pasha Selim, to Rossini's Mustafa, suggested that in Turkey people really did make love differently, under conditions of male despotic power and female subjection. In *Il turco*, however, making love was removed from Turkey to Italy, and under those altered circumstances it turned out that a Turkish man and an Italian woman could achieve a very high degree of romantic and musical compatibility. Fiorilla and Selim sing out the slogan of cultural difference—"*In Italia!*" "*In Turchia!*"—for the purpose of disproving it altogether in the drama and in the music. In the modern world a Turk might be a man like any other, and an Italian a woman like any other.

The dramatic climax of the second act is a costume ball at which, following the poet's advice, Zaida wears the same costume and mask as Fiorilla, while some of the Italians disguise themselves as Turks so that they can be mistaken for Selim. The comedy suggests that Turkishness is ultimately a matter of costume, that the difference between Turks and Europeans is neither racial nor essential, and that a woman might mistake her own husband for a Turk if he wore a robe and turban. Metamorphosis, which was purely a matter of farce in *L'italiana*—Kaimakan and Pappataci—here appears as part of the mystery of romance, and pairs of lovers are mistakenly crossed in the carnivalesque spirit of the masked ball. The ensuing ensemble of mistaken identity uses the recurring phrase "*non è quella, non è questa*" (she's not this one, she's not that one). Stendhal loved the masked ball ensemble and commented that "if music of this quality is to be appreciated in all its perfection, a certain degree of spiritual intoxication is essential in the listener." Philip Gossett suggests that "the masked ball has taken on practically a hallucinatory quality."[51] The references to intoxication and hallucination suggest the potency of the operatic magic at this climactic moment.

Mistaken identities and mismatched lovers have often formed an important aspect of dramatic comedy—as in Shakespeare's *As You Like It* or *A Midsummer Night's Dream*—and also of *opera buffa*, as in the Mozart–Da Ponte masterpieces. In the last act of the *Marriage of Figaro* the Countess and Susanna exchange clothes, misleading both the Count and Figaro in the garden by night. In *Don Giovanni* the conspirators put on masks to go visit Don Giovanni at the end of act 1, and in act 2 Don Giovanni and Leporello exchange cloaks and completely deceive Donna Elvira. The Mozart opera that *Il turco in Italia* echoes most strongly, however, is *Così fan tutte*, and the masked ball with the Italian men in Turkish costume notably recalls the Albanian disguises with which Ferrando and Guglielmo woo one another's lovers. The connection was probably more than accidental, as Mazzolà's libretto of *Il turco in Italia*, set to Seydelmann's music, was performed in Vienna in 1789, just one year before Mozart and Da Ponte created *Così fan tutte* in 1790. Mozart was away on tour when *Il turco* was performed in Vienna in 1789, but replied from Leipzig to a report from Constanze: "A thousand thanks for the account of Seydelmann's opera." Mozart knew Seydelmann personally, as he mentioned in his letter to Constanze, while Da Ponte was well acquainted with Mazzolà, a fellow Venetian.[52] So Mozart and Da Ponte, as they were contemplating *Così fan tutte*, would certainly have been aware of *Il turco in Italia* by Seydelmann and Mazzolà.

Furthermore, Rossini and Romani in 1814, contemplating *Il turco in Italia*, would have been aware of *Così fan tutte*. For *Così fan tutte* was being performed at La Scala in May and June of 1814, just as Rossini was preparing *Il turco in Italia*. In fact, Filippo Galli, Rossini's Turk, sang the part of Guglielmo in *Così fan tutte*, and Rossini's Fiorilla, Francesca Maffei-Festa, sang Fiordiligi. Whether from Mazzolà's influence on Da Ponte, or from Mozart's influence on Rossini, these operas stand in a peculiarly close relation to one another. Bruce Brown, writing about *Così fan tutte*, and Philip Gossett, writing about *Il turco in Italia*, have both taken note of this special connection.[53]

Perhaps the deepest dramatic resemblance between *Così fan tutte* and *Il turco in Italia* lay in both works' utter indifference to the conventional morality of romance. These were comedies in which it seemed anyone could fall in love with anyone, changing partners, and then changing partners again. Part of this libertine amorality included the freedom for European women to fall in love with Ottoman Muslims—whether Albanian or Turkish, whether tenor, baritone, or basso—and to make beautiful music together with them. The lingering spirit of libertinism and religious indifference in *Il turco* looked fondly backward to the eighteenth-century age of Enlightenment.

If *Il turco in Italia* had concluded with the hallucinatory masked ball, the audience would have been left quite uncertain about who would end up with whom—just as in *Così fan tutte*. Instead, the opera continued so as to reunite Selim with Zaida, and to make Fiorilla repent her "capriciousness" and return to Don Geronio.[54] This moral preservation of the marriage tie would also maintain the separation of the European and Turkish spheres, by keeping Fiorilla at home and sending Selim back to Turkey. If they somehow managed to consummate their romantic relation between the scenes of the opera, that potentially scandalous transgression was at least discreetly concealed from the public. In the end, sexual, religious, and cultural proprieties would be precariously preserved.

Fiorilla must demonstrate penitence, in the spirit of the Venetian title of 1794, *La capricciosa ravveduta*, and the finale of *Il turco in Italia* becomes the mirror reflection of the finale of *L'italiana in Algeri*. Instead of the Italians sailing back from Algiers to Italy, now the Turks, Selim with Zaide, sail home from Italy to Turkey. A chorus of Italians, tenors and basses, wish the Turks serene skies and tranquil winds to carry them back across the Mediterranean to their *patria*, their fatherland. Selim takes leave of Italy in the spirit of instant nostalgia, thus bracketing his Italian experience by echoing the excitement of his arrival in the first act:

Cara Italia io t'abbandono,	Dear Italy I abandon you,
Ma per sempre in cor t'avrò.	But will keep you forever in my heart.[55]

Whatever love he may have felt for Fiorilla has dissolved into his love for Italy, as he takes his leave of both the one and the other. Like Goethe or the travelers of the Grand Tour, Selim will carry away from Italy a sense of cultural education and of spiritual enrichment, seasoned with the longing of nostalgia—for there is no hint that he will ever return.

Conclusion: The Departure and Disappearance of Prince Selim

The finale follows the Mozartean *Figaro* formula of begging pardon followed by a declaration of "*tutti contenti*"—here in the most affirmative key of C major. Zaida and Selim, departing, ask pardon of the Europeans: "*Perdonate i nostri errori*" (Pardon our errors). The final ensemble for all soloists, plus chorus, begins with the phrase "*Restate contenti*" (Remain content)— first sung *sotto voce* and then building to *forte* volume, Fiorilla at the top of the treble staff and Selim reaching down to the low C on the bass staff.[56] Turks and Italians will henceforth live separately but contentedly. There is no space on the geopolitical map or operatic stage where Selim and Fiorilla can maintain their spectacular cross-cultural romance and live happily ever after.

On the last vocal note of the opera, a C for all the soloists and the entire chorus, singing the last syllable of *l'amor*, Selim merges into the vocal mass just as he prepares to disappear beyond the maritime horizon.[57] The masked ball suggests that anyone can masquerade as a Turk or as a European, and it is ultimately possible to imagine that Selim might have remained in Italy, shedding his exoticism with his costume and assuming the part of a European for which he seemed so eminently suitable.

Oddly, Rossini and Romani constructed the role so that Selim, though clearly the leading man and title character, enjoys not one single aria of his own in the entire opera. The twenty measures of his opening salutation to Italy lead immediately into a duet with Fiorilla. The twenty measures of his farewell to Italy are neatly embedded in the ensemble finale. It is almost as if he only exists in relation to the other soloists, conjured into existence by their ambivalent fears and fantasies. The poet produces Selim in order to construct the drama, just as Romani and Rossini created the Turkish figure they needed to stand at the center of their *opera buffa*. In fact, Selim's farewell marked the valedictory conclusion of the whole genre of the Turkish *opera buffa*. The dramatic and musical character of Selim functioned in a domain of fantasy that tested the very limits of this operatic genre and challenged the emerging modern assumptions of cultural difference. Rossini's Turk was supremely comfortable among the company of Italians—without the faintest hint of fumbling or hesitation—such that one could scarcely explain how he was fundamentally different. In fact, the Turk in Italy seemed to be as fully European as the Italians whose voices harmonized with his own.

10

MAOMETTO IN NAPLES AND VENICE

The Operatic Charisma of the Conqueror

Introduction: "Conqueror of the world"

Mehmed the Conqueror (Fatih Mehmed Sultan) ruled over the Ottoman empire from 1451 to 1481, and he famously conquered Byzantine Constantinople in 1453. In the fifteenth century, Renaissance Italian statesmen fearfully took note of Mehmed's conquests and reflected upon the reports that he hoped to extend his empire to Italy. Styling himself as the Emperor or Caesar, the political heir to Greece and Rome, he could read both Greek and Latin. Voltaire, in the eighteenth century, noted admiringly that "all the Turkish annals teach us that Mehmed was the best educated prince of his time."[1] After taking Constantinople, he conquered Athens in 1458 and made the Parthenon into a mosque. In 1470 he took Negroponte (today Greek Chalkida), the principal city on the island of Euboea, defeating the Venetians (who had governed there since the Fourth Crusade in the early thirteenth century). Franz Babinger's modern biography of Mehmed observes that from the Venetian perspective the loss of Negroponte was as traumatic as the fall of Constantinople: "The glory and prestige of Venice are destroyed," wrote a Venetian chronicler about the fall of Negroponte.[2] This conquest was the subject of Rossini's opera *Maometto Secondo*.

In 1480, at the end of his life and reign, Mehmed sent an army to Otranto in southern Italy, but his death contributed to the failure of the intended Ottoman conquest of Italy. The sultan himself was fascinated by Italian culture, just as Italian culture was fascinated by him, and he had his portrait painted by the Venetian painter Gentile Bellini (brother of Giovanni), who came to

305

Constantinople in 1479. Mehmed sat posthumously for another Italian portrait in the nineteenth century in Rossini's *Maometto Secondo*. The title allowed him only a numeral, not an epithet, but the opera itself was deeply preoccupied with his role as a conqueror.

The conquest of Constantinople in 1453 immediately created a dark legend surrounding Mehmed, and Aeneas Sylvius Piccolomini, later Pope Pius II, wrote that "those who were present say that the foul leader of the Turks, or to speak more aptly, that repulsive beast, raped on the high altar of Hagia Sophia, before everyone's eyes, the most noble royal maiden and her younger brother, and then ordered them killed."[3] Such hyperbolic fantasies of his barbarousness (which suggested some fascination with his sexuality) did not prevent the Renaissance Italians from making a cooler appraisal of his alarming political qualities. According to one Venetian observer in Constantinople, Mehmed was notably interested in all things European:

> Diligently he seeks information on the position of Italy . . . the seat of the
> Pope, of the Emperor, and how many kingdoms there are in Europe, of which
> he has a map showing the states and provinces. Nothing gives him greater
> satisfaction and pleasure than to study the state of the world and the science of
> war . . . Now, he says, times have changed, so that he would go from the East to
> the West, as the Westerners had gone to the East. The Empire of the world, he
> says, must be one, one faith and one kingdom.[4]

Such interest in European affairs was both flattering and frightening, and with his study of "the state of the world and the science of war," Mehmed might have appeared as an exemplary model for Machiavelli's studiously modern prince. More than three centuries after Mehmed's death, Rossini and his librettist, Cesare Della Valle, made the sultan into an operatic paradigm of the warlike prince, but they also dramatized his fascination with Europe as an aspect of his romantic infatuation with the Venetian heroine of the opera.

In *Maometto Secondo* European opera presented an Ottoman sultan who aspired to conquer Europe, even envisioning universal conquest. "*Del mondo al vincitor*," sings the Muslim chorus, saluting the sultan at his first entrance as the "conqueror of the world." Maometto responds with his determination to overturn empires (*crollar farò gl'imperi*) and triumph over the whole world (*del mondo a trionfar*).[5] It was Filippo Galli who presented himself thus, in the role of Maometto, at the Teatro di San Carlo in Naples, to his loyal Ottoman army on stage and to his appreciative European audience in the boxes. The sultan's brilliant ornamentation of this anthem of world domination—"*del mondo a trionfar*"—was surely intended by Rossini to elicit the amazed admiration of the public. This was a vocal tour de force in which universal conquest became a bel canto project.

Rossini himself, along with the public of 1820, had certainly not forgotten that not long ago they too had responded with enthusiasm to the appeal of a supremely ambitious conqueror, a man who toppled old kingdoms as he established his new empire, a man who conquered in the name of universal ideals. Napoleon was still alive on St. Helena in 1820, and the memory of his military conquests and emancipatory rhetoric was also still alive all over Europe. Even as Rossini was working on his opera in Naples in 1820, a liberal revolution was kindled from the Napoleonic embers. In July the secret society of the Carbonari imposed a constitution upon the Bourbon king Ferdinand of Naples and Sicily, and Rossini was rumored to have written a fighting anthem for the constitutional revolutionaries: "*Inno di guerra dei costituzionali.*" The composer was also, however, reported to be anxious about the unstable political situation, fearful of losing his inspiration, and slow to complete his new opera.[6] The premiere of *Maometto Secondo* finally took place in December, in constitutional Naples, bubbling with liberal sentiment and Napoleonic memories. Habsburg troops, representing the conservative principles of Metternich, marched on Naples and overturned the revolution in March 1821. The liberal public at the opera in December might well have identified the eponymous sultan with the charismatic former French emperor, and the ambivalence that Maometto must surely have evoked, singing of universal conquest on the operatic stage, would have resonated with the still roiling emotional drama of recent historical memory.

Mohammed the Prophet and Mohammed the Conqueror

The subject of Mehmed's conquest of Negroponte in 1470 had been composed as an opera in Hamburg as early as 1696—*Mahumeth II* by Reinhard Keiser—at the moment when Turkish subjects first began to play a significant role on the operatic stage. Yet Mehmed the Conqueror did not appear in the many operas on Ottoman subjects during the eighteenth century, even as Suleiman the Magnificent became the regular subject of musical comedies, like *Les trois sultanes* and its many derivatives.

It was the Napoleonic age of conquest that stimulated operatic interest in Mehmed, with Louis Jadin's *Mahomet II* at the Paris Opéra in 1803—though only for three performances. In Jadin's opera, which had nothing to do with Negroponte, Mehmed virtuously renounces his love for a Christian captive taken at the conquest of Constantinople, and dedicates himself to his own military glory.[7] The opera was surely intended to honor Napoleon after the Peace of Amiens in 1802 and was perhaps also meant as a gesture toward a future alliance between France and the Ottomans, following the failure of Napoleon's Egyptian campaign. Yet not until Napoleon was fully defeated and exiled to St. Helena could Rossini take up the subject of Mehmed the Conqueror and make him sing meaningfully about matters of love and conquest on the operatic stages of Europe.

Behind the figure of Mehmed II, or Mohammed the Conqueror, the European public might also have detected the shadow of Mohammed himself, the Prophet, who created a religion that immediately embarked upon campaigns of military conquest. The numeral of Mehmed II, of course, marked him as the descendant of Mehmed I, a sultan of the earlier fifteenth century, the son of the same Bajazet who was defeated by Tamerlane. Yet the Italian public would surely have known almost nothing about Mehmed I; rather, they would have thought of the "first" Mohammed, the Prophet himself, the founder of Islam. This association would have been reinforced for operagoers by the fact that Rossini's *Maometto Secondo* of 1820 followed by three years Peter Winter's *Maometto* of 1817. The latter was in fact an opera about the life of the Muslim Prophet—perhaps the only such opera—based on the drama by Voltaire and performed in Milan at La Scala, where Rossini definitely saw it.[8]

During the eighteenth century the best-known drama representing the origins of Islam was Voltaire's *Mahomet* of 1741—its full title *Le fanatisme, ou Mahomet le prophète*—one of the great sensations of the Enlightenment. Portraying Mohammed as a hypocritical charlatan who exploited his religious status to satisfy his lusts for women and power, Voltaire offered a strongly anti-Islamic message and dedicated the drama to Pope Benedict XIV. The enlightened public, however, gradually recognized with a collective wink that Voltaire's message about fanatical Islam was equally applicable to fanatical Christianity.

Voltaire's drama begins with the leader of Mecca, Zopire, resisting Mohammed's return to the city in 630 AD, while regarding Mohammed himself as a charlatan of "false marvels" (*faux prodiges*).[9] As a philosophe of the Enlightenment, Voltaire was especially interested in how religion, in its "fanatical" form, inspired people to violence and murder, and he often cited the case of François Ravaillac, the fanatical Roman Catholic who assassinated the French king Henri IV in 1610. The drama *Mahomet* also focuses on how the Prophet uses his religious influence to instigate an assassination. Mohammed provokes the murder of Zopire at the hands of Zopire's own unwitting son, so that the Muslim Prophet might carry out his sexual designs on Zopire's daughter, Palmire. In the final scene she kills herself rather than submit to Mohammed:

> Je meurs.
> Je cesse de te voir, Imposteur exécrable.
> Je me flatte en mourant qu'un Dieu plus équitable
> Réserve un avenir pour les coeurs innocents.
> Tu dois régner; le Monde est fait pour les Tyrans.
>
> I die.
> I cease to see you, hateful impostor.
> I imagine, in dying, that a more equitable god
> Reserves a future for innocent hearts.
> You must reign; the world is made for tyrants.[10]

This uncompromising view of a religious leader as an impostor and a tyrant became uncomfortable for the Roman Catholic public in the eighteenth century once Voltaire's veiled intentions were acknowledged. Today the drama could not be produced without exciting Muslim outrage, and in fact the Geneva production, prepared for Voltaire's tercentennial in 1994, had to be canceled in response to religious protests.

After the Congress of Vienna, in the early years of the post-Napoleonic Restoration, conservative Christian values were preeminent in European politics and supposedly inspired the Holy Alliance of Russia, Prussia, and Austria. The Habsburg emperor Franz, guided by Metternich as chancellor, now governed Lombardy and Venetia in northern Italy, including the great opera houses of La Scala and La Fenice in Milan and Venice, while Vienna also maintained considerable influence throughout the Italian peninsula. In 1817, Peter Winter composed his *Maometto* for La Scala, and it was Felice Romani, the recent librettist of *Il turco in Italia*, who now adapted Voltaire's *Mahomet* to create an opera libretto.

Winter, born in Mannheim in 1754, was Mozart's contemporary and Salieri's pupil, and belonged to the cultural world of the late Enlightenment. Closely associated with the court opera at Munich, Winter created a sequel to Mozart's *Magic Flute*, called *The Labyrinth*, in Vienna in 1798, and it was he who composed *Tamerlan* for Paris in 1802, the operatic sequel that followed the story of Tamerlane after Bajazet's death.[11] *Maometto* came late in Winter's operatic career, and he in his sixties was old enough to share some of the eighteenth-century philosophical and dramatic values of Voltaire. Romani was much younger, born in 1788, and not yet thirty in 1817, but his libretto preserved Voltaire's vision of Mohammed as a scheming hypocrite in quest of power and women. Mohammed was accordingly denounced in the opera's final scene: "*Scellerato! impostor! falso profeta d'un Dio crudel!*" (Villain! impostor! false prophet of a cruel God!).[12]

That Romani's libretto should have resembled the source, Voltaire's *Mahomet*, was hardly surprising. More remarkable, however, were the unexpected similarities between Romani's libretto for Winter's *Maometto* in 1817 and that of Cesare Della Valle for Rossini's *Maometto Secondo* in 1820. The plots, after all, are separated by some eight hundred years, focusing on an Arabian religious leader of the seventh century and an Ottoman sultan of the fifteenth century. Yet both are crucially concerned with sieges carried out against religious and political enemies: Mohammed against Mecca, Mehmed against Negroponte. In both operas the Meccan leader (Zopiro) and the Venetian leader (Erisso) patriotically refuse to surrender to Mohammed/Mehmed, and in both cases history favors the besieging conqueror. In both operas the Muslim leader is in love with the daughter of his military enemy, Palmira in Mecca and Anna in Negroponte, and in both cases the young women dramatically prefer to die in the final act rather than submit. When Rossini rewrote *Maometto Secondo* for Paris as *Le siège de Corinthe* (The siege of Corinth), Anna was renamed "Pamyra" in French, so that she could almost be mistaken for the "Palmire" of Voltaire. Thus the plot of Rossini's opera echoed that of Winter's, and *Maometto Secondo* very roughly resembled its predecessor *Maometto*. Rossini, who saw *Maometto* at La Scala and met with Winter, would have been well aware of these resemblances.

Rossini later spoke to the German composer Ferdinand Hiller about hearing Winter's *Maometto* in Milan in 1817, and noted favorably that "there were some very pretty things in that opera." Rossini also recalled, however, an unpleasant memory of an encounter with Winter himself:

> My chief objection to Winter was his unsavoriness. He was a man of very
> imposing exterior, but cleanliness was not his forte. . . . One day he invited me
> to dinner. We were brought a big dish of meatballs [*polpetti*], and he proceed-
> ed to serve himself and me in the Oriental manner, with his fingers. As far as I
> was concerned, that ended the meal. It was a gruesome incident.[13]

Rossini's comical reminiscence formulated Winter's table manners as Oriental rather than European. This emphasis on Winter's supposedly "Oriental"
unsavoriness may serve as a reminder that both *Maometto* and *Maometto Secondo* were ostensibly dramas of the Orient, and both revolved ambivalently
around issues of Oriental barbarism.

Filippo Galli in Arabia

Maometto opens with a chorus of Meccans praying to their pantheon of
pre-Islamic deities in a style somewhat reminiscent of Mozart's Masonic music: "*Possenti Dei d'Arabia*" (Powerful gods of Arabia). The Masonic resemblance is further suggested by the invocation calling upon those Arabian gods
to defend "the Temple" (*il Tempio*) from the "false rites" of the Muslims, and
Winter thus seemed to establish his musical sympathies on behalf of pagan
polytheism.[14] The Sarastro of this temple is Zopiro, a basso, and none other
than Filippo Galli, the very same basso who performed the role of the Turk in
every one of Rossini's Turkish operas. His prisoner and ward is Palmira, the
object of Mohammed's relentless lust and hypocritical stratagems.

While Galli, formerly Prince Selim, was now Zopiro, the soprano Francesca Maffei-Festa was recast from Rossini's Fiorilla in *Il turco* to Winter's
Palmira in *Maometto*. Therefore, when Rossini saw Winter's *Maometto* at La
Scala in 1817, he would have been listening to singers he knew very well. Rossini particularly admired the religious trio, in which Zopiro prays to his Arab
gods while Palmira and her true love Seide, already Muslim converts, reflect
on their own new Islamic religion and on Mohammed's command to murder
Zopiro.[15]

Rossini might also have admired Winter's chorus of warriors who herald-
ed the appearance of Maometto, for the chorus of Rossinian warriors who
greeted the entrance of Maometto Secondo was notably similar, characterized by the same forcefully driven rhythm and the same triple emphasis in the

musical line.[16] Yet at the moment when each Maometto opened his mouth to sing, it became immediately evident that Winter and Rossini had very different vocal conceptions of their respective eponymous protagonists. For Winter's Maometto was a tenor, and Rossini's Maometto Secondo was, like all the important Rossinian Turks, performed by Filippo Galli, the basso.

The tenor voice of Winter's Mohammed served the very particular characterization of the Prophet suggested by Voltaire in his drama of 1741 and followed by Romani and Winter in their opera of 1817. Voltaire's Mohammed was a dissembling hypocrite, concealing his lusts and ambitions behind a façade of religious piety, even religious populism, which Voltaire characterized as fanaticism. Winter exploited the sweetness of the tenor voice to give his Mohammed all the charms that, according to the sense of the drama, were intended to be entirely false and hypocritical. This compositional strategy made Winter's *Maometto* an unconventional opera, inasmuch as the singing in opera more often affirms the authenticity and sincerity of the operatic characters' emotions.

In Winter's *Maometto* the warmth of the tenor voice became the musical means for conveying treacherous falsity, and the tenor, Domenico Donzelli, had to undertake the difficult task of singing sweetly while dramatically undermining his own musical appeal. Donzelli came from the Bergamo school of tenorial training and was a contemporary of the famous Giovanni Battista Rubini of the same school. Donzelli was only twenty-seven when he took on the role of Mohammed at La Scala, employing a lyrical sound and probably a high *tenorino* head voice. He would later become a famous Rossini tenor, singing the title role of Rossini's *Otello* in Paris in 1825, when his voice had become more dramatic, and he would eventually create the role of Pollione in Bellini's *Norma* at La Scala in 1831.[17] As the Roman proconsul Pollione he would wreak havoc among the religious traditions of the ancient Druids, while as Mohammed he overwhelmed the pagan cults of the pre-Islamic Meccans.

The false seductiveness of Islam was also suggested by Rossini himself, in a very different fashion, when he presented his opera *Armida* at the Teatro di San Carlo in Naples in 1817. Based on Torquato Tasso's Renaissance epic poem *Gerusalemme liberata* and set therefore in the age of the Crusades, Rossini's central figure, Armida, was a sorceress from Damascus and an enemy of the crusaders; she was therefore presumably Muslim, though this was not explicitly mentioned in the libretto by Giovanni Schmidt, which told the story of her enchantment of the Christian knight Rinaldo. In 1817 Armida was already familiar as an operatic subject, since Gluck composed his *Armide* for Paris in 1777, based on the same libretto by Philippe Quinault that Lully had used for his opera *Armide* in 1686. In all these treatments Armida's Muslim identity remained merely implicit, while her combination of sorcery and seduction practiced upon the Christian crusaders was characterized vocally by Rossini with spectacular ornamentation to be executed by the Spanish diva Isabella Colbran (later the female star of *Maometto Secondo*). Colbran's performance in Naples as the seductive Armida coincided in the same year, 1817, with that of Donzelli in Milan as the dissembling Maometto.

The *Gazzetta di Milano*, reviewing the premiere of *Maometto* in 1817, had only praise for Winter's "sweet and energetic melodies" and noted that all the numbers were enthusiastically applauded, with Winter himself summoned to the stage for applause at the end of each act. The hero of the opera, for the *Gazzetta*, was Galli in the role of Zopiro, Mohammed's enemy: "His singing was affecting, pathetic, robust, and always smooth [*spianato*], as reason and taste prescribe. About his companions I can not always say as much."[18] Galli had recently performed the Rossini roles of Selim and Mustafa at La Scala, in 1814 and 1815 respectively, embodying the gallant and the comic faces of Turkishness, though neither represented pious Islam. Now he became the operatic spokesman for resistance to Islam, singing with the voice of basso sincerity in contrast to Mohammed's tenorial dissembling.

In a duet between Mohammed and Zopiro the Prophet remains falsely friendly and fully lyrical: "*Oggi ti bramo amico*" (Today I want you as a friend), sings Mohammed to the rival whose murder he will soon be plotting. The basso Zopiro is more forthright in addressing and condemning Mohammed:

Io patria e Numi onoro,	I honor fatherland and gods,
Tu sprezzi e patria e Dei.	You despise both fatherland and gods.[19]

The Prophet, however, maintains his musical and emotional composure, plotting revenge against Zopiro, and proposing a truce with Mecca that he himself has every intention of breaking. Only at the very end of the opera— after Zopiro has been murdered by Seide, after Seide has denounced Mohammed as a false prophet and a monster, after Palmira has announced her intention to kill herself rather than submit to him—only then does Mohammed reveal his true face and true voice to the people of Mecca. He becomes a fully dramatic tenor as he sings, "*Sì, tremate*" (Yes, tremble).[20] He commands the Meccans to prostrate themselves before him, and in the final choral phrases of the opera they surrender themselves entirely to his will.

"I am not a barbarian"

Mohammed's utter triumph was really the only possible ending for an opera that took its cues from history, since he did in fact establish Islam in Mecca in 630, and after his death in 632 the new religion rapidly expanded its domain beyond Arabia and the Middle East, reaching Spain in 711. Though Muslim successes eroded the territories of the Byzantine empire and the first siege of Constantinople took place as early as 674, the Byzantine capital did not actually fall to a Muslim conqueror until the Ottoman siege of Mehmed II in 1453. Those eight centuries that separated Mohammed the Prophet from Mohammed the Conqueror collapsed into three years on the Italian operatic calendar, separating Winter's La Scala production of 1817 from Rossini's Naples production of 1820. The conquest of Mecca was ancient history already in the nineteenth century, and even the fifteenth-century conquest of Constantinople seemed extremely remote. In 1821, however, the very next year after Rossini's premiere, the Greek revolt against the Ottoman empire suddenly made Mehmed's conquest of Greece seem politically current and relevant.

Like Winter's Maometto, Rossini's was also a Muslim conqueror—but not a hypocrite. As an Ottoman sultan, his interest in power and women could be openly proclaimed without the slightest dramatic incongruity. Galli, now playing the protagonist rather than the victim of Muslim triumph, exuberantly sounded the bass notes of the sultan's hypermasculine political authority and sexual charisma. Indeed, his last Rossinian Turkish outing as Selim in *Il turco in Italia* had already established him as a Turkish romantic hero of the operatic stage, and he now transposed that charisma from the realm of *opera buffa* to the solemnity and grandeur of *opera seria*.

The libretto by Della Valle offered its political sympathies to the embattled Venetians in Greece, but history was on the side of the conqueror, and Rossini's music could not altogether withhold the laurels of triumph. Della Valle based his libretto on his own drama, *Anna Erizo*, in which the Venetian heroine was the title figure, but the opera shifted the eponymous emphasis to

Maometto. An earlier dramatic version of the story dated back to 1783 when Vincenzo Formaleoni wrote *Anna Erizzo ossia La caduta di Negroponte* specifically for Venice as a celebration of Venetian heroism.[21]

The collaboration between Rossini and Della Valle in 1820 was not entirely harmonious, and the latter commented: "My drama counted for nothing; his music for a lot, though it was not much applauded."[22] The plot concerned the conquering sultan's supposed love for the daughter of the Venetian governor of Negroponte, and while such a romance might have appeared entirely operatic, it was loosely based on the most reputable French classical account of Mehmed's reign by Georges Guillet de Saint-George, published in Paris in 1681. Mehmed, according to Guillet, found the young woman "charming" (*charmante*) and promised to show her great favor within his harem, but she preferred a "glorious and heroic" martyrdom.[23] In Rossini's opera the part of Anna was taken at the Naples premiere by Isabella Colbran. In Naples she had already starred in such Rossini works as *Otello*, *Armida*, and *La donna del lago*; by 1820 she was already the composer's lover, and in 1822 she would become Signora Rossini.

Maometto Secondo begins with the Venetian governor or *provveditore*, Paolo Erisso (modified from Erizo or Erizzo), at Negroponte, addressing his Venetian troops in tenor voice as they face the Ottoman siege. He warns that "Maometto threatens fire and death," and identifies the sultan as "the proud conqueror of Byzantium." Calbo, a female contralto singing the role of the Venetian general who loves Erisso's daughter Anna, affirms Venetian defiance and resistance against the "barbarians."[24] Yet when Anna confesses to her father that she is in love with a man she met in Corinth, a man she thought was Venetian—"Uberto," from the island of Mytilene (that is, Lesbos)—she does not suspect that he is in fact the Ottoman sultan under an assumed name. The success of the disguise suggests that by the conventions of the libretto a Venetian and a Turk might be almost indistinguishable in the eastern Mediterranean, where religions and civilizations encountered one another in a heterogeneously mixed domain. Della Valle regarded this mistaken identity as his fictional twist on the historical circumstances; his sources told him Mehmed had loved the daughter of the Venetian governor, but unless they could have met under earlier romantic circumstances before the Ottoman assault, the sultan's attachment would have to be presented on stage as the "filthy spectacle of brutal lust [*libidine*]."[25] Clearly, Della Valle wanted the romance to be more edifying, and the sultan more admirable, than conventionally negative views of the Ottoman conqueror might have allowed.

When the Ottomans break into the fortified city of Negroponte (as the sounds of the cannons are heard offstage), Anna resolves—with her father's approval—to kill herself rather than fall into Ottoman captivity and be left "to the insult of the barbarians" (*de' barbari all'oltraggio*). This brings to a climax the huge trio, or *terzettone*, for Anna, Calbo, and Erisso, which musically dominates the opening scenes of the opera.[26] The insult Anna fears would presumably have involved some sort of Turkish sexual captivity, a familiar operatic subject, but Anna does not know that she herself has already, unwittingly, fallen in love with the Turkish sultan.

Maometto himself finally appears on the scene, according to the stage direction, "surrounded by military and Asiatic pomp." He is also accompanied by a ferocious soldiers' chorus which enthusiastically endorses the destruction of Negroponte. The Turks have entered the city but not yet stormed the Venetian citadel. There is some element of Janissary style in the vocal parts of the Turkish soldiers and in the orchestral accompaniment.

Dal ferro, dal foco	By sword, by fire
nel sangue sommersa	submerged in blood
l'avversa città,	the resistant city,
al mondo suo scempio	its destruction
esempio sarà.	will be an example to the world.[27]

According to the stage directions, soldiers actually attempt to set fire to the city, but Maometto himself restrains them, thus signaling the audience that he is not a man of barbarously unbridled destruction.[28]

The stage picture, with all its Asiatic pomp, offers an image of Oriental despotism surrounding the figure of the sultan: "They all prostrate themselves awaiting his orders." He bids them rise and then launches into the glamorously ornamented aria that immediately establishes his basso charisma, and ultimately welcomes them all into his project of universal conquest:

Crollar farò gl'imperi,	I will make empires collapse,
e volerò con voi	and with you I will fly and
del mondo a trionfar.	triumph over the world.[29]

Maometto almost seems to illustrate his triumph by the brilliance of his vocal runs, up and down the scale. He is enjoying himself as he sings of world conquest, and the chorus likewise salutes him as the "conqueror of the world" with fierce enthusiasm, accompanied by Janissary percussion.[30]

In the opening scenes, Rossini meant for the audience to respond with sympathy to the plight of the Negroponte Venetians—and the contemporary Venetians, after all, were devoted fans of Rossini—but no sooner did Maometto step upon the stage than his musical representation made him immediately compelling, for the audience as well as the chorus. His supreme self-assurance and irresistible imperial prowess surely registered upon the public of the early nineteenth century as at least subliminally Napoleonic. Musicologist Anselm Gerhard has suggested that Gaspare Spontini's opera *Fernand Cortez ou la conquête du Mexique*—created in Paris in 1809 but performed in Naples in 1820—stimulated Rossini to think about the operatic representation of conquest, whether Catholic or Muslim.[31]

In *L'italiana in Algeri* Mustafa was a figure of *opera buffa* whose Turkish swagger was supposed to come across as farcically inflated conceit, but Maometto's operatic self-assurance, by contrast, was something to be taken seriously. After all, he really did conquer Constantinople. In *Maometto Secondo*, when the sultan sings of his joy—"*Oh gioia!*"—in a new prospective triumph at Negroponte, he also recalls the victory at Constantinople in terms that seem to confirm the Christian view of Muslim barbarism: "As in Byzantium, I have seen my steed here again swimming in Christian blood." He expresses a particularly low opinion of Venetians, regarding them as "*sempre infidi*," always treacherous.[32] When Erisso and Calbo are brought before him in chains, Maometto blames them for the bloodshed at Negroponte, as those "who without hope of aid or escape refuse every treaty for the sole delight of spilling more blood." The Venetians' initial conviction of the sultan's barbarism is in effect turned back against themselves for having heedlessly caused unnecessary death and destruction. Maometto, however, proceeds to offer Erisso an unobstructed return to Venice, to see his country again—"*la patria riveder*"—if Erisso will order the remaining Venetian combatants in the citadel of Negroponte to surrender. Erisso, of course, refuses the offer as dishonorable.[33]

At that point, as Erisso is about to be consigned to torture, Anna enters the scene and immediately recognizes Maometto as "Uberto," the man she has loved in Corinth. All four of the principal characters remain "silent," while singing in parentheses of their confused emotions—the former trio of soprano (Anna), contralto (Calbo), and tenor (Erisso) now finally anchored by the addition of a basso (Maometto). Erisso is horrified, while Calbo and a chorus of Venetian women all see Anna as the victim of a "barbarous deception." Yet Anna herself is not quite certain what to think: "*Che penso? che dico?*" (What do I think? what do I say?). As for Maometto, he recognizes that he loves her still, that his soul is filled with a "tender affection," that he is moved by her distress. A chorus of Muslims (*coro di musulmani*) watch their sultan and note his expression of *pietà*, compassion.[34]

The hushed dynamics of this "silent" quartet accompanied by two "silent" choruses—the characters on stage looking inward and singing their thoughts—ends emphatically with a big orchestral flourish that heralds Anna's readiness finally to speak her mind. "*Rendimi il padre, o barbaro*" (Give me back my father, barbarian), she sings out. Anna asks for Calbo as well, claiming that he is her brother, and with brilliant ornamentation she declares that she will kill herself if Maometto does not meet her demand. The same orchestral flourish announces that Maometto is ready with his reply: "*Padre e fratel ti rendo*" (Father and brother I give back to you). Indeed, the sultan personally removes their chains. Maometto now matches Anna's previous ornamentation as he explains why he is making this concession:

Comprendi a sì gran dono	Understand by such a great gift
che un barbaro non sono,	that I am not a barbarian,
ma fido amante ognor.	but a faithful lover always.[35]

The Venetian characters on stage and the Neapolitan public in the opera house watched a Turkish character not only emphatically reject the epithet of "barbarian" but actually disprove it by his actions within the opera. Maometto is apparently no longer the sultan who exults in riding his steed through pools of Christian blood. The power of love has moved him to compassion—*pietà*—and brought him to reject and renounce barbarism altogether. Like Pasha Selim in the *Abduction* he is sufficiently civilized to liberate his captives.

Erisso, the Venetian governor, is not only shocked but also extremely discomfited by Maometto's magnanimity:

Que' ceppi a me rendete,	Give me back those shackles,
la morte io solo attendo . . .	I expect only death . . .[36]

Maometto, however, expects more than that from Anna:

al fianco mio vivrai,	you will live beside me,
se ancor mi sei fedel.	if you remain faithful to me.[37]

The fidelity that Maometto requires of Anna has both romantic and political aspects, and he is in effect proposing some sort of marriage. The ensuing act 1 finale focuses on Anna's distress—*"agitata, confusa, tremante"* (agitated, confused, trembling)—as observed by Maometto and the chorus.[38]

In Della Valle's libretto it is the Ottoman Mehmed, the triumphant conqueror, who—like Tamerlane in Piovene's libretto, a hundred years before—seeks to take as his consort the daughter of the enemy he has defeated. It is the Venetian governor—like Piovene's Bajazet—who is horrified at the idea of his daughter consorting with the enemy and insists that he himself would rather face death. Yet the public in Naples in 1820 would probably not have been watching Maometto and thinking about Tamerlane and Bajazet. Much more likely, they would have been thinking of another conqueror who presumptuously demanded the daughter of his defeated enemy in marriage. In 1809 Napoleon occupied Vienna and decisively defeated the Austrians at the battle of Wagram; in 1810 the daughter of the Habsburg emperor Franz, Archduchess Marie Louise, was given in marriage to Napoleon to replace Josephine as his empress and bear his child and heir. It was a marriage that her Habsburg father regarded as politically necessary but personally distasteful, an act of supreme condescension toward the Corsican adventurer. In 1820 Napoleon was on St. Helena, but Marie Louise was the duchess of Parma and would certainly have been aware of Rossini, while he and his public would have been reciprocally aware of her. The distress of Anna in the act 1 finale—*"agitata, confusa, tremante"*—echoed the circumstances of very recent history, when a beloved daughter had been offered up as a captive bride to placate an aspiring world conqueror.

Turkish and Venetian Disguises

When the curtain rises on act 2, Anna is seated upon the Turkish divan in Maometto's pavilion, surrounded, according to the libretto, by "all the objects of Oriental luxury"—though it was left to the Orientalist imagination of the opera company to specify what those objects might be. She is also now surrounded by young Muslim women (*donzelle musulmane*), "magnificently dressed" and kneeling before her with rich gifts and flasks of perfume. The scene thus already offers a suggestively Oriental scent, even before the orchestra introduces a vaguely Oriental rhythm for the women's chorus. Their words offer a languorous tribute to sensual indulgence, as if to seduce the virtuous Venetian girl:

È follia sul fior degli anni	It is madness in the flower of youth
chiuder l'alma a' molli affetti,	to close the soul to soft sentiments,
e penar fra' tanti affanni	and suffer among so many troubles
d'una rigida virtù.	from a rigid virtue.[39]

In act 1 there was no talk of harems, only of love between a Turkish man and a Venetian woman, but act 2 transforms the entire stage into a harem and immediately raises the familiar operatic issue of what it would mean for a European woman to be loved by an Ottoman sultan. How has this harem of Muslim women suddenly materialized at Negroponte? Where were they during the first act, when the only female chorus was the chorus of Venetian women who expressed their deepest sympathy for Anna? The operatic logic almost seemed to suggest that the Christian Venetian women of the first act had already, in the second, been taken captive for Maometto's harem and had abandoned not only Christianity but also "rigid virtue." Certainly, the female chorus consisted of the same singers, who changed their costumes and their characters with the change of act.

Yet the sultan seems to offer Anna something more than servitude. "You loved Uberto," he reminds her, "and now you see him changed into Maometto." Stagecraft did not have to represent that transformation of the lovable Italian Uberto into the more problematic Turkish conqueror, since Maometto never appears on stage in his Uberto incarnation. The interchangeable identities, however, had to be plausible if the plot was to make any sense. Of course, the role of Maometto was being performed by an Italian, who was singing his lines in Italian, so the question of whether a Turk could impersonate an Italian was to some extent already answered by the reciprocal proof: an Italian could most certainly impersonate a Turk on the operatic stage. "I love you still," declares Maometto. "I want us to be happy together, and I want to make you a queen, yes, the queen of Italy [*sì, d'Italia regina*]." He even offers to place her father and supposed brother alongside her as men of power (*possenti*) within this newly imagined Ottoman Italy.[40] This was the nightmare of the Italian principalities of the fifteenth century, fearing that the Ottomans really did intend to try to extend their empire to Italy, as suggested by the landing at Otranto in 1480. Within the opera Maometto envisions a political and cultural synthesis in which a Turkish sultan might form a Venetian marital alliance and create an Ottoman kingdom of Italy.

Of course there was no kingdom of Italy in the fifteenth century, but the public of 1820 could easily remember the Kingdom of Italy that had been created by a foreign conqueror in very recent history. Napoleon established the Kingdom of Italy in 1805 with himself as king and his stepson Eugène de Beauharnais as viceroy. He also made his brother-in-law Joachim Murat the king of Naples in 1808—and Napoleon's sister Caroline was therefore queen. Murat even attempted to recreate the Kingdom of Italy during the Hundred Days in 1815, and Neapolitans would certainly have remembered Murat during the revolutionary year of 1820. The fantasy of a foreign conqueror establishing a kingdom of Italy, as Maometto proposed within the opera, would not have seemed at all fantastic to the Italian public of the early nineteenth century.

Maometto, while offering to make Anna his queen, cannot keep from reminding her that she is entirely in his power:

> Pensa però che sei già mia conquista,
> e ch'io non trovo ancor chi a me resista.

> But remember that you are already my conquest,
> and that I have not found anyone who can resist me.[41]

Anna immediately accepts the challenge:

> Oggi il ritrovi alfin, quella son io.
> Amava [Amavo] Uberto, un mentitor detesto . . .

> Today at last you have found someone, and it is I.
> I loved Uberto, but I hate a liar . . .[42]

He claims to find Venetians "always treacherous," while the Venetians regard his impersonation of Uberto as a "barbarous deception," and Anna too concludes that he has damned himself as a liar.

The crime would have been a mere peccadillo, royalty traveling incognito, were it not that he had made use of his disguise to violate the Muslim-Christian religious divide that was both fundamental, and at the same time highly permeable, within the eastern Mediterranean scenario of the opera. In *La pietra del paragone* the Turkish disguise was purely farcical, but in *Maometto Secondo* the Turkish sultan wore an Italian disguise in order to deceive an Italian—indeed, to make a romantic conquest of an Italian girl. In *Il turco in Italia* such an impersonation had been completely unnecessary for the Turk to make his conquest, though Turks and Italians were both reciprocally capable of disguising themselves in the context of the masked ball. In *opera buffa* such deceptions offered an entertainment that was all the more potent for being subtly transgressive, but in *opera seria* the cultural and political implications of such cross-dressing and exchange of identities were not only transgressive but fundamentally corruptive. The ease with which Maometto had become an Italian student suggested the ease with which Anna might reciprocally, like all the harem women who rejected rigid virtue, become a Turk.

Denouncing the sultan as a "liar," Anna affirms her own rigid identity as a virtuous Venetian. She refuses to become his queen: "*Regina io teco? Della mia patria a danno?*" (Me, your queen? To the detriment of my fatherland?). Anna emphatically rejects the cultural convergence that he proposes, both in the form of marriage and in the envisioned kingdom of Italy, and she recognizes an inseparable clash of civilizations: "*A separarci, l'universo insorge*" (The universe rises up to separate us). Then she breaks into tears. He, however, instantly replies in her figurative language:

| E Maometto adunque | And so Maometto |
| dell'universo a trionfar già sorge. | already rises to triumph over the universe.[43] |

Ottoman power would both suppress and reconcile the cultural differences that separate them. Maometto's intended conquest of the world suggests a vision of new imperial unity in which old cultural divisions will disappear.

The sultan observes Anna's weeping, and interprets it as a sign of her struggling against her love for him. This she finally admits, and they then embark upon a tender but troubled love duet—before the opera rises up to separate them forever. Their duet leads into a cabaletta of feverish intensity, in which she exclaims, "I love! but I would rather be buried in my tomb than give in to this love." Maometto recognizes that her love is a "desperate love," and he is certain that she cannot ultimately resist "the conqueror of the world."[44] Janissary drumming interrupts them and announces the imminent struggle for the citadel. Maometto entrusts Anna with his own imperial seal, on a ring, so that she might wield his power as if she were already his queen, and then he joins in singing with his soldiers, urging them on to victory in a battle aria of spectacular ornamentation.[45] Rossini's music clearly delineates the two aspects of the Turkish protagonist, who can deploy his basso gloriously on behalf of military conquest or tenderly on behalf of fraught romance. Musically, Maometto is the hero of this opera in spite of himself, even though he is the self-proclaimed enemy of Christian Europe. Anna, after all, admits that she loves him, even if she is about to betray his love in the name of a higher commitment, a betrayal that will also thoroughly upstage him in the opera's conclusion and therefore somewhat unsettle his already ambivalent status as the hero of the piece.

Anna takes the sultan's ring, the mark of his trust in her, and immediately delivers it to Erisso and Calbo, along with (according to the Della Valle libretto) "two turbans and two Turkish cloaks."[46] Thus the two Venetians will be able to disguise themselves as Turks and use the ring with the sultan's seal to rejoin their army in the citadel and lead the resistance to the Turkish assault. Anna then consummates her betrayal of the sultan, the man she loves, by immediately marrying Calbo—with her father performing the rather irregular marriage ceremony at her mother's tomb.

After Erisso and Calbo depart, presumably in their Turkish disguises, Anna remains at the tomb, which is situated beneath the "temple"—that is, the church of Negroponte that was perhaps about to be converted to a mosque after the Ottoman conquest, as in the cases of Hagia Sophia in Constantinople and the Parthenon in Athens. Anna can hear the women in the church praying to "*Nume, cui 'l sole è trono*" (Nume, to whom the sun is a throne).[47] Were these women of Negroponte really Christian at all, or did Della Valle imagine them as ancient Greek pagans who had somehow maintained their paganism through a thousand years of Byzantine and Venetian rule? The women descend into the crypt and give Anna the news that Erisso and Calbo, appearing at the citadel, have managed to bring about the defeat of the Turks.[48] This "defeat" can only have been very temporary, since Della Valle and Rossini both knew with the certainty of history that the Ottomans did in fact conquer all of Greece in the fifteenth century.

In Della Valle's original libretto Anna is supposed to offer Maometto one final declaration of Italian patriotism before killing herself:

> E tu che Italia conquistar presumi,
> impara or tu da un'itala donzella
> che ancora degli eroi la patria è quella.

> And you who presume to conquer Italy,
> you may learn from an Italian girl
> that it is still a fatherland of heroes.[49]

This verse was cut from the composition of the opera. Of course it made no sense: the opera was not set in Italy, and in Greece the Turkish conqueror would be ultimately victorious. Furthermore, Anna's sentiments seemed to evoke the Napoleonic Italian moment that Rossini, Della Valle, and the public certainly remembered—perhaps with some political discomfort in the age of the Restoration.

In 1820 the presumptive conquering army was not Turkish but Austrian, as Metternich prepared to restore the Neapolitan monarchy in the name of the Holy Alliance, and perhaps the Teatro di San Carlo preferred not to feature a potentially provocative patriotic verse. As for Rossini, he may have felt that he had already set this particular verse when he composed the aria *"Pensa alla patria"* for Isabella in *L'italiana in Algeri* in Venice in 1813, though that patriotic aria was also replaced when the opera came to Naples in 1815. The resemblance to the refrain of *"Pensa alla patria"*—in which Italian heroes offered "examples of daring and valor"—may serve as a reminder that in some respects *Maometto Secondo* was the tragic historical inversion of the farcical subject introduced in *L'italiana*: a brave Italian girl and a despotic Turkish ruler.[50] Isabella would trick Mustafa in the spirit of comedy, while Anna would betray Maometto in the spirit of tragedy. In both cases an Italian girl would give lessons to a too presumptuous Turk.

In the final scene of *Maometto Secondo* the Muslim soldiers arrive at the crypt to denounce Anna for her perfidy—*"ecco la perfida"*—while the Christian women praise her loyalty to her country, singing that Italy will never forget *"si bella fedeltà"* (such beautiful loyalty). Maometto appears on the scene to accuse her to her face, *"O perfida!"*—while Anna countercharges, *"O barbaro!"* She tells him that she has married Calbo, to let Maometto know that she has betrayed not only his army but also his love, and then she stabs herself to death with a dagger at her mother's tomb. The final charges between them—*"O perfida!" "O barbaro!"*—echo with supreme ambivalence: Who is true and who is treacherous? Who is barbarous and who is civilized?

The Ottoman subject of *Maometto Secondo* thus presented the public with a difficult dilemma, caught between these radically opposed perspectives in what finally crystallized on stage as an operatic collision of cultural perspectives. The public of Naples in 1820 may not have been entirely comfortable with Mehmed the Conqueror as the tragic hero of the piece, which might have contributed to the fact that, according to Herbert Weinstock, the opera "was not well liked at Naples." Weinstock even wonders whether its lack of success contributed to Rossini's decision to leave Naples. Nevertheless, Rossini remained committed to revising and restaging the opera in the following years.[51]

Rossini in Vienna, Metternich in Venice

Turkishness was one of the subjects through which Rossini negotiated the fraught transition from his early years as a teenage composer in Napoleonic Italy to his status as the preeminent composer of the European Restoration. *L'italiana in Algeri* in 1813 and *Il turco in Italia* in 1814 belonged to the most intense period of Napoleon's collapse, and in 1820, in *Maometto Secondo*, Rossini explored the musical charisma and dramatic tragedy of universal conquest as embodied in the sultan. Rossini came to Restoration Naples in 1819 under the reign of the Bourbon king Ferdinand, and even composed a cantata for the Teatro di San Carlo on the occasion of the Neapolitan visit of the Habsburg emperor Franz.[52] In 1820, however, *Maometto Secondo* was produced in circumstances of revolution and the expectation of Austrian intervention. In 1822 Rossini left Naples to visit Vienna, the Habsburg capital, where Franz together with Metternich presided over the European Restoration and the Holy Alliance.

Rossini came to Vienna in 1822 as a triumphant conqueror, with his operas hugely popular there. One performance of *Matilde di Shabran* that spring was described in the *Allgemeine musikalische Zeitung* as "like an idolatrous orgy," people shouting their enthusiasm as if they had been "bitten by a tarantula."[53] Rossini was honored at a dinner given by Metternich himself, and was struck "at seeing, by comparison, myself treated with such regard by that brilliant Viennese assemblage" while Beethoven, "the greatest genius of the epoch," was "abandoned to such distress." Rossini visited Beethoven in Vienna, and received (as Rossini later recalled) a distinctly conditional, perhaps double-edged, compliment. Beethoven exclaimed: "Ah, Rossini, you are the composer of *Il Barbiere di Siviglia*? I congratulate you; it is an excellent *opera buffa*; I read it with pleasure, and it delighted me. It will be played as long as Italian opera exists. Never try to do anything but *opera buffa*."[54] It was not altogether friendly advice to a composer who had already written a dozen major works of *opera seria* and was about to revise *Maometto Secondo* for Venice before proceeding to Babylonian tragedy in *Semiramide*. Beethoven began composing the Ninth Symphony in 1822 and may have given a thought to Rossini when he inserted a Janissary band, with triangle and cymbals, playing *alla turca* within the "Ode to Joy" of the final movement.[55]

Maometto Secondo would not be heard in Vienna until early the following year, in 1823, which seemed to the *Allgemeine musikalische Zeitung*, considering Rossini's popularity, a rather long delay. Despite the supposed "implausibility" (*Unwahrscheinlichkeit*) of the plot, the soprano Therese Grünbaum was determined to sing the role of Anna, and her husband, Johann Christoph Grünbaum, undertook the translation of the entire libretto into German so that *Mahomet der Zweyte* could be performed at the Kärntnertor Court Theater. The audience was enthusiastic, and the sultan's entrance was described as "*imposant*," while the basso who played the role, Franz Siebert (who also sang Mozart's Osmin in Vienna), was praised not only for his vocal quality but also for his visual appeal: "His costume was absolutely splendid and embellished his anyway well-developed form." In a pre-Freudian typographical slip the *Allgemeine musikalische Zeitung* referred to the role as "Soliman," thus confusing Mehmed with the other great sultan who had actually besieged Vienna itself in 1529. The reviewer was unimpressed by the too predictable presence of Janissary music in such an opera: "People will not be surprised if, in the music under the banners of the victorious crescent moon, the piccolo plays a large roll, and the so-called Gran Cassa [bass drum] becomes very noticeable to the listener, as Rossini wields them very freely and forcefully, often in the middle of the tenderest moments of fervent passion."[56] The dramatic complexity of the opera—the seriousness for which Beethoven doubted Rossini's aptitude—made the Janissary music seem jarring and excessive. It was as if the piccolo and bass drum had escaped from their appropriate sphere, presumably comical, to intrude upon the passion of the Rossinian characters and the absorption of the Viennese audience in this contradictory work with its problematic hero.

When Rossini came to Venice at the end of 1822 for the revised presentation of *Maometto Secondo*, he was at home on the Adriatic but still within the Habsburg monarchy, and the reworked opera was not simply for Venice but for Habsburg Venice, ruled from Vienna. The alteration from the Naples production was very great, most notably the provision of a happy ending, in which Anna does not kill herself but marries the Venetian hero Calbo— without giving any further thought to Maometto! The fall of Negroponte belonged to Venetian history, and so the Venice production of *Maometto Secondo* was a sort of homecoming and had to give satisfaction to the Venetian public. Even in Naples the Venetians had been granted some sort of temporary victory against the Turks as a consequence of Anna's betrayal of the seal, but in Venice the Venetian victory over the Turks at Negroponte became even more emphatic and was celebrated in the happy ending of the opera. The published libretto noted that this production was being staged for the Carnival season of 1822–23, and a preface or warning (*avvertimento*) explained that "in order to remove the horror of the historical catastrophe, the melodrama has been brought to a happy ending [*lieto fine*]."[57] The public was thus to consider itself warned that the opera would not be historically accurate.

To be sure, Mehmed would eventually conquer Greece at some point after the final curtain fell, but that "historical catastrophe" was not to be made obtrusively manifest to the Venetian operatic public in 1822. This pandering to Venetian fantasy in defiance of the facts of Ottoman history received some psychic plausibility from the new turn of contemporary events between the Naples premiere of 1820 and the Venice version two years later. In 1821 the Greek War of Independence began with an uprising against the Ottomans in the Peloponnesus. Mehmed's fifteenth-century conquest of Greece was finally coming undone, and the fantasy of a happy Christian ending to the historical opera found some emotional resonance in the stirrings of contemporary politics. In fact, just seventy-five miles away from Venice, the Congress of Verona was meeting from October to December 1822 as the Holy Alliance attempted to oversee political order and deliberated over the containment of revolutionary rumblings in Italy, in Spain, and in Greece. Rossini himself briefly visited Verona in November and provided two cantatas, one entitled "La Santa Alleanza" (The Holy Alliance), as tokens of his cultural endorsement of the Restoration.[58]

Not only Metternich but also Emperor Franz and Empress Maria Ludovika were present at the Congress of Verona, and they even visited Venice, which they now ruled ever since the defeat of Napoleon. Metternich, whose international conservatism favored the political status quo, was not sympathetic to the Greek struggle against the Ottomans, and at Verona he worked to ensure that the congress would in no way endorse the Greek cause. After the end of the congress Metternich spent ten days in Venice, from December 16 to December 25, Christmas Day, which meant that he just missed being present in the city for the first performance of *Maometto Secondo* on December 26. The emperor and empress were also in Venice in December, attended mass at the Basilica of San Marco, and departed, according to the *Gazzetta Privilegiata di Venezia*, "accompanied by the prayers and by the sentiments of pious gratitude of the Venetians."[59]

The press was carefully censored within the Habsburg monarchy under Metternich's conservative supervision, and he himself may have scrutinized with some interest the report from the Ottoman empire which appeared in the *Gazzetta Privilegiata* on December 24. According to the Venetian newspaper, the Ottoman government was remaining silent about its wars in Persia and Greece, "far from making mention of the terrible defeats of the Turks or the victories of the Greek insurgents."[60] The Habsburg press would have been cautious about expressing explicit sympathy for the Greek insurgents against Ottoman rule as long as Metternich himself was unsympathetic. Yet the revision and reception of *Maometto Secondo* for Venice in 1822 was partly conditioned by the Greek uprising. The Paris transformation of the opera as *Le siège de Corinthe* in 1826 would be even more purposefully premised upon the political developments in Greece.

Overturning History: The Ottomans Defeated at Negroponte

Rossini's revisions for Venice in 1822 added an overture and simplified some of the complex musical structures of the Naples original.[61] In the middle of the second act, however, the plot itself begins to develop differently. After the duet of "desperate love" between Maometto and Anna—sung by Galli and Colbran, as in Naples—the sultan exits without the great battle aria he sang in Naples. Instead, his Turkish confidant Selim offers a recitative of concern, anxious over whether Maometto, "the tamer of Asia, the terror of Europe," might be distracted by love and neglectful of his glory: "*Ah! questo giorno a lui fatal non sia!*" (May this day not be fatal for him!), exclaims Se-lim.[62] This short recitative serves as a transition to the next scene near the walls of Negroponte, where Erisso and Calbo now appear "in Muslim cos-tume," including turbans, given to them by Anna along with Maometto's ring to permit their passage through the city.[63] Erisso throws off his Turkish cos-tume and turban with disgust, and then Maometto appears on the scene and recognizes him.

Diverging ever further from Della Valle's libretto for Naples, Maometto and Calbo were now scripted to fight one another in a duel of personal com-bat over Anna, and Rossini created a trio for them to join with Erisso in the triple expression of masculine rivalry and rage. Calbo and Maometto disap-pear offstage to fight their duel, and the next scene shows Anna preparing to commit suicide at her mother's tomb beneath the temple. Before she can carry out her resolve, however, exultant Venetian soldiers enter, waving flags and singing in chorus:

Vittoria! Vittoria!	Victory! Victory!
Il Veneto valore trionfò.	Venetian valor has triumphed.[64]

The details of the victory remain vague, but Erisso suggests that Calbo has defeated Maometto in personal combat, and that Anna and Calbo might now prepare to live happily ever after. The implication is that Maometto has been killed in the duel and the Turks definitively defeated—as if this were some kind of operatic exercise in counterfactual history.

The chorus celebrates "*la bella pace*" (beautiful peace), while Anna exe-cutes bubblingly brilliant vocal passage work in the concluding aria—"*Fra il padre e fra l'amante*" (Between my father and my lover)—which Rossini lifted from the conclusion of his own earlier opera *La donna del lago* of 1819, based on the poem *The Lady of the Lake* by Sir Walter Scott.[65] (In *La donna del lago* the heroine also attracts the love of a disguised stranger who calls himself "Uberto" and who turns out to be her family's royal enemy, King James V of Scotland, but he gives her up magnanimously in the end.) The Rossinian happy ending for Highland Scotland served equally well for Mediterranean Negroponte, and the Venetian public was able to leave La Fenice in 1822 en-joying not only the triumph of Venetian valor against the Turks but also the triumphant romance of the Venetian hero and heroine. Amazingly, Maom-etto had been eliminated from the conclusion of his own opera, *Maometto*

Secondo, and the Turkish conquest of Greece, with the ensuing centuries of Ottoman rule, were cheerfully erased on the Venetian operatic stage.

The review of the opera, appearing in the *Gazzetta Privilegiata di Venezia* on December 28, actually juxtaposed news from the Greek war with a report from the opera house. On the front page, above the fold, there was news from the Aegean island of Psara where the Greeks had burned a ship from the Turkish fleet; further down the front page, below the fold, was the review of *Maometto Secondo* at La Fenice. Though the opera had been rewritten for Venice—indeed, history itself rewritten for Venice—the reviewer in the *Gazzetta Privilegiata* was very grudging in his opinion of the work and complained that the opening of the Carnival season had not been marked by the presentation of a completely new opera. In spite of its Venetian subject, *Maometto Secondo* was already marked as a Neapolitan product and the reviewer was unable to work up enthusiasm even for Rossini's music. There had been applause for individual numbers, the reviewer conceded, but he preferred to give the credit to the singers than to the composer. He doubted that the Venetian public was any more enthusiastic about the opera than he himself, and he noted that the audience seemed to prefer the ballet that was offered on the same program, based on Voltaire's tragedy *Adelaide du Guesclin*. In fact, the opera received only six performances in Venice.[66]

Three days later, on December 31, *Il Nuovo Osservatore Veneziano* offered a second opinion on the opera, negative on the whole but considerably more detailed. The reviewer thought the public was generally unenthusiastic, responding to most of the numbers with a "cold silence" and to others "with some light indication of disapproval." In this case the reviewer was identified by name, Luigi Prividali, who as a matter of fact had himself served as a librettist for Rossini's *L'occasione fa il ladro* (Opportunity makes the thief) in Venice in 1812. Prividali did not admire the libretto of Della Valle and clearly felt that he himself could have written a better one.[67] Accordingly, the review did not hesitate to ridicule the contradictions of the plot, with Della Valle's libretto censured for "that fatal prolixity of words, always condemnable," and the revised Venetian edition further condemned for the "puerile" unsuitability of the happy ending. There were, however, some kind words for Rossini—"who has already composed so much beautiful music for so many other bad books"—and praise especially for the overture, the women's chorus, the first-act trio, "the grandiose and characteristic entrance of Maometto," and the first-act finale. It was noted with regret that Colbran was indisposed at the premiere and singing below her best.[68]

Prividali commented that "we know this drama suffered here the torture of several variations, but if these did not help make it better, they were not even sufficient to mask its defects." The principal defect, as he saw it, lay in the sultan's own contradictory character on stage:

> Whoever knows from history the famous conqueror of Byzantium would not ever imagine seeing him as the protagonist in this miserable drama, and much less would imagine finding him to be a boring braggart [*noioso millantatore*] who threatens without punishing, and supplicates without obtaining, and does not know how to make himself either feared or loved.[69]

It was almost as if, from Prividali's perspective, Rossini's Maometto seemed a little too much like Mustafa, who had been so completely infatuated with Isabella, the Italian girl in Algiers. Indeed, the epithet "*millantatore*," the braggart, would have fit Mustafa perfectly. Prividali, who collaborated with Rossini in Venice in 1812, probably saw Galli perform the part of Mustafa in Venice in 1813 and could not quite efface that memory when he saw Galli as Maometto in Venice in 1822. The reviewer would have preferred a more Machiavellian hero, one who knew how to make himself both loved and feared. Prividali's lukewarm response to the opera was not derived from any indifference to the figure of Maometto, but rather, if anything, from too great a personal investment, too vivid a preconceived fantasy of the Turkish sultan.

Yet Prividali, though he thought the sultan's character was poorly conceived, could not help admiring Galli in the role:

> Congratulations to Signore Galli who, after having distinguished himself many times in the opposite drama, now portrays with such naturalness the fierce pride of Maometto. As charming as he was in the ridiculous extravagance of Mustafa and the comic caricature of Don Magnifico [in *La Cenerentola*] ... he appears just as terrifying now in the furor of the enamored Ottoman, sustained by the flexible brio of his imposing voice.[70]

Prividali may have felt that Della Valle had made Maometto into a "boring braggart," rather like Mustafa, but the actual performance of Galli seemed to transcend the inconsistencies of the libretto. Galli ultimately succeeded in making Maometto "terrifying" (*terribile*).[71]

Prividali, whatever his mixed feelings about *Maometto Secondo*, entirely disliked the ballet based on Voltaire's *Adelaide di Guesclin*. The reviewer did observe, however, that the choreographer Francesco Clerico was better received in the theater than Rossini. Clerico was some forty years older than Rossini, had been creating ballets for decades all over northern Italy, and remained unrepentantly old-fashioned in his neoclassical (as opposed to Romantic) style. "If a profound conviction caused me to put to death all choreographers," commented Prividali after deploring the ballet, "for the sake of Signore Clerico I would certainly not find myself making an exception to the rule."[72] Such a bizarre comment in the review of a ballet would make no sense at all were it not for the broader context of the review of *Maometto Secondo*. Prividali's fascination with Maometto was such that it seemed incongruous when the operatic sultan was too indulgent—"threatens without punishing"—and the reviewer himself thus seemed to assume the role of Maometto, a more authentically rigorous Maometto, whose threats would be carried out completely. If the sultan-reviewer were to condemn all choreographers to death, then they would all have to die.

Conclusion: Ottoman Magnanimity in Milan

Maometto Secondo was not a triumph in Venice in 1822.[73] In spite of Rossini's best efforts to touch the chords of a lingering Venetian patriotism, the Turkish menace of the fifteenth century was not sufficiently inspirational to rouse the Lion of San Marco in Venice under Habsburg rule. Venice would respond more enthusiastically to Isabella Colbran in the Babylonian setting of *Semiramide* in 1823. On August 16, 1824, *Maometto Secondo* came to La Scala in Milan, performed in the original Naples version and now accompanied by the ballet *Sesostri*, set in ancient Egypt. Did anyone still remember now, three years after his death, that August 15 had once been celebrated in Milan as the grandiose imperial occasion of Napoleon's birthday? The Egyptian ballet might have constituted a subtle Napoleonic allusion for those with long memories and subversive political inclinations.

The review of *Maometto Secondo* in the *Gazzetta di Milano* was dismissive. The reviewer claimed to prefer Winter's *Maometto* (performed at La Scala in 1817) over Rossini's *Maometto Secondo* and, furthermore, to prefer Galli's past performance as Zopiro, the leader of Mecca and enemy of Mohammed, over his current performance as the Turkish sultan. At La Scala in 1824 the sultan made a grand stage entrance on a horse, and the *Gazzetta* commented iron-ically, "It is not to be believed that Galli, who performed Zopiro and covered himself with a glory that no other actor has ever achieved, would have now consented to sacrifice it to the pleasure of mounting a horse." The reviewer even disliked the music ("noisy and confusing instrumentation") and was only willing to praise the exotic sets—Ottoman and Egyptian—for the opera and the ballet.[74]

On August 15 (the day before the first Milan performance), the *Gazzetta di Milano* published on its front page a special report from the Ottoman empire. The newspaper was publishing the text of a letter that had been sent by the commander of the Ottoman forces, Mohammed Emir Pasha, to the Greek military leader, Dimitrios Panourgias. Since the letter was also addressed to the *rayah*, that is, the Christians of Ottoman Greece, it may be regarded as a sort of open letter, now finding its way to an even broader public than the Greek insurgents. The *Gazzetta di Milano* introduced the text by present-ing "the following letter from which radiate sentiments of moderation and magnanimity which, unfortunately, were disregarded."[75] One may wonder whether this sympathetic presentation of the Ottoman letter (consistent with Metternich's hostility to insurgency) allowed for the possibility of an ironic reading, and whether a Grecophile public in Milan might have read with greater antipathy the letter of the Ottoman commander to the rebellious Greeks.

> First of all, we salute you, and then we make known that, contrary to our
> hopes and with the most intense grief, we do not see that the evils of war, and
> the incessant calamities that for three years have weighed and still continue
> to weigh upon you, have yet served as a lesson to abandon your errors, to
> induce you to put an end to your attempts at rebellion, and to obtain, with
> our mediation, the grace of our powerful and fortunate emperor, in order to
> live, like all peoples who have become civilized, tranquil under the shade of his
> imperial protection.[76]

The operatic figure of the generous Turk, indulgent toward those who plotted against him, was as old as Rameau's *Les Indes galantes* from the 1730s, and the figure of the magnanimous pasha received new operatic life with Mozart's *Abduction* in the 1780s: "*Wer so viel Huld vergessen kann!*" Such conventions still lingered in the 1820s and shaped the literary presentation of the Otto-man letter in the *Gazzetta di Milano*, making Mohammed Emir Pasha into an almost operatic figure. What made him most operatic, however, was the resemblance between his text and the imperious demands of Maometto for the surrender of Negroponte, which were about to be sung from the stage of La Scala on the following evening. The contemporary Ottoman letter to the modern Greeks functioned as a sort of aria of introduction to the opera that was about to take the stage.

> Two things seem to trouble your spirits and, unfortunately, keep you from placing yourselves in a state of salutary repentance. First, you hope with the passage of time to exhaust the power of His Highness and thus bring to a conclusion an undertaking as unexecutable as it is crazy [*pazzo*] on every count. However long you persist in your criminal enterprises against such imposing force as that of our sovereign, you will all the more provoke his anger: you will thus put him in absolute necessity of redoubling his efforts in order to subjugate you totally and to humble your foolish arrogance. The second motive that till now has prevented you from abandoning your error is the fear that, in consequence of the evils into which your attempt has precipitated you, the hatred and enmity of His Highness against you could no longer be placated. What an error! The clemency and goodness of His Highness are manifested even in favor of foreigners, and so how much more would he not exercise clemency toward you who are his subjects? Cast out therefore from your spirits this strange thought, correct your errors, and implore sincerely the clemency of His Highness, of which you will quickly receive the most luminous proofs. As plenipotentiary I myself will receive you with open arms, as a father I will care for you; further, from this moment I concede to you a full amnesty for the past. Make haste to reply to this letter. May my words inspire you to salutary sentiments! In the contrary case you will be responsible before God for the blood of the innocent, of the unarmed women and children, which will be shed and which will fall upon your heads.[77]

The menace of the final phrases seemed to conjure the final scenes of *Maometto Secondo*—the Turkish assault upon the city, the chorus of distressed Venetian women—all the inevitably violent consequences of Erisso rejecting Maometto's terms and Anna rejecting his love. The Ottoman letter of 1822 very clearly laid out the operatic alternatives of *Maometto Secondo*: surrender and amnesty on the one hand, subjugation and bloodshed on the other. The revolutionary struggle for independence was not likely to be endorsed publicly in the censored press of Metternich's Milan, and the *Gazzetta* simply commented at the end of the letter, "Panourgias responded to these generous words only with arrogance [*alterigia*] and contempt [*disprezzo*]."[78] The phrase "generous words," however, could have been intended and received ironically, while it was certainly possible to suppose that the Milanese newspaper secretly admired the Greek rebel's defiant contempt.

The contemporary reception of *Maometto Secondo* was partly shaped by the current political situation, and reflected public ambivalence about the eponymous Ottoman conqueror, who was mocked as a contemptibly "boring braggart" in Venice and deemed a mere pretext for bringing a horse onto the stage in Milan. From 1820 in Naples, to 1822 in Venice, to 1824 in Milan, it became increasingly difficult for Galli to convey the romantic charisma of Maometto as a singing Turk. The contemporary Greek War of Independence was gradually making the opera seem irrelevant, so that the publication of the Ottoman pasha's letter in Milan became almost an operatic treatment of contemporary events, both foreshadowing and perhaps overshadowing the opera that was about to appear on the stage of La Scala. In Paris in 1826, when Rossini revised *Maometto Secondo* as *Le siège de Corinthe*, he would boldly bring the contemporary events of the Greek revolution into the literary and ideological framework of the opera.

"I can tell you that from what I have heard of it up to now, it seems to be a masterpiece," wrote Galli about Rossini's opera a week before the premiere in Naples in 1820, "but he has still not completed it."[79] Rossini was working on the opera right up until the last minute, and would be reworking it for the next six years. It was Rossini's last opera on a Turkish subject and therefore also the last Turkish role created for Galli, who sang the role of Maometto not only at the premiere in Naples but also in the revised version for Venice two years later and finally at La Scala in 1824.

Galli had now played Turk after Turk after Turk over the course of a decade, and had explored all the dimensions of Turkishness on the operatic stage. In *La pietra del paragone* in 1812 he played an Italian who adopted Turkish disguise and talked Turkish nonsense (*Tambelloni Kaimacacchi*), but in *Maometto Secondo* he played a Turk who could so seriously and successfully disguise himself as an Italian that he won the heroine's love. In *L'italiana in Algeri* in 1813 Galli played Mustafa, whose farcical sense of his own self-importance invited only the laughing derision of the Italian girl who happened to become his captive. In *Maometto Secondo* a very different Italian girl was so seriously traumatized by her love for the Turkish sultan that she could not suppress its traces even as she betrayed his trust and sacrificed her own life to escape from his power—not just his political power but his romantic power over her. In *Il turco in Italia* in 1814 Galli appeared as a Turk who loved Italy and was irresistible to the Italian woman he courted, even though Selim in Italy possessed none of the despotic power that made Turkish men into masters of the harem. Fiorilla gave him up in the end and remained at home with her Italian husband, but her fantasies certainly followed him back to the Ottoman empire. In *Maometto Secondo* the Italian heroine struggled and failed to eradicate her love for the Turkish sultan, even as he appeared in his most menacing manifestation as the enemy of her family and her country, the aspiring conqueror of the world. Galli would have well understood how to endow Maometto with the necessary charisma to dominate the opera, for no one but Galli was so comprehensively expert in all the ways that operatic Turks could play upon the cultural susceptibilities of the European public.

11

Rossini's Siege of Paris

Ottoman Subjects in the French Restoration

Introduction: Paris Expatriate

In 1824 Rossini moved to Paris, which would become his principal musical home for the rest of the decade, his final decade as an operatic composer. Stendhal published his life of Rossini that same year to hail the conquering composer. His operas had preceded him, and he was already on his arrival probably the most popular composer of the Restoration. At the Théâtre-Italien there had been productions of *L'italiana in Algeri* in 1817 and *Il turco in Italia* in 1820 among other Rossini operas. Then in 1824 Rossini himself became the musical director of the Théâtre-Italien and, as historian James Johnson has observed, made that theater company into "the crown jewel of Restoration society," even overshadowing the Paris Opéra.[1] Rossini consolidated his relation with the Bourbon regime by composing *Il viaggio a Reims* to honor the coronation of Charles X in 1825. In 1826 Rossini prepared for the Paris Opéra the French revision of *Maometto Secondo*: *Le siège de Corinthe*.

Turkish operatic subjects had been important in Paris through the entire eighteenth century, from the Paris fairs to Rameau, Favart, and Grétry. In fact, Grétry's comic opera *La caravane du Caire*, which began as a great success of the ancien régime in 1783, first staged for Louis XVI and Marie Antoinette at Fontainebleau, so far transcended politics that it became the most performed opera of the Napoleonic period, and it still survived into the Restoration. Rossini in Paris thus found many points of past reference for establishing his Turkish subjects in the French repertory. It was, however, the newly potent ideological force of French philhellenism in the decade of the Greek War of

Independence that powerfully shaped the creation and reception of Rossini's *Le siège de Corinthe*, the last important operatic vehicle for the figure of the singing Turk. Rossinian opera in the French Restoration was ultimately transcended by modern colonialism, when Charles X, in almost his last act before falling to the Revolution of 1830, sent not an Italian girl but a French army to conquer Algiers.

Angelica Catalani as Roxelana

In January 1816, half a year after Waterloo, an Ottoman operatic comedy was presented at the Théâtre-Italien, which had been entrusted by the restored Bourbon king Louis XVIII to the direction of the famous Italian soprano Angelica Catalani. She envisioned herself in Turkish comedy, as a sultana, and so she had Favart's eighteenth-century classic *Les trois sultanes* revised and Italianized as *Le tre sultane*—also known as *The Triumph of Roxelana* (Il trionfo di Rosselane)—and fitted with a new operatic score by Italian composer Vincenzo Pucitta. While Favart's work of 1761 was performed with songs, and was regularly revived during both the empire and the Restoration, Pucitta's Italian treatment was more of a fully composed comic opera.[2] Catalani herself assumed the role of Roxelana, the sixteenth-century harem slave and favorite of Suleiman the Magnificent. Historically Ukrainian, Roxelana was conceived as French by Favart for Paris, but now she remained only notionally French for Catalani reimagined her as Italian. The diva first presented the role in London in 1811, and then five years later in Restoration Paris at the Théâtre-Italien.[3]

The performance included contemporary references to suggest that the sixteenth-century sultana Roxelana was, like Angelica Catalani, perfectly familiar with the fashionable places in Restoration Paris. When Roxelana is invited to have sherbet with the sultan, she replies that she only likes sherbet from Tortoni's—the Neapolitan café on the Boulevard des Italiens in Paris.[4] In *Le tre sultane* the farce played upon the permeable meta-theatrical boundary between stage and public, between the sixteenth and the nineteenth centuries, and especially between Turkey and Europe. The opera was in fact being produced by the diva, Mme Catalani, who like Mme Favart in the same role fifty years earlier was able to apply her experience as a star on the European stage to representing Roxelana as the star of the Ottoman harem.

At the end of the opera Roxelana proposes that all the European captives and slaves of the harem be liberated, which Suleiman generously concedes. Roxelana wishes the former captives well—"*Tornate liberi ai patri lari*" (Return free to the lares of your fatherland)—though she herself plans to remain behind in Istanbul as Suleiman's wife. Osmin the eunuch, however, mocked by Roxelana as an "amphibian," cannot help feeling wistful about this emancipation: "*Addio, serraglio bello*," he sings.[5] The emancipation marked, in some sense, the advent of social modernity at the beginning of the nineteenth century, a new world of marriages instead of harems, of women as conjugal partners rather than captives, men as husbands rather than sultanic libertines. "*Addio, serraglio bello*" signaled a sort of farewell to the ancien régime, and amphibian though he was, the eunuch was unlikely to feel comfortable on the terra firma of modern life.

Reviewing the first Paris performance in January 1816, *Le Fidèle Ami du Roi* singled out as especially comical the performance of the eunuch Osmin, who "sang and danced in a very funny manner." The *Fidèle Ami* further saluted Catalani's performance and found that "the various attitudes that she took to charm the sultan produced the same effect on all the spectators."[6] The public thus became Turks for the duration of the performance so that the diva could conquer them too. The *Journal des Débats*, however, did not hesitate to denounce the music as "cold and monotonous, without melody and color," and criticized as inadequate the token efforts to produced "Turkish" percussion effects in the overture. The tenor Gaetano Crivelli had let it be announced at the premiere that he was suffering from a cold, which the *Journal* supposed might have explained the "extreme nonchalance" of his performance as Suleiman: "Although it may be accepted that a sultan should have an air of being bored [*ennuyé*], he exceeded the limits."[7] While acknowledging Catalani as "the greatest singer in Europe," the *Journal* expressed the hope that she would give up the role of Pucitta's sultana and take on the part of Mozart's countess in the *Marriage of Figaro*, as programmed for later in the season.[8]

La Quotidienne further lambasted the libretto for having ruined Favart's eighteenth-century drama thanks to "the Italian translator or rather the Italian mutilator." Yet the *Journal de Paris* observed at the end of January that the Théâtre-Italien remained the "rendezvous of the best society of Paris," and the *Gazette de France* noted that the second and third performances of

the opera played to full houses—"*un monde prodigieux*"—attracted by Catalani in particular.[9] In April she was still performing the work in repertory,
while also taking on the role of Mozart's countess. If for her Pucitta's sultana
provided a vocal warm-up for singing Mozart, for the Parisian public *Le tre
sultane* was above all the crucial preparation for receiving Rossini's *L'italiana
in Algeri* in 1817.

"The most Turkish of Turks": Rossini at the Théâtre-Italien

"All the works of Rossini performed in Paris have been staged in a ridiculous manner," wrote Stendhal in his *Life of Rossini*. "I still remember the first
performance of *L'italiana in Algeri*."[10] That first performance took place at
the Théâtre-Italien on February 1, 1817, and was the first of Rossini's works to
be presented in Paris. The French critics, Stendhal thought, completely failed
to appreciate Rossini's genius in *L'italiana*: "Our grave men of letters in the
Journal des Débats have found the plot of the piece to be mad [*folle*]—not re-
alizing, poor folk, that if it were not mad, it would be unsuited to this type of
music, which is a sort of organized and complete madness [*une folie organisée
et complète*]. If these, our worthy men of letters, want something reasonable
and passionate, let us send them to Mozart."[11] Stendhal embraced *L'italiana*
as brilliant madness, conditioned by the emotional irregularity and irratio-
nality that emerged from the encounter between Europeans and Ottomans.

In the age of the Enlightenment, the great age of Turkishness in European
opera, a Turkish figure such as Mozart's Osmin might serve to dramatize the
tensions surrounding the very idea of reason, as he descended to his lowest
bass notes singing, "*Ich hab' auch Verstand*" (I also have a mind). With the
waning of the Enlightenment, in the aftermath of the Revolution, the relation
of madness and reason became a clinical concern and may have seemed more
problematic as a principle of operatic comedy. Rossini nonsensically scrambled the elements of reason and unreason even as he confused the categories
of European and Turkish character, relishing the interrelated comedy of both
in juxtaposition. In 1817, the year that *L'italiana* came to Paris, Jean-Étienne
Esquirol, the pupil of Philippe Pinel, began to offer a course in psychiatric
illness, *maladies mentales*, at the Salpêtrière Hospital in Paris.[12] It was perhaps
a complicated moment to appreciate the nonsensical "madness" of Mustafa
as a Pappataci.

The reviewer of *L'italiana* in the *Gazette de France* claimed to find the opera vulgar, and especially in comparison to Favart's *Les trois sultanes* of fifty years before.[13] In fact, Rossini's *L'italiana* could be considered a sort of operatic descendant of Favart's work: the Turkish comedy of an Ottoman potentate tamed by an irrepressible European woman, a drama of captivity comically inverted. The *Gazette de France* now denounced *L'italiana* as "*la parade la plus insipide*" (the most insipid *parade*), and observed that "Mustafa is the parody in caricature of [Favart's] Soliman; he loses his head for an Italian slave, a Roxelana of the marketplace, whose manners and language reveal her origin and would suffice to revolt the most Turkish of Turks [*le Turc le plus turc*]."[14] It seems likely that the Italian character of Isabella was part of what made her seem vulgar to the reviewer—a Roxelana of the marketplace—but it was the issue of Turkishness that lay at the very heart of the critical rejection of the opera. The reviewer denied the appeal of Isabella by imagining himself as the most Turkish of Turks, presumed to possess the most vulgar taste in women.

A *parade* was a work of popular theater, including the kind of commedia dell'arte that was staged at the eighteenth-century Paris fairs—where Turkishness was first conceived as French musical comedy. While Favart's conception may have evolved out of those earlier popular works, like *Arlequin sultane favorite*, *Les trois sultanes* now appeared as a model of rococo sophistication, not quite opera but preserving a balance between comedy and music while negotiating the cultural encounter between Ottoman power and French charm. French musical comedy could only dignify its Ottoman subjects by making them—like Soliman—susceptible to European civilization. Bey Mustafa, however, with his eagerness to become a "European" Pappataci, made Europe itself seem ridiculous. *Le Constitutionnel* agreed that *L'italiana* was only "a nasty *parade*" (*une méchante parade*), and the *Journal de Paris*, noting Rossini's youth, thought that not even a schoolboy could have done something "more stupid and more ridiculous."[15]

Il turco in Italia opened in Paris in May 1820, and the *Courrier des Spectacles de Paris* reviewed the premiere by noting that the opera was full of "*bouffoneries*" (clownishness), while praising the music and observing the keen applause of the audience. The *Journal du Commerce* found *Il turco* to be "insipid and ridiculous" but admitted that the audience was responsive, noting special enthusiasm for the number "*Siete Turchi, non vi credo.*" By June 1, the

Journal de Paris declared *Il turco* to be a "triumph" in Paris and noted that it was attracting "a crowd" to the theater.[16]

The *Journal des Théâtres, de la Litterature e des Arts* found the passion of the Turk Selim for Fiorilla perfectly plausible:

> It is easily explained in my eyes, as in those of the parterre, as its object is the pretty Signora Ronzi [Giuseppina Ronzi de Begnis], very worthy of drawing the gaze of a lover, even if he were Asiatic and accustomed to Georgian beauties who disputed for the heart of the master in the seraglios, where they are kept by despotism and voluptuousness. But let us carry on. Selim finds Fiorilla to his taste, and apparently she very much loves Turks.[17]

It was striking how ready the French reviewer was, in this case, to identify with a gallant Turk like Selim in appreciating the charm of an Italian woman like Fiorilla. Such identification would have been impossible with a buffoon like Mustafa in *L'italiana*. In the case of *Il turco*, however, the reviewer found Selim to be a Turkish lover with excellent taste, not "the most Turkish of Turks" but perhaps even the least Turkish of Turks.

The same journal, returning to the subject the next day, had a few more thoughts to offer about Selim as performed by the basso Felice Pellegrini: "He was not sufficiently passionate in the coffee scene . . . I know that it would be easy for Pellegrini to put more fire [*plus de feu*] into the expression of his love."[18] In spite of the stage conventions, this particular Turk was not allowed to be bored, languorous, inertial, or overcome with ennui; he was to be a fiery and passionate Turk, reflecting what was clearly the fire and passion of the French reviewer who would have been very glad to be invited home for coffee with Fiorilla as performed by Signora Ronzi. The identification with Selim was so complete that the reviewer claimed to feel the Turk's passion more fully than the Italian performer on the stage. It was thus the soprano who won over both the Turkish prince on the stage and the French reviewer in the audience, and Signora Ronzi would make further conquests in June, when she began to alternate performances as Rossini's Fiorilla with Mozart's Susanna in the *Marriage of Figaro*.[19]

The year of *Il turco in Italia* at the Théâtre-Italien, 1820, was also the year that a one-act musical vaudeville farce, *L'ours et le pacha* (The bear and the pasha) was first performed at the Théâtre des Variétés on Boulevard Montmartre. Created by the dramatist Eugène Scribe in collaboration with Xavier

Saintine, it was popular during the 1820s when Rossini came to Paris. Alluding to *The Three Sultanas*, the plot concerns a pasha with a French captive named Roxelana, whose husband gains entrance to the harem disguised as a dancing bear, since the pasha "Schahabaham," though he values his harem, is also known to have "favorites" from the court menagerie. *Der Bär und der Bassa*, a German version, was also performed in Vienna in 1820 and Berlin in 1821. The Paris text contained numerous song lyrics to be sung to specified familiar tunes, in the vaudeville manner, with a chorus of Turks to greet the pasha on his entrance: "*Gloire, honneur! honneur à notre pacha!*" (Glory and honor to our pasha!). A penciled production note in a published libretto from 1828 specified that the chorus was to be followed by a march—"*jouer la marche*" (play the march)—very likely in a mock-Turkish style.[20]

In 1792, at the height of the French Revolution, the opera *Les visitandines*, composed by François Devienne, presented the comical abduction of a nun from an oppressive convent in a scenario obviously borrowed from Turkish captivity operas. In 1825, at the height of the Restoration, in the year of Charles's coronation, *Les visitandines* was restaged at the Odéon Theater under the title *Les Français au sérail*, preserving Devienne's music but with the convent now transformed into the seraglio which it had partly represented all along.[21] The presence of operas with Turkish subjects in Paris during the Restoration echoed the operatic dynamics of the ancien régime, including Pucitta's *Three Sultanas*, the operas of Rossini at the Théâtre-Italien, popular parodies like *The Bear and the Pasha*, and even Grétry's perennially revived *Caravan of Cairo*.

Byronic and Rossinian Philhellenism

Rossini was already known in Paris for his Turkish operatic subjects before he first visited Paris in 1823 and then settled there in 1824 for the rest of the decade. Now as director of the Théâtre-Italien, Rossini presided in 1825 over the premiere of his new opera *Il viaggio a Reims* and also productions of his earlier works *La Cenerentola*, *La donna del lago*, and *Semiramide*. In September 1825 Rossini also presented the Italian opera of his German friend Giacomo Meyerbeer, *Il crociato in Egitto* (The Crusade in Egypt), which had had its premiere in Venice at La Fenice the previous year. This was a work with a prominent Islamic subject, set in the age of the Crusades, composed in an Italian style that owed much to Rossini's influence, and sufficiently successful in Paris in 1825 to help make Meyerbeer afterward the preeminent composer of French grand opera in Paris in the 1830s. With its singing sultan, Meyerbeer's *Il crociato in Egitto*, presented by Rossini in Paris in 1825, also prepared the way for Rossini's revision of *Maometto Secondo* as *Le siège de Corinthe* for the Paris Opéra in 1826.

Il crociato is set at the sultanic court of Damietta at the mouth of the Nile on the Mediterranean Sea. The fictional libretto—by Gaetano Rossi, who had written *Tancredi* and *Semiramide* for Rossini—seems to suggest that this is the Sixth Crusade in the thirteenth century, and the sultan would therefore have been a Mameluke sultan of Egypt.[22] He is a basso sultan, preparing to negotiate peace with the crusading knights of Rhodes and undermined by a treacherously scheming tenor Grand Vizier named Osmino. The plot of the opera hinges on the true love, secret marriage, and hidden child of the sultan's daughter Palmide and the man who serves the sultan under the Muslim name of Elmireno but is actually Armando, the nephew of the Christian commander. It would have been difficult for the audience to determine whether Armando betrayed his faith and people by serving the sultan as a Muslim, or whether Palmide betrayed her faith and people by marrying him as a Christian. The libretto allows them to defy the great religious barrier in the age of the Crusades to such an extent that they themselves scarcely know which side they are on, and the boundary between Muslim and Christian worlds seems to dissolve in Meyerbeer's musical treatment of their love. The love between Christian and Muslim in *Il crociato* poses the problem of Mediterranean religious identities as a matter of complex plasticity, comparable to the problematic romance between Maometto and Anna in Rossini's *Maometto Secondo*.

Recomposed to a French libretto by Luigi Balocchi and Alexandre Soumet, *Le siège de Corinthe*—the final metamorphosis of *Maometto Secondo*—became the first French opera of Rossini's new French career. The title immediately indicated that the scene had shifted from Negroponte to Corinth, still within the Greek lands, but the formerly Venetian characters of Della Valle's original Italian libretto now became Greeks in the French treatment. While Negroponte was a name from medieval Venetian history, Corinth, with its famous temple of Aphrodite and eponymous Corinthian columns, was far more evocative of ancient Greece and therefore more meaningful to the European philhellenism of the early nineteenth century. The port city of Missolonghi, where Lord Byron died in 1824, underwent a long siege that ended with the Ottomans taking the city and carrying out a massacre in the spring of 1826. Philhellenes would have been thinking of the siege of Missolonghi when the operatic siege of Corinth commenced at the Paris Opéra in October.

Erisso, the governor of Negroponte in *Maometto Secondo*, became Cléomène, *chef des Grecs* (leader of the Greeks), in *Le siège de Corinthe*; his daughter Anna became the Greek maiden Pamyra, and Calbo became Néoclès, transformed from Venetian to Greek and, vocally, from cross-dressed contralto to manly tenor. No longer Venetians fighting to defend an outpost of the Republic of San Marco in the eastern Mediterranean, Cléomène, Néoclès, and their fighting men now constituted a national Greek resistance to the Ottoman conquest of Corinth—which actually occurred in 1458. This reformulation of the drama created an uncanny encounter between the historical scenario of the fifteenth century and the current nineteenth-century struggle for Greek independence.

The premiere of *Maometto Secondo* in Naples in 1820 was coincidentally followed in 1821 by a rising in Greece against Turkish rule, beginning in the Peloponnesus under the military leadership of Theodoros Kolokotronis. In 1822, as Rossini revised his opera for Venice with a happy ending, the Greeks in Greece affirmed their own hopeful conviction of a happy ending by issuing a declaration of independence. They justified themselves before European opinion by appealing to nineteenth-century philhellenism. "We the descendants of the wise and noble peoples of Hellas, we who are the contemporaries of the enlightened and civilized nations of Europe," began the declaration, "we find it no longer possible to suffer without cowardice and self-contempt the cruel yoke of the Ottoman power which has weighed upon us for more than four centuries."[23] Since the Greek uprising of the nineteenth century was intimately related to the Turkish conquest of the fifteenth century, the intervening four centuries could be conjured away by the performance of *Le siège de Corinthe* on the stage of the Paris Opéra. The audiences who listened to Rossini's singing sultan and operatic Corinthians were themselves being musically mobilized to participate vicariously in the Greek struggle.

"After this prolonged slavery we have determined to take arms to avenge ourselves and our country against a frightful tyranny," affirmed the Greeks of 1822, declaring their independence. "The war which we are carrying on against the Turk . . . is a national war, a holy war, a war the object of which is to reconquer the rights of individual liberty, of property and honor—rights which the civilized people of Europe, our neighbors, enjoy today, rights of which the cruel and unheard-of tyranny of the Ottomans would deprive us."[24] The French libretto for *Le siège de Corinthe* in 1826 echoed the language of the Greek declaration of 1822: the operatic Greeks deploring "the yoke of the tyrant" (*le joug du tyran*), wondering "how to preserve ourselves from a horrible slavery."[25] The libretto looked back to the fifteenth century in order to anticipate the nineteenth century:

La Grèce est libre encor;	Greece is still free;
Nous vaincrons nos tyrans.	We will defeat our tyrants.[26]

Rossini himself and the French public for whom he composed would be able to respond to such a libretto in 1826 as if it were contemporary rather than historical.

To sympathize with the fifteenth-century Venetians of Negroponte when they appeared on the operatic stage in 1820 was a matter of historical nostalgia, but to celebrate Rossinian Greeks in their resistance to Ottoman rule was politically meaningful after the rising of 1821 and the declaration of 1822. Europeans only had to imagine a continuity of Turkish oppression and Greek resistance from the fifteenth to the nineteenth century and accept the convergence of fantasy and history between the operatic stage and the theater of war. In London an adaptation of Mozart's *Abduction from the Seraglio* was prepared for Covent Garden in 1827, and the setting of the opera was now specified as a Greek island, so that even Mozart could be made into a posthumous supporter of Greek freedom against Turkish tyranny. Belmonte was reconceived as an artist who had come to paint the classical ruins of Greece in the spirit of philhellenism.[27]

The Grecian cause had many ardent supporters in Europe, and the most famous philhellene of all was Lord Byron in England. After the Greek declaration of 1822, Byron was inspired in 1823 to set out for Greece to participate in the struggle. He was preparing to participate in a naval expedition against the Turks when he died at Missolonghi in 1824, becoming instantly a romantic martyr of the Greek national cause. Byron's devotion to Greece dated back to his first visit in 1809, at the age of twenty-one; in Athens in 1810 he wrote the poem "Maid of Athens" about a beautiful twelve-year-old Greek girl. In the third canto of *Don Juan* he celebrated "The isles of Greece! The isles of

Greece!" and was inspired by the landscape of Marathon to imagine the over-
throw of the Ottomans:

> The mountains look on Marathon—
> And Marathon looks on the sea;
> And musing there an hour alone,
> I dream'd that Greece might yet be free.[28]

Corinth also inspired in Lord Byron visions of Greek freedom, and in 1816 he
published a long poem under the title "The Siege of Corinth," which almost
certainly inspired the title for Rossini's French libretto.

Byron's poem was an account of the Ottoman siege of Corinth in 1715
in the context of the very last Ottoman-Venetian war that would end with
the peace of Passarowitz in 1718.[29] In the 1820s Corinth was again embattled,
standing on the isthmus that separated Athens from the uprising in the Peloponnesus. Contested between the Ottoman forces and the Greek rebels, the
city suffered serious damage during the course of the war. Rossini, like Lord
Byron before him, would make Corinth into a European emblem of Greek
patriotism and liberty. The *Gazette de France*, in 1826, actually reported on a
completely fictitious meeting and conversation between Byron and Rossini,
as if to suggest that the former had initiated the latter into the mysteries of
the Grecian cause.[30]

In 1826 the Greek war was building to a climax as the sultan sent against
the Greeks the Egyptian troops of Ibrahim Pasha, son of Mehmed (Mohammed) Ali Pasha, the semi-autonomous ruler of Ottoman Egypt. At the same
time the British foreign secretary George Canning took the lead in negotiating an agreement with France and Russia to intervene against the sultan
on behalf of the Greeks. In April 1826 Rossini in Paris helped to prepare for
a fundraising concert for the Greek cause, with some of his own music on
the program, including "*Pensa alla patria*" from *L'italiana*. On this occasion
Italy was irrelevant to Isabella's aria, as the French public was being enjoined
to think of the Greek fatherland.[31] In October the premiere of *Le siège de
Corinthe* was also an occasion for channeling public enthusiasm, not only
for opera but also for Greece. The tenor who sang the part of Néoclès, noting criticism of the opera in the press, compared the critics to Turks, who
were vanquished by the enthusiastic public: "Happily, the public has been
Greek, and some outbursts of drums and trombone—I should say even of

cannon—have not prevented it from coming thrice weekly to admire the denouement of these unhappy Hellenes."[32] In fact, the Greek engagement of the French public was crucial for Rossini's decision to revise and stage the opera for Paris.

In *Maometto Secondo* Anna of Negroponte falls in love with the sultan when she meets him in Corinth in disguise as Uberto, and she supposes him to be Venetian like herself. In *Le siège de Corinthe*, before the opera begins, Pamyra of Corinth has met the sultan in Athens where he is traveling incognito. Later the sultan—Mahomet in French, rather than Maometto in Italian—gives a lyrical account of his visit to Greece, narrated in an almost philhellenic spirit that even seems to echo Byron's "Maid of Athens":

> Une jeune beauté
> se montra dans Athènes à mon oeil enchanté.
> Je marche vers Athènes et mon bonheur commence.

> A young beauty
> appeared in Athens to my enchanted eye.
> I move toward Athens and my happiness begins.[33]

The historical Mehmed the Conqueror did appreciate certain aspects of Greek Byzantium, even as he conquered Constantinople and made it his own capital. He knew the Greek language, was interested in the legacy of Greek antiquity, and, converting Hagia Sophia into a mosque, helped to make Byzantine church architecture a decisive influence on Ottoman mosque architecture.[34] The libretto of *Le siège* went even further, making the sultan into a nineteenth-century romantic in his "enchanted" appreciation of the Greek maiden who inspires his longing for Athens and herself.

When Mahomet and Pamyra finally come face to face in Corinth and recognize one another, he acknowledges that he is still in love, while she, in her father's horrified presence, exclaims, "*Quel jour de douleur!*" (What a day of grief!). The sultan replies with a romantic and political proposition:

> Ce jour peut se changer
> en un jour d'allégresse;
> Qu'elle soit mon épouse
> et je sauve la Grèce.

> This day can change
> into a day of joy;
> Let her become my wife
> and I will save Greece.[35]

Only in French could the word for joy—"*allégresse*"—not only rhyme with but almost enunciate the name of Greece: *la Grèce*. His love for the Greek

Mahomet II, costume design for *Le siège de Corinthe* by artist Hippolyte Lecomte, for the Paris premiere in 1826. The French basso was Henri-Étienne Dérivis, and Lecomte envisioned him not only in full and magnificent costume but in operatic pose, as if about to sing: "*Eh bien! que le soleil, témoin de ma victoire, / Demain cherche Corinthe et ne la trouve pas*" (Well! let the sun, witness of my victory, / Search for Corinth tomorrow and not find it). With kind permission of the Bibliothèque Nationale de France.

maiden makes a philhellene out of Mahomet, who seems to propose some sort of Greek polity even as he is destroying the world of Byzantium. In *Maometto Secondo*, back in 1820, he offered to make Anna the queen of Italy, but in *Le siège de Corinthe*, in 1826, it was the political past, present, and future of Greece that was operatically at stake.

"The dust of Marathon": The Greek Chorus and the French Public

In *Le siège de Corinthe* the most dramatic departure from the Italian original occurs in the penultimate scene preceding Pamyra's suicide. In this scene the Greek elder Hiéros blesses the flags of the Corinthians. Singing in a solemn basso register, he comforts his people for the fall of Byzantium by looking to the Hellenic past and prophesying the glorious neo-Hellenic future:

> O prophétique ivresse!
> Dieu lui-même commande à mes sens agités;
> Il dévoile à mes yeux l'avenir de la Grèce;
> Avant de mourir, écoutez.
>
> O prophetic intoxication!
> God himself commands my agitated senses;
> He reveals to my eyes the future of Greece;
> Before you die, listen.[36]

The singular god invoked in the libretto was not specified—whether pagan or Christian—but seemed to be some sort of oracular deity who inspired prophetic utterances to gratify the philhellenic sensibilities of the public.

The future of Greece that Hiéros prophesies was, of course, the present moment of the performance of the opera, the age of the nineteenth-century Greek War of Independence to which the libretto made specific allusion. Hiéros foresees that after "five centuries of slavery" Greece will "awaken" and rise up against the Ottomans. That future uprising is, however, also inspired by the remote past:

> O Grèce! tous tes fils se lèvent à ton nom..
> Le vent fait voler sur leurs armes
> La poussière de Marathon.

Oh Greece! all your sons rise up at your name.
The wind blows upon their arms
The dust of Marathon.[37]

And the Greek chorus echoes him: "Marathon! Marathon!" Such was the historical fantasy of the European philhellenes in the 1820s—a restaging of the Persian Wars!—and some of the contemporary Greek rebels themselves might have recognized the fantasy, though their struggle would probably have appeared to them more clearly as one of Orthodox Christian subjects against the Muslim sultan.

It was Lord Byron who traveled to Marathon and "dream'd that Greece might yet be free." The prophetic vision of Hiéros looked forward and backward, not only to Marathon but also to Thermopylae:

L'écho sacré des Thermopyles	The sacred echo of Thermopylae
Se souvient de Léonidas.	Recalls Leonidas.[38]

And the chorus responds, "Léonidas! Léonidas!" The Greeks on stage look back a thousand years, from the fall of Corinth in 1458 AD to the battle of the three hundred Spartans against Persia at the pass of Thermopylae in 480 BC. The Paris public of 1826 benefited from the perspective of another five centuries as the features of Mehmed the Conqueror, the Ottoman Turkish sultan, dissolved into those of Xerxes the Great, the Achaemenid Persian Shahanshah, who tried and (unlike Mehmed) failed to conquer Greece.

Thus Rossini composed the philhellene operatic fantasy of Greek history, linking the world of ancient Greece to the contemporary struggle for Greek independence by means of a Turkish subject in an opera that was formerly named for Mehmed the Conqueror. Yet the implicit Turkish protagonist of the French revision was not Mehmed II but Mahmud II, the contemporary sultan who sought to suppress the Greek rising of the 1820s. The Turkish historical subject was now almost overshadowed by the contemporary Greek political drama. The convergence between operatic material and contemporary affairs was disturbingly close for some, like the French critic who commented: "If the new work is a bulletin on Greece, then print it in the *Moniteur*. If it is an opera, then perform it; but choose, for it would be as ridiculous to publish an official tragedy as to sing a diplomatic note."[39] With *Le siège de Corinthe* Rossini found himself at the awkward frontier of the operatic domain, and it was partly for that reason that this would be Europe's last major work of operatic Turkishness.

Hector Berlioz, only twenty-three in 1826, later recalled that the orchestration of *Le siège de Corinthe* had made a great impression. He somewhat facetiously claimed that Rossini's priority was to keep the Paris audience from falling asleep:

> And he put the bass drum [*grosse caisse*] everywhere, as well as the cymbals and the triangle, and the trombones and the ophicleide . . . He made the orchestra burst out with such lightning flashes of sonority and harmony, with such thunderbolts, that the public, rubbing its eyes, took delight in this new genre of emotions . . . From the date of Rossini's arrival at the Opéra, the instrumental revolution in theater orchestras was accomplished. The big noises [*grands bruits*] were used for every purpose and in all works, whatever style was imposed upon them by their subject. Soon the kettledrums, the bass drum, and the cymbals and triangle no longer sufficed.[40]

Berlioz might, for instance, have been thinking of the orchestral explosion that accompanies the invocation by Hiéros, "Oh Greece! all your sons rise up at your name."

Similarly explosive is the rousing national chorus of Greeks who respond to the prophecy of Hiéros and the name of Léonidas:

> Répondons à ce cri de victoire,
> Méritons un trépas immortel.
> Nous verrons dans les champs de la gloire
> Le tombeau se changer en autel.

> Le us respond to this cry of victory,
> Let us deserve an immortal death.
> We will see in the fields of glory
> The tomb transformed into an altar.[41]

It was reported that on the night of the premiere, at the third-act finale, the audience "leaped to its feet as one man at the final notes of the chorus and gave vent to a long shout of admiration"—presumably this same national chorus of the Greeks.[42] Thus the audience, by jumping up and shouting out, actually participated in the national chorus of the Greeks by responding—"*Répondons!*"—in the spirit of the composition itself. Both the chorus on the stage and the public in the hall, in fact, were "responding" not only

to Rossini's music but to the ongoing Greek struggle for national independence against the Ottomans. The spirited rhythm and orchestration of this
Greek choral anthem, celebrating *"les champs de la gloire,"* harkened back to
the Marseillaise, the revolutionary French national anthem created in 1792,
the year of Rossini's birth. A French book of Greek patriotic hymns (*Hymnes
patriotiques des Hellènes*) in the 1820s actually proposed new lyrics to be set to
the tune of the Marseillaise: *"Allons enfants de l'Hellenée!"*[43]

Ideologically, Rossini's two operatic choruses, Greek and Turkish, seemed
to represent very different political principles throughout the opera. From
the very first scene of *Le siège*, the Greek chorus evokes the civic solidarity of
Rousseau's *Social Contract* along with the spirit and rhythm of the Marseillaise:

Jurons tous, oui jurons, par ces armes,
De défendre en ce jour nos remparrts.

We all swear, yes we swear, by these arms,
To defend on this day our ramparts.[44]

The Turkish chorus of the first act sings in a very different spirit to celebrate
the entrance of Mahomet, as if illustrating Montesquieu's discussion of Asiatic despotism in *L'esprit des lois*:

Soumise à ta puissance,	Subject to your power,
L'Asie est dans les fers.	Asia is in chains.[45]

The composition of the choruses in *Le siège* thus became a kind of operatic
work of political theory, with revolutionary nationalism opposed to Asiatic
despotism, but both choruses required an orchestrally explosive militancy,
and the cymbals and triangles of Janissary style were absorbed into percussion arrangements that celebrated Greek freedom. For Rossini, the musical
idol of the Restoration, the subliminal evocation of the Marseillaise underlined his own politically equivocal career, nourished in Napoleonic Italy and
now achieving a sort of royalist apotheosis in Restoration Paris.

It would also have been possible to discern a structural alignment of op-
pressed peoples in Rossini's major works for the Paris Opéra: the Greeks of
Le siège in 1826, the biblical Hebrews of *Moïse et Pharaon* in 1827, and the
medieval Swiss of *Guillaume Tell* in 1829. Such an alignment would also have
implied an equation of operatic despotisms: Ottoman, pharaonic, and final-

ly, terrorizing William Tell, the Austrian Habsburgs, a very current political presence in Restoration Europe. Music historian Benjamin Walton has noted the ambiguity of Rossini's work with reference to such political associations, poised between Revolution and Restoration.[46]

Rossini's Greek chorus—"*Répondons à ce cri de victoire*"—also musically anticipated the Trojan march and chorus that Berlioz would compose in the 1850s. Indeed, the whole prophetic scene of Hiéros, linking the past, present, and future of the Greek nation from the philhellene perspective, was notably related to the much later operatic project of Berlioz, when he followed Aeneas and the Trojans from national tragedy (at the hands of the Greeks, of course) to national destiny in Rome and Italy. Completing *Les Troyens* in 1858, on the eve of Italian national unification, Berlioz had certainly learned something from Rossini about the ways in which opera could stage the metamorphosis of a nation.

Berlioz himself would not be shy about huge orchestral and percussive effects, and his censuring of Rossini was perhaps most interesting for what he did not say about "the kettledrums, the bass drum, and the cymbals and triangle" that "no longer sufficed" for extreme musical emphasis. The named instruments were none other than the basic combination of the Janissary band, the characteristic orchestration of Turkishness dating back to the second half of the eighteenth century. Now Janissary percussion was about to become absorbed into the more generally emphatic percussion section of the nineteenth-century orchestra, even as the Turkish subject of *Maometto Secondo* was somewhat effaced by the Greek drama of *Le siège de Corinthe*.[47]

Already in 1821 Paul Delaroche created a caricature of "Signor Tambou-rossini"—a turbaned Turk playing a bass drum, indicating the Janissary associations of Rossinian percussion. In 1822 critic Auguste Delaforest remarked that Rossini's instrumentation was difficult for Parisians: "The obligatory bass drum, the fifes, the trumpets, were surprising to ears unaccustomed to these warlike instruments." Amédée de Tissot in 1827 was deeply hostile to Rossini, finding that "the continual playing of the bass drum, the timpani, the cymbals" suggested that Rossini was fraternizing with "the lower classes."[48] In fact, Rossini was simply drawing upon the Janissary tradition in classical music, as suggested by the turban in Delaroche's satirical image and even by Delaforest's reference to "warlike instruments"; but for Tissot the problem had begun to appear as a more general matter of modern percussion.

Lith. Villain.

Il Signor Tambourossini ou la nouvelle melodie.

"*Il Signor Tambourossini ou la nouvelle melodie*," by artist Paul Delaroche, published in 1821. The satirical title combined Rossini's name with the word *tambour*, or drum, in this case clearly the *tamburo grande*, the two-headed bass drum closely associated with Janissary percussion in the eighteenth century. This Janissary association is impossible to miss since the drummer is wearing a turban and baggy Turkish trousers. Trampling on the violins that represent "old melody," Signor Tambourossini is offering a "new melody" overwhelmed by brass and percussion, suitable only for the donkey ears of King Midas. The emphatic association of Rossini with Turkishness coincided with a production of *L'italiana in Algeri* in Paris in 1821, and would become even more pointed in 1826, the year of *Le siège de Corinthe*, when one French critic dubbed him "Ibrahim-Rossini-Pasha." With kind permission of the Bibliothèque Nationale de France.

Ludovic Vitet found Rossini to be "like Napoleon" in his orchestration—"all the available instruments are deployed together"—but another critic in 1826 observed that Rossini's Turkish march was particularly marked by the "din of the orchestra" (*tintamarre d'Orchestre*). One of the most hostile French critics, Charles Maurice, denounced Rossini as the Turkish conqueror of the Paris Opéra: "Ibrahim-Rossini-Pasha."[49] It was perhaps fitting, after taking on so many Ottoman subjects, that Rossini himself should appear tinged with Turkishness, the musical counterpart of Mehmed the Conqueror.

Not altogether coincidentally, 1826, the year of *Le siège de Corinthe*, was also the year that Mahmud II in Istanbul, seeking to modernize his army and reform his empire, took the decisive move, in the middle of the Greek war, of abolishing the Janissary corps in the so-called Auspicious Event, Vaka-i Hayriye. The Janissaries, the Ottoman military elite troops since the fourteenth century, were now violently disbanded, and thousands were killed in the struggle. They would be replaced by a new Western-style army.[50] At the same time, the Janissary bands were abolished along with the Janissary corps—to be replaced by Western-style military marching bands. The Janissary music which so captivated Mozart in Vienna would no longer be heard in Istanbul itself, even as Rossini in Paris, who had also once enjoyed and employed Janissary effects, moved toward the effacement of Turkishness within his scoring of percussion. Today it is only possible to hear the performance of a Janissary band—wearing traditional costumes and playing traditional instruments—at the Istanbul military museum.

Conclusion: Beethoven's Janissary Band

In 1824, two years before *Le siège de Corinthe* in Paris, two years before the abolition of the Janissaries in Istanbul, Janissary music received a subtle acknowledgment with the premiere of Beethoven's Ninth Symphony in Vienna. Unmistakably present in the final movement, the "Ode to Joy," was a Janissary band, participating in the general celebration and then finally absorbed into the larger orchestra. Beethoven had presented a Turkish march in 1812 as incidental music for August von Kotzebue's drama *The Ruins of Athens*. Now, in 1824, the Turkish march in the Ninth Symphony was recognizable by its rhythms and its Janissary instrumentation of piccolo, triangle, and cymbals. Harvey Sachs notes that this piece sounds like "a village band approaching from the distance, playing a syncopated, fragmented variation on the 'Joy' theme," for the Turkish march is less sophisticated than the larger orchestral and choral composition. Robert Hatten sees this Turkish passage similarly: "There is a deflation that could be considered humanizing, very much in accord with the message of the choral hymn: 'Alle Menschen werden Brüder.' All styles can be accommodated under one formal roof."[51] If indeed Beethoven intended to embrace Turkishness within the fabric of the "Ode to Joy," it was politically all the more notable in the decade of the Greek War of Independence. Beethoven's text for the Ninth Symphony—Schiller's poem "An die Freude"—dated back to the Enlightenment of the 1780s, the decade of Mozart's *Abduction*, when Pedrillo and Osmin discovered a kind brotherhood in drinking wine and thinking about women. In 1825 Ludwig Fischer, Mozart's original Osmin, died in Berlin at the age of eighty-three, and was memorialized in a contemporary report as "the famous Fischer, formerly the best bass in Germany."[52]

Rossini, as the composer of *Le siège de Corinthe*, enjoyed the partisan enthusiasm of the philhellene public, but he still remained "Ibrahim-Rossini-Pasha," the composer who had made his operatic reputation partly through the transmutation of eighteenth-century Ottoman themes. Even as he developed the musical mystique of the Greek chorus, invoking Thermopylae, Leonidas, and the brotherhood of ancient Spartans, Rossini still preserved for Mahomet the operatic charisma of Turkishness which had played such a potent role on European stages for more than a century. Like the fleeting Janissary moment in Beethoven's Ninth, however, Rossini's Paris representation of the sultan and treatment of the Turkish chorus would soon be seen as the final reformulations of a waning musical tradition.

At the conclusion of *Le siège de Corinthe* Pamyra takes Greek defiance to the operatic extreme, stabbing herself as she rises to a high A, denying herself to Mahomet who witnesses her suicide. The sultan is left alone, and the city of Corinth is in flames. According to the libretto, he is supposed to sing the final lines of the opera "*avec effroi*," with horror, at what he has brought about, with terror for a future (five centuries later) in which his own dynasty will inevitably prove vulnerable to decline and defeat. The swirling violence of the orchestra overwhelms him with a roaring tempest of external destruction and internal anguish:

> Pamyra! Ciel! quelle tempête,   Pamyra! Heaven! what a tempest
> Autour de nous, mugit soudain.   Suddenly roars around us.[53]

His ambition for universal conquest has succumbed to the loneliness of emotional despair, even as he too reaches for a sustained high note on the final syllable, summoning himself from his basso depths and refusing to surrender to the battering of modern history and the Rossinian orchestra. When he invokes the first-person Ottoman plural—the tempest surrounding "us" the Turks, "us" the sultans—does he also suspect that he is to be the last significant Ottoman figure to stand upon the European operatic stage?

12   The Decline and Disappearance of the Singing Turk

Ottoman Reform, the Eastern Question, and the European Operatic Repertory

Introduction: "The Sick Man of Europe"

Le siège de Corinthe was a huge success for Rossini in Paris in 1826 and was performed more than a hundred times in future seasons up until the 1840s, presenting the last important operatic role for a singing Turk.[1] Mehmed—who first became Maometto in Italian, and then Mahomet in French—concluded a century of Ottoman operatic prominence that began with the figure of Bajazet in the Tamerlane scenarios of the late seventeenth and early eighteenth centuries. The curtain of *Le siège* came down on the figure of Mehmed himself confronting the tragedy of Pamyra's suicide and Corinth in flames: "*quelle tempête autour de nous.*" It was not a quiet ending, for Rossini had the orchestra sound the turbulent figure of the military tempest, but there was nevertheless something poignant about Mehmed's isolation within the tempest that he had created but could not control.

The actual Ottomans of 1826 faced no less of a tempest as the European intervention in the Greek War of Independence brought the great naval victory of England, France, and Russia against the Ottoman fleet at the Battle of Navarino in 1827. The modern Eastern Question of post-Ottoman sovereignty was now a matter of European military and diplomatic engagement. In 1830 the French army conquered Algeria, cut its connection to Istanbul, and ruled it as a French colony. In 1832, a diplomatic conference in London made Prince Otto of Bavaria the first king of independent Greece, which still maintained further claims against the Ottoman empire. Serbian uprisings against the Ottomans in 1804 and 1815 had successfully achieved political autonomy, which was formally recognized by Istanbul in 1830 after the Greek War of Independence. Full Serbian independence would not be generally acknowledged until the Congress of Berlin in 1878, when Bulgaria also achieved formal autonomy. Thus, the 1820s and 1830s witnessed major challenges to Ottoman sovereignty, which shaped the political decline and devolution of the Ottoman empire for the rest of the nineteenth century.

The emergence of the Ottoman Turk on the European operatic stage dated back to the period of Ottoman territorial recession in the wars of the 1680s, and the disappearance of the singing Turk from European opera coincided with the modern epoch of Ottoman dismemberment, dating from the Greek struggle of the 1820s. The uncomfortable proximity of opera and international politics was clearly articulated in response to *Le siège de Corinthe*: "If the new work is a bulletin on Greece, then print it in the *Moniteur*. If it is an opera, then perform it."[2] The costumed splendor of magnanimous sultans, farcical pashas, and romantic conquerors on the operatic stage was now confronted with the harsh light of modern international relations in which the Ottoman empire became, in the famous phrase of the Russian tsar Nicholas I, the Sick Man of Europe. There would be very little place for Turkishness in the major operatic works from the 1830s to the 1920s—in Donizetti and Bellini, Verdi and Puccini, Berlioz and Bizet, Wagner and Strauss, the opera composers who came to define the modern repertory.

Operatic Repertory and Ottoman Affairs

Even while seen as the Sick Man of Europe, the Ottoman empire was increasingly perceived as part "of Europe," and the Ottoman reforms of the early nineteenth century created an unmistakable convergence with Europe that also made Turkish figures seem increasingly unfit for the operatic stage. The abolition of the Janissary corps by Mahmud II in 1826, the year of *Le siège de Corinthe*, led to the establishment of a modern army following Western models. The creation of a military school in 1834 was modeled on Napoleon's Saint-Cyr, while the Prussian model was also given a chance when Helmuth von Moltke came to Istanbul in 1835 and became a military adviser to the sultan's army.[3] Mahmud's successor, Abdülmecid I, began his reign in 1839 by inaugurating the age of the Tanzimat reforms with the Hatt-i Sharif of Gülhane, the Edict of the Rose Garden. Coming at the conclusion of a decade of Ottoman losses and concessions in Algeria, Greece, and Serbia, the sultan's edict promised sweeping reforms in Ottoman institutions and also suggested new principles of individual rights without regard to religious difference.

While the Ottoman figures in European opera were never altogether alien to Europe, the new convergence of the Tanzimat period, which would continue from 1839 to 1876, made Turkish subjects less theatrically compelling. Indeed, even the costuming of a Turk was subject to modernization and reform, beginning with the abolition of the Janissaries in 1826 when Ottoman soldiers were outfitted with Western-style uniforms, and this was followed by the encouragement of Western clothing among the general population. Bernard Lewis notes that by decree, beginning in 1829, "robes and slippers gave way to frock-coats and capes, trousers and black leather boots," with the sultan himself leading the way.[4] The most notable reform of costume was the replacement of the turban by the fez, and while the fez would eventually also come to symbolize the Orient, the turban had been the definitive costume element of Turkish characters in European opera. In *Maometto Secondo* Anna brought turbans to her father and to Calbo so that they could disguise themselves as Turks and make their escape.

After the abolition of the Janissary corps with their Janissary bands—the Mehterhane—Western music was also imported for the Ottoman army. In 1831 there was created in Istanbul, as noted by Bernard Lewis, "the Imperial Music School (Muzika-i Humayun Mektebi), the function of which was to provide the new army with drummers and trumpeters to match its tunics and breeches."[5] Western-style musical education at the new school in Istanbul was directed by Giuseppe Donizetti, known as Donizetti Pasha, the brother of Gaetano who remained in Italy and became one of the most celebrated opera composers of the age. Giuseppe had served in the Napoleonic army and even accompanied Napoleon to Elba as a military musician. He moved to Istanbul in 1828 (his brother Gaetano reacting with "astonishment"), led a Western-style military band that played for the sultan, and in 1829 composed in honor of Mahmud II the Mahmudiye March, which became the Ottoman imperial anthem.[6] The success of Donizetti Pasha was reported in a French journal in the 1830s:

> In Constantinople the old Turkish music is dying in agony, and is found only among the dervishes . . . Sultan Mahmud is in love with Italian music and has

introduced it in his guard; it is one of his reforms; the brother of Donizetti is the director of his music.[7]

Donizetti Pasha later composed another march, the Mecidiye, in honor of Mahmud's son and successor Abdülmecid, and was reported also to conduct Rossini marches in Istanbul.[8]

The letters of Giuseppe Donizetti from Istanbul to his father back in Bergamo reported on a visit to the mosque of Hagia Sophia, supposedly forbidden to non-Muslims—achieved at the risk of a good beating (*"il rischio di essere ben bastonato"*). The visit was carried out in Turkish costume (*"con il mio vestiario alla Turca"*) in the company of several men of the seraglio (*"diversi signori del Serraglio"*). In short, it was a kind of comic opera scenario with Donizetti as the harlequin hero, culminating in an ascent to the dome of the great Byzantine monument which he cheerfully vandalized. The whole incident was reported as a matter of pride for those back at home: "that a Bergamo man on August 6, 1830 succeeded in entering Santa Sofia of Constantinople penetrating as far as the cupola and removing with his own hands a piece of the mosaic." In September Donizetti met with Sultan Mahmud II who said "he loves me very much because I am a *bravo maestro*"—which had to be reported to Bergamo, since "I hope this will give much pleasure to all of you and our friends and, I dare say, even to our country [*alla Patria*]." Like Rossini's Isabella in Algiers, Donizetti Pasha was making conquests in Ottoman lands and thinking about *la Patria*.[9] In 1840 he ordered from Giovanni Ricordi, the music publisher in Milan, the piano exercises of Carl Czerny—to provide strict European discipline for Turkish fingers—and also a piano-vocal score of his younger brother's operatic masterpiece *Lucia di Lammermoor*.[10]

For Gaetano Donizetti, the exoticism of the Ottoman empire must have been significantly tempered by the fact that his older brother lived and worked in Istanbul. To the extent that Turkish subjects in European opera depended upon a particular conceptual balance of similarity and difference between Turkey and Europe, the shifting of that balance in the 1830s was probably related to the disappearance of the Turkish figure from the European operatic stage. Among Gaetano Donizetti's operas with Muslim aspects, in *Zoraida di Granata*, composed at the very beginning of his career for the Teatro Argentina in Rome in 1822, the setting was Muslim Spain. In *La favorite*, however, composed for Paris in 1840, with another medieval Spanish setting, the Moors were relegated to the role of offstage enemies. Finally, in *Dom Sébastien Roi de Portugal*, concerning the Portuguese in sixteenth-century Morocco, composed at the very end of Donizetti's career for the Paris Opéra in 1843, a captive Moorish princess—Zayda l'Africaine—converts to Christianity and falls tragically in love with the king of Portugal. Yet Turkishness played a minimal role in Donizetti's tremendous operatic output, and the comparison to Rossini in this regard is striking. Rossini was only five years younger, but his operatic career flourished in the 1810s and 1820s, while Donizetti's most important work was composed in the 1830s. Bellini's *Zaira* of 1829, based on Voltaire's *Zaïre*, was an emphatic failure in Parma, and for Bellini, as for Donizetti, Turkishness also played a minimal role among his contributions to the operatic repertory.

Even the Turkishness of Mozart encountered some public reluctance by the 1830s. In 1838 the music publisher Johann Anton André composed additional music to supplement the fragments of Mozart's *Zaide*, thus making the work hypothetically performable. André had a pedigree that linked him to the eighteenth-century world of operatic Turkishness, for he was the son of the earlier composer Johann André, who had composed *Belmont und Constanze* for Berlin in 1781, the year before Mozart composed the same story as the *Abduction* for Vienna. *Zaide*, however, even after being "completed" in 1838, did not actually come to the stage until 1866, performed in Frankfurt in the year that Prussia vanquished Austria and Bismarck became the master of Germany.[11] By then, Mozart's Sultan Soliman was just a ghost from a long-ago epoch of singing Turks.

In 1840 in Habsburg Milan, a medical doctor named Peter Lichtenthal was cooperating with Karl Mozart, the composer's son, to create an adaptation of the *Abduction* for La Scala. More than half a century after its creation the opera had still never been performed there, and possibly had not been performed in any major Italian opera house. Lichtenthal wanted to make Mozart palatable to "contemporary Italian theatrical taste" and did not hesitate to add new music—for instance, to give the pasha a singing role.[12] By 1840, however, it was too late to interest La Scala or the operatic public in operas on Turkish themes, and the theater did not accept the project. La Scala finally offered its first performance of Mozart's *Il ratto dal serraglio* in 1952, when Maria Callas sang the role of Konstanze in Italian, not long before it was given at the Turkish State Opera in Ankara in 1959.[13]

In Germany in the 1840s there were minor operatic efforts to celebrate the Habsburg hero Prince Eugene of Savoy, who fought against the Turks in the eighteenth century—as in Gustav Schmidt's opera *Prinz Eugen, der edle Ritter* in Frankfurt in 1847, and Julius Becker's *Die Belagerung von Belgrad* in Leipzig in 1848, about the siege of Belgrade in 1717.[14] In Vienna in 1844 the comic opera *Ali Hitsch-Hatsch* was presented by Simon Sechter, a composer of Rossini's generation. The pasha Ali Hitsch-Hatsch rules over an island, and his Ottoman subjects end up abandoning him to go to Habsburg Vienna, while the pasha remains behind alone, too fat to board the boat.[15] Certainly by the 1840s Habsburg Vienna could not take seriously the dramatization of a Turkish foe, and the pasha could therefore only come to Vienna as the ample butt of an operatic farce.

The Operatic Albania of Ali Pasha

In 1827, the year that the Ottoman navy was defeated at Navarino, reframing the whole future of European-Ottoman relations, Joseph von Hammer-Purgstall published in Budapest the first volume of what was arguably the first modern European history of the Ottoman empire: *Geschichte des Osmanischen Reiches*. Hammer had served as an Austrian diplomatic official in Istanbul from 1799, when Selim III was trying to deal with Napoleon in Egypt, to 1807, when Selim was deposed. Hammer's training in languages—Ottoman, Persian, and Arabic—made him the very model of a modern Orientalist, and his critical engagement with the sources and archives enabled him to undertake a modern positivist history of the Ottoman empire. His approach was, in short, entirely antithetical to the dramatic spirit of the operatic tradition.

Beyond Ottoman sources, Hammer stressed the importance of the archives in Venice and Vienna, which for centuries ruled over lands adjacent to the Ottoman empire along the Triplex Confinium:

> Among all European powers only two have been closely historically connected to the Ottoman empire since the earliest times, namely Venice and Austria, and with no other power have the Ottomans so often waged war, so often concluded peace. The state archives of Austria and Venice are therefore also, before those of all other European powers . . . the most important, the richest, and for historical use the most profitable treasuries.[16]

Where once the opera houses of Venice and Vienna had figured prominently as stages for presenting the Ottomans, now the state archives were saluted as the crucial positivist sites of Ottoman discovery. Hammer claimed to renounce both prejudice and sentiment as he introduced the first of his ten volumes:

> Without favor or disfavor [*ohne Vorliebe und Widerwillen*], without preference for persons and peoples, for nations and religions, but with love for the noble and the good, with hatred for the shameful and the bad, without hatred against Greeks or Turks, without preference for Muslims or Christians, but with love for well-regulated strength and well-ordered government, for legal justice and military skill, for beneficent public institutions and scientific development, with hatred against rebellion and oppression, against cruelty and tyranny.[17]

He claimed to be stripping himself of precisely those sentimental "preferences" which had over the course of the previous centuries structured the representation of the Ottoman empire in European culture, including European opera.

Hammer concluded his first volume with an account of Mehmed's conquest of Constantinople and described the sultan, as soon as the walls were breached, hurrying to Hagia Sophia to visit the great church: "Admiringly he gazed at the hundred-and-seven columns of porphyry, granite, serpentine, and many-colored marbles."[18] In Hammer's second volume, published in 1828, he actually related the history of the conquest of Negroponte, the very subject of Rossini's *Maometto Secondo*. The historian mentioned the Venetian governor Erizzo and "his daughter, who did not show herself tractable enough [*nicht geschmeidig genug*] to the tyrant."[19] Hammer could have seen Rossini's *Maometto Secondo* when it was performed in German in Vienna in 1823 as *Mahomet der Zweyte*, followed some years later by *Le siège de Corinthe* which came to Vienna in 1831.[20] The historian's intentions, however, were neither romantic nor dramatic.

In 1827 Hammer dedicated his first volume to the Russian tsar Nicholas I, comparing the Russian tsar and the Ottoman sultan as "masters over diverse tongues and religions."[21] In 1828 Nicholas sent his armies into Moldavia and Wallachia to engage the sultan in southeastern Europe in a Russian-Ottoman war that also advanced the national aims of Greeks and Serbs. In the German city of Münster in 1828 there took place the first performance of Albert Lortzing's one-act Singspiel *Ali Pascha von Janina* set in Ottoman Albania at the beginning of that same decade, an opera whose Turkish setting was virtually contemporary. The historical Ali Pasha began his career as an Albanian bandit, formed an alliance with the pasha of Negroponte, and became a pasha himself in 1787 at the time of the Ottoman war against Russia and Austria. Eventually, ruling over Greek and Albanian lands from his court at Ioannina (today in northwestern Greece), he made himself virtually independent of the sultan in Istanbul. For Ali Pasha of Ioannina, as for Mohammed Ali Pasha of Egypt, the Napoleonic wars became the occasion for establishing autonomy with regard to the sultan. Ali Pasha, for instance, conducted his own independent foreign policy in this period, allying himself first with Napoleon and then changing course to support the British in the Mediterranean.[22]

It was in this period of British alliance that Ali Pasha's court at Ioannina received its most famous visitor and laid its claim to European celebrity with the arrival of the twenty-one-year-old Lord Byron in 1809. He would versify his visit to Ioannina in the second canto of *Childe Harold's Pilgrimage*, which he actually began writing while he was in Albania. The first two cantos were published in England in 1812, and the German translation of Byron's collected works in the 1820s would have formed part of the context for the composition and performance of Lortzing's opera.

Byron gave an account of Ali Pasha in 1809 in a letter to his mother: "He told me to consider him as a father while I was in Turkey, and said he looked on me as his son. Indeed, he treated me like a child, sending me almonds and sugared sherbert, fruit and sweetmeats, twenty times a day."[23] Byron claimed to be aware that Ali Pasha was in fact "a remorseless tyrant, guilty of the most horrible cruelties." The pasha's pampering of the English poet, however, suggested his shrewd capacity, as noted by historian K. E. Fleming, to play to the Orientalism of his European interlocutors, almost to stage himself as an operatic figure.[24]

In 1822 Ali Pasha was killed in a military struggle for authority with Sultan Mahmud II. If Rossini's *Le siège de Corinthe* alluded to the contemporary war for independence in Greece in the 1820s, Lortzing's *Ali Pascha von Janina* was even more acutely embedded in the contemporary affairs of the day. Lortzing, born in Berlin in 1801, began working on the opera in 1823, one year after Ali Pasha's death, and thus effectively took the opera's subject from the current gazettes. Even as Ali Pasha's head was arriving in Istanbul to satisfy the sultan, young Lortzing was already resurrecting him as operatic fantasy. Though the first performance had to wait until 1828, this was another instance of a work that came too close to contemporary history to preserve the carefully wrought perspective of earlier operas on Ottoman historical subjects.

Lortzing composed Ali Pasha as a tyrant, following the conventional dramatic outlines of an eighteenth-century captivity opera, with a plot resembling that of Mozart's *Abduction*. The opera begins with a Frenchman, Bernier, arriving in Albania only to discover that the Greek maiden he loves has been installed in Ali Pasha's harem. Ali Pasha is, inevitably, a basso—the vocal sign of his Ottoman authority—and after being introduced by a grand orchestral flourish, he summons his harem to show off to the visiting Frenchman:

Sieh! Wähnst du dich nicht auf Edens Wiese,
in Mahoms Paradiese?

Look! do you not imagine yourself in Eden's meadow,
in Mohammed's paradise?[25]

A certain set of European conventions about Islam thus structured this opera, including the supposed Koranic conception of paradise as a sort of harem. The basso Ali reaches down to his lowest notes for "*Mahoms Paradiese*" as if to emphasize a certain hypermasculine lewdness. He then commands the women of the harem to unveil themselves so that Bernier can better appreciate their beauty, and the Frenchman immediately recognizes that one of them is his own beloved Arianna.

In the ensuing trio, Ali in his lower register expresses his wrath over the lovers' reunion: "*Mein Zorn.*" It was the same word that Mozart had used in his letter of September 26, 1781, to describe the wrath of Osmin (*der Zorn des Osmin*) and pose the question of how to represent the emotions of outraged Turkish authority. In fact, the resulting aria for Ali Pasha, "*Ha! Schrecklich will ich meine Rache kühlen!*" (Terribly will I take my revenge!), could well have been an aria for Osmin.[26] Ali Pasha's aria is even introduced with emphatic Janissary percussion.

The drama is resolved, however, not by the pasha's magnanimity, as in the *Abduction*, but by French military intervention—entirely appropriate in 1828, one year after Navarino, two years before Algeria. The operatic French triumph becomes greater still when the entire chorus of Albanians pleads with Bernier to take them with him out of Ottoman Albania. Accompanied by solemn woodwinds, the Albanians affirm their longing to go west:

Führe uns nach deinem Lande,	Lead us to your land,
löse unsre Sklavenbande!	loose our bonds of slavery!
Treulich wollen wir dir dienen,	Faithfully we will serve you,
der als Retter uns erschienen.	who has come to us as savior.[27]

This was not exactly an affirmation of freedom, since the escape from slavery was accompanied by a vow of service, as if Albanians in France would inevitably end up as servants.

Bernier grants the Albanians their request to follow him, and as they all prepare to embark, the tempo picks up for a final celebratory chorus, giving thanks for liberation from *Tyrannengewalt* (the violence of tyranny).[28] The tyranny of the Ottomans, however, was considerably compromised in the 1820s as the Greeks fought for their independence, and authentic Frenchmen, not just operatic tenors, participated in the European intervention on behalf of the Greek cause. The notion of Europeans leading Ottoman subjects out of slavery was perhaps even an allusion to the ongoing Greek struggle.

The singing Albanians who abandoned the Ottoman empire at the end of the opera would in real life remain the most loyal of Ottoman subjects during the whole of the nineteenth century. Albania became independent only in 1912, during the Balkan Wars, and at that time Ioannina became part of Greece. Lortzing's Albania was not very specifically Albanian but could have been anywhere in the Ottoman empire according to the conventions of eighteenth-century opera. Nineteenth-century Europe, however, was politically focused on an increasingly precise and specific geography of the Ottoman empire and the Eastern Question.

Bellini and Romani in Parma

In May 1829 Bellini's *Zaira* had its first performance in Parma. In that year the Eastern Question was an urgent matter of European diplomacy; the London Protocol in March determined the parameters of Greek autonomy, while the Russian-Ottoman Treaty of Adrianople in September stipulated Serbian autonomy, a Russian role in the Romanian principalities, and Russian access to the Danube delta and the Black Sea straits. Bellini's *Zaira* was far from current in its subject, based on the eighteenth-century crusader drama of Voltaire, and the failure of the opera in Parma was one indicator of the lingering end to the tradition of Turkish figures on the operatic stage. Voltaire's *Zaïre* of 1732, though set in the age of the Crusades, contributed to the eighteenth-century culture of Turquerie, and one hundred years later Bellini's *Zaira* incongruously coincided with the advent of the modern Eastern Question.

The librettist of *Zaira* was Felice Romani, who had worked with Rossini on *Il turco in Italia* in 1814 and would go on to collaborate further with Bellini on such masterpieces as *La sonnambula* in 1831. Romani, however, was anxious about *Zaira*, and wryly observed in the preface that "for nearly a century theaters have heard the sighs of this most unfortunate maiden; will the public not be bored with their own compassion? And where may I succeed in hiding the lack of novelty in my work; will I be able to bear the comparison with Voltaire?"[29] Filippo Cicconetti, who wrote an early biography of Bellini thirty years later in 1859, noted that the dissatisfaction of the Parma audience at the premiere was "at hearing that style not only different but opposed to that of Rossini, who enjoyed a singular cult among the Parmigiani."[30] Certainly, Bellini's subject—a basso sultan jealously in love with his Christian captive—was one that might easily have roused Rossinian expectations in the public.

The scenario of *Zaira* in fact was not Ottoman Turkish but more generally Islamic Saracen, set in the Holy Land in the thirteenth century in the aftermath of the Seventh Crusade. The Sultan Orosmane could have been a Mameluke, but in the absence of any specific historical identification, the setting of the first scene in "the harem of the sultan" would have immediately signified Turkishness to the operatic public. The stage directions for that scene further specify: "To the sound of Oriental instruments the odalisques weave their dances, the eunuchs burn incense." The opening chorus celebrates Zaira and Orosmane for their approaching marriage, but there is no hint of Mozartean or Rossinian Janissary style in Bellini's setting of Romani's verse:

Egli è il sultan possente,	He is the powerful sultan,
È l'astro d'oriente,	He is the star of the east.
Delle battaglie il folgore,	The thunderbolt of battles,
Terror dell'infedel.	Terror of the infidel.[31]

In fact, the premiere of *Zaira* in May 1829 would have coincided with the Russians crossing the Danube to defeat the army of Sultan Mahmud II in Ottoman Bulgaria.

Orosmane promises to liberate his Christian prisoners, and in the sultan's subterranean dungeons a chorus of prisoners receives the news of their approaching freedom. Possibly inspired by Beethoven's prisoners' chorus from *Fidelio*, Bellini begins with a hushed whisper:

Chi ci toglie ai ceppi nostri?	Who removes our shackles?
Chi ci rende all'alma luce?	Who brings light to our spirits?[32]

The musical crescendo brings the prisoners to the full appreciation of their own emancipation—"*O contento!*"—as the operatic Islamic scenario, once again and now for almost the last time, dramatizes the struggle between Turkish despotism and European liberty.[33] The prisoners' chorus offered yet another allusion to the contemporary Greek struggle and the fantasies of national freedom that it inspired all across Europe in the 1820s.

The first act concludes with Orosmane singing of his jealousy of Zaira, singing in the same basso rage that had overtaken Rossini's Maometto:

Il furor di mia vendetta	The fury of my vengeance
L'Universo scuoterà.	Will shake the universe.[34]

What was once the comical rage of Osmin in Mozart's *Abduction* was now the furious outrage of mighty sultans whose despotic power was frustrated by the plot structures of European opera. It was not something new for those plot structures to turn on the political limitations of the sultan. Now, however, in the 1820s, such an operatic scenario of a sultan in distress coincided uncomfortably with the unoperatic dynamics of the Eastern Question in international affairs, as the actual sultan in Istanbul was compelled to accept the partial dismemberment of his empire according to the dictation of foreign powers.

The basso who sang the role of Orosmane at the premiere in Parma in 1829 was Luigi Lablache, famous for his Rossini roles and especially the comic ones. (He would later create the title role of *Don Pasquale* for Donizetti.) Lablache was also very fat, which may have compromised some of Orosmane's dignity as a tragic romantic hero. Yet like Rossini's Maometto, Bellini's Orosmane finds himself traumatized in the final scene: "*immobile, inorridito, e come fuori di sè*" (immobile, horrified, beside himself), according to Romani's stage direction. Orosmane has murdered Zaira from jealousy, and now he sings of his suffering conscience over her innocent blood. Fully a tragic hero, like Othello, he kills himself as the curtain falls.[35]

Bellini's *Zaira* was chosen to open the new Teatro Ducale in Parma (today's Teatro Regio). The reigning duchess of Parma was Marie Louise, the widow of Napoleon and the daughter of the Habsburg emperor Franz, and probably she was present for the inauguration of the theater and premiere of *Zaira*. Would Marie Louise have felt "compassion" for the heroine—as Romani hoped—or would Zaira have seemed too much like a heroine from the girlhood of Marie Louise's great-grandmother, the Empress Maria Theresa? The premiere has been described as "a fiasco for Bellini," with minimal enthusiasm from the audience.[36]

Zaira was "avenged," according to Bellini, when he borrowed much of the music for a new opera in Venice in 1830, *I Capuleti e i Montecchi*. The brother/sister music for Nerestano and Zaira, mezzo-soprano and soprano, was immediately adaptable for the young lovers Romeo and Juliet. Instead of star-crossed lovers from Christian Europe and the Muslim Orient, the new opera offered a merely local romantic tragedy set in Verona, halfway between Parma and Venice. *Zaira* was perhaps doubly avenged since the music that was hardest to put to use in the new opera was that of the romantic basso sultan. While musically *Zaira* was already a work of attenuated Turkishness—without even the conventional elements of Janissary style—the reassignment of the music to *I Capuleti e i Montecchi* effectively concluded the decade of the 1820s with the definitive elimination of the earlier opera's Turkish subject. *Zaira* was not performed for a century and a half until the revival in Catania—Bellini's hometown—in 1976.

Romani's libretto for Bellini in 1829 belonged to a cluster of Oriental libretti that he wrote around the same time for less brilliant composers. In 1828 his libretto for *Il divorzio persiano* (The Persian divorce), composed by Pietro Generali, was performed at Trieste, and his libretto for *I saraceni in Sicilia* (The Saracens in Sicily), composed by Francesco Morlacchi, was performed in Venice at La Fenice in the same year.[37] Romani's libretto for *Zaira* was set to music once more by Saverio Mercadante for Naples in 1831. Mercadante, coming home to Italy after several years of composing in Spain and Portugal, clearly imagined that Turkishness would be the key to a triumphant return. He created a chorus recognizably in the Janissary style to welcome Orosmane, quite different from the opening of Bellini's *Zaira*. The sultan's entrance as composed by Mercadante seemed closely modeled on Rossinian precedent, and the opening basso phrase—"*Liete voci!*" (Happy voices!)—was almost a musical quotation from Selim's entrance—"*Bella Italia*"—in *Il turco in Italia*.

The stars of Mercadante's show in Naples, Antonio Tamburini as Orosmane and Giuseppina Ronzi de Begnis as Zaira, were very experienced Rossinians; he had sung Mustafa in *L'italiana* in Palermo in 1825, while she had dazzled Paris as Fiorilla in *Il turco* in 1820. Both Tamburini and Ronzi de Begnis apparently gave satisfaction in Mercadante's *Zaira* in Naples, deploying their Rossinian affinities for Turkishness to put across the same operatic subject that had failed for Bellini in Parma two years before. Yet musicologist Jeremy Commons wonders "why the opera did not enjoy a more extensive stage history," why it did not circulate around the operatic centers of Italy, and he concludes that it was "probably simply overtaken and eclipsed by the rich succession of works with which Mercadante followed it."[38]

The waning importance of Turkish themes in European opera coincided with the rise of European music, and even European opera, in Turkey. In 1834 the *Gazzetta Piemontese* in Turin, which was actually edited by the librettist Felice Romani, published a brief (and possibly fictional) travel account of musical life in Istanbul entitled "Donizetti in Costantinopoli," with reference to Donizetti Pasha.[39] The putative traveler, in a boat on the Bosphorus, was amazed to hear the strains of Italian music—"the divine inspirations of Rossini"—wafting across the waters. "Among the many innovations introduced by the sultan is that of having substituted European music for Turkish music," reported the traveler. With regard to the fine arts the Turks had been "savages," and Donizetti Pasha was playing the part of Prometheus, bringing them the fire of European art so that "now the Turks of Istanbul love European music best." Hearing Italian music, the traveler was filled with Italian pride: "Oh Italy!" he exclaimed. "Where has your light not penetrated! It is destiny that in every age the barbarians owe to you alone the lamp of intellect, the sweetness of life."[40] The age of operas on Turkish themes was passing, in part because of the convergence duly noted between Europe and Turkey, and in part because of a newly heightened sense of European cultural imperialism, clearly evident in this Italian report. *The Musical World* in London noted in 1839 that "Italian music has become the rage among Mussulmans, and there is now a brilliant Italian opera at Constantinople."[41]

Donizetti Pasha gave general encouragement to European opera, as it began to be regularly presented in Istanbul: Bellini's *Norma* in the Istanbul Bosco Theater in 1841 (ten years after the Milan premiere), Donizetti's *Lucrezia Borgia* at the Naum Theater in 1844 (eleven years after the Milan premiere), and Rossini's *Barber of Seville* at the Naum in 1845 (almost thirty years after its Rome premiere). When Verdi's *Macbeth* was given in Istanbul in 1848, however, it was only one year after the Florence premiere of 1847 and some considerable integration of Turkey into the world of European opera had been achieved.[42] Indeed, by that point Turks were watching operas about Europeans more than Europeans were watching operas about Turks.

With Italian music wafting across the waters of the Bosphorus, it was as if the sultans in Istanbul had come to incarnate the Italophilia of Rossini's operatic Prince Selim: *"Bella Italia!"* According to one British journal, "the sultan [Abdülmecid], who is exceedingly fond of music, has on several occasions offered Rossini fabulous sums of money, besides all sorts of Turkish decorations and orders of merit, on condition that he would compose him some lyrical work or other."[43] In 1852 Rossini actually did write a military march for Sultan Abdülmecid and was rewarded with the ceremonial order of Nisan-i Iftihar, as if he were being made a "Kaimakan" in the spirit of *L'italiana in Algeri*.

European Empire, Ottoman Reform, and the Advent of Modern Orientalism

Rossinian operatic Turkishness came into being in the political turmoil of Napoleon's final campaign and spectacular collapse, but the operas of 1812, 1813, and 1814—*La pietra del paragone, L'italiana in Algeri, Il turco in Italia*—continued to flourish in the opera centers of the Restoration, including the Théâtre-Italien in Restoration Paris and even in Metternich's Vienna. *Maometto Secondo* belonged entirely to the post-Napoleonic era, evolving from 1820, to 1822, to 1826, from Naples, to Venice, to Paris, in the decade of the Greek struggle. The dramatic issues of authority and conquest permitted Turkishness to function as a running operatic commentary on the historically receding Napoleonic epoch. By 1829, however, when Bellini's *Zaira* failed in the Parma of Marie Louise, the Ottoman empire was engaged in modernizing reform, the leaders of Europe stood ready to preside over Greek independence, and the Bourbon Restoration itself was about to come to an end in Paris with the July Revolution of 1830. Before vanishing from the political scene, however, and making way for a constitutional monarchy, the Bourbon king Charles X inaugurated a new era in European-Ottoman relations by presiding over the military invasion of the Ottoman Regency of Algiers in June 1830. Charles was replaced in July by Louis-Philippe—of the Orléans branch of the Bourbon family—establishing a new political epoch in French and European history, a "bourgeois monarchy" under which the upper middle classes dominated politics, society, and economy. In an important continuity of policy, however, Louis-Philippe persisted in the conquest of Algeria initiated by his dethroned predecessor.

In 1825 a British comic opera titled *The Fall of Algiers* already made the connection between opera and conquest at the Drury Lane Theatre in London. It was a conventional captivity opera, composed by Henry Rowley Bishop and including Janissary percussion, but the eventual rescue of the English captive "Amanda" from the harem of the Bey Orasmin was finally brought about by the theatrical intervention of the British navy, which simply conquered Algiers on stage.[44] This action recalled the British bombardment of Algiers in 1816 but also anticipated the French conquest of 1830, thus setting modern imperialism on the operatic stage. The reviewer in the *London Magazine and Review* felt that the Turkish scenario was predictable but admired the final tableau: "The last scene of Algiers after the bombardment is charmingly painted."[45]

Another perspective on Ottoman Algiers was established in England in 1828 with the publication of the erotic epistolary work *The Lustful Turk or Lascivious Scenes from a Harem* by John Benjamin Brookes (though appearing anonymously).[46] Destined to become a classic of Victorian pornography, the letters described the fate of English female captives in a harem in Algiers, subjected to the explicit brutalities of sexual slavery. Rossini stopped writing operas in 1829 after *Guillaume Tell*, but it is hard to imagine how he would have composed an opera based on *The Lustful Turk* about English girls in Algiers. Mozart believed that Osmin's rage could not become ugly, had to remain musical, but the representation of Turkishness in the late 1820s was gradually developing in ways that made it less susceptible to operatic composition and staging. At the same time, the attribution of pornographic Turkish violence to Algiers in 1828 anticipated the advent of French imperialism in 1830.

The origins of the French invasion dated back to 1827 when contested issues of French business and French debts in North Africa led to a dramatic incident: the French consul was slapped with a fan (or possibly a fly swatter) by Hussein Dey of Algiers. The incident of the fan was worthy of Rossinian operatic farce. The military operations of 1830 then brought about the conquest that Rossini had musically imagined in *L'italiana in Algeri* back in 1813, which had allowed that conquest to be enacted all over Europe during the intervening generation of Rossini's own operatic preeminence. Paul Ennemond de Mont Rond, who actually participated in the French conquest, recorded that "five or six thousand Turks who dominated the Regency, supported by an undisciplined cavalry of Arabs over whom they held a precarious authority, could not hold out long against a perfectly organized army of thirty thousand men." The lesson of the conquest might have been learned at the opera: "The Turks showed themselves to be less terrifying [*terrible*] than their reputation had represented them."[47]

In the end, it was the French who turned out to be terrifying, carrying out the Algerian war of conquest through the 1830s and 1840s with tremendous violence and destruction, accompanied by French colonization and the formal annexation of Algeria to France. Napoleon's invasion of Egypt in 1798 was certainly the crucial precedent, but the Napoleonic occupation of Egypt lasted a brief three years, while the invasion of Algeria in 1830 created a colonial regime that would endure until the 1950s. Taken together with the simultaneous achievement of Greek independence, the conquest of Algeria clearly outlined the implications of the Eastern Question. The lands of the Ottoman empire would become either the targets of foreign imperial ambitions or local national aspirations, and these dynamics of dismemberment would mark the last century of Ottoman history until the final abdication of the last sultan in 1922.

The French invasion and conquest of Algeria in the 1830s coincided with the Ottoman reform in Istanbul, which culminated in the Hatt-i Sharif of Gülhane, the Edict of the Rose Garden of 1839. The edict prescribed Western-style human rights to life, liberty, honor, and justice for Ottoman subjects, with equal rights for non-Muslims.[48] Such a political framework rendered anachronistic the conventions of European opera on Turkish themes, the scenarios of magnanimous despotism or ridiculous autocracy, of tragic Christian subjection or of farcical Turkish humiliation. The newly blatant connection and convergence between Europe and Turkey, whether through European colonial occupation or Turkish modernization and reform, helped to make Ottoman subjects less easily conceivable upon the European operatic stage.

The age of Orientalism was not over by any means; indeed, in the sense suggested by Edward Said, it had only just begun, as the inevitable accompaniment of empire. The occupation of Algeria in 1830 would be followed quickly in 1832 by the arrival of Eugène Delacroix in North Africa, brush in hand, exploring new models and motives for the French painting of Oriental subjects. In the 1820s Delacroix was a French philhellene who painted the tragic allegory of *Greece on the Ruins of Missolonghi* in 1826, the year of Rossini's *Le siège de Corinthe*. In 1834, after visiting Algeria, Delacroix exhibited the painting *The Women of Algiers*, an exotic harem scene infused with the opiated spirit of the hookah in the foreground. The painting has been described as "an iconic representation of Orientalist mastery"—inspired by the painter's own North African experience of the Orient.[49]

In 1830 Benjamin Disraeli recapitulated Lord Byron's trip to Ioannina of twenty years before, and then proceeded to Istanbul. Disraeli, however, encouraged perhaps by a sense of his own Oriental Jewish ancestry, was able to embrace Oriental Turkishness in the spirit of the age of Romanticism:

> I am quite a Turk, wear a turban, smoke a pipe six feet long and squat on a divan . . . I find the habits of this calm and luxurious people entirely agree with my own preconceived opinions of propriety, and I detest the Greek more than ever . . . When I was presented to the Grand Vizier I made up such a costume from my heterogeneous wardrobe that the Turks who are mad on the subject of dress were utterly astounded.[50]

Uninhibited by philhellenism, Disraeli's Turkish fantasies permitted him to costume himself as the star of his very own Turkish opera, in a manner that made actual stagecraft superfluous:

> My Turkish prejudices are very much confirmed by my residence in Turkey. The life of this people greatly accords with my taste which is naturally somewhat indolent and melancholy . . . To repose on voluptuous ottomans and smoke superb pipes, daily to indulge in the luxury of a bath which requires half a dozen attendants for its perfection; to court the air in a carved caique, by shores which are a perpetual scene; this is, I think, a far more sensible life than all the bustle of clubs, all the boring of drawing rooms and all the coarse vulgarity of our political controversies.[51]

He was being purposefully outrageous, but he was also playing a convention-al role that was familiar from the theater: the part of an Ottoman sultan or pasha in voluptuous repose. In this particular scenario the sultan was Disraeli himself, and the Ottoman was merely a piece of furniture, the stage prop on which he reclined to express his sultanic sense of indolence. Maya Jasanoff has noted the presence of a circle of young British expatriates in Ottoman Cairo in the 1820s who similarly lived in an assumed Oriental style, while the irritated British consul declared that "he would not protect any British sub-jects who appeared in Turkish costume."[52]

Disraeli in Istanbul in 1831 enjoyed the spirit of Orientalist fantasy, re-flecting that anyone could be a sultan in the sense that "the meanest mer-chant in the Bazaar looks like a Sultan in an Eastern fairy tale." Yet the sultan himself—Mahmud II—was dressed in European clothes, as Disraeli duly and disapprovingly noted: "He affects all the affable activity of a European Prince, mixes with his subjects, interferes in all their pursuits and taxes them unmer-cifully." Following the sultan's example, "you see the young Turks in uniforms which would not disgrace one of our cavalry regiments."[53] Thus, the operatic role of a truly splendid Ottoman sultan appeared—to Disraeli's Orientalist eye—to be altogether vacant, and he himself, dramatically turbaned, stepped into the breach to occupy and relish the part. Half a century later, as Queen Victoria's Turcophile prime minister, Disraeli would take on the role of sup-porting and sustaining the Ottoman empire in the Eastern Crisis of the 1870s.

Verdi's Revision: From I Lombardi to Jérusalem

The disappearance of the Ottoman operatic subject in the nineteenth cen-tury may be most significantly observed in the work of the most important Italian opera composer of the century, Giuseppe Verdi, whose operas helped define the modern Italian repertory. None of his canonical masterpieces touch on Turkish issues in any fashion, though they find elements of exoticism in cultures ranging from the modern Gypsies to the ancient Egyptians, from the ancient Babylonians to the modern Bostonians. The young Verdi did, howev-er, make use of some Turkish and Islamic materials in two early works of the 1840s—*I Lombardi* and *Il corsaro*—and in these rarely performed and for him unusually unsuccessful works it is possible to discern the very last traces of the long tradition of Turkish subjects on the European operatic stage.

Verdi was born in the village of Le Roncole near Busseto in 1813, a subject of the Napoleonic empire at the very moment when that empire was about to collapse. The composer grew up in the Restoration as a subject of the duchess of Parma, Marie Louise, and continued to live as her subject in Busseto until her death in 1847. *I Lombardi alla prima crociata* (The Lombards on the First Crusade) was performed at La Scala in 1843, but the work was dedicated to Marie Louise of Parma.[54] Based on an epic poem by Tommaso Grossi and crafted into a libretto by Temistocle Solera (who had written Verdi's libretto for *Nabucco* in 1842), *I Lombardi* presented the Muslim governor of Antioch, Acciano, the historical Yaghi-Siyan, who served the Seljuk Turkish sultan Malik Shah. It was Acciano's son Oronte whom Verdi made into the lead romantic tenor of the opera, and the plot turns on Oronte's love for the Christian captive Griselda, culminating in his conversion to Christianity. This conversion of a Muslim to Christianity was very unusual in the operatic repertory, and Verdi himself would make a complete revision, eliminating the Muslim prince and the conversion plot, when he recomposed the opera as *Jérusalem* for Paris in 1847.

The first act of *I Lombardi*, set in Milan, follows a story of attempted fratricide and accidental patricide in the focal Lombard family, and therefore Muslim Antioch in the second act could hardly seem particularly iniquitous by comparison. When the captive Griselda is "rescued" by the crusaders, she actually denounces the whole Christian enterprise of the Crusades:

No! giusta causa, non è d'Iddio	No it is not the just cause of God
La terra spargere, di sangue umano;	To shed human blood over the earth;
È turpe insania, non senso pio,	It is wicked insanity, not pious feeling,
Che all'oro destasi, del musulmano!	To be aroused by Muslim gold![55]

Such sentiments concerning the medieval Crusades and "Muslim gold" were also relevant to nineteenth-century European colonial projects. Rising to the climax of her denunciation, Griselda sings with the emphasis of striking ornamentation, characterizing the Crusades as an "impious holocaust" (*l'empio olocausto*) that could never be approved by God. Appropriately, the Habsburg censors, in the name of religion, raised objections to the first performance in Milan in 1843.[56]

While her fellow Lombards denounce her as sacrilegious, Griselda prophesies over menacing musical figures the terrible future consequences of the

Crusades:

| Veggo di barbari sorger torrenti, | I see torrents of barbarians rising up, |
| D'Europa stringere le genti dome! | To press the subject peoples of Europe![57] |

Thus Solera incorporated into this opera of the Crusades what could only have been a prophesy of the future coming of the Ottomans, here conceived as the Muslim retribution against Europe. The violence of the crusaders was envisioned as in some sense the providential cause of the Ottoman oppressions in southeastern Europe, in such European lands as Serbia and Greece which had only just been emancipated in the early nineteenth century. In the 1840s, of course, the Ottomans remained a presence in Europe, including the lands of Bulgaria, Macedonia, Albania, and Bosnia. The whole operatic tradition of Ottoman subjects was thus implanted in *I Lombardi* as an allusive prophecy of the Ottoman future that was, as Verdi composed, still partially present.

In the third act Oronte is briefly reunited with Griselda for a deathbed conversion to Christianity, which takes place under the auspices of a Christian hermit (who is actually the repentant Milanese parricide from the first act). The tragic-ecstatic trio of love, death, and conversion, which Verdi invested with rapturous musical beauty, was not, however, a triumph of Christianity in the most conventional sense, as when the crusaders celebrated military victory. Rather, the conversion of the dying Muslim prince represented an operatic effort to bridge the gap between the two cultures of the two lovers.

Both Griselda and Oronte explicitly renounce their own peoples and look for a common religious space where they can love each other beyond the grave. A solo violin presides over their search for spiritual transcendence, and the soaring course of the tenor and soprano parts suggests that they have found some spiritual harmony beyond the reach of the Christian hermit with his basso line. By his conversion Oronte's Islamic identity is completely effaced just before his death, and in the final act he appears to Griselda only in a dream, as a vision, through the instrument of a disembodied tenor voice.

In *Jérusalem*, Verdi's French revision of *I Lombardi* for Paris in 1847, Oronte would disappear altogether. The Muslim prince was eliminated from the dramatis personae, and the tenor lead became the French crusader Gaston. With both lovers Christian from the beginning, there could be no question of any sort of romantic conversion, and the musical trio from *I Lombardi* became now, in *Jérusalem*, a trio of religious resolve in which the hermit urged the tenor to maintain his Christian faith.[58] The Islamic aspects of *I Lombardi*, an opera about the Crusades, were thus musically and dramatically marginalized in the revision of the work as *Jérusalem*. The creation and then the elimination of Verdi's Muslim prince over the course of the 1840s was consistent with the effacement of singing Turks, and more generally Muslim figures, from the operatic stage.

Pashas and Corsairs in the Nineteenth Century

In November 1847, when *Jérusalem* was presented in Paris, Verdi was already at work on *Il corsaro*—first performed in Habsburg Trieste in October 1848, with a libretto by Francesco Maria Piave. Verdi envisioned a fully Ottoman scenario and composed roles for a brutal pasha, a harem captive, a eunuch of the harem, and the titular pirate corsair, a heroic tenor part. It was one of Verdi's most striking failures (a "fiasco," according to Verdi biographer Mary Jane Phillips-Matz); the opera was canceled in Trieste after three performances, replaced with Verdi's *Macbeth* and very rarely performed thereafter.[59] Based on Byron's poem *The Corsair*, which was a huge literary success in 1814, Verdi's *Il corsaro* sought to continue operatic themes and conventions that were already rendered anachronistic by the war of Greek independence in the 1820s and seemed all the more incongruous when Verdi put a Turkish pasha on the stage in the year of the European revolutions of 1848.

The opera presents a Mediterranean corsair on a Greek island, vocalizing his hatred of the Turks in a tenor aria with a chorus of corsairs who join in the rousing refrain:

| All'armi, all'armi e intrepidi | To arms, to arms, and intrepidly |
| cadiam, cadiam sull'empia Luna. | let us fall upon the impious Crescent.[60] |

The musical spirit of tenor and chorus anticipated that of "*Di quella pira*" in *Il trovatore* five years later, when Verdi's martial fervor would have nothing to do with Muslims or Turks.

The corsair becomes the prisoner of the Ottoman potentate, Seid Pasha, and is consigned to the dungeon of the pasha's palace at Koroni in the Greek Peloponnesus. The prisoner, however, also wins the romantic sympathy of the pasha's harem captive Gulnara. The jealous pasha, a baritone, therefore plans to devise "new horrible tortures," and addresses the captive corsair in an aria that recalls the bloodthirsty spirit of Osmin, sixty years before, in Mozart's *Abduction*:

Si, morrai di morte atroce,	Yes, you will die an atrocious death,
lenta, infame	slow, infamous,
orrenda morte . . .	horrendous death . . .[61]

There was nothing Mozartean about the music, which seemed to anticipate Rigoletto's "*Si, vendetta*"—later baritone fantasies of personal revenge that would be stripped of any religious or cultural significance.

In 1814 Byron's pasha exults at finding the corsair "fetter'd in my power," and declares that he would not allow such a captive to be redeemed at any price: "if for each drop of blood a gem / were offered rich as Stamboul's diadem."[62] For Byron there was still something spectacularly dramatic to be rendered in the conflict between Turkish power and Christian captivity, especially in the context of Ottoman rule over Greece. One generation later, however, when Verdi and Piave created *Il corsaro* in 1848, the year of liberal revolutions in Europe, the whole scenario had become politically and culturally peripheral. The cruel pasha whom Verdi tried to compose so seriously in Habsburg Trieste in 1848 had already been preceded by Ali Hitsch-Hatsch in Habsburg Vienna in 1844, the farcical pasha who was too fat to board a boat and depart from his island dominion.[63] By the 1840s, it was difficult for the European public to take seriously the dramatization of a Turkish foe.

Verdi, who did not attend the premiere of *Il corsaro* in Trieste, was much preoccupied with the Italian struggle against the Habsburgs in 1848, and the Habsburgs loomed far larger for him (and for Piave) than the Ottomans as a contemporary force of political oppression. The tensions of Verdi's *Il corsaro* were only perfunctorily concerned with religious struggle or Ottoman power, but rather reflected the classic Verdian polarization between an outlaw heroic tenor and a politically powerful, cruelly jealous baritone, already suggested in *Ernani* but soon to receive its most famous formulation in *Il trovatore*. The success of *Il trovatore* in Rome in 1853, with its Gypsy drama set in late medieval Spain, bore no relation to Muslim or Turkish scenarios.

The year of *Il trovatore* was also the year of the outbreak of the Crimean War, and England and France allied themselves with the Ottoman empire against Russia. In Paris there was a revival of Favart's *Three Sultanas* at the

Théâtre des Variétés; the role of Roxelana was taken by Delphine Ugalde, who would later become an Offenbach diva.[64] In 1853 Filippo Galli, Rossini's celebrated basso Turk of the previous generation, died in Paris at the age of seventy, completely destitute.[65]

The Treaty of Paris, which concluded the Crimean War in 1856 (the year that Donizetti Pasha died in Istanbul), coincided with the production at the Paris Opéra of the ballet *Le corsaire*, featuring a thoroughly comical pasha. The future of this ballet would lie in Russia, the enemy of the Ottoman empire and loser of the Crimean War. In St. Petersburg Petipa's choreography of the harem as a living garden (*jardin animé*) and the spectacular celebration of slavery in the figure of the dancing slave made *Le corsaire* into a silent classic of modern Orientalism and helped to consign Verdi's *Il corsaro* to theatrical oblivion. "The deed is done," declares Verdi's harem captive Gulnara after murdering Seid Pasha in his sleep, and just in time. "He was about to wake up." Even Verdi could not reawaken the Ottoman subject in European opera, and indeed there would be no more pashas—cruel or magnanimous, comical or romantic—returning to take the operatic stage.

Subliminal Operatic Traces

While one can trace the sputtering failure of Turkish themes and figures on the operatic stage in the two decades following *Le siège de Corinthe* in Paris in 1826, the second half of the nineteenth century witnessed the virtual disappearance of these themes. A glance at the standard repertory from the nineteenth century confirms that the anthropology of operatic exoticism had abandoned the Ottoman empire: from Bellini's Druids and Bizet's Gypsies to Verdi's Ethiopian slave and Puccini's Japanese geisha. Richard Wagner and Richard Strauss in the German repertory were no more interested in the figure of the singing Turk than their French and Italian contemporaries. Ottoman subjects survived in the emerging operatic repertories of southeastern Europe—Serbian, Croatian, Hungarian—where Ottoman history was most directly relevant to national history. Turkish themes were further preserved in the domain of operetta in the late nineteenth and early twentieth centuries, oriented toward popular entertainment and comical scenarios. The more elevated high culture of grand opera, however, thoroughly eliminated Turkish scenarios from the standard European repertory.

Verdi's *Simon Boccanegra* was first performed in Venice in 1857, in the immediate aftermath of the Crimean War. The titular protagonist is chosen as the doge of Genoa already in the opera's prologue, and presides as doge throughout the three acts, but both the libretto and the dramatis personae specify his earlier career as that of a celebrated *corsaro*, which might have brought to mind Verdi's earlier opera with that title—and also perhaps the ballet *Le corsaire* performed in Paris in 1856. Yet if the seafaring Boccanegra once operated as a crusading corsair against Muslim maritime trade in the late medieval Mediterranean, that plausible implication is never confirmed in the libretto and never becomes meaningful within the opera. The presence of Islam in the work is so subtly implicit as to be virtually subliminal, and altogether undetectable on the operatic stage. In *La forza del destino* of 1862 Fra Melitone comically asks the soldiers if they are Christians or Turks, playing with the name—"*Turchi! Turchi! Turchi!*"—but he only means to reproach their un-Christian conduct on a Sunday.

In Verdi's *Don Carlos*, first performed in its original French version in the Paris of Napoleon III in 1867, the setting of sixteenth-century Spain betrays just a glimpse of the Moorish past that was displaced by the Spanish reconquest in the fifteenth century. At the Spanish court the fatefully beautiful and fiercely jealous Princess Eboli introduces herself with the seductive "song of the veil" (*chanson du voile*) whose lyrics and sensual ornamentations were intended to evoke the Moorish history of the Spanish peninsula. In 1875, the premiere of Georges Bizet's *Carmen* at the Opéra-Comique offered the potent exoticism of the Spanish Gypsy femme fatale, very different from the sultanas of Turkish harem opera.

Meanwhile, in Istanbul Sultan Abdülaziz, far from being an operatic subject, was actually an operatic patron, contributing money to support the opening of Richard Wagner's Bayreuth Festspielhaus in 1876. For *Parsifal* Wagner supposedly considered casting as the self-castrated sorcerer Klingsor the famous Vatican castrato Domenico Mustafà, who was himself partly Turkish by descent—an actual singing Turk—but the composer finally decided to cast Klingsor in the bass-baritone range.[66]

Rossini composed *Otello* for Naples in 1816, which was based on Shakespeare but set in Venice. Verdi's *Otello*, performed at La Scala in 1887, was composed to Arrigo Boito's libretto with the proper Shakespearean setting of Cyprus, thus locating the drama at the geopolitical heart of the eastern Mediterranean struggle between Christian Europe and the Ottoman empire. The tenor's famous entrance, coming ashore in the storm, celebrates the defeat of the Turks: "*Esultate, l'orgoglio musulmano sepolto è in mar*" (Rejoice, for Muslim pride has been buried at sea). In 1570 Cyprus actually fell to the Turks, just one generation before Shakespeare wrote his *Othello* (first performed in 1604). In 1887 the island was still technically subject to Ottoman sovereignty, though it was occupied by the British as a Mediterranean base after the Congress of Berlin in 1878. Verdi and Boito's *Otello* was sensitive to the context of the Ottoman-European encounter, and when Otello stops the soldiers' brawl in the first act, he exclaims: "Am I among Saracens? Or has the Turkish rage been transfused in you [*la turchesca rabbia è in voi trasfusa*]?"[67] Otello himself would soon seem to be transfused with Turkish rage in his violent jealousy. Though Osmin's rage no longer recurred as a familiar feature of European operas, there were traces of Turkishness to be discovered even in Verdi's later operatic work.

With the crises of Bosnia and Bulgaria in the 1870s the Ottoman empire was more than ever a matter of European diplomacy, summed up as the Eastern Question. The Ottomans became a political campaign issue in Britain as William Gladstone mobilized liberal outrage against the Turkish irregular troops, the *bashi-bazouk*s, and Ottoman atrocities in Bulgaria, while Disraeli, backed by Queen Victoria, insisted on supporting the Ottoman empire to counter Russia's imperial ambitions. At the Congress of Berlin in 1878 Disraeli and Bismarck presided over a settlement of balance, as European powers competed for influence while the new states of southeastern Europe sought territory and sovereignty at the expense of the Ottomans. The autonomy of Bulgaria, the full independence of Serbia, Montenegro, and Romania, and the Austrian occupation of Bosnia underlined the political and diplomatic rather than theatrical or exotic aspects of Ottoman recession, and the Balkan Wars of 1912 and 1913 made further military assaults on what remained of the Ottoman empire in Europe.

The Eastern Crisis of the 1870s found little echo in the great opera houses and the established operatic traditions of Europe, but the forging of South Slavic national cultures, directly stimulated by the Ottoman encounters of the decade, also encouraged the creation of some operas of specifically national significance with Ottoman content. One year after the Bosnian uprising of 1875, in the same year as the Bulgarian massacres of 1876, the Croatian composer Ivan Zajc conducted the first performance in Zagreb of what was to become in effect the Croatian national opera, *Nikola Šubić Zrinski*, about the heroic military campaign of the Croatian Zrinski against the Ottomans in the sixteenth century. Born in Habsburg Fiume (or Rijeka, in Croatian) and musically educated in Habsburg Milan, Zajc transformed the Habsburg-Ottoman battle of Szigeth in 1566 into a national Croatian triumph over the Turks, culminating in a choral national anthem, "*U boj, u boj!*" (To battle, to battle!). The opera alternates between a Croatian scenario and the Ottoman camp, including a harem ballet and roles for the historical Grand Vizier (*veliki vezir*) Mehmed Sokolović (sung by a tenor) and the Sultan (*turski car*) Suleiman the Magnificent (sung by a basso), who dies during the campaign, in the opera as in history. The opera's direct national relevance determined its quite precisely delimited reception, then and thereafter, within the Croatian national sphere.[68]

In the year of the Eastern Crisis, 1876, it was an operetta that brought Turkishness to Vienna: *Fatinitza*, by the Dalmatian composer Franz von Suppé. Born in Habsburg Spalato (or Split, in Croatian), Suppé composed principally German-language operettas for Viennese performance. *Fatinitza* was set in the very recent past, in the time of the Crimean War, and thus represented modern politics within the mode of operetta, as if the Eastern Question belonged to the domain of musical fantasy rather than international relations. The story concerns a Russian officer (sung in travesty by a mezzo-soprano) who disguises himself as a Circassian girl ("Fatinitza") and is then taken captive by a Turkish pasha. The farcical relation of the operetta to the operatic tradition of Turkishness was clearly demonstrated by the self-referential circumstance of planning a performance of Mozart's *Abduction* within the story of *Fatinitza*.[69]

Among the many other operettas that touched on Turkish themes, *Der Zigeunerbaron* (The gypsy baron) by Johann Strauss, the most celebrated Viennese operetta composer of all, was performed in Vienna in 1885. Set in post-Ottoman Hungary in the eighteenth century, the operetta features a Gypsy heroine whose status is instantly elevated when it is discovered that she is the daughter of the last Ottoman pasha of Hungary and therefore eligible to marry the Hungarian hero. Nineteenth-century Viennese operetta thus presented the already remote eighteenth-century Habsburg monarchy, including a sentimental reminder of the now fantastically remote seventeenth-century Ottoman presence in Hungary.

In *Nikola Šubić Zrinski* the operatic setting of Suleiman's camp is Ottoman Belgrade in 1566. In post-Ottoman Belgrade in 1903 Stanislav Binički sought to inaugurate a Serbian operatic tradition with a one-act *verismo* opera of village life, *Na Uranku* (At dawn). Two Serbian peasants, Rade and Stanka, are in love with each other, but the Turkish Aga Redžep, a basso, also admires Stanka and tragically intervenes. Binički self-consciously made use of musically Oriental effects—such as the muezzin's Muslim call to prayer—in contrast with an idiom of Serbian folk tunes integrated into the operatic score.[70] As with *Nikola Šubić Zrinski* in Zagreb in 1876, so *Na Uranku* in Belgrade in 1903 presented Ottoman subjects on the operatic stage alongside the Eastern Question in the contemporary public sphere, attempting to create national operatic traditions with Turkish figures cast as national enemies. These were precisely the scenarios that were not present in the established repertories of the leading opera houses of Europe in the later nineteenth and early twentieth centuries.

In the year 1912, when Serbia, Bulgaria, Greece, and Montenegro undertook the first Balkan War to eliminate the Ottoman empire from Europe, *The Three Sultanas* was featured on a poster at Monte Carlo, and Isabelle Moindrot has suggested that the musical comedy was now transformed into something more like a variety show or cabaret act with the lavish display of feathers and turbans.[71] In that same year another venerable Turkish entertainment was rendered dispensable at the premiere in Stuttgart of the first version of Richard Strauss's opera *Ariadne auf Naxos*, composed in collaboration with the Viennese librettist Hugo von Hofmannsthal. In this first version the staging of Molière's drama *Le bourgeois gentilhomme* was followed by an opera about Ariadne and Bacchus—replacing the seventeenth-century musical Turkish ceremony. In 1916, in wartime Vienna, a new version of *Ariadne auf Naxos* eliminated Molière altogether and replaced *Le bourgeois gentilhomme* with the composed prologue—featuring the character of the Composer—which has remained the definitive form of the opera to this day. In April 1918 Hofmannsthal's full dramatic treatment of Molière, *Der Bürger als Edelmann*, was presented in Berlin with Strauss's incidental music, including music for the Turkish ceremony. It was a gesture of respect for French culture—including Turquerie—in that final year of the Great War, but the Berlin public did not respond with enthusiasm, and Hofmannsthal regretfully considered the production to be a failure. When Strauss then attempted to salvage some of his incidental music by creating an orchestral suite, he eliminated the "Turkish" music altogether.[72]

During World War I, while Strauss and Hofmannsthal were revising *Ariadne auf Naxos*, the Ottoman empire was nearing collapse, and Atatürk's modern Turkey would emerge from the imperial ruins after the war. In 1916 a Viennese operetta, *Die Rose von Stambul* by Leo Fall, presented the prewar dilemma of the modern Ottoman Turk, Achmed Bey, whose bold reformist views could only be published behind the French pseudonym of André Léry. Complications develop when Achmed Bey's traditional Turkish fiancée falls in love with the modern European revolutionary Léry, a merely fictive persona. On her honeymoon to Switzerland she finally discovers that her Turkish husband and European fantasy lover are one and the same modern man. The secondary plot of the operetta also involves a twentieth-century abduction from the seraglio.

Coda: After the Ottoman Empire

After World War I the Ottoman empire gave way to modern Turkey, territorially reduced to Asian Anatolia and a small part of European Thrace. Mehmed VI, the last Ottoman sultan, had to give up his throne in 1922. In 1924 Atatürk abolished the Ottoman Caliphate, the supreme Islamic leadership held for centuries by the sultans, and in that same year Giacomo Puccini died, leaving incomplete his final operatic masterpiece, *Turandot*. Set in Beijing and based on an eighteenth-century Venetian drama by Carlo Gozzi, the opera presents the mysterious Prince Calaf who risks his life to answer three riddles for the chance to marry the cruel Chinese princess Turandot. Calaf is a Tartar prince and therefore presumably Muslim, though his religion, like his name, is unknown to the princess. In his famous aria "*Nessun Dorma*" (None may sleep) he sings of conquest at dawn: "*All'alba vincerò*" (At dawn I will conquer).[73] The repeated cry of "*vincerò*" rises to a tenorial high B, as if to conquer the audience in advance of conquering the princess and the kingdom. Subliminally, perhaps, his call to conquest evoked the lost world of the Muslim singing Turk in the European operatic tradition, conjured by Puccini at the moment of the passing of the Ottoman empire. The dethroned Mehmed VI died in Italian exile in 1926 at San Remo, less than two hundred miles from Milan, only three weeks after Arturo Toscanini conducted the posthumous premiere of Puccini's unfinished *Turandot* at La Scala.

Twenty-five years later, one last lingering Turkish figure appeared on the operatic stage—the freakishly bearded lady, Baba the Turk—in Igor Stravinsky's *The Rake's Progress*, first performed in 1951 in Venice, a city that had long been important for the operatic staging of Turkishness. Yet Stravinsky's opera, based on the images of William Hogarth from the 1730s, was deeply imbued with eighteenth-century musical and dramatic values, so that the appearance of Baba may be seen less as a return to Turkishness than an acknowledgment of eighteenth-century fascination with Turkish figures. In the libretto by W. H. Auden and Chester Kallman, Baba proudly narrates the history of her own admirers all over Europe:

> That was in Vienna, no, it must have been Milan
> Because of the donkeys. Vienna was the Chinese fan—[74]

Baba the Turk was admired as a freak in the same cities where singing Turks were admired at the opera throughout the long eighteenth century.

CONCLUSION

The Singing Turk in Chains: Tragedy and Sovereignty

The literally spectacular importance of Ottoman subjects in European opera during the long eighteenth century can only be properly understood in the framework of European-Ottoman relations from the 1680s, after the failed siege of Vienna, to the 1820s, the decade of the successful Greek War for Independence. The creation and performance of those operas constituted one of the manifestations of the changing dynamics of European-Ottoman relations during this long period of transition from the early modern religious clash of Christians against Muslims to the modern diplomatic attention of the European Great Powers to the Ottoman Eastern Question—which led to the Ottoman empire's demolition and demise. The Eastern Question, from the 1820s to the 1920s, focused on the clinical and unoperatic details of how that demise could be best managed through the displacement of the empire by national states while preserving a balance of power in the Middle East and in southeastern Europe.

Baroque opera, Martha Feldman has argued, was centrally concerned with issues of power and sovereignty, not only affirming the power of the prince in court spectacles but also challenging power and analyzing sovereignty by mobilizing a commercial public through the vocal charisma of opera stars who were also players in a political drama. Early modern operas, according to Feldman, reflected "a set of absolutist claims about a cosmic order wherein the benign sovereign stands in for God, the heroic youth for the ideal enlightened subject or the sovereign whom he sometimes succeeds as heir, and the dramatis personae as a whole for the hierarchy of the socio-political order."[1] Operas about Turks represented a level in between the cosmic order and the sociopolitical order, namely the international order, and in fact throughout the eighteenth century such operas were closely attuned to the development of relations between European states and the Ottoman empire. The Turks who were driven back from the walls of Vienna in 1683 reappeared almost immediately on the operatic stages of Venice and Hamburg in 1689 and 1690 in the figure of the captive Sultan Bajazet. At the same time the Ottoman boundaries which receded with the treaties of Karlowitz and Passarowitz in 1699 and 1718 were artistically reconfigured within European theaters—not military but musical—in the first decades of the eighteenth century. The distress of wounded sovereignty could be sung out before the European public, most often by the tragic figure of Bajazet whose political abjection was charismatically compensated in operatic triumph.

Operatic treatments of Bajazet's captivity popped up all over northern Italy in the early eighteenth century—Venice, Florence, Rome, Udine, Livorno, and Ancona—and in 1719, notably one year after the peace of Passarowitz, Agostino Piovene and Francesco Gasparini, librettist and composer, rewrote their opera *Tamerlano* as *Il Bajazet* for Reggio Emilia. Now, after a whole generation of European-Ottoman warfare on the Triplex Confinium, with the Habsburgs and Venetians advancing irregularly, sometimes losing but mostly gaining territory at Ottoman expense, Piovene and Gasparini created an unprecedented musical suicide for a tenor impersonating the Ottoman sultan. That same tenor, Francesco Borosini, went to London in 1724 to perform the same part for Handel, who created around him one of the masterpieces of baroque opera, culminating in the noble, tragic, beautiful, and inspirational death scene of a Muslim Turk.

The context of Handel's other masterpieces of that moment—*Giulio Cesare* and *Rodelinda*—confirm the deeply political concerns of his operatic preoccupations, musical studies in sovereignty that charted the passions accompanying the rise and fall, collapse and betrayal, triumph and captivity of princes. The shifting of tempo and harmony, rhythm and dynamics, represented the emotional climate of shifting circumstance and contingent power in a dramatic scenario of competing sovereignties. In contrast to the brilliant display arias of the triumphant conqueror Tamerlano, the musical abjection of Bajazet reflected the humbling of the Ottoman empire in the age of Karlowitz and Passarowitz and explored the dark emotional penumbra of degraded sovereignty, demonstrating that even despotic sultans might come to grief. From the 1720s to the 1760s Bajazet would sing his political despair in multiple musical versions in London, Venice, Naples, Hamburg, Milan, Mantua, Turin, Florence, Ljubljana, Verona, Vicenza, Modena, Bologna, Lisbon, Rome, Parma, Munich, Prague, and Copenhagen. The eighteenth century would conclude with one last staging of Bajazet's captivity in 1799, composed by Gaetano Marinelli, in Venice, where the whole phenomenon began.

The cantata performed in Rome in 1717 to celebrate the Habsburg military victories of Eugene of Savoy musically conjured the figure of a sultan in chains:

Dell'Asia il fier Tiranno,	The proud tyrant of Asia,
Dimmi, ch'è in ceppi avvinto	Tell me that he is in chains[2]

The current Sultan Ahmed III had suffered defeat by the Habsburgs when Eugene captured Belgrade in 1717, but Ahmed was not at all in chains, and was in fact about to embark upon the brilliant "Tulip Period" in Ottoman culture, a cultural florescence with intimations of European rococo influence. Furthermore, Belgrade would be recaptured by the Turks in 1739. The chained Asiatic tyrant of the cantata was thus merely a metaphor for the Ottoman setback—but found dramatic expression in the operatic staging of Bajazet's captivity from earlier Ottoman history. The same cantata, saluting the Habsburg emperor Charles VI, also revealed the fundamental reason behind the emerging operatic phenomenon:

Per lui respira	For him breathes
Italia bella,	Beautiful Italy,
Ne più sospira	And no more sighs
Per lo timor.	For fear.[3]

In this same spirit, operas about Turks marked the end of an age of fear that dated back to the fifteenth century, when Mehmed II conquered Constantinople and an Ottoman army landed at Otranto in Italy. For Vienna, too, the dissipation of fear dated from the lifting of the siege of the city in 1683, followed by the rolling back of the frontier in southeastern Europe. It now became possible for Europeans to reconceive the infidel Ottoman scourge in the form of the singing Turk who could excite sympathy and even admiration, especially when he appeared on stage in captivity.

The Magnanimous Singing Turk: Comedy and Absolutism

In Paris the Ottomans never appeared as fearful as they did from Vienna or Venice, not just because of the greater remoteness but also because France had been historically the implicit ally of the sultans against the common Habsburg enemy. Musical Turkishness actually made its appearance in France in the generation preceding the siege of Vienna, with Lully's Turkish ceremony music for Molière's *Le bourgeois gentilhomme* presented as comedy before the court of Louis XIV in 1670. Even as Bajazet was establishing himself as a tragic hero of the Italian operatic stage during the early decades of the eighteenth century, subversively transforming Ottoman military defeat into moral and musical triumph, comical Ottoman subjects were emerging with parallel political impact in the popular theatrical arena of the Paris fairs. Ordinary men and women at the fairs watched musical comedies that featured their own theatrical hero, Arlequin or Harlequin, as he braved the dangers of the Muslim Ottoman world and emerged indomitable in spirit. The Turks were only comically intimidating in such works as *Arlequin Grand Vizir* at St. Germain in 1713, *Arlequin Mahomet* at St. Laurent in 1714, and *Arlequin sultane favorite* at St. Germain in 1715.

In France the recession of the Ottoman empire was no cause for celebration since French ascendance in Europe was undermined by Habsburg victory, but musical comedies about Turks still offered subversive messages to popular audiences. Power and authority were cheerfully ridiculed when an omnipotent sultan lustfully removed the veil from his captive concubine only to reveal the comical face of Arlequin. The year 1715, when Arlequin appeared as the "favorite sultana," was actually a year of Ottoman military success when Ahmed III reconquered the Greek Morea from Venice. Much more important than the vicissitudes of the sultan, however, was the death of Louis XIV in 1715, after a reign of seventy-two years. Dissenting voices against royal absolutism could already be heard in the last years of his reign and would quickly multiply under the regency that followed his death, creating the cultural foundation for the French Enlightenment.

As the king lay dying, Arlequin sang out from the Ottoman scenario of *Arlequin sultane favorite*:

Sous la puissance d'un Tyran	Under the power of a tyrant
Nous voici donc Esclaves . . .	Here we are slaves . . .[4]

The tyrant explicitly invoked was the Ottoman sultan, but the people of Paris would have appreciated the sentiment in relation to their own political circumstances, even as they laughed at an Ottoman world where Arlequin had to live without wine, where he worried about being made into a eunuch. The fears were not real fears, however, as Pierrot reassured the public: "*Les Turcs m'ont pris mais je n'ai rien à craindre*" (The Turks have taken me, but I have nothing to fear).[5] Face to face with the sultan, caught in the embarrassing disguise of a sultana, Arlequin knew what he had to do. He had to make the sultan laugh: "*Riez donc, Monsieur Mustapha.*"[6] The sultan was invited to join with the laughing public, partly because the joke was not really, or not entirely, at the sultan's expense.

The musical comedy of Turkishness which emerged at the Paris fairs would proliferate in the operatic world of the eighteenth century, and always as a vehicle for the comic appreciation of European issues and principles. The Turks who became objects of ridicule according to the conventions of *opera buffa* could always be recognized—behind their veils or moustaches, beneath their turbans or robes—as representatives of European foibles, vices, emotions, and prejudices. The features of Harlequin would remain recognizable in this operatic tradition, and it is not difficult to identify him in Mozart's *Abduction* in the role of Pedrillo, getting drunk with Osmin and joining the Turkish overseer in an intoxicated tribute to pretty girls of every kind: "*Es leben die Mädchen, die Blonden, die Braunen!*" In Vienna in 1782, approaching the centennial of the Turkish siege, comic opera suggested that the public now had nothing to fear from the Turks.

In Paris in 1783 Grétry presented in a similar spirit his hugely successful comic opera *La caravane du Caire*, making Turkishness a major theme in the decade that led up to the French Revolution. Grétry's opera would go from triumph to triumph under the ancien régime, during the Revolution, in the age of Napoleon, and into the Restoration with the political values of each epoch finding some point of reference in the comedy of Turkishness. Exotic scenes from the *La caravane du Caire*—with camels, tents, and turbans—were even printed on the fabrics of the late eighteenth century, so that operatic themes passed from the musical to the visual arts, and the spectacular sets of the theater became items of everyday décor.[7] Far from frightening, Turkishness could be comically entertaining on the operatic stage and piquantly charming as an adornment of the domestic interior.

The Ottoman sultan at the Paris fairs was not, in the end, a fearsome figure. He freed his European captives and invited Arlequin to remain freely in Turkey—an invitation that Arlequin freely declined, for what was life without wine? The magnanimity of the sultan in the musical comedy of 1715 already anticipated the emergence of the figure of the "generous Turk" who turned up in one opera after another in the eighteenth century, especially after the type received its most explicit formulation in the scene of "Le Turc généreux" within the operatic framework of Rameau's *Les Indes galantes* in Paris in 1735. Rameau's Osman Pasha demonstrated his generosity by renouncing the French captive whom he loved and liberating her to return to France with her French lover. Not only generous but emotionally sensitive, Osman withdrew from the stage for the musical finale so that the rejoicing lovers and supporting chorus would not have their celebration marred by the melancholy regret of his unrequited love and lonely isolation.

The dramatic principle of the generous Turk was that his generosity had to come as a surprise at the end of the opera, for it was the presumption of his cruelty that drove the dramatic and musical tensions of the work, which were finally resolved by the unexpected revelation of his magnanimity. In this sense, the operatic figure of the generous Turk recapitulated the recent history of European-Ottoman relations, in which the historically fearsome sultans and pashas, whether magnanimous or not, ceased to be international objects of terror. On the stage they could now provoke sympathy and even pity, as in the tragic case of Bajazet or the sentimental case of Osman Pasha, an omnipotent authority who finally recognized that he could command anything but the love of his captive.

Yet the conceit of Turkish generosity in the matter of Christian captives was by no means historically consistent with the international circumstances of the 1730s. While there was a significant decline in the Mediterranean piracy of the Barbary corsairs dating from the 1680s, when the French navy of Louis XIV made several concerted assaults on Algiers—at the same time that the Habsburgs were forcing an Ottoman retreat in southeastern Europe—still large numbers of European captives were being taken and sold as slaves within the Ottoman empire in the eighteenth century. Sometimes they were liberated but rarely as a matter of generosity, for such piracy was embedded in the Mediterranean economy and emancipation was usually an economic transaction produced by organized ventures in ransoming.

The celebration of generous Turkish pashas on the operatic stage was generally intended as an indirect tribute to European princes and the principle of monarchical authority. A fashion for Turquerie was already present at the court of Louis XV in the 1730s, when Jean-Marc Nattier painted "Mademoiselle de Clermont Dressed as a Sultana" and Carle Van Loo painted "The Grand Turk Giving a Concert to His Mistress." Beneath the Turkish costume and turban of Rameau's generous pasha it would have been very possible to discern the features of the young Louis XV, who also enjoyed playing pasha with a harem of mistresses. Fifty years later in the 1780s, Mozart composed Turkish choruses of tribute to the magnanimous Pasha Selim, who mirrored from the stage the emperor in the audience, Joseph II, the most radical practitioner of enlightened absolutism in the eighteenth century. Rameau's pasha pleaded to be remembered—"*Souvenez-vous d'Osman*"—and Mozart's pasha was celebrated by a final vaudeville declaring the utmost contempt for anyone who could ever forget his supreme benevolence (*Wer so viel Huld vergessen kann*). The operatic figure of the generous Turk was sympathetically intended with reference to the Ottoman empire but also validated the governing principle of European monarchical authority, especially with the advent of the age of enlightened absolutism.

The Singing Turk in Violent Rage: Extreme Operatic Emotions

Operas on Turkish subjects thus provided the opportunity for the choral or ensemble celebration of absolutism while at the same time defining a standard for the virtuous exercise of absolute power in its Ottoman manifestation, presumed to be maximally absolute. The individual singing Turks on the operatic stage were, however, more likely to be characterized by the extreme emotion that was both an aspect of their Turkishness, a product of frustrated Ottoman authority, and a common human characteristic that the enlightened European public could easily appreciate. In the history of the emotions, eighteenth-century society and culture acknowledged the fundamental relation of passionate sensibility and individual character, while also recognizing that explosive emotions had to be controlled according to mannerly conventions.

In the many operas about Bajazet that followed Piovene's libretto, including Handel's *Tamerlano* in London in 1724, the Sultan Bajazet sang of his rage and humiliation in captivity, expressing the strongest emotions. In *Scanderberg*, at the Paris Opéra in 1735, the Sultan Amurat sang out his jealousy of the eponymous Albanian hero:

Regnez Haine, Fureur,	Reign hate and fury,
Regnez jalouse Rage . . .	Reign jealous rage . . .[8]

In Hasse's *Solimano* in Dresden in 1753 (and then in multiple later settings of the same libretto), Suleiman the Magnificent very nearly condemned his own son to death, his raging resentment stoked by the provocations of the sultana Roxelana.

Operas about Turkish sultans allowed for the baroque musical expression of furious rage, aggravated by the presumption of absolute sultanic omnipotence; with the musical and dramatic disciplining of such extreme emotions, the operatic development became a course of self-civilization, a taming of Turkish emotional violence. Mozart seemed to understand this implicitly in the surviving fragments of *Zaide* when his Sultan Soliman expressed, in a complex musical scene of *melologo* combined with aria, the diverse aspects of his tenor rage at Zaide's flight: "*Zaide entflohen!*" The aria form provided a musical setting for Soliman's psychological insight into his own politically leonine condition:

Der stolze Löw' lässt sich zwar zähmen,
er nimmt von Schmeichler Fessel an.
Doch will man sklavisch ihn beschämen,
steigt seine Wut bis zum Tyrann.

The proud lion lets himself be tamed,
he accepts the chain from the flatterer.
But if someone wants to humiliate him as a slave,
his fury rises to the point of making him a tyrant.[9]

Operas about Ottoman power were particularly interesting vehicles for composing and staging the musical expression of such fury, which was also inseparable from an implicitly embedded political theory of absolutism. The singing operatic sultan was governed by a calculus of emotions which exercised a tyrannical hold upon him even as they made him into a tyrant.

Mozart, however, when he was working on the *Abduction* a few years later, also understood that music had the effect of moderating the passions, not just in the sense that the magic flute could soothe the savage beasts, but rather inasmuch as musical form inevitably set aesthetic limits upon the ugly excesses of emotion. Trying to explain to his father the basic principle of Osmin's first-act aria, Mozart theorized: "A person who gets into such a violent rage oversteps all order, measure, and object; he no longer knows himself"—but "passions, violent or not, must never be expressed to the point of disgust, and music must never offend the ear."[10] Music itself was the means of containing Turkish rage, the basis of an enlightened ordering of extreme passions. Pasha Selim also had a fierce temper, and frustrated at Konstanze's romantic resistance, he threatened her with "tortures of all kinds" (*Martern aller Arten*), though it was she, and not he, who transmuted that violent phrase into an aria of musical beauty. The speaking pasha was removed from the strictly musical emotions of the opera, but he disciplined himself to become a generous Turk in the final scene and received the musical tribute to his magnanimity.

Osmin, however, expressed sentiments of violence that conformed to early modern images of Turkish cruelty as "monstrous barbarians" (*immanes barbari*). Such was the perspective of Cardinal Basilios Bessarion, the great Renaissance patron of Greek learning in Rome, writing at the time of the Ottoman conquest of Constantinople in 1453: "Men have been butchered like cattle, women abducted, virgins ravished, and children snatched from the arms of their parents. If any survived so great a slaughter, they have been enslaved in chains so that they might be ransomed for a price, or subjected to every kind of torture."[11] This Renaissance account was largely consistent with Osmin's rage, centuries later:

Erst geköpft, dann gehangen,	First beheaded, then hung,
dann gespiesst auf heisse Stangen,	then impaled on hot stakes,
dann verbrannt, dann gebunden,	then burned, then bound,
und getaucht, zuletzt geschunden.	then drowned, then flayed.[12]

Yet even as Janissary percussion further excited the furious intensity of the aria, as if heating the stakes, Mozart prepared to stabilize the musical spirit of the piece as Osmin sang "*Ich hab' auch Verstand*"—reminding both himself and the public of his human reason, and returning on the lowest note to the low F which confirmed the tonality of the aria as a whole. The operatic public, listening to the musical raging of Osmin while observing the emotional self-control of the pasha, participated through the Ottoman scenario in an enlightened demonstration of the expression and mastery of the human emotions.

Osmin of course was not a sultan or a pasha but an overseer, and his rage derived from the fact that he was both autocrat and underling, the absolute master of the captives, the abject slave of the pasha. Earlier versions of this character bore little emotional relation to Osmin, as in the case of his predecessor Osmin in *Zaide*, who served Sultan Soliman and sang a cheerful aria with a laughing refrain. The even earlier Osmin who served Sultan Soliman in Favart's *Three Sultanas* was a merely token force of comical resistance to Roxelana's European influence, and all the more comical for the fact that he was designated in the libretto as "the kislar-aga or chief of the eunuchs"— with Roxelana entirely contemptuous of this "amphibious monster."[13]

The most important literary precedent for the rage of Mozart's Osmin may be found among the harem eunuchs of Isfahan, as described by Montesquieu in the *Persian Letters*. Montesquieu's chief eunuch wrote about the women of the harem:

> I never forget that I was born to command over them, and it is as if I become a man again on the occasions when I now give them orders. I hate them, now that I can face them with indifference, and my reason allows me to see all their weakness. Although I keep them for another man, the pleasure of making myself obeyed gives me a secret joy . . . The seraglio for me is like a little empire, and my desire for power, the only emotion which remains to me, is to some extent satisfied.[14]

The eunuch was for Montesquieu the repository of an emotional hoard of hatred implicit in the autocratic system of Persia. Such a person was simultaneously omnipotent within the harem and impotent everywhere else, both master and slave at the same time, such that the exaltation of mastery grated always against the humiliation of subjection.

The emotional complex of hatred, frustration, and rage of Montesquieu's Persian eunuchs was reconstructed and set to music half a century later when Mozart created the figure of Osmin. An audience familiar with the conventions of the Ottoman (or Persian) harem might suspect that Osmin, as the guardian of the pasha's female captives, was supposed to be a eunuch. Mozart's assignment of the deepest and most extreme musical range to Osmin was in part a practical matter of exploiting the talent of an available performer, Ludwig Fischer. It was also, however, the perfect evasive musical maneuver to distract the public from the distasteful possibility that Osmin really had to be a eunuch, according to the logic of the Ottoman circumstances. Mozart knew relatively little about eunuchs (even if some of his friends and colleagues were castrati), but he knew everything he needed to know about the psychology of being an underling. Living in the service of the archbishop of Salzburg—feeling as powerless as a eunuch—made him perfectly familiar with the rage of Osmin. The challenge of trying to contain Osmin's rage within a pleasing musical form was also the challenge of humanizing Osmin's extreme Turkish emotions, so that he was not just a "monstrous barbarian," and finally the challenge of becoming an emotionally disciplined and civilized adult for Mozart himself.

The Militant Singing Turk:
Janissary Style and Ottoman Conquest

The Janissary percussion that Mozart used to underscore Osmin's violent outbursts against the Christian intruders emulated the militant spirit of authentic Janissary bands, encouraging the Ottoman armies to fight fiercely against the enemy. The besieged Viennese population of 1683 would have heard Janissary music outside the walls of the city, and one hundred years later the security of the city was such that Janissary music could be performed for entertainment in Vienna—in the Prater, for instance, where a Janissary band performed in 1781—and then within the walls, at the Hoftheater in the Michaelerplatz, when Mozart inserted Janissary elements into the score of the *Abduction*. The introduction of Janissary bands at European courts took place during the first half of the eighteenth century, especially at the Saxon court of Dresden, and it would be plausible to suggest that certain European courts were actually cultivating a sultanic style of absolutism, culturally confirmed by the presence of Turkish Janissary bands. The fact that the Saxon Wettins, Augustus II and Augustus III, were constrained to govern Poland as kings severely limited by the republican institutions of the Polish-Lithuanian Commonwealth would only have made them all the more eager to celebrate themselves as absolute sultans in Dresden.

The midcentury employment of Janissary instruments and *alla turca* style in opera may also have begun in Dresden with Hasse's *Solimano* of 1753, and continued through Gluck's and Haydn's treatments of the musical pilgrims in the 1760s and 1770s in Vienna and Esterháza, culminating in Mozart's *Abduction* in the 1780s which began in Vienna and traveled all over the German lands. By the end of the decade the Janissary style reached Stockholm with Joseph Kraus's *Soliman II*, a Swedish treatment of Favart's *Three Sultanas*. While the characteristic percussion in an overture was sufficient to signal an Ottoman scenario, the Janissary style in opera also continued the courtly tradition of affirming sultanic absolutism: as in Mozart's choruses celebrating Pasha Selim (performed at the Austrian court of Joseph II), and in Kraus's *Soliman II*, celebrating Suleiman the Magnificent (at the Swedish court of Gustav III).

While the presence of Janissary bands at European courts in the early eighteenth century coincided with ongoing European warfare against the Ottoman empire and borrowed the spirit of Ottoman militancy, the later Ottoman musical presence in European opera coincided with the unprecedented half century of Habsburg-Ottoman peace between 1739 and 1787, punctuated by the Russian-Ottoman war from 1768 to 1774. Janissary instrumentation and *alla turca* style now became not only militantly emphatic but festively entertaining and therefore perfectly appropriate for comic opera. Both Gluck and Haydn used Janissary accents for the comical aria of the Kalender in *Les pèlerins de la Mecque* and *L'incontro improvviso*, underlining the comical nature of the Muslim mendicant who thought mostly about eating and drinking. Mozart used the Janissary accents in the aria of Osmin's violent rage but stipulated in his letter of September 26, 1781, that rage would be "rendered comical" by the use of Turkish music—the rage that was both Turkish and universal according to the Mozartean comedy of the human emotions.[15] Bence Szabolcsi's argument that Viennese *alla turca* style was to some extent borrowed from surviving Hungarian Ottoman folk music suggests the extent to which some elements of Turkishness were simultaneously internal and external to the Habsburg monarchy in the eighteenth century, and therefore to European culture as a whole.[16]

The Russian-Ottoman war of 1768 to 1774, which Vienna and the German courts watched from a neutral but attentive perspective, belonged to the period that Franco Venturi has described as "the first crisis" of the ancien régime, bringing the advent of revolutionary modernity.[17] In 1768 Haydn presented

Lo speziale at Esterháza, located in the Hungarian lands of what had once been the Ottoman frontier; the comical finale turned on a matter of Turkish disguise, while the principal apothecary of the title fantasized about a medical mission to Turkey. In 1775 when the Russian-Ottoman war was over, the Habsburg monarchy acquired, through opportune statecraft rather than military conquest, the Ottoman province of Bukovina; its detachment from Ottoman Moldavia—a sort of prologue to the modern Eastern Question—coincided with Haydn's enthusiastic deployment of Janissary style in *L'incontro improvviso* at Esterháza in 1775. Indeed, the very name of "Bukovina" now came into usage to describe this territory, invented as much as annexed by the Habsburgs, who would create a quintessentially Habsburg city at Czernowitz, marking the emergence of a new geopolitical space on the now negotiable European-Ottoman border. For Haydn at Esterháza this border became a sphere of creative cultural play, as it would be for Mozart in Vienna, with Janissary style serving as one means of negotiating and crossing the operatic frontier a century after the Ottoman defeat at Vienna and expulsion from Hungary.

Rossini's extravagant sense of operatic play was all-embracing, and it easily incorporated the Ottoman themes of the eighteenth century, which were historically enhanced by the Napoleonic interlude that so brilliantly demonstrated the dramatic intricacies—serious and comical—of sultanic aspirations to absolute power and universal empire. Venice's peace with the Ottoman empire was even older than Vienna's, dating all the way back to Passarowitz in 1718, the musical age of Gasparini and Handel. Rossini, not Venetian but definitely Adriatic, could compose on Ottoman themes with almost a century of Adriatic peace behind him, though the issue of Barbary piracy remained alive up until the very commencement of his operatic career. The second American Barbary War in 1815 and the British bombardment of Algiers in 1816 came only after Rossini had comically conquered Algiers in 1813 with *L'italiana in Algeri* and acknowledged the charm of an Ottoman prince in *Il turco in Italia* in 1814. The cast of *L'italiana* in Venice was even supposed to have included a female singer who had been ransomed from captivity in Algiers.

Yet all of Rossini's operas on Turkish subjects have a certain valedictory character—especially when viewed in historical retrospect—and may be seen as taking leave of and definitively concluding the Turkish tradition in European opera. *L'italiana in Algeri* offered a ludicrously farcical view of the

Ottoman Bey Mustafa, which in no way prevented the Italian public from recognizing in him a cartoon of preposterous masculine arrogance in Italy and throughout Europe. Isabella's vision of Mustafa as a bird in a cage (*in gabbia è già il merlotto*) absolutely reversed the operatic conception of the Christian captive as the caged singing bird, and the "conquest" of the bey was so complete that he had to surrender even his own Turkishness when he allowed himself to be ridiculously inducted into the secret European society of the Pappataci.[18] *Il turco in Italia* reversed the dynamics of *L'italiana*, for it was a Turk who now came to "conquer" Italy, in the merely romantic sense, by exercising his Rossinian musical charisma. The formerly terrifying possibility of a Turkish conquest of Italy, dating back to the Renaissance, was no longer really imaginable, and even the fear of North African pirates along the Italian coast was increasingly attenuated, so that Prince Selim was greeted as a fascinating guest. Furthermore, he himself arrived as a confirmed Italophile as if visiting on the Grand Tour, saluting Italy's irresistible appeal—"*Bella Italia, alfin ti miro*"—even as he demonstrated his own irresistibility.[19]

In their duet Selim and Fiorilla sang about the incongruity of love across cultures—"*In Italia certamente non si fa l'amor così*," "*In Turchia sicuramente non si fa l'amor così*"—but Rossini made them so musically compatible as they harmonized together that the public could not fail to recognize that the Turk and the Italian made love in exactly the same way.[20] Both *L'italiana in Algeri* and *Il turco in Italia* concluded with finales in which the Turks and Italians took leave of one another, Isabella leading the Italians on their escape from Algiers, Prince Selim wistfully taking leave of Fiorilla to return to Turkey. Both resolutions involved a dramatic separation of cultural spheres with a choral harmonizing that seemed to undermine that separation. The harmony of the Turkish and Italian choruses might be heard as a final tribute to the early modern correspondences of the Braudelian Mediterranean, even as it became the modern Mediterranean to be transformed by imperialism in the nineteenth century and mass immigration in the twentieth century.[21]

Aftermath: The Disappearance of the Singing Turk

The final and most audacious Rossinian Ottoman subject was Mehmed the Conqueror, the sultan whose conquest of Constantinople in 1453 traumatized the Renaissance Italian courts. It was, above all, the end of the Napoleonic epoch which made it possible to contemplate with philosophical appreciation the rise and fall of a conqueror of such staggering ambition. Rossini's *Maometto Secondo* allowed the sultan to stand on the stage of San Carlo in Naples in 1820 and sing, in the basso voice of Filippo Galli, his elaborately ornamented program of universal domination—just because the world of the Restoration was reassured to think that such a song could never sustain itself, that such a domination would eventually pass, whether over centuries in Turkey or over decades in France. By the time Rossini reconceived *Maometto Secondo* for Paris in 1826 as *Le siège de Corinthe*, the public could already listen with conviction to the Rossinian musical hymns to Thermopylae, Leonidas, and Greek independence.

The staging of the most fearsome conqueror in Ottoman history was an operatic enterprise precariously at risk of troubling the public. The eventual convergence between Greek resistance to the Turkish conqueror on stage in Paris and the Greek struggle for independence in the French gazettes of the 1820s produced a politically remarkable parallel of present and historical circumstances that ultimately destabilized the fictive conventions of operatic representation. The actual achievement of Greek independence, the full articulation of the Eastern Question, and the clinical acknowledgment of Turkey as the Sick Man of Europe made the Ottoman empire in the 1830s a peculiarly unoperatic subject after more than a century's procession of singing Turks. In 1830 the French occupation of Ottoman Algeria brought a new style of modern imperialism to European-Ottoman relations and a new style of European Orientalism to Western perspectives on Turkey. Modern Orientalism of the Other was in fact very different from the operatic idiom of the Enlightenment in which Europeans and Turks were closely connected by a set of overlapping cultural, musical, vocal, and personal resemblances.

From the 1680s to the 1820s, singing Turks constituted an important presence on the operatic stages of Europe, but they then disappeared from the mainstream repertory of nineteenth-century European opera. While Donizetti and Bellini both made early attempts at composing medieval Muslim subjects in the 1820s, *Zoraida* and *Zaira* respectively, neither would occupy a significant place in those composers' contributions to the repertory. Donizetti, in fact, would take Filippo Galli from his Rossinian Turkish roles and cast him not as a sultan with a harem but, very aptly, as King Henry VIII in *Anna Bolena* in 1830. Verdi's Muslim and Turkish efforts confirm the conclusion of the tradition. *I Lombardi* in 1843, with its tenor role for a Muslim prince, was revised for Paris as *Jérusalem*—without the Muslim prince. *Il corsaro* in 1848, with its Byronic Turkish tale of a heroic Christian corsair and a cruel Ottoman pasha, was among Verdi's most notable operatic failures. For the rest of the nineteenth century the presence of the Ottomans in European opera was either subliminal or submerged. One notable landmark was the failure in 1840, despite the enthusiastic support of Mozart's own son, to obtain an Italian premiere in Milan for the *Abduction*.

Rossini had relished the Mozartean style of Janissary music when orchestrating *L'italiana*, even turning the voices of the first-act finale into a human percussion ensemble of bells and drums. The Janissary accents in the music of *Maometto Secondo*, however, were largely eliminated in *Le siège de Corinthe*, thus fully absorbing the Janissary instruments into the modern percussion section. This was even more evident in the work of Beethoven, who allowed a Janissary band to make one very small appearance in the last movement of the Ninth Symphony in the 1820s, a subtle reminder of the former importance of such Turkish ensembles.

The year of *Le siège de Corinthe* in Paris, 1826, was also the year that Mahmud II abolished the Janissary corps in Istanbul in the context of Ottoman military reform. The Janissary bands in Istanbul, with their *mehter* music, were eliminated at the same time, and "Donizetti Pasha" presided over a new Western style of military music for the Ottoman empire. "The universe rises up to separate us," sang the heroine of *Maometto Secondo* to the sultan she could not help loving.[22] In fact, however, by the 1820s (as opposed to the operatic scenario of the fifteenth century) there was already a convergence taking place between Turkey and Europe, facilitated by Ottoman reform, European imperialism, international commerce, and reciprocal diplomatic engagement. In the 1720s Handel's Bajazet was permitted to sing on stage of his deep dynastic pride in "the blood of the Ottomans." His pride exercised its spell upon the public, who listened as he sang of his "triumph" in death: "è questa morte il mio trionfo eletto" (this death is my chosen triumph).[23] The triumph that he was able to achieve in circumstances of extreme abasement made Bajazet operatically compelling as a singing sultan, and in fact his tragedy became a musical triumph.

Rameau's Osman Pasha, in "Le Turc généreux" of the 1730s, was defeated not in battle but in love, and he aspired only to the very modest triumph of being remembered: "*Souvenez-vous d'Osman.*"[24] On this note of musical melancholy, almost fading away, he gave a demonstration of refined sensibility to the European public, and, like Bajazet, indicated through his Ottoman experience how to respond to circumstances of adversity. The European operatic tradition did in fact create an enormous cultural monument for commemorating, and thus remembering, the Ottoman empire by setting to music the scenarios of European-Ottoman relations and establishing at the center of European operatic culture the figure of the singing Turk. Osman Pasha's phrase of self-effacement, his plea to be remembered, offers an apt perspective on the operatic repertory of Ottoman subjects, which was destined to be largely forgotten in the nineteenth and twentieth centuries as pashas and sultans, with their harems and captives, disappeared from the operatic stages of Europe.

Notes

Introduction

1. Nancy Bisaha, *Creating East and West: Renaissance Humanists and the Ottoman Turks* (Philadelphia: University of Pennsylvania Press, 2004), 28–29; John Bohnstedt, "The Infidel Scourge of God: The Turkish Menace as Seen by German Pamphleteers of the Reformation Era," *Transactions of the American Philosophical Society* 58:9 (1968), 1–58; Preserved Smith, *The Life and Letters of Martin Luther* (New York: Houghton Mifflin, 1914), 412; Orhan Koloğlu, *Le Turc dans la presse française* (Beirut: Al-Hayat, 1971), 20; see also Almut Höfert, *Den Feind beschreiben: "Türkengefahr" und europäisches Wissen über das Osmanische Reich 1450–1600* (Frankfurt: Campus Verlag, 2003); Paul Levin, "From 'Saracen Scourge' to 'Terrible Turk': Medieval, Renaissance, and Enlightenment Images of the 'Other' in the Narrative Construction of 'Europe,'" Ph.D. dissertation, University of Southern California, 2007.

2. Stendhal, *Vie de Rossini* (Paris: Michel Lévy Frères, 1854), 55; Stendhal, *Life of Rossini*, trans. Richard Coe (Seattle: University of Washington Press, 1970), 72; all translations are my own unless otherwise cited in the notes, and in some cases, as with Stendhal, I have adjusted an existing translation with reference to the original.

3. *Constructing Border Societies on the Triplex Confinium*, ed. Drago Roksandić and Nataša Stefanac (Budapest: Central European University, History Department Working Paper Series, 2000); *Tolerance and Intolerance on the Triplex Confinium*, ed. Egidio Ivetić and Drago Roksandić (Padua: Cooperativa Libreria Editrice, Università di Padova, 2007).

4. Franco Venturi, *The End of the Old Regime in Europe, 1768–1776: The First Crisis*, trans. R. Burr Litchfield (Princeton: Princeton University Press, 1989).

5. Thomas Betzwieser, *Exotismus und "Türkenoper" in der französischen Musik des Ancien Régime* (Laaber: Laaber-Verlag, 1993); Bruce Brown, *Gluck and the French Theatre in Vienna* (Oxford: Clarendon Press, 1991); Thomas Bauman, *W. A. Mozart: Die Entführung aus dem Serail* (Cambridge: Cambridge University Press, 1987); Matthew Head, *Orientalism, Masquerade, and Mozart's Turkish Music* (London: Royal Musical Association, 2000); there have also been exceptionally valuable contributions by Eve Meyer,

"Turquerie and Eighteenth-Century Music," *Eighteenth-Century Studies* 7:4 (Summer 1974), 474–88; Eric Rice, "Representations of Janissary Music (*mehter*) as Musical Exoticism in Western Compositions, 1670–1824," *Journal of Musicological Research* 19 (1999), 41–88; Edmund Bowles, "The Impact of Turkish Military Bands on European Court Festivals in the 17th and 18th Centuries," *Early Music* 34:4 (2006), 533–59; Mary Hunter, "The *Alla Turca* Style in the Late Eighteenth Century: Race and Gender in the Symphony and the Seraglio," in *The Exotic in Western Music*, ed. Jonathan Bellman (Boston: Northeastern University Press, 1998), 43–73; Françoise Dartois-Lapeyre, "Turcs et turqueries dans les représentations en musique," in *Turcs et turqueries (XVIe-XVIIIe siècles)* (Paris: Presses de l'Université Paris-Sorbonne, 2009), 163–215; Michael Pirker, "Die Türkische Musik und Mozarts *Entführung aus dem Serail*," in *Die Klangwelt Mozarts: Eine Ausstellung des Kunsthistorischen Museums* (Vienna: Kunsthistorisches Museum, 1991), 133–48; and Giovanni Morelli, "Povero Bajazetto: Osservazioni su alcuni aspetti dell'abbattimento tematico della 'paura del turco' nell'opera veneziana del Sei-Settecento," in *Venezia e i turchi: Scontri e confronti di due civiltà* (Milan: Electa, 1985), 280–93; issues of musical exoticism are explored in the books of Anke Schmitt, *Der Exotismus in der deutschen Oper zwischen Mozart und Spohr* (Hamburg: Verlag der Musikalienhandlung Karl Dieter Wagner, 1988); Adrienne Ward, *Pagodas in Play: China on the Eighteenth-Century Italian Opera Stage* (Lewisburg, PA: Bucknell University Press, 2010); and Ralph Locke, *Musical Exoticism: Images and Reflections* (Cambridge: Cambridge University Press, 2009); valuable dissertations include those of Miriam Whaples, "Exoticism in Dramatic Music, 1600–1800," Ph.D. dissertation, Indiana University, 1958; and Margaret Griffel, "Turkish Opera from Mozart to Cornelius," Ph.D. dissertation, Columbia University, 1975; as well as the M.A. thesis of Christoph Yew at Osnabrück, 2009, published as *The Turk on the Opera Stage: A History of a Musical Cliché* (Munich: GRIN Verlag, 2009); there are very important edited volumes, including those of the Don Juan Archiv based on conferences in Vienna and Istanbul, *Ottoman Empire and European Theatre*, vol. 1, *The Age of Mozart and Selim III*, ed. Michael Hüttler and Hans Weidinger (Vienna: Hollitzer, 2013); and *Ottoman Empire and European Theatre*, vol. 2, *The Time of Joseph Haydn: From Sultan Mahmud I to Mahmud II*, ed. Michael Hüttler and Hans Weidinger (Vienna: Hollitzer, 2014); and two volumes of collected studies concerning the cultural and historical implications of the siege of Vienna, *Geschichtspolitik und "Türkenbelagerung": Kritische Studien zur "Türkenbelagerung"*, vol. 1, ed. Johannes Feichtinger and Johann Heiss (Vienna: Mandelbaum, Kritik & Utopie, 2013); and *Der erinnerte Feind: Kritische Studien zur "Türkenbelagerung"*, vol. 2, ed. Johannes Feichtinger and Johann Heiss (Vienna: Mandelbaum, Kritik & Utopie, 2013); cultural history and criticism have been particularly valuable for appreciating issues of exoticism in the European-Ottoman context, notably the work of Alain Grosrichard, *Structure du sérail: La fiction du despotisme asiatique dans l'Occident classique* (Paris: Seuil, 1979), translated as *The Sultan's Court: European Fantasies of the East*, trans. Liz Heron (London: Verso, 1998); Ruth Bernard Yeazell, *Harems of the Mind:*

Passages of Western Art and Literature (New Haven: Yale University Press, 2000); Paolo Preto, *Venezia e i turchi* (Florence: G. C. Sansoni, 1975); and Nebahat Avcioglu, *Turquerie and the Politics of Representation, 1728–1876* (Burlington, VT: Ashgate, 2011).

6. Fatma Müge Göçek, *East Encounters West: France and the Ottoman Empire in the Eighteenth Century* (Oxford: Oxford University Press, 1987); Daniel Goffman, *The Ottoman Empire and Early Modern Europe* (Cambridge: Cambridge University Press, 2002); Juan Cole, *Napoleon's Egypt: Invading the Middle East* (New York: Palgrave Macmillan, 2007); see also Eric Dursteler, *Venetians in Constantinople: Nation, Identity, and Coexistence in the Early Modern Mediterranean* (Baltimore: Johns Hopkins University Press, 2006).

7. Linda Colley, *Captives: Britain, Empire, and the World, 1600–1800* (New York: Anchor Books, 2002); Robert Davis, *Christian Slaves, Muslim Masters: White Slavery in the Mediterranean, the Barbary Coast, and Italy, 1500–1800* (New York: Palgrave Macmillan, 2003); Molly Greene, *Catholic Pirates and Greek Merchants: A Maritime History of the Mediterranean* (Princeton: Princeton University Press, 2010).

8. Martha Feldman, *Opera and Sovereignty: Transforming Myths in Eighteenth-Century Italy* (Chicago: University of Chicago Press, 2007); James Johnson, *Listening in Paris: A Cultural History* (Berkeley: University of California Press, 1995); Victoria Johnson, *Backstage at the Revolution: How the Royal Paris Opera Survived the End of the Old Regime* (Chicago: University of Chicago Press, 2009); David Chaillou, *Napoléon et l'opéra: La politique sur la scène 1810–1815* (Paris: Fayard, 2004); Benjamin Walton, *Rossini in Restoration Paris: The Sound of Modern Life* (Cambridge: Cambridge University Press, 2007); Michael Steinberg, *Listening to Reason: Culture, Subjectivity, and Nineteenth-Century Music* (Princeton: Princeton University Press, 2004).

9. Charlotte Colding Smith, *Images of Islam, 1453–1600: Turks in Germany and Central Europe* (London: Pickering & Chatto, 2014), 69–75 and 88–90; Hartmut Bobzin, "'Aber itzt hab ich den Alcoran gesehen Latinisch': Gedanken Martin Luthers zum Islam," in *Luther zwischen den Kulturen*, ed. Hans Medick and Peer Schmidt (Göttingen: Vandenhoeck & Ruprecht, 2004), 264–65.

10. Larry Wolff, "Discovering Cultural Perspective: The Intellectual History of Anthropological Thought in the Age of Enlightenment," in *The Anthropology of the Enlightenment*, ed. Larry Wolff and Marco Cipolloni (Stanford: Stanford University Press, 2007), 3–32.

11. Fernand Braudel, *The Mediterranean and the Mediterranean World in the Age of Philip II*, 2 vols., trans. Siân Reynolds (New York: Harper & Row, 1973).

12. Peter Stearns, "Modern Patterns in Emotions History," in *Doing Emotions History*, ed. Susan Matt and Peter Stearns (Urbana: University of Illinois Press, 2014), 20–22; Susan Matt, "Recovering the Invisible: Methods for the Historical Study of the Emotions," in *Doing Emotions History*, 44–45; William Reddy, *The Navigation of Feeling: A Framework for the History of the Emotions* (Cambridge: Cambridge University Press,

2001), 161–72; Nicole Eustace, *Passion Is the Gale: Emotion, Power, and the Coming of the American Revolution* (Chapel Hill: University of North Carolina Press, 2008), 171–96; see also Norbert Elias, *The Civilizing Process*, vol. 1, *The History of Manners*, trans. Edmund Jephcott (New York: Urizen Books, 1978); Peter Stearns and Carol Stearns, "Emotionology: Clarifying the History of Emotions and Emotional Standards," *American Historical Review* 90:4 (October 1985), 813–36.

13. Joan-Pau Rubiés, "Oriental Despotism and European Orientalism: Botero to Montesquieu," *Journal of Early Modern History* 9:1–2 (2005), 162; Lucette Valensi, *Birth of the Despot: Venice and the Sublime Porte*, trans. Arthur Denner (Ithaca: Cornell University Press, 1993).

14. Cole, *Napoleon's Egypt*, 125–27.

15. Goffman, *Ottoman Empire and Early Modern Europe*, 224–25.

Chapter 1: The Captive Sultan

1. Francesco Gasparini, *Il Bajazet* (Reggio, 1719), ed. Martin Ruhnke, in *Die Oper: Kritische Ausgabe von Denkmälern der Operngeschichte*, vol. 3 (Munich: G. Henle Verlag, 1985), 7–8.

2. Winton Dean and John Merrill Knapp, *Handel's Operas 1704–1726* (1987; reprint, Woodbridge, UK: Boydell Press, 2009), 534–35.

3. Galina Yermolenko, "Roxolana in Europe," in *Roxolana in European Literature, History, and Culture*, ed. Galina Yermolenko (Burlington, VT: Ashgate, 2010), 35–36.

4. Michèle Longino, *Orientalism in French Classical Drama* (Cambridge: Cambridge University Press, 2002), 109–46.

5. Christopher Marlowe, *Tamburlaine*, act 3, scene 3 (Mineola, NY: Dover, 2002), 34–35.

6. Marlowe, *Tamburlaine*, act 4, scene 4, 49.

7. William Shakespeare, *Henry IV, Part 2*, act 5, scene 2; see also Richard Hillman, "'Not Amurath an Amurath Succeeds': Playing Doubles in Shakespeare's Henriad," *English Literary Renaissance* 21:3 (September 1991), 161–89.

8. Jacques Pradon, *Tamerlan, ou la mort de Bajazet*, in *Les oeuvres de Mr. Pradon, divisées en deux tomes*, vol. 1 (Paris: La Compagnie des Libraires Associés, 1744), 99 and 104.

9. Erwin Neumann, "Tamerlan und Bajazet: Eine Antwerpener Tapisserien-Serie des 17. Jahrhunderts," in *Miscellanea Jozef Duverger: Bijdragen tot de Kunstgeschiedenis der Nederlanden*, vol. 2 (Ghent: Vereniging voor de Geschiedenis der Textielkunsten, 1968), 819–35.

10. Pradon, *Tamerlan*, 142.

11. Ibid., 183.

12. Peter Burke, *The Fabrication of Louis XIV* (New Haven: Yale University Press, 1992), 138–39.

13. Nicholas Rowe, *Tamerlane: A Tragedy in Five Acts*, in *The British Theatre; or A Collection of Plays, which are acted at the Theatres Royal, Drury Lane, Covent Garden, and*

Haymarket, vol. 10 (London: Longman, Hurst, Rees, and Orme, 1808), 13; Xavier Cervantes and Guy Le Thiec, "Sur les théâtres de l'histoire: Tamerlan et Bajazet en France et en Angleterre (1529–1724)," in *Rêver d'Orient, connaître l'Orient: Visions de l'Orient dans l'art et la littérature britanniques*, ed. Isabelle Gadoin and Marie-Élise Palmier-Chatelain (Lyon: ENS Éditions, 2008), 160–61; Dean and Knapp, *Handel's Operas 1704–1726*, 531.

14. Rowe, *Tamerlane*, 6 and 20.

15. Ibid., 28 and 45.

16. Andrea Sommer-Mathis, "Türckische Tragödia und Christliche Comödia: Die 'Türkenfeiern' 1683 in Europa," in *Geschichtspolitik und Türkenbelagerung*, ed. Johannes Feichtinger and Johann Heiss (Vienna: Mandelbaum, 2013), 91–92.

17. Sommer-Mathis, "Türckische Tragödia und Christliche Comödia," 96 and 101.

18. Silvia Dallinger, "Was macht ein Pascha auf einem Esel? Die zweite Wiener Türkenbelagerung als gegenwärtige Vergangenheit," in Feichtinger and Heiss, *Geschichtspolitik und Türkenbelagerung*, 169–71.

19. John Warrack, *German Opera: From the Beginnings to Wagner* (Cambridge: Cambridge University Press, 2004), 38; Eve Meyer, "Turquerie and Eighteenth-Century Music," *Eighteenth-Century Studies* 7:4 (Summer 1974), 475; Anke Schmitt, *Der Exotismus in der deutschen Oper zwischen Mozart und Spohr* (Hamburg: Verlag der Musikalienhandlung Karl Dieter Wagner, 1988), 114–15; Sommer-Mathis, "Türckische Tragödia und Christliche Comödia," 104–5; Margaret Griffel, "Turkish Opera from Mozart to Cornelius," Ph.D. dissertation, Columbia University, 1975, 196; Dorothea Schröder, "Cara Mustapha oder Aufstieg und Ende eines Tyrannen," in *Italian Opera in Central Europe 1614–1780*, vol. 3, *Opera Subjects and European Relationships*, ed. Norbert Dubowy et al. (Berlin: Berliner Wissenschafts-Verlag, 2007), 333–39.

20. Sommer-Mathis, "Türckische Tragödia und Christliche Comödia," 106; *Allgemeine Theater-Revue*, ed. August Lewald, Zweiter Jahrgang (Stuttgart und Tübingen: Verlag der J.G. Cotta'schen Buchhandlung, 1836), 37–38.

21. Sommer-Mathis, "Türckische Tragödia und Christliche Comödia," pp. 107–8.

22. Ibid., 107n31.

23. Ellen Harris, *Handel as Orpheus: Voice and Desire in the Chamber Cantatas* (Cambridge: Harvard University Press, 2004), 39; Roger Freitas, "An Erotic Image of the Castrato Singer," in *Italy's Eighteenth Century: Gender and Culture in the Age of the Grand Tour*, ed. Paula Findlen, Wendy Wassyng Roworth, and Catherine Sama (Stanford: Stanford University Press, 2009), 211.

24. Giulio Cesare Corradi (libretto) and Marc'Antonio Ziani (music), *Il gran Tamerlano: Drama per musica, da rappresentarsi nel famosissimo Teatro Grimano di SS. Gio. e Paulo l'Anno 1689* (Venice: Nicolini, 1689), 3–5.

25. Ibid., 6.

26. Ibid., 9–10.

27. Ibid., 8 and 74.

28. Christian Heinrich Postel (libretto) and Johann Philipp Förtsch (music), *Bajazeth und Tamerlan, in einem Sing-Spiel vorgestellt* (Hamburg: Hamburger Gänsemarkt Oper, 1690) preface, n.p.

29. Ibid., act 1, scene 1, n.p.

30. Ibid., act 1, scene 2, n.p.

31. Ibid., act 1, scene 2, n.p.

32. Ibid., act 1, scene 4, n.p.

33. Ibid., act 2 and act 3, n.p.

34. Reinhard Keiser, *Mahumeth II* (Hamburg: Hamburger Gänsemarkt Oper, 1696). The catalogue of the Austrian National Library locates the performance in Hamburg in 1696 and attributes the composition to Keiser, who did compose many operas for the Hamburg Theater am Gänsemarkt. The libretto has been attributed to Heinrich Hinsch.

35. Claudio Sartori, *I libretti italiani a stampa dalle origini al 1800*, 7 vols. (Cuneo: Bertola & Locatelli Editori, 1990–94), vol. 5, 295.

36. William Holmes, *Opera Observed: Views of a Florentine Impresario in the Early Eighteenth Century* (Chicago: University of Chicago Press, 1994), 31–32; Domenico Pietropaolo and Mary Ann Parker, *The Baroque Libretto: Italian Operas and Oratorios in the Thomas Fisher Library at the University of Toronto* (Toronto: University of Toronto Press, 2011), 150.

37. Antonio Salvi (libretto) and Alessandro Scarlatti (music), *Il gran Tamerlano: Drama per musica, rappresentato nella Villa di Pratolino* (Florence: Nella Stamperia di Sua Altezza Reale, per Anton Maria Albizzini, 1706), 35.

38. Ibid.

39. Edward Joseph Dent, *Alessandro Scarlatti: His Life and Works* (London: Edward Arnold, 1905), 106–7.

40. Salvi and Scarlatti, *Il gran Tamerlano*, 35.

41. Alfred Dürr and Richard Jones, *The Cantatas of J. S. Bach: With Their Librettos in German-English Parallel Text* (Oxford: Oxford University Press, 2005), 231–32.

42. Saverio Franchi, *Drammaturgia Romana,* vol. 2 *(1702–1750)* (Rome: Edizioni di Storia e Letteratura, 1997), 128–29.

43. *Cantata: Nelle presenti vittorie riportate dall'armi cesaree contro il turco,* cantata d'Ignazio di Bonis, posta in musica dal Sig. Giuseppe Amadori (Rome: per Francesco Gonzaga, in Via Lata, 1717), 4.

44. Handel, *Tamerlano* (London, 1724), libretto (Florence: Teatro del Maggio Musicale Fiorentino, 2001), act 1, scene 1, 41.

45. Gasparini, *Il Bajazet* (Reggio, 1719), in *Die Oper*, ed. Ruhnke, vol. 3, 21 and 36–40; *Il Trace in catena: Drama per musica da rappresentarsi nella sala de' Signori Capranica* (Rome: Bernabò, 1717).

46. *Cantata: Nelle presenti vittorie* (Rome, 1717), 4.

47. Ibid., 7–9.

48. Dennis Libby, "Paita, Giovanni," in *The New Grove Dictionary of Opera*, ed. Stanley Sadie, vol. 3 (Oxford: Oxford University Press, 1997), 828; "Giovanni Paita," *Quell'usignolo: Le site des premiers interprètes baroques et classiques*, http://www.quellusignolo.fr/tenors/paita.html

49. Sartori, *I libretti italiani*, vol. 5, 296.

50. Paolo Preto, *Venezia e i turchi* (Florence: G. C. Sansoni, 1975), 25–66; see also Filomena Viviana Tagliaferri, "Subjects in Between: Three Different Ways of Translating Experience by Italian Travelers in Late 17th, Early 18th Century Ottoman Space," *Cahiers de la Méditerranée* 88 (2014), 329–51.

51. Piovene (libretto) and Gasparini (music), *Tamerlano: Tragedia per musica, da rappresentarsi nel Teatro Tron di San Cassiano* (Venice: Marino Rossetti, 1710 *more veneto* [by Venetian custom], actually 1711); Piovene (libretto) and Gasparini (music), *Bajazette: Tragedia per musica, da rappresentarsi nel Teatro Grimani di San Samuele, l'Anno 1723, per la Fiera dell'Ascensione* (Venice: Marino Rossetti, 1723).

52. Dean and Knapp, *Handel's Operas, 1704–1726*, 534; C. Steven LaRue, *Handel and His Singers: The Creation of the Royal Academy Operas, 1720–1728* (Oxford: Clarendon Press, 1995), 19 and 48–49; Reinhard Strohm, "Handel and His Italian Opera Texts," in *Essays on Handel and Italian Opera*, ed. Reinhard Strohm (Cambridge: Cambridge University Press, 1985), 50.

53. LaRue, *Handel and His Singers*, 47–50, 58–60; Dean and Knapp, *Handel's Operas, 1704–1726*, 534–37; Gasparini, *Il Bajazet* (Reggio, 1719), in *Die Oper*, ed. Ruhnke, vol. 3, 51.

54. Michael Talbot and Kurt Markstrom, "Piovene, Agostin," *The New Grove Dictionary of Opera*, vol. 3, 1016.

55. Piovene (libretto) and Gasparini (music), *Tamerlano* (Venice, 1710/1711), "al lettore," 5–6; Piovene (libretto) and Gasparini (music), *Bajazette* (Venice, 1723), "al lettore," 5–6.

56. Handel, *Tamerlano* (London, 1724), libretto, act 1, scene 1, 39.

57. Piovene (libretto) and Gasparini (music), *Tamerlano* (Venice, 1710/1711), "al lettore," 6; Piovene (libretto) and Gasparini (music), *Bajazette* (Venice, 1723), "al lettore," 6.

58. Peter Gay, *The Enlightenment: The Rise of Modern Paganism* (New York: Alfred A. Knopf, 1966).

59. Handel, *Tamerlano* (London, 1724), libretto, act 1, scene 1, 41; Gasparini, "Forte e lieto," and Handel, "Forte e lieto," *Three Baroque Tenors* (CD; Ian Bostridge, with Bernard Labadie and The English Concert) (EMI, 2010), tracks 5 and 6.

60. Dean and Knapp, *Handel's Operas, 1704–1726*, 539; see also Reinhard Strohm, "Francesco Gasparini's Later Operas and Handel," in Strohm, *Essays on Handel and Italian Opera*, 80–92.

61. Luigi Rossi, "Lamento di Mustafà e Bajazet," text (CD liner notes), in *Lamenti Barocchi*, vol. 1 (Sergio Vartolo, Cappella Musicale di S. Petronio) (Naxos, 1995), 10.

62. Ibid., 11.

63. Ibid., 13.

64. Ibid., 15.

65. Giovanni Morelli, "Povero Bajazetto: Osservazioni su alcuni aspetti dell'abbattimento tematico della 'paura del turco' nell'opera veneziana del Sei-Settecento," in *Venezia e i Turchi: Scontri e confronti di due civiltà* (Milan: Electa, 1985), 280; see also Rolando Minuti, *Oriente barbarico e storiografia settecentesca: Rappresentazioni della storia dei Tartari nella cultura francese del XVIII secolo* (Venice: Marsilio, 1994).

66. Handel, *Tamerlano* (London, 1724), libretto, act 2, scene 9, 66.

67. Dean and Knapp, *Handel's Operas 1704–1726*, 80; Donald Burrows, *Handel*, 2nd ed. (Oxford: Oxford University Press, 2012), 31–32.

68. Lady Mary Wortley Montagu, "Verses written in the Chiosk of the British Palace, at Pera, overlooking the city of Constantinople," in *The Letters and Works of Lady Mary Wortley Montagu*, vol. 2, ed. Lord Wharncliffe (London: George Bell and Sons, 1887), 464–66.

69. Handel, *Tamerlano* (London, 1724), libretto, act 3, scene 1, 77.

70. Dean and Knapp, *Handel's Operas, 1704–1726*, 340.

71. Handel, *Tamerlano* (London, 1724), libretto, act 3, scene 8, 89.

72. Lady Mary Wortley Montagu, *The Turkish Embassy Letters*, ed. Malcolm Jack (London: Virago Press, 1994), 161; Anthony Hicks, "Tamerlano," *The New Grove Dictionary of Opera*, vol. 4, 642.

73. Handel, *Tamerlano* (London, 1724), libretto, act 3, scene 8, 90.

74. Dean and Knapp, *Handel's Operas, 1704–1726*, 542.

75. Handel, *Tamerlano* (London, 1724), libretto, act 3, scene 8, 90.

76. Dean and Knapp, *Handel's Operas, 1704–1726*, 542–46.

77. Handel, *Tamerlano* (London, 1724), libretto, act 3, scene 10, 92.

78. Ibid.; Dean and Knapp, *Handel's Operas, 1704–1726*, 549.

79. Handel, *Tamerlano* (London, 1724), libretto, act 3, scene 11, 96.

80. Ellen Harris, *George Frideric Handel: A Life with Friends* (New York: Norton, 2014), 112.

81. Frédéric Delaméa, "The Noble Death-Pangs of Vivaldian Opera" (CD liner notes) in Vivaldi, *Bajazet* (Fabio Biondi, Europa Galante) (EMI Records/Virgin Classics, 2005), 17.

82. Henry Laurens, *Les origines intellectuelles de l'expédition d'Égypte: L'orientalisme Islamisant en France, 1698–1798* (Istanbul and Paris: Editions Isis, Institut Français d'Études Anatoliennes, 1987), 171–72; see also John Stoye, *Marsigli's Europe, 1680–1730: The Life and Times of Luigi Ferdinando Marsigli* (New Haven: Yale University Press, 1994).

83. Delaméa, "Noble-Death Pangs of Vivaldian Opera," 13–15.

84. Vivaldi, *Bajazet* (Verona, 1735), libretto (CD liner notes) (EMI Records/Virgin Classics, 2005), act 3, scene 10, 142.

85. Morelli, "Povero Bajazetto," 293.

86. Michael Talbot and Kurt Markstrom, "Piovene, Agostin," *New Grove Dictionary of Opera*, vol. 3, 1016; Dean and Knapp, *Handel's Operas 1704–1726*, 531–32; *Cyclopedia of Music and Musicians*, ed. John Denison Champlin, vol. 3 (New York: Charles Scribner's Sons, 1899), 456; Gasparini, *Il Bajazet* (Reggio, 1719), in *Die Oper*, ed. Ruhnke, vol. 3, 42–44; Cervantes and Le Thiec, "Sur les théâtres de l'histoire: Tamerlan et Bajazet," 172–74.

87. Metoda Kokole, "The 'Comedia Italiana in Musica' (1660) and the Opera *Il Tamerlano* (1732) in Ljubljana," in *Italian Opera in Central Europe*, vol. 1, *Institutions and Ceremonies*, ed. Melania Bucciarelli, Norbert Dubowy, and Reinhard Strohm (Berlin: Berliner Wissenschafts-Verlag, 2006), 60–66.

88. Dean and Knapp, *Handel's Operas 1704–1726*, 556–57.

89. *Tamerlan: Opera en trois actes, représenté pour la première fois, sur le Théâtre de l'Opéra, le 27 Fructidor an X, les paroles sont de M. Morel, la musique est de M. Winter* (Paris: Chez Roullet, 1815), 1.

90. *Tamerlán*, Národní Divadlo Praha, 1.12.1977 Premiere, http://vis.idu.cz/ProductionDetail.aspx?id=18320&tab=photo&print=1

Chapter 2: The Generous Turk

1. Molière, *Le bourgeois gentilhomme*, ed. Jean Thoraval (Paris: Bordas, 1984), 100.

2. Georgia Cowart, *The Triumph of Pleasure: Louis XIV and the Politics of Spectacle* (Chicago: University of Chicago Press, 2008), 101–2 and 112–13.

3. Molière, *Le bourgeois gentilhomme*, 98; Michèle Longino, *Orientalism in French Classical Drama* (Cambridge: Cambridge University Press, 2002), 111–15, 138–43; Françoise Dartois-Lapeyre, "Turcs et turqueries dans les représentations en musique," in *Turcs et turqueries: XVIe-XVIIIe siècles* (Paris: Presses de l'Université Paris-Sorbonne, 2009), 181–82; see also Nicholas Dew, *Orientalism in Louis XIV's France* (Oxford: Oxford University Press, 2009); Miriam Whaples, "Early Exoticism Revisited," in *The Exotic in Western Music*, ed. Jonathan Bellman (Boston: Northeastern University Press, 1998), 12–13.

4. James Anthony, "L'Europe galante," *The New Grove Dictionary of Opera*, ed. Stanley Sadie (Oxford: Oxford University Press, 1997), vol. 2, 87–88; *L'Europe galante*, http://www.musicologie.org/Biographies/campra_andre.html.

5. Dartois-Lapeyre, "Turcs et turqueries dans les représentations en musique," 189–93; Adrienne Ward, *Pagodas in Play: China on the Eighteenth-Century Italian Opera Stage* (Lewisburg, PA: Bucknell University Press, 2010), 173–79; Thomas Betzwieser, *Exotismus und "Türkenoper" in der französichen Musik des Ancien Régime* (Laaber: Laaber-Verlag, 1993), 202–3, 208–11, 226–31.

6. Bent Holm, *The Taming of the Turk: Ottomans on the Danish Stage 1596–1896* (Vienna: Hollitzer, 2014), 123–25.

7. C. D. Rouillard, "Un 'Arlequin Grand Visir' joué à Paris en 1687 et ses échos au théâtre de la foire," *Revue de la Société d'Histoire du Théâtre* 28:3 (1976), 203–19; Dar-

tois-Lapeyre, "Turcs et turqueries dans les représentations en musique," 190; Holm, *Taming of the Turk*, 125–31.

8. *Arlequin Mahomet: Pièce d'un acte, par Monsieur le S[age], representée à la Foire de S. Laurent* (Paris, 1714); Daniel Heartz, "Terpsichore at the Fair: Old and New Dance Airs in Two Vaudeville Comedies by Lesage," in *From Garrick to Gluck: Essays on Opera in the Age of Enlightenment* (Hillsdale, NY: Pendragon Press, 2004), 142.

9. Daniel Heartz, *Music in European Capitals: The Galant Style 1720–1780* (New York: Norton, 2003), 701–2; Thomas Crow, *Painters and Public Life in Eighteenth-Century Paris* (New Haven: Yale University Press, 1987), 65–66; Dartois-Lapeyre, "Turcs et turqueries dans les représentations en musique," 189–93; see also Betzwieser, *Exotismus und "Türkenoper" in der französichen Musik des Ancien Régime*, 201–17.

10. *Arlequin sultane favorite, pièce en trois actes, par Monsieur le T[ellier], representée à la Foire de S. Germain* (Paris, 1715), act 1, scene 2.

11. Ibid., act 1, scene 3.

12. Ibid., act 2, scene 12.

13. Ibid., act 2, scene 12.

14. Ibid., act 1, scene 7.

15. Ibid., act 3, scene 9.

16. *Arlequin au sérail: Comédie en un acte en prose, representée pour la première fois le 29 mai 1747, par M. Saint-Foix* (Paris, 1747); *Arlequin esclave à Baghdad, ou le calife généreux: Comédie en un acte, en prose et vaudevilles, par le citoyen T. L. Vallier* (Paris, An VII, 1798–99); *Arlequin odalisque: Comédie-parade en un acte, en prose, melée de vaudevilles, par Citoyen Auger* (Paris, An VIII, 1800); Bent Holm, "The Staging of the Turk: The Turk in the Danish Theatre of the Eighteenth Century," in *Ottoman Empire and European Theatre*, vol. 1, *The Age of Mozart and Selim III*, ed. Michael Hüttler and Hans Weidinger (Vienna: Hollitzer, 2013), 408; Matthias Pernerstorfer, "The Second Turkish Siege of Vienna (1683) Reflected in Its First Centenary," in *Age of Mozart and Selim III*, 526–27; Johann Heiss, "Die Ereignisse zum hundertjährigen Jubiläum 1783," in *Geschichtspolitik und Türkenbelagerung*, ed. Johannes Feichtinger and Johann Heiss (Vienna: Mandelbaum, 2013), 71–72; Holm, *Taming of the Turk*, 108–9.

17. Fatma Müge Göçek, *East Encounters West: France and the Ottoman Empire in the Eighteenth Century* (Oxford: Oxford University Press, 1987), 72.

18. Rouillard, "Un 'Arlequin Grand Visir' joué à Paris," 215.

19. Orlin Sabev, "European Printers in Istanbul during Joseph Haydn's Era: Ibrahim Müteferrika and Others," in *Ottoman Empire and European Theatre*, vol. 2, *The Time of Joseph Haydn: From Sultan Mahmud I to Mahmud II*, ed. Michael Hüttler and Hans Weidinger (Vienna: Hollitzer, 2014), 197–201.

20. Marianne Roland Michel, "Exoticism and Genre Painting in Eighteenth-Century France," in *The Age of Watteau, Chardin, and Fragonard: Masterpieces of French Genre Painting*, ed. Colin Bailey (New Haven: Yale University Press, 2003), 110; Göçek, *East*

Encounters West, 44–46; see also Auguste Boppe, "Les 'Peintres de Turcs' au XVIIIᵉ siècle," *Gazette des Beaux-Arts* (Paris, 1905), 43–55 and 220–30.

21. Ulrich Marzolph, ed., *The Arabian Nights in Transnational Perspective* (Detroit: Wayne State University Press, 2007), 288; Laura Gonzenbach, *Fiabe siciliane* (Rome: Donzelli editore, 1999), xxiv.

22. James Anthony, "Printed Editions of André Campra's *L'Europe galante*," *Musical Quarterly* 56:1 (January 1970), 64–66.

23. Göçek, *East Encounters West*, 47; see also Orhan Koloğlu, *Le Turc dans la presse française* (Beirut: Al-Hayat, 1971), 151–52.

24. Koloğlu, *Le Turc dans la presse française*, 135.

25. Nebahat Avcioğlu, *Turquerie and the Politics of Representation, 1728–1876* (Burlington, VT: Ashgate, 2011), 45–46, 62–70.

26. Voltaire, *Zaïre*, ed. Claude Blum (Paris: Librairie Larousse, 1972), 62; see also Daniel Winkler, "Crusaders, Love, and Tolerance: Tragic and Operatic Taste in and around Voltaire's *Zaïre* (1732)," in *Time of Joseph Haydn*, 445–61.

27. Robert Davis, *Christian Slaves, Muslim Masters: White Slavery in the Mediterranean, the Barbary Coast, and Italy, 1500–1800* (New York: Palgrave Macmillan, 2003), 23; Linda Colley, *Captives: Britain, Empire, and the World, 1600–1800* (New York: Anchor Books, 2002), 44 and 53.

28. Voltaire, *Essai sur les Moeurs*, ed. René Pomeau (Paris: Garnier Frères, 1963), vol. 2, 807–8; see also Alain Grosrichard, *Structure du sérail: La fiction du despotisme asiatique dans l'Occident classique* (Paris: Seuil, 1979), translated as *The Sultan's Court: European Fantasies of the East*, trans. Liz Heron (London: Verso, 1998); Ruth Bernard Yeazell, *Harems of the Mind: Passages of Western Art and Literature* (New Haven: Yale University Press, 2000); Esin Akalin, "The Ottoman Seraglio on European Stages," in *Age of Mozart and Selim III*, 339–73; Koloğlu, *Le Turc dans la presse française*, 84–87 and 105–6.

29. Graham Sadler, "*Les Indes galantes*," in *The New Grove Dictionary of Opera*, vol. 2, 795–96.

30. François Lesure, "Rameau et l'opéra-ballet" (CD liner notes), in Rameau, *Les Indes galantes* (Orchestre Jean-François Paillard) (Erato, 1974), 13–14; Dartois-Lapeyre, "Turcs et turqueries dans les représentations en musique," 196–97.

31. Jean-Philippe Rameau, *Les Indes galantes* (CD liner notes; Orchestre Jean-François Paillard) (Erato, 1974), act 1, "Le Turc généreux," libretto, scene 1, 48; Rameau, *Les Indes galantes, par M. Rameau, représenté en 1735* (Paris, 1735), musical score, 74; in the original score Osman sings of Emilie's "useless ardors" (*inutiles ardeurs*), presumably for the man she loves, though in other texts her ardors become "useless griefs" (*inutiles douleurs*).

32. Rameau, *Les Indes galantes*, act 1, "Le Turc généreux," libretto, scene 4, 58.

33. Ibid., 60.

34. Rameau, *Les Indes galantes* (Paris, 1735), musical score, 113.

35. Rameau, *Les Indes galantes*, act 1, "Le Turc généreux," libretto, scene 4, 60.

36. Ibid.; Rameau, *Les Indes galantes* (Paris, 1735), musical score, 113.

37. Sadler, "*Les Indes galantes*," 795–96; Bruce Brown, *Gluck and the French Theatre in Vienna* (Oxford: Clarendon Press, 1991), 186–89.

38. Rameau, *Les Indes galantes*, act 1, "Le Turc généreux," libretto, scene 4, 62; *Les Indes galantes* (Paris, 1735), musical score, 113–14.

39. Rameau, *Les Indes galantes* (Paris, 1735), musical score, 125.

40. Ibid., 125–26.

41. Rameau, *Les Indes galantes*, act 1, "Le Turc généreux," libretto, scene 5, 64; *Les Indes galantes* (Paris, 1735), musical score, 141; see also Timothy Taylor, "Peopling the Stage: Opera, Otherness, and New Musical Representations in the Eighteenth Century," *Cultural Critique* 36 (Spring 1997), 61–63.

42. Colley, *Captives*, 76–77.

43. Colley, *Captives*, 53–54 and 80–81; Davis, *Christian Slaves, Muslim Masters*, 150–53, 170, and 178–79; Holm, "Staging of the Turk," 405.

44. Colley, *Captives*, 80–81.

45. Davis, *Christian Slaves, Muslim Masters*, 182–83.

46. Colley, *Captives*, 99–101.

47. Rameau, *Les Indes Galantes*, act 3, "Les fleurs," libretto, scene 3, 90.

48. Ibid., 92.

49. Antonio Salvi (libretto) and Antonio Vivaldi (music), *Scanderbeg, dramma per musica, da rappresentarsi in Firenze, nel Teatro degl'Illustriss. SS. Accademici Immobili, posto in Via della Pergola, nel Estate dell'Anno MDCCXVIII* (Florence: Da Anton Maria Albizzini, 1718); H.C. Robbins Landon, *Vivaldi: Voice of the Baroque* (Chicago: University of Chicago Press, 1993), 55.

50. Salvi and Vivaldi, *Scanderbeg*, act 3, scene 7, 56; see also Oliver Schmitt, *Skanderbeg: Der neue Alexander auf dem Balkan* (Regensburg: Friedrich Pustet Verlag, 2009).

51. Salvi and Vivaldi, *Scanderbeg*, act 2, scene 9, 40–41.

52. Ibid., act 3, scene 9, 58.

53. Lois Rosow, "Scanderberg," *The New Grove Dictionary of Opera*, vol. 4, 199; Dartois-Lapeyre, "Turcs et turqueries dans les représentations en musique," 207–8.

54. Philip Weller, "Chassé (de Chinais), Claude Louis Dominique," *The New Grove Dictionary of Opera*, vol. 1, 824–25.

55. François Francoeur (music) and François Rebel (music), *Scanderberg, tragédie représentée pour la première fois par l'Académie Royale de Musique, 27 octobre 1735* (Paris: L'Imprimerie de Jean-Baptiste-Christophe Ballard, 1735), act 1, scene 1.

56. Ibid., act 4, scene 6.

57. Betzwieser, *Exotismus*, 422–24; see also Margaret Griffel, "Turkish Opera from Mozart to Cornelius," Ph.D. dissertation, Columbia University, 1975, 125–26.

58.   Francoeur and Rebel, *Scanderberg* (Paris, 1735), act 5, scene 5.

59.   François Francoeur (music) and François Rebel (music), *Scanderberg, tragédie représentée devant Leurs Majestés à Fontainebleau le 22 octobre 1763* (Paris: L'Imprimerie de Christophe Ballard, 1763), act 5, scene 6.

60.   Francoeur and Rebel, *Scanderberg* (Fontainebleau, 1763), act 5, scene 6.

61.   Ibid., act 5, scene 7.

Chapter 3: The Triumphant Sultana

1.   Thomas Betzwieser, *Exotismus und "Türkenoper" in der französichen Musik des Ancien Régime* (Laaber: Laaber-Verlag, 1993), 217 and 432.

2.   Paolo Preto, "Il mito del Turco nella letteratura veneziana," in *Venezia e i Turchi: Scontri e confronti di due civiltà* (Milan: Electa, 1985), 143; see also Preto, *Venezia e i Turchi* (Florence: G. C. Sansoni, 1975).

3.   Carlo Goldoni (libretto), *Lugrezia Romana in Costantinopoli, dramma comico, da rappresentarsi in musica dalla Compagnia de' Comici nel Teatro Grimani di San Samuele, il carnevale dell'anno 1737* (Venice: Alvise Valvasense, 1737), preface, to the reader.

4.   Ibid., act 1, scene 1.

5.   Ibid., act 1, scene 1 and scene 2.

6.   Ibid., act 2, scene 9.

7.   Ibid., act 1, scene 11.

8.   Ibid., act 2, scene 11.

9.   Ibid., act 3, scene 5.

10.   Ibid., act 3, scene 8.

11.   *Osmano Re di Tunisi, tragicommedia del D. C. G.* [Carlo Goldoni?], *ad uso della Compagnia de' Comici del celebre Teatro Grimani di San Samuele in Venezia* (Venice, 1740); Anna Scannapieco, "Alla ricerca di un Goldoni perduto: 'Osmano Re di Tunisi,'" *Quaderni Veneti* 20 (1994), 9–56.

12.   Marianne Roland Michel, "Exoticism and Genre Painting in Eighteenth-Century France," in *The Age of Watteau, Chardin, and Fragonard: Masterpieces of French Genre Painting*, ed. Colin Bailey (New Haven: Yale University Press, 2003), 111; see also Auguste Boppe, "Les 'Peintres de Turcs' au XVIIIe siècle," *Gazette des Beaux-Arts* (Paris, 1905), in two parts, 226–27.

13.   Perrin Stein, "Amédée Van Loo's Costume Turc: The French Sultana," *Art Bulletin* 78:3 (September 1996), 419–20.

14.   Christian Baulez, "Le goût turc: François Rémond et le goût turc dans la famille royale au temps de Louis XVI," *L'Objet d'Art: Magazine de Collection* 2 (December 1987), 36–39; Charlotte Vignon, "Turkish Taste at the Court of Marie-Antoinette," *The Frick Collection: Members' Magazine* (Spring/Summer 2011), 8–13.

15.   Daniel Heartz, *Music in European Capitals: The Galant Style 1720–1780* (New York: Norton, 2003), 703–9.

16. Paul Salvatore, *Favart's Unpublished Plays: The Rise of the Popular Comic Opera* (New York: Institute of French Studies, 1935), 280.

17. Salvatore, *Favart's Unpublished Plays*, 80–88.

18. Isabelle Moindrot, "The 'Turk' and the 'Parisienne': From Favart's *Soliman Second, ou Les trois sultanes* (1761) to *Les trois sultanes* (Pathé, 1912)," in *Ottoman Empire and European Theatre*, vol. 1, *The Age of Mozart and Selim III*, ed. Michael Hüttler and Hans Weidinger (Vienna: Hollitzer, 2013), 433.

19. James Johnson, *Listening in Paris: A Cultural History* (Berkeley: University of California Press, 1995), 105–6.

20. Boppe, "Les 'Peintres de Turcs' au XVIIIᵉ siècle," 226–29; see also Galina Yermolenko, "Roxolana in Europe," in *Roxolana in European Literature, History and Culture*, ed. Galina Yermolenko (Burlington, VT: Ashgate, 2010), 23–55; David Hammerbeck, "*Les trois sultanes*: French Enlightenment Comedy and the Veil," *Journal of Dramatic Theory and Criticism* 18:2 (Spring 2004), 55–78.

21. Leslie Peirce, *The Imperial Harem: Women and Sovereignty in the Ottoman Empire* (New York: Oxford University Press, 1993), 61.

22. Ibid., 61–62.

23. Ibid., 63.

24. Joan Landes, *Women and the Public Sphere in the Age of the French Revolution* (Ithaca: Cornell University Press, 1988), 17–90.

25. Charles-Simon Favart, *Soliman Second ou Les trois sultanes, comédie en trois actes et en vers* (Paris: Chez Didot, 1772), 3.

26. Favart, *Soliman Second ou Les trois sultanes* (1772), 20, 29, 36.

27. Vignon, "Turkish Taste at the Court of Marie-Antoinette," 12–13; Boppe, "Les 'Peintres de Turcs' au XVIIIᵉ siècle," 229.

28. Françoise Dartois-Lapeyre, "Turcs et turqueries dans les représentations en musique," in *Turcs et turqueries: XVIᵉ–XVIIIᵉ siècles* (Paris: Presses de l'Université Paris-Sorbonne, 2009), 200; Eve Meyer, "Turquerie and Eighteenth-Century Music," *Eighteenth-Century Studies* 7:4 (Summer 1974), 478n15.

29. Moindrot, "'Turk' and the 'Parisienne,'" 434.

30. Ibid., 437.

31. Favart, *Soliman Second ou Les trois sultanes* (1772), 4 and 11.

32. Ibid., 17.

33. Ibid., 18.

34. Ibid., 18.

35. Ibid., 19.

36. Ibid., 22–24.

37. Yermolenko, "Introduction," in *Roxolana in European Literature, History and Culture*, 2.

38. "Air que chant Mme Favart s'accompagnant de la harpe dans le role de Rox-

elane," in *Soliman Second ou Les trois sultanes, representé sur le Théâtre de la Comédie Italienne, le 9 Avril 1761, mis en musique de M. Gibert, les paroles sont de M. Favart* (Paris: Chez M. le Menu, 1761?), 9; Favart, *Soliman Second ou Les trois sultanes* (1772), 41.

39. Favart, *Soliman Second ou Les trois sultanes* (1772), 40.

40. Ibid., 37.

41. Ibid., 49.

42. Ibid., 57.

43. Ibid., 57.

44. Robert Darnton, *Forbidden Best-Sellers of Pre-Revolutionary France* (New York: Norton, 1995), 137–66.

45. *Il Trionfo di Solimano ovvero Il trionfo maggiore è vincere se stesso, dramma per musica, da rappresentarsi in Firenze, nel Teatro degl'Illustriss. SS. Accademici Immobili, posto in Via della Pergola, sotto la protezione dell'Altezza Reale il Serenissimo Gio. Gastone, Gran Principe di Toscana* (Florence: Da Anton Maria Albizzini, 1719).

46. Margaret Griffel, "Turkish Opera from Mozart to Cornelius," Ph.D. dissertation, Columbia University, 1975, 166–67.

47. Sven Hansell, "Migliavacca, Giovanni Ambrogio," *The New Grove Dictionary of Opera*, 4 vols., ed. Stanley Sadie, vol. 3 (Oxford: Oxford University Press, 1997), 381–82; David Perez, *Solimano*, introduction by Howard Mayer Brown (New York/London: Garland, 1978), preface.

48. Giovanni Ambrogio Migliavacca (libretto) and Johann Adolph Hasse (music), *Solimano, dramma per musica, da rappresentarsi nel Teatro della Regia Elettoral Corte de Dresda* (Dresden: Stamperia Regia per la Vedova Stössel, 1753); Giovanni Battista Lampugnani (music), *Solimano, dramma per musica, da rappresentarsi nel Real Teatro di S. Cecilia dell'Unione de' Musici nell'autunno di quest'anno 1763* (Palermo: Antonino Toscano, 1763); *Solimano: Dramma per musica da rappresentarsi nel Teatro di S. M. B.* (pasticcio) (London: G. Woodfall, 1758).

49. Migliavacca and Hasse, *Solimano* (Dresden, 1753); Domenico Fischietti (music), *Solimano, dramma per musica, da rappresentarsi nel Teatro Giustinian di San Moisè nel carnevale 1755* (Venice: Modesto Fenzo, 1755); *Solimano* (pasticcio) (London, 1758); Lampugnani, *Solimano* (Palermo, 1763); Baldassare Galuppi (music), *Il Solimano* (Venice: Modesto Fenzo, 1769); Jennifer Griesbach, "*Solimano* ('Suleyman'): *Dramma per musica* in three acts by David Perez," *The New Grove Dictionary of Opera*, vol. 4, 447.

50. Migliavacca and Hasse, *Solimano* (Dresden, 1753), 9–10.

51. Rudolph Erich Raspe, *Soliman der Zweyte, oder, Die drey Sultaninnen, in drei Handlungen, aus dem Französischen des Herrn Favart* (Hamburg?, 1765); Karl Starke (libretto), *Soliman der Zweyte, oder, Die drey Sultaninnen, ein Lustspiel* (Vienna: Gedruckt bey Johann Thomas Edlen von Trattnern, 1770).

52. Yermolenko, "Roxolana in Europe," 40–41.

53. Bent Holm, "The Staging of the Turk: The Turk in the Danish Theatre of the

Eighteenth Century," in *Age of Mozart and Selim III*, 410–12; see also Bent Holm, *The Taming of the Turk: Ottomans on the Danish Stage 1596–1896* (Vienna: Hollitzer, 2014), 111–17.

54. *Mozart's Letters, Mozart's Life*, ed. and trans. Robert Spaethling (New York: Norton, 2000), letter of December 30, 1774, 50.

55. Lady Mary Wortley Montagu, *The Turkish Embassy Letters*, ed. Malcolm Jack (London: Virago Press, 1994), letter of April 1, 1717, 59; Ruth Bernard Yeazell, *Harems of the Mind: Passages of Western Art and Literature* (New Haven: Yale University Press, 2000), 17–19, 22–24.

56. Isaac Bickerstaffe, *The Sultan, or a Peep into the Seraglio: A Farce in Two Acts*, 2nd ed. (London: C. Dilly, 1787), 21; see also Esin Akalin, "The Ottoman Seraglio on European Stages," in *Age of Mozart and Selim III*, 353–61.

57. Giovanni Bertati (libretto), *Il Serraglio di Osmano, dramma giocoso per musica* (Venice: Antonio Casali, 1785), 13; Luigi Nerici, *Storia della Musica in Lucca*, in *Memorie e documenti per servire alla storia di Lucca*, vol. 12 (Lucca: Tipografia Giusti, 1880), 340; see also *Pagine dedicate al compositore Giuseppe Gazzaniga: Il Serraglio di Osmano*, http://www.italianopera.org/compositori/G/c2182002.html; *Almanacco di Gherardo Casaglia*, http://www.amadeusonline.net

58. Bertati, *Il Serraglio di Osmano*, 63.

59. Ian Woodfield, *Performing Operas for Mozart: Impresarios, Singers, and Troupes* (Cambridge: Cambridge University Press, 2011), 75.

60. Bertil van Boer, "*Soliman II, eller De tre sultaninnorna*: A Gustavian Turkish Opera" (CD liner notes), in Joseph Martin Kraus (music), *Soliman II* (Philip Brunelle) (Virgin Classics, 1992), 7.

61. Kraus, *Soliman II* (CD liner notes), libretto, act 3, 36–41.

62. Suna Suner, "The Earliest Opera Performances in the Ottoman World and the Role of Diplomacy," in *Age of Mozart and Selim III*, 189–92; see also Holm, "Staging of the Turk," 419–20.

63. Erich Duda, "Mozart's Pupil and Friend: Franz Xaver Süssmayr's Sinfonia Turchesca, *Il turco in Italia*, and *Soliman der Zweite*," in *Age of Mozart and Selim III*, 545–46; Griffel, "Turkish Opera from Mozart to Cornelius," 297–311; Franz Xaver Süssmayr (music), *Soliman der Zweite, oder, Die drey Sultaninnen, ein Singspiel, nach dem Französischen des Herrn Favart bearbeitet von Franz Xaver Huber, aufgeführt auf den k. k. Hoftheatern* (Vienna: J. B. Wallishauser, 1799); Franz Xaver Süssmayr (music), *Soliman der Zweite*, Musikhandschrift, Partitur, Musiksammlung, Österreichische Nationalbibliothek, KT.419.

64. Afred Loewenberg, *Annals of Opera 1597–1940*, 3rd ed. (London: John Calder, 1978), 1 October 1799, *Soliman der Zweite*; s.v. "Willmann, Magdalena," *A Dictionary of Music and Musicians*, ed. George Grove, vol. 4 (London: Macmillan, 1889), 461; Peter Clive, *Beethoven and His World: A Biographical Dictionary* (Oxford: Oxford University Press, 2001), 399–400.

65. Yermolenko, "Roxolana in Europe," 42.

66. Stanford Shaw, *History of the Ottoman Empire and Modern Turkey*, vol. 1, *Empire of the Gazis: The Rise and Decline of the Ottoman Empire 1280–1808* (Cambridge: Cambridge University Press, 1976), 246–47.

67. Favart, *Soliman Second ou Les trois sultanes* (1772), 59.

Chapter 4: The Turkish Subjects of Gluck and Haydn

1. Voltaire and Catherine, *Correspondence*, in *Documents of Catherine the Great: The Correspondence with Voltaire and the Instruction of 1767*, ed. W. F. Reddaway (1931; New York: Russell & Russell, 1971), Voltaire's letter of November 15, 1768, 20; *Oeuvres complètes de Voltaire*, vol. 53, *Correspondance avec l'Impératrice de Russie* (Paris: Chez E. A. Lequien, 1822), 27; see also Larry Wolff, *Inventing Eastern Europe: The Map of Civilization on the Mind of the Enlightenment* (Stanford: Stanford University Press, 1994), 211–15; Andrei Zorin, *By Fables Alone: Literature and State Ideology in Late-Eighteenth–Early-Nineteenth Century Russia*, trans. Marcus Levitt (Boston: Academic Studies Press, 2014), 30–36.

2. W. Daniel Wilson, "Turks on the Eighteenth-Century Operatic Stage and European Political, Military, and Cultural History," *Eighteenth-Century Life* 9 (January 1985), 81–82.

3. Tom Standage, *The Turk: The Life and Times of the Famous Eighteenth-Century Chess-Playing Machine* (New York: Berkley Books, 2002), 22–30.

4. Cevad Memduh Altar, "Wolfgang Amadeus Mozart im Lichte Osmanisch-Österreichischer Beziehungen," *Revue belge de musicologie* 10 (1956), 144.

5. Frank Huss, "*Auf türkische Art prächtig aufgeputzt*: The Visit to Vienna by the Extraordinary Ottoman Envoy, Chaddi Mustafa Efendi, in the Year 1748," in *Ottoman Empire and European Theatre*, vol. 1, *The Age of Mozart and Selim III*, ed. Michael Hüttler and Hans Weidinger (Vienna: Hollitzer, 2013), 277–82; Suna Suner, "Of Messengers, Messages, and Memoirs: Opera and the Eighteenth-Century Ottoman Envoys and their Sefâretnâmes," in *Ottoman Empire and European Theatre*, vol. 2, *The Time of Joseph Haydn: From Sultan Mahmud I to Mahmud II*, ed. Michael Hüttler and Hans Weidinger (Vienna: Hollitzer, 2014), 104–5.

6. Thomas Betzwieser, "Ottoman Representation and Theatrical *Alla Turca*: Visiting an Unknown Viennese Source of 'Turkish' Incidental Music," in *Age of Mozart and Selim III*, 469–92.

7. Michael Yonan, *Empress Maria Theresa and the Politics of Habsburg Imperial Art* (University Park: Pennsylvania State University Press, 2011), 136.

8. Bruce Brown, *Gluck and the French Theatre in Vienna* (Oxford: Clarendon Press, 1991), 186–89; see also Suner, "Of Messengers, Messages, and Memoirs," 110–16.

9. Brown, *Gluck and the French Theatre in Vienna*, 294.

10. Brown, *Gluck and the French Theatre in Vienna*, 186–89; see also Virginia Aksan, *An Ottoman Statesman in War and Peace: Ahmed Resmi Efendi, 1700–1783* (Leiden: E. J. Brill, 1995).

11. Brown, *Gluck and the French Theatre in Vienna*, 186–89.

12. Adrienne Ward, *Pagodas in Play: China on the Eighteenth-Century Italian Opera Stage* (Lewisburg, PA: Bucknell University Press, 2010), 169–71; Daniel Heartz, *Haydn, Mozart, and the Viennese School, 1740–1780* (New York: Norton, 1995), 152–53; Yonan, *Empress Maria Theresa and the Politics of Habsburg Imperial Art*, 127.

13. Eve Meyer, "Turquerie and Eighteenth-Century Music," *Eighteenth-Century Studies* 7:4 (Summer 1974), 486.

14. Karl Signell, "Mozart and the *Mehter*," *Turkish Music Quarterly* 1:1 (Summer 1988), 9–15.

15. Uwe Baur, "Figurinen zu Mozarts Oper *Die Entführung aus dem Serail* (Koblenz 1787)," *Acta Mozartiana* 49 (2002), notebooks 1–2, 53–72.

16. William Parmentier, "The *Mehter*: Cultural Perceptions and Interpretations of Turkish Drum and Bugle Music throughout History," in *Age of Mozart and Selim III*, 290–91.

17. Meyer, "Turquerie and Eighteenth-Century Music," 485; Nurhan Atasoy, "Processions and Protocol in Ottoman Istanbul," in *The Sultan's Procession: The Swedish Embassy to Sultan Mehmed IV in 1657–1658 and the Rålamb Paintings*, ed. Karen Ådahl (Istanbul: Swedish Research Institute in Istanbul, 2006), 172–73.

18. Mary Hunter, "The *Alla Turca* Style in the Late Eighteenth Century: Race and Gender in the Symphony and the Seraglio," in *The Exotic in Western Music*, ed. Jonathan Bellman (Boston: Northeastern University Press, 1998), 44; Edmund Bowles, "The Impact of Turkish Military Bands on European Court Festivals in the 17th and 18th Centuries," *Early Music* 34:4 (2006), 546–48. See also Alina Witkowska, *Muzyka na dworze Augusta II w Warszawie* (Warsaw: Arx Regia Zamek Królewski, 1997), 129–42; according to Witkowska, Janissary bands may already have been present in late-seventeenth-century Poland under King Jan Sobieski, the hero of the siege of Vienna.

19. Bowles, "Impact of Turkish Military Bands," 549–50 and 558n64.

20. Walter Preibisch, "Quellenstudien zu Mozart's *Entführung aus dem Serail*: Ein Beitrag zu der Geschichte der Türkenoper," in *Sammelbände der Internationalen Musikgesellschaft* 10:3 (April–June 1909), 436–37; Margaret Griffel, "Turkish Opera from Mozart to Cornelius," Ph.D. dissertation, Columbia University, 1975, 167.

21. Bowles, "Impact of Turkish Military Bands," 553 and 559, n66; see also D. Doran Bugg, "The Role of Turkish Percussion in the History and Development of the Orchestral Percussion Section," Ph.D. dissertation, Louisiana State University, 2003, 1–7.

22. Giambattista Toderini, *Letteratura Turchesca*, vol. 1 (Venice: Giacomo Storti, 1787), 238–40.

23. Hunter, "*Alla Turca* Style in the Late Eighteenth Century," 49–50; Harrison Powley, "Janissary Music (Turkish Music)," in *Encyclopedia of Percussion*, ed. John Beck (London: Taylor & Francis, 1995), 195–200.

24. Matthew Head, *Orientalism, Masquerade, and Mozart's Turkish Music* (London: Royal Musical Association, 2000), 82; see also Bowles, "Impact of Turkish Military

Bands," 553; Meyer, "Turquerie and Eighteenth-Century Music," 484–86; Griffel, "Turkish Opera from Mozart to Cornelius," 99 and 102.

25. Eric Rice, "Representations of Janissary Music (*Mehter*) as Musical Exoticism in Western Compositions, 1670–1824," *Journal of Musicological Research* 19 (1999), 64–65; Christoph Yew, *The Turk on the Opera Stage: A History of a Musical Cliché* (Munich: GRIN Verlag, 2009), 15–20.

26. Henry George Farmer, "Oriental Influences on Occidental Military Music," *Islamic Culture* 15:2 (April 1941), 239; s.v. "Trenck, Franz, Freiherr von der (1711–1749)," in *Encyclopaedia Britannica*, 11th ed., vol. 27 (Cambridge: Cambridge University Press, 1911), 245–46; Bowles, "Impact of Turkish Military Bands," 546–54.

27. Rice, "Representations of Janissary Music," 64–65; Head, *Orientalism, Masquerade, and Mozart's Turkish Music*, 57–58; Bowles, "Impact of Turkish Military Bands," 553–54; Griffel, "Turkish Opera from Mozart to Cornelius," 7 and 101–2.

28. Hunter, "*Alla Turca* Style in the Late Eighteenth Century," 45; Robert Winter, "Orthodoxies, Paradoxes, and Contradictions: Performance Practices in Nineteenth-Century Piano Music," in *Nineteenth-Century Piano Music*, ed. R. Larry Todd (New York: Routledge, 2004), 38–39; Farmer, "Oriental Influences on Occidental Military Music," 240; Bugg, "Role of Turkish Percussion," 22–23.

29. Brown, *Gluck and the French Theatre in Vienna*, 386–87 and 396–97; Griffel, "Turkish Opera from Mozart to Cornelius," 127–28.

30. Rice, "Representations of Janissary Music," 65–67; Hunter, "*Alla Turca* Style in the Late Eighteenth Century," 46–47.

31. Brown, *Gluck and the French Theatre in Vienna*, 417.

32. Alain-René Le Sage and Jacques-Philippe d'Orneval, *Les pèlerins de la Mecque, pièce en trois actes, représentée par l'Opéra-Comique du Sieur Francisque, à la Foire Saint Laurent* (Paris, 1726); Daniel Heartz, *Music in European Capitals: The Galant Style 1720–1780* (New York: Norton, 2003), 701–2; see also Heartz, "Terpsichore at the Fair: Old and New Dance Airs in Two Vaudeville Comedies by Lesage," in *From Garrick to Gluck: Essays on Opera in the Age of Enlightenment*, ed. John Rice (Hillsdale, NY: Pendragon Press, 2004), 135–58.

33. Brown, *Gluck and the French Theatre in Vienna*, 416–17.

34. Heartz, *Haydn, Mozart, and the Viennese School*, 387.

35. Christoph Willibald Gluck, *Les pèlerins de la Mecque ou La rencontre imprévue*, libretto (CD liner notes), *Les pèlerins de la Mecque* (Münchener Rundfunkorchester, Leopold Hager) (Orfeo, 1991), act 1, scene 2, no. 2; see also *La rencontre imprévue, opéra bouffon tiré des Pèlerins de la Mecque, redigé par M. Dancourt, & mis en musique par M. le Chevalier Gluk* [*sic*], *représenté au Théâtre Français de la Haye, le 24 Septembre 1768* (Amsterdam/The Hague: Chez Constapel et Le Febure, 1768), 4.

36. Gluck, *Les pèlerins de la Mecque*, libretto, act 1, scene 2, no. 3; see also *La rencontre imprévue, opéra bouffon tiré des Pèlerins de la Mecque*, 6–7.

37. Gluck, *Les pèlerins de la Mecque*, libretto, act 1, scene 4, no. 5; see also *La rencontre imprévue, opéra bouffon tiré des Pèlerins de la Mecque*, 10.

38. Le Sage and d'Orneval, *Les pèlerins de la Mecque* (Paris, 1726), act 1, scene 2.

39. Ibid., act 1, scenes 2 and 4.

40. Gluck, *Les pèlerins de la Mecque*, libretto, act 1, scene 5, no. 6; see also *La rencontre imprévue, opéra bouffon tiré des Pèlerins de la Mecque*, 11; this latter version, published in Amsterdam and The Hague in 1768, contains Osmin's response *"castrato, castrata."*

41. Gluck, *Les pèlerins de la Mecque*, libretto, act 3, scene 2, no. 23; see also *La rencontre imprévue, opéra bouffon tiré des Pèlerins de la Mecque*, 40.

42. Gluck, *Les pèlerins de la Mecque*, libretto, act 3, scene 2, no. 23; see also *La rencontre imprévue, opéra bouffon tiré des Pèlerins de la Mecque*, 40.

43. Haydn, *L'incontro improvviso*, libretto (CD notes), *L'incontro improvviso* (Orchestre de Chambre de Lausanne, Antal Dorati) (Philips, 1980), act 1, 58–60.

44. Haydn, *L'incontro improvviso*, libretto, act 1, 68; see also Hunter, *"Alla Turca* Style in the Late Eighteenth Century," 58–62.

45. Brown, *Gluck and the French Theatre in Vienna*, 411.

46. Montesquieu, *Persian Letters*, trans. C. J. Betts (London: Penguin, 2004), letters 117 and 118, 213; Voltaire, *Philosophical Dictionary*, trans. Theodore Besterman (London: Penguin, 2004), s.v. "Abbé," 16.

47. David Sorkin, *The Religious Enlightenment: Protestants, Jews, and Catholics from London to Vienna* (Princeton: Princeton University Press, 2011), 226; Johann Pezzl, *Sketch of Vienna*, in H.C. Robbins Landon, *Mozart and Vienna* (New York: Schirmer Books, 1991), 58; Matthew Head, "Haydn's Exoticisms: 'Difference' and the Enlightenment," in *The Cambridge Companion to Haydn*, ed. Caryl Clark (Cambridge: Cambridge University Press, 2005), 81; Matthew Head, "Interpreting 'Abduction' Opera: Haydn's *L'incontro improvviso*, Sovereignty, and the Esterház Festival of 1775," in *Time of Joseph Haydn*, 319–20.

48. Brown, *Gluck and the French Theatre in Vienna*, 412–13; see also Bruce Brown, "Gluck's *Rencontre imprévue* and Its Revisions," *Journal of the American Musicological Society*, vol. 36, no. 3 (Autumn 1983), 498–518.

49. "Informationen zur Uraufführung," in *Die unvermuthete Zusammenkunft oder Die Pilgrimme von Mekka*, Gluck-Gesamtausgabe.de, http://www.gluck-gesamtaus gabe.de/gwv/werkregister/eintrag/die-unvermuthete-zusammenkunft-oder-die-pil grime-von-mecca.html

50. Gluck, *Les pèlerins de la Mecque*, libretto, act 3, scene 10, no. 33; see also *La rencontre imprévue, opéra bouffon tiré des Pèlerins de la Mecque*, 56–57.

51. Gluck, *Les pèlerins de la Mecque*, libretto, act 3, scene 10, no. 34; see also *La rencontre imprévue, opéra bouffon tiré des Pèlerins de la Mecque*, 60.

52. Bent Holm, "Occidental Portraits in Oriental Mirrors: The Ruler Image in the Eighteenth-Century *Türkenoper* and Gluck's *La rencontre imprévue*," in *Time of Joseph*

Haydn, 506–7; Bent Holm, *The Taming of the Turk: Ottomans on the Danish Stage 1596–1896* (Vienna: Hollitzer, 2014), 140–43.

53. Haydn, *L'incontro improvviso*, libretto, act 3, 158.

54. Heartz, *Haydn, Mozart, and the Viennese School*, 386; Head, "Interpreting 'Abduction' Opera," 324–28; Necla Çikigil, "Haydn's Humour Reflected in *Lo speziale* (1768) and *L'incontro improvviso* (1775)," in *Time of Joseph Haydn*, 311.

55. Parmentier, "*Mehter*," 299.

56. Larry Wolff, *Venice and the Slavs: The Discovery of Dalmatia in the Age of Enlightenment* (Stanford: Stanford University Press, 2001), 25–75; see also "Venice and the Slavs of Dalmatia: The Drama of the Adriatic Empire in the Venetian Enlightenment," *Slavic Review* 56:3 (Fall 1997), 428–55.

57. Carlo Goldoni, *Lo speziale: Dramma giocoso per musica*, in *Edizione completa dei testi per musica di Carlo Goldoni*, www.librettidopera.it (2005), act 1, scenes 3 and 4, 8–9; Haydn, *Lo speziale*, libretto (CD liner notes), *Der Apotheker/Lo speziale* (Deutsche Kammerakademie Neuss am Rhein, Johannes Goritzki) (DeutschlandRadio, 2000), act 1, scene 2, 22; see also Head, "Haydn's Exoticisms," 77.

58. Wolff, *Venice and the Slavs*, 82–83.

59. Goldoni, *Lo speziale*, act 1, scene 13, 21; Haydn, *Lo speziale*, libretto, act 1, scene 9, 28.

60. Goldoni, *Lo speziale*, act 1, scene 13, 21; Haydn, *Lo speziale*, libretto, act 1, scene 9, 28.

61. Carlo Goldoni, *Lo Speziale: The Apothecary, a Comic Opera as Perform'd at the King's Theatre in the Hay-Market. The Music of the First Act by Signor Pallavicini: The Second and Third by Signor Fischietti* (London: W. Griffin, 1769).

62. Thomas Bauman, *W. A. Mozart: Die Entführung aus dem Serail* (Cambridge: Cambridge University Press, 1987), 27–32; Ulf Schlawinski, "Wenn ich eine gute Oper hören will, gehe ich nach Esterhaza" (CD liner notes), in Haydn, *Der Apotheker/Lo speziale* (DeutschlandRadio, 2000), 8.

63. Goldoni, *Lo speziale*, act 1, scene 10, 18; Haydn, *Lo speziale*, libretto, act 1, scene 7, 26; Karl Geiringer, *Haydn: A Creative Life in Music* (Berkeley: University of California Press, 1982), 243; Larry Wolff, "Turkish Travesty in European Opera: Haydn's *Lo speziale* (1768)," in *Time of Joseph Haydn*, 283–90.

64. Haydn, *Lo speziale*, libretto, act 3, scene 4, 41.

65. Ibid.; Goldoni, *Lo speziale*, act 3, scene 6, 51; Head, "Haydn's Exoticisms," 78–79 and 91–92; Heartz, *Haydn, Mozart, and the Viennese School*, 375–76; Caryl Clark, "Encountering 'Others' in Haydn's *Lo speziale* (1768)," in *Time of Joseph Haydn*, 294–300; Caryl Clark, *Haydn's Jews: Representation and Reception on the Operatic Stage* (Cambridge: Cambridge University Press, 2009), 114–26; Clark argues further that Sempronio himself may have been intended by Haydn to be seen and heard as implicitly Jewish, which might have conditioned the apothecary's interest in things Turkish.

66. Goldoni, *Lo speziale*, act 3, scene 2, 43–44.

67. Ibid., 44.

68. Casanova, *Histoire de ma vie*, ed. Francis Lacassin, vol. 1 (Paris: Robert Laffont, 1993), 295–97.

69. Goldoni, *Lo speziale*, act 3, scene 6, 50.

70. Ibid.

71. Goldoni, *Lo speziale*, act 3, scene 7, 51.

72. Goldoni, *Lo speziale*, act 3, scene 8, 52.

73. Ibid.

74. Miriam Whaples, "Early Exoticism Revisited," in *Exotic in Western Music*, 23.

75. Larry Wolff, *Inventing Eastern Europe: The Map of Civilization on the Mind of the Enlightenment* (Stanford: Stanford University Press, 1994), 113–14.

76. Goldoni, *Lo speziale*, act 3, scene 8, 52; Haydn, *Lo speziale*, libretto, act 3, scene 6, 40; Paolo Preto, *Venezia e i Turchi* (Florence: G. C. Sansoni, 1975).

77. Parmentier, "*Mehter*," 300–01; Bugg, "Role of Turkish Percussion," 32–33.

78. Niccolò Jommelli, *La schiava liberata: Dramma serio-comico per musica, da rappresentarsi nel Real Teatro dell'Ajuda in occasione di festeggiarsi il felicissimo giorno natalizio di Sua Reale Maestà l'Augustissima Signora D. Marianna Vittoria Regina Fedelissima nella primavera dell'anno 1770* (Lisbon: Stamperia Reale, 1770), 40; Hermann Abert, *Niccolo Jommelli als Opernkomponist* (Tutzing: Hans Schneider, 1991), 438.

79. Marita McClymonds, "Jommelli's Last Opera for Germany: The Opera Seria-Comica *La schiava liberata* (Ludwigsburg 1768)," *Current Musicology*, no. 39 (Spring 1985), 7–20.

80. Ibid., 15.

81. Manuel Carlos de Brito, *Opera in Portugal in the Eighteenth Century* (Cambridge: Cambridge University Press, 1989), 40–41; Baldassare Galuppi, *Solimano: Dramma per musica, da rappresentarsi nel nuovo Teatro di Padova in occasione della fiera dell'anno 1768* (Venice: Stamperia Fenzo, 1768).

82. Jommelli, *La schiava liberata*, 12.

83. Heartz, *Music in European Capitals*, 569–70.

84. Georg Joseph Vogler, *Der Kaufmann von Smyrna: Eine Operette in einem Aufzuge* (Mannheim: C. F. Schwan, 1771), 9–11.

85. Thomas Bauman and Paul Corneilson, "Kaufmann von Smyrna, Der," in *The New Grove Dictionary of Opera*, 4 vols., ed. Stanley Sadie, vol. 2 (Oxford: Oxford University Press, 1997), 963–64; see also Griffel, "Turkish Opera from Mozart to Cornelius," 200–204.

86. Vogler, *Der Kaufmann von Smyrna*, 19–20.

87. Mozart, *Die Entführung aus dem Serail: Partitura* (Budapest: Könemann, 1995), act 3, 245.

88. *Mozart's Letters, Mozart's Life*, ed. and trans. Robert Spaethling (New York: Nor-

ton, 2000), letters of November 20, 1777, and February 22, 1778, 97 and 133; Paul Corneilson, "Vogler, Georg Joseph," in *The New Grove Dictionary of Opera*, vol. 4, 1036–37.

89. Bauman and Corneilson, "Kaufmann von Smyrna, Der," 963–64.

90. Vogler, *Der Kaufmann von Smyrna*, 43; Sébastien-Roch Nicolas de Chamfort, *Le marchand de Smyrne: Comédie en un acte et en prose, représentée pour la première fois le Vendredi 26 Janvier 1770* (Paris: Chez Delalain, 1770), 21.

91. Vogler, *Der Kaufmann von Smyrna*, 75.

92. Milan Postolka, "Holý, Ondřej František," in *The New Grove Dictionary of Opera*, vol. 2, 743–44; Johann Jakob Moser, *Beyträge zu dem neuesten europäischen Gesandtschaffts-Recht* (Frankfurt: Varrentrapp Sohn und Wenner, 1781), 87; Paul Corneilson, *The Autobiography of Ludwig Fischer: Mozart's First Osmin* (Malden, MA: Mozart Society of America, 2011), 57; see also Bistra Dontschewa, "Der Türke im Spiegelbild der deutschen Literatur und des Theaters im 18. Jahrhundert," Ph.D. dissertation, Munich, 1944, 57–60; and Griffel, "Turkish Opera from Mozart to Cornelius," 212–14.

93. *Il figlio del Gran Turco: Dramma giocoso per musica, ad uso del Real Teatro di Colorno nell'autunno dell'anno 1774* (Parma: Stamperia Reale, 1774).

94. *Catalogue of the Molière Collection in Harvard College Library*, ed. Thomas Franklin Currier and Ernest Lewis Gay (Cambridge: Library of Harvard University, 1906), 23 and 67.

95. *Il figlio del Gran Turco*, 59–60.

96. Ibid., 62.

97. Ibid., 63.

98. Ibid., 69.

99. Ibid., 73.

Chapter 5: Osmin in Vienna

1. Johann Pezzl, *Sketch of Vienna*, in *Mozart and Vienna*, ed. H.C. Robbins Landon (New York: Schirmer Books, 1991), 86–87; Johann Pezzl, *Skizze von Wien*, ed. Gustav Gugitz and Anton Schlossar (Graz: Leykam Verlag, 1923), 246.

2. Johann Pezzl, *Chronik von Wien*, ed. Franz Ziska (Vienna: Carl Armbruster, 1824), 192–93.

3. Alfred Einstein, *Mozart: His Character, His Work*, trans. Arthur Mendel and Nathan Broder (New York: Oxford University Press, 1962), 458–59; Matthew Head, *Orientalism, Masquerade, and Mozart's Turkish Music* (London: Royal Musical Association, 2000), 1–2; Peter Kivy, *Osmin's Rage: Philosophical Reflections on Opera, Drama, and Text* (London: Royal Musical Association, 2000); Mary Hunter, "The *Alla Turca* Style in the Late Eighteenth Century: Race and Gender in the Symphony and the Seraglio," in *The Exotic in Western Music*, ed. Jonathan Bellman (Boston: Northeastern University Press, 1998), 59–60.

4. Thomas Bauman, *W. A. Mozart, Die Entführung aus dem Serail* (Cambridge: Cambridge University Press, 1987), 27–35; see also Walter Preibisch, "Quellenstudien

zu Mozarts *Entführung aus dem Serail*: Ein Beitrag zu der Geschichte der Türkenoper," *Sammelbände der Internationalen Musikgesellschaft* 10:3 (April–June 1909), 430–76.

5. Bauman, *W. A. Mozart, Die Entführung aus dem Serail*, 103–4.

6. Head, *Orientalism, Masquerade, and Mozart's Turkish Music*, 74; Michael Malkiewicz, "Wolfgang Amadeus Mozarts Skizzenblatt zu *Le gelosie del serraglio*," in *Prima la Danza! Festschrift für Sibylle Dahms*, ed. Sibylle Dahms, Gunhild Oberzaucher-Schüller, Daniel Brandenburg, and Monika Woitas (Würzburg: Königshausen & Neumann, 2004), 112–13, 120–22.

7. Derek Weber, "From *Zaide* to *Die Entführung aus dem Serail*: Mozart's 'Turkish' Operas," in *Ottoman Empire and European Theatre*, Volume 1, *The Age of Mozart and Selim III*, ed. Michael Hüttler and Hans Weidinger (Vienna: Hollitzer, 2013), 636; Einstein, *Mozart*, 452–53.

8. Franz Joseph Sebastiani (libretto) and Joseph Friberth (music), *Ein musikalisches Singspiel genannt: Das Serail, oder, Die unvermuthete Zusammenkunft in der Sclaverey zwischen Vater, Tochter und Sohn* (Botzen: Karl Joseph Weiss, 1779); Neil Zaslaw, "Zaide" (CD liner notes), in Mozart, *Zaide* (Academy of Ancient Music, Paul Goodwin) (Harmonia Mundi, 1998), 4–5.

9. Mozart, *Zaide*, libretto (CD liner notes) (Harmonia Mundi, 1998), act 1, 10.

10. Ibid., 11.

11. Nicholas Till, *Mozart and the Enlightenment: Truth, Virtue and Beauty in Mozart's Operas* (London: Faber & Faber, 1992), 56–59; see also Daniel Heartz, *Haydn, Mozart, and the Viennese School, 1740–1780* (New York: Norton, 1995), 684–86; see also Marianne Tråvén, "Getting Emotional: Mozart's 'Turkish' Operas and the Emotive Aspect of Slavery," in *Age of Mozart and Selim III*, 618–20.

12. Mozart, *Zaide*, libretto, act 2, 18.

13. Heartz, *Haydn, Mozart, and the Viennese School*, 682.

14. *The Letters of Mozart and His Family*, ed. Emily Anderson, 3rd ed. (New York: Norton, 1985), letter of Leopold Mozart, December 11, 1780, 685.

15. *Mozart's Letters, Mozart's Life*, ed. and trans. Robert Spaethling (New York: Norton, 2000), letter of April 18, 1781, 244.

16. Bauman, *W. A. Mozart, Die Entführung aus dem Serail*, 9–10.

17. *Mozart's Letters, Mozart's Life*, letter of April 28, 1781, 245.

18. Gustav Friedrich Wilhelm Grossmann (libretto), *Adelheit von Veltheim, oder, Der Bassa von Tunis: Ein Singspiel in vier Akten, aufgeführt im k. k. Nationaltheater* (Vienna: Logemeister, 1781). There was new music for Vienna, possibly by Giuseppe Sarti, or possibly by Joseph Sardi (*"Die Musik dazu ist neu, vom Herrn Sardi"*).

19. Margaret Griffel, "Turkish Opera from Mozart to Cornelius," Ph.D. dissertation, Columbia University, 1975, 225–26.

20. Hermann Abert, *W. A. Mozart*, trans. Stewart Spencer (New Haven: Yale University Press, 2007), 653–54; Thomas Bauman, *North German Opera in the Age of Goethe*

(Cambridge: Cambridge University Press, 1985), 191–93; Bistra Dontschewa, "Der Türke im Spiegelbild der Deutschen Literatur und des Theaters im 18. Jahrhundert," Ph.D. dissertation, Munich, 1944, 77–80; *Almanacco di Gherardo Casaglia*, September 23, 1780, *Adelheit von Veltheim*, amadeusonline.net; Grossmann and Sarti, *Adelheit von Veltheim* (Vienna, 1781), 2.

21. Bauman, *W. A. Mozart, Die Entführung aus dem Serail*, 65; Clemens Zoidl, "A Royals' Journey in 1775: The Vienna Official Press Review," in *Ottoman Empire and European Theatre*, Volume 2, *The Time of Joseph Haydn: From Sultan Mahmud I to Mahmud II*, ed. Michael Hüttler and Hans Weidinger (Vienna: Hollitzer, 2014), 417.

22. Michael Pirker, "Die Türkische Musik und Mozarts *Entführung aus dem Serail*," in *Die Klangwelt Mozarts: Eine Ausstellung des Kunsthistorischen Museums* (Vienna: Kunsthistorisches Museum, 1991), 134.

23. Bence Szabolcsi, "Exoticisms in Mozart," *Music and Letters* 37:4 (1956), 328–30; see also Griffel, "Turkish Opera from Mozart to Cornelius," 275–76; Heartz, *Haydn, Mozart, and the Viennese School*, 683.

24. Bauman, *W. A. Mozart, Die Entführung aus dem Serail*, 63–64; see also Miriam Whaples, "Exoticism in Dramatic Music, 1600–1800," Ph.D. dissertation, Indiana University, 1958; Pirker, "Die Türkische Musik und Mozarts *Entführung aus dem Serail*," 139; see also Karl Signell, "Mozart and the Mehter," *Turkish Music Quarterly* 1:1 (Summer 1988), 9–15.

25. Heartz, *Haydn, Mozart, and the Viennese School*, 628.

26. *Letters of Mozart and His Family*, letter of Leopold Mozart, October 6, 1777, 297; Hans-Peter Kellner, "The Sultan of Denmark: Voltaire's *Zaïre* and King Christian VII, Madness and Enlightenment," in *Time of Joseph Haydn*, 482–85; Nadja Kayali, "Mozart's 'Orient' on Stage," in *Age of Mozart and Selim III*, 654–55.

27. *Mozart's Letters, Mozart's Life*, letter of August 1, 1781, 276; Mozart, *Briefe*, ed. Horst Wandrey (Zurich: Diogenes, 1988), 284–85.

28. *Mozart's Letters, Mozart's Life*, letter of August 1, 1781, 276–77; Mozart, *Briefe*, ed. Wandrey, 284–85.

29. *Mozart's Letters, Mozart's Life*, letter of August 1, 1781, 277; Mozart, *Briefe*, ed. Wandrey, 284–85.

30. Hunter, "*Alla Turca* Style in the Late Eighteenth Century," 50–52; Till, *Mozart and the Enlightenment*, 102–5; Paul Corneilson, *The Autobiography of Ludwig Fischer: Mozart's First Osmin* (Malden, MA: Mozart Society of America, 2011), 11.

31. Cesare Questa, *Il Ratto dal Serraglio: Euripide, Plauto, Mozart, Rossini* (Bologna: Patron Editore, 1979), 21–27.

32. *Letters of Mozart and His Family*, letter of Mozart to his father, December 5, 1781, 781.

33. Volkmar Braunbehrens, *Mozart in Vienna, 1781–1791*, trans. Timothy Bell (New York: Grove Weidenfeld, 1989), 60–63; Tom Standage, *The Turk: The Life and Times of the*

Famous Eighteenth-Century Chess-Playing Machine (New York: Berkley Books, 2002), 40–41.

34. *Mozart's Letters, Mozart's Life,* letter of October 19, 1782, 333.

35. *Mozart's Letters, Mozart's Life,* undated letter of September 1781, 284; Bauman, *W. A. Mozart, Die Entführung aus dem Serail,* 33.

36. *Mozart's Letters, Mozart's Life,* letter of September 26, 1781, 287.

37. Ibid., 286.

38. Ibid., 287; Mozart, *Briefe,* ed. Wandrey, 299.

39. Mozart, *Zaide,* libretto, act 2, 17.

40. Mozart, *Die Entführung aus dem Serail: Partitura* (Budapest: Könemann, 1995), act 3, 276.

41. Mozart, *Zaide,* libretto, act 2, 18.

42. Ibid., 20–21; see also Jean-Victor Hocquard, *L'enlèvement au Sérail* (Paris: Aubier-Montaigne, 1980), 45–46.

43. Mozart, *Zaide,* libretto, act 2, 20–21.

44. *Mozart's Letters, Mozart's Life,* letter of September 26, 1781, 285–86; Mozart, *Briefe,* ed. Wandrey, 297.

45. Corneilson, *Autobiography of Ludwig Fischer,* 8–9; "Informationen zur Uraufführung," in "Gluck Gesamtausgabe," *Die unvermuthete Zusammenkunft oder Die Pilgrimme von Mekka,* http://www.gluck-gesamtausgabe.de/gwv/werkregister/eintrag/die-unvermuthete-zusammenkunft-oder-die-pilgrime-von-mecca.html

46. Mozart, *Briefe,* ed. Wandrey, 297.

47. Ibid., 299.

48. *Mozart's Letters, Mozart's Life,* letter of September 26, 1781, 286; Mozart, *Briefe,* ed. Wandrey, 297–98; see also Bauman, *W. A. Mozart, Die Entführung aus dem Serail,* 67.

49. Henry Laurens, *Les origines intellectuelles de l'expédition d'Égypte: L'Orientalisme Islamisant en France, 1698–1798* (Istanbul/Paris: Editions Isis, Institut Français d'Études Anatoliennes, 1987), 63–65; s.v. "Tott, François, baron de," *Biographie Universelle: ancienne et moderne,* ed. Louis-Gabriel Michaud, Volume 42 (Paris: Delagrave, 1870–73), 6–8; see also Larry Wolff, *Inventing Eastern Europe: The Map of Civilization on the Mind of the Enlightenment* (Stanford: Stanford University Press, 1994), 69–70.

50. *Mozart's Letters, Mozart's Life,* letter of October 13, 1781, 288–89; *Mozarts Briefe,* ed. Ludwig Nohl (Salzburg: Verlag der Mayrischen Buchhandlung, 1865), 327.

51. Peter Stearns, "Modern Patterns in Emotional History," in *Doing Emotions History,* ed. Susan Matt and Peter Stearns (Urbana: University of Illinois Press, 2014), 20–21; see also William Reddy, *The Navigation of Feeling: A Framework for the History of the Emotions* (Cambridge: Cambridge University Press, 2001), 141–72.

52. Marie-Claude Lambotte, "Franz Xaver Messerschmidt's 'Character Heads': The Conflicting Nature of the Mirror Relation," in *Franz Xaver Messerschmidt,* ed. Maria Pötzl-Malikova and Guilhem Scherf (New York: Neue Galerie, 2010), 56–63; see also

Antonia Boström, *Messerschmidt and Modernity* (Los Angeles: J. Paul Getty Museum Publications, 2012).

53. Mozart, *Die Entführung aus dem Serail: Partitura*, act 1, 48–54; see also Head, *Orientalism, Masquerade and Mozart's Turkish Music*, 1–10; Hocquard, *L'enlèvement au Sérail*, 78–83; Stearns, "Modern Patterns in Emotional History," 20–21.

54. Mozart, *Die Entführung aus dem Serail: Partitura*, act 1, 55–58; see also Bauman, W. A. *Mozart, Die Entführung aus dem Serail*, 70; and Pirker, "Die Türkische Musik und Mozarts *Entführung aus dem Serail*," 140–41; and Benjamin Perl, "Mozart in Turkey," *Cambridge Opera Journal* 12:3 (2001), 227; and Timothy Taylor, "Peopling the Stage: Opera, Otherness, and New Musical Representations in the Eighteenth Century," *Cultural Critique* 36 (Spring 1997), 77–80. The libretto of 1782 clearly states "gespiesst auf heisse Stangen" though modern grammar might prefer "auf heissen Stangen"

55. Charlotte Colding Smith, *Images of Islam, 1453–1600: Turks in Germany and Central Europe* (London: Pickering & Chatto, 2014), 1–3, 41–45, 57–62, 181n1.

56. Hunter, "*Alla Turca* Style in the Late Eighteenth Century," 44, 67–68.

57. Preibisch, "Quellenstudien zu Mozarts *Entführung aus dem Serail*," 441.

58. Montesquieu, *Persian Letters*, trans. C. J. Betts (New York: Penguin Books, 1985), 9th letter, 50–51; Voltaire, *The History of Charles XII*, trans. Tobias Smollett, in *The Works of M. de Voltaire*, Volume 11 (London: J. Newbery, R. Baldwin, W. Johnston, 1762), 10.

59. Mary Wortley Montagu, *The Works*, 6th ed., Volume 5 (London: Longman, Hurst, 1817), 150.

60. Voltaire, *Candide*, in *Candide, Zadig, et autres contes* (Paris: Editions Jean-Claude Lattès, 1988), ch. 12, 56.

61. Giovanni Bertati, *Il Serraglio di Osmano, dramma giocoso per musica* (Venice: Antonio Casali, 1785), 13.

62. Christoph Friedrich Bretzner, *Belmont und Constanze, oder Die Entführung aus dem Serail* (Leipzig: Carl Friedrich Schneider, 1781), in *Die Entführung aus dem Serail: Faksimile-Ausgabe zur Geschichte des Librettos*, ed. Gerhard Croll and Ulrich Müller (Salzburg: Verlag Ursula Müller-Speiser, 1993), 21.

63. *Mozart's Letters, Mozart's Life*, letter of March 17, 1781, 234; Mozart, *Briefe*, ed. Wandrey, 246–47.

64. *Mozart's Letters, Mozart's Life*, letter of March 24, 1781, 235; Mozart, *Briefe*, ed. Wandrey, 249.

65. *Mozart's Letters, Mozart's Life*, letter of April 4, 1781, 239; Mozart, *Briefe*, ed. Wandrey, 254–55.

66. *Mozart's Letters, Mozart's Life*, letter of April 11, 1781, 242.

67. *Mozart's Letters, Mozart's Life*, letter of May 9, 1781, 247; Mozart, *Briefe*, ed. Wandrey, 257.

68. *Mozart's Letters, Mozart's Life*, letter of May 9, 1781, 248; Mozart, *Briefe*, ed. Wan-

drey, 260; see also Braunbehrens, *Mozart in Vienna*, 29–41; Maynard Solomon, *Mozart: A Life* (New York: Harper Collins, 1995), 241–48.

69. *Mozart's Letters, Mozart's Life*, letter of June 2, 1781, 259.

70. *Mozart's Letters, Mozart's Life*, letter of June 9, 1781, 260–62; Mozart, *Briefe*, ed. Wandrey, 271–73.

71. Solomon, *Mozart*, 248.

72. Mozart, *Die Entführung aus dem Serail: Partitura*, act 2, 98–99; Stephanie (libretto) and Mozart, *Die Entführung aus dem Serail* (Vienna: Logenmeister, 1782), in *Die Entführung aus dem Serail: Faksimile-Ausgabe zur Geschichte des Librettos*, 22–23.

73. Gerhard Croll, "Preface," in Mozart, *Die Entführung aus dem Serail*, Bärenreiter Urtext, ed. Gerhard Croll (Kassel: Bärenreiter, 1982), xxx–xxxi.

74. Mozart, *Die Entführung aus dem Serail: Partitura*, act 2, 105–7.

75. Derek Beales, *Joseph II*, Volume 2, *Against the World 1780–1790* (Cambridge: Cambridge University Press, 2009), 287.

76. Linda Colley, *Captives: Britain, Empire, and the World, 1600–1800* (New York: Anchor Books, 2002), 127–30; Robert Davis, *Christian Slaves, Muslim Masters: White Slavery in the Mediterranean, the Barbary Coast, and Italy, 1500–1800* (New York: Palgrave Macmillan, 2003), 36.

77. Davis, *Christian Slaves, Muslim Masters*, 125–26; Colley, *Captives*, 57.

78. *Mozart's Letters, Mozart's Life*, letter of September 26, 1781, 287; Mozart, *Briefe*, ed. Wandrey, 300.

79. Colley, *Captives*, 117 and 124.

80. Stephanie and Mozart, *Die Entführung aus dem Serail* (Vienna, 1782), act 2, 35–36.

81. Pirker, "Die Türkische Musik und Mozarts *Entführung aus dem Serail*," 142–43; see also Perl, "Mozart in Turkey," 224–25; and Hocquard, *L'enlèvement au Sérail*, 128–30.

82. Matthew Head, "'In the Orient of Vienna': Mozart's 'Turkish' Music and the Theatrical Self," in *Age of Mozart and Selim III*, 607.

83. *Mozart's Letters, Mozart's Life*, letter of January 22, 1783, 340; letter of March 12, 1783, 345; Braunbehrens, *Mozart in Vienna*, 109 and 182.

84. Head, "In the Orient of Vienna," 607.

85. Johann Heiss, "Die Ereignisse zum hundertjährigen Jubiläum 1783," in *Geschichtspolitik und Türkenbelagerung*, ed. Johannes Feichtinger and Johann Heiss (Vienna: Mandelbaum, 2013), 71–72.

86. Ibid., 62–63 and 82–83.

87. Ibid., 64–65; see also Anke Schmitt, *Der Exotismus in der deutschen Oper zwischen Mozart und Spohr* (Hamburg: Verlag der Musikalienhandlung Karl Dieter Wagner, 1988), 114–15.

88. Matthias Pernerstorfer, "The Second Turkish Siege of Vienna (1683) Reflected in Its First Centenary," in *Age of Mozart and Selim III*, 526–27; Heiss, "Die Ereignisse zum hundertjährigen Jubiläum 1783," 69–72.

89. Larry Wolff, "Muslims, Christians, and Mozart," *The New York Times*, 24 April 2016.

90. Cevad Memduh Altar, "Wolfgang Amadeus Mozart im Lichte osmanisch-öster-reichischer Beziehungen," *Revue belge de musicologie* 10 (1956), 148; see also Pirker, "Die Türkische Musik und Mozarts *Entführung aus dem Serail*," 146.

91. Szabolcsi, "Exoticisms in Mozart," 332.

92. Corneilson, *Autobiography of Ludwig Fischer*, 39.

93. Ibid., 13–14.

Chapter 6: "To honor the Emperor"

1. Mary Hunter, "The *Alla Turca* Style in the Late Eighteenth Century: Race and Gender in the Symphony and the Seraglio," in *The Exotic in Western Music*, ed. Jonathan Bellman (Boston: Northeastern University Press, 1998), 64.

2. Joan-Pau Rubiés, "Oriental Despotism and European Orientalism: Botero to Montesquieu," *Journal of Early Modern History* 9:1–2 (2005), 160–64; Lucette Valensi, *Birth of the Despot: Venice and the Sublime Porte*, trans. Arthur Denner (original French edition 1987; trans. Ithaca: Cornell University Press, 1993); see also Asli Çirakman, "From Tyranny to Despotism: The Enlightenment's Unenlightened Image of the Turks," in *International Journal of Middle East Studies* 33:1 (2001), 49–68.

3. Derek Beales, "Mozart and the Habsburgs," in Beales, *Enlightenment and Reform in Eighteenth-Century Europe* (London: I. B. Tauris, 2005), 90–116; see also Derek Beales, *Joseph II*, vol. 2, *Against the World 1780–1790* (Cambridge: Cambridge University Press, 2009); Volkmar Braunbehrens, *Mozart in Vienna 1781–1791*, trans. Timothy Bell (New York: Grove Weidenfeld, 1989).

4. *The Letters of Mozart and His Family*, ed. Emily Anderson, 3rd ed. (New York: Norton, 1985), letter of January 11, 1778, 444–45; Mozart, *Briefe*, ed. Horst Wandrey (Zurich: Diogenes, 1988), 115.

5. *Mozart's Letters, Mozart's Life*, ed. and trans. Robert Spaethling (New York: Norton, 2000), letter of November 12, 1778, 193–94; Mozart, *Briefe*, ed. Wandrey, 210.

6. Mozart, *Zaide*, libretto (CD liner notes), in Mozart, *Zaide* (Academy of Ancient Music, Paul Goodwin) (Harmonia Mundi, 1998), act 2, 17.

7. Ibid., 18–19.

8. Ibid., 20.

9. Ibid., 21.

10. Franz Joseph Sebastiani (libretto) and Joseph Friberth (music), *Ein musikalisches Singspiel genannt: Das Serail, oder, Die unvermuthete Zusammenkunft in der Sclaverey zwischen Vater, Tochter und Sohn* (Botzen: Karl Joseph Weiss, 1779), act 2, scene 17.

11. Ibid.

12. Mozart, *Die Entführung aus dem Serail: Partitura* (Budapest: Könemann, 1995), act 1, 68–69; see also Jean-Victor Hocquard, *L'enlèvement au sérail* (Paris: Aubier-Mon-

taigne, 1980), 63–64; Gerhard Croll, "Preface," in Mozart, *Die Entführung aus dem Serail,*
Bärenreiter Urtext, ed. Gerhard Croll (Kassel: Bärenreiter, 1982), xli.

13. Braunbehrens, *Mozart in Vienna,* 226–66.

14. *Mozart's Letters, Mozart's Life,* letter of November 20, 1782, 334.

15. Stephanie and Mozart, *Die Entführung aus dem Serail* (Vienna: Logenmeister,
1782), in *Die Entführung aus dem Serail: Faksimile-Ausgabe zur Geschichte des Librettos,*
ed. Gerhard Croll and Ulrich Müller (Salzburg: Verlag Ursula Müller-Speiser, 1993), 15.

16. Ibid., 17.

17. Timothy Taylor, "Peopling the Stage: Opera, Otherness, and New Musical Representations in the Eighteenth Century," *Cultural Critique* 36 (Spring 1997), 67.

18. Stephanie and Mozart, *Die Entführung aus dem Serail* (Vienna, 1782), act 2, 29–30.

19. Mozart, *Die Entführung aus dem Serail: Partitura,* act 3, 244. The libretto has
Osmin exclaiming "O!" but this is more often written and sung as "Ha!"

20. Stephanie and Mozart, *Die Entführung aus dem Serail* (Vienna, 1782), act 3, 60.

21. Linda Colley, *Captives: Britain, Empire and the World, 1600–1850* (New York:
Anchor Books, 2004), 23–134.

22. Stephanie and Mozart, *Die Entführung aus dem Serail* (Vienna, 1782), act 3, 60.

23. Christoph Friedrich Bretzner, *Belmont und Constanze, oder Die Entführung aus
dem Serail* (Leipzig: Carl Friedrich Schneider, 1781), in *Die Entführung aus dem Serail:
Faksimile-Ausgabe zur Geschichte des Librettos,* act 3, 69; see also Cesare Questa, *Il Ratto
dal Serraglio: Euripide, Plauto, Mozart, Rossini* (Bologna: Patron Editore, 1979), 84–85.

24. Stephanie and Mozart, *Die Entführung aus dem Serail* (Vienna, 1782), act 3, 64.

25. Ibid., 65.

26. Thomas Bauman, *W. A. Mozart, Die Entführung aus dem Serail* (Cambridge:
Cambridge University Press, 1987), 33.

27. Mozart, *Die Entführung aus dem Serail: Partitura,* act 3, 271–72.

28. Ibid., 275–76; Beales, *Joseph II,* vol. 2, 214–38; Braunbehrens, *Mozart in Vienna,*
310–16.

29. Mozart, *Die Entführung aus dem Serail: Partitura,* act 3, 276–79.

30. Ibid., 280–85.

31. *Mozart's Letters, Mozart's Life,* letter of July 20, 1782, 314–15; Mozart, *Briefe,* ed.
Wandrey, 324.

32. Braunbehrens, *Mozart in Vienna,* 158–69.

33. *Mozart's Letters, Mozart's Life,* letter of July 20, 1782, 315; Mozart *Briefe,* ed. Wandrey, 324.

34. *Mozart's Letters, Mozart's Life,* letter of September 26, 1781, 286; Mozart, *Briefe,*
ed. Wandrey, 298.

35. *Mozart's Letters, Mozart's Life,* letter of July 20, 1782, 315; Mozart *Briefe,* ed. Wandrey, 325.

36. Bastiaan Blomhert, "Wolfgang Amadeus Mozart: The Donaueschingen *Harmo-*

niemusik of *Die Entführung aus dem Serail*" (CD liner notes), in Mozart, *Die Entführung aus dem Serail: Harmoniemusik* (Amadeus Winds) (L'Oiseau-Lyre, 1990); see also Bastiaan Blomhert, "The *Harmoniemusik* of *Die Entführung aus dem Serail* by Wolfgang Amadeus Mozart: Study about Its Authenticity and Critical Edition," Ph.D. dissertation, University of Utrecht, 1987.

37. *Mozart's Letters, Mozart's Life*, letter of July 27, 1782, 316–17; Ludwig Nohl, *Mozarts Briefe* (Salzburg: Verlag von Ludwig Taube, 1867), letter of July 27, 1782, 367.

38. *Mozart's Letters, Mozart's Life*, letter of July 27, 1782, 317.

39. *Mozart's Letters, Mozart's Life*, letter of July 31, 1782, 318; Mozart, *Briefe*, ed. Wandrey, 328.

40. *Mozart's Letters, Mozart's Life*, letter of August 7, 1782, 321.

41. Bauman, *W. A. Mozart, Die Entführung aus dem Serail*, 103.

42. Richard Taruskin, "Pashkevich, Vasily Alexeyevich," *The New Grove Dictionary of Opera*, 4 vols., ed. Stanley Sadie, vol. 3 (Oxford: Oxford University Press, 1997), 899–900.

43. Beales, *Joseph II*, vol. 2, 341; Johann Heiss, "Die Ereignisse zum hundertjährigen Jubiläum 1783," in *Geschichtspolitik und Türkenbelagerung*, ed. Johannes Feichtinger and Johann Heiss (Vienna: Mandelbaum, 2013), 59–60; Johann Pezzl, *Marokkanische Briefe: Aus dem Arabischen* (Frankfurt/Leipzig: Johann Paul Krausischen Buchhandlung, 1784), 9–10.

44. David Charlton, "Zémire et Azor," in *The New Grove Dictionary of Opera*, vol. 4, 1224; *Catalogue of Opera Librettos Printed before 1800*, vol. 2, Library of Congress, Music Division, ed. Oscar George Theodore Sonneck (Washington: U.S. Government Printing Office, 1914), 1317; Bauman, *W. A. Mozart, Die Entführung aus dem Serail*, 10.

45. André Grétry, *La caravane du Caire, opéra en trois actes* (Paris: Chez de Lormel, 1785), 6.

46. Ibid., 6.

47. Ibid., 15.

48. Ibid., 18–19.

49. Ibid., 19–20.

50. Bernard Lewis, *The Emergence of Modern Turkey*, 2nd ed. (Oxford: Oxford University Press, 1968), 47–49.

51. David Charlton, "Caravane du Caire, La," *The New Grove Dictionary of Opera*, vol. 1, 728.

52. "La Caravane du Caire," ca. 1785–1790, textiles-printed, French, accession number 26.233.24, The Metropolitan Museum of Art, The Collection Online, http://metmuseum.org/collection/the-collection-online/search/221854; and "La Caravane du Caire," early 19th century, textiles-printed, French, accession number 31.130.7, The Metropolitan Museum of Art, The Collection Online, http://www.metmuseum.org/collection/the-collection-online/search/222538

53. Grétry, *La caravane du Caire*, 38.

54. Bent Holm, *The Taming of the Turk: Ottomans on the Danish Stage 1596–1896* (Vienna: Hollitzer, 2014), 150–53.

55. *Mozart's Letters, Mozart's Life*, letter of March 29, 1783, 346; Mozart, *Briefe*, ed. Wandrey, 348.

56. *Mozart's Letters, Mozart's Life*, letter of April 12, 1783, 348.

57. Lewis, *Emergence of Modern Turkey*, 49.

58. Bauman, *W. A. Mozart, Die Entführung aus dem Serail*, 103.

59. Da Ponte and Mozart, *Così fan tutte*, act 1, scene 11, in Lorenzo Da Ponte, *Memorie/Libretti mozartiani* (Milan: Garzanti, 1981), 622.

60. Johann Pezzl, *Sketch of Vienna*, in H.C. Robbins Landon, *Mozart and Vienna* (New York: Schirmer Books, 1991), 65–66.

61. Da Ponte and Mozart, *Le nozze di Figaro*, act 1, scene 8, in *Memorie/Libretti mozartiani*, 426.

62. Braunbehrens, *Mozart in Vienna*, 314–16.

63. Larry Wolff, *Inventing Eastern Europe: The Map of Civilization on the Mind of the Enlightenment* (Stanford: Stanford University Press, 1994), 134–39.

64. Ibid.

65. Pezzl, *Sketch of Vienna*, 162.

66. Ibid., 162–63.

67. Maynard Solomon, *Mozart: A Life* (New York: Harper Collins, 1995), 432.

68. Uwe Baur, "Figurinen zu Mozarts Oper *Die Entführung aus dem Serail* (Koblenz 1787)," *Acta Mozartiana* 49 (2002), notebooks 1–2, 53–72.

69. Matthew Head, "In the Orient of Vienna: Mozart's 'Turkish' Music and the Theatrical Self," in *Ottoman Empire and European Theatre*, vol. 1, *The Age of Mozart and Selim III*, ed. Michael Hüttler and Hans Weidinger (Vienna: Hollitzer, 2013), 607.

70. Beales, "Mozart and the Habsburgs," 103–4.

71. Ibid., 104–05.

72. Ibid., 108.

73. Ibid.

74. Ibid.

75. Pezzl, *Sketch of Vienna*, 178–79.

76. Ibid.

77. Beales, "Mozart and the Habsburgs," 104 and 115; Solomon, *Mozart: A Life*, 432.

78. Suna Suner, "Of Messengers, Messages, and Memoirs: Opera and the Eighteenth-Century Ottoman Envoys and their Sefâretnâmes," in *Ottoman Empire and European Theatre*, vol. 2, *The Time of Joseph Haydn: From Sultan Mahmud I to Mahmud II*, ed. Michael Hüttler and Hans Weidinger (Vienna: Hollitzer, 2014), 123–24.

79. Jane Girdham, "The Siege of Belgrade," *The New Grove Dictionary of Opera*, vol. 4, 365–66; Emre Araci, "Help for the Turk: Investigating Ottoman Musical Represen-

tations in Britain from the Late Eighteenth to the Mid Nineteenth Century," in *Age of Mozart and Selim III*, 378; Margaret Griffel, "Turkish Opera from Mozart to Cornelius," Ph.D. dissertation, Columbia University, 1975, 188–90.

80. Stanford Shaw, *Between Old and New: The Ottoman Empire under Sultan Selim III, 1789–1807* (Cambridge: Harvard University Press, 1971), 13–27 and 180–256.

81. Talat Halman, *Rapture and Revolution: Essays on Turkish Literature* (Syracuse: Syracuse University Press, 2007), 120; Suna Suner, "The Earliest Opera Performances in the Ottoman World and the Role of Diplomacy," in *Age of Mozart and Selim III*, 196–97; Bülent Aksoy, "Musical Relationships between Italy and Turkey through Turkish Eyes," in *Giuseppe Donizetti Pascià: Traiettorie musicali e storiche tra Italia e Turchia*, ed. Federico Spinetti (Bergamo: Fondazione Donizetti, 2010), 66; see also Günsel Renda, "Selim III as Patron of the Arts," in *Age of Mozart and Selim III*, 823–30.

82. Solomon, *Mozart: A Life*, 469–71.

83. Benjamin Perl, "Mozart in Turkey," *Cambridge Opera Journal* 12:3 (2001), 234.

84. H.C. Robbins Landon, *1791: Mozart's Last Year* (New York: Schirmer Books, 1988), 107–9.

85. Braunbehrens, *Mozart in Vienna*, 316.

86. Da Ponte and Mozart, *Don Giovanni*, act 1, scene 5, in *Memorie/Libretti mozartiani*, 522.

87. Perl, "Mozart in Turkey," 229–31.

88. Mozart, *Die Entführung aus dem Serail: Partitura*, act 3, 282–92; *Letters of Mozart and His Family*, letter of January 11, 1778, 444–45; Mozart, *Briefe*, ed. Wandrey, 115.

Chapter 7: The Ottoman Adventures of Rossini and Napoleon

1. Stendhal, *Vie de Rossini* (Paris: Michel Lévy Frères, 1854), 1; Stendhal, *Life of Rossini*, trans. Richard Coe (Seattle: University of Washington Press, 1970), 3.

2. Herbert Weinstock, *Rossini: A Biography* (New York: Limelight Editions, 1987), 6–7.

3. Henry Laurens, *Les origines intellectuelles de l'expédition d'Égypte: L'Orientalisme Islamisant en France, 1698–1798* (Istanbul/Paris: Editions Isis, Institut Français d'Études Anatoliennes, 1987), 187–90.

4. Edward Said, *Orientalism* (New York: Knopf, 1979), 80–88 ; Juan Cole, *Napoleon's Egypt: Invading the Middle East* (New York: Palgrave Macmillan, 2007), 245–46.

5. Maya Jasanoff, *Edge of Empire: Lives, Culture, and Conquest in the East, 1750–1850* (New York: Vintage Books, 2006), 138–39; Cole, *Napoleon's Egypt*, 128; see also Alexandre Lhaa, "Performing Turkish Rulers on the Teatro Alla Scala's Stage: From the Late Eighteenth to the Mid Nineteenth Century," in *Ottoman Empire and European Theatre*, vol. 1, *The Age of Mozart and Selim III*, ed. Michael Hüttler and Hans Weidinger (Vienna: Hollitzer, 2013), 321–22.

6. Cole, *Napoleon's Egypt*, 126–28; Jasanoff, *Edge of Empire*, 144–46.

7. Cole, *Napoleon's Egypt*, 125–27; see also Orhan Koloğlu, *Le Turc dans la presse française* (Beirut: Al-Hayat, 1971), 202–14.

8. Jasanoff, *Edge of Empire*, 145–46.

9. Bernard Lewis, *The Emergence of Modern Turkey*, 2nd ed. (London: Oxford University Press, 1968), 58–61.

10. *L'enlèvement du Serail, imité de l'allemand par le Citoyen Moline, redigé par I. Pleyel, musique de W. A. Mozart, arrangé pour le clavecin par C. G. Neefe* (Bonn: Chez N. Simrock, 1798?), conserved in the Bibliothèque Nationale de France, Paris, Département de la Musique.

11. Ibid., 23–28.

12. Ibid., 123.

13. Cole, *Napoleon's Egypt*, 189.

14. *L'enlèvement du Serail*, 83–86.

15. Ibid., 140–51.

16. Miriam Whaples, "Early Exoticism Revisited," in *The Exotic in Western Music*, ed. Jonathan Bellman (Boston: Northeastern University Press, 1998), 19.

17. Vittoria Crespi Morbio, ed., *La Scala di Napoleone: Spettacoli a Milano 1796–1814* (Turin: Umberto Allemandi, 2010), 20.

18. Alexandre Lhaa, "Performing Turkish Rulers on the Teatro Alla Scala's Stage," 319–22.

19. Jeremiah McGrann, "Of Saints, Name Days, and Turks: Some Background on Haydn's Masses Written for Prince Nikolaus II Esterhazy," *Journal of Musicological Research* 17:3–4 (1998), 195–210.

20. Anke Schmitt, *Der Exotismus in der deutschen Oper zwischen Mozart und Spohr* (Hamburg: Verlag der Musikalienhandlung Karl Dieter Wagner, 1988), 131–33.

21. Lewis, *Emergence of Modern Turkey*, 56–64; Cole, *Napoleon's Egypt*, 31.

22. Lewis, *Emergence of Modern Turkey*, 70–72.

23. Tom Standage, *The Turk: The Life and Times of the Famous Eighteenth-Century Chess-Playing Machine* (New York: Berkley Books, 2002), 105–7.

24. Alexander de Groot, "Dragomans' Careers: The Change of Status in Some Families Connected with the British and Dutch Embassies at Istanbul, 1785–1829," in *Friends and Rivals in the East: Studies in Anglo-Dutch Relations in the Levant from the Seventeenth to the Early Nineteenth Century*, ed. Alastair Hamilton, Alexander de Groot, and Maurits van den Boogert (Leiden: Brill, 2000), 243–44; Çetin Sarikartal, "Two Turkish-Language Plays Written by Europeans at the Academy of Oriental Languages in Vienna during the Age of Haydn," in *Ottoman Empire and European Theatre*, vol. 2, *The Time of Joseph Haydn: From Sultan Mahmud I to Mahmud II*, ed. Michael Hüttler and Hans Weidinger (Vienna: Hollitzer, 2014), 149–52.

25. *Hadgi Bektache ou La création des Janissaires, drame en langue Turque en trois*

actes, par [Thomas] Chabert (Vienna: Chez Antoine Schmid, 1810), "avant propos," conserved in the Bibliothèque Nationale de France, Paris.

26. s.v. "Reichardt, Johann Friedrich," in *A Dictionary of Musicians: From the Earliest Ages to the Present Time*, vol. 2 (London: Sainsbury, 1824), 344–45.

27. Peter Winter, *Tamerlan, opera en trois actes; représenté pour la première fois, sur le Théâtre de l'Opéra, le 27 Fructidor an X [14 September 1802]; les paroles sont de M. Morel; la musique est de M. Winter* (Paris: Chez Roullet, 1815), 1.

28. Winter, *Tamerlan*, 41; Théodore de Lajarte, *Bibliothèque Musicale du Théâtre de l'Opéra: Catalogue historique, chronologique, anecdotique* (Paris: D. Jouaust, 1878; reprint, Hildesheim: Georg Olms Verlag, 1969), vol. 2, 26–27; see also Isabelle Moindrot, "*Tamerlan*: A 'Turkish' Opera by Peter von Winter for the Paris Opera (1802)," in *Time of Joseph Haydn*, 521–36.

29. Alexander Broadley and John Holland Rose, *Napoleon in Caricature, 1795–1821*, vol. 1 (London: John Lane, 1911), 190.

30. Peter von Winter, *Zaira, a serious opera in two acts, as represented in the King's Theatre in the Haymarket* (London: printed by P. Da Ponte & J. B. Vogel, and sold by L. Da Ponte, 1805); Rodney Bolt, *The Librettist of Venice: The Remarkable Life of Lorenzo Da Ponte* (New York: Bloomsbury, 2006), 392.

31. Crespi Morbio, *La Scala di Napoleone*, plate 6.

32. *Le médecin Turc, opéra-bouffon en un acte, paroles de MM. Armand-Gouffé et Villiers, musique de M. Nicolò Isouard, représenté pour la première fois, à Paris sur le Théâtre de l'Opéra-Comique, le 27 Brumaire an 12* (Paris: Chez Madame Cavanagh, ci-devant Barba, an XII-1803); Margaret Griffel, "Turkish Opera from Mozart to Cornelius," Ph.D. dissertation, Columbia University, 1975, 155–56.

33. Louis Jadin, *Mahomet II, tragédie-lyrique en trois actes, représentée pour la première fois sur le Théâtre de l'Opéra, en Thermidor, an XI [1803]; les paroles sont du C[itoyen] Saulnier; la musique est du C[itoyen] Louis Jadin; les ballets sont du C[itoyen] Gardel* (Paris: Chez Ballard, an XI-1803), 5.

34. Ibid., 54.

35. Ibid.

36. Pierre Baour de Lormian, *Mahomet II, tragédie en cinq actes et en vers, représentée pour la première fois sur le Théâtre Français, le 9 mars 1811; e le 12 du même mois au palais des Tuileries devant LL. MM. II. et RR.* (Paris: Chez J. N. Barba, 1811).

37. *Arlequin Odalisque, comédie-parade en un acte et en prose, mêlée de vaudevilles; représentée pour la première fois, sur le Théâtre des Troubadours, le 15 Messidor, an VIII [4 July 1800]; par le Citoyen [Louis-Simon] Auger* (Paris: Au magasin des pièces de théâtre, 1800?); *Arlequin à Maroc, ou la pyramide enchantée, Théâtre des Jeunes Artistes, 11 Thermidor, an XII [30 July 1804]; par J. B. [Jean-Baptiste-Augustin] Hapdé; musique de M. [François] Foignet fils* (Paris: Chez Barba, an XII-1804).

38. Isabelle Moindrot, "The 'Turk' and the 'Parisienne': From Favart's *Soliman Second, ou Les trois sultanes* (1761) to *Les trois sultanes* (Pathé, 1912)," in *Age of Mozart and Selim III*, 428n5 and 447–52.

39. *Mahomet Barbe-Bleue, ou La terreur des Ottomanes, imitation burlesque de Mahomet II, en prose et en un acte, mêlée de couplets* (Paris: Chez Madame Veuve Duminil-Lesueur, 1811), 16.

40. Ibid., 10.

41. Schmitt, *Der Exotismus in der deutschen Oper*, 438.

42. *Les Pages au Sérail, vaudeville en deux actes de Messieurs [Emmanuel] Théaulon et [Armand] Dartois, représenté sur le Théâtre du Vaudeville, le 17 Juin 1811* (Paris: Imprimerie de J. B. Sajou, 1811), 5.

43. David Chaillou, *Napoléon et l'Opéra: La politique sur la scène 1810–1815* (Paris: Fayard, 2004), 8–10; see also James Johnson, *Listening in Paris: A Cultural History* (Berkeley: University of California Press, 1995), 165–81.

44. Chaillou, *Napoléon et l'Opéra*, 314–16.

45. Ibid., 124.

46. Crespi Morbio, *La Scala di Napoleone*, 37–39, and plates 95 and 97; Giampiero Tintori, *Cronologia: Opere, balletti, concerti 1778–1977* (Gorle: Grafica Gutenberg, 1979), June 1, 1805, "Cantata alla presenza di Napoleone"; Monica Guerzoni, "Federici, Vincenzo," in *Dizionario Biografico degli Italiani*, vol. 45 (Rome: Istituto della Enciclopedia Italiana, 1995).

47. Crespi Morbio, *La Scala di Napoleone*, plate 97.

48. Johann Simon Mayr, *Tamerlano, melodramma serio in due atti del Sig. Luigi Romanelli, da rappresentarsi sul Teatro alla Scala per la prima opera di carnevale dell'anno 1813 [26 dicembre 1812]; musica di Giovanni Simone Mayr [Johann Simon Mayr]* (Milan: Tipografia dei Classici Italiani, 1812?), 8.

49. Tintori, *Cronologia*, August 16, 1808, September 26, 1812, December 26, 1812.

50. Rossini, *La pietra del paragone*, act 1, scenes 10 and 17, in *Tutti i libretti di Rossini*, ed. Mario Beghelli and Nicola Gallino (Milan: Garzanti, 1991), 117 and 123.

51. Stendhal, *Vie de Rossini*, 71; Stendhal, *Life of Rossini*, 96.

52. Weinstock, *Rossini*, 31.

53. *Il serraglio, melodramma buffo in due atti obbligato alla musica dell'opera francese Les Visitandines del signor Devienne, rappresentato il giorno 17 gennaio dell'anno 1810 da una brigata di amici nella villa del sig. XXX ricorrendo l'anniversario del matrimonio di sua figliola maritata a Parigi* (Milan: Tipografia Bonfanti, 1810).

54. Rossini, *La pietra del paragone*, act 1, scene 17, in *Tutti i libretti di Rossini*, 123–24.

55. Stendhal, *Vie de Rossini*, 72; Stendhal, *Life of Rossini*, 96.

56. Elizabeth Forbes, "Galli, Filippo," in *The New Grove Dictionary of Opera*, 4 vols., ed. Stanley Sadie, vol. 2 (Oxford: Oxford University Press, 1997), 328–29.

57. Griffel, "Turkish Opera from Mozart to Cornelius," 19.

58. Stendhal, *Vie de Rossini*, 72; Stendhal, *Life of Rossini*, 96–97; Weinstock, *Rossini*, 31.

59. Stendhal, *Vie de Rossini*, 73; Stendhal, *Life of Rossini*, 97.

60. Stendhal, *Vie de Rossini*, 67; Stendhal, *Life of Rossini*, 91; Richard Osborne, "Rossini's Life," in *The Cambridge Companion to Rossini*, ed. Emanuele Senici (Cambridge: Cambridge University Press, 2004), 13–14; Rossini, *La pietra del paragone*, act 1, scene 8, in *Tutti i libretti di Rossini*, 116.

61. Schmitt, *Der Exotismus in der deutschen Oper*, 130.

62. Stendhal, *Vie de Rossini*, 69; Stendhal, *Life of Rossini*, 93.

63. Stendhal, *La Chartreuse de Parme* (Paris: Garnier-Flammarion, 1964), 39.

64. David Laven, *Venice and Venetia under the Habsburgs 1815–1835* (Oxford: Oxford University Press, 2002), 50.

65. Weinstock, *Rossini*, 32.

66. Standage, *The Turk*, 111–13.

67. Lord Byron, *Don Juan* (London: Thomas Allman, 1846), Fifth Canto, 130.

Chapter 8: Pappataci and Kaimakan

1. Stendhal, *Vie de Rossini* (Paris: Michel Lévy Frères, 1854), 55; Stendhal, *Life of Rossini*, trans. Richard Coe (Seattle: University of Washington Press, 1970), 72.

2. *Giornale Dipartimentale dell'Adriatico*, May 24, 1813.

3. Herbert Weinstock, *Rossini: A Biography* (New York: Limelight Editions, 1987), 39.

4. Giuseppe Ortolani, *Settecento: Per una lettura dell'abate Chiari* (Venice: Fontana, 1905), 510–11; Paolo Preto, "Il mito del turco nella letteratura veneziana," in *Venezia e i Turchi: Scontri e confronti di due civiltà* (Milan: Electa, 1985), 139.

5. Thomas Bauman, *W. A. Mozart, Die Entführung aus dem Serail* (Cambridge: Cambridge University Press, 1987), 115.

6. Stendhal, *Vie de Rossini*, 38; Stendhal, *Life of Rossini*, 50.

7. David Chaillou, *Napoléon et l'Opéra: La politique sur la scène 1810–1815* (Paris: Fayard, 2004), 286–87; see also James Parakilas, "How Spain Got a Soul," in *The Exotic in Western Music*, ed. Jonathan Bellman (Boston: Northeastern University Press, 1998), 146.

8. Chaillou, *Napoléon et l'Opéra*, 307.

9. Chaillou, *Napoléon et l'Opéra*, 231–35.

10. Mozart, *Die Entführung aus dem Serail*, act 1, in J. D. McClatchy, *Seven Mozart Librettos* (New York: Norton, 2011), 158–59; Stephanie and Mozart, *Die Entführung aus dem Serail* (Vienna: Logenmeister, 1782), in *Die Entführung aus dem Serail: Faksimile-Ausgabe zur Geschichte des Librettos*, ed. Gerhard Croll and Ulrich Müller (Salzburg: Verlag Ursula Müller-Speiser, 1993), 10–11.

11. Paul Corneilson, *The Autobiography of Ludwig Fischer: Mozart's First Osmin* (Malden, MA: Mozart Society of America, 2011), 39.

12. Robert Davis, *Christian Slaves, Muslim Masters: White Slavery in the Mediter-*

ranean, the Barbary Coast, and Italy, 1500–1800 (New York: Palgrave Macmillan, 2003), 23; see also Linda Colley, *Captives: Britain, Empire, and the World, 1600–1800* (New York: Anchor Books, 2002); and Roderick Cavaliero, *Ottomania: The Romantics and the Myth of the Islamic Orient* (2010; London: I. B. Tauris, 2013), 65–79.

13. Rossini, *L'italiana in Algeri, dramma giocoso per musica da rappresentarsi nel Teatro a S. Benedetto, la Primavera dell'Anno 1813. Musica del Sig. Giovacchino Rossini di Pesaro* (Venice: Casali Stampatore, 1813), 6.

14. Davis, *Christian Slaves, Muslim Masters*, 29.

15. Larry Wolff, "Venice and the Slavs of Dalmatia: The Drama of the Adriatic Empire in the Venetian Enlightenment," *Slavic Review* 56:3 (Fall 1997), 428–55.

16. Jon Meacham, *Thomas Jefferson: The Art of Power* (New York: Random House, 2012), 365–66; see also Brian Kilmeade and Don Yaeger, *Thomas Jefferson and the Tripoli Pirates: The Forgotten War That Changed American History* (New York: Sentinel, 2015).

17. Weinstock, *Rossini*, 406; Richard Osborne and John Black, "Anelli, Angelo," in *The New Grove Dictionary of Opera*, 4 vols., ed. Stanley Sadie, vol. 1 (Oxford: Oxford University Press, 1997), 133.

18. Angelo Anelli (libretto) and Luigi Mosca (music), *L'italiana in Algeri, dramma giocoso per musica da rappresentarsi nel R. Teatro alla Scala, l'autunno dell'anno 1808* (Milan: Società Tipografica de' Classici Italiani, 1808), 22; Paolo Fabbri, "Librettos and Librettists," in *The Cambridge Companion to Rossini*, ed. Emanuele Senici (Cambridge: Cambridge University Press, 2004), 55.

19. D. Doran Bugg, "The Role of Turkish Percussion in the History and Development of the Orchestral Percussion Section," Ph.D. dissertation, Louisiana State University, 2003, 38–40; *A Descriptive Catalogue of the Musical Instruments Recently Exhibited at the Royal Military Exhibition, London, 1890* (London: Eyre & Spottiswoode, 1891), 233.

20. Bauman, *W. A. Mozart, Die Entführung aus dem Serail*, 115 and 129n30.

21. Rossini, *L'italiana in Algeri: Vocal Score*, ed. Azio Corghi (Milan: Ricordi, 1982), 14–15.

22. Ibid., vi and 15–18.

23. Ibid., 20–26.

24. Ibid., 27–29.

25. Voltaire, *Essai sur les moeurs*, ed. René Pomeau, vol. 2 (Paris: Garnier Frères, 1963), 807–8.

26. Rossini, *L'italiana in Algeri: Vocal Score*, 39.

27. Ibid., 41.

28. Ibid., 70–76.

29. Ibid., 77–79.

30. Stendhal, *Vie de Rossini*, 53; Stendhal, *Life of Rossini*, 69.

31. Rossini, *L'italiana in Algeri: Vocal Score*, 85–86.

32. Ibid., 107.

33. Ibid., 117.

34. Ibid., 123–26.

35. Ibid., 130–31.

36. Ibid., 132–35.

37. Ibid., 136.

38. Ibid., 137–43.

39. Mosca, *L'italiana in Algeri* (partitura), in *L'italiana in Algeri*, ed. Paolo Fabbri and Maria Chiara Bertieri (Pesaro: Fondazione Rossini, 1997), 255–72.

40. Rossini, *L'italiana in Algeri: Vocal Score*, 177.

41. Ibid., 179–80.

42. Ibid., 189–194.

43. Margaret Griffel, "Turkish Opera from Mozart to Cornelius," Ph.D. dissertation, Columbia University, 1975, 92.

44. Rossini, *L'italiana in Algeri: Vocal Score*, 237–38.

45. Ibid., 259.

46. Ibid., 145.

47. Aldo Castellani and Albert Chalmers, *Manual of Tropical Medicine*, 3rd ed. (New York: William Wood, 1919), ch. 44, "Pappataci Fever," 1254–55.

48. Rossini, *L'italiana in Algeri: Vocal Score*, 351–66.

49. Ibid., 415–16.

50. Johann Wolfgang von Goethe, *Italian Journey*, trans. W. H. Auden and Elizabeth Mayer (San Francisco: North Point Press, 1982), 43, 132, 190.

51. Auguste Creuzé de Lesser, *Voyage en Italie et en Sicile, fait en 1801 et 1802* (Paris: Chez P. Didot l'aîné, 1806), 75, 96, 110, 115; see also Nelson Moe, *The View from Vesuvius: Italian Culture and the Southern Question* (Berkeley: University of California Press, 2002), 37–57.

52. *Giornale Dipartimentale dell'Adriatico*, May 24, 1813.

53. Stendhal, *Rome, Naples, et Florence en 1817* (Paris: Delaunay, 1817), 168–70.

54. Rossini, *L'italiana in Algeri: Vocal Score*, 378.

55. Ibid., 380–81.

56. Rossini, *Tancredi, melodramma eroico per musica, l'estate del 1816* (Livorno: Pietro Meucci, 1816?) act 1, scene 4, 7.

57. Stendhal, *La Chartreuse de Parme* (Paris: Garnier-Flammarion, 1964), 39–40.

58. Stendhal, *Vie de Rossini*, 50; Stendhal, *Life of Rossini*, 65.

59. Azio Corghi, "Prefazione," *L'italiana in Algeri: Vocal Score*, xix–xx; Philip Gossett, "Transmission versus Tradition," in *Divas and Scholars: Performing Italian Opera* (Chicago: University of Chicago Press, 2006), 89–97; *L'italiana in Algeri* (Turin: Derossi, 1813); *L'italiana in Algeri* (Trieste: Governiale, 1814); *L'italiana in Algeri* (Florence: Giuseppe Fantosini, 1814); *L'italiana in Algeri* (Ancona: Baluffi, 1814); *L'italiana in Algeri* (Ferrara: Francesco Pomatelli, 1815).

60. *Giornale Dipartimentale dell'Adriatico*, May 24, 1813.

61. Ibid.

62. Corghi, "Prefazione," xxii; Gossett, "Transmission versus Tradition," 90–91.

63. *Il Corriere Milanese*, August 13, 1815.

64. *Il Corriere Milanese*, August 11, 1815.

65. Ibid.

66. *Il Corriere Milanese*, August 15, 1815.

67. Weinstock, *Rossini*, 43–45; Richard Osborne, *Rossini* (1986; Oxford: Oxford University Press, 2001), 21; Cesare Questa, *Il ratto dal serraglio: Euripide, Plauto, Mozart, Rossini* (Bologna: Patron Editore, 1979), 144–50.

68. Rossini, *L'Italiana in Algeri: Vocal Score*, appendix 4, 514. I am grateful to Marco Cipolloni and Karl Appuhn for consulting with me about the possible meanings of this verse.

69. Weinstock, *Rossini*, 44–45.

70. Stendhal, *Vie de Rossini*, 55; Stendhal, *Life of Rossini*, 72.

71. Rossini, *L'italiana in Algeri: Vocal Score*, 421–27.

72. Ibid., 440–41.

73. Ibid., 442–43.

Chapter 9: An Ottoman Prince in the Romantic Imagination

1. Stendhal, *Vie de Rossini* (Paris: Michel Lévy Frères, 1854), 113; Stendhal, *Life of Rossini*, trans. Richard Coe (Seattle: University of Washington Press, 1970), 146.

2. Stendhal, *Vie de Rossini*, 116; Stendhal, *Life of Rossini*, 151.

3. *Corriere Milanese*, August 14, 1814.

4. Ibid.

5. Herbert Weinstock, *Rossini: A Biography* (New York: Limelight Editions, 1987), 41.

6. Philip Gossett, "*Il turco in Italia*: Poor Relation or Noble Scion?" (CD liner notes), in Rossini, *Il turco in Italia* (Neville Marriner, Academy of St. Martin in the Fields), (Philips, 1992), 13.

7. Fiamma Nicolodi, "Da Mazzolà a Romani (e Rossini)," in *Il turco in Italia*, ed. Fiamma Nicolodi (Pesaro: Fondazione Rossini, 2002), x–xiii and xlii; Erich Duda, "Mozart's Pupil and Friend: Franz Xaver Süssmayr's *Sinfonia Turchesca, Il turco in Italia*, and *Soliman der Zweite*," in *Ottoman Empire and European Theatre*, vol. 1, *The Age of Mozart and Selim III*, ed. Michael Hüttler and Hans Weidinger (Vienna: Hollitzer, 2013), 548–51.

8. Margaret Bent, "Prefazione," in Rossini, *Il turco in Italia: Vocal Score*, 2 vols. (Milan: Ricordi, 2000), vol. 1, xvi–xviii; Weinstock, *Rossini*, 494; Fiamma Nicolodi and Paolo Trovato, "La tradizione primo ottocentesca dei libretti (1814–1830)," in *Il turco in Italia*, ed. Nicolodi, lxiii–lxvi; Margaret Griffel, "Turkish Opera from Mozart to Cornelius," Ph.D. dissertation, Columbia University, 1975, 183n60; Alfred Loewenberg, *Annals of Op-*

era 1597–1940, 3rd ed. (London: John Calder, 1978), 1814: *Il turco in Italia*, online, http:// archive.org/stream/AnnalesOfOpera1597–1940/AnnalsOfOpera_djvu.txt

9. Robert Davis, *Christian Slaves, Muslim Masters: White Slavery in the Mediterranean, the Barbary Coast, and Italy, 1500–1800* (New York: Palgrave Macmillan, 2003), 35.

10. Davis, *Christian Slaves, Muslim Masters*, 45; Paul Corneilson, *The Autobiography of Ludwig Fischer: Mozart's First Osmin* (Malden, MA: Mozart Society of America, 2011), 39.

11. Montesquieu, *Persian Letters*, trans. C. J. Betts (New York: Penguin Classics, 1973), 23rd letter, 71.

12. Johann Wolfgang von Goethe, *Italian Journey*, trans. W. H. Auden and Elizabeth Mayer (San Francisco: North Point Press, 1982), 195 and 198.

13. *Giornale Italiano*, August 22, 1814.

14. Ibid.

15. *Corriere Milanese*, August 19, 1814.

16. Rossini, *Il turco in Italia: Vocal Score*, vol. 1, 18.

17. Ibid., 62.

18. Ibid., 63–65.

19. Mazzolà, *Il turco in Italia* (Vienna, 1789), in *Il turco in Italia*, ed. Nicolodi, 22.

20. Mazzolà, *Il turco in Italia* (Vienna, 1789), and Mazzolà, *La capricciosa ravveduta, dramma giocoso per musica da rappresentarsi nel nobilissimo Teatro Giustiniani in San Moisè* (Venice, 1794), in *Il turco in Italia*, ed. Nicolodi, 22 and 89.

21. Rossini, *Il turco in Italia: Vocal Score*, vol. 1, 65–67.

22. Ibid., 71 and 186.

23. Ibid., 81–82.

24. Ibid., 83–85.

25. Stendhal, *Life of Rossini*, 146.

26. *Corriere Milanese*, August 25, 1814.

27. Ibid.

28. Rossini, *Il turco in Italia: Vocal Score*, vol. 1, 87- 91; see also Alessandro Roccatagliati, *Felice Romani librettista* (Lucca: Libreria Musicale Italiana, 1996), 167–69.

29. Rossini, *Il turco in Italia: Vocal Score*, vol. 1, 98–100.

30. Ibid., 102.

31. Ibid., 107.

32. Mazzolà, *Il turco in Italia* (Vienna, 1789), act 1, scene 6, and Mazzolà, *La capricciosa ravveduta* (Venice, 1794), act 1, scene 7, in *Il turco in Italia*, ed. Nicolodi, 36 and 100.

33. Fernand Braudel, *The Structures of Everyday Life: Civilization and Capitalism*, vol. 1 (New York: Harper & Row, 1982), 256–57; Danilo Reato, *La bottega del caffè: I caffè veneziani tra '700 e '900* (Venice: Arsenale Editrice, 1991), 13–15, 24–27, 44–46.

34. Rossini, *L'italiana in Algeri*, in *Tutti i libretti di Rossini*, ed. Marco Beghelli and Nicola Gallino (Milan: Garzanti, 1991), 215.

35. Rossini, *Il turco in Italia: Vocal Score*, vol. 1, 130–31.

36. Ibid., 132–34.

37. Ibid., 135–36.

38. Ibid., 138–39.

39. Stendhal, *Vie de Rossini*, 113; Stendhal, *Life of Rossini*, 147.

40. Stendhal, *Vie de Rossini*, 114; Stendhal, *Life of Rossini*, 147–48.

41. *Allgemeines bürgerliches Gesetzbuch für die gesammten Deutschen Erbländer der Oesterreichischen Monarchie*, part 1 (Vienna: Aus der k. k. Hof und Staatsdruckerey, 1811), 6–7.

42. Weinstock, *Rossini*, 339; *Onoranze Fiorentine a Gioachino Rossini: Inaugurandosi in Santa Croce il Monumento al Grande Maestro*, ed. Riccardo Gandolfi (Florence: Tipografia Galletti & Cocci, 1902), letter of March 23, 1866, 107.

43. Bent, "Prefazione," xvi–xvii.

44. Rossini, *Il turco in Italia: Vocal Score*, vol. 1, 190–91.

45. *Corriere Milanese*, August 16, 1814.

46. Ibid.

47. Rossini, *Il turco in Italia: Vocal Score*, vol. 2, 313–14; see also Roccatagliati, *Felice Romani librettista*, 178–80.

48. Stendhal, *Vie de Rossini*, 115; Stendhal, *Life of Rossini*, 150.

49. Rossini, *Il turco in Italia: Vocal Score*, vol. 2, 362–63.

50. Ibid., 364–69.

51. Ibid., 453; Stendhal, *Life of Rossini*, 151; Gossett, "*Il turco in Italia*: Poor Relation or Noble Scion?" 18.

52. *The Letters of Mozart and His Family*, ed. Emily Anderson, 3rd ed. (New York: Norton, 1985), letter of May 16, 1789, 926; Rodney Bolt, *The Librettist of Venice: The Remarkable Life of Lorenzo Da Ponte* (London: Bloomsbury, 2006), 53.

53. Bruce Brown, *W. A. Mozart, Così fan tutte* (Cambridge: Cambridge University Press, 1995), 166; Gossett, "*Il turco in Italia*: Poor Relation or Noble Scion?" 14–15; see also Nicolodi, "Da Mazzolà a Romani (e Rossini)," lvi–lix.

54. Gossett, "*Il turco in Italia*: Poor Relation or Noble Scion?" 15.

55. Rossini, *Il turco in Italia: Vocal Score*, vol. 2, 520.

56. Ibid., 523–27.

57. Ibid., 535.

Chapter 10: Maometto in Naples and Venice

1. Voltaire, *Essai sur les moeurs*, ed. René Pomeau, vol. 1 (Paris: Garnier Frères, 1963), 817.

2. Franz Babinger, *Mehmed the Conqueror and His Time*, trans. Ralph Manheim, ed. William Hickman (Princeton: Princeton University Press, 1978), 280–84.

3. Nancy Bisaha, *Creating East and West: Renaissance Humanists and the Ottoman Turks* (Philadelphia: University of Pennsylvania Press, 2004), 63.

4. Bernard Lewis, *Istanbul and the Civilization of the Ottoman Empire* (1963; Norman: University of Oklahoma Press, 1972), 26–27.

5. Gioachino Rossini, *Maometto II, dramma per musica in due atti, testi di Cesare della Valle* (Naples, 1820), www.librettidopera.it, act 1, scene 4, 15.

6. Herbert Weinstock, *Rossini: A Biography* (New York: Limelight Editions, 1987), 102–3; Marco Beghelli, "Quando Maometto sbarcò a Venezia," in *Maometto Secondo*, ed. Michele Girardi (Venice: Fondazione Teatro La Fenice, 2005), 28.

7. Louis Jadin, *Mahomet II* (Paris: Chez Ballard, an XI-1803).

8. Weinstock, *Rossini*, 74–75; Weinstock's biography of Rossini confuses the subject of Winter's opera, identifying it as *Maometto II* when it was simply *Maometto*, but Weinstock clearly indicates that Rossini was present for a performance of Winter's opera.

9. Voltaire, *Le fanatisme ou Mahomet le Prophète* (Amsterdam: Jacques Desbordes, 1743), act 1, scene 1, 3.

10. Voltaire, *Le fanatisme ou Mahomet le Prophète*, act 5, scene 4, 104.

11. Linda Tyler, "Winter, Peter von," in *The New Grove Dictionary of Opera*, 4 vols., ed. Stanley Sadie, vol. 4 (Oxford: Oxford University Press, 1997), 1165–66.

12. Peter von Winter, *Maometto, melodramma tragico in due atti, del Sig. Felice Romani, da rappresentarsi nel Regio Teatro alla Scala, il carnevale dell'anno 1817* (Milan: Stamperia di Giacomo Pirola, 1817), 42.

13. Weinstock, *Rossini*, 75; Ferdinand Hiller, *Aus dem Tonleben unserer Zeit*, vol. 2 (Leipzig: Hermann Mendelssohn, 1868), 60–61.

14. Winter, *Maometto* (Milan, 1817), 9.

15. Weinstock, *Rossini*, 75; see also Winter, *Maometto* (Milan, 1817), 36.

16. Winter, *Maometto* (Milan, 1817), "*La città che a te si schiude*," 18; Rossini, *Maometto II* (Naples, 1820), "*Del mondo al vincitor*," act 1, scene 4, 15.

17. Elizabeth Forbes, "Donzelli, Domenico," in *The New Grove Dictionary of Opera*, vol. 1, 1228.

18. *Gazzetta di Milano*, January 31, 1817.

19. Winter, *Maometto* (Milan, 1817), 22.

20. Ibid., 43.

21. Paolo Preto, "Il mito del Turco nella letteratura veneziana," in *Venezia e i Turchi: Scontri e confronti di due civiltà* (Milan: Electa, 1985), 139.

22. Beghelli, "Quando Maometto sbarcò a Venezia," 29.

23. Georges Guillet de Saint-George, *Histoire du règne de Mahomet II, Empereur des Turcs*, vol. 2 (Paris: Chez Denys Thierry et Claude Barbin, 1681), 177–79.

24. Rossini, *Maometto II* (Naples, 1820), act 1, scene 1, 4–5.

25. Beghelli, "Quando Maometto sbarcò a Venezia," 33.

26. Rossini, *Maometto II* (Naples, 1820), act 1, scene 3, 13.

27. Ibid., act 1, scene 4, 14.

28. Ibid., 14.

29. Ibid., 14–15.

30. Ibid.

31. Anselm Gerhard, "Lo scontro delle civiltà e il nuovo ordine del melodramma: l'importanza della tinta turca nel *Maometto II* di Rossini," in *Maometto Secondo*, ed. Girardi, 9; Miriam Whaples, "Early Exoticism Revisited," in *The Exotic in Western Music*, ed. Jonathan Bellman (Boston: Northeastern University Press, 1998), 19.

32. Rossini, *Maometto II* (Naples, 1820), act 1, scene 4, 16.

33. Ibid., act 1, scene 5, 16–17.

34. Ibid., act 1, scene 6, 19–20.

35. Ibid., 20.

36. Ibid., 20.

37. Ibid., 21.

38. Ibid.

39. Ibid., act 2, scene 1, 22.

40. Ibid., act 2, scene 2, 23.

41. Ibid.

42. Ibid.; concerning *amava* vs. *amavo*, see Joseph Baretti, *English and Italian Dictionary*, 1st Leghorn ed. (Leghorn [Livorno]: J. P. Pozzolini, 1829), part 2, 27.

43. Rossini, *Maometto II* (Naples, 1820), act 2, scene 2, 23.

44. Ibid., 25.

45. Ibid., 27.

46. Ibid., act 2, scene 4, 29.

47. Ibid., act 2, scene 5, 32–33.

48. Ibid., act 2, scene 5, 33–34.

49. Gerhard, "Lo scontro delle civiltà," 13; Reto Müller, "*Maometto II* (Venice Version)," (CD liner notes), in Rossini, *Maometto II*, 1822 Venice Version (Brad Cohen, Czech Chamber Soloists, Brno) (Naxos, 2004), 5.

50. Rossini, *L'italiana in Algeri: Vocal Score*, ed. Azio Corghi (Milan: Ricordi, 1982), 380–81.

51. Weinstock, *Rossini*, 103–4; Richard Osborne, *Rossini* (1986; Oxford: Oxford University Press, 2001), 48–49.

52. Osborne, *Rossini*, 45.

53. Ibid., 56–57.

54. Weinstock, *Rossini*, 120–22.

55. Nicholas Mathew, "Beethoven and His Others: Criticism, Difference, and the Composer's Many Voices," *Beethoven Forum* 13:2 (Fall 2006), 149–50.

56. *Allgemeine musikalische Zeitung*, 7:10–11 (February 1823), 77–82.

57. Rossini, *Maometto Secondo, melo-dramma eroico da rappresentarsi nel Gran Teatro La Fenice, nel Carnovale 1822–23* (Venice, 1822), "Avvertimento," 4; see also Gian Giuseppe Filippi, "Mehmet II al-Fatih e la battaglia di Negroponte," in *Maometto Secondo,* ed. Girardi, 57–58.

58. Osborne, *Rossini,* 59–60.

59. Ulrike Tischler, *Die habsburgische Politik gegenüber den Serben und Montenegrinern 1791–1822* (Munich: Oldenbourg, 2000), 219n522; *Gazzetta Privilegiata di Venezia,* December 24, 1822.

60. *Gazzetta Privilegiata di Venezia,* December 24, 1822.

61. Müller, "*Maometto II* (Venice Version)," 5–6.

62. Rossini, *Maometto Secondo* (Venice, 1822), act 2, scene 3, 39.

63. Ibid., act 2, scene 4, 39.

64. Ibid., act 2, scene 8, 47.

65. Müller, "*Maometto II* (Venice Version)," 7.

66. *Gazzetta Privilegiata di Venezia,* December 28, 1822; Gerhard, "Lo scontro delle civiltà," 21.

67. *Il Nuovo Osservatore Veneziano,* December 31, 1822.

68. Ibid.

69. Ibid.

70. Ibid.

71. Ibid.

72. Ibid.

73. Weinstock, *Rossini,* 128.

74. *Gazzetta di Milano,* August 19, 1824; see also Rossini, *Maometto Secondo, melodramma serio, da rappresentarsi Nell' I. R. Teatro alla Scala, l'autunno dell'anno 1824* (Milan: Tipografia di Giacomo Pirola, 1824).

75. *Gazzetta di Milano,* August 15, 1824.

76. Ibid.

77. Ibid.

78. Ibid.

79. Weinstock, *Rossini,* 103.

Chapter 11: Rossini's Siege of Paris

1. James Johnson, *Listening in Paris: A Cultural History* (Berkeley: University of California Press, 1995), 184–85.

2. Isabelle Moindrot, "The 'Turk' and the 'Parisienne': From Favart's *Soliman Second, ou Les trois sultanes* (1761) to *Les trois sultanes* (Pathé, 1912)," in *Ottoman Empire and European Theatre,* vol. 1, *The Age of Mozart and Selim III,* ed. Michael Hüttler and Hans Weidinger (Vienna: Hollitzer, 2013), 439.

3. Andrea Lanza, "Pucitta, Vincenzo," in *The New Grove Dictionary of Opera,* 4

vols., ed. Stanley Sadie, vol. 3 (Oxford: Oxford University Press, 1997), 1173–74; Elizabeth Forbes, "Catalani, Angelica," in *The New Grove Dictionary of Opera*, vol. 1, 771.

4. Vincenzo Pucitta, *Le tre sultane, dramma giocoso in tre atti* (Paris: Théâtre Royal Italien, l'Imprimerie de Hacquet, 1816), 10–11.

5. Pucitta, *Le tre sultane* (Paris, 1816), 53.

6. *Le Fidèle Ami du Roi*, January 24, 1816, in Jean Mongrédien, *Le Théâtre-Italien de Paris 1801–1831: Chronologie et documents*, 8 vols. (Lyon: Symétrie, 2008), vol. 3 (1809–1816), 636–37.

7. *Journal des Débats*, January 24, 1816, in Mongrédien, *Le Théâtre-Italien*, vol. 3, 637–38.

8. Ibid.

9. *La Quotidienne*, January 27, 1816; *Journal de Paris*, January 31, 1816; *Gazette de France*, February 1, 1816, in Mongrédien, *Le Théâtre-Italien*, vol. 3, 640–43.

10. Stendhal, *Vie de Rossini* (Paris: Michel Lévy Frères, 1854), 20; Stendhal, *Life of Rossini*, trans. Richard Coe (Seattle: University of Washington Press, 1970), 27.

11. Stendhal, *Vie de Rossini*, 57–58; Stendhal, *Life of Rossini*, 76.

12. Jan Goldstein, *Console and Classify: The French Psychiatric Profession in the Nineteenth Century* (Chicago: University of Chicago Press, 1987), 129–30; see also Michel Foucault, *Madness and Civilization: A History of Insanity in the Age of Reason* (New York: Vintage, 1988).

13. *Gazette de France*, February 2, 1817, in Mongrédien, *Le Théâtre-Italien*, vol. 4 (1817–1821), 28–29.

14. Ibid.

15. *Le Constitutionnel*, February 3, 1817; *Journal de Paris*, February 4, 1817, in Mongrédien, *Le Théâtre-Italien*, vol. 4, 29–31.

16. *Courrier des Spectacles de Paris*, May 24, 1820; *Journal du Commerce*, May 25, 1820; *Journal de Paris*, June 1, 1820, in Mongrédien, *Le Théâtre-Italien*, vol. 4, 405–16.

17. *Journal des Théâtres, de la Litterature e des Arts*, May 25, 1820, in Mongrédien, *Le Théâtre-Italien*, vol. 4, 411–12.

18. *Journal des Théâtres, de la Litterature e des Arts*, May 26, 1820, in Mongrédien, *Le Théâtre-Italien*, vol. 4, 414.

19. *Journal des Théâtres, de la Litterature e des Arts*, June 11, 1820, June 20, 1820, in Mongrédien, *Le Théâtre-Italien*, vol. 4, 419–422.

20. Eugène Scribe and Xavier Saintine, *L'ours et le pacha* (Paris: Baudouin Frères, Pollet, et Barba, 1828), 26 and 34; Anke Schmitt, *Der Exotismus in der deutschen Oper zwischen Mozart und Spohr* (Hamburg: Verlag der Musikalienhandlung Karl Dieter Wagner, 1988), 151.

21. Mark Everist, *Music Drama at the Paris Odéon, 1824–1828* (Berkeley: University of California Press, 2002), 202–3.

22. Giacomo Meyerbeer, *Il crociato in Egitto, melo-dramma eroico, testi di Gaetano*

Rossi, musiche di Giacomo Meyerbeer, prima esecuzione: 7 marzo 1824, Venezia, www.librettidopera.it; see also Claudio Toscano, "Mamma li turchi! percorsi esotici nell'opera italiana di primo ottocento," in *Giuseppe Donizetti Pascià: Traiettorie musicali e storiche tra Italia e Turchia,* ed. Federico Spinetti (Bergamo: Fondazione Donizetti, 2010), 92–98.

23. "Proclamation of Independence Issued by the Greek National Assembly" (January 27, 1822), in *Readings in European History,* ed. James Harvey Robinson, vol. 2, *From the Opening of the Protestant Revolt to the Present Day* (Boston: Ginn and Company, 1906), 555.

24. Ibid.

25. Rossini, *Le siège de Corinthe, tragédie lyrique en trois actes de Luigi Balocchi et Alexandre Soumet* (Paris, 1826), in Rossini, *Le siège de Corinthe* (CD liner notes) (Paolo Olmi, Orchestra e Coro del Teatro Carlo Felice di Genova) (Nuova Era, 2002), libretto, act 1, scene 1, 25.

26. Ibid., 26.

27. Thomas Bauman, *W. A. Mozart, Die Entführung aus dem Serail* (Cambridge: Cambridge University Press, 1987), 111–15; Emre Araci, "'Help for the Turk': Investigating Ottoman Musical Representations in Britain from the Late Eighteenth to the Mid Nineteenth Century," in *Age of Mozart and Selim III,* 379–80.

28. Lord Byron, *Don Juan,* third canto, in *English Romantic Writers,* ed. David Perkins (New York: Harcourt, Brace & World, 1967), 878.

29. Lord Byron, *The Siege of Corinth,* in *The Siege of Corinth: A Poem & Parisina: A Poem* (London: John Murray, 1818); see also Roderick Cavaliero, *Ottomania: The Romantics and the Myth of the Islamic Orient* (2010; London: I. B. Tauris, 2013), 90–95.

30. Benjamin Walton, *Rossini in Restoration Paris: The Sound of Modern Life* (Cambridge: Cambridge University Press, 2007), 146–47.

31. Walton, *Rossini in Restoration Paris,* 127–31.

32. Herbert Weinstock, *Rossini: A Biography* (New York: Limelight Editions, 1987), 150–55.

33. Rossini, *Le siège de Corinthe* (Paris, 1826), act 1, scene 7, 31.

34. Bernard Lewis, *Istanbul and the Civilization of the Ottoman Empire* (1963; Norman: University of Oklahoma Press, 1972), 26–27 and 103–4.

35. Rossini, *Le siège de Corinthe* (Paris, 1826), act 1, scene 9, 32.

36. Ibid., act 3, scene 6, 46.

37. Ibid.

38. Ibid.

39. Walton, *Rossini in Restoration Paris,* 114.

40. Weinstock, *Rossini,* 154; *Journal des Débats,* Hector Berlioz, feuilleton, February 6, 1853.

41. Rossini, *Le siège de Corinthe* (Paris, 1826), act 3, scene 6, 46.

42. Weinstock, *Rossini*, 154.

43. Walton, *Rossini in Restoration Paris*, 108 and 126.

44. Rossini, *Le siège de Corinthe* (Paris, 1826), act 1, scene 1, 26.

45. Ibid., act 1, scene 6, 30.

46. Walton, *Rossini in Restoration Paris*, 185. See also Anselm Gerhard, *The Urbanization of Opera: Music Theater in Paris in the Nineteenth Century* (Chicago: University of Chicago Press, 1998), 68–83.

47. James L. Moore, "How Turkish Janizary Band Music Started Our Modern Percussion Section," *Percussive Notes* 2:4 (1965), 2–13; see also D. Doran Bugg, "The Role of Turkish Percussion in the History and Development of the Orchestral Percussion Section," Ph.D. dissertation, Louisiana State University, 2003.

48. Walton, *Rossini in Restoration Paris*, 14–16.

49. Ibid., 149 and 153.

50. Bernard Lewis, *The Emergence of Modern Turkey*, 2nd ed. (London: Oxford University Press, 1968), 78–80; Noel Barber, *The Sultans* (New York: Simon & Schuster, 1973), 134–36.

51. Harvey Sachs, *The Ninth: Beethoven and the World in 1824* (New York: Random House, 2010), 157–58; Robert Hatten, "On Narrativity in Music: Expressive Genres and Levels of Discourse in Beethoven," *Indiana Theory Review* 12 (Spring–Fall 1991), 89; Bugg, "Role of Turkish Percussion," 33–36.

52. Paul Corneilson, *The Autobiography of Ludwig Fischer: Mozart's First Osmin* (Malden, MA: Mozart Society of America, 2011), 8.

53. Rossini, *Le siège de Corinthe* (Paris, 1826), act 3, scene 6, 47.

Chapter 12: The Decline and Disappearance of the Singing Turk

1. Herbert Weinstock, *Rossini: A Biography* (New York: Limelight Editions, 1987), 153.

2. Benjamin Walton, *Rossini in Restoration Paris: The Sound of Modern Life* (Cambridge: Cambridge University Press, 2007), 114.

3. Bernard Lewis, *The Emergence of Modern Turkey*, 2nd ed. (Oxford: Oxford University Press, 1968), 80–95.

4. Ibid., 102.

5. Ibid., 84.

6. Kemal Karpat, *The Politicization of Islam: Reconstructing Identity, State, Faith, and Community in the Late Ottoman State* (New York: Oxford University Press, 2001), 227; Emre Araci, "Giuseppe Donizetti at the Ottoman Court: A Levantine Life," *Musical Times* 143:1880 (Autumn 2002), 50; Federico Spinetti, "Introduzione," in *Giuseppe Donizetti Pascià: Traiettorie musicali e storiche tra Italia e Turchia*, ed. Federico Spinetti (Bergamo: Fondazione Donizetti, 2010), xiii–xxv.

7. *Le ménestrel* (Paris), December 18, 1836; Araci, "Giuseppe Donizetti at the Otto-

man Court," 51; Emre Araci, "From Napoleon to Mahmud: The Chequered Career of the Other Donizetti," in *Giuseppe Donizetti Pascià*, 3–9.

8. Araci, "Giuseppe Donizetti at the Ottoman Court," 52–53.

9. Giuseppe Donizetti, letters of August 10, 1830, and September 10, 1830, in *Giuseppe Donizetti Pascià*, 152–56.

10. Giuseppe Donizetti, letter of March 11, 1840, in *Giuseppe Donizetti Pascià*, 172.

11. Derek Weber, "From *Zaide* to *Die Entführung aus dem Serail*: Mozart's 'Turkish' Operas," in *Ottoman Empire and European Theatre*, vol. 1, *The Age of Mozart and Selim III*, ed. Michael Hüttler and Hans Weidinger (Vienna: Hollitzer, 2013), 636; Alfred Einstein, *Mozart: His Character, His Work*, trans. Arthur Mendel and Nathan Broder (New York: Oxford University Press, 1962), 452–53.

12. Thomas Bauman, *W. A. Mozart, Die Entführung aus dem Serail* (Cambridge: Cambridge University Press, 1987), 115.

13. Suna Suner, "The Earliest Opera Performances in the Ottoman World and the Role of Diplomacy," in *Age of Mozart and Selim III*, 214.

14. Anke Schmitt, *Der Exotismus in der deutschen Oper zwischen Mozart und Spohr* (Hamburg: Verlag der Musikalienhandlung Karl Dieter Wagner, 1988), 116.

15. Schmitt, *Der Exotismus*, 151.

16. Joseph von Hammer-Purgstall, *Geschichte des Osmanischen Reiches*, vol. 1 (Budapest: C. A. Hartleben; Vienna: Anton Strauss, 1827), xxv–xxvi.

17. Ibid., xxvii–xxviii.

18. Ibid., 553–57.

19. Joseph von Hammer-Purgstall, *Geschichte des Osmanischen Reiches*, vol. 2 (Budapest: C. A. Hartleben; Vienna: Anton Strauss, 1828), 98–100.

20. Weinstock, *Rossini*, 503 and 506.

21. Hammer-Purgstall, *Geschichte des Osmanischen Reiches*, vol. 1, dedication.

22. K. E. Fleming, *The Muslim Bonaparte: Diplomacy and Orientalism in Ali Pasha's Greece* (Princeton: Princeton University Press, 1999), 3–35; see also Schmitt, *Der Exotismus*, 135–37.

23. Lord Byron, letter to his mother, from Preveza, November 12, 1809, in *English Romantic Writers*, ed. David Perkins (New York: Harcourt, Brace & World, 1967), 925–26; see also Lord Byron, *Childe Harold's Pilgrimage*, canto 2 (Philadelphia: Henry Carey Baird, 1854).

24. Lord Byron, letter to his mother, from Preveza, November 12, 1809, 926; Fleming, *Muslim Bonaparte*, 120–21 and 156–80.

25. Albert Lortzing, *Ali Pascha von Janina* (Münster, 1828), libretto (CD liner notes), (Jan Stulen, Kölner Rundfunkorchester) (Musikproduktion Dabringhaus und Grimm, 1989), 33.

26. Lortzing, *Ali Pascha von Janina* (Münster, 1828), libretto, 34; Mozart, *Mozart Briefe* (Zurich: Diogenes, 1988), letter of September 26, 1781, 297–98; see also Peter Kivy,

Osmin's Rage: Philosophical Reflections on Opera, Drama, and Text (London: Royal Musical Association, 2000).

27. Lortzing, *Ali Pascha von Janina* (Münster, 1828), libretto, 38.

28. Ibid.

29. Felice Romani, "Proemio dell'autore" (The author's preface), (CD liner notes), in Bellini, *Zaira* (Paolo Olmi, Orchestra e Coro del Teatro Massimo "Bellini" di Catania), (Nuova Era, 1991), 11 and 21.

30. Filippo Cicconetti, *Vita di Vincenzo Bellini* (Prato: Tipografia F. Alberghetti, 1859), 47.

31. Vincenzo Bellini, *Zaira* (Parma, 1829), libretto (CD liner notes), (Nuova Era, 1991), act 1, scene 1, 25.

32. Ibid., act 1, scene 8, 30.

33. Ibid.

34. Ibid., act 1, scene 15, 38.

35. Ibid., act 2, scene 14, 48.

36. Friedrich Lippmann, "Zaira Yesterday and Today," in Bellini, *Zaira* (Parma, 1829), (CD liner notes), (Nuova Era, 1991) 13; see also Simon Maguire and Elizabeth Forbes, "Zaira," in *The New Grove Dictionary of Opera*, 4 vols., ed. Stanley Sadie, vol. 4 (Oxford: Oxford University Press, 1997), 1202.

37. John Black, "Romani, Felice," in *The New Grove Dictionary of Opera*, vol. 4, 19; Pietro Generali, *Il divorzio Persiano, o sia, Il gran bazzarro di Bassora, melodramma in due atti, da rappresentarsi nel Teatro Grande di Trieste, il Carnovale dell'Anno 1828* (Trieste: Dalla Tipografia Weis, 1828); Francesco Morlacchi, *I Saraceni in Sicilia, ovvero Eufemio di Messina, melodramma serio di Felice Romani, da rappresentarsi nel Gran Teatro La Fenice, il Carnovale dell'Anno 1828* (Venice: Dalla Tipografia Casali, 1828); Alessandro Roccatagliati, *Felice Romani librettista* (Lucca: Libreria Musicale Italiana, 1996), 30n24.

38. Jeremy Commons, "'All his knowledge and study of his art': Mercadante's *Zaira*" (CD liner notes), in Mercadante, *Zaira* (Naples, 1831), (David Parry, London Philharmonia Orchestra) (Opera Rara, 2002), 17–19; see also Michael Rose, "Mercadante, Saverio," in *The New Grove Dictionary of Opera*, vol. 3, 335.

39. "Donizetti in Costantinopoli: Frammento di un viaggio inedito in Oriente," in *Miscellanee del Cavaliere Felice Romani tratte dalla Gazzetta Piemontese* (Turin: Tipografia Favale, 1837), 9–12; Roccatagliati, *Felice Romani librettista*, 37–40; Araci, "Giuseppe Donizetti at the Ottoman Court," 53. Music historian Emre Araci has raised the fascinating possibility that the traveler-author might have been Felice Romani himself, as the piece was signed with the initials F.R. and was later published together with his *Miscellanee* from the *Gazzetta Piemontese*; there does not, however, seem to be other clearly confirming evidence that Romani actually made such a trip to Istanbul, and the travel account may well have been a literary fiction. I am grateful to Philip Gossett, Emre Araci, and Alessandro Roccatagliati for consulting with me about this historical puzzle.

40. "Donizetti in Costantinopoli," 9–12.

41. Emre Araci, "'Each Villa on the Bosphorus Looks a Screen New Painted, or a Pretty Opera Scene': Mahmud II Setting the Ottoman Stage for Italian Opera and Viennese Music," in *Ottoman Empire and European Theatre*, vol. 2, *The Time of Joseph Haydn*, ed. Michael Hüttler and Hans Weidinger (Vienna: Hollitzer, 2014), 625–26.

42. Suner, "Earliest Opera Performances in the Ottoman World," 202–3; Araci, "Giuseppe Donizetti at the Ottoman Court," 53–54; for Ottoman Egypt, see also Adam Mestyan, "Sound, Military Music, and Opera in Egypt during the Rule of Mehmet Ali Pasha," in *Time of Joseph Haydn*, 650–51.

43. Araci, "Giuseppe Donizetti at the Ottoman Court," 56n26.

44. Margaret Griffel, "Turkish Opera from Mozart to Cornelius," Ph.D. dissertation, Columbia University, 1975, 190–92.

45. *London Magazine and Review* 1 (February 1825), 288–89.

46. Steven Marcus, *The Other Victorians: A Study of Sexuality and Pornography in Mid-Nineteenth-Century England* (New Brunswick, NJ: Transaction, 2009), 197–216.

47. Paul Ennemond de Mont Rond, *Conquête de l'Algérie de 1830 a 1847*, vol. 1 (Paris: Imprimerie de E. Marc-Aurel, 1847), 55 and 67.

48. Lewis, *Emergence of Modern Turkey*, 84–85, 106–8.

49. Daniel Varisco, *Reading Orientalism: Said and the Unsaid* (Seattle: University of Washington Press, 2007), 380n46; Roderick Cavaliero, *Ottomania: The Romantics and the Myth of the Islamic Orient* (London: I. B. Tauris, 2013), 32–33; see also Vincent Gille, "L'air du temps: Sources et contexte des *Orientales*," in *Les Orientales: Maison de Victor Hugo* (Paris: Musées, 2010), 50–55.

50. Robert Blake, *Disraeli's Grand Tour: Benjamin Disraeli and the Holy Land, 1830–31* (New York: Oxford University Press, 1982), 47.

51. Ibid., 57.

52. Maya Jasanoff, *Edge of Empire: Lives, Culture, and Conquest in the East, 1750–1850* (New York: Vintage Books, 2006), 289–91.

53. Blake, *Disraeli's Grand Tour*, 55; see also Cavaliero, *Ottomania*, 173–79.

54. Mary Jane Phillips-Matz, *Verdi: A Biography* (1993; New York: Oxford University Press, 1996), 145–46.

55. Giuseppe Verdi, *I Lombardi alla prima crociata, dramma lirico di Temistocle Solera, posto in musica dal Sig. Maestro Giuseppe Verdi, da rappresentarsi nell'I. R. Teatro alla Scala, il carnevale MDCCCXLIII* (Milan: Gaspare Truffi, 1843), act 2, scene 9, 21.

56. Phillips-Matz, *Verdi*, 140–46.

57. Verdi, *I Lombardi* (Milan, 1843), act 2, scene 9, 22.

58. Roger Parker, "*Jérusalem*," in *The New Grove Dictionary of Opera*, vol. 2, 893–94.

59. Phillips-Matz, *Verdi*, 243–44.

60. Giuseppe Verdi, *Il corsaro* (Trieste, 1848), libretto (CD liner notes), (Lamberto Gardelli, New Philharmonia Orchestra) (Philips 2005), 23.

61. Verdi, *Il corsaro* (Trieste, 1848), libretto, 38–39.

62. Lord Byron, *The Corsair: A Tale*, 7th ed., canto 3 (London: John Murray, 1814), 69.

63. Schmitt, *Der Exotismus*, 151.

64. Isabelle Moindrot, "The 'Turk' and the 'Parisienne': From Favart's *Soliman Second, ou Les trois sultanes* (1761) to *Les trois sultanes* (Pathé, 1912)," in *Age of Mozart and Selim III*, 439–40. Moindrot notes that Offenbach, looking back fondly at the age of Louis XV from the perspective of the Second Empire, even considered creating an operetta about Madame Favart herself.

65. Paola Campi, "Galli, Filippo," *Dizionario Biografico degli Italiani*, vol. 51 (1998), http://www.treccani.it/enciclopedia

66. Araci, "'Each Villa on the Bosphorus," 629; s.v. "Castrato," in *Oxford Dictionary of Music*, ed. Michael Kennedy and Joyce Bourne (Oxford: Oxford University Press, 2006), 158.

67. Verdi, *Otello* (Milan, 1887), www.librettidopera.it, act 1, scene 2, 11.

68. Koraljka Kos, "Zayc, Ivan," in *The New Grove Dictionary of Opera*, vol. 4, 1203–4.

69. Zdravko Blažeković, "Political Implications of Croatian Opera in the Nineteenth Century," in *Music-Cultures in Contact: Convergences and Collisions*, ed. Margaret Kartomi and Stephen Blum (Basel: Gordon and Breach, 1994), 51; Gottfried Franz Kasparek, "Franz von Suppé: Operette mit Italianità" (CD liner notes), in Franz von Suppé, *Fatinitza* (Vinzenz Praxmarer, Franz Lehar Orchester) (Classic Produktion Osnabrück, 2007), 8–9.

70. Jana Minov, "Stanislav Binički Opera *Na Uranku*: Genesis of Critical Analysis of the First Serbian Opera," unpublished research paper, Arizona State University, 2011, 34–64; Tatjana Marković, "The Ottoman Other in Southeast European Nineteenth-Century Opera," paper presented at New York University, Center for European and Mediterranean Studies, March 2011.

71. Moindrot, "'Turk' and the 'Parisienne,'" 443.

72. *A Working Friendship: The Correspondence between Richard Strauss and Hugo von Hofmannsthal*, trans. Hanns Hammelmann and Ewald Osers (New York: Random House, 1962), Hofmannsthal to Strauss, letter of July 8, 1918, 304–5; Jack Stein, "Adaptations of Molière-Lully's *Le bourgeois gentilhomme* by Hofmannsthal and Strauss," *Comparative Literature Studies* 12:2 (June 1975), 101–21.

73. Giacomo Puccini, *Turandot, libretto di Giuseppe Adami and Renato Simoni* (Milan: La Scala), act 3, 26, http://www.teatroallascala.org/en/season/opera-ballet/2010–2011/turandot.html

74. W. H. Auden and Chester Kallman (libretto) and Igor Stravinsky (music), *The Rake's Progress*, act 2, scene 3, http://documents.mx/documents/the-rakes-progress-libretto.html

Conclusion

1. Martha Feldman, *Opera and Sovereignty: Transforming Myths in Eighteenth-Century Italy* (Chicago: University of Chicago Press, 2007), 23.

2. *Cantata: Nelle presenti vittorie riportate dall'armi cesaree contro il Turco, cantata d'Ignazio di Bonis, posta in musica dal Sig. Giuseppe Amadori* (Rome: Per Francesco Gonzaga, in Via Lata, 1717), 4.

3. *Cantata: Nelle presenti vittorie* (Rome, 1717), 7–9.

4. *Arlequin sultane favorite, pièce en trois actes, par Monsieur le T[ellier], representée à la Foire de S. Germain* (Paris, 1715), act 1, scene 3.

5. Ibid., act 1, scene 2.

6. Ibid., act 3, scene 9.

7. Metropolitan Museum of Art, fabric "La Caravane du Caire," Petitpierre et frères, 1785–1790, accession number 26.233.24; fabric "La Caravane du Caire," early 19th century, accession number 31.130.7.

8. François Francoeur and François Rebel, *Scanderberg, tragédie représentée devant Leurs Majestés à Fontainebleau le 22 octobre 1763* (Paris: L'Imprimerie de Christophe Ballard, 1763), act 4, scene 6.

9. Mozart, *Zaide* (CD liner notes), libretto (Paul Goodwin, Academy of Ancient Music) (Harmonia Mundi, 1998), act 2, 20.

10. *Mozart's Letters, Mozart's Life*, ed. and trans. Robert Spaethling (New York: Norton, 2000), letter of September 26, 1781, 286; Mozart, *Briefe*, ed. Horst Wandrey (Zurich: Diogenes, 1988), 297–98.

11. Nancy Bisaha, *Creating East and West: Renaissance Humanists and the Ottoman Turks* (Philadelphia: University of Pennsylvania Press, 2004), 2 and 189.

12. Mozart, *Die Entführung aus dem Serail: Partitura* (Budapest: Könemann, 1995), act 1, 55–58; see also Thomas Bauman, *W. A. Mozart, Die Entführung aus dem Serail* (Cambridge: Cambridge University Press, 1987), 70; Michael Pirker, "Die Türkische Musik und Mozarts *Entführung aus dem Serail*," in *Die Klangwelt Mozarts: Eine Ausstellung des Kunsthistorischen Museums* (Vienna: Kunsthistorisches Museum, 1991), 140–41; and Benjamin Perl, "Mozart in Turkey," *Cambridge Opera Journal* 12:3 (2001), 227.

13. Charles-Simon Favart, *Soliman Second ou Les trois sultanes, comédie en trois actes et en vers* (Paris: Chez Didot, 1772), 17.

14. Montesquieu, *The Persian Letters*, trans. C. J. Betts (New York: Penguin, 1985), 9th letter, 50–51.

15. *Mozart's Letters, Mozart's Life*, letter of September 26, 1781, 286; Mozart, *Briefe*, ed. Wandrey, 297–98.

16. Bence Szabolcsi, "Exoticisms in Mozart," *Music and Letters* 37:4 (1956), 328–30.

17. Franco Venturi, *The End of the Old Regime in Europe, 1768–1776: The First Crisis*, trans. R. Burr Litchfield (1979; Princeton: Princeton University Press, 1989).

18. Rossini, *L'italiana in Algeri: Vocal Score*, ed. Azio Corghi (Milan: Ricordi, 1982), 137–43.

19. Rossini, *Il turco in Italia: Vocal Score*, 2 vols. (Milan: Ricordi, 2000), vol. 1, 83–85; Stendhal, *Vie de Rossini* (Paris: Michel Lévy Frères, 1854), 113; Stendhal, *Life of Rossini*, trans. Richard Coe (Seattle: University of Washington Press, 1970), 146.

20. Rossini, *Il turco in Italia: Vocal Score*, vol. 2, 364–69.

21. Fernand Braudel, *The Mediterranean and the Mediterranean World in the Age of Philip II*, 2 vols., trans. Siân Reynolds (New York: Harper & Row, 1973).

22. Rossini, *Maometto II, dramma per musica in due atti, testi di Cesare della Valle* (Naples, 1820), www.librettidopera.it, act 2, scene 2, 23.

23. Handel, *Tamerlano* (London, 1724), libretto (Florence: Teatro del Maggio Musicale Fiorentino, 2001), act 2, scene 9, 66; act 3, scene 10, 92.

24. Jean-Philippe Rameau, *Les Indes galantes* (CD liner notes), libretto (Orchestre Jean-François Paillard) (Erato, 1974), act 1, "Le Turc généreux," scene 4, 60; Rameau, *Les Indes galantes, par M. Rameau, représenté en 1735* (Paris, 1735), musical score, 113.

Index

The Abduction from the Seraglio (Mozart): antecedent works, 140, 141–42, 149, 150, 153, 159–61, 172; Belmonte character, 154, 180, 191, 198–99, 201; Berlin performance, 182 (fig.); Blonde character, 154, 178–79, 183, 202; cast of first performances, 158, 204; commission, 147; composition, 1, 153, 156–59, 161–71; costumes, 166 (fig.), 194, 196 (fig.); costumes of Janissary band, 115 (fig.), 116 (fig.), 117, 194; drinking duet of Osmin and Pedrillo, 82, 124, 180–86, 183 (fig.), 218, 231–32, 270, 393; final scene, 4, 199–203, 200 (fig.), 226, 232, 395; first performance, 49, 147, 148 (fig.), 158, 188–89, 194, 201, 203, 204; influence, 101, 257, 270; Koblenz production, 115 (fig.), 116 (fig.), 117, 166 (fig.), 194, 196 (fig.), 219; Konstanze character, 154, 158, 171, 191, 193–94, 195, 197, 198; libretto, 152, 153–54, 156, 158, 165, 199–201, 433n54, 436n19; overture, 5, 155, 159; Paris performance (1798), 228, 231–32; Pedrillo character, 123, 154, 169, 175, 180–84, 253; performance at La Scala, 363, 404; performances around Europe, 157, 206–7, 215, 219, 224, 231, 346; plot, 198–99, 212, 253; political occasion, 156–58, 207; power relations, 174–78; public reception, 1, 203–4, 205, 206; singers, 158, 179, 204; slavery issue, 178–79, 180, 181, 184; success, 149, 194–95, 205, 206; Turkish chorus, 5, 158, 159, 188, 194, 195 (fig.), 226; Turkish musical elements, 5, 154–55, 158–59, 164–65, 188, 202–3, 204–5, 226, 399, 400; wind instrumentation, 204–5. *See also* Osmin character; Selim, Pasha

Abdülaziz, Sultan, 383

Abdülhamid I, Sultan, 142, 223

Abdülmecid I, Sultan, 360–61, 373

Les Abencérages (Cherubini), 252–53

Abington, Fanny, 99, 100

Absolutism: in Europe, 10, 399; in France, 10, 58, 392; musical associations, 399–400; of sultans, 97, 392–93, 396. *See also* Despotism; Louis XIV; Napoleon Bonaparte

Absolutism, enlightened: in *L'incontro improvviso*, 127; of Joseph II, 127, 128, 189–90, 201, 221, 226, 395; in Scandinavia, 101, 214; of Selim III, 223

Abu Hassan (Weber), 239–40

Académie Royale, *see* Paris Opéra

Adelaide du Guesclin (Voltaire), 330, 331–32

Adelheit von Veltheim (Neefe), 153, 231

Adriatic Sea, 4, 15, 32, 73, 227, 327, 401